Helping and Healing Our Families

Helping and Healing Our Families

PRINCIPLES AND PRACTICES INSPIRED BY
"THE FAMILY: A PROCLAMATION TO THE WORLD"

CRAIG H. HART

LLOYD D. NEWELL

ELAINE WALTON

DAVID C. DOLLAHITE

EDITORS

JULIE H. HAUPT

MANAGING EDITOR

HILARY M. HENDRICKS
LISA BOLIN HAWKINS

CONSULTING EDITORS

SCHOOL OF FAMILY LIFE
BRIGHAM YOUNG UNIVERSITY

DESERET BOOK COMPANY

Dedicated to

President Gordon B. Hinckley

Champion of the family

© 2005 School of Family Life, Brigham Young University

DESERET BOOK is a registered trademark of Deseret Book Company.

Visit us at deseretbook.com

Library of Congress Cataloging-in-Publication Data

Helping and healing our families : principles and practices inspired by
    The family : a proclamation to the world / edited by Craig H. Hart
    ... [et al.].
        p.   cm.
Includes bibliographical references and index.
ISBN 1-59038-485-7 (hardbound : alk. paper)
    1. Family—Religious life.   2. Church of Jesus Christ of Latter-day Saints—Doctrines.   I. Hart, Craig H., 1957–   .
BX8643.F3H44   2005
248.4'89332—dc22
                                                                                          2005015383

Printed in the United States of America   72076
Publishers Printing, Salt Lake City, UT

10   9   8   7   6   5   4   3   2   1

Contents

SECTION V: MAINTAIN AND STRENGTHEN THE FAMILY

Acknowledgments

The editors gratefully acknowledge the exceptional professionalism and hard work of our three assisting editors: Julie Haupt, managing editor, and Hilary Hendricks and Lisa Hawkins, consulting editors. They have been central to this volume from the beginning and have contributed extraordinary judgment and wise counsel. We also thank source checkers Kirk Shaw and Emily Ellsworth, who have diligently worked to ensure the accuracy of source citations in the volume.

We express our appreciation to James Harper, director of the Brigham Young University School of Family Life, for his oversight and counsel on this project; and to Susanne Olsen, associate director of curriculum for the school, for her continued support. From the outset of the first volume, *Strengthening Our Families: An In-Depth Look at the Proclamation on the Family,* Alan Hawkins encouraged the creation of these resources for families. Without his work and vision, this volume might never have come to be. We express thanks to LaRita Johnson and the secretarial staff of the School of Family Life for their valuable assistance.

At the beginning of this project, many focus group participants—including parents, BYU faculty teaching the Family Life 100 course, local priesthood leaders from various parts of the United States, ward Relief Society presidents, and friends—provided input that guided our selection of topics to be covered in this volume. We gratefully acknowledge their wisdom, experience, and suggestions, which contributed to our decision to organize the book into short chapters and essays covering a wide breadth of topics.

We appreciate those at Deseret Book who have brought this volume to fruition, including Chris Schoebinger (product director), Jay Parry (editor), Lisa Mangum (editorial assistant), Tonya Facemyer (typographer), Richard Erickson (art director), and Ken Wzorek (designer). We also thank the many individuals who assisted us throughout the project by reading manuscripts and providing valuable feedback.

Most especially, we thank all the authors, who have volunteered countless hours of unpaid time on this project. We have been impressed by their insights and expertise, touched by their sincerity and worthy desires to help families, and grateful for their consecrated efforts. Royalties from the sale of *Helping and Healing Our Families* will be donated to the BYU School of Family Life to support teaching, scholarship, and outreach.

Finally, we express profound appreciation to our spouses and children for their support, their encouragement, and their love, which keep us striving to help and heal families.

THE FAMILY

A PROCLAMATION TO THE WORLD

THE FIRST PRESIDENCY AND COUNCIL OF THE TWELVE APOSTLES OF THE CHURCH OF JESUS CHRIST OF LATTER-DAY SAINTS

WE, THE FIRST PRESIDENCY and the Council of the Twelve Apostles of The Church of Jesus Christ of Latter-day Saints, solemnly proclaim that marriage between a man and a woman is ordained of God and that the family is central to the Creator's plan for the eternal destiny of His children.

ALL HUMAN BEINGS—male and female—are created in the image of God. Each is a beloved spirit son or daughter of heavenly parents, and, as such, each has a divine nature and destiny. Gender is an essential characteristic of individual premortal, mortal, and eternal identity and purpose.

IN THE PREMORTAL REALM, spirit sons and daughters knew and worshiped God as their Eternal Father and accepted His plan by which His children could obtain a physical body and gain earthly experience to progress toward perfection and ultimately realize his or her divine destiny as an heir of eternal life. The divine plan of happiness enables family relationships to be perpetuated beyond the grave. Sacred ordinances and covenants available in holy temples make it possible for individuals to return to the presence of God and for families to be united eternally.

THE FIRST COMMANDMENT that God gave to Adam and Eve pertained to their potential for parenthood as husband and wife. We declare that God's commandment for His children to multiply and replenish the earth remains in force. We further declare that God has commanded that the sacred powers of procreation are to be employed only between man and woman, lawfully wedded as husband and wife.

WE DECLARE the means by which mortal life is created to be divinely appointed. We affirm the sanctity of life and of its importance in God's eternal plan.

HUSBAND AND WIFE have a solemn responsibility to love and care for each other and for their children. "Children are an heritage of the Lord" (Psalms 127:3). Parents have a sacred duty to rear their children in love and righteousness, to provide for their physical and spiritual needs, to teach them to love and serve one another, to observe the commandments of God and to be law-abiding citizens wherever they live. Husbands and wives—mothers and fathers—will be held accountable before God for the discharge of these obligations.

THE FAMILY is ordained of God. Marriage between man and woman is essential to His eternal plan. Children are entitled to birth within the bonds of matrimony, and to be reared by a father and a mother who honor marital vows with complete fidelity. Happiness in family life is most likely to be achieved when founded upon the teachings of the Lord Jesus Christ. Successful marriages and families are established and maintained on principles of faith, prayer, repentance, forgiveness, respect, love, compassion, work, and wholesome recreational activities. By divine design, fathers are to preside over their families in love and righteousness and are responsible to provide the necessities of life and protection for their families. Mothers are primarily responsible for the nurture of their children. In these sacred responsibilities, fathers and mothers are obligated to help one another as equal partners. Disability, death, or other circumstances may necessitate individual adaptation. Extended families should lend support when needed.

WE WARN that individuals who violate covenants of chastity, who abuse spouse or offspring, or who fail to fulfill family responsibilities will one day stand accountable before God. Further, we warn that the disintegration of the family will bring upon individuals, communities, and nations the calamities foretold by ancient and modern prophets.

WE CALL UPON responsible citizens and officers of government everywhere to promote those measures designed to maintain and strengthen the family as the fundamental unit of society.

This proclamation was read by President Gordon B. Hinckley as part of his message at the General Relief Society Meeting held September 23, 1995, in Salt Lake City, Utah.

PREFACE

Family life holds the promise for our greatest happiness in this life and the next. While family life includes much joy, it also involves discovering, solving, and working through the problems of everyday living. Many families face daunting challenges arising from divorce, single parenting, mental illness, long-term health problems and physical disabilities, death, marital and parent–child conflict, wayward children, and children with special needs—to name a few. The purpose of this volume is to provide hope, principles, practices, and eternal perspectives in addressing these issues.

This volume is based upon prophetic principles of marriage and family life, particularly doctrines taught in "The Family: A Proclamation to the World."[1] At the creation of the School of Family Life at Brigham Young University, President Boyd K. Packer delivered a charge that BYU faculty produce textbooks on the family that would be worthy of a great university. He admonished faculty to fill these books with moral and spiritual truths in full harmony with the restored gospel. These books were to help students and others be good spouses and parents.[2] The concerted efforts of 125 authors, including faculty across many disciplines at Brigham Young University and individuals with professional and personal experience in topics related to family life, culminate here in an offering that responds to this apostolic charge. In addition, publication of this book coincides with the tenth anniversary of "The Family: A Proclamation to the World," which President Gordon B. Hinckley introduced in a general Relief Society Meeting in September 1995.[3] With this volume, we celebrate proclamation principles and the blueprint they provide for success in family life.

In 2000, *Strengthening Our Families: An In-Depth Look at the Proclamation on the Family* was published, edited by David C. Dollahite from the School of Family Life at BYU. This seminal volume demonstrated that proclamation principles are well supported by conceptual and empirical scholarship. A primary objective in this second, companion volume is to provide concrete ideas and real-world examples to assist couples and families.

Three years of preparation, discussion, and careful planning by the editorial board, along with the efforts of talented authors (each with considerable expertise and experience in the designated topic area), have combined to produce this work. The eighty-four chapters and essays contained herein provide a rich variety of topics to help and heal families. Chapters incorporate prophetic statements and scholarly research; essays primarily focus on personal experiences of Latter-day Saints. To achieve this breadth, the chapters and essays are necessarily short. However, most list additional reading, cross references, or other resources that can provide further help. (Articles from the *Ensign* can be read and printed, free of charge, at www.lds.org.)

As the insights, experiences, and testimonies of Latter-day Saints are shared in this book, we hope readers will be reminded of God's love for each individual, and of His great plan of happiness for marriages and families. We hope you will gain inspiration for your own circumstances as the principles of successful family life are explicated. President Ezra Taft Benson explained how principles might be translated into action:

> Usually the Lord gives us the overall objectives to be accomplished and some guidelines to follow, but he expects us to work out most of the details and methods. The methods and procedures are usually developed through study and prayer and by living so that we can obtain and follow the promptings of the Spirit.[4]

Additionally, as you read about challenges you have not personally confronted, we hope this volume can help you to grow in empathy and become better equipped to help others who struggle or have become discouraged. While the practical suggestions for strengthening families apply most directly to families in North America, the doctrinal principles can be applied to all families. We have written with Latter-day Saint readers in mind, but we invite our friends of other faiths to consider the volume's faith-based approach to creating, sustaining, and healing family relationships.

It is our sincere desire that the principles and practices in this volume will help families move closer to the ideals set forth in the family proclamation and, in the process, find greater happiness and joy in family life.

> Craig H. Hart
>
> Lloyd D. Newell
>
> Elaine Walton
>
> David C. Dollahite

NOTES

1. First Presidency and Council of Twelve Apostles (1995, November), The family: A proclamation to the world, *Ensign, 25*(11), 102.

2. See D. C. Dollahite (2000), Introduction: The proclamation as prophetic guidance for strengthening the family; in D. C. Dollahite, ed., *Strengthening Our Families: An In-Depth Look at the Proclamation on the Family* (Salt Lake City: Bookcraft), 3.

3. Gordon B. Hinckley (1995, November), Stand strong against the wiles of the world, *Ensign, 25*(11), 98–101.

4. Ezra Taft Benson (1974), *God, Family, Country: Our Three Great Loyalties* (Salt Lake City: Deseret Book), 381.

CHAPTER 1

HEAVENLY FATHER'S FAMILY-CENTERED PLAN

CRAIG H. HART, LLOYD D. NEWELL, ELAINE WALTON,
DAVID C. DOLLAHITE, JULIE H. HAUPT, AND HILARY M. HENDRICKS

The family is central to the Creator's plan for the eternal destiny of His children. . . .
In the premortal realm, spirit sons and daughters knew and worshiped God as their Eternal Father
and accepted His plan by which His children could obtain a physical body and gain earthly experience to progress
toward perfection and ultimately realize his or her divine destiny as an heir of eternal life.[1]
—"The Family: A Proclamation to the World"

As we anticipated our mortal existence and "shouted for joy" (Job 38:7), we were taught about our Heavenly Father's great plan of happiness. We must have learned then that families are at the center of God's plan and that family relationships would be central to our happiness as His children. President Gordon B. Hinckley explained, "God is the designer of the family. He intended that the greatest of happiness, the most satisfying aspects of life, the deepest joys should come in our associations together and our concerns one for another as fathers and mothers and children."[2]

"The Family: A Proclamation to the World" teaches us that Heavenly Father's plan of happiness includes providing an opportunity for His children to "obtain a physical body" and "gain earthly experience to progress toward perfection and . . . eternal life."[3] Elder Merrill J. Bateman listed family as a main purpose of creation:

> There are three major purposes for the earth's creation and the mortal experience. The first is to obtain a physical body (see Abraham 3:26). The second is to grow spiritually by keeping the Lord's commandments (see Abraham 3:25). The third is to initiate an eternal family (see D&C 131:1–4; 132:19). Thus, the physical body, spiritual growth, and family are the grand prizes of mortality.[4]

These three "grand prizes" of mortal life are made possible within the context of family relationships. In this chapter we share principles that will help Latter-day Saints consider family life as a preparation for eternal glory and view exaltation as a family endeavor.

THE "GRAND PRIZES" OF MORTALITY AND FAMILY RELATIONSHIPS

Our Father in Heaven has provided each of His children with an opportunity to be part of a family. Speaking of families, President James E. Faust said: "I wish to define *family* very broadly. In the Church we have traditional families and single-parent families. Furthermore, each single member is considered to be, in a sense, a Church family. We also have ward families in which the bishop serves as a spiritual father."[5] All Latter-day Saints can reap great blessings of family interaction as they serve their extended families, ward families, and others (see essay A4).

While family situations are sometimes less than ideal, Elder Neal A. Maxwell gave this encouragement: "There are no perfect families, either in the world or in the Church, but there are many good families. My spiritual applause also goes to those heroic parents—left alone by death or divorce—who are righteously and 'anxiously engaged' in nurturing and providing for their families, often against such heavy odds."[6]

Each child of God belongs to His eternal family.

The proclamation declares, "Each is a beloved spirit son or daughter of heavenly parents, and, as such, each has a divine nature and destiny."[7] This destiny, for the faithful, includes returning to live again with God.

Obtain a physical body. The first of the three "grand prizes" of mortality is the opportunity to obtain a physical body. The proclamation teaches that "the means by which mortal life is created [are] divinely appointed."[8] Through these means children can be welcomed by their families, provided for physically, and nurtured with love. Loving relationships can support God's spirit children as they move from the spirit world to the mortal world. God's command that "the sacred powers of procreation are to be employed only between man and woman, lawfully wedded as husband and wife"[9] provides for the optimal condition in which His children may receive their physical bodies. Children who are born to a father and mother who are married and committed to their family are more likely to be successful in many aspects of their mortal existence[10] (see essay C2 on the advantages of marriage).

Seek spiritual growth. The proclamation speaks of the second "grand prize" in declaring that we come to mortality to "gain earthly experience to progress toward . . . eternal life."[11] Family relationships help us make sense of our earthly experience and provide many opportunities for spiritual growth.

As we begin our life on earth, our early childhood experiences are centered in family life. Parents and other loved ones form the basis of a child's understanding of self and others, home, and the outside world (see chapter 3). Throughout childhood and adolescence, families help children frame their experiences, ideally in a context of love and support (see chapter 16). As they become adults, children support and nurture others, filling their own earthly experience with meaningful interaction and love. Thus, family can provide a loving context for finding meaning in mortal experiences and for confronting problems both inside and outside the family (see chapter 28).

Family life offers daily opportunities for spiritual growth. As family members learn to communicate with one another, sacrifice for each other, and worship God together (see chapters 29 and 30), each is strengthened spiritually. Family challenges provide opportunities to exercise patience, faith, and other qualities that help to prepare us for eternal life.

Initiate an eternal family. Eternal life is the quality of life that God Himself enjoys. He lives in a family unit, and He wants us to experience all the glory and joy of His life. Since eternal life is familial, the third prize of mortality involves learning how to create and nurture eternal marital and family relationships.

The abilities developed through our interactions with family members prepare us for exaltation. Elder Dallin H. Oaks taught, "Exaltation is an eternal family experience, and it is our mortal family experiences that are best suited to prepare us for it."[12] In family life, we learn and experience many of the lessons of mortality. Elder Henry B. Eyring taught: "Eternal life means to become like the Father and to live in families in happiness and joy forever. . . . Family life here is the schoolroom in which we prepare for family life there."[13] In fact, the family is the only temporal institution that will be carried into the eternities.[14] Elder Bateman stated: "Salvation is a one-by-one process, whereas exaltation is accomplished two-by-two and in family groupings. . . . The most important relationships in mortality—those of the family—are meant for eternity."[15] These eternal relationships are intended to bring us joy both here and hereafter.

FINDING JOY IN FAMILY LIFE

In the context of family, agency underlies joy and progress. Our own choices and the choices of those we love have the opportunity to bring great joy. Meaningful family experiences include cradling a first grandchild, seeing the smile of a child fresh from the waters of baptism, listening to the short phrases of a teen's expression of testimony, or benefiting from the generosity of an extended family member. Taking time to ponder on our blessings, to rejoice in that which we have received, and to treasure these precious moments is essential to finding joy amid the struggles. (Essay E3 shares other examples of finding joy.)

Our own choices and the choices of those we love will surely bring a measure of sorrow and disappointment. That is part of the process and growth of mortality (see chapter 26). When we experience the pain of difficult family situations, it can help to remember that marriage and family life bring rewarding and joyful experiences, as well as times of sorrow. Through the gospel, we can abide in the hope that circumstances can improve, that present trials will pass, and that repentance can bring renewal. Elder Oaks taught that our responses to adversity "will inevitably shape our souls and ultimately determine our status in eternity."[16] Bishop Richard C. Edgley reminded us:

> There are few of us, if any, who don't walk the refiner's fire of adversity and despair, sometimes known to others but for many quietly hidden and privately endured. Most of the heartache, pain, and suffering we would not choose today. But we did choose. We chose when we could see the complete plan. We chose when we had a clear vision of the Savior's rescue of us. And if our faith and understanding were as clear today as it was when we first made that choice, I believe we would choose again.[17]

Finding joy in family life when our current circumstances do not match our expectations requires that we look for the beauty that does exist in our family relationships. President Hinckley lamented that "too many who come to marriage [believe] that everything must be precisely right at all times, that life is a series of entertainments." Instead, he emphasized, "Marriage is beautiful when beauty is looked for and cultivated."[18] Recognizing the precious gift of one another in our lives helps us gain perspective and gives us hope to carry on. President Hinckley also counseled family members to look for eternal worth in each other and in their relationships:

> Wives, look upon your husbands as your precious companions and live worthy of that association. Husbands, see in your wives your most valued asset in time or eternity, each a daughter of God, a partner with whom you can walk hand in hand, through sunshine and storm, through all the perils and triumphs of life. Parents, see in your children sons and daughters of your Father in Heaven, who will hold you accountable for them. Stand together as their guardians, their protectors, their guides, their anchors.[19]

One Latter-day Saint couple, when newly married, had many dreams for idyllic family moments. After several children joined their family, they occasionally remarked to each other, "Remember those times we always dreamed of? This is one of them." During many other moments when life was not sailing very smoothly, the same couple looked at each other with smiles and said, "Remember those times we always dreamed of? This is definitely not one of them!" Another couple reflected after many years of marriage that it was their good times, but most especially their hard times, that brought them together and strengthened their love.

Our greatest joy and consolation in times when all seems lost is the steady assurance that Heavenly Father loves us and is aware of our individual circumstances. We can have confidence that He will help us "realize [our] divine destiny as [heirs] of eternal life."[20] Agency is essential to God's plan; thus, when the choices of others hurt us deeply, the Lord is able to "consecrate [our] afflictions for [our] gain" (2 Nephi 2:1–3). Elder Maxwell reminded us: "Of course, we cannot know the meaning of all things *right now!* But we can know, *right now,* that God knows us and loves us individually!"[21] Surely, family life teaches us and stretches us in ways that prepare us to live again with God.

Facing Challenges in Family Life

Considering the central place of family in the happiness of God's children, we can predict that the forces of evil would have combined against the sacred institutions of home and family. In our modern day, "the traditional family is under heavy attack."[22] President James E. Faust noted: "In recent times, society has been plagued with a cancer. I speak of the disintegration of many of our homes and families. Confusion and disorder are all too common in society, but we must not permit them to destroy our families."[23] Latter-day Saint scholar Truman G. Madsen stated, "Too many want gratification without love, love without covenants [marriage], marriage without partnership, partnership without children, children without care or concern, care and concern only for what is convenient."[24]

We have been instructed in the safeguards that will help protect our families in these "perilous times" (see 2 Timothy 3:1–7). Our safeguards include family prayer, family home evening, family and personal scripture study,[25] and temple worthiness and attendance (see chapter 18). Families can provide refuge from the evil influences that swirl outside and threaten from the inside (see chapter 13 and chapter 25 for examples). Yet, even when families work diligently to live the principles and commandments that have been given, the trials of mortality come. President Gordon B. Hinckley noted:

> Stormy weather occasionally hits every household. Connected inevitably with the whole process is much of pain—physical, mental, and emotional. There is much of stress and struggle, of fear and worry. For most, there is the ever-haunting battle of economics. There seems never to be enough money to cover the needs of a family. Sickness strikes periodically.

Accidents happen. The hand of death may reach in with dread stealth to take a precious one. But all of this seems to be part of the processes of family life. Few indeed are those who get along without experiencing some of it. It has been so from the beginning.[26]

It has been so from the beginning because challenges and adversity are integral to the tests of mortality. This test of mortality is designed to bring out the best in us and to help "prove" us (Abraham 3:25). President Lorenzo Snow taught of our instruction in the spirit world: "There is no doubt that we saw and understood clearly there that, in order to accomplish our exaltation and glory, this was a necessary experience: and however disagreeable it might have appeared to us, we were willing to conform to the will of God, and consequently we are here."[27]

Elder Maxwell delineated three causes of the suffering we experience: (1) those things that happen as a result of our own mistakes and sins or the actions of others; (2) those trials that come to us in the course of daily living, for the Lord "sendeth rain on the just and on the unjust" (Matthew 5:45), and (3) the challenges that come to us for the purpose of teaching us (see Hebrews 12:6; Mosiah 23:21). In the latter category, whether the Lord gives us a particular individual or family trial or simply declines to remove it, the results are the same, according to Elder Maxwell.[28]

An understanding of the Eternal Father's plan of happiness assists us as we wrestle with the vicissitudes of life. Elder Ballard advised, "The only satisfying answers . . . come from the comforting perspective of faith in our Heavenly Father and his eternal plan for our happiness."[29] And we are promised that those who "put their trust in God shall be supported in their trials, and their troubles, and their afflictions, and shall be lifted up at the last day" (Alma 36:3).

KEEPING FAMILY PRIORITIES CENTRAL

Many activities, responsibilities, and other stressors can draw us away from keeping family life central in our lives, swallowing up time and energy that are better devoted to our families. Worldly distractions abound as a frenzied culture of careerism and amusement pulls individuals apart into separate interests and activities. Family members must be vigilant in guarding couple and family time and energy in such a culture. In addition, Church leaders have warned us that active Latter-day Saints can sometimes become so involved in Church activities that they do not adequately attend to marital and family life.[30]

In a general conference address, President Boyd K. Packer empathized with the "many members [who] face conflicts as they struggle to balance their responsibility as parents together with faithful activity in the Church." His answer to handling the conflict of balance was to envision parenthood as the most sacred and important of Church callings. "Devotion to the family and devotion to the Church are not different and separate things," he taught. "I . . . encourage leaders to carefully consider the home lest they issue calls or schedule activities which place an unnecessary burden on parents and families."[31] He also taught that "every call, every service in the Church brings experience and valuable insights which carry over into family life."[32]

Parents must wisely consider family time and their children's needs as they choose from the many worthy school, community, and extracurricular activities in which family members might participate. (See chapter 31 and essay A2 for ideas on balancing priorities to place family first.) Elder Ballard counseled: "Remember [that] too much of anything in life can throw us off-balance. At the same time, too little of the important things can do the same thing."[33] Latter-day Saint scholar Brent L. Top observed: "It may be that the worst thing we can give our children is the opportunity to participate in an additional sport, music lesson, or other activity that demands money and time away from the family. Teaching our children how to live 'quiet, sane,' and balanced lives may be one of the most vital things we can do for them in these frenzied last days."[34]

In making "family-friendly" decisions in daily life, it is crucial that we prayerfully determine our priorities and do all things "in wisdom and order" (Mosiah 4:27).[35] In so doing, we will gain confidence in the decisions we are making and avoid the temptation to feel guilty when this prayerful determination indicates that some duties and opportunities will best be served in another season of our lives. Elder Oaks wrote that members should not feel guilty when attention to family responsibilities keeps them from, for example, "submitting as many group sheets or attending the temple as frequently" as others.[36] "This kind of guilt comes not from insufficient efforts, but from insufficient vision," he taught. "For example, a mother with several young children may be furthering the mission of the Church most profoundly in all three of its dimensions [proclaim the gospel, redeem the dead, and perfect the Saints] in her own home when she helps her children to prepare for missions, when she teaches them to revere the temple and prepare to make covenants there, and when she shows them how to strive for perfection in their personal lives."[37]

Finally, Elder Maxwell counseled: "Preserve yourselves and your marriages and families in order to serve more individuals and for longer! People-fatigue can overtake us all, especially the conscientious, if we are not wise. . . . We unwisely often write checks against our time accounts as we never would dare do, comparably, against our bank accounts."[38] Faithful service in the Church can bring many blessings into family life. Through the inspiration of the Holy Ghost, we can learn how best to further God's work in every season and circumstance, while maintaining family life as a central priority.

CONCLUSION

Our Heavenly Father's plan centers on families. "The Family: A Proclamation to the World" emphasizes the importance of eternal marriage and family relationships. In that inspired document, we can find the guidance we seek as we experience the grand prizes of mortality—our physical bodies, spiritual growth, and the opportunity to participate in a family that may be ours for eternity. In working through the challenges of our day and the challenges facing our individual families, we can "press forward with a steadfastness in Christ, having a perfect brightness of hope, and a love of God and of all men." We can seek the everlasting joy of exaltation with our families in the celestial kingdom of God. "Wherefore, if ye shall press forward, feasting upon the word of Christ, and endure to the end, behold, thus saith the Father: Ye shall have eternal life" (2 Nephi 31:20).

NOTES

1. First Presidency and Council of Twelve Apostles (1995, November), The family: A proclamation to the world, *Ensign*, 25(11), 102.

2. Gordon B. Hinckley (1991, May), What God hath joined together, *Ensign*, 21(5), 74.

3. First Presidency and Council of Twelve Apostles (1995), 102.

4. Merrill J. and Marilyn S. Bateman (2003, January 14), Mortality and our eternal journey; BYU Devotional Address; available at http://speeches.byu.edu

5. James E. Faust (2005, March 1), Where is the Church?; BYU Devotional Address; available at http://speeches.byu.edu

6. Neal A. Maxwell (1994, May), Take especial care of your family, *Ensign*, 24(5), 89.

7. First Presidency and Council of Twelve Apostles (1995), 102.

8. Ibid.

9. Ibid.

10. K. M. Harris, F. F. Furstenberg Jr., and J. K. Marmer (1998), Paternal involvement with adolescents in intact families: The influence of fathers over the life course, *Demography*, 35, 201–216; L. J. Waite and M. Gallagher (2000), *The Case for Marriage* (New York: Doubleday); see studies recently summarized in B. H. Maher, ed. (2004), *The Family Portrait: A Compilation of Data, Research and Public Opinion on the Family*, 2d ed. (Washington, D.C.: Family Research Council).

11. First Presidency and Council of Twelve Apostles (1995), 102.

12. Dallin H. Oaks (2000, November), The challenge to become, *Ensign*, 30(11), 33.

13. Henry B. Eyring (1998, February), The Family, *Ensign*, 28(2), 10, 15.

14. See A. Theodore Tuttle (1969, December), *Improvement Era*, 107; as quoted in D. K. Judd, G. L. Dorius, and D. C. Dollahite (2000), Families and the great plan of happiness, in D. C. Dollahite, ed., *Strengthening Our Families: An In-Depth Look at the Proclamation on the Family* (Salt Lake City: Bookcraft), 11. Elder Tuttle stated: "The family is the most important relationship in this life. . . . This is the one eternal unit which can exist in the presence of God."

15. Bateman (2003).

16. Dallin H. Oaks (1995, January 17), Adversity; BYU Devotional Address; available at http://speeches.byu.edu

17. Richard C. Edgley (2002, May) For thy good, *Ensign*, 22(5), 65.

18. Hinckley (1991), 73, 74.

19. Ibid, 74.

20. First Presidency and Council of Twelve Apostles (1995), 102.

21. Neal A. Maxwell (2002, November), Encircled in the arms of His love, *Ensign*, 32(11), 18.

22. Gordon B. Hinckley (2004, January 10), Standing strong and immovable; address delivered in a Worldwide Leadership Training Meeting (Salt Lake City: The Church of Jesus Christ of Latter-day Saints), 20.

23. James E. Faust (2004, January 10), Challenges facing the family; address delivered in a Worldwide Leadership Training Meeting (Salt Lake City: The Church of Jesus Christ of Latter-day Saints), 1.

24. Quoted in T. Walch (2004, April 3), Expo offers advice on raising kids, *Deseret Morning News*, B5.

25. Faust (2004), 2–3.

26. Hinckley (1991), 72.

27. C. J. Williams, ed. (1984), *The Teachings of Lorenzo Snow* (Salt Lake City: Bookcraft), 92–93.

28. Neal A. Maxwell (1999), *All These Things Shall Give Thee Experience* (Salt Lake City: Bookcraft; reprint), 93.

29. M. Russell Ballard (1995, May), Answers to life's questions, *Ensign*, 25(5), 22.

30. Elder Robert D. Hales gave specific advice for bishops in preserving their family time: "I promise if you will put your wife and your family first, you will not only be a better husband and father, you will become a better bishop." He also counseled those in leadership positions: "Generally, do not spend more than two

nights a week away from your home on your calling—and one of those evenings should be spent visiting in the homes of the members. Tell your family in advance when you will be home, and keep your word no matter what—so that your car will drive into the driveway at the time you have said you would be there. . . . Spend time each week with your wife and with each of your children." Robert D. Hales (2003, June 21), The calling and responsibilities of a bishop; address delivered at a Worldwide Leadership Training Meeting (Salt Lake City: The Church of Jesus Christ of Latter-day Saints), 10.

31. Boyd K. Packer (1998, November), Parents in Zion, *Ensign, 28*(11), 23. President Packer also cautioned: "Remember, when you schedule a youngster, you schedule a family—particularly the mother."

32. Packer (1998), 23. Some examples of involving family members in callings include using a family council to discuss ways family members can support each other in their Church responsibilities. On traveling assignments, take an older child along and use the travel time as special one-on-one time together. In a family with teenaged children, spend time in family home evenings doing Young Women and Scouting or Duty to God requirements together.

33. M. Russell Ballard (1987, May), Keeping life's demands in balance, *Ensign, 17*(5), 16.

34. B. L. Top (2005, April), A balanced life, *Ensign, 35*(4), 28.

35. President Hinckley specifically counseled priesthood holders regarding the order of their priorities: "Each of us has a fourfold responsibility. First, we have a responsibility to our families. Second, we have a responsibility to our employers. Third, we have a responsibility to the Lord's work. Fourth, we have a responsibility to ourselves." Excellent counsel on how to balance these important priorities is offered. See Gordon B. Hinckley (2003, June 21), Rejoicing in the privilege to serve; address delivered in a Worldwide Leadership Training Meeting (Salt Lake City: The Church of Jesus Christ of Latter-day Saints), 22.

36. Dallin H. Oaks (1989, June), Family history: In wisdom and order, *Ensign, 19*(6), 7.

37. Ibid.

38. Neal A. Maxwell (1993, August 25), Wisdom and order; addresses delivered at the 1993 Annual University Conference; in Neal A. Maxwell (2004), *The Inexhaustible Gospel* (Provo, UT: Brigham Young University), 228–229.

CHAPTER 2

STANDING IN HOLY PLACES—
AS INDIVIDUALS AND FAMILIES

ROBERT L. MILLET

We are responsible for the home we build. We must build wisely,
for eternity is not a short voyage. . . . The thoughts we think, the deeds we do, the lives we live influence
not only the success of our earthly journey; they mark the way to our eternal goals.[1]
—*President Thomas S. Monson*

I like to think of the home as a sanctuary. A sanctuary is a holy place, a place where sacred things are felt and experienced—a place where men, women, and children are linked to the divine and thus reacquainted with those tender and sweet associations we once knew. A sanctuary is also a defense, a refuge, a covert from the storms that descend upon all of us, whether in the form of temptation or false and degrading beliefs and practices. The disciples of Christ are commanded to "stand . . . in holy places, and be not moved, until the day of the Lord come; for behold, it cometh quickly, saith the Lord" (D&C 87:8; see also 45:32).

FOUNDATIONAL TRUTHS

God lives, He listens, and He longs for us to live in such a manner as to gain peace and happiness, both individually and as families. He has a plan for His sons and daughters. Life is meant to be lived in harmony with that divine system of salvation. Misery and unhappiness are the inevitable results of seeking to do things in our own way. Jesus of Nazareth is the Son of God, the Savior and Redeemer of humankind, the One sent of the Father to "bind up the broken-hearted" and liberate the captives (Isaiah 61:1). That upon which Christ places His hand, whether a distraught individual or a dysfunctional family, is healed and re-created.

From the beginning, Satan and his minions have sought to "deceive and to blind" men and women, "to lead them captive at his will, even as many as would not hearken" unto the voice of God (Moses 4:4). In the words of Elder Dallin H. Oaks:

Satan's most strenuous opposition is directed at whatever is most important to the Father's plan. Satan seeks to discredit the Savior and divine authority, to nullify the effects of the Atonement, to counterfeit revelation, to lead people away from the truth, to contradict individual accountability, to confuse gender, to undermine marriage, and to discourage childbearing (especially by parents who will raise children in righteousness).[2]

These truths about God, Satan, Jesus Christ, and our eternal nature are fundamental. They are essential to understanding individuals and families. They should be basic to any efforts to rectify the wrongs of society and minister to the wounded and scarred souls all about us. We ignore them at our peril. Most of our efforts to deal with social-emotional problems, to provide therapeutic remediation—independent of those absolute truths—will be at best deficient. I agree with C. S. Lewis, who observed that once we begin to mature spiritually, we realize that everything that really needs to be done in our souls can be done only by God.[3] Elder Jeffrey R. Holland, as a member of the Seventy, said:

We need to turn to God. We need to reaffirm our faith, and we need to reassert our hope. Where necessary we need to repent, and certainly we need to pray. It is the absence of spiritual fidelity that has led us to moral disarray in the twilight of the twentieth century. We have sown the wind of religious skepticism, and we are reaping the whirlwind of existential despair.

Without our religious faith, without recognizing the reality and necessity of spiritual life, the world makes no sense, and a nonsense world is a place of horror. Only if the world has meaning at a spiritual level is it possible for human beings to keep going, to keep trying.[4]

To teach and practice solely according to the teachings of men, without the clarifying and illuminating lenses of the Restoration, is to live beneath our privileges and to wander at dusk when we could walk in the light of the noonday sun (D&C 95:6).

THE STORMS THAT RAGE

Every person, every marriage, and every family builds a house of faith. We do so knowingly or unknowingly. And every builder soon learns that a good building with a bad foundation is worse than useless; it is dangerous. There are certain ideologies, certain trends in our society to which I feel the doors of our hearts and our homes must be forever closed if we expect to enjoy the approbation of heaven.

1. *An obsession with self.* Everyone wants to be at peace, to feel good inside, to have a positive outlook on life. Everyone wants to find contentment in his or her labors and a feeling of satisfaction in accomplishments. But there are limits here; we can become obsessed with *me, my* will, *my* wishes, *my* happiness, and *my* well-being.

We live in a day when the religious solutions to problems and questions, if they are given any credence at all, are among the least and last considered. We are reminded continually of what a tense and stress-filled world we live in. The complexity of life and the competition to not only stay afloat but also get ahead have resulted in a host of psychophysiological disorders, maladies that would have been unknown to our forebears. Many people preoccupy themselves needlessly with self-inspections; they are compulsively taking their own emotional or spiritual temperatures to assure that they are happy or stable or "together" or worthy. Others spend a lifetime (and too often a fortune) seeking to love themselves or to "find themselves."

2. *False teachings about men and women.* Over the last four decades, we have observed widespread consideration of ideas and worldviews that are destructive of individuals and families. Many men, for example, have been told that they must be stoic, stern, and macho. They have been instructed to guard their feelings, hide their emotions, and maintain a cool exterior. Some have imbibed the poisonous notion that the great indicator of success in life is to be found outside the home, to be ascertained in terms of portfolios, chrome, real estate, business contacts, or academic degrees. Some have become so ensnared by their work—that which is intended, at best, to be a means to an end—that they have abrogated their responsibilities toward home and children.

Some have given way to carnal urges, learned to re-label sin as psychology, and tragically surrendered to that excuse we have come to know as the "midlife crisis." Far too many men in the Church have missed the mark in leading their families, have taken license from what they would call the patriarchal order of government, and have become tyrannical and dictatorial in their leadership of the home. Truly, the vicious but versatile father of lies rages in the hearts of some while he pacifies others (see 2 Nephi 28:20–21).

There can be no question but that women have been the object of abuse and indignity for centuries and that even today many women—in and out of the Church—live under circumstances that range from the uncomfortable to the intolerable. Men have too often been cruel and uncaring, insensitive to women—their needs, their desires, and their voices. In that sense, women must make the effort to reassert their value and their critical place in society. Sadly, however, many women have turned to brands of radical feminism that have brought more heartache than help. One woman wrote:

> Being "just a housewife" still gets you no respect, especially from [radical] feminists. . . . For a movement dedicated so stridently to choice, they are remarkably selective in the choices they are willing to allow other women to make. . . . You cannot declare the primary work of most women throughout most of history to be beneath serious consideration without sending women the covert message that it is really women who are beneath serious consideration.[5]

In general we could say that men and women, in and out of the Church, have been taunted by and titillated with views concerning man, woman, priesthood, and family that are at odds with the revealed word and thus with "things as they really are, and . . . as they really will be" (Jacob 4:13). Confusion and conflict have ensued, and a few have forsaken the faith because they chose to give heed to seductive voices. No person who revolts against the divinely established role and calling he or she was given before the foundations of this earth were laid can be happy or find real fulfillment, not here or in eternity.

3. *An erosion of moral absolutes.* One Christian writer has observed: "If the stability of buildings depends largely upon their foundations, so does the stability of human lives. The search for personal security is a primal instinct, but many fail to find it today. Old familiar landmarks are being obliterated. Moral absolutes which were once thought to be eternal are being abandoned."[6] In recent years we have sown the wind and now reap the whirlwind as far as standards of behavior are concerned. People clamor for rights and recognition in society while few speak of our moral responsibilities to society. We permit and even promote lewdness and perversion in the name of openness and acceptance.

The erosion of moral absolutes is highly correlated with what we consume in terms of literature, movies, music, and entertainment of many kinds. Young people in our day need not search out alleys and backstreets to become involved in the lurid and the obscene; they need only pay the box office price, flip the television channel, or rent the DVD. As movie critic Michael Medved has written, "Hollywood's crisis is, at its very core, a crisis of values. It's not 'mediocrity and escapism' that leave audiences cold, but sleaze and self-indulgence. . . . Hollywood no longer reflects—or even respects—the values of most American families. On many of the important issues in contemporary life, popular entertainment seems to go out of its way to challenge conventional notions of decency."[7]

4. *A failure to hearken to prophetic counsel.* Too often the Saints have treated lightly prophetic counsel on how to solve social and emotional problems, as well as how to strengthen marriages and families. Sometimes we have not prepared ourselves to be taught by the Lord through His servants. And sometimes, sadly, we ignore or reject the living oracles because their instruction comes in conflict with our own training, background, or orientation. This is perilous. It places us in a position to lose light and deny ourselves and those we serve consummate spiritual privileges. To the Prophet Joseph Smith, the Lord said: "And all they who receive the oracles of God, let them beware how they hold them lest they are accounted as a light thing, and are brought under condemnation thereby, and stumble and fall when the storms descend, and the winds blow, and the rains descend, and beat upon their house" (D&C 90:5).

Among the most important prophetic counsel given to address the unique challenges and temptations in our time is "The Family: A Proclamation to the World."[8] As with all prophetic principles, doctrines from the family proclamation must not remain on the printed page but must be written on the "fleshy tables" of our hearts and homes (see 2 Corinthians 3:3).

A SURE FOUNDATION

Most of the answers to life's most troublesome questions are simpler than we think. These answers call for a retrenchment, a return to our spiritual and moral moorings, a return to virtue, a return to the faith of our fathers and mothers. Here I suggest some simple principles of truth and righteousness upon which we must build our lives if we are to stand in holy places and be not moved.

1. *Losing ourselves.* "I receive not honour from men," Jesus said (John 5:41). Jesus' sense of personal worth seemed to be inextricably tied to His commitment to His mission and His complete submission to the will of His Father. In the self-centered culture that surrounds us, we must follow the example of the Savior and lose ourselves in service to our family members—our husband or wife, mother and father, sons and daughters, sisters and brothers. Jesus went about doing good. His eye was single to the glory of God (see John 5:30; 6:38; 7:16; 8:29; 10:30). His compassion for others often overrode His personal desires. We must go about doing good to the members of our near and extended families and to other families in our stewardship and influence.

As President Ezra Taft Benson explained, "a wholesome view" of self "is best established by a close relationship with God."[9] Surely a more significant undertaking than discovering ourselves is coming to know God and gaining His approval. We can feel and become all that we were intended to feel and be, but it will come about in the Lord's own way, through laboring in His cause, serving others, and seeking through Him to become a "new creature" in Christ (see 2 Corinthians 5:17). The Savior's commission to "love thy neighbour as thyself" (Matthew 19:19) has little to do with loving oneself; it has much to do with loving others as one would desire to be loved, to fulfill the Golden Rule (see Matthew 7:12; 3 Nephi 14:12).

2. *Accepting absolute truths.* While in the "true and living church" (D&C 1:30) specific policies or programs may change from time to time, certain truths and practices are set, fixed, and immutable. They may not be altered by time or opinion. They are eternal absolutes. Without absolute truths, without set and established principles and practices within our personal and social experience, life would have little meaning, and, in fact, there would be few things on which we could depend with certainty. President Rex E. Lee explained to BYU students that "there is nothing more important for each of you to do than build a firm, personal testimony that there are in this life some absolutes, things that never change, regardless of time, place, or circumstances. They are eternal truths, eternal principles—and . . . they are and will be the same yesterday, today, and forever."[10]

No matter the regularity of society's chants or the decibels of special interest groups' demands, some things are forever proper and right, and some things are eternally wrong. Popular vote or consensus is not the means of ascertaining truth. We turn instead to the scriptures, to revelation, to those called and anointed to make known to the Church and the world the mind and voice and will of the Lord. President Spencer W. Kimball testified: "The world may have its norm; the Church has a different one. . . . The world may countenance premarital sex experiences, but the Lord and his church condemn in no uncertain terms any and every sex relationship outside of marriage."[11]

3. *Receiving the Lord's servants.* There is a power associated with loyalty to the Lord's anointed servants. God has called and empowered prophets to lead us, revelators to dispense saving truths, and seers to discern and prepare us for the challenges and storms that are on the horizon. Those we sustain as seers are endowed with divine power to see things "afar off" (D&C 101:54), things that are "not visible to the natural eye" (Moses 6:36).

Threats to marriages and family, threats to the stability of personal life and society, threats to the foundations of our nation and world—these are the things an omniscient God makes known to His chosen servants, almost always many years before the storm arrives. For example, the family home evening program was revealed in the early part of the twentieth century, long before the attacks on family life and family time that have so devastated contemporary families. The wisest among us learn to prepare ourselves and our homes against the stormy assault when things are calm and dry and sunny. Acceptance of the Lord's servants is a sure sign of the depth of our commitment to the Lord and His plan; as President Harold B. Lee testified so often, you are not fully converted until "you see the power of God resting upon the leaders of this Church and that testimony goes down into your heart like fire."[12]

CONCLUSION

It has occurred to me many times that one of the most important gifts to be sought for and acquired in this complex age is the gift of discernment—not only the capacity to distinguish good from evil, as important as that is, but also the ability to discern what matters from what doesn't matter quite so much. I shudder at the possibility that I might finish my life and then have the Lord explain to me that I had spent my time laboring largely in secondary causes. Marriage and family responsibilities are primary causes that should occupy much of our spiritual attention, much of our time and energy. Nothing is more important here or hereafter than marriage and family life. The devil doesn't need to persuade us to steal or lie or commit adultery. You and I need merely undersell, understate, and thus underestimate the powers, appropriateness, and relevance of the gospel, the importance of marriage and family. The devil wins when we stand idly by, choosing to not get involved in making a worthwhile difference for marriage and family life—our own and others'.

I reaffirm that the hope of the world lies in the person and powers of Jesus Christ, who is the Hope of the Ages. He is the "Wonderful Counsellor."[13] There are, as latter-day prophets have declared, many tight places through which the people of the covenant will be required to pass in the days ahead. Peace and protection and progress will be ours as we stand in holy places as individuals and families, as we learn to be selective, as we sift and sort through the sordid and even the subsidiary. Some things simply matter more than others. The family is the most important unit in time and in eternity, and the home is the most sacred of all the holy places in which we are privileged to stand. Of this eternal institution, the Lord might well say, as He did to Moses: "Put off thy shoes from off thy feet, for the place whereon thou standest is holy ground" (Exodus 3:5).

ABOUT THE AUTHOR

Robert L. Millet is Richard L. Evans Professor of Religious Understanding and former dean of Religious Education at Brigham Young University. He and his wife, Shauna, are the parents of six children and the grandparents of five.

ADDITIONAL READING

Bruce C. Hafen and Marie K. Hafen (1994), *The Belonging Heart: The Atonement and Relationships with God and Family* (Salt Lake City: Deseret Book).

Jeffrey R. Holland (1993, November), Look to God and live, *Ensign, 23*(11), 13–15.

Dallin H. Oaks (1991), *The Lord's Way* (Salt Lake City: Deseret Book).

NOTES

Adapted from an address delivered at the BYU Family Expo, Brigham Young University, Provo, Utah, 4 April 1994. The full version of this address is printed in Robert L. Millet (2000), *Selected Writings of Robert L. Millet* (Salt Lake City: Deseret Book), 296–310.

1. Thomas S. Monson (2001, October), Hallmarks of a happy home, *Ensign, 31*(10), 3.

2. Dallin H. Oaks (1993, November), The great plan of happiness, *Ensign, 23*(11), 72.

3. See C. S. Lewis (1952), *Mere Christianity* (New York: Macmillan), 141.

4. Jeffrey R. Holland (1993, November), Look to God and live, *Ensign, 23*(11), 13–14.

5. O. Papazoglou (1992, January), Despising our mothers, despising ourselves, *First Things, 19*, 18–19.

6. J. Stott (1991), *Life in Christ* (Wheaton, IL: Tyndale House), 22.

7. M. Medved (1992), *Hollywood vs. America* (New York: HarperCollins), 10.

8. First Presidency and Council of Twelve Apostles (1995, November), The family: A proclamation to the world, *Ensign, 25*(11), 102.

9. Ezra Taft Benson (1986, May), Cleansing the inner vessel, *Ensign, 16*(5), 6.

10. Rex E. Lee (1992, January 14), Things that change, and things that don't; BYU Devotional Address; in *BYU 1991–92 Fireside and Devotional Speeches* (Provo: Brigham Young University Publications), 54; available at http://speeches.byu.edu

11. Spencer W. Kimball (1977), *Faith Precedes the Miracle* (Salt Lake City: Deseret Book), 175.

12. Harold B. Lee (1973, September 11), Be loyal to the royal within you; BYU Devotional Address; in *Speeches 1973* (Provo: Brigham Young University Publications), 90; available at http://speeches.byu.edu

13. D. W. Parry, J. A. Parry, and T. M. Peterson (1998), *Understanding Isaiah* (Salt Lake City: Deseret Book), 96; "Wonderful Counsellor" is an interpretation of Isaiah 9:6 ("and his name shall be called Wonderful, Counsellor . . .") based on the Hebrew reading of those words.

The Family and the Kitchen Sink

The Jeff and Juanita Hill Family

Most of what we say and do while washing the dishes is not particularly meaningful or bonding. At cleanup time our kitchen is filled with short utterances by children who would rather be somewhere else. Listen in: "I get to rinse!" "Throw me the rag!" "Where's Seth?" "Would you *please* get in here and work?!" "Who forgot to start the dishwasher?!" "Amanda's supposed to do that!" "Not me!"

However, the kitchen sink is a rendezvous place for our family to do something productive nearly every day. In fact, mealtime and cleanup afterwards are probably the most frequent activities that we share together as a whole family. It's also true that though we've sometimes struggled with the routine, the dishes have helped us to tell stories, have fun, develop talents, work together, sacrifice, discuss meaningful questions, and deal with challenges. Actually, many family members will admit it's sometimes quite pleasant to do the dishes. And every once in a while we experience something profound.

What We've Learned from the Kitchen Sink

In the beginning Mom did all the dishes. She didn't like that. And in an epoch before any child now living at home can remember, she created The Ten Minutes. This means that after meals everybody has to help do the dishes, clean the kitchen, and straighten the living room. It doesn't matter if you want to do it or not, you just do it. Everyone helps. The reason it's called The Ten Minutes is that we used to work as fast as we could, and if we finished the dishes in less than ten minutes, Mom and Dad would put 50 cents in the Disneyland fund jar. The oldest kids remember actually going to Disneyland, but that was a long time ago. For this essay Dad talked to all the family members about their thoughts, then

arranged those thoughts to show the benefits of family work.

The kitchen sink creates a regular place and time for family storytelling. Abby (20) remembers, "We like to kid Mom about the time we discovered a royal mess in the kitchen cupboard. There was a half a gallon of ice cream melted all over everything. Yuck! When we asked who would do such a silly thing, Mom got this sheepish look on her face and confessed. She had been snitching a treat while reading her book earlier that afternoon and we kids burst unexpectedly through the door from school. Not wanting to be caught in the act, she had thrown the carton of ice cream in the cupboard and promptly forgot about it. We laughed and laughed about it then, and we've laughed about it many, many times since. Mom still gets the same sheepish grin every time we tell the story."

Doing dishes can be wholesome recreation. Seth (7) describes what he likes about doing the dishes: "Dad does something kind of fun. If you have to wipe off the table he yells at you, 'High Low?! Fast Slow?!' He means: 'How do you want the dish rag?' I always say, 'High Fast,' and he throws the rag so high and so fast! Man, you have to jump so good to get it. When I miss it, I throw it back and he throws it at me again. Sometimes it gets me all wet Then I hit him and get him wet That's the funnest!"

The Ten Minutes helps us develop our talents. The dishes have helped our family learn to sing better. We sing hymns, Primary songs, show tunes, nonsense songs, everything. Both Emily (15) and Jeff (24) credit some of their love for playing the piano to The Ten Minutes. Jeffrey explains, "If we went in the living room and played Church hymns on the piano, we were excused from the kitchen. I didn't especially enjoy playing the piano, but I enjoyed doing the dishes even less. So The Ten Minutes provided me many hours of practice time on the piano. As I grew, I learned to love playing the piano." Emily agrees, "Now I like to play the piano for hours every day."

The Ten Minutes teaches us to work together respectfully. Aaron (22) reminds us that through the years there were many modes of operation for doing the dishes, such as working together at breakneck speed for ten minutes, completing one task and then being excused, or dividing into teams. Hannah (17) and Emily think the family learned how to deal with disagreements by deciding together which of these strategies to use.

> *Hannah:* Dad felt strongly we should just happily work together until the dishes were all done, no matter how long it took, and no matter how hard anyone worked. But I wanted to have my job, get it done, and get out of there.
> *Emily:* It wasn't fair for me to have to wait for those who weren't working. I have better things to do with my time than do the dishes.
> *Hannah:* So we talked about it and worked it out. Everyone in the family got a day to be in charge. On Dad's day we could do it his way, and on our days we could do it our way. We're all happy with this, at least most of the time.

The Ten Minutes teaches us that no one is too young to help. Mom remembers, "We were so excited when our first two-year old, Sarah, learned to empty the dishwasher. She considered it great fun, and we enjoyed her antics. We now have a grandson, Jeffrey, who just turned one. His dad proudly announced that he is already unloading the silverware for them. Though we've seen how little Jeffrey does it. Most of the silverware ends up on the floor."

The kitchen sink teaches us to sacrifice. Hannah stated, "I learned there are things that you don't want to do, that you just have to do. You can choose to fight and complain, or you can choose to be happy."

The kitchen sink teaches us that many hands make light work. Sarah (26) remembers the first time Mom and Dad left her with the children overnight. "I thought it would be great not to do The Ten Minutes. Then it was late at night and I had to do all the dishes by myself. It took *forever.* I appreciated The Ten Minutes much more."

The Ten Minutes provides the setting for discussing meaningful questions. There was the poignant time Amanda (12) found out her kitten had died. We discussed the important question, "Is there an afterlife for cats?" Dad remembers, "Another important question we have discussed at the kitchen sink is, 'What is a date, really?' My daughters seem to think a date is

when a guy comes over all dressed up and takes you to the prom or something. I think a date is anytime you participate in any social activity with a specific member of the opposite sex. We have talked and talked about this." Mom remembers, "A couple of days ago Abby and I were left to finish the dishes. We talked about what marriage is like. It gave me a chance to tell her that marriage can be really hard, and that you have to work every day at it if you want to be happy."

Amanda recalls personal time with her mom: "I remember I would often be standing alone with Mom at the sink doing breakfast dishes after everybody else had left for school or work. Most of the time I complained to myself, 'Why do I have to do this?' But sometimes I thought it was neat to talk alone with Mom."

The kitchen sink helps us process big family challenges. The Ten Minutes has been a stabilizing influence in our family lately. Dad remembers, "A few years ago Juanita was diagnosed with a serious cancer. We've had to deal with difficult medical treatments, extraordinary fears, and a host of challenges. All these astonishing changes threatened to disorient our family. But the dishes were still there, just like they always had been. Every evening our family still gathered around the kitchen sink as The Ten Minutes called to us. As we engaged in this comfortable routine, we could leave our worries behind and find comfort in just being together doing something. It helped us feel that God was still in His heaven and still cared for us."

Conclusion

For most of our family members, most of the time, doing the dishes is simply that—doing the dishes. But the kitchen sink has provided a setting for some meaningful conversations and treasured experiences. These simple routines have created memories, built family bonds, and taught us to work together. We have learned to tell stories, have fun, develop talents, sacrifice, and deal with challenges. Though most of what we do around the kitchen sink is mundane, the sum of it all has provided a powerful context for connection.

ABOUT THE AUTHORS

The Jeff and Juanita Hill family consists of fifteen souls living in Orem and Provo, Utah; Seattle, Washington; and heaven—Jeff (Dad), Juanita (Mom), Aaron (22), Abby (20), Hannah (17),

Emily (15), Amanda (12), Seth (7) Away: Sarah (26) and Joel with Eva (1); Jeff (24) and Jenny with Jeffrey (1); Heidi (in heaven). Together they enjoy walking, talking, reading, eating, hiking, biking, playing, praying, laughing, camping, jogging, Frisbee, mountains, Maui, beaches, picnics, and Liverpool rummy. And sometimes they enjoy doing the dishes together.

Juanita passed away on April 21, 2005. Now as we do dishes together, she feels ever so close. We can still hear her voice encouraging us as we do The Ten Minutes. In this way, every day, she is with us.

ADDITIONAL READING

Kathleen Slaugh Bahr, et al. (2000), The meaning and blessings of family work; in David C. Dollahite, ed., *Strengthening Our Families: An In-Depth Look at the Proclamation on the Family* (Salt Lake City: Bookcraft), 177–189.

Kathleen Slaugh Bahr (2001), The sacred nature of everyday work, *Meridian Magazine;* available at http://www.meridian magazine.com.

Orson Scott Card (1978, August), The elbow-grease factor: How to teach your children to love work, *Ensign, 8*(8), 60–63.

E. Jeffrey Hill (1998, July), Doing dishes with Daddy, *Ensign, 28*(7), 24–25.

Melanie Silvester (2003, February), The day the dishwasher broke, *Ensign, 33*(2), 18–19.

E S S A Y   A 2

A KEY TO SIMPLICITY IN FAMILY LIFE

MARY K. DOLLAHITE

The clarity of the air after rain. Or a deep sense of peace and security. That's what simplicity feels like to me.

With ten people under the Dollahite roof—a retired grandpa, a university professor, a homemaker, a college student, a high school senior, a sophomore, an eighth-grader, a fourth-grader, a home-schooled first-grader, and a preschooler—a lot of our time and energy is spent cooking, cleaning, and coordinating schedules. I asked in family home evening the other day how we were doing, managing a busy family. The teenaged girls answered, "What? Isn't chaos normal!?" The boys thought life was fine. The three-year-old was focused on balancing chess pieces on top of one another.

I hear a lot of advice for handling the natural chaos of everyday family life. "Expert" voices advise us on time management, house organization, child discipline and education, and on spousal and parent-child relationships. My testimony of the eternal nature of family leads me to believe that there is a way to simplify family life and to feel joy in the daily effort of the balancing act—an act as seemingly impossible as standing one chess piece on another.

A DIVINE MODEL

Of course, keeping the commandments is the preliminary step to simplicity in family life. Given that, we are then prepared to learn through the prophets and in the temple that we are God's children and that this earth was created for us to learn to be more like He is. He teaches us that it is important for us to have choices, to learn accountability, and to exercise our agency wisely. As our Father, He teaches us how to be a family. He helps us make and keep covenants that will build and bind our families into the eternities. When we bring the principles and inspiration of the temple home and follow the Lord's eternal pattern for families as revealed in the proclamation, clarity and simplicity begin to emerge in an otherwise complex and temporal family life.

Principle 1: Require a recommend. The temple recommend can be viewed as a teaching tool in defining what influences do and do not belong in the temple. In a similar way, a "home recommend" can guide the family as to what does and does not belong in the family home. Reducing and eliminating extraneous "stuff" (i.e., excessive belongings, clutter, overcommitments, and unnecessary activities) goes a long way in simplifying family life. Focus will return and remain on what's most important: family relationships.

The first part of simplifying the home could be establishing guidelines to distinguish between good and bad. In our homes, we want to minimize dealing with the effects of the bad. When our oldest was three years old she came in from the playground with a new word. When I asked her what it meant, she said she didn't know. When I explained the meaning of the word to her, she said she didn't need that word. Watching our use of the "S" word (*stupid*) or the "D" word (*dumb*) reduces contention, stress, and disciplining time in our family.

A second part of simplifying emphasizes finding satisfaction when we have enough for our needs, so that instead of striving for more possessions, we have more energy and time for family. "Wherefore, do not spend money for that which is of no worth, nor your labor for that which cannot satisfy" (2 Nephi 9:51). My mother taught me a way to recognize that I am satisfied with the possessions we already have. When I go shopping, I put what I think I need or want in my shopping cart. I "own" it for several minutes. Then, if I think we still want to trade family money for it, give space to it, and budget family time to take care of it, I'll buy it. Often, owning the thing for a few minutes is enough. We like "things," but we're realizing that more than things, we'd rather have more time and shared experiences with each other.

A third part of simplifying helps us make the decisions between two or more good choices, choosing activities that will bring more joy to our families. We know that Adam and Eve, the first family, made a hard choice: "Adam fell that man might be; and men are, that they might have joy" (2 Nephi 2:25). Most often, scheduling conflicts are between seemingly small, everyday activities, such as when our fun-loving second daughter willingly postpones an activity with friends to be home when we need to be away with another child, or when Dad chooses to coach the nine-year-old's basketball game instead of attending a Saturday professional meeting.

Principle 2: Design a family plan. The Father's plan of happiness as experienced in the temple and expressed in the proclamation has a clear and positive goal: to help us return to His presence as eternal families. If we don't have a plan, then others outside our home will have plenty of plans for us. Having clear and positive plans in our earthly families can simplify family life by helping us focus our family time and resources with confidence.

In our home we've witnessed the peace and sense of security of knowing what we're going to study in family home evening. Part of our family plan is to take the thirteen months before each child's baptism to study each of the thirteen Articles of Faith. We thought we'd hear "I'm bored" and "I know this already" comments from older kids by the fourth and fifth times around. But now that we're starting on our sixth thirteen-month series, we find family blessings we hadn't anticipated. For example, we hear our older children looking forward to the next series, anticipating the discussions with confidence, asking new questions pertinent to their present ages and experiences, and sharing with their soon-to-be-baptized sibling their own testimony and faith-building experiences.

Principle 3: Teach accountability. In the temple I see the principle of accountability taught over and over. I understand how requiring a "home recommend" and having a plan would simplify family life. Now I ask why the Father, who teaches about families and makes the way home clear, emphasizes accountability as we complete divinely ordained assignments.

The Lord established the teaching pattern: "For he will give unto the faithful line upon line, precept upon precept; and I will try you and prove you herewith" (D&C 98:12). As part of the proving, "It is required of the Lord, at the hand of every steward, to render an account of his stewardship, both in time and in eternity" (D&C 72:3). On reflection, I realize that when I learn "line upon line" and know I'm going to be held accountable, I stay more focused. When I turn around and teach "line upon line," I am more confident and don't try to teach everything all at once.

Right now our first-grader is learning to read. He is literally learning to read line by line. Each day he learns a few new words. I confirm for him which words he knows and then help him with hard ones he doesn't understand or has forgotten. Some days he's happy just to be done; other days his joy is focused on the "well done" from me. As he looks to me, I take the opportunity to let him know that I think he's doing well, and that I'm on his side cheering for him.

We have opportunities every day to practice reporting on our stewardships, such as during family home evening, family mealtimes, and during bedtime stories and late-night teenager chats. Rather than just "Did you have a good time?" we try to ask "What did you learn?" and "How did the activity go compared to how you planned?" When we practice our parental listening side of the principle and look for times to express love, we see our children grow in responsibility and confidence, and family life goes more smoothly.

CONCLUSION

Creating simplicity in family life is not easy. We live in a world full of sound, color, and activity, both in and out of the home, and in a material world where the focus is on individuals, not families. Our efforts to "declutter" before some object or thought even crosses our threshold, to establish and enjoy the strength of a family plan, and to forge generational connections through trust earned by lovingly teaching accountability will allow us to focus more on our family and our eternal relationships.

I'm grateful that I am a child of God. I'm grateful that as His child I can learn more from Him about how to be a family. One of my hopes in patterning family life on the principles we learn from the prophets and in the temple is that when our children enter the Lord's sacred house, they will feel like they're coming home.

I joy in knowing that family life has a divine purpose, that there is a divine pattern, and that the balancing act is possible.

ABOUT THE AUTHOR

Mary K. Dollahite earned a B.A. and JD from BYU. When she's not attempting to declutter the house and schedules, you'll find her talking with teenaged girls, reading to Primary-aged boys, listening to her husband's storytelling, or taking family photographs.

ADDITIONAL READING

William R. Bradford (1992, May), Unclutter your life, *Ensign*, 22(5), 27–29.

Jack D. Brotherson and Sean E. Brotherson (2000), Temple covenants and family relationships; in David C. Dollahite, ed., *Strengthening Our Families: An In-Depth Look at the Proclamation on the Family* (Salt Lake City: Bookcraft), 251–252.

Kathleen H. Hughes (2004, November), Out of small things, *Ensign, 34*(11), 109–111.

Kristine Manwaring (2000), My home as a temple; in David C. Dollahite, ed., *Strengthening Our Families: An In-Depth Look at the Proclamation on the Family* (Salt Lake City: Bookcraft), 94–96.

E S S A Y   A 3

BALANCED GOSPEL LIVING

LISA BOLIN HAWKINS

We have been asked to do many things as members of The Church of Jesus Christ of Latter-day Saints: pray, study the scriptures, attend the temple, serve in callings, work on family history, engage in provident living, be missionaries, beautify our homes, become educated and skilled, take good care of our bodies, enhance our marriages, rear righteous children, serve "as witnesses of God at all times" (Mosiah 18:9), and "do many good things of [our] own free will" (D&C 58:27).

I've probably left out some things. When you consider the reward for working on these opportunities—eternal life with our Father in Heaven—you may long to do everything right now. However, God has also revealed that we are not required to run faster

than we have strength (Mosiah 4:27). That's a lesson I learned when I was younger.

When I was baptized at age 17, I wanted to thank the Lord by doing everything I could to build up the kingdom. Because (obviously) the entire planetary population hadn't joined the Church because they just didn't know about it yet, I sent referral cards to the missionaries for everyone I knew, including immediate and extended family. No one joined the Church. I don't think I did any harm, but I had become a bit of a fanatic. I was running (trying to convert the world) faster than I had strength (knowledge of effective missionary work).

We need to avoid fanaticism and take a balanced approach, using effective means to fulfill the requirements of gospel living. As you look at the list in the first paragraph of this essay, you may see or add your favorite gospel requirement. My personal favorite is family history work. And yet the Lord might be displeased if I spent time, money, or took advantage of others to search for the dead at the expense of my responsibilities to the living. If a child is sick, or I've promised to take a meal to a neighbor family, or my husband wants to talk, no one—not the child, the family, my husband, or my ancestors—will accept the excuse that I was spending time with Richard, Duke of Burgundy, instead.

Testimonies can be undermined when people don't keep their promises, especially if they use one responsibility to avoid another. We can't use the gospel as an excuse to ignore our stewardships. The following excuses could hurt someone's testimony: "Sorry I didn't do the laundry; I was praying." "Get someone else to help with your homework; I'm reading the scriptures." "I know she has a cold—she'll be okay in the nursery; that's probably where she got it. I have a lesson to teach and if you stay home from church with her, you'll miss the sacrament." This type of selfish spirituality is a form of hypocrisy.

Occasionally, in times of trial or confusion or joy, the Holy Spirit may prompt us to spend more time in prayer, scripture study, and service. But the Lord doesn't take over the other things we need to do. If I thought that God would watch my young children while I did my visiting teaching, that could lead to tragedy. Miracles happen, but not on demand. The old excuse, "the dog ate my homework," is more believable than "I thought God would do my homework." Using our righteousness as a shield to avoid our responsibilities can hurt us and others.

We can also unwisely use our gospel opportunities as swords when we call people to lopsided battles. As we march in defense or pursuit of some gospel principle, it's possible to cut other principles out of our lives or make them too complicated. The Prophet Jacob called this "looking beyond the mark" and testified that true prophets spoke so that people could understand them (Jacob 4:13–14). We can take their words at face value, without looking for hidden messages meant for a special, more sophisticated group of Church members. The self-chosen few may want to initiate their families into these "mysteries," thus upsetting the balance of their children's developing faith. The sacred simplicity of the gospel has joy and depth enough for any seeker of truth.

Ironically, it may be your favorite gospel opportunity that becomes your downfall.[1] An overzealous approach to constitutional government could lead to accusations that those who disagree with your political party are unrighteous. Your children could easily pick up the idea that people who oppose your way of thinking are evil or should not have the right to express their views—thus undermining their understanding of the constitutional form of government that you cherish.

Perhaps you want to donate time or money to a worthwhile charity, but you place yourself in spiritual danger when you look beyond those who need you most. Charles Dickens wrote of Mrs. Jellyby, whose efforts to help the natives of "Borrioboola-Gha" took all her time, leaving her house dirty and cold and her husband and children miserable.[2] She was looking far beyond the mark to assist others, while ignoring those who had first claim on her love and care.

These dangers began with righteous gifts and desires: the admiration of an inspired form of government, the desire to give to those in need. But when we "call ourselves" to go beyond the mark and attempt to persuade others that we have stewardship over things we do not, danger arises. In the examples, those false stewardships are over the political choices of others and over strangers in need when family needs are neglected.

Another way that we can lose our balance in living the commandments is to add requirements that haven't been revealed. For example, the Word of Wisdom (D&C 89) is a revelation about health. A family could focus on one phrase—"wheat for man" (D&C 89:17)—and interpret the phrase to mean only whole wheat (never refined flour), grown on your own land blessed for the purpose, is acceptable. These rules aren't stated in the revelation. They may be harmless. But if the family begins to think they are living a higher law, they may begin to think others are living a lesser law, and unrighteous judgment begins.

Other families may decide not to have a television set or Internet connection, because they've been warned that unsavory and evil material is available through these media. A decision like this one is not wrong, but it can become wrong if the family begins to believe it's a commandment and condemns other families for making a different choice. Other "enhanced" commandments could range from the false idea that bread for the sacrament must be home-baked, not store-bought, to the idea that the Holy Spirit will dwell in the home more readily if the home is decorated a certain way and everyone talks in whispers, so it is like a temple.[3] These enhanced commandments go beyond the mark and may interfere with family life. Worse, members of the family may become so careful about the enhanced commandments, which are usually easy to measure, that they forget the real, important commandments about loving and serving God and others. Sadly, following our own mediocre "commandments" and ignoring the great commandments and promises of the Lord may deprive us of the ability to hear the promptings of the Spirit. Instead we strew the path with meaningless obstacles and use those obstacles as a basis to unrighteously judge others.

There are more gospel opportunities than time to fulfill them all at once, but we can put our energy to good use and please our Heavenly Father by remembering a few things:

• Pray to our Heavenly Father, seeking the promptings of the Holy Ghost for counsel on spending our time and energy wisely.

• Ponder the examples in the scriptures to understand "going beyond the mark"—Why was Uzzah killed when he steadied the Ark of the Covenant? (See 2 Samuel 6:1–7.) What does the Savior teach about "going beyond the mark" with respect to Sabbath observance? (See Matthew 12:1–21.)

• Look to our latter-day prophets and apostles as examples of balanced gospel living.

• Cultivate humility, the great protector against pride.[4]

• Reread your patriarchal blessing to help you determine your priorities.

• Talk about balanced gospel living with your family.

• Decide what you can do now and what must wait for later, pray about your choices, and if you feel the approval of the Spirit, don't feel guilty that you can't do it all.

Our Father in Heaven doesn't want us to feel burdened by His commandments. The Savior said, "My yoke is easy, and my burden is light" (Matthew 11:30). And the opportunities we have to serve in the home, in the Church, and in the world are not meant to be mournful slogs around an unavoidably wicked earth. Although we face trials, they are not the result of earnestly keeping the commandments or humbly pursuing our talents and opportunities within the gospel. A balance among our responsibilities can be consecrated service to God, our families, and our neighbors—consecrated service that will bring us joy.

ABOUT THE AUTHOR

Lisa Bolin Hawkins earned a B.A. and J.D. from BYU and currently teaches in the BYU School of Family Life and in the honors program. She and her husband, Alan, are the parents of two children and the grandparents of one.

NOTES

1. Dallin H. Oaks (1994, October), Our strengths can become our downfall, *Ensign, 24*(10), 11.

2. Charles Dickens (1964), *Bleak House* (New York: New American Library; reprint), chapter 4.

3. Kristine Manwaring (2000), My home as a temple; in David C. Dollahite, ed., *Strengthening Our Families: An In-Depth Look af the Proclamation on the Family* (Salt Lake City: Bookcraft), 94–96.

4. Oaks (1994), 11.

E S S A Y   A 4

BEING SINGLE IN THE CHURCH

KATE L. KIRKHAM

Many years ago as a young single adult living away from my parents' home, I imagined that being single was a one-time thing—something everyone experienced and then "singleness" was gone. Now I know that being single is based on many different circumstances and that the temptation to be dismayed about being single can come from many sources.

Apprehension, doubt, fear, and discouragement are words used to define *being dismayed*.[1] Conver-

Counsel for Young Adults

"Let us face the fact that in this life some of you will marry, some of you may not. . . . For those who do not marry, this fact of life must be faced squarely. But continuous single status is not without opportunity, challenge, or generous recompense."[2]

—President Gordon B. Hinckley

"In large measure the Church exists to strengthen families. I wish to define *family* very broadly. In the Church we have traditional families and single-parent families. Each single is considered in a sense to be a Church family. We also have ward families in which the bishop is a spiritual father. . . . Certainly not all families can, but I am persuaded that families with enough internal caring, discipline, commitment, and love, somehow, someway, can handle the majority of their problems. . . . I would urge members of extended families, grandparents, uncles, aunts, nephews, nieces, cousins, to reach out in concern, to succor."[3]

—President James E. Faust

"We have special admiration for the unsung but unsullied single women among whom are some of the noblest daughters of God. These sisters know that God loves them, individually and distinctly. They make wise career choices even though they cannot now have the most choice career. Though in their second estate they do not have their first desire, they still overcome the world. These sisters who cannot now enrich the institution of their own marriage so often enrich other institutions in society. They do not withhold their blessings simply because some blessings are now withheld from them."[4]

—Elder Neal A. Maxwell

"To you single women . . . who wish to be married, I say this, '*Do not give up hope. And do not give up trying. But do give up being obsessed with it.* The chances are that if you forget about it and become anxiously engaged in other activities, the prospects will brighten immeasurably.'"[5]

—President Gordon B. Hinckley

"I hope that every woman who finds herself in [these] circumstances . . . is . . . blessed with an understanding and helpful bishop, with a Relief Society president who knows how to assist her, with home teachers who know where their duty lies and how to fulfill it, and with a host of ward members who are helpful without being intrusive."[6]

—President Gordon B. Hinckley

Box A 4.1

sations about fundamental differences between individuals (i.e., being married or single) can create such apprehension that a real discussion is avoided. And then an opportunity to express or experience pure charity is lost. Ward members and leaders who seek to better understand the experiences of being a single adult in a family-focused church may be helped by considering three factors: (a) the implications of identity differences, (b) our shared challenge to fully live the gospel, and (c) the value of extended family relationships. I write based on my experience as one who has not married, but the principles apply to the many conditions of being single.

AND WHO ARE YOU?

My sister, her husband, their two children, and I entered the Independence, Missouri, Visitor's Center, with the two kids dashing past the guide first. He turned to my sister and said, "You must be the mother of these beautiful children." To my brother-in-law, who was next, he said: "You must be the father of these beautiful children." As I passed, he looked from them to me and said, "And who are you?"

As a single adult in the Church, understanding how I fit in takes effort. Defining who I am in conversation with others is a continuous adventure. When I first returned to live in Utah after a decade working on the East Coast, some treated me only as my father's daughter. To others I was the career woman. My sister heard me referred to as "your sister who has the degree." At family reunions, I was the one asked to bring soft drinks. Now when one of the newest generation asks me, "Are you my second grandma?" it is an easier question than "What happened to your husband?"

I have learned that the effort to get past the label or assumptions some offer as casually as a greeting is worthwhile. First, those who seem to have made a judgment about me because I am single may actually want to get to know or include me but feel awkward because of our different experiences. Second, I, too, make assumptions about others based on their circumstances. For example, sometimes I wrongly assume that married women will know more about nurturing, that they feel sorry for me, or that they always have someone who is paying attention to their needs.

Personal energy is required to get past the distance of differences. If the effort is two-way, the cost is shared. If the effort is one-way, the end goal can become shaped by the amount of effort and take the form of a survival strategy—just make it through the meeting, event, or weekend. The effort can also take the form of combat, a battle to change the other person's thinking. However, the process of defining who I am is not finished by just confronting an attitude or by surviving a conversation with someone (such as those offering advice on what I should do if I really want to be married). I must seek to make a contribution in my ward because of who I am—not just seek to be comfortable with an identity based on what I am not.

Ward leaders and members can benefit by focusing on opportunities of single members to bless the lives of others and continue their personal development. In a worst-case scenario, competition develops between circumstance and contributions: Perhaps some married women see themselves as sacrificing self for family service and view single members as having numerous opportunities for self-development. Some single sisters focus on their disappointment in not being able to have a family and miss seeing how they can develop themselves through service. In the best-case ward scenario, married and single sisters work together to benefit from each others' knowledge, skills, opportunities, and service.

LIVING THE GOSPEL TO THE FULLEST WITH BIFOCAL VISION

Every Latter-day Saint has the same challenge and obligation: live the gospel to the fullest in the context of day-to-day circumstances. I experience my single life as an act of faith—believing that some day the blessings of eternal marriage will be mine (if I live worthily). I need to put gospel teachings fully into my life now. Being single is not an excuse to limit my development in gospel knowledge, obedience to commandments, or efforts to do good works.

Living the gospel daily does require a bifocal vision on my part and on the part of others around me: seeing the day-to-day and seeing the eternal possibilities. This same principle operates for those who are now single, for example, because they are widowed. If I focus on the fact that they will one day join their companions again, I may assure them through the eternal lens, but the immediate challenge of being alone may need just as much attention.

I find it difficult to be appreciated as an active ward member (attending and statistically counted) and yet invisible as a single person in a family-focused ward (relationships avoided, needs not known, or talents not used). A bifocal lens perspective can help make our context whole—who we are in the eternal perspective and who we are as we face today's circumstances.

The second great commandment to love our neighbor as ourselves (see Matthew 22:39) is a necessary condition for creating an inclusive ward that values all members. To love is to give our attention to others. We learn what matters to them, what discourages them, what causes them to feel lonely in addition to the aloneness that comes with being single. For every single person I have met, there are moments that bring their different state in sharp contrast to those around them; moments that are not "seen" unless we attend to another's experience and not just to our perception of their experience. Each fall, just as the leaves turn, the flowers are gone, and my yard begs to be prepared for winter, I feel more alone than at any other season or holiday. The experience is as simple as not having another pair of hands to hold the leaf bag open and as complex as the implication of winter that draws us closer to home. When I have tried to explain how this moment is so defining for me, I get immediate offers for help with yard work. More than an offer of helping hands, my deeper need is for companionship.

EMBRACING THE EXTENDED FAMILY DYNAMICS

Church members most often reference the nuclear family and the tasks of righteous parenting. These parenting tasks are enormously important and demanding. And, because I don't have children, I have more time to attend to the way in which extended family relationships continue to affect parenting across the generations. One family's code of "YSLM" (you sound like Mother) was a shorthand way of identifying patterns of behavior that were intentionally or unintentionally being repeated in the next family generation. Siblings often can see these dynamics more clearly than can a spouse. Single individuals play an important role in family learning by talking about their insights, experiences, and relationships among their extended family network. Admittedly, I can be dismayed by the complexity of feelings, history, and relationships. But what better opportunity to apply the principles of the gospel than with our own relatives with whom we will associate eternally?

I continue to seek ways to be involved with my extended families: I create traditions, such as giving an annual spring party to which all are invited, getting involved with family reunions, initiating phone calls to others in our extended family, and hosting family travel.

The relationships with extended family members are not a substitute for one's own family in mortal life, but they are a real crucible for living the gospel that can influence generations of family members. I hope that extended family members (or ward members) do not assume that singles can or should be assigned certain tasks, based on the fact that they are single, without considering other factors such as personality or finances. For example, my choice to provide care for my elderly parents in my home came after much planning by all.

As single members we can define who we are, live the gospel to the fullest extent we can in mortality, and invest in the eternal network of family relationships. When we seek "first the kingdom of God and his righteousness" (3 Nephi 13:33), we will be blessed with the promptings and guidance we need to find joy and happiness here and hereafter. We can trust that the Lord's promise in Isaiah 41:10 also applies to us: "Fear thou not; for I am with thee."

ABOUT THE AUTHOR

Kate L. Kirkham, Ph.D., is an associate professor in the Department of Organizational Leadership and Strategy and director of the William G. Dyer Institute at Brigham Young University. She finds great joy in family relationships as a daughter, sister, aunt, niece, and "in-law."

ADDITIONAL READING

Cynthia Doxey, et al. (2000), Single adults and family life; in David C. Dollahite, ed., *Strengthening Our Families: An In-Depth Look at the Proclamation on the Family* (Salt Lake City: Bookcraft), 227–238.

Kathy Grant (2002, June), Singles in the ward family, *Ensign*, 32(6), 44–48.

Kimberly D. Nelson (2005, January), My classroom, *Ensign*, 35(1), 36–38.

Rebecca M. Taylor (2005, January), A different path, *Ensign*, 35(1), 38–39.

NOTES

1. This phrase is the opposite of the Lord's admonition in Isaiah 41:10 to "be not dismayed." See also R. Keen and J. Ellis (1985), How firm a foundation, *Hymns* (Salt Lake City: The Church of Jesus Christ of Latter-day Saints), 85: "Fear not, I am with thee; oh, be not dismayed," which adapts the scripture in Isaiah.

2. Gordon B. Hinckley (1997, March), A conversation with single adults, *Ensign*, 27(3), 60.

3. James E. Faust (2005, March 1) Where is the church? BYU Devotional address; available at http://speeches.byu.edu

4. Neal A. Maxwell (1978, May), The women of god, *Ensign*, 8(5), 11.

5. Gordon B. Hinckley (1997), 60.

6. Gordon B. Hinckley, (1996, November), Women of the church, *Ensign*, 26(11), 69.

ESSAY   A 5

ONE FAMILY'S JOURNEY TO ZION

KATE JENKINS

Having traveled the world many times over, President Gordon B. Hinckley has visited with Saints of every culture and circumstance, yet his instruction and counsel remains constant across the miles: "The tremendous progress of the Church in which all Latter-day Saints share is but the lengthened shadow of the faith and sacrifices of the devoted early Saints, the pioneers. . . . It is good to reflect upon the work of those who labored so hard and gained so little in this world, but out of whose dreams and early plans, so well nurtured, has come a great harvest of which we are the beneficiaries. Their tremendous example can become a compelling motivation for us all, for each of us is a pioneer in his own life, often in his own family, and many pioneer daily in trying to establish a gospel foothold in distant parts of the world."[1]

Whether the posterity of pioneers or the first of a family to discover the gospel, every member of the Church is a pioneer in his or her own right, traveling the plains of mortality toward spiritual Zion. Perth, Australia, possibly the farthest inhabited location from Salt Lake City, the center of Zion, was my birthplace and, for many years, my home. Though it was more than a hundred years before my time that the gospel came to Australia, it has not yet been one lifetime since the gospel came to my family. I am the first person in my line to be born into the Church, as both my paternal and maternal grandparents' conversion occurred when my father and mother were each two years of age. All four of my grandparents are the first living members of their families to have accepted the gospel, and each has left a priceless legacy of faith and endurance through their pioneering examples; however, the focus of this essay will be on the challenges and experiences of my father's family.

My father's father, gentle and quiet by nature, was sent away to war as a young man, from which he returned broken and silent. On meeting my highly extroverted grandmother, he was drawn out of this shell long enough to marry and begin a family, but there were difficulties from the beginning. My grandmother had also sustained emotional injury, somewhat earlier in life, enduring years of sexual abuse by a family member, making it extremely difficult for her to maintain normal, healthy relationships throughout her life. Yet, despite her private pain, she immediately embraced the gospel when it was presented to her by two tracting missionaries, and a few months later my grandfather followed suit.

Even though my grandmother was always passionate about her faith and determinedly ensured her entire family attended church regularly, my father recalls that, on the home front, there was little application of the principles being taught. As a consequence of the many challenges in my grandparents' personal lives, there was much anger and frustration expressed in ways that had long-term destructive effects for their children. Home was not a haven of peace, and my father left as early as he was able. Though somewhat lacking in personal direction and desire, he eventually found himself on a mission, where he was blessed to gain a testimony of the truthfulness of the Book of Mormon. It was also while serving in the city of Perth that he met my mother, his future wife.

My mother has often told me that in the early period encompassing her courtship and temple marriage to my father, she felt that she was living a real-life fairytale. In her eyes, despite any minor disturbances to their wedded bliss, my father was about as perfect as he could be, and so it came as a shock when, after some years and the addition of three children to the family, their relationship became strained, as my father began to exhibit outwardly the symptoms of a lifelong struggle with severe depression.

It is a credit to my father that he was quick to seek professional help for his illness, during the course of which he uncovered and confronted many of the early events that had contributed to his condition. For a long time he struggled to overcome feelings of bitterness and resentment at having been raised in a family where the gospel was a relatively recent discovery, practiced on little more than a superficial level, a thin skin of dogma masking confusion, aggression, and pain. Why had he not been one of those assigned such a glorious heritage and bloodline as the Saints in "Zion," he wondered, with their strong, righteous pioneer forebears? It took time and much healing before my father found answers to his questions and reasons for life's seeming inequalities.

From the perspective that life is a race in which all of humanity is competing, there is much in mortality that could appear as favoritism on the part of God. How fortunate we are to have the illuminating truths of the gospel, which teach us that each individual is on his own journey, aided not only by a loving Father in Heaven, but by devoted family members and friends. With that strength and support, my father has come to understand his importance and potential in the eyes of God and to realize that the path of eternal progression lies in working as a family toward the goal of complete harmony and unity with God and with one another. And, just as the pioneers of old, our family has known joy in the journey toward Zion.

Nevertheless, one of the greatest challenges in life is to discover and maintain this familial peace and perfection, and this can be most difficult when the storms are raging, not on the outside, but deep within. For the pioneers who trekked across the plains, many of the obstacles to the success of their journey were plainly visible and pushed them to their physical limits. The bitterness of cold, the pangs of hunger, the weight of their carts as they traveled over inhospitable and unbroken terrain. For my father, the weight of depression was as onerous to carry as the burden of the heaviest handcart, being dragged over the steepest, rockiest circumstances life could present. He felt he had inherited a terrible load from parents who had had their "wagons" packed with a multitude of unwanted encumbrances, seemingly hindering our family's progress. Yet, like the pioneers as they crossed the plains, he was not left to push this heavy load alone.

My mother, though she added some items of her own to their collection of "excess baggage," has been a caring and constant companion to my father, without which our family's journey would have become impossible. Together they have pushed and pulled and sorted the various hefty items, slowly and painfully discarding those discovered to be of little or no worth and keeping only the things most essential for survival. It is not surprising that the items most resolutely retained in their handcart are those that uphold the principles listed in the proclamation as being the foundation upon which happiness can be achieved in family life. Implementing these principles years before they were ever organized in the form of the proclamation, my parents faithfully maintained vital traditions of church attendance, family home evening, family and personal prayer and scripture study, and "wholesome recreational activities,"[2] from which dedication the blessings have continued to flow.

They also demonstrated, through their mutual determination to succeed in their marriage relationship, the application and necessity of "repentance, forgiveness, respect, love, [and] compassion"[3] between family members. My parents have taught through their actions that achieving true happiness takes effort and that everyone needs to push the handcart together, in the same direction, for any significant progress to be made. A family member focused on any alternative goal, and pulling toward whatever it may be, can make it extremely difficult for the group to move Zion-ward, particularly if the member is a parent, with their stronger influence and

position of responsibility. How grateful I am that my parents were united in faith and purpose as they covenanted to raise a family in righteousness. I know that generations to come will look to my father and mother, and my grandparents, and will "arise up, and call [them] blessed" (Proverbs 31:28) for the great work they have accomplished.

To my mind, it is evident that just as the faithful pioneer Saints of yesteryear were enabled to survive on their journeys because of the things that they carried with them, we too are able to progress by using the things that we carry within ourselves. Through applying gospel principles and keeping our gaze determinedly fixed on our eternal goal, we can discover and come to understand our shortcomings and, as promised in Ether, the Lord will "make weak things become strong" (Ether 12:27). I gain great strength to face the challenges in my own life, to push my own handcart alongside my righteous husband (a convert and faithful pioneer in his family), as I reflect on the example of those who have traveled before me, who had already covered so much of the distance between spiritual Babylon and Zion before my feet ever even touched hard dirt. Because of their faith and endurance, it may yet be in my lifetime that our family will know the joy and peace of perfect unity and oneness with God, the vision of which spurs us ever onward. Then, when comes that day when the "watchmen upon the mount Ephraim shall cry, Arise ye, and let us go up to Zion unto the Lord our God" (Jeremiah 31:6), we will be ready to heed the call, having already made the journey in our hearts and homes.

ABOUT THE AUTHOR

Kate Jenkins is a devoted wife, stay-at-home mother, and occasional writer and composer. She and her "Kiwi" husband, Craig, live in Perth, Australia, with their 2-year-old daughter, Mekyja Joy.

NOTES

1. Gordon B. Hinckley (1989), *Faith: The Essence of True Religion* (Salt Lake City: Deseret Book), 102.

2. First Presidency and Council of Twelve Apostles (1995, November) The family: A proclamation to the world, *Ensign*, 25(11), 102.

3. Ibid.

CHAPTER 3

THE RELATIONAL NATURE OF ETERNAL IDENTITY

LARRY J. NELSON AND DAVID A. NELSON

All human beings—male and female—are created in the image of God.
Each is a beloved spirit son or daughter of heavenly parents, and, as such, each has a divine nature and destiny.
Gender is an essential characteristic of individual premortal, mortal, and eternal identity and purpose.[1]
—"The Family: A Proclamation to the World"

Each of us is a child of God. Satan, however, would like nothing more than to blind Heavenly Father's children to their true identity. In the Pearl of Great Price we read that the Lord appeared to Moses and repeatedly referred to him as "my son" (Moses 1:4, 6, 7). As soon as the Lord departed, Satan came to Moses and immediately took aim at his identity by saying, "Moses, son of man, worship me" (Moses 1:12). Fortunately, Moses had a firm grasp on his eternal identity and responded boldly, saying, "I am a son of God" (Moses 1:13). This scriptural account affirms that God is our Father and we are all His children, and that every individual needs to recognize his or her own eternal worth in order to be able to withstand the attempts of the adversary to weaken his or her sense of eternal identity.

This chapter focuses on the divine nature and destiny of every individual. In particular, this chapter will address how one's sense of worth and eternal identity develops within the context of relationships, including with Heavenly Father and between parents and children. We will consider (a) the unchanging nature of our divine worth as children of God, (b) the difference between how God sees our worth and how each of us esteems that worth in ourselves, (c) how families can assist children in building a strong sense of their eternal identity and individual worth, and

(d) how gender influences the development of our mortal and eternal identity.

ETERNAL IDENTITY: THE INFINITE WORTH OF A CHILD OF GOD

One of the prevailing questions asked by human beings is "Who am I?" People often settle on answers to this question based on worldly distinctions such as occupation, nationality, or political affiliation. While there is nothing wrong with these aspects of identity, they do not explain who we really are. Our true identity includes knowledge of our royal lineage and our glorious potential. Our true identity includes being a son or daughter of heavenly parents with the potential to inherit all that the Father has (3 Nephi 11:33).

When we look at a family portrait, we often point out the characteristics of parents found in their children ("You have your father's eyes and your mother's smile"). If we were able to look through the veil for just a moment, we would recognize that we have developing traits of our heavenly parents. Parley P. Pratt taught:

> An intelligent being, in the image of God, possesses every organ, attribute, sense, sympathy, affection of will, wisdom, love, power and gift, which is possessed by God himself. But . . . these attributes are in embryo, and are to be gradually developed.[2]

The truth of our divine origin and destiny provides insight into our past, gives purpose to our present state, and increases hope for a glorious future. It affirms that every individual is of infinite worth. One's mistakes and weaknesses might affect one's worthiness but never one's worth.[3] No one can take away another person's worth. Nothing can change the worth of a soul in the sight of God (see D&C 18:10).

EARTHLY IDENTITY AND SELF-WORTH: SEEING THROUGH A GLASS, DARKLY

While there is nothing that can change the worth of a soul in the sight of God, unfortunately not every person has that same view of him- or herself. An important task of mortality is to recognize the worth within ourselves. Too many individuals suffer throughout their lives with feelings of self-doubt and worthlessness. Like Moses, we need to come to see ourselves as God sees us so we can withstand the adversary's attacks on our identity. Elder Russell M. Nelson taught that the gospel of Jesus Christ declares "joy to be part of our divine destiny." In order to feel joy, he said, you "must feel good about yourself—not in any sense of conceit, but simply a proper esteem for yourself, well deserved."[4]

In the social science literature, the nature of how one perceives oneself has commonly been referred to as *self-esteem*. Some Latter-day Saint scholars and writers have attacked the notion of self-esteem when used as a synonym to self-love or when it focuses primarily on comparisons with others, worldly status, or a preoccupation with self.[5] For our purposes, however, we define self-esteem as nothing more than the overall value one places on the self as a person.[6] In other words, we may say self-esteem is the extent to which a person has come to see him- or herself as the Lord sees him or her. Again, we want to make it very clear that a person's worth *never* changes in the sight of God, but, unfortunately, individuals vary significantly in their ability to recognize that worth in themselves. Therefore, we will use the term self-esteem to reflect the changing extent to which individuals see themselves in a positive light (in the words of Elder Nelson, "feel good about yourself"[7]) to distinguish it from our true personal worth, which is how God sees us and which never changes. To reiterate, acquiring for ourselves the perspective that God has for each of us is an essential requirement of mortality. Elder Neal A. Maxwell emphasized this when he taught, "Since self-esteem controls ultimately our ability to love God, to love others, and to love life, nothing is more central than our need to build justifiable self-esteem."[8]

These statements by Church leaders tell us how important a justified, proper view of oneself is to our development in mortality. Many individuals' self-perceptions are not accurate or proper—they do not see themselves the way their loving Father in Heaven sees them. Social comparison is the primary measure of their self-worth. They only feel good about themselves if they perform better than others, possess more of something (e.g., money, property, strength), or otherwise vaunt themselves above others. In other words, the worldly approach to self-esteem is not based on divine worth but rather derived from competition with others.[9]

Social comparison is a foundation bound to crumble. Regardless of our talents, possessions, or characteristics, there is always someone we perceive to be prettier, smarter, more spiritual, stronger, or wealthier. Thus, the only way to maintain positive self-regard, if based on comparisons to others, is to consistently be the best (a goal difficult to maintain), put others down, or avoid interaction with those who may outperform us and damage our fragile self-esteem. As a result, a feeling of competitiveness rather than connectedness is introduced. This approach to seeking identity undermines our ability to form strong, loving relationships.

A highly capable student related how her sense of worth was based solely on how she measured up to her peers. Despite graduating first in her high school class and being accepted into one of the top medical schools, she considered herself a failure when she found herself ranked 11th in her class of 45. She became depressed, anxious, and began avoiding interactions with others. Although the pursuit of excellence is laudable, it should not be so consuming that it becomes a stumbling block in our eternal progression. We should *do* our best, but we need not *be* the best to ensure our worth. If entering Heavenly Father's kingdom was based on such a competition, in which only "the best" were eligible, perhaps only the Savior would be allowed entrance.

Family relationships can also influence our feelings about ourselves. Some struggle to feel good about themselves as they deal with the bitter effects of divorce or an unhappy marriage, the heartbreak of wayward children, or lack of opportunity to marry. We should try to not let discouragement overcome us if our current family circumstances do not fit the ideal that we are striving for. The Lord's promises will be fulfilled as we seek to live the commandments and deal constructively with the adversity common to mortal life. President Gordon B. Hinckley spoke words of comfort consistent with this doctrine when he assured parents in the raising of children: "[Children] may do . . . some things you would not want them to do, but be patient, be patient. You have not failed as long as you have tried. Never forget that."[10] Thus, we need to remember that our worth is not, nor should our self-esteem be, based on our marital status, family structure, or the choices of our children.

In the end, sense of worth is inextricably intertwined with the mission of our Savior. Christ's Atonement helps each of us to overcome deficiencies as we develop toward completeness (Ether 12:27). In this way, each child of God is individually succored by a loving Father. Only through Christ will we return to God and gain exaltation. As we develop a testimony of Christ's Atonement, we realize the worth Christ sees in us to make such a sacrifice. Thus, our relationship with Deity is what matters now and in eternity.

DEVELOPING JUSTIFIED SELF-ESTEEM: A PROGRESSION

The ability to recognize one's worth does not come all at once. Building self-esteem is a process that occurs over time and within the context of relationships. The use of the word *build* conveys the notion of a process. Child development research emphasizes that self-perceptions gradually unfold as the individual develops and matures within warm and nurturing relationships, most importantly with parents. The development of one's sense of self begins in infancy with the basic understanding of oneself as separate from others and continues to develop and become increasingly complex throughout one's life. For example, children tend to define themselves according to simple characteristics such as gender and physical characteristics ("I'm a big boy") and abilities ("I can run fast"). As children mature into adulthood, they will expand the list to include more abstract dimensions of identity such as moral behavior, career orientation, political views, and religious beliefs.

Across development, the nature of these self-assessments is heavily influenced by the feedback children receive from adults and peers. For example, starting at about age six, children develop the ability to compare their own qualities, abilities, and performance with those of their peers. Children begin to internalize what others say about them—and not all of it is positive. As a result, children start to develop some negative self-evaluations. As children enter late childhood and adolescence, social comparison increases. Teenagers are increasingly concerned with how they look and behave. Ideally, young people eventually come to accept their strengths and limitations and realize that lack of ability in an area does not make their worth as a person any less.

Many struggle, however, with developing proper self-perceptions. Some children feel negative about themselves as early as age four[11] and some individuals continue to base their self-perceptions on the opinions of others well into adulthood.[12] For some people it appears quite easy to have healthy self-esteem, while others struggle to feel good about themselves. Parents, teachers, and leaders can do much to help children develop a positive sense of self.

PARENTING THAT STRENGTHENS A CHILD'S POSITIVE SELF-PERCEPTIONS

Parents play a critical role in both the general development of their children's self-perceptions and in helping children see their eternal identity. Children's developing sense of themselves is heavily influenced by the words and actions of others. Hence, children who are loved and valued, particularly in the context of loving familial relationships, come to see themselves in a positive light, while children who experience abuse and neglect develop negative self-perceptions.[13] The following paragraphs describe specific ways parents can foster positive self-esteem.

Respond to your children's needs. To help infants begin to understand that their actions affect others (personal agency), parents should respond promptly and appropriately to their children. When parents respond to crying infants, for example, babies learn to equate their actions (crying) with a response (parents' coming closer) and will come to see themselves as agents. As parents respond, infants learn they have a sense of control in getting their needs met As this process continues, children begin to feel that others are concerned about them and love them, which instills a sense of worth (i.e., "I must be important because Mommy and Daddy love me"). Some believe that responding "slavishly" to an infant's cries will spoil the child and produce a miniature tyrant or a child who is highly dependent. Research actually demonstrates that children of parents who respond promptly and appropriately are more independent and confident in their capabilities. They have developed a sense of self that allows them to venture confidently into the world around them.[14]

Express delight in your children's early accomplishments. Let your children see and hear that you notice their achievements and are pleased with them. As noted earlier, children's earliest self-perceptions are based on their physical abilities, so complimenting their performance leads to a positive foundation of self-perceptions. For young children, you can show your pleasure through smiles, nodding your head, clapping, or hugging them. Be sure to verbally share your enthusiasm as well. Older children will notice when you do things like displaying their artwork on the refrigerator or wearing the paper tie they made you in preschool. Do not take your child's accomplishments for granted just because every other child can do it; it is a new accomplishment for your child.

Focus on effort, process, and progress. As children get older, continue to praise good outcomes, but start to focus more on effort, process, and progress. They need to understand that neither success nor worth are based on outcomes (i.e., who wins the game, who gets the highest grades). Acknowledge your children's best effort: "You shouldn't be disappointed with your grade because you sure worked hard." Focus on the process rather than the outcome: "Your team lost the game, but didn't you have a lot of fun?" Help your children focus on internal rewards rather than the external praise: "It may not have won first prize, but didn't it feel good to build that model all by yourself?" Help them notice the progress they are making: "See how much better you are doing? You only fell once this time." In times of difficulty, disappointment, and failure, parents also need to point out children's strengths and give specific examples of successes. They can emphasize that working harder will produce results. Many parents can illustrate this best by relating personal experiences in which hard work paid off. In contrast, focusing on the child's weaknesses as unchangeable ("You just aren't good at this, are you?") undermines motivation to do better and hampers self-esteem.

Provide support and encouragement. Parents need to help their children succeed. There is a fine balance in this because children need to feel a sense of having accomplished a difficult task on their own but might need some appropriate support from parents to achieve it. Parents should not set their children up to fail by giving them tasks that are beyond their abilities. Rather, provide a task challenging enough to merit a sense of accomplishment when completed. Parents can offer encouragement, stay positive and pleasant, and provide suggestions.

Parents should also provide honest feedback. While it is beneficial to be extremely positive with young children (ages 0–5), as children enter elementary school it is important not to shower them with praise that includes lies or exaggerations. They have a good sense of when they have or have not done well, and feigned positive feedback will teach them not to believe you. Instead, provide gentle and loving and specific feedback that points out what went wrong as well as what went right. Make sure children know that all people, including adults, make mistakes and need to learn and improve.

Provide freedom to make choices. As noted previously, it is important that children attempt things on their own. Parents should not shelter children from potentially positive experiences just because there is a risk of failure. Research has shown that parents who are overprotective in their parenting tend to have children who, as young as age four, feel poorly about themselves.[15] Overprotective parenting includes (a) constantly stepping in to do things for children, (b) repeatedly telling children not to try things because they might fail or get hurt, or (c) promoting children's complete dependence upon their parents. These parental behaviors convey a sense that children are incompetent ("Mommy always says I will hurt myself or mess things up") and incapable of progress. While some uncaring parents harshly criticize their children's abilities ("Why can't you get anything right?"), some loving parents mistakenly transmit the same message by not allowing children to explore and try things on their own.

Do not make your love conditional. Parents should never make their love contingent on their children's good behavior or performance. Children should know that a parent's love is constant, ever present, and does not change according to their behavior. There are only a few times recorded in the scriptures in which we hear directly from our Father in Heaven. In each instance, the Father introduces the Savior by declaring, "Behold my Beloved Son, in whom I am well pleased" (3 Nephi 11:7). Note that the Father separates His love for His Son ("my Beloved Son") and His view of His behavior ("in whom I am well pleased"). Parents should follow this example and distinguish between love and behavior (i.e., "We love you but we aren't pleased with what you did"). In showing unwavering love for their children, parents set an example of the type of love that our Heavenly Father shares. It will be easier for children to come to understand that God's love for them is constant and ever-present, too.

Teach about divine heritage and potential. Parents have the additional opportunity to teach children to incorporate their eternal worth into their view of themselves by helping them understand that (a) Heavenly Father loves and values each of His children, completely and without reservation, regardless of our imperfections; (b) the proper use of agency will help us develop a strong relationship with Heavenly Father and lead us back to His presence; and (c) we can only become perfect and complete like our heavenly parents through the Savior's loving Atonement for us. As children develop both cognitively and spiritually, and through their relationships with parents, they become able to gradually incorporate God's view of them into their own emerging sense of self.

IMPROVING SELF-ESTEEM REQUIRES RELATIONSHIPS

Improving self-esteem must occur with a focus on improving relationships with Jesus Christ, family members, and others. The most important relationship must exist with our Savior. As we come closer to our Savior, we come to feel His love for us and gain a clearer understanding of our heritage and destiny. Too often people who struggle with self-esteem turn inward and disconnect from interaction with and service to others. In contrast, a focus on self is no longer possible when we reach out to others. Rather than worrying that others may be better than we are, we are led to sincerely wish for and rejoice in their successes and accomplishments. As we serve others we also begin to love them and develop a perspective of the worth our Father in Heaven sees in them. When we begin to see divine worth in others, it becomes easier to see it in ourselves.

GENDER AS AN ESSENTIAL CHARACTERISTIC OF ETERNAL IDENTITY

Another essential aspect of our eternal identity is gender.[16] In the world today, there is a tendency to either exaggerate or diminish the role of gender in our lives. Children are bombarded with confusing messages about gender. Elder Boyd K. Packer advised, "Be careful lest you unknowingly foster influences and activities which tend to erase the masculine and feminine differences nature has established."[17] A gospel foundation allows us to consider gender in a way that uplifts rather than undermines eternal progression and enhances our sense of worth and purpose.

While we know little regarding the role of gender in our premortal existence, we know that our spirits were distinctly male or female. Elder Packer taught: "The scriptures and teachings of the apostles and prophets speak of us in premortal life as sons and daughters, spirit children of God. Gender existed before, and did not begin at mortal birth."[18] We also know that God loved all of His children—male and female—and did not set one above the other. Therefore, male-female relationships on earth should be based on equality and respect. For example, as President Hinckley stated: "In the marriage companionship there is neither inferiority nor superiority. The woman does not walk ahead of the man; neither does the man walk ahead of the woman. They walk side by side as a son and daughter of God on an eternal journey."[19]

Finally, we know that our Father in Heaven's purpose is to bring to pass the eternal life of all of His children (Moses 1:39). His divine plan called for children to grow in family units in which mothers and fathers would have certain divine roles that would interact in a synergistic manner to provide children the optimal setting for their development. As with gender, He did not designate one divine role (provide and protect or nurture) to be more or less important than another. (Chapters 19 and 20 discuss the stewardships of fathers and mothers; chapter 7 and essay B4 describe ways to maintain equal partnership in marriage.)

It is common to attribute certain traits to males, such as leadership, ambition, activity, independence, self-confidence, and competitiveness; while ascribing other traits to females, such as emotional sensitivity and expressivity, nurturing ability, connectedness, and empathy. Studies have tested whether these differences are in fact real. Results tend to show that differences are not as great as we tend to believe. However, studies also demonstrate that significant differences do exist, on average, for some attributes.[20]

We do not know for certain where all gender differences originate. Some differences predate our mortal existence. Elder Henry B. Eyring observed, "We know that in the premortal world we were men or women with unique gifts because of our gender."[21]

Further, our genetic endowment and social environment may either inhibit or facilitate the development of premortal characteristics. For example, biology plays some role in the mortal manifestation of gender. Male and female hormones have been found to be directly related to numerous behaviors and abilities such as moodiness, verbal skills, spatial abilities, play styles, and aggression.[22]

However, the association between hormones and behavior is typically small and the socialization impact of the child's relationships appears to be greater. In particular, a child's gender significantly determines how that child is perceived and treated by others. For example, parents report holding different expectations for boys (e.g., achievement, exploration, competition, and emotional control) than girls (e.g., warmth, reliance on others, emotional sensitivity).[23] Parents also hold different attitudes for each gender, such as whether it is more appropriate for girls to play with "boy" toys than for boys to play with "girl" toys.[24] Peers also send important gender messages. For example, young boys are intolerant of cross-gender play in their male peers.[25]

While it may be interesting to explain the origin of gender differences, it is more important to realize they exist, are part of our eternal identity, and serve important roles in our Heavenly Father's plan of happiness. Sister Sheri L. Dew explained this well:

> [Satan] would have us believe men and women are so alike that our unique gifts are not necessary, or so different we can never hope to understand each other. Neither is true. Our Father knew exactly what He was doing when He created us. He made us enough alike to love each other, but enough different that we would need to unite our strengths and stewardships to create a whole. Neither man nor woman is perfect or complete without the other.[26]

Men and women, and the best qualities possessed by each, have the same divine origin. Further, our Savior, Jesus Christ, is the perfect example of how various traits can merge together to complete divine nature. He possesses the positive characteristics that we tend to attribute to men (e.g., leader, assertive, persistent, decisive), and those we tend to attribute to women (devoted to others, empathetic, gentle, nurturing, kind). He was an assertive, decisive leader, protector, and provider when He cleansed the money changers from His Father's house (Matthew 21:12–13), calmed the raging sea (Mark 4:36–41), and fed the multitudes (John 6:5–14). In other

instances, we read of He who wept with Mary over the loss of her brother Lazarus (John 11:19–36), held and loved children (Luke 18:15–17; 3 Nephi 17:21–25), and cared for the needs of the sick and afflicted (Luke 7:1–17; 3 Nephi 17:5–10). Elder Bruce Hafen said:

> The world has long tried to convince men that it is not manly to be refined, kind, or spiritually sensitive. This suggests that the hands of a "real" man would be out of place holding the hand of a child, soothing the fevered brow of a sick wife, or being placed on someone's head to give a needed blessing. But when we think of the hands of Joseph Smith or Brigham Young, Moses, Peter, or the Savior himself, we see strong, masculine hands in the posture of blessing, serving, and loving in gentleness and tenderness.[27]

With the Savior's attributes in mind, we may want to reconsider how we think about men and women. Rather than speaking of masculine and feminine traits, we should perhaps focus on Christlike traits, as a mix of these qualities prepare us for eternal life. In other words, regardless of whether certain characteristics tend to come more naturally or require effort to develop, both men and women need to acquire the qualities that will enable them to become more like Jesus Christ. The optimal way for children to develop these Christlike qualities is to be reared by a mother and father who are keeping marital covenants. By experiencing the strengths of both parents, children can learn many Christlike qualities and come to understand their own eternal identity as children of God.

Children should be helped to develop all of the competencies and Christlike qualities that will make them complete. We should be careful not to allow our conceptions of gender to stand in the way of a child's development. For example, boys should not be discouraged from displaying proper emotion because we perceive emotion to be a predominantly female attribute. Empathy is a strong deterrent to physical aggression and antisocial behavior (behaviors that are more common in boys). Similarly, girls should not be discouraged from pursuing talents that are more typically encouraged in boys, such as mathematical ability.

Some of the attributes that come more naturally to boys or girls can be liabilities, particularly with peers. For example, the greater sensitivity and relationship focus of girls makes them more susceptible to the damaging effects of behaviors meant to exclude or denigrate relationships, such as gossip. Boys, in contrast, tend to be more avid risk takers, which can promote development of various competencies. However, they are consequently more open to negative peer pressure to engage in risky or harmful behavior. Awareness of gender differences, therefore, can help focus parenting on supporting children's unique needs.

CONCLUSION

"Who am I?" The proclamation provides the answer: Every person is a son or daughter of heavenly parents with the potential to become like them. Therefore, every individual is endowed with infinite worth that cannot be enhanced or diminished by any action or behavior. Unfortunately, coming to see ourselves the way our Father in Heaven sees us is a process that leaves many faltering under misguided notions of self-esteem. Gender is an essential element that defines who we are and will influence our development through the eternities. Misconceptions about gender can distort our identity and self-esteem. Fortunately, there are steps parents can take to help their children develop a proper, justified view of themselves and, more important, a sense of their eternal identity and worth as sons and daughters of God and heirs to all He has. Such a view of oneself is developed in the context of warm, nurturing parent-child relationships and, in turn, lays the foundation for future loving, supportive marital relationships.

ABOUT THE AUTHORS

Larry J. Nelson is an assistant professor of marriage, family, and human development at BYU. He received his Ph.D. from the University of Maryland. His research interests are in social and self-development during early childhood and emerging adulthood. He and his wife, Kimberly, have three children: Jessica, Carrie, and Isaac.

David A. Nelson is an assistant professor of marriage, family, and human development at BYU. He received his Ph.D. in child psychology from the Institute of Child Development at the University of Minnesota. His research is focused on childhood social cognition and aggression. He and his wife, Emily, have three children: Jessica, Joshua, and Christian.

ADDITIONAL READING

Allen E. Bergin (2002), *Eternal Values and Personal Growth* (Provo, UT: BYU Studies).
Barbara Day Lockhart and Shirley E. Cox (2000), The divine nature of each individual; in David C. Dollahite, ed., *Strengthening Our Families: An In-Depth Look at the Proclamation on the Family* (Salt Lake City: Bookcraft), 217–226.

Eleanor E. Maccoby (1998), *The Two Sexes: Growing Up Apart, Coming Together* (Cambridge, MA: Harvard University Press).
Lloyd D. Newell (1992), *The Divine Connection: Understanding Your Inherent Worth* (Salt Lake City: Deseret Book).

NOTES

1. First Presidency and Council of Twelve Apostles (1995, November), The family: A proclamation to the world, *Ensign*, 25(11), 102.
2. Parley P. Pratt (1978), *Key to the Science of Theology*, Classics in Mormon Literature (Salt Lake City: Deseret Book), 61.
3. B. D. Lockhart and S. E. Cox (2000), The divine nature of each individual; in D. C. Dollahite, ed., *Strengthening Our Families: An In-Depth Look at the Proclamation on the Family* (Salt Lake City: Bookcraft), 217–226.
4. Russell M. Nelson (1986, November), Joy cometh in the morning, *Ensign, 16*(11), 67–70.
5. H. W. Goddard (2002, April), Getting past self-esteem, *Marriage & Families*, 24–29; J. E. Faulconer (1993, June), Self-image, self-love, and salvation, *Latter-day Digest, 2*(3), 7–26; Esther Rasband (1998), *Confronting the Myth of Self-Esteem: Twelve Keys to Finding Peace* (Salt Lake City: Deseret Book).
6. S. Harter (1999), *The Construction of the Self* (New York: Guilford Press).
7. Nelson (1986), 67–70.
8. Neal A. Maxwell (1967), *A More Excellent Way: Essays on Leadership for Latter-day Saints* (Salt Lake City: Deseret Book), 90.
9. See Ezra Taft Benson (1989, May), Beware of pride, *Ensign, 19*(5), 4–7.
10. Gordon B. Hinckley (1997), *Teachings of Gordon B. Hinckley* (Salt Lake City: Deseret Book), 422.
11. R. J. Coplan, L. C. Findlay, and L. J. Nelson (2004), Characteristics of preschoolers with lower perceived competence, *Journal of Abnormal Child Psychology, 32,* 399–408.
12. Harter (1999).
13. S. Toth, D. Cicchetti, J. Macfie, and R. N. Emde (1997), Representations of self and other in the narratives of neglected, physically abused, and sexually abused preschoolers, *Development and Psychopathology, 9,* 781–796.
14. M. D. S. Ainsworth, M. C. Blehar, E. Waters, and S. Wall (1978), *Patterns of Attachment: A Psychological Study of the Strange Situation* (Hillsdale, NJ: Erlbaum).
15. L. J. Nelson, C. H. Hart, S. F. Olsen, and C. C. Robinson (2000, July), Behavioral and relational correlates of low self-perceived competence in preschoolers; presented in R. Coplan and H. Chen (Chairs), Recent Issues in the Study of Inhibition, Shyness, and Social Withdrawal in Childhood, a paper symposium presented at the 16th Biennial Meeting of the International Society for the Study of Behavioral Development, Beijing, China.
16. First Presidency and Council of Twelve Apostles (1995), 102.
17. Boyd K. Packer (1998, May), The Relief Society, *Ensign*, 28(5), 72.
18. Boyd K. Packer (1993, November), For time and all eternity, *Ensign*, 23(11), 21–23.
19. Gordon B. Hinckley (2002, May), Personal worthiness to exercise the priesthood, *Ensign*, 32(5), 52–59.
20. See S. Golombok and M. Hines (2002), Sex differences in social behavior; P. K. Smith and C. H. Hart, eds., in *Blackwell*

Handbook of Childhood Social Development (Oxford: Blackwell), 117–136; D. N. Ruble and C. L. Martin (1998), Gender development, in W. Damon and N. Eisenberg, eds., *Handbook of Child Psychology* (New York: John Wiley & Sons), 933–1016. These reviews of scientific literature suggest that girls tend to perform better in verbal skills and reading comprehension, tend to show greater concern about appearance and to demonstrate more helping behaviors, and tend to be more socially oriented, sensitive, and better able to decode emotions. Boys tend to show greater self-confidence and assertiveness and to perform better in spatial tasks. The authors note, however, that these differences are small to moderate at best.

21. Henry B. Eyring (1998, February), The family, *Ensign, 28*(2), 10.

22. D. N. Ruble and C. L. Martin (1998), Gender development, 933–1016.

23. L. Brody (1999), *Gender, Emotion, and the Family* (Cambridge, MA: Harvard University Press); C. Leaper (2000), Gender, affiliation, assertion, and the interactive context of parent-child play, *Developmental Psychology, 36,* 381–393; P. J. Turner and J. Gervai (1995), A multidimensional study of gender typing in preschool children and their parents: Personality, attitudes, preferences, behavior, and cultural differences, *Developmental Psychology, 31,* 759–772.

24. N. K. Sandnabba and C. Ahlberg (1999), Parents' attitudes and expectations about children's cross-gender behavior, *Sex Roles, 40,* 249–263.

25. D. Carter and L. A. McCloskey (1984), Peers and the maintenance of sex-typed behavior: The development of children's conceptions of cross-gender behavior in their peers, *Social Cognition, 2,* 294–314.

26. Sheri L. Dew (2001, November), It is not good for man or woman to be alone, *Ensign, 31*(11), 12–15.

27. B. C. Hafen and M. K. Hafen (1994), *The Belonging Heart: The Atonement and Relationships with God and Family* (Salt Lake City: Deseret Book), 235.

Latter-day Saint Families at the Dawn of the Twenty-first Century

R I C H A R D J . M C C L E N D O N A N D B R U C E A . C H A D W I C K

Further, we warn that the disintegration of the family will bring upon individuals, communities,
and nations the calamities foretold by ancient and modern prophets.[1]
—"The Family: A Proclamation to the World"

Prophetic counsel has emphasized that social stability and individual happiness can only thrive within communities where marriage and family are a priority.[2] Modern social science confirms the teachings of the prophets. In their widely acclaimed book, *The Case for Marriage,* Linda Waite and Maggie Gallagher reviewed a large research literature and found compelling scientific evidence that married individuals have better health, finances, and happiness. When compared to singles, cohabiters, or divorcees, those who are married live longer, suffer less illness, recover faster when sick, have less depression and anxiety, and commit suicide less often. Married people have greater financial security. They also have children who grow up to be physically and emotionally healthier and who are less likely to be delinquent than children who are raised in single-parent homes.[3]

In spite of this supportive evidence, marriage is on the decline in America. Some have suggested that factors such as modernization, the change in divorce laws, and increased educational opportunities for women have contributed to this shift.[4] Consequently, marital status in the United States over the past several decades has dramatically changed so that not only are people marrying at a later age, but divorce, which peaked in 1979, continues to affect nearly half of all families.[5] Recent data from the U.S. Census indicate that the percentage of married-couple house-

holds with children under 18, normally referred to as the "traditional family," is at an all-time low of 24 percent compared to 45 percent in the 1960s.[6]

President Gordon B. Hinckley observed:

As I look to the future, I see little to feel enthusiastic about concerning the family in America and across the world. Drugs and alcohol are taking a terrible toll, which is not likely to decrease. Harsh language, one to another, indifference to the needs of one another—all seem to be increasing. There is so much of child abuse. There is so much of spouse abuse. There is growing abuse of the elderly. All of this will happen and get worse unless there is an underlying acknowledgment, yes, a strong and fervent conviction, concerning the fact that the family is an instrument of the Almighty. It is His creation. It is also the basic unit of society.[7]

How are Latter-day Saint families doing? Are the trends of the world making their way into the families of the Church? In seeking to answer this, we investigated several familial factors among Latter-day Saints. First, we explored factors relating to marriage among members of the Church as well as their peers across the United States. Second, we compared data on divorce among Latter-day Saints and those not of our faith. Finally, we looked within Latter-day Saint families to learn more about their characteristics. Overall, we sought to clarify what we know and don't know about the familial health of Latter-day Saints at the dawn of the twenty-first century.

DATA

Data from three different random samples were used in this analysis. The first came from a survey in 1999 of 6,000 men and women from the United States who served missions for the Church. The sample was divided between those who had been back from their missions two, five, ten, and seventeen years, respectively. The age of the respondents ranged from 23 to 45 years old. Sixty-seven percent of the men and 84 percent of the women responded to the survey, making a combined response rate of 73 percent.[8]

The second survey was conducted in 2000 and collected data from 6,000 LDS men and women in the United States who did *not* serve a mission. The survey was mailed to the same age groups as those of the returned-missionary survey. Only 12 percent of the men and 31 percent of the women responded, making a combined response rate of 20 percent. Further analysis showed that the extremely low response rate for non-returned-missionary men was mainly due to high rates of Church inactivity.[9] Therefore, any findings reported in this chapter on non-returned-missionary men may only be generalizable for those who are more active in the Church.

The third sample represents the general population of men and women throughout the United States and comes from the 1998 and 2000 General Social Survey (GSS). The GSS is conducted by the National Opinion Research Center (NORC) at the University of Chicago. It collects interviews from a national sample of adult men and women. The response rates for 1998 and 2000 were 76 percent and 70 percent, respectively.[10] We selected the men and women in the GSS survey between the ages of 24 and 41, which matches the age range of the LDS samples.

It is important to note here that findings in this study often show that on average those who served missions tend to have greater marital success and happiness than those who did not serve. Recognizing this, we believe it would be a mistake to assume that missionary service alone is the sole cause of greater success in marriage and successful avoidance of divorce. It's highly likely that other factors are involved that not only lead to stronger marriages later in life, but also make a difference in whether a person chooses to go on a mission in the first place (e.g., ado-

lescent religiosity, positive personality characteristics). So, on the one hand, we in no way want to minimize the real changes that may result from missionary service, yet we must acknowledge that successful marriages may also be attributed to adolescent factors that were not measured.

MARRIAGE

Over the past three decades, marital status in the United States has changed dramatically, and the divorce rate continues to remain relatively high. How do Latter-day Saint marriages compare to these national trends? Table 1 compares the current marital status of men and women by about age 40.[11] Significantly more Latter-day Saint men, both returned missionary and non-returned missionary, are married compared to men across the United States. Ninety percent of the returned-missionary men and 63 percent of the non-returned-missionary men are currently in their first marriage, with 7 percent and 18 percent who are remarried, respectively. Fifty percent of men nationally are in their first marriage and 11 percent are remarried. Relatively few returned-missionary men are single (1 percent) or are currently divorced or separated (2 percent). Twelve percent of the non-returned-missionary men are single and 8 percent are divorced or separated. By contrast, almost one-fourth (22 percent) of the men from the GSS sample have never married, 11 percent are remarried, and 16 percent are currently divorced or separated.

By age 40, returned-missionary and non-returned-missionary women are also significantly different in their marital status from women across the nation. Seventy-six percent of returned-missionary women and 77 percent of non-returned-missionary women are in their first marriage. According to the GSS, 49 percent of the women in the national sample are in their first marriage. Only about 3 percent of non-returned-missionary women are still single as compared to 11 percent of returned-missionary-women and 15 percent of women nationally (11 percent—whites only). Twice as many non-returned-missionary women (14 percent) have remarried compared to returned-missionary women (7 percent). The rate of divorce for both groups is the same (6 percent). The data in Table 1 demonstrate that members of the Church are significantly more likely to be in their first marriage and less likely to be single, remarried, or divorced .

Single-Parent Households

The increase of divorce since the 1970s has brought with it a rise in single-parent families. In 1990, the percentage of children under age 18 living in a one-parent home in the United States (whites only) was around 19 percent.[12] Most of these are being raised by their mothers. This percentage is much smaller for Latter-day Saints. In 1992, Tim Heaton reported that the percentage of LDS children being raised in single-parent families in the United States was around 5 percent.[13] These figures have probably increased about 1 or 2 percent over the past 15 years.

Age at First Marriage

A significant trend in marriage patterns in the United States, which also affects Latter-day Saints, is the age at which couples marry. The median age at first marriage in the United States has fluctuated during the past century. For example, in 1900, the median age at which a man married was about 26 years old; a woman married around age 22. These ages steadily dropped until the 1950s, when the median age for men was 22 and for women, age 20. Since then, the median age at first marriage has dramatically increased. In 2003, the median age for men was 27 and women, around 25.[14]

Figure 1 shows the median age at first marriage for both LDS and U.S. men and women from 1980 to

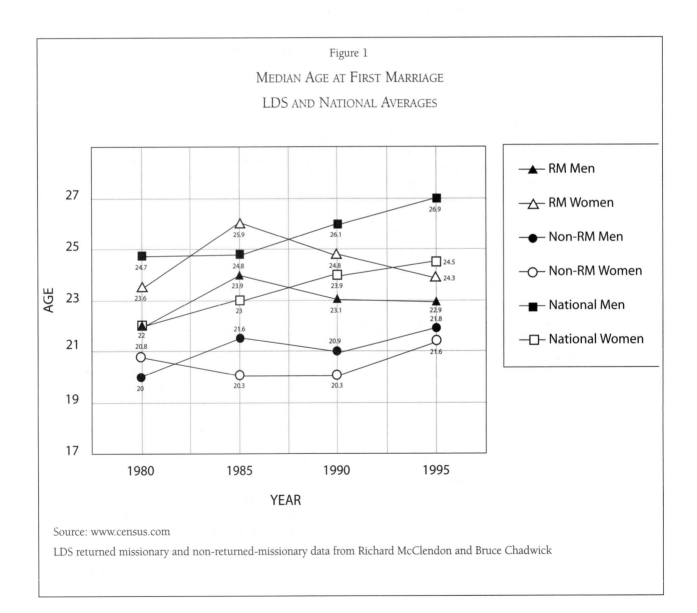

Figure 1

MEDIAN AGE AT FIRST MARRIAGE

LDS AND NATIONAL AVERAGES

Source: www.census.com

LDS returned missionary and non-returned-missionary data from Richard McClendon and Bruce Chadwick

Table 1

MARITAL STATUS: LDS AND NATIONAL DATA

Category	MEN[1]				WOMEN[2]			
	Returned Missionary (1999)	Non-Returned Missionary[3] (2000)	GSS All[4] (1998/2000)	GSS Whites Only[5] (1998/2000)	Returned Missionary (1999)	Non-Returned Missionary[6] (2000)	GSS All[7] (1998/2000)	GSS Whites Only[8] (1998/2000)
	N = 417	N = 96	N = 121	N = 103	N = 256	N = 139	N = 128	N = 105
Single—never married	1%	12%	22%	19%	11%	3%	15%	11%
Married, first marriage	90%	63%	50%	52%	76%	77%	49%	52%
Remarried	7%	18%	11%	10%	7%	14%	15%	15%
Divorced or Separated	2%	8%	16%	18%	6%	6%	20%	21%
Widowed	1%	0%	3%	1%	0.4%	0%	1%	1%
Total*	101%	101%	102%	100%	100%	100%	100%	100%

*Totals may not equal 100% due to rounding.

[1] Data is from specific age cohorts who are ages 38 and 39 years old.

[2] Data is from specific age cohorts who are ages 40 and 41 years old.

[3] Non-RM men's sample is significantly different at the .001 level when compared to the RM men.

[4] General Social Survey (GSS) men's sample (all races) is significantly different at the .001 level when compared to RM men and at the .05 level when compared to non-RM men.

[5] GSS men's sample (whites only) is significantly different at the .001 level when compared to RM men and is not significantly different when compared to non-RM men.

[6] Non-RM women's sample is significantly different at the .001 level when compared to the RM women.

[7] GSS women's sample (all races) is significantly different at the .001 level when compared to either the RM women or non-RM women.

[8] GSS women's sample (whites only) is significantly different at the .001 level when compared to either the RM women or non-RM women.

Table 2

MARITAL HAPPINESS: LDS AND NATIONAL DATA*

	Men[1]				Women[2]			
Category	Returned Missionary (1999)	Non-Returned Missionary (2000)	GSS All (1998/2000)	GSS Whites Only (1998/2000)	Returned Missionary (1999)	Non-Returned Missionary (2000)	GSS All (1998/2000)	GSS Whites Only (1998/2000)
	N = 1376	N = 246	N = 154	N = 123	N = 948	N = 522	N = 250	N = 213
1 = Not Too Happy	7%	10%	4%	4%	6%	10%	2%	2%
2 = Pretty Happy	31%	43%	42%	42%	30%	38%	37%	35%
3 = Very Happy	62%	47%	55%	55%	64%	53%	61%	63%
Total**	100%	100%	101%	101%	100%	101%	100%	100%
Mean	2.54[3]	2.35[4]	2.51	2.5	2.57[5]	2.41[6]	2.59	2.62

**Totals may not equal 100% due to rounding.

*The RM and non-RM scales were collapsed to fit the same categories as the General Social Survey (GSS) scales. The question for RM and non-RM samples was: All things considered, how happy is your marriage? Categories are: 1=Very unhappy, 2=Unhappy, 3=Mixed, 4=Happy, 5=Very happy. The question for GSS sample was: Taking things all together, how would you describe your marriage? Would you say that your marriage is very happy, pretty happy, or not too happy?

[1] Data is from specific age cohorts who are between ages 24 and 40 years old.

[2] Data is from specific age cohorts who are between ages 25 and 41 years old.

[3] RM men's sample is significantly different at the .001 level when compared to the non-RM men, but is not significantly different to each of the GSS men's samples (all and whites only).

[4] Non-RM men's sample is significantly different at the .05 level when compared to each of the GSS men's samples (all and whites only).

[5] RM women's sample is significantly different at the .001 level when compared to the non-RM women, but is not significantly different from the GSS women's samples (all and whites only).

[6] Non-RM women's sample is significantly different at the .001 level when compared to each of the GSS women's samples (all and whites only).

1995. Figures in 1995 show that the median age for first marriage among returned-missionary men is about 23, while non-returned-missionary men marry around age 22. The median age of first marriage for returned-missionary women is 24, non-returned-missionary women are much younger, marrying between 21 and 22. Thus, on average, LDS men in 1995 married about 4.5 years younger than their male peers nationally and LDS women married 1.5 years younger than women across the United States.

LDS data for the last 10 years is unavailable. However, we do have information on men and women nationally. For example, the median age at marriage for men has not increased over the past decade, but the rate for women has increased almost a full year. So, if the same pattern is found for Latter-day Saints, we would suppose that the age at first marriage for LDS women has increased, while age for LDS men has remained the same since 1995.

Marital Happiness

Marital happiness in the United States has consistently been found to be extremely high. Since the GSS began surveying in 1973, the percentage of those who say they are either "very happy" or "pretty happy" in their marriages has hovered around 97 percent.[15] Marital happiness among Latter-day Saints is also very high (see Table 2). Our analysis found that returned-missionary marriages were not significantly different in marital happiness than marriages nationally. Marital happiness among non-returned-missionary marriages was also very high, although lower when compared to the other two groups for both men and women.

Given prophetic counsel concerning eternal marriage and the principles of the proclamation, we are convinced that religious factors heighten marital happiness among Latter-day Saints. Our research confirmed this by showing that among three of the four LDS groups we studied, religiosity was clearly related to marital happiness. Those who more often read their scriptures, pray privately, and hold family scripture study, family prayer, and family home evening regularly are happier in their marriages. Being temple worthy and holding strong personal religious beliefs are also related to happier marriages.[16] We recognize that there may also be a number of other nonreligious factors that lead to marital happiness, but for Latter-day Saints, religiosity appears to be salient.

LDS Marital Characteristics

Table 3 shows several marital characteristics of LDS couples. These are whether both spouses are members of the Church, whether they were married in the temple, and under what circumstances the spouses met When asked whether his or her spouse was LDS, almost every married returned missionary said yes (men—99 percent; women—98 percent). Eighty-three percent of the non-returned-missionary men and 92 percent of the women had an LDS spouse.

The vast majority of returned missionaries (men—97 percent; women—96 percent) are currently sealed to their spouses, either through an original temple sealing or a sealing that took place after a civil marriage. Nearly two-thirds of the non-returned-missionary men (64 percent) have been sealed in the temple, as have around three-fourths of the non-returned-missionary women (78 percent).

One characteristic of mate selection that is unique in the LDS culture is where a person meets his or her spouse. We found that a Church meeting or activity was the most popular place for returned-missionary men and women as well as non-returned-missionary women to meet their future spouse. On the other hand, non-returned-missionary men generally found their spouses at a social or school event or some place other than a Church meeting. This may be due in part to being less active in Church attendance during their young adult years.[17]

DIVORCE

Given the emphasis the Church places on marriage, a significant and often-asked question is: What is the divorce rate among Latter-day Saints, especially for those with a temple marriage?[18] Unfortunately, information necessary to provide an exact answer to this is not available. However, researchers have done their best to produce some type of estimate. For example, in the late 1970s, Stan Albrecht, Howard Bahr, and Kristen Goodman conducted a divorce study of individuals (various religious affiliations) who lived in the Intermountain West. These researchers compared divorce rates by varying types of marriage settings (e.g., civil marriage, church marriage, temple marriage, other). Given the high rate of Latter-day Saints living in Utah, they included "temple marriage" as a category and assumed that only LDS members would select this response. In the end, they found that 7 percent of Church members

		RM Men N = 1631	Non-RM Men N = 257	RM Women N = 1091	Non-RM Women N = 529
Question	**Response**				

Table 3

LDS COURTSHIP AND MARRIAGE

Question	Response	RM Men N = 1631	Non-RM Men N = 257	RM Women N = 1091	Non-RM Women N = 529
Is your spouse a member of the LDS Church?	Yes	99%	83%	98%	92%
	No	1%	16%	2%	8%
	Total*	100%	99%	100%	100%
What type of ceremony did you have for your current marriage?	Temple sealing	91%	29%	91%	65%
	Civil marriage first, then temple sealing later	6%	35%	5%	13%
	Civil marriage	4%	36%	4%	22%
	Total*	101%	100%	100%	100%
What were you doing when you met your spouse?	Church meeting or activity	41%	18%	40%	32%
	Social event (not Church-related)	14%	22%	10%	17%
	School event (not Church-related)	11%	20%	7%	12%
	Work-related activity	8%	14%	10%	15%
	Other	26%	26%	33%	24%
*Totals may not equal 100% due to rounding.	Total*	100%	100%	100%	100%

who had originally had a temple marriage were either now divorced or were divorced and now remarried.[19] Thirty-five percent of the sample (includes all religious affiliations) who had originally married civilly were either currently divorced or remarried. Among those who were originally married in a church or synagogue, 15 percent were either divorced or remarried, and for those whose original marriage was classified in the "other" category, 21 percent had terminated these marriages.[20]

Given the differences in these rates, divorce rates of temple marriages were about five times lower than civil marriages, two times lower than church- or synagogue-type marriages, and three times lower than those who married in other settings.[21]

A study conducted by Tim Heaton and Kristen Goodman in the early 1980s compared divorce rates

between Latter-day Saints and members of other religious denominations who were white and age 30 and older. They found that Latter-day Saints had the lowest rate of divorce compared to other religious denominations including Catholics, liberal and conservative Protestants, and those with no religious preference. They reported that around 14 percent of LDS men and 19 percent of LDS women had been divorced at the time of the study. Twenty percent of Catholic men had divorced, as had 23 percent of Catholic women. Other religions reported higher percentages than the Catholics, with the highest percentage of divorce found to be among those who claimed no religious preference. Nearly 40 percent of the men and 45 percent of the women from this category had divorced.[22]

Heaton and Goodman also looked at the relationship between Church attendance and divorce. They found about 10 percent of active LDS men were divorced, while 22 percent of the LDS men who attended Church meetings less frequently were divorced. Fifteen percent of active LDS women were divorced as compared to 26 percent for those who did not go to church as often. Thus, LDS men and women who attended Church meetings regularly were about half as likely to be divorced as those who went to church only occasionally and about four to five times less than men and women nationally.[23]

Finally, Heaton and Goodman showed the proportion of members who had divorced from a temple marriage as compared to a non-temple marriage. Of those who had originally married in the temple, about 5 percent of the men and 7 percent of the women had been divorced. Around 28 percent of non-temple-married men and 33 percent of non-temple-married women were divorced.[24] Thus, temple marriages were about 5 times less likely to end in divorce than non-temple marriages.[25]

Follow-up research by Tim Heaton, Stephen Bahr, and Cardell Jacobson assessed data from the 1990s and suggested that the divorce rate gap between Latter-day Saints and their national peers is narrowing. Specifically, they estimated that the lifetime divorce rate for Latter-day Saints married in the temple may be two-thirds of the national average of divorce, or around 30 percent.[26]

We recently did our own assessment of divorce among Latter-day Saints from data collected between 1999 and 2001. Table 4 shows the marital status by about age 40 among ever-married LDS men and women and national men and women. Returned-missionary men ranked lowest in divorce at 9 percent. This is in comparison to 29 percent of non-returned-missionary men and 38 percent of men nationally. This shows that returned-missionary men are around three times less likely to divorce than non-returned-missionary men and a little over four times less likely than men nationally. Non-returned-missionary men are about three-fourths as likely to divorce as men nationally.

As for women, returned missionaries have a divorce rate of 15 percent, while non-returned missionaries are higher at 21 percent, and U.S. women are the highest compared to all other categories with 48 percent (whites only—45 percent) who have been divorced. Thus, returned-missionary women are about three-fourths less likely to divorce than non-returned-missionary women and slightly over three times less likely than women nationally. Marriages for non-returned-missionary women are just under half as likely to end in divorce as their national peers of the same age.

If the above rates represent divorce by age 40, is it possible to calculate a lifetime divorce rate? Many scholars believe that the current lifetime divorce rate in the United States is now around 50 percent.[27] Assuming that the proportion of divorce between Church members and their U.S. peers is similar across the life span, we estimate that the current lifetime divorce rate for returned-missionary men is around 12 percent[28] and for the women, around 16 percent. The lifetime rate for non-returned-missionary men is around 38 percent[29] and around 22 percent for non-returned-missionary women. These figures include both civil and temple marriages combined.

What then would be the divorce rate of temple marriages only? We, like previous researchers, must also estimate this figure. First of all, we know that returned missionaries represent a relatively active sub-group in the Church and, because almost all of them eventually attain a temple marriage (see Table 3), we believe that their lifetime divorce rate, which we reported earlier as 12 percent for the men and 16 percent for the women, would represent the lifetime divorce rate for temple marriages among typically active Latter-day Saints. Thus, our estimation of the lifetime divorce rate for those with temple marriages is somewhere in the teens and probably no higher than 20 percent.

LDS FAMILY CHARACTERISTICS

Family Size

We found a relatively high fertility rate among LDS men and women, which confirms the long-held notion that Latter-day Saint families are generally larger than those across the nation. Non-returned-missionary women have the highest number of children with an average of 3.92 per household, followed by returned-missionary women at 3.83. Returned-missionary men had an average of 3.75 children per household, with non-returned-missionary men the lowest among the LDS groups at 3.31. Compare these to men and women across the United States, where men average 1.73 children and women 1.99 per household, respectively.[30] With all LDS groups averaging 3+ children by their early thirties, this is almost twice the rate of their peers across the United States.

Table 4

MARITAL STATUS AMONG EVER-MARRIED MEN AND WOMEN: LDS AND NATIONAL DATA

Category	MEN[1]				WOMEN[2]			
	Returned Missionary (1999)	Non-Returned Missionary[4] (2000)	GSS All[5] (1998/2000)	GSS Whites Only[6] (1998/2000)	Returned Missionary (1999)	Non-Returned Missionary[7] (2000)	GSS All[8] (1998/2000)	GSS Whites Only[9] (1998/2000)
	N = 411	N = 85	N = 101	N = 88	N = 229	N = 135	N = 122	N = 101
First marriage	91%	71%	59%	61%	85%	79%	52%	55%
Ever divorced[3]	9%	29%	38%	38%	15%	21%	48%	45%
Widowed	1%	0%	3%	1%	0.4%	0%	1%	1%
Total*	101%	100%	100%	100%	100%	100%	101%	101%

*Totals may not equal 100% due to rounding.

[1] Data is from specific age cohorts who are 38 and 39 years old and have ever married.

[2] Data is from specific age cohorts who are 40 and 41 years old and have ever married.

[3] Includes those who are divorced, separated, remarried, and widows who had ever been divorced.

[4] Non-RM men's sample is significantly different at the .001 level when compared to the RM men.

[5] GSS men's sample (all races) is significantly different at the .001 level when compared to the RM men and is not significantly different when compared to the non-RM men.

[6] GSS men's sample (whites only) is significantly different at the .001 level when compared to the RM men and is not significantly different when compared to the non-RM men.

[7] Non-RM women's sample is not significantly different when compared to the RM women.

[8] GSS women's sample (all races) is significantly different at the .001 level when compared to either the RM women or the non-RM women.

[9] GSS women's sample (whites only) is significantly different at the .001 level when compared to either the RM women or the non-RM women.

Family Religious Behavior

Family religious behavior such as family scripture study, family prayer, and family home evening are shown in Table 5. As can be seen, 74 percent of the men and 79 percent of the women who served missions hold regular family prayer. Around 40 percent of the non-returned-missionary men hold regular family prayer, as do 62 percent of the non-returned-missionary women.

Family scripture study occurs less often than family prayer. Nearly half (46 percent) of the returned-missionary women say they hold family scripture study at least a few times a week. Returned-missionary men are next at just over one-third (36 percent). Non-returned-missionary women are at 33 percent, and only about 18 percent of the non-returned-missionary men have family scripture study several times a week.

Finally, more than half of the families of returned-

Table 5					
LDS Family Religious Practices					
Family Practices	**Response**	**RM Men** N = 1678	**Non-RM Men** N = 282	**RM Women** N = 1129	**Non-RM Women** N = 561
During the past year, how often did you pray as a family?	Every day/A few times a week	74%	40%	79%	62%
	About once a week/2 to 3 times a week/About once a month	15%	22%	13%	16%
	Less than once a month/Not at all	10%	38%	7%	22%
	Total	99%	100%	99%	100%
During the past year, how often did you study the scriptures as a family?	Every day/A few times a week	36%	18%	46%	33%
	About once a week/2 to 3 times a week/About once a month	36%	29%	32%	30%
	Less than once a month/Not at all	27%	53%	21%	37%
	Total	99%	100%	99%	100%
During the past year, how often did you hold family home evening?	Every day/A few times a week	55%	29%	63%	48%
	About once a week/2 to 3 times a week/About once a month	15%	12%	12%	15%
	Less than once a month/Not at all	29%	58%	24%	36%
	Total	99%	99%	99%	102%

missionary men (55 percent) and women (63 percent) hold regular family home evening. For families of women who did not serve a mission, the rate is around 48 percent. Twenty-nine percent of the men in this category are having regular home evenings with their families.

CONCLUSION

Our findings suggest that many members of The Church of Jesus Christ of Latter-day Saints are living the principles as found in "The Family: A Proclamation to the World."[31] Research shows significant differences in several marital factors of Latter-day Saints compared to their peers throughout the United States. A higher percentage of Latter-day Saints are married, fewer are divorced or single, they have more children per family, they marry earlier in life, and they have comparable marital happiness to those across the nation. Such an enduring social structure within the Church is encouraging given the anti-family sentiments that seem to be sweeping across America through various media and political platforms. If families are to receive the help and healing they need, they must continue to follow the prophetic counsel of both past and present prophets—that the family is the fundamental institution of society and that love and respect within marriage will create lasting happiness for families and stability in society.

ABOUT THE AUTHORS

Richard J. McClendon is a visiting assistant professor of sociology and an adjunct professor of ancient scripture at Brigham Young University. He received a Ph.D. in sociology at Brigham Young University.

Bruce A. Chadwick is a professor of sociology at Brigham Young University and has published numerous books and articles. He is a past recipient of the Karl G. Maeser Distinguished Research Award at BYU and holds the Maeser Professorship in General Education. He and his wife, Carolyn, are the parents of three sons and grandparents of seven.

ADDITIONAL READING

Tim B. Heaton, Stephen J. Bahr, and Cardell K. Jacobson (2004), *A Statistical Profile of Mormons: Health, Wealth, and Social Life* (Lewiston, NY: Edwin Mellen Press).

Richard J. McClendon and Bruce A. Chadwick (2004), Latter-day Saint returned missionaries in the United States: A survey on religious activity and postmission adjustment, *BYU Studies,* 43(2), 131–156.

NOTES

1. First Presidency and Council of Twelve Apostles (1995, November), The family: A proclamation to the world, *Ensign*, 25(11), 102.

2. Gordon B. Hinckley (2004, November), The women in our lives, *Ensign, 34*(11), 82–85; Ezra Taft Benson (1982, November), Fundamentals of enduring family relationships, *Ensign, 12*(11), 59–61; Spencer W. Kimball (1980, November), Families can be eternal, *Ensign, 10*(11), 4–5.

3. L. J. Waite and M. Gallagher (2000), *The Case for Marriage: Why Married People Are Happier, Healthier, and Better Off Financially* (New York: Doubleday).

4. R. J. Gelles (1995), *Contemporary Families: A Sociological View* (Thousand Oaks, CA: Sage), 389–396; R. Stark (2004), *Sociology,* 9th ed. (Belmont, CA: Wadsworth), 383.

5. Stark (2004), 381–382; Gelles (1995), 393.

6. E. Schmitt (2001, May 15), For first time, nuclear family drops below 25% of households, *New York Times*, A1, A20.

7. Gordon B. Hinckley (1997, November), Look to the future, *Ensign, 27*(11), 69.

8. In the winter and spring of 1999, four random samples were generated of 1,000 men and 500 women who had been back from their missions for two, five, ten, and seventeen years. A final sample of 4,884 returned missionaries (3,082 men and 1,802 women) from the United States was produced. Data were then collected via standard mail survey procedures which included four separate mailings.

9. To understand such a low response rate we called the bishops of a sample of 230 nonrespondents. Most bishops indicated that the nonrespondent in their ward either did not consider him- or herself a member of the Church or was completely inactive. Because of their alienation from the Church they probably saw little reason to participate in the study.

10. General Social Survey 1972–2002 Cumulative Datafile (2003); available at http://sda.berkeley.edu:7502/D3/GSS02/Docyr/gs020013.htm

11. This comparison was based on men, ages 38 and 39, and women, ages 40 and 41. The two LDS samples have a disproportionate number of whites when compared to the more varied racial makeup of the GSS sample. This demographic difference could relate to the differences in marital status outcomes. Thus we show as GSS categories in Table 1, Table 2, and Table 4 all races together and whites only.

12. U.S. Bureau of the Census (1992), Current Population Reports, P23–180, *Marriage, Divorce, and Remarriage in the 1990's* (Washington, D.C.: U.S. Government Printing Office).

13. T. B. Heaton (1992), Vital statistics, in *Encyclopedia of Mormonism,* Daniel H. Ludlow, ed. (New York: Macmillan), 4:1533.

14. U.S. Bureau of the Census (2003), Estimated median age at first marriage, by sex: 1890 to present; available at http://www.census.gov/population/socdemo/hh-fam/tabMS-2.pdf

15. General Social Survey 1972–2002 Cumulative Datafile (2003).

16. The correlations for these relationships range from .06 to .17. Although these are relatively small, they are significant, and the fact that several religiosity factors are significant shows the importance of religiosity's influence on keeping LDS couples happy in marriage. Non-returned-missionary men did not show

the same pattern as the other groups. Further research would be required to ferret out the reasons for this outcome.

17. D. A. Janson, (2002), *Religious Socialization and LDS Young Adults,* doctoral dissertation, Brigham Young University, 117.

18. This is referring to the civil divorce rate and not the dissolution of temple sealings.

19. S. L. Albrecht, H. M. Bahr, and K. L. Goodman (1983), *Divorce and Remarriage: Problems, Adaptations, and Adjustments* (Westport, CT: Greenwood Press), 80–81.

20. President Spencer W. Kimball, in a 1976 devotional address to students at Brigham Young University, stated that about 10 percent of temple marriages were dissolved by divorce. This is slightly higher than what Albrecht, Bahr, and Goodman found. See Spencer W. Kimball (1976, September 7), Marriage and divorce; BYU Devotional Address; available at http://speeches. byu.edu; Albrecht, Bahr, and Goodman (1983), 80–81.

21. Our assessment assumes that most of those who remarried were originally divorced rather than widowed.

22. T. B. Heaton and K. L. Goodman (1985), Religion and family formation, *Review of Religious Research, 26*(4), 349.

23. Ibid., 352.

24. Ibid., 354.

25. Ibid., 353.

26. T. B. Heaton, S. J. Bahr, and C. K. Jacobson (2005), *A Statistical Profile of Mormons: Health, Wealth, and Social Life* (Lewiston, NY: Edwin Mellen Press), 105.

27. We recognize that there continues to be an ongoing debate among scholars predicting an accurate lifetime divorce rate estimate. Some see it at or lower than 50 percent while others suggest it to be higher. Part of the problem is that there are a number of different ways to calculate the rate and each has its own strengths and weaknesses. See Stark (2004), 381–382; General Social Survey 1972–2002 Cumulative Datafile (2003). We use the 50 percent estimate as a matter of convenience in comparing LDS to national rates. If the national rate is in fact higher or lower, then our LDS estimate would also represent that shift.

28. This rate was calculated by taking the estimated lifetime divorce rate for U.S. men (50 percent) and multiplying it times the divorce rate of returned missionary men by age 40 (9 percent). The product was then divided by the divorce rate for U.S. men by age 40 (38 percent). This produced a quotient of .12 or 12 percent. The lifetime divorce rate for the other LDS samples were also calculated by this equation.

29. As we mentioned earlier, there was a very low response rate of non-returned missionaries to the survey and the main reason is likely disassociation from the Church. Because Church activity and marital stability are inversely associated, the divorce rate reported here (36 percent) may in fact be higher if we could include data from the nonrespondents. In other words, those who did not respond to the survey may have a higher rate of divorce than those who did respond.

30. Analysis is based on married, divorced, or separated persons between ages 35 and 44.

31. First Presidency and Council of Twelve Apostles (1995), 102.

CHAPTER 5

PROGRESSING TOWARD AN ETERNAL MARRIAGE RELATIONSHIP

THOMAS B. HOLMAN, ABBY VIVEIROS, AND JASON S. CARROLL

This will be the most important decision of your life, the individual whom you marry. . . .
Marry the right person in the right place at the right time.[1]
—President Gordon B. Hinckley

Since the creation of the world, the Lord, through His prophets, has continually emphasized the importance of marriage in the divine plan of happiness. The sacred ordinance of celestial marriage is essential to becoming like our heavenly parents and inheriting a fulness of eternal life. The ancient prophet Moses recorded that after the Lord God placed Adam in the Garden of Eden, He declared "that it was not good that the man should be alone; wherefore, I will make an help meet for him" (Moses 3:18). The New Testament apostle Paul taught, "neither is the man without the woman, neither the woman without the man, in the Lord" (1 Corinthians 11:11). In a revelation given to the Prophet Joseph Smith, we learn that "marriage is ordained of God unto man. Wherefore, it is lawful that he should have one wife, and they twain shall be one flesh, and all this that the earth might answer the end of its creation" (D&C 49:15–16). In modern times, "The Family: A Proclamation to the World" reaffirms these prophetic testimonies, stating that marriage is "ordained of God" and "is essential to His eternal plan" for the eternal destiny of His children.[2]

Current societal trends reveal that there are a number of pitfalls in today's dating and courtship culture that require young adults to approach marriage with an even greater degree of faith and steadfastness than was required in previous generations. In fact, for some single Latter-day Saints, following the prophets'

counsel to form a righteous marriage relationship may feel like a daunting, if not overwhelming, task. In this chapter we discuss several of the pitfalls of current dating practices in today's society and how those pitfalls influence dating patterns among Latter-day Saint young adults. Finally, we review prophetic principles of progressing toward an eternal marriage relationship with faith and confidence.

CURRENT SOCIAL TRENDS

Several demographic shifts during the last fifty years have contributed to changing societal views about what makes a person an adult and what is needed to be ready for marriage. One of the most dramatic changes influencing marriage preparation in the United States has been the emergence of a new life stage between adolescence and adulthood that has been labeled "emerging adulthood."[3] This life stage is the result of a substantial increase in the median age at first marriage for both men and women over the last 30 years. Since 1970, the median age of marriage in the United States has risen from 21 years for females and 23 for males to 25 and 27 years for females and males, respectively.[4] This tendency to delay marriage has created a period of nearly 10 years in the family life cycle in which most young adults have left adolescence and are beginning to view themselves as adults, but have not yet entered into the commitments and lifestyle patterns of married adult life.

Scholars have noted that the culture of dating that young adults experience today is markedly different than the one experienced by their parents and grandparents. In particular, there has been an erosion of traditional courtship patterns, and the new dating culture appears to be one that lacks any socially defined norms, rituals, and relationship milestones to guide young people toward marriage. Without the formal structure of traditional courtship, a number of dating pitfalls have emerged: (1) a growing pessimism about marriage, (2) a focus on personal independence before and after marriage, (3) widespread sexual permissiveness, and (4) high rates of couples living together before marriage.

Pessimism about marriage. Despite the growing trend to delay marriage, recent research indicates that having a successful, lifelong marriage is still a highly valued goal for the majority of young adults. In fact, 92 percent of young adults in the United States rate "having a good marriage" as quite or extremely important to them.[5] However, having grown up in a society saturated with divorce, many young people are becoming increasingly pessimistic about their chances of having a happy marriage. Nearly 1 in 3 young adults today agree with the statement that "one sees so few good or happy marriages that one questions it as a way of life." Simply put, when it comes to marriage, many young adults today have high aspirations but low expectations.

Getting ahead before getting wed. The responsibilities of adulthood in past generations centered on caring for one's spouse, providing for a family, and nurturing children—all of which involved duties toward others. However, recent research reveals that young people no longer consider marriage and parenthood to be criteria for adulthood.[6] In contrast, many young adults today report that becoming an adult occurs when a person accepts responsibility for oneself, achieves financial independence, and becomes an independent decision maker. For the most part, these new markers of perceived adulthood carry a theme of self-sufficiency and self-reliance compared to the traditional, other-oriented criteria of the past. This type of "independent ethic" to life may hinder young adults' willingness to embrace the "interdependent ethic" needed for spouses to become one in marriage and family life.

Hanging out and hooking up. One of the most dramatic changes in the dating culture is the disappearance of dating. Put another way, the "dating" culture has become a "hanging out" culture. Several studies have found that traditional dating, where a man asks a woman out on a date and pays for the evening's events, is becoming rare.[7] The common pattern these days is for young women and men to informally "hang out"—in a group or with just each other—rather than go on planned dates. With these patterns becoming widespread and accepted, young adults frequently report that even when they have "hung out" with a friend of the opposite sex for a long period of time, they still do not know whether they are a couple. This type of ambiguity in dating often leaves young adults with few widely recognized norms to guide and support them as they try to move forward toward love, commitment, and marriage.

Sexual permissiveness. Along with hanging out, today's dating culture is one often characterized by casual attitudes toward sexual relationships. Even though premarital sexual behavior has been shown to be a significant risk factor limiting future marital success,[8] single life in American culture has become synonymous with sexual experimentation in noncommittal romantic relationships.[9] A study of 1,000 college young women showed that a form of getting together, called "hooking up," is becoming widespread and accepted. Hooking up occurs when a young man and woman get together for the sole purpose of some kind of physical encounter, often full sexual expression, with no further expectations for the relationship.[10] One research team characterized today's dating and mating culture as "sex without strings, relationships without rings."[11]

Women complain about young men being "commitment phobic," and there is evidence to support that view. One study of young men suggested several reasons so many are unwilling to marry. Some of these reasons include: (1) they can get sex without marriage, (2) they can enjoy the benefits of having a wife by cohabiting rather than marrying, (3) they want to avoid divorce and its financial risks, (4) they fear that marriage will require too many changes and compromises, (5) they are waiting for the perfect soul mate and she hasn't yet appeared, (6) they face few social pressures to marry, and (7) they want to enjoy single life as long as they can.[12]

Acceptance of cohabitation. Recent research also indicates that emerging adults are increasingly embracing the idea that a couple needs to live together before marriage to test their relationship and see if they are ready for marriage. Recently, 62 percent of young adults reported in a survey that they believe living together before marriage is a good way to avoid eventual divorce.[13] In fact, more than half of all marriages in America today are preceded by cohabitation.[14] However, studies on cohabitation and later marital success have consistently found that couples who cohabit before marriage are *more* likely to divorce than couples who do not cohabitate before marriage.[15]

Parental attitudes about marriage. One final trend worth mentioning is the shifting views parents are offering to their young adult children when it comes to marriage preparation. Overall, there has been a lack of involvement by parents and lack of awareness about what hooking up or dating means for college students in today's world.[16] The espousal by many of a "personal independence ethic" of adult living may be encouraging emerging adults to develop self-focused identities and may be communicating the message that marriage is an unstable foundation for adult life and happiness. In addition, the encouragement of delayed marriage by parents may be exposing their children to additional marital risk factors such as cohabitation and premarital sexual behavior. Simply put, parents may be preparing their children for divorce rather than marriage.

DATING PATTERNS AMONG LATTER-DAY SAINT YOUNG ADULTS

Although many of the trends emerging in the larger dating culture have not become widespread among Latter-day Saints, there are some signs that the "hanging-out culture" of the day is becoming increasingly common among many young adult members of the Church. While the median age of first marriages among Latter-day Saints is still lower than national averages, Latter-day Saint young adults on average are marrying later than their parents and grandparents (see chapter 4 for statistical information on average age of first marriage among Latter-day Saints). Of those who do marry, too many later choose divorce.

Given the messages they are receiving and their experiences in the broader culture, it is not surprising that many young adults are confused, afraid to make commitments, and too often turning their ears to the messages of the world. There, they look for peace, for intimacy, for joy where it everlastingly can never be found. For example, a recent study of unmarried Brigham Young University students showed that "fear of making a mistake" was a factor influencing nearly 60 percent of those who are delaying marriage.[17] So

PREMARITAL RESOURCES

Just as you wouldn't invest in a major purchase or engage in a life-changing event without studying all the details, you shouldn't enter into marriage without first researching it. Many resources are available to help guide you. Be cautious, however, in your choosing; not all are wholesome or accurate. Brigham Young University's School of Family Life is a safe place to begin. The School houses some helpful online resources.

Before Forever Premarital Resources (http://beforeforever.byu.edu) provides comprehensive information about ways not only to prepare for the wedding, but also for your marriage. Devotionals on the topic of marriage are listed, as are LDS book references, talks given by family life scholars, and *Ensign* articles pertaining to marital issues. Worksheets about finances, mate selection, family traditions, and other topics are available to personalize your own preparation. Other useful resources and referrals are available to help plan your marriage.

The RELATE Institute (http://www.relate-institute.org) provides questionnaires individuals and couples can take to assess personal readiness for marriage or evaluate the strengths and weaknesses in a current relationship. After completing the questionnaire, a report is generated that provides feedback on "red flag" areas to be aware of, charts and graphs reflecting various issues related to marriage, and interpretation guidelines that include suggestions to improve your chances for a healthier and stronger marriage. The cost for each questionnaire is minimal.

Forever Families (http://foreverfamilies.net) provides practical, scholarly, and sacred information for strengthening individuals, marriages, and families that is organized around themes of "The Family: A Proclamation to the World." For example, the section on marriage preparation includes articles that provide helpful information from both scholarly and theological points of view.

Many LDS family scholars have written insightful books to guide you through the process of marriage preparation. We recommend you read and study these books. Not only are they enjoyable to read, you will learn much about the various components of marriage.

Box 5.1

what can be done to move toward a marriage relationship with confidence and trust?

Do not fear. First and foremost, "be of good cheer, and do not fear" (D&C 68:6). Elder Richard G. Scott advised: "You have a choice. You can wring your hands and be consumed with concern for the future or choose to use the counsel the Lord has given to live with peace and happiness."[18] Questions such as "When is the right time for me to marry?" or "How do I know if this is the right person to marry?" can cause a great deal of fear, doubt, and uncertainty. Concerning this topic, Elder Jeffrey R. Holland stated:

> I would like to have a dollar for every person in a courtship who knew he or she had felt the guidance of the Lord in that relationship, had prayed about the experience enough to know it was the will of the Lord, knew they loved each other and enjoyed each other's company, and saw a lifetime of wonderful compatibility ahead—only to panic, to get a brain cramp, to have total catatonic fear sweep over them. They "draw back," as Paul said [Hebrews 10:38], if not into perdition at least into marital paralysis. . . . Face your doubts. Master your fears. "Cast not away therefore your confidence" [Hebrews 10:35]. Stay the course and see the beauty of life unfold for you.[19]

One young man said this about overcoming the fear to make a commitment: "When Cheryl and I first started dating, I wondered if I really wanted to stop dating other girls. I was becoming more confident with dating and having more fun than ever before. I wasn't sure if I wanted this to end quite yet Then I thought about how much I had grown to love Cheryl and realized that I didn't want to fall in love with anyone else. When I made that realization, my goals regarding marriage became clear."[20] The scriptures remind us: "If ye are prepared ye shall not fear" (D&C 38:30).

Sometimes, even after dating someone for an extended amount of time, uncertainty may remain. The Lord will not leave you during this crucial time of decision making. Whatever fears you may have, seek the Lord to help overcome them and you will have peace.

In seeking answers, it is important to remember that ofttimes the Lord will answer these prayers for guidance as He answers most prayers—through the still small voice. Too many times, we overlook the peace the Lord provides as an answer because we're too busy waiting for thunder to boom. One of the authors was praying concerning the person she wanted to marry but wasn't receiving an answer in the way she wanted: "I expected the Lord to tell me in a big, booming voice that this person was the right man to marry. I didn't understand why I wasn't receiving a confirmation this way. After expressing this concern

to my brother, I prayed and went to bed. Later, I heard my door slowly open and a voice say in a deep, booming manner, 'YES!' I chuckled at my brother's attempt to help, but most importantly, I realized that the Lord had answered my prayers through the still small voice and by giving me peace about my decision."

Elder John H. Groberg taught the importance of true love and provided insights about seeking a temple marriage. The first step is to gain a testimony that marrying in the temple is what the Lord wants you to do. Next, make a promise that you will do everything in your power to make this happen. And finally, seek to marry the right person at the right time and in the right place. Elder Groberg stressed, once you know the marriage is right, don't delay unreasonably.[21]

Marry the right person. The idea of "the right person" must not be confused with the idea of a soul mate, a one-and-only. There is no such thing (see chapter 7). The right person, according to Elder Bruce R. McConkie, "is someone for whom the natural and wholesome and normal affection that should exist does exist. It is the person who is living so that he or she can go to the temple of God and make the covenants that we there make."[22]

Research shows that a right person should generally have values and characteristics similar to yours. Look for someone who is emotionally, mentally, and spiritually similar to you. Search for someone who helps you be your best and holds true to the highest values. President Ezra Taft Benson suggested asking these important questions: "Does he [she] have a strong testimony? Does he [she] live the principles of the gospel and magnify his priesthood? Is he [she] active in his [her] ward and stake? Does he [she] love home and family, and will he [she] be a faithful husband [wife] and a good father [mother]?"[23] There are plenty of good singles who can answer "yes" to these questions.

One young adult explained how her choice in marriage was influenced by gospel commitment: "When I became friends with [my future husband], I did not consider him a romantic interest. He didn't match up very well with all those lists I had made about my ideal spouse. But I enjoyed his friendship because he made me laugh and always treated me with great respect. When I saw his commitment to the Lord, to working hard, and to serving others— then I fell in love. We couldn't be happier!"[24]

There are many desirable qualities to look for in

a mate. The Lord expects you to be wise in choosing characteristics that are most important, but also understand that the list should be realistic. If your list describes in detail traits of Cinderella or Prince Charming, you may be waiting a long time to find your fairytale spouse. Furthermore, before you start holding others up to scrutiny to see if they are worthy of you, maybe you should work first on becoming a right person yourself. As Elder Richard G. Scott has said: "I suggest that you not ignore many possible candidates who are still developing these attributes, seeking the one who is perfected in them. You will likely not find that perfect person, and if you did, there would certainly be no interest in you. These attributes are best polished together as husband and wife."[25]

Marry in the right place. A marriage solemnized in the temple is the highest ordinance—an essential ordinance—of the gospel that must not be compromised. President Gordon B. Hinckley stated: "There is no substitute for marrying in the temple. It is the only place under the heavens where marriage can be solemnized for eternity."[26] Marrying in the right place also includes doing it with the right attitude—with an emphasis on the holy sealing ordinance and other temple covenants. As you kneel across from your chosen mate at the altar of the temple, you are sealed to one another with a covenant and a promise of eternal life and posterity. This simple, short sealing is of the most profound importance for you, for your children, and for generations to come.

We often see brides and grooms—and parents—who are stressed and troubled about many things in preparing for the marriage, such as the reception, wedding dress, tuxedos, invitations, and pictures. Although the reception and other parts of the wedding celebration are a great way for family and friends to share in this important occasion, the most careful preparations should be made for the most important part of the day—entering into the marriage covenant and reflecting upon the promises and blessings that will be made in the house of the Lord.

Marry at the right time. President Hinckley has this counsel about timing:

> I hope you will not put off marriage too long. I do not speak as much to the young women as to the young men whose prerogative and responsibility it is to take the lead in this matter. Don't go on endlessly in a frivolous dating game. Look for a choice companion, one you can love, honor, and respect, and make a decision.[27]

One young woman, although not certain about the exact timing of when she'd marry, understood that she needed to prepare herself so she would feel ready when that time came. She explained, "[Beginning when I was a teenager], I learned skills that would help my marriage. . . . For instance, I learned how to cook and budget Most importantly, I attended institute classes and tried to listen to the counsel of the Brethren to prepare myself to be a better individual. I also worked on my communication skills with my friends and roommates. Now that I'm married, I can say that learning and practicing these skills beforehand have greatly helped my marriage."[28]

For some single adults, marriage may not occur in this life. Only the Lord knows the exact timeline of life events, including marriage. Sister Sheri L. Dew recounted how she dealt with this issue of desiring marriage in the temple while waiting on the Lord's timing:

> My solution initially to my heartbreak was to exercise so much faith that the Lord would have to give me what I wanted—which was a husband. Believe me, if fasting and prayer and temple attendance automatically resulted in a husband, I'd have one. Well, the Lord hasn't even yet given me a husband; but He did heal my heart. . . . There is power in God the Father and His Son Jesus Christ—power that we may access through the word, the Holy Ghost, the priesthood, and the ordinances of the holy temple.[29]

Conclusion

As you prepare for a celestial marriage, have faith that God will help you find a wonderful person and establish a happy family—in His way and in His time. Prayer and personal revelation are keys in inviting the Lord to help us as we seek a temple marriage. Elder Henry B. Eyring promised, "As we read of what the proclamation tells us about the family, we can expect, in fact we must expect, impressions to come to our minds as to what we are to do, and we can be confident it is possible for us to do according to those impressions."[30] Although current marital trends may look discouraging, remember the Lord's desire that we marry the right person at the right time in the right place. The Lord does not give commandments that cannot be obeyed (1 Nephi 3:7). Approach the Lord with your concerns about moving toward eternal marriage, and have faith—expect that impressions will come and that you can do whatever the Lord tells you. Don't be afraid, don't give up, and don't become discouraged. Wherever you are, the Lord stands ready and willing to help you.

ABOUT THE AUTHORS

Thomas B. Holman is professor and chair of Marriage, Family, and Human Development in the School of Family Life at Brigham Young University. He has published widely in the area of mate selection and marital quality. He is married to the former Linda Nicholls and they are the parents of five children and grandparents of five.

Abby Viveiros is currently finishing her master's degree at Brigham Young University in marriage, family, and human development. Her interests lie in premarital education and marital quality. Abby and her husband, David, are the parents of two children.

Jason S. Carroll is assistant professor of marriage, family, and human development in the School of Family Life at Brigham Young University. He is widely published in the areas of marriage readiness, marital quality, and marriage education. He and his wife, Stefani, are the parents of Garret, Austin, Lindsey, and Caleb.

NOTES

1. Gordon B. Hinckley (1999, February), Life's obligations, *Ensign, 29*(2), 2.

2. First Presidency and Council of Twelve Apostles (1995, November), The family: A proclamation to the world, *Ensign, 25*(11), 102.

3. J. J. Arnett (2000), Emerging adulthood: A theory of development from the late teens through the twenties, *American Psychologist, 55,* 469–480.

4. U.S. Census Bureau (2003), *Statistical Abstract of the United States, 2003* (Washington, D.C.: U.S. Census Bureau); available at http://www.census.gov/population/socdemo/hh-fam/tabMS-2.pdf. See statistical information specifically related to Latter-day Saints in chapter 4 of this volume.

5. B. D. Whitehead and D. Popenoe (1999), Changes in teen attitudes toward marriage, cohabitation and children: 1975–1995; available at http://marriage.rutgers.edu/Publications/pubteena.htm

6. J. J. Arnett (1998), Learning to stand alone: The contemporary American transition to adulthood in cultural and historical context, *Human Development, 41,* 295–315.

7. Only 50 percent of college women report that they have been asked out on six or more dates, and one-third said they have only been asked on two or fewer dates. See Independent Women's Forum (2001), Hooking up, hanging out, and hoping for Mr. Right—College women on dating and mating today, http://www.iwf.org/campuscorner/pdf/hookingup.pdf. See also Dallin H. Oaks (2005, May 1), The dedication of a lifetime; CES Fireside Address; available at http://speeches.byu.edu

8. T. B. Heaton (2002), Factors contributing to increasing marital stability in the United States, *Journal of Family Issues, 23,* 392–409.

9. Independent Women's Forum (2001).

10. Ibid.

11. B. D. Whitehead and D. Popenoe (2000), The state of our unions 2000: The social health of marriage in America; available at http://marriage.rutgers.edu

12. B. D. Whitehead and D. Popenoe (2002), The state of our unions 2002: The social health of marriage in America; available at http://marriage.rutgers.edu

13. B. D. Whitehead and D. Popenoe (2001), The state of our unions 2001: The social health of marriage in America; available at http://marriage.rutgers.edu

14. L. Bumpass and H. H. Lu (2000), Trends in cohabitation and implications for children's family contexts in the United States, *Population Studies, 54,* 29–41.

15. J. Teachman (2003), Premarital sex, premarital cohabitation, and the risk of subsequent marital dissolution among women, *Journal of Marriage and Family, 65,* 444–455.

16. Independent Women's Forum (2001).

17. B. A. Chadwick, B. L. Top, R. J. McClendon, and L. Smith (not yet published), Dating BYU style; manuscript in possession of the authors.

18. Richard G. Scott (2004, May), How to live well amid increasing evil, *Ensign, 34*(5), 100.

19. Jeffrey R. Holland (1999, March 2), Cast not away therefore your confidence; BYU Devotional Address; available at http://speeches.byu.edu

20. Andrew Arnott, personal communication, 20 December 2004.

21. John H. Groberg (2001, December 4), The other side of heaven; BYU Devotional Address; available at http://speeches.byu.edu

22. Bruce R. McConkie (1955, September 30), in conference report, 13.

23. Ezra Taft Benson (1988, November), To the single adult sisters of the Church, *Ensign, 18*(11), 97.

24. Hilary Hendricks, personal communication, 15 October 2004.

25. Richard G. Scott (1999, May), Receive the temple blessings, *Ensign, 29*(5), 26.

26. Hinckley (1999), 2.

27. Gordon B. Hinckley (1990, March), Thou shalt not covet, *Ensign, 20*(3), 6.

28. Stacee Seegmiller, personal communication, 3 January 2005.

29. Sheri L. Dew (2003, December 9), You were born to lead, you were born for glory; BYU Devotional Address; available at http://speeches.byu.edu

30. Henry B. Eyring (1998, February), The family, *Ensign, 28*(2), 10.

CHAPTER 6

THE COVENANT OF MARRIAGE

DANIEL K JUDD AND ANN N. MADSEN

The family is ordained of God. Marriage between man and woman is essential to His eternal plan.[1]
—*"The Family: A Proclamation to the World"*

While marriage has been a vital part of all civilized cultures throughout the history of the world, the "new and everlasting covenant of marriage" (D&C 131:2), as revealed by the Lord through the Prophet Joseph Smith, is a distinguishing feature of the restored gospel of Jesus Christ. President Gordon B. Hinckley explained, "Marriage may be eternal through exercise of the power of the everlasting priesthood in the house of the Lord."[2] President Spencer W. Kimball stated: "Civil marriage is an earthly *contract,* dissolved by the death of either party. Eternal celestial marriage is a sacred *covenant* between man and woman, consecrated in the holy temple by servants of God who hold authoritative keys. It bridges death; it includes both time and eternity."[3]

Elder Bruce C. Hafen illustrated one of the differences between contractual marriage and covenant marriage. He stated:

> When troubles come, the parties to a *contractual* marriage seek happiness by walking away. They marry to obtain benefits and will stay only as long as they're receiving what they bargained for. But when troubles come to a *covenant* marriage, the husband and wife work them through. They marry to give and to grow, bound by covenants to each other, to the community, and to God.[4]

While there are those in our contemporary cul-ture who define marital and family associations in terms of contract relationships, and many nations are in the process of allowing the redefinition of what constitutes a marriage and a family, latter-day prophets continue to articulate the definition established by the Lord. Elder Richard G. Scott clearly explained why the covenant of marriage is between one man and one woman:

> In the Lord's plan, it takes two—a man and a woman—to form a whole. Indeed, a husband and wife are not two identical halves, but a wondrous, divinely determined combination of complementary capacities and characteristics. . . . When used as the Lord intends, those capacities allow a married couple to think, act, and rejoice as one—to face challenges together and overcome them as one, to grow in love and understanding, and through temple ordinances to be bound together as one whole, eternally. That is the plan.[5]

The marriage covenant includes God as the principal partner in the relationship. Placing God at the center of marriage is another major difference between the covenant of marriage and a marriage contract. Bishop Keith B. McMullin of the Presiding Bishopric explained:

> When I married my dear wife, I knew I would always be number two in her life. This is because she loves God more than she loves me. Over the years my

understanding and appreciation for the paramount importance of this "first and great commandment" [Matthew 22:36–38] has deepened. You see, because she loves God more than anything else, she is able to love me more than everything else. . . . As we center our love first and foremost in God, the Eternal Father, the capacity emerges within us to love all the works of His hands. . . . Temple covenants protect and preserve us.[6]

TEMPLE COVENANTS

"A covenant is a sacred promise," Elder F. Burton Howard stated. "We promise to do some things, and God binds Himself to do others. To those who keep the covenant of marriage, God promises the fullness of His glory, eternal lives, eternal increase, exaltation in the celestial kingdom, and a fullness of joy." Elder Howard also described some of what is required of the covenant couple:

> This means that the parties to the marriage covenant agree to invite God into their marriage, to pray together, to keep the commandments, to keep wants and passions within certain limits that the prophets have outlined. It means to be equal companions and to be just as true and pure outside the home as inside the home.[7]

Covenants are guideposts along the path we are to travel and include the promise of future blessings. Covenants define the "way of holiness" (Isaiah 35:8) and the "rod of iron" (1 Nephi 8:19). These holy promises bring us closer and closer to the Lord and to one another. Strength comes from knowing that there are others who share our values and will help us keep our commitments.

The grace of Christ, the obedience of His children, and the binding of God and His children together are accomplished as a couple enters into and keeps temple covenants. As a man and woman approach the altar of the temple, prepared to covenant with God that they will work to create an eternal marriage, they are bound together in love and commitment as their marriage begins. Knowledge of one's own and discovery of the other's unknown habits and minor faults are tempered by the desire to build a celestial relationship. As time goes by and trials come, commitment to the marriage covenant helps husbands and wives to sustain and lift each other.[8] Elder Spencer J. Condie shared the following story of a couple who overcame serious differences to build an eternal relationship:

A few years ago my wife, Dorthea, and I were walking across the grounds of a temple in a foreign land when we met a very radiant, cheerful, silver-haired sister. Her cheerful, Christlike countenance seemed to set her apart from those around her, and I felt inclined to ask her to explain why she looked so happy and content with life.

"Well," she said with a smile, "several years ago I was in a hurry to get married, and quite frankly, after a few months I realized I had married the wrong man." She continued, "He had no interest in the Church as he had initially led me to believe, and he began to treat me very unkindly for several years. One day I reached the point where I felt I could go on no longer in this situation, and so in desperation I knelt down to pray, to ask Heavenly Father if He would approve of my divorcing my husband.

"I had a very remarkable experience," she said. "After I prayed fervently, the Spirit revealed a number of insights to me of which I had been previously unaware. For the first time in my life, I realized that, just like my husband, I am not perfect either. I began to work on my intolerance and my impatience with his lack of spirituality.

"I began to strive to become more compassionate and loving and understanding. And do you know what happened? As I started to change, my *husband* started to change. Instead of my nagging him about going to church, he gradually decided to come with me on his own initiative.

"Recently we were sealed in the temple, and now we spend one day each week in the temple together. Oh, he's still not perfect, but I am so happy that the Lord loves us enough to help us resolve our problems."[9]

Continued expressions of love for spouse, with increased attention to one's own behavior and spiritual progress, can help couples overcome differences. (Essay H5 shares encouragement for those with family members who do not participate fully in Church activity.)

THE FOUNDATION OF A STRONG MARRIAGE

The foundation upon which an eternal marriage and family grows and thrives is Jesus Christ. All other temporal foundations will eventually fail. The Book of Mormon prophet Helaman taught his sons, Nephi and Lehi, "that it is upon the rock of our Redeemer, who is Christ, the Son of God, that ye must build your foundation" (Helaman 5:12). As we make and keep sacred covenants that bind us to God, our temple sealing becomes a viable force in our daily lives. We slowly learn to acquire the attributes of the Savior, helping us be more like Him. As we come closer to God we come closer to one another and we find our marriage growing into an eternal partnership. We learn to love with that unfailing love known in the scriptures as *charity,* "the pure love of Christ" (Moroni 7:47). Elder Marvin J. Ashton explained:

> Perhaps the greatest charity comes when we are kind to each other, when we don't judge or categorize someone else, when we simply give each other the benefit of the doubt or remain quiet Charity is accepting someone's differences, weaknesses, and shortcomings; having patience with someone who has let us down; or resisting the impulse to become offended when someone doesn't handle something the way we might have hoped. Charity is refusing to take advantage of another's weakness and being willing to forgive someone who has hurt us. Charity is expecting the best of each other.[10]

A careful study of Mormon's discourse on charity (Moroni 7:45–48; see also 1 Corinthians 13:1–13) reveals a pattern for forgiveness. When we have made up our minds to forgive, we are determined to be kind, not puffed up, and to leave envy and jealousy behind. We decide not to be easily provoked, nor to think evil or be suspicious. We are determined not to rejoice in iniquity, but rather to rejoice in the truth. The prophet Jacob explains that the Spirit speaks the truth of "things as they really are, and of things as they really will be" (Jacob 4:13). Hence, the Spirit can reveal to us knowledge of things as they were during the moment of hurt or offence, and of things as they now *really* are at the present moment, when we may have grown in understanding. Then we can glimpse, again through the Spirit, "things as they *really* will be" as we envision with a "perfect brightness of hope" (2 Nephi 31:20) a sanctified, celestial relationship.

After receiving the illuminating principles of the gospel, Elder Parley P. Pratt experienced an increase in his ability to love:

> I had loved before, but . . . now I loved—with a pureness—an intensity of elevated, exalted feeling, which would lift my soul from the transitory things of this groveling sphere and expand it as the ocean. I felt that God was my heavenly Father indeed; that Jesus was my brother, and that the wife of my bosom was an immortal, eternal companion: a kind, ministering angel. . . . In short, I could now love with the spirit and with the understanding also.[11]

Couples who seek the gift of charity through prayer, righteous living, and gospel study will grow together in understanding and love.

Growing Together

There is a rhythm of giving and receiving between the parties in a covenant marriage. Equal partners are constantly repenting of their own sins and learning to give for the good of the other. There are few experiences more inspiring than watching two people bring out the best in each other. We can give the benefit of the doubt to those we love and in return receive their forgiveness for our sins and weaknesses. When we forgive everyone, everything, every time, we lighten our own burdens. When we refuse to forgive, we burn the bridge that we ourselves must cross. We can give up cherished notions, and we can learn to care more for the person than for our own long-held perfect idea of what he or she ought to be. Fixing ourselves becomes the priority rather than attempting to fix others. Eventually, we will find we are able to give all in consecration, but it is a process that takes much practice and prayer.

There is a sweetness, a joy, in overcoming one's own sins and weaknesses and, at the same time, giving constant encouragement by adding our faith as our spouse strives to do the same. Giving and receiving teaches us to be one. Maintaining this eternal perspective changes the petty to the profound in a moment. The very thought of the Savior and all He gave for us[12] serves as a constant invitation to love and to change.

The Savior described why faultfinding in marriage doesn't work. He encouraged us to "first cast out the beam out of thine own eye; and then shalt thou see clearly to cast out the mote out of thy [spouse's] eye" (Matthew 7:5). Seeing clearly, we can witness our spouse's development with joy and avoid the "I told you so" that plagues so many marriages. Finding truth together and then being willing to act upon it takes courage. Saying "I'm truly sorry" takes practice. We must stand ready to lift, never to push back down, and to receive in love—always an ally, never an enemy. The feeling that "I'm on your side" is vital.

In the marriage covenant we are each other's constant context.[13] There will be times when we lift and times when we must lean on one another when the journey is wearying. Be so near to those whom you love, that when they weep you taste the salt of their tears. We can always smile in love and understanding in good times and in bad. And sometimes we can laugh or cry, but always together. The Lord instructed, "I say unto you, be one; and if ye are not one ye are not mine" (D&C 38:27). The cord of oneness grows stronger and stronger as spouses help each other through the trials of life: "Me lift thee and thee lift me, and we'll both ascend together."[14]

The Ideal Family and the Doctrine of Eternal Marriage

There is a story told of a young boy who walks into the foyer of a large office building with his father and sees a clock that is so high on the wall no one can reach it. To make any adjustments or to service the clock, workmen must use a tall ladder. The boy asks his father, "Why is the clock set so high, where nobody can reach it?" "It's simple," answers the boy's father, "the clock used to be lower, within reach of everybody. People would pass by, look at their watch, and adjust the clock to match their watch. When they moved the clock higher, people would look at it and adjust their watches accordingly."[15] (See D&C 1:16; Deuteronomy 12:8; Proverbs 12:15.)

Though some object to the high standards exacted by the marriage covenant, we need to keep this sacred relationship as a clock high on the wall, an immovable ideal that helps to guide our progress. Elder Richard G. Scott said:

> Throughout your life on earth, seek diligently to fulfill the fundamental purposes of this life *through the ideal family*. While you may not have yet reached that ideal, do all you can through obedience and faith in the Lord to consistently draw as close to it as you are able. Let nothing dissuade you from that objective. If it requires fundamental changes in your personal life, make them. . . . If you have lost the vision of eternal marriage, rekindle it. If your dream requires patience, give it. . . . Living a pattern of life as close as possible to the ideal will provide much happiness, great satisfaction, and impressive growth while here on earth regardless of your current life circumstances.[16]

Trying to have the ideal marriage and family can be challenging and is often discouraging, but it is important to remember that in mortality the ideal marriage isn't perfect. President Spencer W. Kimball helps us understand: "While marriage is difficult, and discordant and frustrated marriages are common, yet real, lasting happiness is possible, and marriage can be more an exultant ecstasy than the human mind can conceive. This is within the reach of every couple, every person."[17] If we are true to the covenants we have made, through the Atonement of Christ, we will one day be part of an ideal marriage.

We should also remember that provision will be made for those who have not had the opportunity to create their own eternal marriage and family in this life. President Gordon B. Hinckley spoke plainly to the women of the Church:

> Some of you, unfortunately, will never marry in this life. That turns out to be the case sometimes. If that happens, do not spend your life grieving over it. The world still needs your talents. It needs your contribution. The Church needs your faith. It needs your strong, helping hand. Life is never a failure until we call it such. There are so many who need your helping hands, your loving smile, your tender thoughtfulness. I see so many capable, attractive, wonderful women whom romance has passed by. I do not understand it, but I know that in the plan of the Almighty, the eternal plan which we call God's plan of happiness, there will be opportunity and reward for all who seek them.[18]

There is a voice in each of us, married or single, that whispers to us that we can become like the Lord Jesus Christ. His path is simple and direct; in fact, He calls it *strait* (narrow, bounded).[19] Loving and serving one another helps us stay on the path. Married or single, we can develop godly traits as we stay on this Christ-led way. Faithfulness to sacred covenants between a man, a woman, and God allows marriage to exist through mortality into an eternal world beyond.

ABOUT THE AUTHORS

Daniel K Judd is an associate professor of ancient scripture at BYU. He is married to Kaye Seegmiller Judd and they are the parents of four children and one grandchild. He currently serves as first counselor in the Sunday School general presidency.

Ann N. Madsen teaches courses in ancient scripture at BYU. She taught for five years at the BYU Center for Near-Eastern Studies in Jerusalem. She served with her husband, Truman G. Madsen, as he presided over the New England Mission. They are the parents of four children, sixteen grandchildren, and five great-grandchildren.

ADDITIONAL READING

Douglas E. Brinley and Daniel K. Judd, eds. (2004), *Living a Covenant Marriage: Practical Advice from Thirteen Experts Who've Walked in Your Shoes* (Salt Lake City: Deseret Book).

Bruce C. Hafen (1996, November), Covenant marriage, *Ensign*, 26(11), 26–28.

Gordon B. Hinckley (1991, May), What God hath joined together, *Ensign*, 21(5), 71–74.

NOTES

1. First Presidency and Council of Twelve Apostles (1995, November), The family: A proclamation to the world, *Ensign, 25*(11), 102.

2. Gordon B. Hinckley (1998, November), What are people asking about us? *Ensign, 28*(11), 71.

3. Spencer W. Kimball (1995, February), Temples and eternal marriage, *Ensign, 25*(2), 42, emphasis added.

4. Bruce C. Hafen (1996, November), Covenant marriage, *Ensign, 26*(11), 26.

5. Richard G. Scott (1996, November), The joy of living the great plan of happiness, *Ensign, 26*(11), 73–74.

6. Keith B. McMullin (2003, October 21), Make God and His kingdom the center of your life; BYU Devotional Address; available at http://speeches.byu.edu

7. F. Burton Howard (2003, May), Eternal marriage, *Ensign, 33*(5), 93.

8. Hafen (1996), 26–28.

9. Spencer J. Condie (1993, November), A mighty change of heart, *Ensign, 23*(11), 15.

10. Marvin J. Ashton (1992, May), The tongue can be a sharp sword, *Ensign, 22*(5), 19.

11. Quoted in Truman G. Madsen (2001), *Five Classics* (Salt Lake City: Eagle Gate), 81.

12. Bernard of Clairvaux (attributed) and John B. Dykes (1985), Jesus, the very thought of Thee, *Hymns* (Salt Lake City: The Church of Jesus Christ of Latter-day Saints), 141.

13. See Claudia Clayton (2004, April 6), Agency and context; BYU Devotional Address; available at http://speeches.byu.edu

14. John Greenleaf Whittier; quoted in Sterling W. Sill (1974), *That Ye Might Have Life* (Salt Lake City: Deseret Book), 268.

15. Rabbi Irving Lehrman; quoted in M. Gold, *Family: A Spiritual Guide;* in D. K Judd, ed. (2003), *Taking Sides: Clashing Views on Controversial Issues in Religion* (Guilford, CT: McGraw-Hill/Dushkin), 140.

16. Richard G. Scott (2001, May), First things first, *Ensign, 31*(5), 7; emphasis in original.

17. Quoted in E. L. Kimball, ed. (1982), *Teachings of Spencer W. Kimball* (Salt Lake City: Bookcraft), 305–306.

18. Gordon B. Hinckley (2003, November), To the women of the Church, *Ensign, 33*(11), 114.

19. Merriam-Webster's Collegiate Dictionary (2003), 10th ed., s.v. "strait." See Matthew 7:13–14; 2 Nephi 31:17–20.

CHAPTER 7

LOVING AND CARING FOR EACH OTHER IN MARRIAGE

JASON S. CARROLL AND ELIZABETH VANDENBERGHE

Husband and wife have a solemn responsibility to love and care for each other.[1]
—"The Family: A Proclamation to the World"

Amid the advice a particularly famous devil offers to his apprentice demon on driving humans further into mischief lies a gem on wrecking marriages. In C. S. Lewis's *The Screwtape Letters,* Screwtape admonishes young nephew Wormwood that "humans can be made to infer the false belief that the blend of affection, fear, and desire which they call 'being in love' is the only thing that makes marriage either happy or holy."[2] Screwtape explains that this form of deception keeps men and women from recognizing the deeper nature and purposes of marriage that involve "the intention of loyalty to a partnership for mutual help, for the preservation of chastity, and for the transmission of life."[3] Promoting the delusion that "being in love" is the foundation of marriage is the primary means by which these devils keep spouses from realizing that when God "described a married couple as 'one flesh' [He] did not say 'a happily married couple' or 'a couple who married because they were in love.'"[4]

But isn't "being in love" the key factor of a successful marriage? Aren't love, romance, and happiness the cornerstones of good marriage? How we answer these questions largely depends on the sources we turn to for insight into what makes marriage work. This chapter explores how prophetic teachings on marriage differ from many perspectives of marriage perpetuated in popular culture and discusses how gospel principles offer spouses a sure and effective

way to maintain a loving, lasting marriage. Building upon these principles, we discuss some general practices spouses can use to strengthen their marriage relationships.

PERSPECTIVES ON MARRIAGE

Screwtape's tactic of leading people to believe that marriage should be primarily based on the emotional state of "being in love" seems to be particularly effective in our individualistic, consumer-driven, media-saturated culture. Contrary to the assumptions of couples in previous centuries, many people at this point in history seem to believe that being in love is the only rationale for a couple to come together and stay together in marriage. Misguided perceptions and expectations about what constitutes a good marriage often lead to dissatisfaction and divorce. For example, a wife reads a magazine article and learns that her marriage is "unhealthy" because she and her husband don't use "I feel" to express emotions, sometimes don't talk at all, and occasionally find themselves in an argument. A husband drawn to the outdoors struggles with his wife's lack of enthusiasm for kayaking and rappelling. He wonders how long he can love someone unable to share his passions. Another couple disagrees about the same things over and over again—some of them involving important facets of life. So when problem-solving techniques don't help them always see eye to eye, they begin to believe that something must be wrong with their marriage.

Actually, what may be wrong are these couples' expectations and perceptions. In a recent study, Latter-day Saint marriage counselors estimated that 71 percent of couples experience problems with "unrealistic expectations of marriage or spouse"—a problem area more frequently reported than problems with communication, finances, decision making, or sexual intimacy.[5] In this section, we compare the views of the world with the views of the gospel in three areas critical to marriage: love, romance, and happiness.

LOVE: PREDESTINED MATCH VS. CHOSEN COMMITMENT

We live in the age of so-called "soul mate marriage," where love is frequently portrayed as a seamless matching with your "other half" and couple relationships are seen as a pathway to personal happiness. In a national survey of single young adults, 94 percent agreed with the statement that "when you marry you want your spouse to be your soul mate, first and foremost" and 88 percent also agreed that "there is a special person, a soul mate, waiting for you somewhere out there."[6] Founded on the belief of predestined love, marriage today is often portrayed as an effortless and conflict-free relationship, filled with romantic intimacy and emotional togetherness that can meet our every need and desire.

While soul mate love may work for Hollywood films or romance novels, most couples making marriage work in the real world will tell you that maintaining their relationship requires work, patience, personal growth, compromise, commitment, and sacrifice. President Spencer W. Kimball warned Latter-day Saints to not be led astray by soul mate culture when he said, "'Soulmates' are fiction and an illusion; and while every young man and young woman will seek with all diligence and prayerfulness to find a mate with whom life can be most compatible and beautiful, yet it is certain that almost any good man and any good woman can have happiness and a successful marriage if both are willing to pay the price."[7] President Kimball continued by teaching a four-step "never failing" formula for forming a happy and eternal marriage: (1) proper and wise mate selection, (2) great unselfishness, (3) continued courtship and consideration, and (4) complete faithfulness to the gospel of Jesus Christ.

Soul mate beliefs and unrealistic expectations can lead disillusioned partners to believe that any marital problems that arise must stem from having made a "faulty match" and that the only line of recourse is to "unmatch" and "rematch" again with someone else who must be their "real" soul mate. However, the proclamation on the family teaches us that sustained love in marriage is not primarily a process of matching or finding—above all it is about becoming and choosing. The word *love* appears five times in the proclamation, each time linked with an action word such as "to love and care" or "to love and serve." The language of the proclamation suggests that love falls within the scope of our agency. Love is something we do, something we can control, and ultimately something we can choose—if not, God could not command us to "love one another" (John 13:34).[8] President Spencer W. Kimball taught:

> [Divine love] is not like that association of the world which is misnamed love, but which is mostly physical attraction. . . . The love of which the Lord speaks is not only physical attraction, but also faith, confidence, understanding, and partnership. It is devotion and companionship, parenthood, common ideals and standards. It is cleanliness of life and sacrifice and unselfishness. This kind of love never tires nor wanes. It lives on through sickness and sorrow, through prosperity and privation, through accomplishment and disappointment, through time and eternity.[9]

Relationships founded on divine love are based on the realistic expectation that the type of companionship needed to sustain marriage must be nurtured, repaired, and chosen on a daily basis as marriage partners seal themselves to each other with their commitment, selflessness, patience, and sacrifice.

POPULAR ROMANCE VS. GENUINE CONCERN

Romance is a popular topic for relationships today. Messages of how marriages "turn stale" or "lose their spark" abound, often coming from media and advertising sources. Couples are led to believe that the foundation of marriage lies in keeping the emotional feelings of romance and passion alive. In contrast, President Gordon B. Hinckley taught that "true love is not so much a matter of romance as it is a matter of anxious concern for the well-being of one's companion."[10] He explained that this type of love and respect for one's spouse "comes of recognition that each of us is a son or daughter of God, endowed with something of His divine nature, that each is an individual entitled to expression and cultivation of individual talents and deserving of forbearance, of patience, of understanding, of courtesy, of thoughtful consideration."[11] Through a gospel lens, romance is appropriately seen as spouses' intentional, day-to-day efforts to love and care for each other. This perspective views romance as a means to marital unity and oneness, rather than an end in itself.

THE HAPPINESS OF THE WORLD VS. THE JOY OF CHRIST

Perhaps nowhere in our Father's plan is happiness more intended to be a part of our lives than in our marriage and family relationships. However, the peace and joy promised to us by Christ are quite different from the happiness envisioned in popular culture. Jesus taught the Apostles about the Comforter and explained to them the divine pattern of finding peace and joy. He said, "Peace I leave with you, my peace I give unto you: not as the world giveth, give I unto you. Let not your heart be troubled, neither let it be afraid" (John 14:27). At this time, the Savior also told his Apostles, "These things have I spoken unto you, that my joy might remain in you, and that your joy might be full" (John 15:11). Peace, joy, love, and other life experiences are best understood as gifts from the Spirit, and often we will need the Holy Spirit to reveal to us the path that we must follow to fully receive of the Lord's peace and joy.

Peace and joy can be felt in marriage in spite of differences and difficulty. For example, the joy of Christ sustains a middle-aged couple who are staying up, waiting for a teenager to come home late—again; who have weathered the husband's unemployment for eighteen months when the computer industry took a downturn; who survived the wife's three pregnancies requiring bed rest; who keep mopping up their flooding basement after every large thunderstorm; who've never figured out how to fully resolve her need for an active social life and daily communication with his need for solitude and quiet reading time; and who are committed, loyal, forgiving, honest, and generous partners who realize that family life can be difficult as well as pleasurable. This couple's joy springs from their devotion to the Lord and to each other, not from worldly measures of success or happiness.

PRINCIPLES OF MARRIAGE

Prophets have provided guiding principles upon which to build our marriage relationships. Here we discuss three overarching principles for maintaining an eternal marriage: (1) fostering equal partnership, (2) developing marital virtues, and (3) handling differences in marriage constructively.

Fostering Equal Partnership

We live in a time of increased recognition of the need for equality between spouses in marriage. This must be pleasing to our Father in Heaven. The proclamation on the family declares that "all human beings—both male and female—are created in the image of God" and that "each is a beloved spirit son or daughter of heavenly parents."[12] However, the culture of our day often promotes a type of equality in marriage that is based on the idea that there should be no distinction between men and women in family life. Secular voices tell couples that equality in marriage is best accomplished when spouses spend proportionate time in the workforce, divide all household chores evenly, and maintain similar, yet separate financial earnings.[13] In contrast, the Lord's plan for marital equality lies in recognizing the unique and irreplaceable stewardships both husbands and wives have in family life and that these divine responsibilities can only be fully accomplished in a marriage of equals. "One of the most revolutionary aspects of the restored gospel is its ability to help us envision difference without hierarchy, distinctiveness without inequality."[14]

One area of possible confusion for Latter-day Saint couples is how to integrate the proclamation's counsel for fathers to "preside over their families in love and righteousness" with the teaching that "fathers and mothers are obligated to help one another as equal partners."[15] Is it possible to have one spouse preside in the home and yet truly live a pattern of equal partnership? The answer is yes. This is exactly what the Lord holds as the divine pattern of oneness in marriage (Genesis 2:22–24; D&C 42:22). Perhaps some of the confusion with blending these principles stems from the use of the term *preside* within the Church to refer to positions where one individual has been called to serve in an authoritative stewardship over others. Because of this, some have interpreted "presiding" to mean that after equal counsel, equal consent is not necessary because the husband, the presider, has the right to the final say.

However, it is an error to infer that the principle of presiding in marriage and family life means the same thing that it does within the Church. President Boyd K. Packer contrasted the distinct line of authority in the Church with the co-stewardship relationship of husband and wife: "In the home it is a partnership with husband and wife equally yoked together, sharing in decisions, always working together."[16] Both spouses are entitled to revelation for their family—their mutual stewardship. Thus marriage requires a unique form of presiding and partnership (see Box 7.1). Essay B4 describes ways husbands and wives can support each other in an equal partnership.

Developing Marital Virtues

A second principle for finding Christ's promised joy in our marriage relationships is to develop the attributes of a virtuous spouse. Recently, marriage scholar and therapist Blaine Fowers explained what years of counseling and research have taught him to be the foundation of a successful marriage. He wrote, "The best way to have a good marriage is to be a good person."[17] In particular, Fowers described four "marital virtues" that all spouses need to develop for the good of their marriages: friendship, generosity, fairness, and loyalty. In a gospel context, these virtues are best understood as aspects of charity, "the pure love of Christ" (Moroni 7:47).

Friendship. Caring, helpfulness, and companionship characterize the lasting marriage. Unfortunately, many spouses fall into a pattern of "parallel marriage" where they share a home together, but they do not share a life together. Studies find that lasting marriages are ones in which spouses create a deep friendship through shared interests, activities, values, and conversation. Just knowing personal details like each other's favorite movies, most-disliked tasks, or hoped-for dreams creates intimacy and emotional bonding. Pursuing common goals, in particular, like creating a business, cultivating music in family life, or learning a new hobby, gives marriage meaning. Fostering friendship in our marriages also creates an environment of positive feelings that helps spouses push out negative thoughts that may compete for mental space in a marriage.

Generosity. Generosity helps spouses concentrate on their partner's good qualities and brings genuine love to their marriage. Generosity can bolster spouses during the typical ups and downs of marriage and

---

PROPHETIC TEACHINGS ON PRESIDING IN EQUAL PARTNERSHIP

"A man who holds the priesthood accepts his wife as a partner in the leadership of the home and family with full knowledge of and full participation in all decisions relating thereto. Of necessity there must be in the Church and in the home a presiding officer. By divine appointment, the responsibility to preside in the home rests upon the priesthood holder. The Lord intended that the wife be a helpmeet for man (*meet* means equal)—that is, a companion equal and necessary in full partnership. Presiding in righteousness necessitates a shared responsibility between husband and wife; together you act with knowledge and participation in all family matters. . . . Each partner must be considerate and sensitive to the other's needs and desires."[18]

—President Howard W. Hunter

"When there is a family decision to be made that affects everyone, you and your wife together will seek whatever counsel you might need, and together you will prayerfully come to a unified decision. If you ever pull priesthood rank on her you will have failed."[19]

—President Boyd K. Packer

"Now a word to you sisters who are married. In a very substantial way, you sisters make our homes a refuge of peace and happiness in a troubled world. A righteous husband is the bearer of the priesthood, which priesthood is the governing authority of the home. But he is not the priesthood; he is the holder of the priesthood. His wife shares the blessings of the priesthood with him. He is not elevated in any way above the divine status of his wife. President Gordon B. Hinckley in last April's general priesthood meeting stated: 'In the marriage companionship there is neither inferiority nor superiority. The woman does not walk ahead of the man; neither does the man walk ahead of the woman. They walk side by side as a son and daughter of God on an eternal journey.' "[20]

—President James E. Faust

"Some of you have noticed the absence of Sister Hinckley. For the first time in 46 years, since I became a General Authority, she has not attended general conference. . . . It is a somber time for me. We've been married for 67 years this month. . . . We've walked together side by side through all of these years, coequals and companions through storm and sunshine."[21]

—President Gordon B. Hinckley

Box 7.1

serves as damage repair when there are differences or conflict in the relationship. For instance, a wife becomes regularly discouraged with her husband's lack of intellectual interests. He's happy going to basketball games and rarely cracks a book. She, however, reads vociferously and finds herself demeaning him mentally for being unable to philosophize with her. A perpetual problem? Probably so. A potential for divorce or separation? Not when generosity steps in. It gives the wife enough charity of spirit to see past and forgive her husband's failings while simultaneously realizing his good qualities. Maybe he doesn't read Dostoevsky, she realizes, but he willingly cares for the children and he works hard to provide for the family. And besides, she concludes, he puts up with her sloppy housekeeping and tendency to overspend. Why should she think he has to be perfect? (Charity in marriage is further discussed in chapter 6.)

Each of us is revealed in our marriage relationship. All of our faults and our virtues are laid open in this most intimate of relationships. Spouses stand on sacred ground as they respond to each other's shortcomings and imperfections. There is something very powerful when spouses are each other's strongest supporters—when they rally to each other's side, rather than turn away; encourage, rather than criticize; see the best in each other, rather than the worst; and lift each other up, rather than push each other down.

Fairness. Fowers' "virtue of fairness" could be envisioned by Latter-day Saints as the day-to-day application of equal partnership. Spouses need to learn how to shoulder the work and difficulties of marriage and family life together and to rely on the mutual strengths each brings to the relationship. Perhaps nowhere is the degree of fairness more displayed in a marriage than in a spouse's participation, or lack thereof, in housework. Having a fair marriage does not mean dividing up the chores with an exact number, with the husband changing the baby's diaper this time and the wife the next, he weeding the garden on Thursday and she on Saturday. Rather it consists of both spouses giving their all to the relationship and having an overall sense of fairness. The full measure of intimacy in marriage requires husbands and wives to be equals. However, as one marriage expert puts it, "spouses who have confidence in the fairness of their arrangements generally perceive justice in their relationships in a global way and do not need to struggle over their equality on a daily basis."[22]

Fairness in a relationship also goes hand-in-hand with compromise and trade-offs. Both spouses need to agree on where they will live, how many children they will have, and what goals they will pursue. Marriages get out of balance if one spouse is constantly giving up his or her dreams so that the other can exclusively pursue his or her agenda. Research also shows that there is a greater sense of fairness in marriages when spouses recognize and express appreciation for sacrifices made by their spouse for the sake of the relationship.[23]

Loyalty. Fowers emphasized the importance of a steadfast commitment to one's relationship in spite of difficulties that inevitably arise in marriage. President Gordon B. Hinckley has advised spouses to be "fiercely loyal" to one another.[24] This type of loyalty fosters selflessness and sacrifice, ultimately the key virtues of marital perseverance. Ironically, satisfaction more often results when couples stick it out through tough times, not when they break up. A recent national study found that unhappily married adults who divorced were typically not any happier than unhappily married people who stayed married. Even more dramatic, the researchers also found that two-thirds of unhappily married spouses who stayed married reported that their marriages were happy five years later. In addition, the most unhappy marriages reported the most dramatic turnarounds: among those who rated their marriages as very unhappy, almost 8 out of 10 who avoided divorce were happily married five years later.[25]

As we practice these four virtues, we begin to view marriage not merely as a means to our own personal happiness, but rather as a partnership of charity that invites us to live outside ourselves for the good of our spouse and others. The perspective of one spouse interviewed by Fowers captures this approach to marriage: "I think a lot less about what I get out of the relationship and more about what I can give to it. I think a lot about how I can keep our togetherness going and about how it is good for our children. We are a couple in love, and we have lived through a lot of difficult times. We work through those problems together and always come back to that love. I've seen it grow stronger and deeper as a result."[26]

Learn to Handle Differences Constructively

During the last twenty years, marriage scholars have primarily focused on the ways that couples deal with differences and handle conflict in their relationships. Numerous studies have shown that what distinguishes marriages that succeed from those that don't is not the number of differences in the relationship, but rather the way in which differences are handled. Nearly 70 percent of the problems couples report in their relationship can be labeled as "perpetual problems," meaning that they often never get fully resolved.[27] Successful marriage is more about accepting and handling differences constructively than it is about solving problems or creating a conflict-free relationship. Research by marriage scholar John Gottman and others points to three simple questions couples can ask themselves to evaluate if they are handling differences constructively.

1. *"When discussing differences, do we stay focused on resolving the problem?"* Often when couples discuss problem areas in their relationship—such as balancing the budget, dealing with extended families, or disciplining children—they begin to argue and their conversations veer into other areas of complaint. Spouses should strive to set the pattern of discussing differences in ways that focus on finding solutions, not winning arguments.

2. *"Do we manage our emotions during conflictual exchanges?"* When spouses allow themselves and their partners to become flooded with emotions during discussions, they rarely address their differences in a positive way.[28] Spouses need to learn to bring up concerns in the relationship in non-blaming ways and to find ways to soothe themselves and each other during discussions so that negative emotions stay in check.

3. *"Do we maintain respect and concern for one another during an argument?"* Scholars have found that spouses in successful marriages maintain high levels of respect and mutual regard for one another—even during an argument. Sometimes spouses allow arguments to degrade into episodes of criticism and personal attack. This type of negative blaming can have lasting detrimental effects on couple unity, prompting some spouses to withdraw emotionally from the relationship.[29] Maintaining respect and concern for one another sends the message that your relationship is more important than the problems you are currently facing and that you are on the same side in finding ways to constructively deal with your differences.

Sometimes differences in marriage can lead one or both spouses to try to control the other through using aggressive or abusive behavior. This type of inappropriate behavior may include verbal criticism, psychological manipulation, spiritual coercion, and physical abuse. Both men and women are capable of being hurtful and aggressive in marriage, especially when we recognize forms of "relational aggression" (personal insults, coercion, blackmail, spreading gossip, love withdrawal) as destructive forms of abusive behavior.[30] The proclamation clearly warns that individuals "who abuse spouse or offspring . . . will one day stand accountable before God."[31] Such behavior represents an unrighteous effort to exercise control or dominion over another (D&C 121:36–37). The irony of using harsh means to compel others toward what we view as righteous ends is evident within the principles of the restored gospel. The Lord counsels us that appropriate influence is practiced "only by persuasion, by long-suffering, by gentleness and meekness, and by love unfeigned" (D&C 121:41). Anyone in a marriage relationship characterized by controlling behavior should counsel with ecclesiastical leaders, trusted friends, and wise family members to find ways to end these destructive patterns. (Chapter 35 discusses preventing and healing from abuse).

PRACTICES TO STRENGTHEN MARRIAGE

Building upon the perspectives and principles of marriage available in the gospel of Jesus Christ, couples can develop patterns and practices that will help strengthen their marriage relationship. When discussing practices to strengthen marriage, we should keep in mind that no two couples are exactly the same. Nor do all marriages face the same situations and circumstances. Each couple needs to mutually determine what specific practices need to be applied to their relationship at a specific time.

Prioritize Your Marriage

For most families, hectic schedules seem to be the norm. Feelings of being over-scheduled have become so widely held that scholars have coined the phrase "time famine" to describe how many couples and families feel "starved for time" together.[32] Living such hectic schedules, many spouses have become too busy for their marriages. With child rearing, work commitments, Church callings, and other aspects of managing day-to-day life, many spouses do not make their marriage a daily priority.

Prophets and apostles have counseled us to make our marriage relationship our highest priority and to make sure that our commitment to the relationship is demonstrated not only in our words, but also in our daily and weekly schedules. The appointments we have with our spouse are sacred and we should give them at least the same priority in our schedule as we give to work or Church appointments. Of course, work, Church, and other commitments are important and will require the sacrifice of marriage and family time occasionally, but we should be mindful not to set the pattern of letting important matters take precedence over essential ones. In counsel given to husbands, President Ezra Taft Benson taught: "Nothing except God himself takes priority over your wife in your life—not work, not recreation, not hobbies. . . . What does it mean to 'cleave unto her'? It means to stay close to her, to be loyal and faithful to her, to communicate with her, and to express your love for her."[33] If other commitments take precedence over the marriage relationship on a regular basis, it might be time to prayerfully reevaluate one's commitments, as noble and worthwhile as they may be.

Our efforts to prioritize time for our marriages do not have to be large to have great benefits. A recent study found that couples who devoted five extra hours a week to their marriage reported having a better relationship than couples who did not spend this time together. During these five hours, couples primarily attended to four things: (1) learning about each other's life that day, (2) having a stress-reducing conversation at the end of each day, (3) doing something every day to express genuine affection and appreciation, and (4) having a weekly date together.[34]

Spiritualize Your Marriage

The prophets have frequently counseled married couples to build their lives around the practices of gospel living. By doing this, couples recognize the need for the Spirit of the Lord to be in their hearts and in their homes as they grow together in marriage. President Spencer W. Kimball taught:

> If two people love the Lord more than their own lives and then love each other more than their own lives, working together in total harmony with the gospel program as their basic structure, they are sure to have great happiness. When a husband and wife go together frequently to the holy temple, kneel in prayer together in their home with their family, go hand in hand to their religious meetings, and both are working together for the building up of the Kingdom of God, then happiness is at its pinnacle.[35]

The importance of religious practices to bring the Spirit into our lives is a particularly important aspect of managing the ups and downs that occur in every marriage. Elder Jeffrey R. Holland taught:

> In a final injunction to us He [Christ] said, "A new commandment I give unto you, That ye love one another; as I have loved you" (John 13:34). Of course such Christlike staying power in romance and marriage requires more than we naturally have. It requires *an endowment from heaven.* Remember Mormon's promise—that such love, the love we each yearn for and cling to, is bestowed upon true followers of Christ (see Moroni 7:48). You want capability and safety in dating and romance, in married life and eternity? Be a true disciple of Jesus. Be a genuine, committed, word-and-deed Latter-day Saint. *Believe that your faith has everything to do with your romance, because it does.* You separate dating from discipleship at your peril. Or to phrase that more positively, Jesus Christ, the Light of the World, is the only lamp by which you can successfully see the true path of love and happiness for you and your sweetheart.[36]

A couple's increased effort to live God's commandments will bring to their marriage a greater measure of divine love and true joy.

As with all aspects of life, Christ teaches us to center our marriages in Him. The Savior instructs: "Abide in me, and I in you. As the branch cannot bear fruit of itself, except it abide in the vine; no more can ye, except ye abide in me" (John 15:4). As we learn to view marriage according to the pattern of the Lord and strive to incorporate His teachings, we will realize the fullness of love and joy available to our marriage relationships through the Savior and His gospel.

ABOUT THE AUTHORS

Jason S. Carroll is assistant professor of marriage, family, and human development in the School of Family Life at Brigham Young University. He is widely published in the areas of marriage readiness, marital quality, and marriage education. He and his wife, Stefani, are the parents of Garret, Austin, Lindsey, and Caleb.

Elizabeth VanDenBerghe, MA, is a writer trying to put her interest in marriage and family theories into practice with her husband, Jed, and children, John, William, Christian, Grace, Anika, Benjamin, Samuel, and Andrew. Every once in a while, she succeeds.

ADDITIONAL READING

Bruce C. Hafen (1996, November), Covenant marriage, *Ensign, 26*(11), 26–28.

Gordon B. Hinckley (1971, June), Except the Lord build the house, *Ensign, 1*(6), 71–72.

Spencer W. Kimball (1977, March), Oneness in marriage, *Ensign, 7*(3), 3–5.

Lynn G. Robbins (2000, October), Agency and love in marriage, *Ensign, 30*(10), 16–22.

NOTES

1. First Presidency and Council of Twelve Apostles (1995, November), The family: A proclamation to the world, *Ensign, 25*(11), 102.

2. C. S. Lewis (1959), *The Screwtape Letters* (New York: Macmillan), 83.

3. Ibid., 83–84.

4. Ibid., 82.

5. R. F. Stahmann and T. R. Adams (1997), LDS counselor ratings of problems occurring among LDS premarital and remarital couples; unpublished manuscript in possession of authors, Brigham Young University.

6. B. D. Whitehead and D. Popenoe (2001), *Who Wants to Marry a Soulmate;* The National Marriage Project (Rutgers University); available at http://marriage.rutgers.edu

7. Spencer W. Kimball (1976), *Marriage and Divorce* (Salt Lake City: Deseret Book), 16.

8. H. M. Bahr, A. S. Loveless, and I. F. Beutler (2000), Love, respect, and compassion in families; in D. C. Dollahite, ed., *Strengthening Our Families: An In-Depth Look at the Proclamation on the Family* (Salt Lake City: Bookcraft), 167–176.

9. Edward L. Kimball, ed. (1982), *The Teachings of Spencer W. Kimball* (Salt Lake City: Bookcraft), 248.

10. Gordon B. Hinckley (1971, June), Except the Lord build the house, *Ensign, 2*(6), 71.

11. Ibid.

12. First Presidency and Council of Twelve Apostles (1995), 102.

13. A. DeMaris and M. A. Longmore (1996), Ideology, power, and equity: Testing competing explanations for the perception of fairness in household labor, *Social Forces, 74,* 1043–1071; R. L. Blumberg and M. T. Colman (1989), A theoretical look at gender balance of power in the American couple, *Journal of Family Issues, 10,* 225–250; see also Hawkins, et al. (2000), Equal partnership and the sacred responsibilities of mothers and fathers, in D. C. Dollahite, ed., *Strengthening Our Families: An In-Depth Look at the Proclamation on the Family* (Salt Lake City: Bookcraft), 63–82.

14. Hawkins, et al. (2000), 66.

15. First Presidency and Council of Twelve Apostles (1995), 102.

16. Boyd K. Packer (1998, May), The Relief Society, *Ensign, 28*(5), 73.

17. B. J. Fowers (2000), *Beyond the Myth of Marital Happiness* (San Francisco: Jossey-Bass), 23.

18. Howard W. Hunter (1994, November), Being a righteous husband and father, *Ensign, 24*(11), 49.

19. Quoted in C. Broderick (1986), *One Flesh, One Heart: Putting Celestial Love into Your Temple Marriage* (Salt Lake City: Deseret Book), 32.

20. James E. Faust (2002, November), You are all heaven sent, *Ensign, 32*(11), 110.

21. Gordon B. Hinckley (2004, May), Concluding remarks, *Ensign, 34*(11), 103.

22. Fowers (2000), 187.

23. A. J. Hawkins, C. M. Marshall, and S. M. Allen (1998), The orientation toward domestic labor questionnaire: Exploring dual-earner wives' sense of fairness about family work, *Journal of Family Psychology, 12*(2), 244–258.

24. Gordon B. Hinckley (1997), *Teachings of Gordon B. Hinckley* (Salt Lake City: Deseret Book), 328–329.

25. L. J. Waite, D. Browning, W. J. Doherty, M. Gallagher, Y. Luo, and S. M. Stanley (2002), *Does Divorce Make People Happy? Findings from a Study of Unhappy Marriages* (New York: Institute for American Values).

26. Fowers (2000), 19.

27. J. M. Gottman and J. S. Gottman (1999), The marriage survival kit: A research-based marital therapy; in R. Berger and M. T. Hannah, eds., *Preventive Approaches in Couples Therapy* (Philadelphia: Brunner/Mazel).

28. J. M. Gottman, L. F. Katz, and C. Hooven (1997), *Meta-emotion: How Families Communicate Emotionally* (Hillsdale, NJ: Lawrence Erlbaum).

29. J. M. Gottman (1999), *The Seven Principles for Making Marriage Work* (New York: Crown Publishers).

30. C. H. Hart, D. A. Nelson, C. C. Robinson, S. F. Olsen, and M. K. McNeilly-Choque (1998), Overt and relational aggression in Russian nursery-school-age children: Parenting style and martial linkages, *Developmental Psychology, 34,* 687–697.

31. First Presidency and Council of Twelve Apostles (1995), 102.

32. J. de Graaf (2003), *Take Back Your Time: Fighting Overwork and Time Poverty in America* (San Francisco: Berrett-Koehler); W. J. Doherty (2001), *Take Back Your Marriage: Sticking Together in a World That Pulls Us Apart* (New York: Guilford Press).

33. Ezra Taft Benson (1987, November), To the fathers in Israel, *Ensign, 17*(11), 48.

34. J. M. Gottman (1999).

35. Spencer W. Kimball (1977, March), Oneness in marriage, *Ensign, 7*(3), 3.

36. Jeffrey R. Holland (2003, October), "How do I love thee?" *New Era, 33*(10), 4.

CHAPTER 8

FINANCIAL STEWARDSHIPS AND FAMILY RELATIONSHIPS

BERNARD PODUSKA AND LUCY BEUTLER

Avoid the philosophy and excuse that yesterday's luxuries have become today's necessities. They aren't necessities unless we oursleves make them such. . . . It is essential for us to live within our means.[1]
—President Thomas S. Monson

One of the challenges of mortal life is wise management of our resources. The Apostle Paul proclaimed, "We brought nothing into this world, and it is certain we can carry nothing out. And having food and raiment let us be therewith content" (1 Timothy 6:7–8). During our brief mortal existence we never truly own anything—the Lord merely asks us to assume a sacred stewardship over the possessions that He entrusts to our care.

According to "The Family: A Proclamation to the World," married couples ideally balance their stewardship with regard to family resources as follows:

> By divine design, fathers are to preside over their families in love and righteousness and are responsible to provide the necessities of life and protection for their families. Mothers are primarily responsible for the nurture of their children. In these sacred responsibilities, fathers and mothers are obligated to help one another as equal partners.[2]

Each couple or parent with children takes circumstances into account and plans stewardships with reference to this prophetic pattern. Individual circumstances may require adaptation after prayerful consideration.

Families require basic necessities, but the acquisition of things should never take precedence over the spiritual. Henry David Thoreau noted, "Money is not required to buy one necessary of the soul."[3] Nor can

it buy happiness, respect, love, or security. Still, money can buy housing, education, pay for a mission or a trip to the temple, and provide for a secure retirement. Children learn the importance and unimportance of money from their parents. Parental conversations—or arguments—about money can influence children's attitudes. Imagine a mother and father arguing over money. Their children overhear one of the parents say, "If we can't get these bills under control, I'm calling it quits." A second family is also having financial difficulties, but their children hear the parents making comments such as, "Well, we'll scrape by on love and faith, even if we don't have much money." The children in the second family are learning that security is to be found in relationships and faith in God.

Pay Tithes and Offerings First

Many Latter-day Saints make payment of tithing, fast offerings, and other contributions the first item on the list of bills to be paid, because these contributions are our most important expenditure. Paying tithing provides the spiritual strength necessary to cope with a financial crisis successfully, as well as other spiritual and temporal problems. During financial difficulties, a couple may be tempted not to pay tithing, because the money could be used for payments that seem more urgent. In truth, it is during the hard times that we cannot afford to stop paying our tithing. President Gordon B. Hinckley reminded us: "We *can* pay our tithing. It is not so much a matter of money as it is a matter of faith."[4]

Jesus taught: "Therefore take no thought, saying, What shall we eat? or, What shall we drink? or, Wherewithal shall we be clothed? . . . for your heavenly Father knoweth that ye have need of all these things. But seek ye first the kingdom of God, and his righteousness; and all these things shall be added unto you" (Matthew 6:31–33).

Living the law of tithing, by seeking first the kingdom of God, establishes a family financial policy that blesses our immediate family and the next generation. These blessings are more often spiritual rather than temporal: love and peace in the home, the gift of faith, trust in the Lord—rather than financial gain. President Gordon B. Hinckley taught: "Now, do not get me wrong. I do not say that if you pay an honest tithing you will realize your dream of a fine house, a Rolls Royce, and a condominium in Hawaii. *The Lord will open the windows of heaven according to our need, and not according to our greed.*"[5]

Children who see their parents pay tithing and who pay their own tithing establish a testimony of correct principles before facing the wiles of the world that may result in chronic indebtedness. They create patterns of discipline in their lives. Elder Robert D. Hales counseled:

> Too often we as parents do not teach and encourage our children to live this law [of tithing] because their contribution only amounts to a few cents. But without a testimony of tithing, they are vulnerable. In their teenage years, they become attracted to clothes, entertainment, and expensive possessions and risk losing the special protection that tithing provides.[6]

Tithes and offerings can establish a pattern of gratitude toward God that helps youth survive a culture that seems to encourage selfishness and to foment dissatisfaction. Because of unnecessary teen employment and gifts of substantial discretionary income to teenage children, important years that should be spent focusing on personal development may be replaced with years of indiscriminant consumption. Teens may buy into the market culture, measuring themselves and others not by what they can contribute, but rather by what they possess.[7] In order to avoid this pattern of behavior, parents can help their teens learn to distinguish between needs and wants.[8] Needs are limited to basic foods, shelter, and medical care; everything else falls into the category of wants, such as designer jeans, exotic sports shoes, and cool-looking cars.

Using Temporal Resources to Bless Families

One pitfall that may ensnare teenagers, single adults, and couples is credit card debt. At interest rates of 19 or 20 percent or more, a debt can quickly grow into a source of despair. Our culture encourages us to get what we want now and pay later—a dangerous plan. Unless the credit card owner can limit its use and pay the bill entirely each time, thus avoiding interest, a couple may decide to have no credit cards, or perhaps one that is left at home except in situations where an emergency may arise. Imagine the difference when an engaged couple plans their future and their combined credit card debt is $30,000. Then think of the couple who bring to their marriage thousands of dollars in savings because they have avoided the impulse purchases or spending beyond their incomes that so often accompany the use of credit. Many people are happy and their finances more stable because they have not given in to the "buy now, pay later" philosophy.

Although we are living during a time of unprecedented prosperity, we may spend more than we earn and act as if a day of reckoning will never come. As a result, "consumer credit increased . . . to $1.76 trillion, and household debt now stands at 110 percent of annual disposable income, up from 76 percent in 1986."[9] In addition, more than 1.7 million individuals declared personal bankruptcy in 2003.[10] In Utah, in 2003, it was 1 in every 36 families.[11] Elder Wirthlin admonished: "Remember this: debt is a form of bondage. . . . When we make purchases on credit, they give us only an illusion of prosperity. We think we own things, but the reality is, our things own us."[12]

Husband and wife complement each other as they make decisions together about the family's current and future needs. For example, one family may choose to use half of all financial increases to enhance the quality of life while designating the other half as savings for their children's education, the couple's retirement, or missions for the couple and their children. Another family may decide to do without a car for a time, walking and using public transportation instead, so that the father can return to school and increase his employment potential.

Planning for the Future

A couple makes similar decisions with regard to obtaining adequate medical and life insurance and deciding which expenditures are a priority and which must wait. Some decisions, by their nature, are best begun as early as possible. A great deal more will be available for retirement to the couple who begins saving at a younger age, due to compounding interest. Similarly, a couple should contribute enough to get all available matching funds from an employer. Other employer-sponsored benefits, such as flexible spending accounts that save before-tax dollars for medical expenses and childcare, can save the family from paying taxes on income spent towards those costs.

Families whose breadwinner is not eligible for insurance or a retirement plan through work must consider carefully how they can obtain these benefits on their own. Individual plans may be more costly, but illness, disability, or death of either parent can undermine the financial stability of a family without insurance. Further, if parents reach retirement without savings, their children may struggle financially to support their parents and provide for their own children.

Money may also be needed to pay for professional advice about finances, wills, or trusts for the parents (see additional readings for more information on wills and trusts). Parents of young children may not have a lot of money for their children to inherit if both parents died in the same accident. However, the parents should agree on the persons who would rear the children in case of such a tragedy. The same people or someone else may be appointed to manage the children's inherited money on the children's behalf. Such decisions are best recorded in the parents' wills and in trust documents.

Further, even if there are no minor children, a parent's money and property should be distributed at death as the couple has agreed, usually to the surviving spouse and then, at the survivor's death, among the children or to another designated recipient, such as an organization or university. Establishing a trust fund for educational or other purposes can be an excellent way to distribute resources. If the parents die without a will (intestate), the surviving children may be surprised to learn that when a person dies without a will, the government has essentially written a will through laws that apply in that case.

Wants and Needs

After the future responsibilities are provided for and the current bills are paid, families may have some money left over. While this money could be saved for a large bill that the parents know is coming, or to increase emergency funds on hand, there will almost always be someone in the family who wants to make a purchase. Again, the ability to distinguish between needs and wants is essential when trying to live within a budget (see additional reading for more information on budgeting). A need is something required for survival. It provides a means to go on living. A want, on the other hand, is something that provides greater convenience, enrichment, or pleasure. Personal wants and needs must be carefully weighed against the needs of the family. Far too often, members of the family will use the word "need" when asking for permission to make a purchase—"I need a new dress," or "I need a new fishing reel"—because the word *need* implies a demand for gratification. In contrast, the word *want* lacks such an implied demand. Having members of the family make this distinction can be both financially responsible as well as enlightening.

At times a couple may decide to spend money on experiences that enhance a marriage or build family memories: a brief getaway for husband and wife to enjoy time together away from the children, a family vacation to a national park or an extended family reunion, music or dance lessons, the opportunity for a family member to take a trip—the list of worthwhile experiences is long. Each couple must decide the worth of such experiences, as well as of other affordable things, compared to the other needs of the family.

Preserving Relationships

The financial principle that "Nothing is worth the relationship" provides sound advice. No thing should ever take precedence over the emotional well-being of another or the interpersonal closeness in our relationships.

President Spencer W. Kimball, in his book *Marriage,* wrote:

> The marriage that is based upon selfishness is almost certain to fail. The one who marries for wealth or the one who marries for prestige or social plane is certain to be disappointed. The one who marries to satisfy vanity and pride or who marries to spite or to show up another person is fooling only himself. But the one who marries to give happiness as well as

receive it, to give service as well as to receive it, and looks after the interests of the two and then the family as it comes will have a good chance that the marriage will be a happy one.[13]

Family finances are among the leading sources of marital contention and divorce.[14] In most cases, the disagreements focus on the issues of allocation and control. When allocating limited resources, some interests might be fully funded while others are left to languish. As a consequence, the issue of who controls the allocations becomes important.

In order to maintain harmony in marriage, the couple may decide to allocate and control their money together. If one partner is given responsibility over allocation, he or she must exercise that privilege with love rather than power. That partner needs to ask two questions about each allocation:

1. Does this decision consider my spouse's feelings?

2. Is the decision I prefer based on love rather than power?

Early in marriage, it may be best for a couple to work together on finances until they know each other's feelings about money. Later, one partner could take over the everyday financial tasks, consulting the other when important concerns or choices (defined by the couple) are involved. When presenting a financial decision to the other partner, it may be helpful to use the phrase, "How would you feel . . . ?" about a potential allocation. This places the feelings and welfare of the other above the desire to satisfy individual needs or wants.

Each partner should consider the other partner's contribution to be as valuable as his or her own. Each spouse contributes vital nonmonetary resources to the home—the question of who is earning the actual paycheck is of less importance than an appreciation for each spouse's contributions and a willingness to be flexible when circumstances and love require it. As a family becomes more prosperous, they are faced with the need to cope with the increased stewardship responsibilities that accompany the accumulation of wealth. To "whom much is given much is required" (D&C 82:3). Unfortunately, the availability of large amounts of discretionary income can lead to conspicuous consumption, overindulgence, and pandering to insatiable demands, thereby lending credence to the adage, "Children are more likely to survive poverty than wealth." However, prosperity can also offer greater opportunities to make charitable contributions, to enhance the lives of others, and to support missionary and welfare needs.

Using Family Resources to Bless Others

An important consideration in planning the use of family resources is the family's ability to bless the lives of others. Families can do this through donating money, as they pay fast offerings and other contributions to the Church. There are also many reputable charities that do good in the community and the world. But donating money is not the only way to help others. Children may be able to participate as the family donates time to local schools, shelters, programs for the poor, and literacy efforts. Children can sort outgrown clothing and other items for the family to donate to a shelter workshop or similar charity. Teens can donate baby-sitting to a couple who can then have a date night or go to the temple. The family can "adopt" an elderly or lonely neighbor and include that person in family activities. Donations can be made to the Church's humanitarian relief efforts (see www.lds.org/ldsfoundation). The Relief Society compassionate service leader will undoubtedly have a list of opportunities to serve, and other opportunities are waiting for family members who ask for guidance in their prayers.

Financial Decisions Reflect a Couple's Basic Values

People may seek money to survive and wealth to promote the service of others. Or they may value wealth because they believe it will protect them and buy security. In the latter case, as a consequence, they may not feel a need to seek or rely on God. President Spencer W. Kimball counseled, "Whatever thing a man sets his heart and his trust in most is his god; and if his god doesn't also happen to be the true and living God of Israel, that man is laboring in idolatry."[15] Family members could make it a regular practice to examine their hearts to see that they remain focused on our Heavenly Father. If acquiring and maintaining their material resources outstrips their time and energy for building the kingdom of God and fostering healthy family relationships, then it might be time to reassess priorities.

The Lord admonishes: "Before ye seek for riches, seek ye for the kingdom of God. And after ye have obtained a hope in Christ ye shall obtain riches, if ye seek them; and ye will seek them for the intent to do good—to clothe the naked, and to feed the hungry, and to liberate the captive, and administer relief to the sick and the afflicted" (Jacob 2:18–19). God loves us, and wants us to turn to Him, rather than to a bank account, as a means of solving our problems and fulfilling the righteous desires of our hearts. Indeed, He is the only source of such fulfillment.

More than ever before, today's family must adhere to the adage, "You can never get enough of what you don't need, because what you don't need can never satisfy you." The prophet Haggai addressed this situation quite clearly when he declared: "Now therefore thus saith the Lord of hosts; Consider your ways. Ye have sown much, and bring in little; ye eat, but ye have not enough; ye drink, but ye are not filled with drink; ye clothe you, but there is none warm; and he that earneth wages earneth wages to put it into a bag with holes. Thus saith the Lord of hosts; Consider your ways" (Haggai 1:5–7).

When we manage our resources wisely, however much we have, with hearts ready to serve and trust the Lord, care for our families, and help others, we can experience many blessings as the windows of heaven open upon us (see Malachi 3:10). Those blessings may not always take the form of increased financial resources, but they will satisfy our souls as only our Heavenly Father can.

ABOUT THE AUTHORS

Bernard Poduska recently retired from BYU as an associate professor and associate chair of the Marriage, Family, and Human Development program. He is the author of *For Love and Money* and *Until Debt Do Us Part*. He is the husband of Barbara Poduska, father of five children, and grandfather of ten.

Lucy Beutler is a homemaker, college instructor, and member of the Young Women General Board. She is the wife of Ivan F. Beutler, mother of six, and grandmother of nine.

ADDITIONAL READING

W. Steve Albrecht (1988, December), Making money your ally, *Ensign, 18*(12), 49–52.

James E. Faust (1982, November), The blessings we receive as we meet the challenges of economic stress, *Ensign, 12*(11), 87–90.

Bernard Poduska (2000), Meeting the temporal needs of the family; in David C. Dollahite, ed., *Strengthening Our Families: An In-Depth Look at the Proclamation on the Family* (Salt Lake City: Bookcraft), 97–99.

Jane Bryant Quinn (1997), Willing makes it so; in *Making the Most of Your Money* (New York: Simon & Schuster), 100–129.

Jane Bryant Quinn (1997), A spending plan that works; in *Making the Most of Your Money* (New York: Simon & Schuster), 160–177.

NOTES

1. Thomas S. Monson (2005, May), Constant truths for changing times, *Ensign 35*(5), 20.

2. First Presidency and Council of Twelve Apostles (1995, November), The family: A proclamation to the world, *Ensign, 25*(11), 102.

3. H. D. Thoreau (1854), *Thoreau: Walden and Other Writings,* Joseph Wood Krutch, ed. (Boston: Ticknor and Fields; reprint, New York: Bantam, 1962), 347; page number is to the reprint.

4. Gordon B. Hinckley, (1989, December), The sacred law of tithing, *Ensign, 19*(12), 4; emphasis in original.

5. Ibid.

6. Robert D. Hales (2002, November), Tithing: A test of faith with eternal blessings, *Ensign, 32*(11), 28–29.

7. L. Steinberg and E. Cauffman (1995), The impact of employment on adolescent development, in R. Vasta, ed., *Annals of Child Development* (London: Jessica Kingsley), 11:133.

8. Joe J. Christensen (1999, May), Greed, selfishness, and overindulgence, *Ensign, 29*(5), 9.

9. L. Dobbs (2003, July 21), In hock to the hilt, *U.S. News & World Report,* 36.

10. E. Warren and A. W. Tyagi (2003), *The Two Income Trap: Why Middle-Class Mothers and Fathers Are Going Broke* (New York: Basic Books), 33; D. Anderton (2004, March 26), Utah still ranks first in bankruptcy filings, *Deseret Morning News.*

11. Anderton (2004).

12. Joseph B. Wirthlin (2004, May), Earthly debts, heavenly debts, *Ensign, 34*(5), 40–41.

13. Spencer W. Kimball (1978), *Marriage* (Salt Lake City: Deseret Book), 44.

14. R. O. Blood Jr. and D. M. Wolfe (1968), Husbands and wives; in R. E. Bell, *Studies in Marriage and the Family* (New York: Thomas Y. Crowell), 58–92.

15. Spencer W. Kimball (1976, June), The false gods we worship, *Ensign 6*(6), 4.

CHAPTER 9

INTIMACY IN MARRIAGE

ROBERT F. STAHMANN AND KEVIN M. MARETT

*We . . . declare that God has commanded that the sacred powers of procreation are
to be employed only between man and woman, lawfully wedded as husband and wife.
We declare the means by which mortal life is created to be to divinely appointed.*[1]
—*"The Family: A Proclamation to the World"*

Intimacy in marriage and family life are expressed in many forms, most of which are nonsexual. Intimacy includes shared social, spiritual, emotional, intellectual, and affectional experiences. These may include religious activities, social events, leisure activities, sports, sharing personal hopes and dreams, and even eating. Couples in a serious premarital relationship probably become appropriately intimate with their partner doing most of these things before the wedding. These forms of intimacy are right and necessary for the relationship to become meaningful and to develop beyond a mere friendship. During courtship, when each is getting to know the other in increasingly intimate ways, sexual intimacies must be curtailed and reserved until marriage.

THE IMPORTANCE OF APPROPRIATE INTIMACY

For parents and children, an intimate family relationship is one of caring, mutual trust, and acceptance. "Caring" is showing genuine concern for each family member's well-being. "Mutual trust" is the feeling that one family member will not be harmed or hurt by another. "Acceptance" is the recognition or approval of each other. An intimate family relationship also models and teaches appropriate nonsexual affection and physical contact. The tender touching or holding between a parent and child conveys an intimate expression of mutual love, caring, and support between the two. While this touching is a personal and intimate physical relationship, it is not a sexual relationship. Any sexual involvement between the parent and child is a grievous sin and would destroy intimacy. A family relationship that is appropriately intimate provides the foundation for healthy sexual intimacy in the parents' marriage and sets an example for their children's future marriages.

In a loving and joyful marriage, partners are intimate with each other and are nonsexually and sexually fulfilled and nurtured. An intimate sexual relationship is an important aspect of marriage. It helps keeps marriage vital. When couples experience difficulty relating to each other sexually, small problems seem larger, and the marriage itself may suffer.[2] President Spencer W. Kimball quoted the Reverend Billy Graham, who stated:

> The Bible celebrates sex and its proper use, presenting it as God-created, God-ordained, God-blessed. It makes plain that God himself implanted the physical magnetism between the sexes for two reasons: for the propagation of the human race, and for the expression of that kind of love between man and wife that makes for true oneness. His command to the first man and woman to be "one flesh" was as important as his command to be "fruitful and multiply."[3]

PREMARITAL CHASTITY BUILDS TRUST

When complete trust exists between husband and wife, the strongest emotional, spiritual, and sexual relationship occurs. When couples make a commitment to control their sexual appetites, desires, and passions until they are married, trust for each other will increase significantly. Trust allows each partner to feel safe and secure. Sexual intimacy prior to marriage can result in having less trust in each other after the wedding.[4] Some segments of society suggest otherwise: that sexual intimacy before marriage is desirable because it feels good, it is natural, and it provides the opportunity to really get to know each other. Such "natural man" reasoning completely denies the spiritual dimension to intimacy and trust. In Latter-day Saint marriages, this spiritual trust is perhaps the most important aspect of the relationship. Focusing on this spiritual trust provides a more meaningful context to the somewhat abrupt transition from the total absence of sexual intimacy before marriage to the total expression of sexual intimacy after marriage.

With increased trust comes an increased security in the relationship. This increased trust and security helps couples weather the emotional, physical, financial, and other challenges that every marriage encounters. Individuals whose sexual behavior before marriage is consistent with their personal value system will have easier marital adjustments than those individuals whose premarital sexual behavior was in opposition to their personal value system.[5]

REPENTANCE AND FORGIVENESS

While ideally both partners will have remained chaste prior to marriage, in reality this may not be the case. Fortunately, our Heavenly Father's plan allows individuals to repent and be forgiven, even though such repentance may take time and involve Church discipline. For those who have truly repented, Heavenly Father forgives their sins and remembers them no more (D&C 58:42). The couple should do the same. The plan of repentance permits the repentant individual or couple to build their marriage around current mutual trust and fidelity. Once repentance and forgiveness have occurred, it is not necessary or appropriate to discuss (or remember) those past events, with very few exceptions. If there has been previous sexual experience, testing for sexually transmitted diseases may be appropriate and may warrant disclosure.

Some couples believe that if they truly want to be honest with each other then there needs to be full and total disclosure of any past sexual (or other) transgressions. If the sexual problem is currently still a problem, like pornography addiction or homosexual tendencies, then that needs to be brought up and openly discussed. It is important for the couple together to determine how much of a problem remains, what has been done to resolve the problem, and what is currently being done to eliminate the problem. Honesty and disclosure are important when coupled with love and kindness. Generally speaking, after disclosure occurs, what has been done in the past and resolved in the past needs to stay in the past as the couple moves ahead, building their loving eternal marriage.

ABSTINENCE BEFORE MARRIAGE

Pam Stenzel, a popular speaker at high schools and universities across the nation, has a simple yet compelling question to help youth make the decision as to whether or not they should engage in sex: "Are you married?" If married, then engage in sex with your husband or wife. If not married, then abstinence is the only answer God will ever give. Couples who live together without being married and are sexually active do not have an easier or better sexual adjustment in marriage than couples who are not sexually involved before marriage.[6] Issues of lack of commitment and trust are often present in relationships for people who cohabit. When individuals in a relationship are not willing to make a marital commitment to each other for a lifetime (let alone eternally), they may not feel that they are the most important person in their partner's life.[7]

Additionally, there are significant research findings about cohabitation that demonstrate the negative effects of that experience.[8] For example:

• Cohabitation before marriage increases the risk of divorce after marriage. Studies show that cohabiting couples who marry each other are 46 percent more likely to divorce than couples who marry but have not cohabited first.

• Cohabitation increases the risk (especially for women and children) of physical and sexual violence in the relationship.

• Cohabiting couples report lower levels of happiness and general well-being than married couples report.

• Financially, cohabiting partners often live and

behave more like single persons than like a married couple. Joint budgeting and joint career goals are largely absent.

SEXUAL FIDELITY AFTER MARRIAGE

After marriage, a strong monogamous relationship between partners who are sexually faithful to each other provides a safe harbor. This security plays a key role in rejuvenating both partners as they face the everyday world outside their marriage. Both partners feel secure, loved physically, and cherished emotionally and sexually. This security is the result of commitment, which began with both partners' having been morally clean and chaste before the wedding. When a partner is unfaithful, trust is violated and the emotional security needed for a strong sexual relationship is impossible to achieve, at least until a new trust and commitment can be built (see chapter 14). Infidelity strikes the marriage a serious and often fatal blow. David Mace, longtime marriage counselor and writer, pointed out that "the sexual side of marriage is closely linked with the emotional and personal elements in the relationship. . . . What the married couple have to achieve, therefore, is a sex relationship that expresses, sustains, and renews their deepest and most tender feelings for each other."[9] Sexual fidelity is essential as couples work together to build and intensify their unconditional love for each other.

THE IMPORTANCE OF THE SEXUAL RELATIONSHIP WITHIN THE BONDS OF MARRIAGE

Within the bonds of marriage, sexual relations allow the couple to grow together. For a married couple, sexual feelings and actions are righteous and good. When a married couple unites in the act of sexual love, they experience an exclusively intimate union shared only with each other. Sexual intimacy provides bonding, uniting, and enrichment that are vitally important to marriage. President Spencer W. Kimball quoted the Reverend Billy Graham, who said, "Sex can be a . . . creative force more powerful than any other in the fostering of a love, companionship, [and] happiness."[10] A married couple should strive to communicate openly and learn to satisfy each other both emotionally and sexually. Sexual intimacy is not the same as having a strong sexual drive and should not be interpreted as a sexual "need" that has to be fulfilled "or else." It is not sexual intimacy if it involves coercion, manipulation, or anything else that separates the sexual act from the person.

One spouse may have a stronger desire for sexual intimacy, but that does not obligate the other spouse to fulfill that desire. Marriage is not a license to require or demand sexual intimacy, but, rather, sexual intimacy is a way to strengthen the social, spiritual, emotional, intellectual, and affectional aspects of marriage. There are a variety of medical and psychological situations where physical intimacy may not be possible or desirable. It is also important to be able to respect and honor the other's desire to refrain from sexual relations because of hormonal cycles, illness, fatigue, physical problems, or other pressing reasons. Each person in the relationship is responsible for his or her own body and consequently has the right to determine whether or not he or she wants to or is able to engage in sexual relations. Any attempt to use sexual intimacy to manipulate or coerce or to satisfy selfish lusts is counterproductive to achieving true oneness. Sacrifice is a divine principle and nowhere is it more relevant than in the sexual intimacies within marriage. Putting the physical needs of your spouse ahead of your own is a major part of what makes marriages work. In a strong and loving relationship there should be no coercion or neglect, no pressure or vindictive withholding. Love and respect for the spouse may prompt opportunities to fulfill the other's desires even when one's own desire is lacking or absent.

Sexual intimacy can bring a married couple closer or push them apart. A good sexual relationship, kept within the proper boundaries, will help keep marriage strong and will improve the marital relationship. A couple can be functioning well in everything else, but if one or both are unhappy in their intimate affectional and sexual relationship, they can be quite unhappy in marriage. A strong sexual relationship will improve marriage because it will help reduce the importance of other problems.[11] In addition, it will help bind a couple together such that they can work on other challenges as a team. Being able to give and receive physical pleasure allows both wife and husband to develop the closeness and intimacy necessary to become one in both heart and purpose.

Couples may decide to read a book on sexual intimacy to help them gain a greater knowledge and understanding of human sexuality. Although there are many books available on that subject, most contain at least some suggestions and recommendations that are not in harmony with Church standards. The married couple might visit a bookstore or library together and browse through books on sexuality and marital intimacy, selecting a book that seems to address the questions or topics of interest or importance to them. Then, as they read the book together and find information that is helpful, they can use that. Also, as they find material that is offensive or not relevant to them, they can ignore that and use only that which uplifts and strengthens their marital relationship. A reading list that the authors believe is in harmony with Latter-day Saint standards is provided at the end of this chapter to help those interested in gaining additional information on this subject. LDS and Christian bookstores have books that are more in line with Church standards than do general bookstores. Married couples should carefully select a resource that both feel comfortable with. Should they experience persistent problems with sexual intercourse, they may wish to consult a sex therapist or a physician specializing in sexual dysfunction.

Note that while the relationship must be strong and secure even before sexual intimacy can be fully enjoyed, expressing love through sexual intimacy can dramatically improve the marital relationship. For example, one partner's openness to having sex will often increase the other partner's feelings of love and gratitude. Communicating and expressing love for each other during sexual intimacy will often strengthen emotional closeness in other aspects of the marriage and allow for a more satisfying sexual experience. Newly married couples especially should talk to each other and express sexual likes and dislikes as they work together to create a mutually satisfying sexual relationship. For example, men are often visually oriented and easily aroused at the onset of sexual intimacy. Women, on the other hand, may need to spend more time talking and sharing their day as they relax and emotionally and physically prepare for this intimacy. There is a popular misconception that if a couple are truly in love with each other, they will somehow just know what sexually pleases the other without saying a word—this in spite of the fact that neither has any sexual experience to speak of. Good communication during sex should be related to the experience at hand and not involve other issues that, although important, are not appropriate in such a situation. The ideal is to use sexual intimacy as a means of enjoying the marriage relationship, rather than using the marriage relationship as a means of enjoying sexual intimacy.

A positive sexual relationship between a husband and wife increases their attraction for each other, stimulates greater energy, and promotes better health.[12] Additionally, a strong, intimate bond between a husband and wife can be a powerful resource for resisting temptation (see 1 Corinthians 7:2–5). In short, a loving and enjoyable sexual relationship is a blessing from God.

CONCLUSION

What spouses consider to be a loving and enjoyable sexual relationship is for them to determine as they are guided by their love and respect for one another and by the Spirit. The processes of dialogue, obtaining information, and prayer are important. Defining and discovering appropriate sexual intimacy is one of the joys of marriage. There will be frustrations and misunderstandings, but that is normal. We have been reminded by a prophet that "it is not love if it manipulates; it is selfishness; it is irresponsibility."[13] President Howard W. Hunter said:

> Keep yourselves above any domineering or unworthy behavior in the tender, intimate relationship between husband and wife. . . . Tenderness and respect—never selfishness—must be guiding principles in the intimate relationship between husband and wife. Each partner must be considerate and sensitive to the other's needs and desires. Any domineering, indecent, or uncontrolled behavior in the intimate relationship between husband and wife is condemned by the Lord.[14]

If spouses disagree regarding an intimate sexual behavior, they should not engage in that behavior until they agree on what is appropriate. Communication, love, respect, and caring are all important in developing appropriate sexuality in marriage. Inappropriate influences by media or other sources must be excluded from the couple's intimate relationship.

Typically, Latter-day Saint couples enter marriage having disciplined themselves to resist sexual thoughts and actions prior to marriage, then find that in marriage an open expression of sexual intimacy is appropriate, expected, and desired. Just as other forms of intimacy took time to develop, so, too, will sexual intimacy take more than the honeymoon to develop. Intimacy is a process, not an event. Because of the personal, private nature of sexual intimacy, individuals may come to the marriage in different states of readiness to develop this intimacy. Past experiences (having been embarrassed or having been physically or sexually abused), lack of knowledge, incorrect information, and naïveté may all complicate the process. True sexual intimacy includes the attributes of charity—patience, kindness, compassion, unselfishness, and discipline—which will assist couples as they learn together.

Marriage is a living entity. Marriage is an eternal process. As a marriage relationship is cultivated and nourished, it will thrive. The intimate sexual relationship, as an important part of marriage, also needs nurturing. Remember that sexuality is just one form of being intimate and should not be allowed to overshadow the emotional, spiritual, social, intellectual, and affectional aspects of intimacy within a marriage. Sexual intimacy is part of the divine plan to help husband and wife become one in purpose and have the kind of relationship that will last throughout the eternities and bring true joy and happiness.

ABOUT THE AUTHORS

Robert F. Stahmann, Ph.D., is a professor and chair of the Marriage and Family Therapy graduate program at BYU. He and his wife, Kathy, have five children and five grandchildren.

Kevin M. Marett, Ph.D., is an associate professor and director of the School of Social Work at BYU. He and his wife, Lori, are the parents of six children.

ADDITIONAL READING

Brent A. Barlow (1986, September), They twain shall be one: Thoughts on intimacy in marriage, *Ensign, 16*(9), 49–53.

Tim and Beverly LaHaye (1998), *The Act of Marriage: The Beauty of Sexual Love*, revised ed. (Grand Rapids, MI: Zondervan).

Stephen E. Lamb and Douglas E. Brinley (2000), *Between Husband and Wife: Gospel Perspectives on Marital Intimacy* (American Fork, UT: Covenant Communications).

Robert F. Stahmann, Wayne R. Young, and Julie G. Grover (2004), *Becoming One: Intimacy in Marriage* (American Fork, UT: Covenant Communications).

Joseph B. Stanford (2000), Procreation and the sanctity of life; in

David C. Dollahite, ed., *Strengthening Our Families: An In-Depth Look at the Proclamation on the Family* (Salt Lake City: Bookcraft), 215–216.

Wendy L. Watson (2000), Personal purity and marital intimacy; in David C. Dollahite, ed., *Strengthening Our Families: An In-Depth Look at the Proclamation on the Family* (Salt Lake City: Bookcraft), 60–62.

NOTES

1. First Presidency and Council of Twelve Apostles (1995, November), The family: A proclamation to the world, *Ensign, 25*(11), 102.

2. R. F. Stahmann, W. R. Young, and J. G. Grover (2004), *Becoming One: Intimacy in Marriage* (American Fork, UT: Covenant Communications).

3. Spencer W. Kimball (1974, May), Guidelines to carry forth the work of God in cleanliness: A plea to forsake the ways of the world, *Ensign, 4*(5), 7.

4. Stahmann, Young, and Grover (2004).

5. R. F. Stahmann and W. J. Hiebert (1997), *Premarital and Remarital Counseling: The Professional's Handbook* (San Francisco: Jossey-Bass).

6. P. Stenzel, with C. Kirgiss (2003), *Sex Has a Pricetag: Discussions About Sexuality, Spirituality, and Self-Respect* (Grand Rapids, MI: Zondervan).

7. L. J. Waite and M. Gallagher (2000), *The Case for Marriage: Why Married People Are Happier, Healthier, and Better Off Financially* (New York: Doubleday).

8. J. H. Larson (2001, January) The verdict on cohabitation vs. marriage, *Marriage & Families*, 7–12; T. D. Olson (2000), Chastity and fidelity in marriage and family relationships, in D. C. Dollahite, ed., *Strengthening Our Families: An In-Depth Look at the Proclamation on the Family* (Salt Lake City: Bookcraft), 50–59; D. Popenoe and B. D. Whitehead (1999), *Should We Live Together?: What Young Adults Need to Know About Cohabitation Before Marriage* (New Brunswick, NJ: National Marriage Project).

9. David R. Mace (1958), *Success in Marriage* (Nashville: Abingdon), 47, 48.

10. Kimball (1974), 8.

11. Stahmann, Young, and Grover (2004).

12. Waite and Gallagher (2000).

13. Spencer W. Kimball (1981, September), Thoughts on marriage compatibility, *Ensign, 11*(9), 46.

14. Howard W. Hunter (1994, November), Being a righteous husband and father, *Ensign, 24*(11), 51.

CHAPTER 10

TRANSITIONS IN MARRIAGE AND FAMILY LIFE

SUSANNE FROST OLSEN AND TERRANCE D. OLSON

We are promised uplifting sunshine and nourishing rain in times of slower growth or
serious setbacks, if only we stretch out our hand, mind, and heart to receive renewing energy and
strength through the power of the Atonement of Jesus Christ.[1]
—Elder Dieter F. Uchtdorf

To be mortal is to face changes, to meet transitions. The manner in which we respond to transitions, be they positive or negative, sought or avoided, planned or a surprise, is grounded in the manner of man or woman we are and by the person we can become. We experience times when we feel nearly overcome by joy or by grief. Yet, the outcome of transitions ultimately lies in who we are, not what the transition is. President Ezra Taft Benson reminded us:

> The Lord works from the inside out. The world works from the outside in. . . . The world would mold men by changing their environment. Christ changes men, who then change their environment. The world would shape human behavior, but Christ can change human nature.[2]

The scriptures sustain the idea that what is within us, not what is "out there," determines the quality of our responses to earthly circumstances. First, "all things work together for good to them that love God" (Romans 8:28). Second, no matter what events we might face, the Lord will not allow us to face more than we can bear, even if those events include injustices (1 Corinthians 10:13). The Lord recounted disastrous events that the Prophet Joseph Smith had already experienced and said, "Know thou, my son, that all these things shall give thee experience, and shall be for thy good" (D&C 122:7). The scriptures

help us understand that the obedient will not necessarily escape trials or challenges, but that they will not be overwhelmed by them (see Alma 36:3).

Surely one of the most unexpected transitions in the life of Stella Harris Oaks was the death of her husband after eleven years of marriage. Already no stranger to intense life transitions, Stella thus embarked upon a decade of significant challenge, commitment, and effort to provide for, nurture, and rear her children. With the help of family members, she sought and completed a quality education. She blessed her family by her example and provided them with a secure foundation of gospel living. She became an influence for good in her community. The key to her success in meeting life's challenges is illustrated in her own description of an experience she had as she watched her husband become weaker and lose ground:

> One June night I knelt alone in prayer, utterly spent, wondering at that midnight hour how humble one had to be to receive an answer to one's pleading. It was just at that moment that I felt an envelopment of the spirit of peace, a profound assurance that God is over all and that it was his will that was in command and not mine. I could finally say, "Thy will be done," and feel the peace. . . . I relaxed in my faith and discovered that I had a new trust in the Lord. . . . I was given to know that the Lord loved me and that I would be made equal to my mission. I felt an encircling love

that has sustained me ever since that great moment of change in my life. I have had continual hardships and challenges but always the sure knowledge that Jesus is the Christ, our Redeemer, and that he sustains us through the opposition that must arise in all things.[3]

PREDICTABLE TRANSITIONS IN MARRIAGE AND FAMILY LIFE

Changes in our lives may come in the form of myriad transition moments or as dramatic events. They can be viewed as invitations to drop to our knees or as provocations to shake our fists at the heavens. By being true to our covenants, it is possible to experience stress without despair, despite challenging circumstances. Not all changes are negative, just as not all changes are chosen, anticipated, or inevitable. However, change and transition require making adjustments. The choice is ours to do our best with current circumstances or become overwhelmed and abandon our capacity to make these necessary adjustments. Although some individuals may struggle with discouragement, even the little events of everyday life offer us opportunities to bring our best to the task of transitions.

For example, to our everyday interactions with our children, we can bring our best. Harshness and rejection can be abandoned, even when children's choices bring about undesirable changes to the family structure. President Gordon B. Hinckley described two parents' reactions when their teenaged son became rebellious. The father's response was to scold and threaten, whereas his mother, even after the boy left home, "kept his room tidy, his bed made, and the food he liked in the refrigerator. She told him that whenever he felt like coming home, he was welcome."[4] Although many months passed, the day came when the boy returned home to sleep occasionally.

> He began to improve his appearance. He stayed home more. . . . He abandoned some of his bad habits. . . . Our children are never lost until we give up on them! Love, more than any other thing, will bring them back into the family fold. . . . Reprimands without love will not accomplish it. Patience, expressions of appreciation, and that strange and remarkable power that comes with love and prayer will eventually win through.[5]

As in this example, the qualities that prepare us to handle transitions in life are manifest in our way of being with each other.

This way of being also translates into how we respond to more dramatic transitions. Family researchers classify family changes or transitions into two broad categories. *Non-normative,* or unanticipated, transitions are generally unexpected, unplanned, and unforeseen. A broken engagement, divorce, unanticipated job loss, a spouse's losing his or her testimony, bankruptcy, the birth of a child with a disability, a family member going to war, mental or physical illness, miscarriage, a stillborn birth, or early death due to an accident or illness are all examples of non-normative, or unexpected, family transitions.[6]

In contrast, *normative,* predictable transitions are those that occur as part of everyday life or normal developmental processes. These are changes that are expected, anticipated, and often chosen, such as going to school, becoming employed, graduating from high school, getting married, having a child, becoming a grandparent, retiring, and aging.[7] Although these predictable changes are often chosen (or "volitional"[8]), we may not see the panoramic consequences of our choices until we begin to experience them. Yet, the more we imagine possible consequences and seize the opportunity to plan for them, the more we can minimize the negative stress that may accompany them.

Normative, or predictable, transitions can also be surprising and possibly disruptive at times. Family scholar Pauline Boss explained that these transitions can be particularly difficult when they involve an individual's entering or leaving the family, resulting in a disruption in the existing state of affairs.[9] For example, even though marriage is a happy event for couples, they often must accommodate each other's differences, including coming to understand the value of those differences. Along with the joy new parents feel in the birth of a child, they also experience disruption in their lives as their routines change, sleep is lost, and the baby's demands require a reorganization of household duties. In both of these situations, over time, family members come to recognize that the sacrifices they have made for each other have blessed their lives many times over.

The "empty nest" years and retirement provide an example of how normative transitions may be unsettling to family members. A new retiree, Chuck, became irritable and impatient after the departure of his youngest son for dental school and his own retirement from 38 years at the cement plant. A comment by his wife, Gretta, reminded him that his problem did not lie in this double-barreled transition, but in his unwillingness to tell the truth about it to himself.

Gretta had been silent, mostly, when Chuck would mutter resentfully about every little thing. Then one day she said, "You planning to work with that cement in your head while it is still wet, or are you just going to watch it set up like concrete and become a hard old man?" Chuck stopped in his tracks—physically and verbally. He didn't have to ask what she meant. He started chuckling. "I've already been hard on you. Sorry. Thanks for catching me in time." This couple found a way to allow this normative transition to be a starting point for attending to their marital partnership in ways that restored their faith in their own agency and in life's new opportunities.

PROCLAMATION PRINCIPLES AND FAMILY TRANSITIONS

Principles from the proclamation help us to understand the place of transitions in the plan of salvation and provide guidelines to family members experiencing change. Change, transitions, and the opportunities connected with them have been associated with our Heavenly Father's plan from the beginning, as reiterated in the proclamation: "In the premortal realm, spirit sons and daughters . . . accepted His plan by which His children could obtain a physical body and *gain earthly experience to progress toward perfection* and ultimately realize his or her divine destiny as an heir of eternal life. The divine plan of happiness enables family relationships to be perpetuated beyond the grave."[10] Thus, transitions are an inherent part of the earthly experience of progressing to become what God desires us to be.

Adam and Eve experienced transition as they left the Garden of Eden and became mortal. This blessing of mortality was a condition created by their own choice, and they soon discovered that earth life would include experiencing pain, joy, sorrow, and injustice, and being confronted by good and evil (see Moses 5:11). This was part of our Heavenly Father's eternal plan, and Adam and Eve knew that in His love and mercy, He would not abandon them in their new circumstances. That evil should triumph was not in the plan.

The proclamation also reminds us of our Heavenly Father's love and His desires for us: "Each is a beloved spirit son or daughter of heavenly parents, and, as such, each has a divine nature and destiny."[11] This truth becomes an essential resource in times of transition. The proclamation asserts that in fulfilling our divine destinies, being married and having a family are "central to the plan," "essential," and "ordained of God."

Because the transition to marriage and family life is a change that is chosen and anticipated, it may be perceived as a fairly easy transition. Research indicates, however, that couples making this transition have identified specific areas that may be problematic during the first years of marriage. These areas include financial issues, sexual relationships, balancing job and family, expectations about household tasks, parents-in-law, time spent with spouse, and communication and conflict resolution.[12]

President Gordon B. Hinckley told of a couple who came to him for counseling after being married for only six months. As the couple visited with him separately, each dwelt on the other's faults—"she didn't do the dishes before she left for work" and "he didn't put away his clothes." President Hinckley's analysis of the problem was that these individuals focused more on each other's shortcomings than good qualities. Although they could have spoken more positively to each other, they chose not to. Their negative outlook and attitude, along with "careless and sour words" destroyed their marriage. President Hinckley lamented, "With criticism and shouting, they had violated the most sacred of all relationships."[13] Sadly, instead of taking the opportunity to become closer as a new couple in the face of challenges, they grew apart.

Parenting researchers Carolyn and Philip Cowan described some of the changes and transformations that take place in the developing family system during the transition to parenthood. Changes may occur in the quality of relationships in families the new parents grew up in, in the new parents' couple relationship, in the quality of the relationship developed between the parents and the baby, in the balance between social support and life stress in the emerging family, and in the distress or well-being of the baby and parents as individuals.[14] In the transition to parenthood, family members may have to identify new ways of working together and getting along.

The proclamation also teaches that "successful marriages and families are established and maintained on principles of faith."[15] We can meet life's transitions in a faithful way when we have given our hearts to God. We can be optimistic and sufficiently humble, and we can retain a sense of humor. For example, Sister Marjorie Pay Hinckley exemplified these characteristics in her parenting and in the advice she gave to others.[16] In describing her own experience as a new mother, daughter Kathleen Barnes noted that she had always wanted to be a mother and had assumed that motherhood would be as easy for her as it appeared to be for Sister Hinckley. However, when her first child arrived,

> I was ill prepared for what I faced. This tiny little six-pound bundle instantly took total control of my life. She determined when I could sleep, when I could eat, when I could shower, clean my house, do my laundry, where and if I could go anyplace. Not only that, everything I did was done in a state of complete fatigue. About six weeks into this I looked around one day and knew that this was not the life I had planned. And suddenly I desperately wanted out. Motherhood was not all it was cracked up to be. . . . "I've had it!" I cried to my mother. "I'm not cut out to be a mother! I can't do this the rest of my life. . . . I want my old life back!" She listened quietly as I unloaded for several tearful minutes. Then, quite unexpectedly, she started to laugh. "Well, guess what, dear," she said through her laughter. "It's too late!"[17]

Sister Hinckley responded to her daughter with love in a humorous way, but her response was grounded in her faith that our Heavenly Father could help this young mother in this challenging transition. When we are faithful, we look at transitions with patient faith. Elder Richard G. Scott described how this might happen:

> Gratefully, in His perfect love, [God] has provided a way for us to resolve . . . challenges while growing in strength and capacity. I speak of the sustaining power of faith in times of uncertainty and testing. God has given us the capacity to exercise faith, that we may find peace, joy, and purpose in life. However, to employ its power, faith must be founded on something. There is no more solid foundation than faith in the love Heavenly Father has for you, faith in His plan of happiness, and faith in the capacity and willingness of Jesus Christ to fulfill all of His promises.[18]

Elder Russell M. Nelson described how his wife exemplified patient faith:

> With the arrival of our fourth child we felt further the pinch of poverty; but I can never remember any murmurings from my sweet wife, even though I felt that she was being imposed upon, as were the children. . . . It seems amazing to me that a woman could genuinely be as selfless as she has been, for all she ever wanted was enough to provide for the children that were so near and dear to us. . . . Indeed, if I were to sum up in one scripture the faith of my beloved companion, I would say the twenty-third Psalm would be my selection: "The Lord is my shepherd; I shall not want."[19]

In transitions of affliction, the quality of our response determines the impact and meaning of the transition itself. We can respond with patience or resentment; with charity or selfishness; with concern for others or with withdrawal. Our perception of a transition and the meaning we attach to it comes from within, and yet we are spiritually expanded through the experience itself. Latter-day Saint family scholars have reminded us that our perspective and frame of reference are important.[20] Just how do we view transitions? Do we see every change as being some kind of loss and suppose that we can count on confronting troubles every day? Do we see transitions as being inherently debilitating or ruinous or even automatically beneficial? Can we "come out of the world" regarding how we see the meaning of family transitions? Do our meanings come to us through eyes of faith?

In addition to faith, resources of individuals, the family, and the community can assist family members in adapting to the transitions in marriage and family life. These resources may include traits, abilities, or characteristics of the individuals in the family, the family as a whole, or the community.[21] Examples are a spirit of love and nurturing, flexibility, and extended family support.

Moreover, our success in adapting to life changes will be grounded in our willingness to meet these changes. President Gordon B. Hinckley counseled: "Looking at the dark side of things always leads to a spirit of pessimism, which often leads to defeat. Let us replace our fears with faith."[22] As we approach changes with soberness, confidence, and faith, and learn from them, we can be assured that the Lord is available to us, knows our names, and has not abandoned us. Often people with limited abilities are able to adapt to changes because of their honest hearts, their willingness to work hard, and their positive attitudes.

One mother learned that difficulties arising from the marriage of her daughter could be tempered by a determination to show love and to trust the Lord. Lani's daughter was married in the temple to Bentley, a young man who was raised in a less-active family. At first Lani and her son-in-law seemed to get along, but gradually he took offense at family habits, became critical of family members, and withdrew from most family activities. Initially, the behavior of her son-in-law hurt Lani. She resented the way he was tearing her family apart. However, throughout this period Lani constantly sought the Lord for help. Over time, she developed a greater understanding of her son-in-law's circumstances and personal trials. She returned love and patience for Bentley's resentment. Although family relationships are still not perfect, Lani has a sense of peace and knowledge that she is being helped by our Heavenly Father to draw upon the best within her to encourage beneficial family relationships during this time of transition.

Conclusion

Thomas L. Campbell has discussed how the Chinese character signifying *crisis* is composed of two symbols, one representing danger, and the other, opportunity.[23] A family who responds in patient faith—with a conscience "void of offense" (D&C 135:4)—is better prepared to weather any crisis, great or small, than a family who can only find loss in the trials and tribulations of this life. Through faith in the Lord Jesus Christ there is reason for the hope that is (or can be) within us (see 1 Peter 3:15). President Ezra Taft Benson reminded us: "When you choose to follow Christ, you choose the Way, the Truth, the Life—the right way, the saving truth, the abundant life (see John 14:6)."[24] If, in the midst of our personal frailties and challenges, we choose to turn our hearts to Christ, we will be able to acknowledge the availability of sorrow over despair, of humility over resentment, of determination and perseverance over a sense of martyred helplessness. Only then will we come to see how, with the Lord's help, all things work together for our good.

ABOUT THE AUTHORS

Susanne Frost Olsen is associate director of the School of Family Life and a faculty member in the Marriage, Family, and Human Development program. She currently serves as Primary president in the Orem Utah Suncrest Tenth Ward.

Terrance D. Olson is a member of the BYU Marriage, Family, and Human Development faculty who has focused on developing, delivering, and evaluating programs that invite individuals to live lives that promote a quality future. He serves in the Young Men program in his Orem ward.

ADDITIONAL READING

Virginia H. Pearce, ed. (1999), *Glimpses into the Life and Heart of Marjorie Pay Hinckley* (Salt Lake City: Deseret Book).

Richard G. Scott (2003, May), The sustaining power of faith in times of uncertainty and testing, *Ensign, 33*(5), 75–77.

Susan W. Tanner (2003, May), Did I tell you . . . ? *Ensign, 33*(5), 73–75.

NOTES

1. Dieter F. Uchtdorf (2002, October), Making choices for eternity, *Ensign, 32*(10), 26.

2. Ezra Taft Benson (1989, July), Born of God, *Ensign, 19*(7), 2.

3. L. R. Hartshorn (1975), Thy will be done; in *Remarkable Stories from the Lives of Latter-day Saint Women, volume 2* (Salt Lake City: Deseret Book), 183–184.

4. Gordon B. Hinckley (2000), *Standing for Something: 10 Neglected Virtues That Will Heal Our Hearts and Homes* (New York: Times Books), 156.

5. Ibid., 157.

6. See other chapters and essays in this volume, specifically chapters on chronic illness, death, and grieving (chapter 32), blended families (chapter 22), and children with special needs (chapter 23), and essays on surviving the death of a child (essay G5), spousal infidelity and betrayal (essay C1), single-parent dating and remarriage (essay E4), and spiritual crises (essay C4).

7. P. Boss (2002), *Family Stress Management: A Contextual Approach*, 2d ed. (Thousand Oaks, CA: Sage); P. C. McKenry and S. J. Price (2000), *Families & Change: Coping with Stressful Events and Transitions*, 2d ed. (Thousand Oaks, CA: Sage).

8. Boss (2002).

9. Ibid.

10. First Presidency and Council of Twelve Apostles (1995, November), The family: A proclamation to the world, *Ensign, 25*(11), 102; emphasis added.

11. Ibid.

12. G. S. Risch, L. A. Riley, and M. G. Lawler (2003), Problematic issues in the early years of marriage: Content for premarital education, *Journal of Psychology and Theology, 31*, 253–269.

13. Hinckley (2000), 106.

14. C. P. Cowan and P. A. Cowan (1995), Interventions to ease the transition to parenthood: Why they are needed and what they can do, *Family Relations, 44*, 412–423.

15. First Presidency and Council of Twelve Apostles (1995), 102.

16. V. H. Pearce, ed. (1999), *Glimpses into the Life and Heart of Marjorie Pay Hinckley* (Salt Lake City: Deseret Book), 3.

17. Ibid., 113–114.

18. Richard G. Scott (2003, May), The sustaining power of faith in times of uncertainty and testing, *Ensign, 33*(5), 75–76.

19. Russell M. Nelson (1979), *From Heart to Heart: An Autobiography* (Salt Lake City: Quality Press), 61, 89.

20. J. Carroll, et al. (2000), The family crucibles of illness, disability, death, and other losses; in D. C. Dollahite, ed., *Strengthening Our Families: An In-Depth Look at the Proclamation on the Family* (Salt Lake City: Bookcraft), 278–292.

21. McKenry and Price (2000), 9–10.

22. Hinckley (2000), 101–102.

23. T. L. Campbell (2000), Physical illness: Challenges to families; in P. C. McKenry and S. J. Price, eds., *Families & Change: Coping With Stressful Events and Transitions* (Thousand Oaks, CA: Sage), 154–182.

24. Benson (1989), 2.

Joys and Challenges of Marrying Later in Life

Camille Fronk

I never intended to be a marital anomaly. As a Latter-day Saint young adult in northern Utah, I expected to marry and become a mother by my mid-twenties. But after one quarter of college, besides dating, I discovered a love for school and chances to see the world. So by my 23rd birthday, I was a college graduate, a returned missionary—and a dating casualty. My "professional-dater" friends told me I needed to flirt, play down my academic interests, and make "trapping" a man my top priority. I couldn't do it. Tricking someone into liking me felt deceptive, manipulative, and miserable.

In the meantime, I received experience with learning to recognize direction from the Spirit. For example, at age 24, when I received an offer to teach seminary full-time, I longingly hoped for a more traditional route to follow. But I felt the divine tug to accept the job, becoming the only woman in Utah at the time in that occupation. Amazingly, ability beyond my natural talents led me through doors of opportunity with a success I never before imagined. One scripture seemed to explain the phenomenon and propel me toward some unknown destination: "As often as thou hast inquired thou hast received instruction of my Spirit. If it had not been so, thou wouldst not have come to the place where thou art at this time" (D&C 6:14).

By my mid-forties, I had a master's degree in Near Eastern Studies, a Ph.D. in sociology of the Middle East, continuing status (tenure) as an associate professor of ancient scripture at Brigham Young University, and a passport stamped for a plethora of places that bore no cultural resemblance to my hometown. I will not delineate ways my life had become foreign to my youthful dreams, but I was grateful to God for a surprisingly fulfilling journey. Don't misunderstand; at times I longed for companionship and felt frustrated with my career path, but I sensed what President Ezra Taft Benson promised: "God . . . can make a lot more out of [our] lives than [we] can."[1]

Through mutual friends, I became acquainted with Paul Olson, an ophthalmologist whose wife had passed away two years earlier. Our first date was not accompanied by trumpets and hallelujahs. In fact, it felt like dozens of other first dates I had experienced. Long after leaving the restaurant, however, Paul continued our conversation, wanting to better understand me. I obliged, thinking this would be the last time I saw him. Undoubtedly, I underestimated his charm.

When people asked him, "Aren't you intimidated by her?" he was mystified and answered, "She knows more about scriptures than I do; I know more about eyes than she does." He was comfortable with his own identity and so could actively pursue me. At first, I hesitated at his invitations to get together again. Finally, he asked me why and whether he should take my delayed responses personally. I confessed my fear of commitment which had nothing to do with him. The next time I saw him, he asked, "Tell me about this 'fear of commitment.'" He listened while I struggled to psychoanalyze my idiosyncrasies, and then observed, "It isn't commitment you fear but overcommitment because you will do whatever you commit." Instantly, I had lost yet another subconscious sabotage-the-relationship tactic.

Early on, I recognized Paul's positive characteristics: honesty and openness, patience, and a most disarming sense of humor. During subsequent months, my awareness of those qualities only intensified and increased. Still, I could not admit what I was feeling. I convinced myself that I should search for unseen problems, which must surely exist, because no man could be this good. Others' reactions would help me discern whether or not I was being objective: someone who cared about me but didn't know Paul, his children, or my family.

While on assignment in Alberta, I stayed with friends who, at my request, analyzed the relationship. Here was a couple who married 50 years before in the same temple where they now presided. He had unflinchingly supported her during her leadership assignments and she was a true helpmeet for him in his Church responsibilities. They were a happy and contributing couple who had never become bitter because of childlessness. I concluded they would be ideal marriage counselors for me. During a most entertaining discussion, they listed "essential qualities" of a good husband and I was to rate Paul somewhere between 1 and 10 for each one. Without knowing Paul, they named his strongest characteristics one after another. After I announced, "10," for the tenth time in a row, the man exclaimed, "What are you waiting for? Let's plan the wedding."

Paul has two children. Emily was married and employed out of state, using her MBA education until the birth of her first child. Dave had just graduated from BYU and begun a job in Salt Lake City. If Paul posed no impediments to our relationship, certainly, I surmised, one or both of his children would object.

When Paul introduced me to Dave, I learned we had already met About three months before my first date with Paul, I spoke to the sister missionaries at the Missionary Training Center. As an MTC employee, Dave provided graphics support for my talk. After my remarks, this nice young man offered me a video recording of my presentation. When I declined, Dave took the recording home to his dad with the invitation, "You can date this one." I would later learn that Dave became my greatest advocate. When Paul and I had dated about four months and were seeing each other nearly every day, Dave and I went to dinner to talk straight—without Paul's buffering influence. He wanted to see if my intentions toward his father were sincere; I wanted to see his reaction to the possibility of my joining his family. Along the way, I discovered how easy it was to genuinely love and delight in Dave—and that Paul was as even-tempered, generous, and sincere at home as he was with me. Dave learned that I had fallen in love with his father.

If I could have changed one circumstance in our courtship, I would have found a way to meet Emily earlier. As it happened, introductions occurred a month before our marriage and two months before the birth of her child. Paul and Dave both assured me, however, that she trusted their judgment and was equally supportive of the match. I have since found a kindred spirit in Emily, finding topics to discuss with equal passion and delight.

Finally, when my parents and siblings gave an enthusiastic thumbs-up after meeting Paul, I acknowledged my feelings and gladly accepted his marriage proposal. Marrying at age 48 suddenly seemed the best of all worlds. When God writes the script, there are no marital anomalies—only evidences that His promises far exceed our greatest dreams.

We chose a quiet wedding. I felt no need for a multitude to witness what was clearly a miracle from God. On the contrary, this sense of belonging and being loved was so sacred that I didn't want it spoken of casually. No reception or dinner embellished the day; we had a lifetime ahead of us for celebrations. Instead, we quietly slipped away for the rest of the week while Dave inconspicuously mailed stacks of announcements. I was back teaching the following week when friends discovered our news in their mailboxes.

Elder Boyd K. Packer suggested to women "who are slipping past the usual age for marriage" that "marriage may well come to you as a September song and be twice more precious for the waiting."[2] I was warned, right up to the hour we were married, that I would have a rough adjustment. How difficult is it to learn to be waited on and cherished at every turn? Living alone supposedly makes one selfish and inflexible to another's habits and lifestyle. But it can also make one appreciative of power in partnership, shared responsibilities, and emotional security. For me, marriage in the autumn of life is at least "twice more precious for the waiting."

Years of following the path less traveled have taught me much about welcoming change and surmounting challenges. Within six months of marriage, we sold both of our homes, designed and built a new home together, and became grandparents. In each case, we communicated personal opinions, combined our talents and faith, and found opportunities to grow together. Additional twists and turns will surely come as mortality necessitates, but I do not fear. More than ever before, I hear the Savior's witness, "As often as thou hast inquired thou hast received instruction of my Spirit. If it had not been so, thou wouldst not have come to the place where thou art at this time" (D&C 6:14).

ABOUT THE AUTHOR

Camille Fronk, Ph.D., is an associate professor of ancient scripture at Brigham Young University. She is married to Paul F. Olson, a Provo ophthalmologist.

ADDITIONAL READING

Dallin H. Oaks (2002, January 29), Timing; BYU Devotional Address; in *Brigham Young University 2001–2002 Speeches* (Provo: Brigham Young University Press), 187–193; available at http://speeches.byu.edu

NOTES

1. Ezra Taft Benson (1988), *Teachings of Ezra Taft Benson* (Salt Lake City: Bookcraft), 361.

2. Boyd K. Packer (1963, November 3), Eternal love; BYU Fireside; available at http://speeches.byu.edu

Essay B2

Differing Expectations in Gospel Living

Amy Hardison

Twenty-seven years ago, my husband and I stepped onto a Christmas tree lot, ready to buy our first Christmas tree as a newly married couple. My husband walked over to an elegant tree with few, sparse branches. To me, it looked like a pole with a handful of green toothpicks sticking out of it. I walked over to the kind of tree my family had always had, a full, lush fir. To my husband, my tree looked like a bush on steroids. I looked at his tree and then at mine and realized we would need to do a lot of compromising in order to achieve unity in our marriage. Christmas trees would prove the easiest.

Most couples must grapple with multiple differences, from where to squeeze the toothpaste, to how to give children allowances, to how and where to celebrate holidays. No areas of life are exempt: not communication, not physical intimacy, not even religion. It is quite possible for a husband and wife who are both active, dedicated, righteous members of the Church to differ on how to live the gospel of Jesus Christ.

A steadfast, righteous couple may differ on how to keep the Sabbath day holy, what words are acceptable or offensive, how frequently to attend the temple, what programs are appropriate to watch on television, when—or if—family activities should take precedence over a fireside or other auxiliary activity, and for which physical activities it is or is not appropriate to wear one's temple garment. These differences may arise from different practices in a couple's families of origin, different levels of commitment to gospel principles, and different personality styles. Even a couple who agrees on how to live the gospel in their own home may face the complication of differing values in their extended family.

Resolving differences on how to live the gospel may be particularly challenging for several reasons. As human beings, we tend to approach life with a right or wrong orientation. While we may not admit it, we usually think we know the right way to do things. In teaching my institute classes, I have asked my students how many of them know the right way to drive a car or clean a house or conduct some aspect of family life. Inevitably, they grin and nod in affirmation. We have great fun sharing our individual right ways until I give them the assignment to spend a week setting aside their rightness in order to live in unity. Everyone sobers up quickly. It is hard to set aside our notions about the right way to drive a car. It is even harder to do so in issues regarding religious observance. First of all, we feel strongly about such issues. In addition, our religious observance consists of both divinely mandated rights and wrongs that should not be bent in the slightest and personal rights and wrongs that allow some flexibility. It is not always easy to determine which is which. Distinguishing between preferences and principles takes humility.

Another difficulty is that matters of religion and spirituality are matters of consequence. Though we may really like big, bushy Christmas trees, we recognize that getting a spindly one won't influence our eternal salvation. It is far more difficult to compromise when it feels like we are compromising our spiritual integrity. Consequently, we may be less willing to compromise in issues of religious observance than in other areas of our marriages. Finally, when faced with a spouse or extended family with different ideas, we may feel we are in the difficult position of choosing between two good things: family or principles. In spite of the difficulties involved, it is essential to work out these differences if we are to achieve unity and harmony in marriage.

A key to resolving differences in marriage, including how we live the gospel, is communication. One idea for initiating communication is to make a list of the gospel principles you consider inviolable. When you finish, compare your list with your spouse's list. Note the similarities—and celebrate. It is too easy to focus on the differences. Next, tackle the issues for which you differ. Discuss why you feel the way you do. Can you trace your attitudes back to the way you did things in your family of origin? Have you come to your current feelings through personal experience? Explain why it is important to you. Of course, sharing your feelings is only half the process. You must also listen, really listen. This means listening without judgment, listening with empathy, listening without internally debating what your spouse is saying. True listening is a journey into another's heart and experience. "Listening is a strenuous but silent activity. . . . [It] requires a submersion of the self and immersion in the other. This isn't always easy."[1]

Having truly listened to one another, it might be beneficial to take a brief hiatus. Pray about your lists. Seek divine guidance. You might want to include in your prayers such things as "What can I do to make my spouse's life less frustrating?" and "What am I not seeing that Thou wouldst have me see?" Such requests are not for the timid. However, we must remember that God has a vested interest in our success. He is omniscient and wise. He can and will reveal what we need to do to make our marriages strong and sweet And He will probably reveal your weaknesses to you and your spouse's weaknesses to him or her—not the other way around.

Once you have pondered and prayed over your lists, talk to your spouse and negotiate a compromise. This negotiation must be done with integrity and respect. Avoid coercion, guilt trips, and manipulation. Personal inspiration or priesthood office should not be used as a spiritual trump card to get one's own way. In addition, remember that giving up is not the same thing as compromising. If your compromise leaves you feeling resentful or like a martyr, keep talking until you find a compromise you can both support.

It might be helpful to step back and look at your list and learn something from it as a whole. What does it reveal about your commitment to the gospel? Are there things you consider negotiable that should really be inviolable? Is it time to step up to a higher level of obedience? On the other hand, if your list goes on for ten pages, you might want to consider whether you are living the gospel with a letter-of-the-law mentality. Do you tend to be a little too rigid? Of course, there is nothing wrong with being "steadfast and immovable" (Mosiah 5:15), but we must be wary of being inflexible in matters of human relations. We live in families, not petri dishes. We must take into consideration those with whom we live. In matters of personal relationships, it is usually more important to be effective than to be right. In this case, effectiveness means having a family that loves being together and loves the gospel. An approach that is too heavy-handed may thwart this ultimate objective.

Many couples have successfully negotiated their differences in how to live the gospel. The following are examples of how different couples worked out compromises regarding keeping the Sabbath day holy. In citing these, I am not supporting one particular adherence. In many homes, husbands and wives differ on whether they should watch television, specifically sports, on Sunday. In one home, the husband agreed to watch sporting events without the volume. He could see the game, but the noise did not fill the home. In another home, the husband and wife agreed on the things they both wanted to do on the Sabbath, such as writing to family members who lived far away, reading the *Friend* to their children, and making cards for missionaries. By the time they do these things, the time for television watching is naturally diminished. In other homes, couples agreed to a limited amount of television time or that they would only watch television in the evening. In one home, the husband watched sports while the wife read, wrote in her journal, and did the things she saw fitting for the Sabbath day. The interesting thing about this last compromise is that in some instances, a couple might agree to disagree. In other words, occasionally an acceptable compromise is for each person to do what works for him or her.

In working out compromises, it is important to see it as a process, one that might need refining and adjustments as you go along. For instance, one family who has extended family members who aren't members of the Church agreed to attend the family swimming parties on Sunday, but decided to wear their Sunday clothes and not swim. They soon learned that wearing their Sunday clothes made the extended family uncomfortable. They then decided to attend the family gatherings in casual clothes, but held firm to their commitment not to swim.

Finally, a few words to those who feel that by making compromises on how they live the gospel, they are living beneath their spiritual privileges and responsibilities:

Nagging doesn't work. Express your feelings and then let go. Letting go disallows subtle forms of disapproval, such as condescending sighs and reproving looks, and even unspoken, internal censure. Instead of overt or covert badgering, set an example. One wife who wished her husband was more diligent in his personal scripture study made a personal goal that she would not miss a day of her own scripture study. Eventually, her husband followed her example.

Keep perspective. If your spouse is an outstanding father or mother, faithful to his or her temple covenants, kind and considerate, but not as diligent in his or her Church calling as you would wish, don't let what's missing color everything. Focus on all the great things that he or she does and express your appreciation for those things.

Choose your battles carefully. Our homes should be havens of peace, not battlegrounds. Anger, resentment, and discord drive away the Spirit. In fact, bitter words, hostile feelings, and barbed criticism may actually be more sinful in the eyes of God than the behavior that triggers them.

Learning to live in love and harmony with another person who has different views on everything from Christmas trees to the Sabbath day is not easy. It is, however, essential if we are to achieve unity and satisfaction in our marriages. Moreover, an important role of the gospel is to teach us to be more like Christ, more loving, more service-oriented, less self-absorbed. Thus, working out our marital differences is not just something we must endure. It is sanctifying.

ABOUT THE AUTHOR

Amy Hardison is an instructor at the Tempe Arizona Institute. She and her husband, Steve, are the parents of four children.

ADDITIONAL READING

M. Catherine Thomas (1996), Enduring marriage; in *Spiritual Lightening* (Salt Lake City: Bookcraft), 75–92.

M. Catherine Thomas (1996), Living the spirit of At-one-ment; in *Spiritual Lightening* (Salt Lake City: Bookcraft), 59–64.

Joe J. Christensen (1995, May), Marriage and the great plan of happiness, *Ensign, 25*(5), 64–66.

NOTE

1. Michael P. Nichols (1995), *The Lost Art of Listening* (New York: Guilford Press).

E S S A Y   B 3

RESOLVING MARITAL DIFFERENCES

KENNETH W. MATHESON

Dealing with differences is part of every marital relationship. Elder Joe J. Christensen wrote: "Any intelligent couple will have differences of opinion. Our challenge is to be sure that we know how to resolve them."[1]

Spouses must learn to avoid thinking that one spouse is right and the other wrong, that one opinion is better than the other, or that all differences must be brought to immediate resolution. In some situations, couples learn to live without resolving certain differences, and simply agree to disagree. In one such case, the husband was an avid sports fan, but his wife wasn't. He wanted to attend and enjoy football games with her on Saturdays, but her response was that she could accomplish more by staying at home. Initially, the husband personalized the lack of willingness on the wife's part to spend time with him. However, as they discussed the situation, he soon realized that it had nothing to do with him, but more to do with her preferences and the use of her time. He continues to attend with members of his family and she is satisfied to spend the time involved in her projects. They have learned to adjust to the situation and allow each other the freedom to pursue their own preferences.

Based on my experience in counseling with couples and families, I have found that understanding and implementing the following principles will help couples better deal with the inevitable differences in their marriages.

Differences are normal and are essential for personal growth and couple cohesiveness. A wife once told her husband, "If you were more loving like me, we wouldn't have so many differences and arguments in our marriage." When differences are present, it is natural for a spouse to try to change the other to his or her way of thinking. President Brigham Young, speaking to the elders of the Church, emphasized a great principle that applies to dealing with differences in marriage effectively. He stated: "We should not look upon ourselves as an infallible standard for others. . . . Is it wisdom for each Elder to strive to mould and fashion all others precisely according to himself in all the views and notions he possesses? Is this the way? No, it is not."[2]

When differences do need to be resolved, the process of change shouldn't be viewed as negative, but rather as being essential to character growth. Elder Boyd K. Packer stated: "Marriage is not without trials of many kinds. These tests forge virtue and strength. The tempering that comes in marriage and family life produces men and women who will someday be exalted."[3]

Differences are best resolved in an environment of mutual love, consideration, and the application of Christlike attributes. In order to deal effectively with differences in any relationship, especially marriage, each individual must strive to demonstrate Christlike attributes. These attributes include patience, kindness, love, cooperation, respect, humility, forgiveness, understanding, courtesy, consideration, trust, commitment, and obedience to gospel principles.

When serious differences go unresolved, it is usually because one or both of the partners lacks one of the above-mentioned positive attributes, or because of stubbornness, pride, or selfishness. For example, a husband was demanding, always had to be right, and was self-centered. In turn, his wife gradually felt devalued and smothered and began to withdraw into herself. One afternoon, the husband received the strong impression that he needed to let the Lord be more involved in the marriage. Then as he tried to reach out to his wife, he realized that if he would worry more about her feelings, their marriage would improve. It is amazing what can happen to a relationship when one becomes humble and is more concerned about the welfare of the spouse than the self. Based on the husband's efforts, the wife began to see him differently, forgave his previous unrighteous demands, and began to look forward to their time together. Elder Loren C. Dunn remarked: "People will always have opposing views, and I suppose there will always be conflict and even misunderstanding; but the principle of *mutual respect* mixed with charity and forgiveness can lay the foundation for the resolving of differences and the solving of problems."[4]

Resolving differences together increases spirituality. If a Latter-day Saint couple were asked how they could increase their spirituality, they would probably suggest studying the scriptures, attending the temple more frequently, holding effective family home evenings, or praying more meaningfully and consistently together. President Ezra Taft Benson gave additional ideas: "Rely on the Lord, the teachings of the prophets, and the scriptures for guidance and help, particularly when there may be disagreements and problems. Spiritual growth comes by solving problems together—not by running from them. . . . The more we serve one another, the greater is our spiritual and emotional growth."[5]

Acknowledge the effort the spouse makes to meet needs and expectations. Every person has a need to be loved, appreciated, valued, and accepted. When one spouse is trying to meet the expectations of the other, it is important to reward the efforts positively, even though the performance may not be perfect. An example of this might be, "I appreciate the effort you've made in helping me clean the windows," rather than, "Is that the best you can do? I'd better just do it myself." When one spouse acknowledges the other's effort, the other spouse is likely to try again.

View the problem as being separate from the spouse. Calmly discussing problems together—details, facts, timelines, outcomes—in the spirit of cooperation, respect, and love is vital to understanding each other. Accusing, blaming, labeling, or attacking each other is not helpful in resolving differences. Learn to separate the content of the problem from the emotion; be hard on the problem and easy on the person. For example, "Dear, we can work together to solve these financial problems," would be a more appropriate response than, "Dear, if you would work harder and not be so lazy, we wouldn't be in the financial fix we're in." When a spouse feels attacked, he or she will personalize a criticism, feel hurt, and most likely desire to strike back.

I occasionally hear a husband respond to his wife by stating that a particular problem "is yours, not mine." Any problem in marriage affects both partners; thus, problems are best solved together. The focus should not be on who is right, but on what is right.

Create an atmosphere of caring through positive communication. To have effective communication in a marriage, a sincere feeling of caring for each other must be present and perceived by both spouses. Caring is the single most important quality to improve personal, in-depth communication. Because an atmosphere of caring is lacking in their relationship, some couples can't discuss deep emotional issues without ending up in an argument. Both partners have a responsibility to make the atmosphere of communication psychologically safe so that sharing personal feelings will continue. Communication is more an attitude than a skill.

Emphasize the positive aspects of the marital relationship. We all would prefer to receive compliments, especially from our spouse, even though it seems easier to point out the negative aspects of our spouse's behavior. President Gordon B. Hinckley taught that if we emphasized the virtues and not the vices in our homes, there would be "more of happiness."[6] John M. Gottman, a respected social science researcher, found that couples who stay married emphasize the positive with each other more than the negative. Among the things he learned was that for every negative interaction that occurs in a relationship, there need to be at least five positive interactions to offset it.[7]

Seek help when needed. A marital relationship may become so damaged that the couple find it difficult to salvage on their own. If repeated attempts to improve the marriage always end up in an argument, or if not knowing what to do becomes an issue, the couple might consider getting outside help. The couple's bishop can provide insights and inspiration. Wise, carefully chosen marriage counselors may also lend support. Ultimately, the couple has the responsibility and power to improve their marriage, but another person might be needed to assist them.

Involve the Savior more in the marital relationship. The Savior can heal relationships, soften hearts, and make weak things strong (Ether 12:27). Through personal revelation, husbands and wives may realize that the Savior is interested in the success of their marriage. The example and teachings of the Savior bring the ultimate source of power to resolve differences and to heal wounded hearts.

Remember, God can heal sick and troubled relationships just as He can heal sick bodies. He wants us to develop Christlike qualities and become more like Him. By developing His characteristics in our lives, we can better overcome differences in our relationships, and thus He can better assist us to achieve our goal of eternal life.

ABOUT THE AUTHOR

Kenneth W. Matheson, DSW, is a professor in the School of Social Work at Brigham Young University and a licensed clinical social worker and marriage and family therapist. He and his wife, Marlene, are the parents of seven children.

ADDITIONAL READING

John M. Gottman and Nan Silver (1999), *The Seven Principles for Making Marriage Work* (New York: Three Rivers).

Spencer W. Kimball (1978), *Marriage* (Salt Lake City: Deseret Book).

David H. Olson and Amy K. Olson (2000), *Empowering Couples: Building on Your Strengths*, 2d ed. (Minneapolis: Life Innovations).

NOTES

1. Joe J. Christensen (1995, May), Marriage and the great plan of happiness, *Ensign, 25*(5), 65.

2. Brigham Young (1861), in *Journal of Discourses, 9*, 121, 122.

3. Boyd K. Packer (1981, May), Marriage, *Ensign, 11*(5), 15.

4. Loren C. Dunn (1991, May), Before I build a wall, *Ensign, 21*(5), 83; emphasis added.

5. Ezra Taft Benson (1992, July), Salvation—A family affair, *Ensign, 22*(7), 2, 4.

6. Gordon B. Hinckley (1998, May), Living worthy of the girl you will someday marry, *Ensign, 28*(5), 51.

7. J. M. Gottman and N. Silver (1994), *Why Marriages Succeed or Fail* (New York: Simon & Schuster), 29, 57, 61.

ESSAY B 4

SIDE BY SIDE: SUPPORTING ONE ANOTHER IN EQUAL PARTNERSHIP

SEAN AND KRISTEN BROTHERSON

The principle or doctrine of supporting one another in a marriage partnership is lived out in the challenging realities of mortal life. We have sometimes wondered about the "what ifs" of history that might have turned on the hinge of marital support. For example, what if Sariah had told the prophet Lehi in no uncertain terms that she was not going to pack up and ride off into the wilderness? Or what if Joseph had abandoned Mary, the mother of Jesus, rather than supporting her when she became pregnant with the Son of God? And what if Ezra Taft Benson and Flora Smith Amussen had not each willingly supported the other during missionary service? We do not know. But we do know that, at its heart, marriage is designed as a partnership of love and that giving one another support and commitment brings spouses together on the common ground of equal companionship before the Lord.

God set the pattern for the marital partnership when He indicated that "they twain shall be one flesh" (D&C 49:16). Sister Patricia Holland noted that the scriptures reinforce that imagery, with Eve's creation from Adam's rib figuratively showing that she was taken "from his side, under his arm, close to his heart," such that "husband and wife were to be united in every way, side by side."[1] We have learned it is important to support one another in equal partnership in at least four vital areas: (1) spiritual companionship, (2) temporal responsibilities, (3) marital decisions, and (4) eternal commitments.

SUPPORTING ONE ANOTHER AS SPIRITUAL COMPANIONS

Supporting one another in marriage begins first with uniting our lives as spiritual companions. This means that we must prepare ourselves for spiritual guidance, give heed to one another's counsel, and trust one another's inspiration.

Many years ago a young couple, Todd and Katherine,[2] met and married at Brigham Young University. After graduation they accepted a promising position with a company in California. They looked forward to the future, but after several years of wanting to begin a family, their second bedroom was still stacked with old college textbooks; the crib they had purchased in anticipation of a future child sat unused. This sweet mother-in-waiting, spiritually in tune, came to know with every maternal instinct God had given her that a child was waiting to come to their family. A child they needed to find. Trusting her instincts and heeding her suggestion that they seek to adopt, Todd supported Katherine as she led out in the search for a child to bless their home. The process was laborious, time consuming, and expensive. Yet they supported one another with faith, fasting, prayer, priesthood blessings, and temple attendance. Together they sought the fulfillment of her inspiration. Small and large miracles occurred and they were able to adopt a baby boy within months of the spiritual guidance that had prompted their search.

A few years later Todd felt impressed to consider going to graduate school despite his good job. It was Katherine's turn to heed his counsel and trust his inspiration. Soon, much like Lehi and Sariah, they left their comfortable home and headed to the "wilderness" of the East Coast and a new life of student housing, penny-pinching, and "casserole surprise." In this instance, a faithful father and husband commenced a spiritual process that would lead their family to new opportunities and experiences. Mutual support as spiritual companions is at the heart of the marital partnership.

This couple began a pattern early in marriage of supporting one another as spiritual companions. They prayed together, studied the scriptures, attended the temple, and trusted in the inspiration each received. Each took seriously the responsibility to be spiritually prepared, to support each other's inspiration, and to seek guidance together in meeting personal, work, church, or family challenges. Elder Neal A. Maxwell said of his wife, Colleen, that her "spiritual antenna" was "more highly attuned" than his own and so he "learned to pay attention over the years when she had those impressions and feelings."[3] Husbands and wives who support each other as spiritual companions will help one another become more Christlike.

SUPPORTING ONE ANOTHER IN TEMPORAL RESPONSIBILITIES

Home life requires that husbands and wives fulfill many common, everyday responsibilities—washing the dishes, doing laundry, cooking meals, running after children. The equal partnership of marriage functions best when spouses also support one another in performing these temporal responsibilities.

When our first daughter was born, Kristen took the semester off from both school and work in order to stay home with our new baby. It was a difficult transition for both of us. We had a newborn to care for, nobody was getting much sleep, and our lives suddenly seemed to diverge. After several weeks when each of us felt unappreciated, exhausted, and overwhelmed, Sean came home one day and was met at the door by a beleaguered spouse. Kristen then proceeded to conduct a tour of our small apartment in order to point out everything that she had accomplished that day. It didn't take long to realize that Sean was not giving enough appreciation for all of the work she had been doing around the house. We repeated this exercise a few times as needed. About a year later our roles reversed, and Sean stayed home taking care of our one-year-old daughter while Kristen worked toward her graduate degree. It wasn't long before she was met at the door one night and taken on a similar tour of our little home in order to point out everything that was accomplished during the day. Home life is most meaningful when the tasks we must perform as spouses and parents are shared with caring consideration for one another.

Neither of us has forgotten the lesson we learned as new parents. Though some of our work may be different, our efforts in the home are equally important, and mutual support is essential to achieving our goal of having an eternal family. We expect that if we wish to be together in the next life, then we must serve and support each other in all of the mundane, practical home and family responsibilities in this life.

SUPPORTING ONE ANOTHER IN MARITAL DECISIONS

At times married couples struggle with fully supporting each other in important decisions that will affect their marriage and family. Extending mutual support on key decisions can require patience, discussion, compromise, and humility—but it is vital to a healthy marriage.

Some friends of ours were recently faced with a difficult decision concerning their family's future. Jack was working for an international accounting firm in the Midwest and was traveling extensively. Marie was feeling increasingly overwhelmed with the responsibilities of caring for a young family of six children largely on her own. Jack began searching for a new job that would require less travel, allow more flexibility, and perhaps move them closer to their extended family in the West. After several months of interviewing, Jack was offered the job of his dreams—in Georgia. Jack felt this was the right opportunity, but the concerns affecting his decision were mostly professional. He informed his would-be employers that Marie would need to fly out and see how she felt before making any decisions. Marie made the trip with a list of questions about housing, schools, Church locations, and other family-oriented factors. The ingredients for her decision focused more on family concerns and quality of life. Each provided the other with the time and opportunity to explore the issues, and then they discussed their thoughts and feelings. Their support for each other in decision making eased the challenge that their family faced and highlights the process of supporting each other as true partners in marriage.

Patience, discussion, humility—these elements are the foundation for mutual support in decision making. The Lord has said, "I say unto you, be one; and if ye are not one ye are not mine" (D&C 38:27). There is power in oneness within marriage, and such oneness can only be reached when husbands and wives counsel together and provide mutual support in important family decisions.

SUPPORTING ONE ANOTHER IN ETERNAL COMMITMENTS

We commit ourselves in marriage to love our spouse with all our heart and cleave to none else—this is a commitment that prepares us for eternity. We must be prepared in marriage to keep such commitments, and covenants, by giving full support when the times of trial demand it of us.

Among the Hawaiian Islands is the small island of Molokai. On an isolated peninsula sits Kalaupapa, the remote location where those who contracted leprosy were sent to suffer and die, usually far from family and friends. Jonathan Napela and his wife, Kitty, were early Hawaiian converts to the Church. At a time when Kalaupapa was still a place of fear and misery, Kitty Napela contracted leprosy and was sentenced to live out her days in the remote leper colony. Who knows what she must have felt? She faced the prospect of illness, starvation, pain, violence, and isolation. She would be separated from the husband of her youth and from her family.

Jonathan Napela faced a decision. A brief historical narrative about the Kalaupapa colony summarizes:

> Some people considered it an expression of love—the ultimate sacrifice. Going willingly to Kalawao, into isolation, to help a husband, wife, or child diagnosed with leprosy. . . . Known as *na kokua,* or helpers, these people provided loving care that could not have been provided another way. Their presence served to eliminate loneliness and pain. . . . One of the most prominent kokua was Jonathan H. Napela, a Hawaiian who accompanied his sick wife Kitty to Kalawao in 1873. An elder in The Church of Jesus Christ of Latter-day Saints . . . Jonathan Napela eventually contracted Hansen's disease (leprosy) and died within isolation.[4]

How did Jonathan choose? He chose Kitty. He chose Kalaupapa. He chose his own death by leprosy. He chose support in an eternal commitment. He chose love.

Our decisions may not be so momentous. And yet we choose daily. We choose to curb our tongue—or not. We choose to stay with a sickly spouse—or not. We choose to reserve some time just to talk—or not. Jonathan Napela chose sacrificial love. Christ, in His commitment to us, chose sacrificial love. Marriage requires sacrificial love. We face the world together in marriage, as Adam and Eve once did, and we, too, may walk hand in hand as we make our solitary way.[5] We can seek to be equally yoked as husband and wife. This requires that we seek to move ahead together rather than individually. Being equally yoked means we look out for each other, rather than looking out for ourselves, and bear one another's burdens (Mosiah 18:8).

We have made commitments. We have made covenants. We can choose to support one another in an equal partnership, as God intends, and receive His promise that our marriage will be ours for eternity. We bless one another as we pledge ourselves to support each other as husband and wife in spiritual companionship, temporal responsibilities, marital decisions, and eternal commitments.

ABOUT THE AUTHORS

Sean and Kristen Brotherson are the parents of five children and love being married to each other. Sean works as an assistant professor and family life educator at North Dakota State University and has a Ph.D. in family studies. Kristen works as a homemaker and has an M.A. in humanities and art history.

ADDITIONAL READING

Alan J. Hawkins, et al. (2000), Equal partnership and the sacred responsibilities of mothers and fathers; in David C. Dollahite, ed., *Strengthening Our Families: An In-Depth Look at the Proclamation on the Family* (Salt Lake City: Bookcraft), 63–82.

Sara Brown Neilson (1994, December), Consider the shoe, *Ensign,* 24(12), 30–31.

Russell M. Nelson (1987, November), Lessons from Eve, *Ensign,* 17(11), 86–89.

NOTES

1. Jeffrey R. Holland and Patricia T. Holland (1989), *On Earth As It Is in Heaven* (Salt Lake City: Deseret Book), 107.

2. Names have been changed.

3. Bruce C. Hafen (2002), *A Disciple's Life: The Biography of Neal A. Maxwell* (Salt Lake City: Deseret Book), 199.

4. Kalaupapa National Historic Park website, section on "Na Kokua, the helpers of Kalaupapa"; available at http://www.nps.gov/kala/docs/start.htm, June 11, 2004.

5. See John Milton (1674), *Paradise Lost,* 12.649–650: "They hand in hand with wandring steps and slow, / Through *Eden* took their solitarie way." Ray Flannagan, ed. (1998), *The Riverside Milton* (New York: Houghton Mifflin), 710.

KEEPING MARRIAGE RELATIONSHIPS STRONG THROUGH THE YEARS

ED J. AND PATRICIA P. PINEGAR

Which phase of marriage is best? Right now! As we thought back over our years together and analyzed what it was that made each phase we were in the best, we returned over and over again to our family. Despite the difficult moments every marriage and family encounter, we have discovered that love deepens and our marriage relationship is strengthened when we are united in working together to teach and bless our children and grandchildren. True joy comes in seeing the happiness of those you love the most. When your marriage is strong, your family can be strong. When your family is strong, your marriage will be happy.

Take Saturdays as an example. We set up a couple of card tables with coloring supplies, blocks, and games. We spread out a picnic quilt and get down the basket of soft balls and we're ready for the grandchildren to arrive on Sunday evening. Retirement and downsizing haven't cramped our style. Our children who live in the area gather on Sunday evening to have a sandwich, chips, and a bowl of ice cream with chocolate sauce. Our home pulsates with noisy love and laughter and an occasional tear from a little one. It is our favorite time of the week. We call it "joy and rejoicing in our posterity"; that is, joy and rejoicing in the happiness of others.

How have we done it? Partway through our married life, we identified a tool that helped our relationship deepen and our family be strengthened. We had recently moved into our dream home. Our family was growing and we were trying to do all of the things suggested by our Church leaders. I was feeling somewhat overwhelmed and discouraged with the seemingly endless, usually thankless, tasks of changing diapers, washing, ironing, cooking, cleaning, helping with homework, and starting over again. In a tender moment, Ed teased me about my possible future role as the chief vacuumer in the eternities. That was not

what I wanted to hear—that was not what I wanted to do in the eternities. Ed's comment moved me to action. I spent a day away from home fasting and praying, reviewing my life, and identifying what was really important to me. That experience was so comforting and so empowering that I returned home and shared my day with Ed.

Because of that experience we began to make plans and set weekly, monthly, and yearly goals. As we prioritized our lives, our purposes became united. We found ourselves equally yoked in a common cause. Our weekly planning meetings were especially effective and tender when we attended the temple, enjoyed lunch in the cafeteria, and then worked on our planning and evaluating. We remember shedding tears during our first evaluation as we shared our personal goals and needs. We really hadn't addressed our relationship before. We discovered that just existing in a marriage is not really wonderful. A good marriage relationship takes work; it takes effort, caring, understanding, and patience. With our regularly scheduled and ongoing planning sessions we created a safe environment to help us listen to each other's needs, discuss the needs of our family and each child, and share our deepest concerns. Our annual planning sessions were especially fun. Spending a full day together—or even better, an overnight at Bear Lake or Sundance—was rejuvenating for both of us and gave us time to map out the entire year.

Some of the results of these planning sessions are described below.

Family scripture time. We decided that we needed to have a better format for scripture time. I suggested that Ed make scripture time as exciting for our children as he did for his seminary classes. Ed spent several hours on Sunday choosing a topic that would be helpful for the children to study and finding scriptures to support that topic.

Fun together. We had always had a date night as a couple but decided we needed to do more fun things together. Ed took a day off in the middle of the week so we could ski together. Later we found mutual interest in hiking and identifying wildflowers.

Family council. Having family council once a month allowed the children an opportunity to share their needs and wants and to help plan what they wanted to have happen with the family. I had decided it would be wonderful for the children to wake up listening to classical music. It was during one of the family council meetings that my morning classical music was voted down 6 to 2. You can't win them all! During family council we decided on some of our Pinegar family absolutes, such as "be totally honest" and "no contention." We all voted and the children set the consequences.

Parent-child interviews. Ed would interview and counsel each child each month, providing a blessing when appropriate. He and the children experienced tender times and I wanted to be involved, too. For a while I spoke with each child before they visited with Ed. I played a game with them: They repeated and finished a sentence I started (e.g., "I wish Mommy wouldn't . . ." or "It makes me sad when . . ."). One of the rules was that I could not make any excuses or any denials. As I listened, I found out about concerns they had, feelings they had hidden, or frustrations that I was unaware of. I learned a lot.

What have we learned from our challenges? Keep trying. Trying is the key to keeping marriage relationships strong. The hard times we experienced were always more difficult when our priorities were neglected. We worked through broken dryers, car trouble, flooded basements, miscommunication—the kinds of challenges that every couple will face. No one is immune to the trials and tribulations in the test of life. Below are the priorities that made a difference for us.

Selflessness. President Hinckley has condemned selfishness as the cause of the destruction of marriage. He said:

> There are too many broken homes among our own. The love that led to marriage somehow evaporates, and hatred fills its place. Hearts are broken, children weep. Can we not do better? Of course, we can. It is selfishness that brings about most of these tragedies. If there is forbearance, if there is forgiveness, if there is an anxious looking after the happiness of one's companion, then love will flourish and blossom.[1]

He also promised, "If you will make your first concern the comfort, the well-being, and the happiness of your companion, sublimating any personal concern to that loftier goal, you will be happy, and your marriage will go on through eternity."[2]

Prayer and scripture study. We simply cannot be one in all things and succeed without prayer.[3] President Howard W. Hunter gave the following counsel:

> When we talk to young people facing marriage, we tell them of the great value that will come to their lives if, as husband and wife, they will kneel and pray together. When little ones join them in family prayer and take their turn as they grow old enough to speak, they will learn lessons that will stay with them all of their lives. What a great blessing we are passing by if we do not take the time to kneel with our families in family prayer.[4]

The word of God has the power to change lives (see Alma 31:5). Reading the scriptures aloud together gives time to not only hear the word but to discuss the word and its power in our lives.

Family home evening. Family home evening, when faithfully practiced, will keep marriage relationships and families strong. Even in our empty nesting years, we make it a priority to share time in a gospel-oriented session. We read the *Ensign* together, have a family home evening with other empty nesters once a month, and visit with our children. In every phase, as husband and wife plan family events together, their families will grow together in purpose and love.

Time together. Togetherness becomes one of the keys to a strong marriage. Eat together, read together, play together, shop together, work together, raise your children together. Whenever possible, do all things together. Worshipping and serving together in the temple is renewing. We can receive strength, answers to our prayers, and inspiration as to the things we should do (see D&C 97:13–14). The empty nester years are terrific.

When we're talking about building relationships through all phases of married life, why do we always come back to the family? Family is our work and our glory, as it is for our heavenly parents. Feeling a oneness in purpose, with a time, place, and way to make family goals happen, is a joyous experience. As we build a strong marriage relationship, the blessings overflow into the family unit. Never suppose that you stand alone as a couple, for this would supplant the true purpose of marriage and the divine destiny for which it was intended. Make your marriage and family eternal.

ABOUT THE AUTHORS

Ed J. Pinegar, BS, DDS, practiced dentistry in Provo, Utah. He taught religion at Brigham Young University and the Institute of Religion at Utah Valley State College. The author of many LDS books, he has been recognized for his teaching and service.

Patricia P. Pinegar and her husband, Ed, have eight children, thirty-four grandchildren, and three great-grandchildren. She was Primary general president for five years. The Pinegars are presently teaching together at the Joseph Smith Academy in Nauvoo.

ADDITIONAL READING

F. Burton Howard (2003, May), Eternal marriage, *Ensign, 33*(5), 92–94.

Judy Abbott (1995, March), Trust that deepens through the years, *Ensign, 25*(3), 23–25.

NOTES

1. Gordon B. Hinckley (1997, November), Look to the future, *Ensign, 27*(11), 69.

2. Gordon B. Hinckley (1997), *Teachings of Gordon B. Hinckley* (Salt Lake City: Deseret Book), 329.

3. See 1 Peter 3:7; Alma 13:28; 34:17–27; Moroni 7:48; 10:4; D&C 90:24.

4. Howard W. Hunter (1997), *Teachings of Howard W. Hunter,* C. J. Williams, ed., (Salt Lake City: Bookcraft), 146.

Chapter 11

Breaking the Chain of Negative Family Influences

Roberta L. I. Magarrell and Dean E. Barley

Acts [of others] may cause pain, anguish, even physical harm, but they cannot destroy your eternal possibilities in this brief but crucial life on earth. . . . Your attitude can control the change for good in your life. It allows you to have the help the Lord intends you to receive. No one can take away your ultimate opportunities when you understand and live eternal law.[1]
—Elder Richard G. Scott

What a blessing it is to be raised in a strong, healthy family where the marital relationship is one of complete fidelity and mutual support, where parents provide for their children's physical and spiritual needs, and where the children are taught to love and serve each other, to keep the commandments, and to be law-abiding citizens.[2] However, many are not blessed with such a home and may struggle with the cumulative effects of negative family influences, including addictions, abuse, violence, mental illness, unstable relationships with caregivers, enmeshment or estrangement (see definitions in chapter 37), poverty, and crime. There also may be more subtle negative influences such as materialism, competitiveness, apostasy, or psychological control.

Fortunately, the transmission of negative family patterns from one generation to the next does not always occur. Not everyone who has been abused becomes an abusive parent, nor does everyone with divorced parents have a marriage that ends in divorce.[3] Many who come from stressful, destructive, or dysfunctional homes are able to end the chain of detrimental family influences in their own lives and in the lives of their children. For example, in the scriptures we read of how Abraham chose a path different from that of his father (see Abraham 1:4–5). People who overcome negative family influences can be called "transitional persons,"[4] meaning that they make positive transitions in their own lives and in their family lines. Converts to the Church often choose to leave behind unwanted family traditions and patterns and become transitional characters for the generations that follow. How does this occur? What enables one to rise above potentially destructive family experiences?

Regardless of the particular negative patterns one is working to overcome, the majority of transitional people do the following as an ongoing process throughout the various stages of their lives:

- question their circumstances;
- become aware of changes that need to be made;
- desire to make things different;
- arrive at an enlightened understanding that allows for new possibilities for themselves and their families;
- devise specific strategies and action plans;
- believe that their own efforts can make a difference;
- act on their plans;
- receive help and learn from others;
- have spiritual experiences that move them forward in the desired direction;
- learn to forgive;
- express a sense of mission that motivates them to help others; and
- learn from any backsliding or relapses.

This challenging process requires persistence, a

willingness to look at oneself and others through God's eyes, and the ability to ask for and receive help when necessary. Transitional characters may continue in the change process across their life spans. The transitional process as described in the steps just named can be helpful in dealing with difficulties of varying degrees of severity that may be encountered in nuclear and extended family relationships. The following experiences illustrate the process.

MARGARET

Margaret grew up terrified of her father. He would verbally and physically abuse her mother, her older sister, and Margaret The worst part was not knowing what would trigger his outbursts. Margaret's parents divorced when she was seven years old, but her sister, Nell, continued to beat Margaret almost daily and to call her negative names of every kind. Margaret's mother was working and could not afford child care; she was also chronically exhausted and depressed. By the time Margaret was nine, she had accepted that she was worthless and deserved the treatment she received, and she felt constant anxiety during court-ordered visits with her father.

At age 14, Margaret grew taller than Nell and the beatings stopped. Their father moved to another state. Margaret began to read the Bible her maternal grandparents had given her. She wanted to please God by being baptized (John 3:1–7; 14:15). She investigated every church, philosophy, and organization she could find. At last, she obtained a copy of the Book of Mormon from the library, read it, and prayed about it. By now she was 17, and with her mother's permission, she was baptized. A year later she went to BYU and met the young man she would marry. He was kind and soft-spoken, and Margaret began to realize that her sharp words could harm others. She had already resolved never to physically abuse her children, and she added to that a resolve to speak to them without sarcasm, criticism, and other damaging verbal tactics.

Margaret is a transitional person. She began by questioning her circumstances: "How can I escape this? How can I create something different? How do I reject a family lifestyle that is harming me and create a better lifestyle for myself and my future family?" Transitional people become aware of the unwanted consequences for themselves and their loved ones and they form a desire to make things different. They gain an enlightened understanding that opens up new pos-

sibilities for their lives and provides a fresh view of themselves and their families.

With this new understanding, transitional people often develop specific strategies and action plans to protect themselves or to lead their lives in different directions. This often requires conscious, sustained effort to change hurtful family patterns of interaction, especially if family members are opposed to such changes.

DEBORAH

Deborah's parents disciplined her with what she later called "mind games." If she did something to displease them, they would stop speaking to her, would ignore her, and would refuse to respond to her attempts to discuss the problem or to apologize. Finally, right before bedtime, her parents would tell her they had acted with her best interests at heart, that they loved her, and that she should feel guilt for their pain because she had forced them to behave in a way that made them feel terrible. Deborah would often become physically ill or be unable to sleep after these "disciplinary sessions." She began holding back emotionally and finally stopped listening to or caring about her parents' attempts to control her through their twisted form of "love."

Her best friend's family helped her see a healthier pattern of discipline and realize that her parents' behavior was abnormal and unhealthy. Over the years, she began to create a healthy philosophy of life around which she organized her thoughts and actions. She determined that she would set standards different from those of her parents for acceptable behavior. She would make good choices and exercise self-control, rather than be controlled by her parents' withdrawal of attention and love.[5]

Transitional people conclude that they need not remain a victim of circumstances, but can deliberately make a difference in their own lives and the lives of their loved ones. Transitional people believe in their autonomy and feel empowered to change their own lives in significant ways, even in the face of extreme hardship, and they act on their plans. This action entails choosing a destination and doing what needs to be done to get there. This frequently includes more earnestly turning to the Lord in fervent prayer, seeking to follow spiritual promptings, increasing positive time with family members, learning to substitute healthier alternative behaviors, making new friends, joining a self-help group, or talking with a close friend or relative. As their actions begin to produce desired results, transitional people are encouraged to continue their efforts. To accomplish this, transitional people may need to overcome their own fears or learn new skills. This often requires turning to others for support and an example.

BARBARA

Barbara's single mother was heavily into drugs, and Barbara suffered much from neglect during the times when her mother was oblivious to her needs. She stated that her movement forward was gradual in some areas and very fast in others. There were lots of people in the right place at the right time. One of these people was her sister, to whom she could talk openly in her later teens about some areas in her life. That sister had a positive outlook on life and was transitioning forward herself. Watching her sister do this helped Barbara to see that she could face difficult issues. Her sister validated her, accepted her, loved her, and did not judge her. Another helpful person was a grandmother who loved her, was very accepting of her, and showed confidence in her. Her Young Women leaders also provided listening ears and good examples.

In spite of a poor parental example, Barbara was able to use the support and examples of other people around her and did not allow herself to become paralyzed by her past. Transitional people are often assisted by helpful people (friends, immediate or extended family members, ecclesiastical leaders, teachers, mentors) who can offer encouragement, support, and a concrete example of new skills helpful in making necessary changes. Transitional people may also receive help through reading good books and by participating in seminars, workshops, or support groups. Many people who have been through extremely negative family experiences and who continue to struggle with difficulties benefit from professional help. They explore the appropriate use of available resources (such as therapists or medications). In addition to aid from others, transitional people frequently report spiritual experiences that move them forward.

ANDREW AND FRANCIE

Andrew and Francie had each grown up in wealthy homes where they were provided everything a child and then teen could want. Each received a car for his or her 16th birthday. They met at college (tuition paid by their parents) and their similar backgrounds contributed to their attraction. After their temple wedding, they and their families and friends enjoyed two lavish wedding receptions at their parents' homes. When they returned from a honeymoon in Hawaii, they lived in the condo that Andrew's parents had purchased for them to help them get started. Francie and Andrew enjoyed shopping for new furniture and helping the decorator with designs for the condo. Almost before they knew it, they had three children, Andrew had a well-paying job, and they owned a beautiful home.

Andrew and Francie went to see a financial planner after their third child was born. They came away from their meeting believing that it had been helpful for planning the future, but troubled as they considered whether they were too focused on material pursuits. The couple kept returning to something their oldest child had said when the news of the tragic earthquake and tsunami in the Indian Ocean became known. "Dumb people," they were surprised to hear their son say. "Why didn't they just get on the yacht and get away?" Andrew's yacht, a favorite for family vacations, was at a marina near their home. Francie and Andrew didn't know whether to be unhappier that their son thought everyone had access to a yacht or that he had referred to the suffering victims of the natural disaster as "dumb" because they didn't know how to get away—especially when they had no warning.

Andrew and Francie decided that their children might benefit from less parental generosity and more opportunities to see how the family's time and money could benefit others. During a temple session the next day, their covenants seemed more individual and meaningful than ever. They prayed together about what they could do, made plans, and called the family together. They discussed tithes and offerings with the children, went through closets and storage spaces looking for items to donate, talked more about the tsunami during family home evening, and made a large donation to the Red Cross for tsunami relief. They also pledged to serve meals at the local homeless shelter one night a week. They considered ways to involve the children better in daily chores and to help them contribute to their own college savings accounts, and they looked for opportunities to spend more time as a family.

Quite often the result of spiritual experiences is a "transitional leap" commonly evidenced by deeper, more significant changes in behaviors and the way one views the world. These experiences make it easier to let go of the past and to look more to the present and the future. Frequently the transitional person begins to dismiss a false sense of responsibility for family problems or can better see his or her part in the family pattern. A new sense of identity and an increased feeling of self-worth can emerge. Transitional people may feel more at peace with themselves, those around them, and with God. They often conclude that God lives and loves them, which can help them to forgive their offenders, where that is needed.

DOUG

Doug experienced family violence at the hand of his alcoholic father. Doug said that he loves his dad and knows that his father had many negative family experiences growing up. He stated: "I came to a point where I knew I had to forgive what he did to me if I wanted my sins forgiven. I'm sure it was little bit by little bit. I started to see things differently. During high school and [my] mission, I forgave my dad out of duty, because it was right to do that, and I felt a lot of peace at that. Since, I've attended college. I've learned a lot more about why he is the way he is and I forgive him more out of pity. The reason I was able to forgive was because I learned how to pray for understanding of how important someone is to Heavenly Father, including my dad. So, I came to understand that I could love my dad. I could have charity for him. Over time, it was one of the most beautiful miracles I've had in my life. Then finally I was able to love myself, too."

Often transitional people work through a process of forgiving that can allow them to move forward with their lives without harboring resentment. This does not necessarily mean reconciliation with an abuser or harmful family member, but it can mean no longer living as a victim or holding family members to blame for one's own decisions. Often, transitional people are aided in the process of forgiveness by their own religious convictions and through more closely understanding the offender in the context of the offender's own history (empathy). Along with spiritual experiences, many people leaving behind negative family influences feel a sense of mission to help others.

Doug stated: "I started studying the teachings of Christ and for the first time in my life, I decided to try these things and see if they work. I discovered that the teachings of Christ worked. I discovered that there's power in them. Life's not easy. There's still lots of pain in my life, but at least I know what I'm supposed to do. I started focusing more on charity and on the life of Christ and to heal and uplift others, and not to judge. Everyone's walked a different path to get to where they are, and I need to be sensitive to that."

This sense of mission is often future-oriented. There is a growing desire to accomplish something for themselves and their posterity. Transitional people often look beyond their own needs: They reach out in love and service to others. They demonstrate a desire to contribute and to share their talents and abilities. This sense of mission to help others can aid the transitional person to stay focused on what is important. It also adds purpose and meaning to past suffering and to present and future action plans. In spite of this, for those seeking to make significant changes, progress is often punctuated with episodic relapses or backsliding.

CAROLYN

Carolyn was severely abused sexually and had an extremely traumatic time from early childhood to adulthood. As a youth she set some standards for herself and decided never to have sex before she was married. Then, within two months of making this decision, she was pregnant and having an abortion. After the abortion she saw a counselor and spent two weeks in a hospital. A short time after discharge she helped the counselor to produce a video about her struggles, which was then used to help other struggling young women.

Later she met a young man who valued her for who she was. She stated: "He gave me back my self-respect. He treated me like I was of worth and that there was more to me than just anatomy. I didn't have anyone else like that." They both went away to different colleges. Her behavior slipped some and during the Christmas season she went into a state of depression, which included a crisis of faith. She then had an experience "that gave me faith in a higher power, that there was really something there."

She made further progress at college but began drifting. She quit in her junior year to take time to focus on herself and work through some things. She made progress through service to others. She then returned to the university and continued her healing through family-related courses. She gained further education and entered the helping field where she has successfully assisted children of abuse in the healing process.

The entire process for the transitional person is usually not one of consistent progression. Often there are starts and stops with occasional backsliding into prior unwanted patterns. As Elder Richard G. Scott observed: "Changing a profoundly embedded pattern of life can be very difficult. . . . Persistent faith in the Savior and obedience will see you through such hardships to greater blessings. The scriptures illustrate how conviction and faith can overcome traditions in conflict with God's plan, bringing blessings to individuals, and even generations of people."[6]

In summary, those working to overcome a wide range of negative family influences often do the following: question their circumstances, become aware of changes that need to be made, have a desire to make things different, turn to God in fervent prayer, arrive at an enlightened understanding that allows for new possibilities for themselves and their families, come up with specific strategies and action plans, believe that their own efforts can make a difference, act on their plans, receive help and learn from others, continue to have spiritual experiences that move them forward in the desired direction, learn to forgive, have a sense of mission that motivates them to help others, and learn from any backsliding or relapses. As individuals have the courage to move through the difficult and demanding process of breaking the chain of negative family influences, they can create new patterns that will bless and heal for generations to come.

ABOUT THE AUTHORS

Roberta L. I. Magarrell, Ph.D., is an assistant professor in the BYU School of Family Life and the faculty director and coordinator of the school's Academic Internship program. She and her husband, James, have four sons and six grandchildren.

Dean E. Barley, Ph.D., licensed psychologist, LCSW, is the associate director for clinical services at the BYU Comprehensive Clinic. He and his wife, Karren, have seven children.

ADDITIONAL READING

The journey to healing (1997, September), *Ensign, 27*(9), 19–23.
Name withheld (2000, February), Dispelling the darkness of abuse, *Ensign, 30*(2), 37–41.
Name withheld (2001, September), Let it end with me, *Ensign, 31*(9), 61–63.
Richard G. Scott (1992, May), Healing the tragic scars of abuse, *Ensign, 22*(5), 31–33.

NOTES

1. Richard G. Scott (1992, May), Healing the tragic scars of abuse, *Ensign, 22*(5), 31.
2. First Presidency and Council of Twelve Apostles (1995, November), The family: A proclamation to the world, *Ensign, 25*(11), 102.
3. R. Magarrell (1994), *Becoming a Transitional Character,* doctoral dissertation, Brigham Young University, 6–12.
4. A. E. Bergin (2002), *Eternal Values and Personal Growth: A Guide on Your Journey to Spiritual, Emotional, and Social Wellness* (Provo, UT: BYU Studies), 229–232.
5. For more information about parents' use of control, see B. K. Barber (2002), *Intrusive Parenting: How Psychological Control Affects Children and Adolescents* (Washington, D.C.: American Psychological Association).
6. Richard G. Scott (1998, May), Removing barriers to happiness, *Ensign, 28*(5), 86.

CHAPTER 12

WHEN MARRIAGES ARE THREATENED BY ADDICTION

JEFFRY H. LARSON AND LANAE VALENTINE

Addiction to any substance enslaves not only the physical body but the spirit as well. . . .
Each one who resolves to climb that steep road to recovery must gird up for the fight
of a lifetime. But a lifetime is a prize well worth the price.[1]
—*Elder Russell M. Nelson*

Addiction is defined as the compulsive and out-of-control use of any substance or activity that leads to adverse consequences in a person's life and that produces unpleasant physical or emotional symptoms, or both, when the use of the substance or activity is stopped.[2] For a person struggling with addiction, the substance or activity is used in a never-ending search for relief from uncomfortable underlying emotions (e.g., anxiety and depression), distraction from life's seemingly overwhelming problems and crises, physical or emotional comfort, excitement, or a sense of power or control. The purpose or function of most addictions is to put a buffer between addicted people and awareness of their feelings. Many things can be used addictively, such as alcohol, illicit and prescription drugs, food, sex, work, spending, gambling, or pornography. Many who would never dream of becoming addicted to a substance like alcohol or nicotine may not realize that they are in fact addicted to work, stress, eating, perfectionism, or extreme caretaking.

Sometimes loved ones wonder why addicted people continue to do things they know are harmful and why they go to such great effort to engage in their addictive substance or activity even though the consequences can be terribly self-destructive. The addictive process is powerfully reinforced by a comforting sensation of well-being induced by the addictive substance or behavior. Unfortunately, the process is accompanied by the atrophy of the addicted person's other interests and abilities and the general deterioration of his or her life situation. Life increasingly revolves around the addiction. Compulsion, craving, enslavement, and obsession come to characterize the addicted person's experience.

HOW TO RECOGNIZE ADDICTIVE BEHAVIOR IN SELF OR OTHERS

Among the key characteristics of addiction are feelings of being "driven" to get a fix—above all else, out-of-control behavior exemplified by no sense of personal power to stop using the substance or activity and by subsequent negative consequences that pile up. The addicted person generally focuses his or her life first on getting and consuming the substance or activity (almost every day, though some use their substances or engage in addictive activities in sporadic binges). Spouse, children, extended family, friends, and coworkers take second place. Their lives are tragically affected by the addicted person's compulsive, selfish, out-of-control behavior. Negative consequences such as marital conflict, violence, separation, divorce, and unemployment can result from untreated addictions.

Sometimes addictions can be difficult to detect early because of the tendency to deny or minimize the frequency or seriousness of the addictive behavior. Addicted persons swear they do not have a problem with drinking, working, eating, or spending, for example, and claim they can stop using the substance or doing the activity when they wish. Yet there are some recognizable patterns that manifest themselves over time. Clears signs of addiction include (1) the growing use of the substance or behavior to achieve the same amount of relief or benefit, (2) a persistent desire or unsuccessful effort to cut down on or control the use of the substance or activity, (3) spending a great deal of time in activities necessary to obtain or engage in the addictive substance or activity, and (4) continuing to engage in the addictive activity despite knowledge of destructive consequences.

How Addictions Affect Marriage

Not only will addicted persons suffer emotionally, physically, and spiritually from their addictive behavior, but so will their spouses. Addictions damage nearly every aspect of marriage, including trust, roles, intimacy and affection, feelings, conflict resolution, parenting, and safety. Trust erodes as the addicted person fails to live up to normal marital and family responsibilities and as dishonesty is used to hide and deny the addiction. As addicted spouses become more distracted and insensitive to the needs of the family, nonaddicted spouses tend to take up the slack, leaving them feeling overburdened. Intimacy and affection suffer since trust is the basis of feeling love toward one another and wanting to be emotionally and sexually intimate.

Time spent in the addictive behavior robs the couple of time spent together. Marital communication breaks down, and blaming and fighting begin. When addicted persons are not using their substance or activity, they are often irritable, anxious, fatigued, depressed, and either noncommunicative or angry and hostile. With frequent communication breakdowns, resolving conflicts becomes nearly impossible; both spouses lose faith in their ability to resolve even simple problems.

Parenting suffers as the addicted spouse does less parenting and the nonaddicted spouse does more to compensate. The spouse and children resent the addicted person's absence at important family rituals such as parent-teacher meetings, concerts, sports events, and even family meals. Children come to mistrust the addicted parent. Hurt feelings, anger, and a sense of rejection or abandonment abound in family members as they sense the addicted person loves the addiction more than he or she loves family members.[3]

In some families, addicted persons may lose the ability to function in other roles, too, such as a career. They frequently lose their jobs due to chronic absenteeism, health-related problems, poor job performance, and poor interpersonal relationships at work. Often a nonworking spouse must seek full-time employment to save the family from financial disaster.

The emotional dimension of marriage perhaps suffers most. Instead of love and security, the marriage atmosphere changes to fear, insecurity, guilt, and anger. Safety often becomes a problem, as the co-occurrence of family violence with such addictions as drug and alcohol abuse is well documented and all too frequently experienced by the innocent. Importantly, addictive behaviors affect a person's ability to feel the Spirit. Elder Boyd K. Packer noted that inspiration comes more often as a feeling than a sound. He stressed, "If someone 'under the influence' can hardly listen to plain talk, how can they respond to spiritual promptings that touch their most delicate feelings?"[4] For this reason, addictive habits make it difficult to respond appropriately to a spouse or to guide children effectively.

Marital Breakdown Due to Addictions

Marital breakdowns can occur as "addiction runs counter to the essence and purpose of being a couple. It increases personal isolation, creates dividing conflicts, enhances egotism, and destroys intimacy."[5] Generally, when an addiction is created, addicted persons gradually abandon their primary relationships with their spouses and children for a relationship with a substance or an activity.[6] As the addiction grows, these individuals detach more and more from their spouses and children. They may still profess that the marriage is most important, yet their increasing isolation and neglect of family relationships speaks otherwise. The nonaddicted spouse feels hurt, afraid, and angry. Both spouses become increasingly anxious about the situation. As this happens, addicted spouses react by falling further under the spell of the substance or activity.[7]

Nonaddicted spouses try to reduce their anxiety by seeking more power and control in the relationship. They may try to keep the addicted person away from the activity, mend fences the addicted person has broken, or make excuses to others for the spouse's irresponsible behavior. The nonaddicted spouses want their old marriage back—a return to what was. Unfortunately, these responses actually harm the relationship more.

make it to work, an enabling spouse may call the workplace to explain that the spouse is sick and unable to be at work. This simply serves to enable the addicted person to continue to drink irresponsibly.

A healthier and more supportive response by the spouse would be to consider letting the addicted person suffer the natural consequences. Careful consideration is necessary because the consequences may be potentially dire in some circumstances. However, experiencing negative consequences can help a person eventually "bottom out" and seek treatment for the addiction. Rescuing or shielding another from experiencing the impact of self-destructive behavior is not loving. Some enabling behaviors that nonaddicted spouses must learn to check include the following:

- protecting the spouse from the natural consequences of behavior;
- keeping secrets about the spouse's behavior from others in order to keep peace;
- making excuses for the spouse's behavior to family, coworkers, and friends;
- bailing the spouse out of trouble (debts, jobs, legal authorities);
- blaming others for the addicted person's behavior;
- giving money that is undeserved or unearned;
- making threats that have no follow-through or consistency;
- taking care of the addicted person (doing what he or she should be expected to do); and
- attempting to control (using guilt and shame to get the spouse to change, monitoring, checking up, policing, punishing).

Nonaddicted spouses, as much as the persons struggling with addiction, often need treatment to learn that they are not responsible for their spouse's recovery, that they can't control or manipulate them to change, and that their happiness and self-esteem are not dependent upon their spouse's behavior. Nonaddicted spouses can learn to remove the focus from their spouse's behavior and deal with their own emotions, thoughts, and behaviors. As they learn to focus on their own needs and well-being, they begin to establish limits and boundaries that protect them and their children. Core recovery skills the enabling spouse must learn include (1) letting go of control, (2) learning to validate self, (3) learning to feel and express feelings, (4) learning to identify needs, and (5) learning to set limits and boundaries.

One wife said, "I finally learned that I could not

These natural responses by the nonaddicted spouse to the addicted spouse are referred to collectively as codependency in popular literature. Codependency is caretaking, support, and love gone awry. It leads the nonaddicted spouse to do things perceived to be supportive or helpful for the addicted spouse, when in reality they are harmful and only encourage the addiction to flourish. For example, if the addicted person has a hangover and is unable to

make my happiness and well-being dependent upon my husband's behavior. Otherwise I would be on a constant roller coaster—happy when I thought he was having a good day and devastated when I thought he was doing badly. I finally learned that my real happiness and security rest in the Savior and His Atonement. I don't know yet what the outcome with my husband will be, but my salvation is not dependent upon him." This woman recognized that, while difficult experiences might need to be overcome and problems resolved, she could rely upon the Savior, develop positive skills, and make good choices despite her husband's behavior.

When addicted spouses refuse to admit they have a problem or refuse to do anything about the problem, it is common practice to conduct an intervention. An intervention is a confrontation of self-destructive behavior by the addicted person's loved ones. It is often professionally facilitated, although that is not a requirement. It involves the family, friends, and other important people in the addicted person's life confronting the self-destructive behavior and setting boundaries with the person. These interventions are examples of "tough love," recognizing that true love requires that boundaries be respected.

SOLUTIONS FOR OVERCOMING ADDICTIONS

Overcoming addictions may require several solutions implemented simultaneously. The addict should be involved in individual or group treatment focused on (1) abstinence, (2) altering addictive patterns of thought and behavior, and (3) building spirituality.

Total abstinence or moderation. Becoming abstinent may first require detoxification for individuals dangerously addicted to alcohol and some drugs (e.g., cocaine). Detoxification is available at most hospitals and inpatient rehabilitation clinics. For addictive substances and behaviors from which one should not totally abstain, such as food, spending, sex, or work, addicts must learn moderation and balance as they learn to use these substances and activities appropriately in their lives.

Altering addictive patterns. Individual and group therapy should focus on breaking through denial and altering addictive behavioral cycles and addictive thinking patterns. For example, people with addictions must learn to combat permission-giving beliefs such as, "I worked hard today so I deserve to have a beer tonight," or "I can go on a spending spree or have an eating

binge; I've earned it." In addition, if the addict has an emotional problem related to the addiction such as an anxiety disorder or depression, this should be treated in individual and group psychotherapy.

In many instances, people with addictions can learn skills to alter anxious or depressive beliefs and thoughts. They can learn new habits and ways to self-nurture and self-soothe, such as exercise, relaxation, yoga, creative outlets, hobbies, volunteerism, and other healthy ways to connect to others. Sometimes environmental changes are required, such as switching jobs, finding new friends, or even moving. If anti-depressant or anti-anxiety medication is warranted, it also may be cautiously prescribed. (It is important to work with a medical doctor who has expertise in treating addictions, because some medications, like those for anxiety, may be addictive as well.)

Building spirituality. The addict may be helped by a twelve-step recovery program like Alcoholics Anonymous, Narcotics Anonymous, Gamblers Anonymous, or Sexaholics Anonymous (see Box 12.1). In these no-cost support groups, people with addictions find fellowship with others and learn to use twelve steps to sobriety. These self-help programs essentially offer the spiritual component to treatment. Twelve-step programs provide recovering people with hope, a nonjudgmental support group, feedback, a sense of belonging, mutual empathy, structure, a chance to help others, and a spiritual foundation. "Since addiction is fueled by a lack of meaning and purpose in life, the spiritual aspect of self-help programs can be an antidote."[8]

In some communities, LDS Family Services Substance Abuse Recovery Groups have been organized based on the Alcoholics Anonymous model of recovery. Scriptures that support each of the twelve steps are included in the program. The first three steps encourage faith in Jesus Christ. Steps 4 through 7 are the steps in the repentance process. Steps 8 through 9 focus on good works and restitution based on conversion to gospel principles. Finally, steps 10 through 12 help the addicted person avoid relapse by encouraging humility. If LDS groups are not available, spouses may attend a twelve-step group called Al-Anon while teenagers attend Alateen groups to understand and provide support as the addicted person seeks recovery. The content of all twelve-step groups is confidential and group members use first names only. As people with addictions and their families begin the recovery process, pondering Mosiah 7:33

and Mosiah 29:20 can be especially powerful and encouraging.[9]

INTERVENTION THROUGH MARITAL AND FAMILY THERAPY

Marital and family therapy can be a key element in improving marriage relationships that have suffered the strain of addictive behaviors. In treatment, both spouses are simultaneously working on improving themselves and the marriage. Children are included in family therapy when appropriate to work on their issues of mistrust, fear, anger, confusion, or anxiety created by the addiction and the other parent's responses to it. This comprehensive approach has proven effective in the treatment of addictions and the rehabilitation of the marriage relationship.

In marital therapy the couple learns how to do the following:

- Break through denial. Sometimes the sober spouse is in worse denial than the person with the addiction. In therapy one learns to talk about the real problems and the real issues.
- Stop any violent behavior and establish safety. This includes establishing healthy boundaries and attaching consequences to unacceptable behavior.
- Stop enabling cycles to help the addicted person suffer the natural consequences of addiction and eventually break out of denial.
- Stop blaming and attempts to control or change each other, and instead focus on self-improvement. Nonaddicted spouses need to ask themselves, "If my spouse no longer had an addiction, how would I be living my life? Where would my time, energy, and focus be?"
- Rebuild trust in the relationship and learn to express honest thoughts and feelings.
- Increase positive couple and family interactions, such as caring behaviors, showing respect, rituals without the addictive substance present, couple time together, and increasing couple recreation and leisure activities. Improve marital intimacy and affection.
- Communicate and resolve conflict in a healthy manner by learning new skills and expressions of love and closeness. Learn how to request behavior changes in the marriage, negotiate, and compromise without manipulation or power struggles. Learn to be direct, honest, and to the point.
- Forgive each other for past hurts, disappointments, betrayals of trust, rejection, and neglect.
- Establish new, healthier roles in the family, including shared parenting and a fair balance of work and family responsibilities.
- Work together as a team to help the addicted person maintain sobriety and avoid a relapse. Develop a relapse response plan in case it occurs. Learn to see relapse as an opportunity to learn instead of a failure.
- Develop healthier rules to live by. Learn that it's okay to be human, to make mistakes, or to "rock the boat." In other words, it's okay that people will not always agree with what we think or feel or that we might disrupt the status quo or disappoint someone.

CONCLUSION

Addictions can actually be viewed as a tool for self-discovery because they give tangible feedback that something is amiss. Whenever people crave food, or sex, or drugs, or start thinking their thighs are too fat, or start wanting to count fat grams, it is usually a signal that they are having some uncomfortable feeling or they are in some uncomfortable situation. Once they become aware of these signals, they have an ideal opportunity to look at the underlying negative feelings and the original unresolved issues to which those feelings might be related. They then can learn how to process their feelings in a healthy way that won't be detrimental to body and spirit.

One woman said, "My eating disorder forced me to look deep within myself, to come home, and to realize that there was something very beautiful and powerful that lay beneath all of the outward self-hatred and criticism. My enemy was actually my friend—she showed me parts of myself I never knew existed and taught me to love all of myself." Another woman confided, "It may seem strange to say this, but my husband and I have actually communicated more and grown closer because of his addiction. I think our marriage will be better once we work through this." In spite of the easily accessible addictions that flourish in our society, there are many excellent resources to assist individuals, couples, and families in recovery. There is a reason to hope and work towards recovery. As Elder Nelson reminded us, "Each one who resolves to climb that steep road to recovery must gird up for the fight of a lifetime. But a lifetime is a prize well worth the price."[10]

ABOUT THE AUTHORS

Jeffry H. Larson, Ph.D., LMFT, is former chairperson and a professor in the Marriage and Family Therapy program at Brigham Young University and teaches a graduate-level addictions and violence course. He and his wife, Diana, have four children.

LaNae Valentine, Ph.D., LMFT, is the director of Women's Services and Resources at Brigham Young University and specializes in the treatment of women's issues.

NOTES

1. Russell M. Nelson (1988, November), Addiction or freedom, *Ensign, 18*(11), 6.

2. A. M. Washton and D. Boundy (1989), *Willpower's Not Enough: Understanding and Recovering from Addictions of Every Kind* (New York: Harper and Row), 13.

3. M. Elkin (1984), *Families Under the Influence* (New York: W. W. Norton), 56.

4. Boyd K. Packer (1979, November), Prayers and answers, *Ensign, 9*(11), 19.

5. C. Nakken, (2000), *Reclaim Your Family from Addiction* (Center City, MN: Hazelden Foundation), 141.

6. M. E. Edwards and D. Steinglass (1995), Family therapy treatment outcomes for alcoholism, *Journal of Marital and Family Therapy, 21,* 475–509.

7. Nakken (2000), 141.

8. Washton and Boundy (1989), 165.

9. For additional help, see C. L. Player (2005, January), When a loved one struggles with addiction, *Ensign 35*(1), 62–66.

10. Nelson (1988), 6.

CHAPTER 13

OVERCOMING THE DESTRUCTIVE INFLUENCE OF PORNOGRAPHY

RORY C. REID AND JILL C. MANNING

*If there be any within the sound of my voice who are [involved in pornography] . . . may
you plead with the Lord out of the depths of your soul that He will remove from you the addiction which enslaves
you. And may you have the courage to seek the loving guidance of your bishop and,
if necessary, the counsel of caring professionals.[1]*
—President Gordon B. Hinckley

Pornography consumption, including through the Internet, is devastating marriages and families at an unprecedented rate.[2] Some experts have labeled this problem "a hidden public health hazard exploding, in part because very few are recognizing it as such or taking it seriously."[3] Dr. Paul Birch stated that pornography is a sign of "an inappropriate perspective on the sacred gift of sexuality."[4] Indeed,

> the real problem in our society is not the proliferation of pornography . . . [but] that our understanding of the true nature of sexual relationships is becoming increasingly polluted. We have traded that which is of most worth for something less—life-giving, commitment-solidifying, joy-producing sexuality for transient, sensual, immediate gratification.[5]

Sadly, Latter-day Saint marriages are not immune to this epidemic. Latter-day prophets have offered repeated counsel to avoid pornographic material. President Gordon B. Hinckley warned:

> Pornography is everywhere with its seductive invitation. You must turn away from it. It can enslave you. It can destroy you. Recognize it for what it is—tawdry and sleazy stuff. . . . Life is better than that which is so frequently portrayed. Nature is better than that. Love is better than that.[6]

PROTECTING FAMILIES FROM THE EPIDEMIC OF PORNOGRAPHY

Pornography is so pervasive in our society that it is naïve to expect to be completely protected from exposure to it. A more realistic approach is to prepare ourselves to respond to pornography in ways that can minimize its harmful effects. Certainly preventative measures, such as establishing boundaries for proper Internet use, installing computer filters, keeping computers in frequently traveled areas of the home, supporting organizations that work against pornography, and participating in grass-roots efforts to raise the standard of decency in our local communities all contribute to protecting our families.

Perhaps the more effective defense against pornography, however, is the climate we cultivate in our homes around important issues such as human intimacy, communication, media standards, conflict, stress, and emotions. An open, honest, and respectful climate can be a powerful buffer against pornography's influence. Couples can fortify their homes and marriages through obedience to gospel truths and by adopting the principles outlined in the proclamation.[7]

Because children are being exposed to sexual information early,[8] rigorous efforts should be made to arm children with truths about sexuality so they can combat the fraudulent messages they encounter from other sources. Elder M. Russell Ballard has admonished:

> Parents need to teach children to avoid any pornographic photographs or stories. Children and youth need to know from parents that pornography of any kind is a tool of the devil; and if anyone flirts with it, it has the power to addict, dull, and even destroy the human spirit. . . . Talk to [children] plainly about sex and the teaching of the gospel regarding chastity. Let this information come from parents in the home in an appropriate way.[9]

PORNOGRAPHY AND FIDELITY

Pornography consumption of any kind constitutes a form of infidelity. Emotional fidelity, a commitment of heart and mind, is undermined by the consumption of pornography as thoughts and feelings turn from one's spouse toward objects, people, or practices outside the marriage covenant. Breaches of fidelity, both emotional and physical, destroy trust, respect, and marital intimacy on all levels. Such breaches threaten the stability of marriages, families, and communities. (See essay C5.)

Pornography has many devastating effects on individual development and marriage relationships. Some of the most common effects can be the following:

- Decreased trust and feelings of betrayal
- Distorted views of sexual intimacy
- Decreased emotional, spiritual, and physical intimacy
- Decreased sensitivity, tenderness, and kindness
- Financial instability, including loss of employment
- Loss of priesthood leadership in the home
- Decreased mental and physical health
- Increased hopelessness, depression, guilt, shame
- Increased acceptance of sexually oriented humor and media
- Strained communications and increased marital conflict
- Increased risk of divorce

Because pornography affects so many core dimensions of individual worth and marriage, both partners must be committed to tackling the effects together if the marriage is to be preserved. (Essay C3 shares one couple's experience.)

One of the lies the "adult entertainment" industry wants couples to believe is that pornography can enhance sexual relationships. Research has demonstrated that pornography diminishes intimacy in marriage.[10] Pornography is, at best, a pitiable counterfeit of God-ordained marital intimacy and pales in comparison to the potential for marriage expressed by President Spencer W. Kimball, who taught that "marriage can be more an exultant ecstasy than the human mind can conceive."[11]

SUGGESTIONS FOR INDIVIDUALS STRUGGLING WITH PORNOGRAPHY'S INFLUENCE

Pornography consumption can become an addictive habit. Elder Richard G. Scott stated: "The tragic pattern is so familiar. It begins with a curiosity that is fueled by its stimulation and is justified by the false premise that when done privately, it does no harm to anyone else. Lulled by this lie, the experimentation goes deeper, with more powerful stimulations, until the web closes and a terribly immoral, addictive habit is formed." Elder Scott concluded, "For many, that addiction cannot be overcome without help."[12]

Overcoming the destructive influence of pornography is a complex process. Individuals who have successfully overcome pornography problems report that professional help, ecclesiastical direction, family support, and a recommitment to spirituality were instrumental in generating hope and fostering recovery. The following suggestions can be a starting point for individuals impacted by pornography.

Acknowledge the problem. Many individuals minimize the extent of their pornography habit because of feelings of shame or an unwillingness to give up the pleasure associated with their behavior. The Lord's way, however, requires that we fully acknowledge and confess our faults to Him (see Psalm 32:5; Alma 38:14 and 39:13; D&C 5:28). Such confession is really an exercise in self-awareness as we acknowledge to ourselves that which is already transparent to God. In addition to confessing sexual transgressions to one's bishop, Church leaders usually encourage confession to and seeking forgiveness from one's spouse. Many individuals fear a disclosure to their spouse may jeopardize their marriage. Research indicates most marriages stay intact if both partners are willing to work through the problem together.[13]

Be willing to give away all sins. Are you willing to "give away" all your sins to know God (Alma 22:18)?

Doing so includes abandoning the secrecy and isolation used to perpetuate pornography use. It involves identifying and responding differently to triggers that precipitate acting out. It means severing all "hooks" that could enable you to return to the behavior. Many people run from temptation but leave a forwarding address. Like Ananias and his wife, have you "kept back part of the price" (Acts 5:2) required to come unto Christ? The Old Testament stories of Achan and Gehazi (see Joshua 7:18–26; 2 Kings 5:20–27) teach us the importance of giving up everything the Lord requires if we are to receive His promised blessings. Failure to do so will result in our condemnation—our ability to progress will stop.

Be accountable. Part of taking responsibility for our behavior includes being accountable to self, God, and others. The pattern of reporting to others is a principle of eternal progression. Ecclesiastical leaders, a spouse, and trusted friends can provide an invaluable network of support that can abolish secrecy and increase motivation to change. Developing a network of support to which one is accountable is an integral part of recovery. Learning to interact and rely on others is the antithesis of the isolating and disconnecting influence habitual pornography use can have. The scriptures teach that "two are better than one. . . . For if they fall, the one will lift up his fellow: but woe to him that is alone when he falleth; for he hath not another to help him up" (Ecclesiastes 4:9–10). When interacting with members of a support network, individuals may consider reporting the presence or absence of their behavior, steps they've taken to make positive change, and how they are meeting life's challenges differently.

Seek the Lord's help. Individuals can turn to God to find reservoirs of strength beyond their own. A recommitment to spirituality and to one's relationship to Heavenly Father is a vital part of the recovery process. The scriptures repeatedly teach us that "his arm is extended to all people who will repent and believe on his name" (Alma 19:36). God understands the pain and suffering of those who have developed a pornography habit. In the hymn "Where Can I Turn for Peace?" we sing, "Who, who can understand? He, only One."[14] Christ does understand us. He knows us better than we know ourselves. He has promised relief from pain for those who repent (D&C 19:16). The spirit of discouragement, hopelessness, and despair is used by the adversary to prevent us from repenting and receiving the healing offered through Christ's Atonement.

Ecclesiastical leaders can assist us in accessing the Lord's help as we navigate the process of repentance and recommit to gospel truths. These truths can play a powerful role in redirecting attention from pornography to that which will empower us to realize our true potential. Seeking the Lord's help can occur through genuine and sincere prayer, repentance, sacrifice, and feasting upon the words of Christ. As we come to the Lord with a broken heart and contrite spirit, He will extend "lovingkindness and tender mercies" (Psalm 103:4; see also 1 Nephi 8:8). President Boyd K. Packer taught: "True doctrine, understood, changes attitudes and behavior. The study of the doctrines of the gospel will improve behavior quicker than a study of behavior will improve behavior."[15]

Seek professional help. Carefully chosen professional help[16] can assist couples in developing new coping strategies for dealing with conflict, stress, lack of self-confidence, unresolved issues from the past, and for healing the effects of pornography use. A combination of individual, couple, and group therapy has been helpful for many couples working through pornography problems.

Develop positive goals. Positive goals have four characteristics. First, they are incompatible with the inappropriate behavior—the goal and the behavior cannot occur simultaneously. Second, the goal is something about which a person feels passionate. Third, the goal can be realistically achieved. Finally, the goal has its own built-in reward system—accomplishing the goal will feel satisfying. It is helpful to state goals using affirmative language. For example, "I will live the law of chastity" would be preferable to "I must stop my pornography use." One common positive goal among individuals with pornography problems is "I will be honest with myself and others."

Take one day at a time. People can become discouraged and overwhelmed when they fixate on the many changes necessary to repair and heal the damage caused by their consumption of pornography. Although an eternal perspective can be helpful, it can also be daunting when we realize how much further we have to go.[17] The children of Israel learned to rely on the Lord one day at a time when their supply of manna was rationed daily as they journeyed through the wilderness (Exodus 16:11–35). This is a valuable lesson for recovery. Focusing on incremental change and what can be done today is the most effective foundation for tomorrow's success.

Develop an emergency kit. Emergency kits are used

when cravings to act out become so intense they are difficult to ignore. These kits include small items and resources that can be used in a wide range of settings to combat temptation and ground a person in reality when intrusive thoughts arise. A variety of items need to be included in these kits because one item seldom works in every situation. Examples of items include photographs of loved ones, a temple recommend, phone numbers of members of one's support network, gift certificates for wholesome activities, inspirational quotes or scriptures that have personal meaning, a patriarchal blessing, letters of encouragement (you can include a letter to yourself), a list of the consequences of continued pornography use, music, a journal, helpful concepts gleaned from therapy or conversations with a religious leader, and so forth.

Suggestions for Spouses of Individuals Struggling with Pornography

The discovery or disclosure of a pornography problem can be devastating to a spouse. (See Box 13.1 on dealing with suspicions that a spouse may be involved in pornography.) Many spouses report feeling a range of intense emotions such as anger, betrayal, confusion, despair, rage, disgust, denial, hopelessness, powerlessness, worthlessness, and shame.

A literal reading of the Lord's standard of fidelity implies that consumption of pornography is a form of adultery. "Whosoever looketh on a woman to lust after her hath committed adultery with her already in his heart" (Matthew 5:28). Some spouses even report that consumption of pornography is more devastating to them than a "real life" affair because affairs seldom involve the distorting and deviant themes portrayed in pornography, and they tend to be shorter in duration.

Even though a spouse's need for support is equally important, it is common for spouses to be overlooked by caregivers as attention is directed toward the partner with the pornography problem. Subsequently, spouses may need to initiate a support system of their own so they can receive the help they need to resolve their pain. When spouses receive support, prognosis for a positive outcome is significantly enhanced for both partners. Although a growing number of women are consuming pornography, the following suggestions are directed toward women since the majority of individuals involved in pornography are men.

Clarify roles and responsibilities. Many women will erroneously blame themselves for their partner's pornography use, thinking that if they were more physically attractive or more sexual, their husbands would not be turning to pornography. This is a lie! The majority of pornography users have had a long history of consumption prior to meeting their spouse and have brought this problem into their marriage. Women must clarify who is responsible for the pornography problem: A spouse is never responsible for her partner's choice to use pornography! Further, a husband's pornography use is not a reflection of a wife's sexuality, attractiveness, or personality traits but rather of his inability to cope with challenges in healthy ways. Wives are not responsible for the problem and are not responsible for fixing it. A wife's role in a husband's healing process is to seek help for herself, support her husband's efforts to abandon his behavior, and, in time, be open to trusting again as positive changes occur.

Seek support. The embarrassment and shame associated with a husband's pornography use often alienates a wife from reaching out to others. She may fear the consequences of disclosing the problem or fear that people may not understand. Women should carefully select people in whom they can confide during this emotionally taxing time. Sources of support may include family, friends, ecclesiastical leaders, and professional counselors. Support and guidance regarding difficult decisions about the marriage should always be sought from Heavenly Father.

Develop boundaries. Establishing healthy boundaries with a spouse involves clarifying limits and implementing structures that help your husband be his best self while protecting you from further impropriety and disregard for the marriage. When violations of sexual intimacy have occurred, a wife may wish to change the degree of sexual intimacy she's comfortable with in order to protect herself from feeling hurt, used, or objectified by her husband. Husbands need to be sensitive to the fact that their behavior impairs the relationship from moving forward as it once did and that new ideas of "normal" will need to be negotiated as trust is restored and healing occurs. This is a process that takes time, and women should not be pressured to have sexual contact they do not feel comfortable with. Other boundaries may involve reevaluating computer usage, business travel, type of employment, communication, and therapy. Contact with ecclesiastical leaders may change as husband and wife work on the process.

Care for yourself. Fostering a Christlike relationship towards oneself is paramount to well-being. The Lord commanded "love thy neighbor as thyself" (D&C 59:6), yet many love their neighbors at the expense of self. If this becomes a habitual pattern, the ability to help others is impaired because our own needs become neglected and the energy and clarity of mind needed to tackle the diverse issues that accompany pornography problems is compromised. Examples of self-care can include proper nutrition, exercise, sleep, wholesome recreational activities, meditation, maintaining healthy boundaries, and attending to one's spiritual and social health.

Allow time for restoring trust. Many men erroneously assume that trust can be restored quickly following a disclosure of their behavior. One husband had a 20-minute conversation with his wife about his problem and a week later, when she wanted to discuss it further, responded, "Do we have to rehash this again?" The answer is a resounding yes! Men who frequently turn to pornography as a quick fix for coping with stress or challenges often attempt to resolve the breach of trust in their marriages with the same quick-fix mentality. This does not work. Rushing the process of restoring trust and healing is incongruent with the pace and nature of mature, loving relationships (chapter 14 discusses restoring trust in cases of infidelity). Just as men will need time to abandon their pornography habit successfully, women need time to work through the process of being open to trusting again—trusting that her partner will remain faithful, that her grievances will be addressed, and that she will not regret recommitting to the relationship.[18] Men need to understand that it is their responsibility to restore trust in action-oriented ways because they breached the trust. It can be helpful for a husband if his wife outlines a road map of the changes that are necessary for her to have renewed confidence in the relationship.

Allow time for forgiveness. Forgiveness, like trust, takes time and should not be rushed. Often people feel the need to forgive because it's the "Christian thing to do." Although this is true, authentic forgiveness cannot occur without a person's working through the issues of pain and suffering. Sometimes this may involve allowing themselves to experience emotions such as anger and using such feelings in productive ways—such as creating new relationship boundaries and clarifying priorities. Underestimating

---

SIGNS OF A POSSIBLE PORNOGRAPHY PROBLEM

Suspicions often arise long before an inappropriate behavior is discovered in marriages. When there is a disturbance in the spiritual climate of a home, we should explore the meaning of these changes and seek divine guidance on how to act. Some signs that may indicate a problem with pornography follow. Keep in mind that some of these signs may be associated with issues other than pornography.

1. Loss of interest in sexual relations or insatiable sexual appetite
2. Introduction of unusual sexual practices in the relationship
3. Diminished emotional, physical, social, spiritual, and intellectual intimacy
4. Neglect of responsibilities
5. Increased isolation (such as late night hours on the computer); withdrawal from family
6. Easily irritated, irregular mood swings
7. Unexplained absences
8. Preference for masturbation over sexual relations with spouse
9. Unexplained financial transactions
10. Sexual relations that are rigid, rushed, without passion, and detached

Box 13.1

---

the process of genuine forgiveness can have devastating consequences. As Janis Abrahms Spring, a nationally recognized psychologist who specializes in working with couples confronting infidelity, states:

> [Forgiveness] given rashly or prematurely . . . buries the pain alive, and robs you and your partner of the chance to confront the lessons of [betrayal] and properly redress each other's wounds. . . . The problem with *expedient forgiveness*—forgiveness granted without any attitudinal or emotion change toward the offender—is that it's likely over time to exacerbate feelings of depression and grief, and feed an underlying aggression toward your partner. . . . The result is a relationship ruled by resentment, petty squabbles, numbness, surface calm, and self-denial—a relationship lacking in both vitality and authenticity.[19]

WOMEN AND PORNOGRAPHY

Gender differences in pornography consumption are gradually narrowing. Although research shows pornography consumption is significantly higher among men than women, there are growing numbers of women who are turning to pornography, especially on the Internet Women are also overrepresented among cybersex addicts.[20] Traditionally, it has been believed that men are more visually stimulated than women and subsequently more prone to becoming involved with pornography. Since the advent of the Internet, this assumption is rapidly becoming outdated. Over the past several decades the adult entertainment industry has challenged traditional stereotypes through deliberate efforts to target female consumers. More females are in executive roles within the adult entertainment industry and are directing the production and distribution of pornography catered for women. It is expected that female consumers will increase if current trends continue.

Although women are increasingly being visually stimulated by pornography in a similar manner as men, women's preference for sexually acting out is more often manifest in online chat rooms where they seek opportunities to connect with others. It is important to note that women are significantly more likely than men to meet their online partners in real life (80 percent vs. 33.3 percent), and frequently these encounters result in sexual affairs.[21] These off-line meetings are extremely risky and in some cases the women have been sexually assaulted.

It is critical that ecclesiastical leaders, family, and friends do not ignore the increasing problem of women's involvement in pornography. Although there are common issues that need to be addressed for both men and women who develop habitual pornography problems, there are some differences unique to each gender, and subsequently, specialized professional help should be sought for women who have been unsuccessful in their attempts to abandon pornographic material.

Conclusion

Despite the magnitude of issues related to pornography problems, overcoming pornography's influence is possible. Many couples who have paid the price of recovery indicate that their marriage was worth saving and that working through the process fostered increased honesty and openness in their marriage (see essay C2). Although the task may seem daunting, help is available and reservoirs of strength beyond our own can be accessed through the power of the Atonement of Jesus Christ.

ABOUT THE AUTHORS

Rory C. Reid, MSW, works as a therapist for the Provo Counseling Center and the Salt Lake Counseling Center treating individuals with compulsive sexual behavior. He teaches part time for Brigham Young University and Utah Valley State College. He has formerly worked for the Utah State Prison Sex Offender Program and LDS Family Services.

Jill C. Manning, MS, is a marriage and family therapist who has practiced in hospital, school, and private practice settings, as well as for LDS Family Services. Her research interests are in finding effective therapeutic approaches for families impacted by pornography.

ADDITIONAL READING

Paul James Birch (2002, September), Pornography use: Consequences and cures, *Marriage & Families,* 18–25; available at www.marriageandfamilies.byu.edu
Victor B. Cline and Brad Wilcox (2002, September), The pornography trap, *Marriage & Families,* 10–17; available at www.marriageandfamilies.byu.edu
Names withheld (2001, February), Breaking the chains of pornography, *Ensign, 31*(2), 55–59.
Dallin H. Oaks (2005, May), Pornography, *Ensign, 35*(5), 87–90.
Rory C. Reid (2005, February), The Road Back: Abandoning Pornography, *Ensign 35*(2), 46–51.

NOTES

1. Gordon B. Hinckley (2004, November), A tragic evil among us, *Ensign, 34*(11), 62.
2. B. W. McCarthy (2002), The wife's role in facilitating recovery from male compulsive sexual behavior, *Sexual Addiction & Compulsivity, 9,* 275–284; J. P. Schneider (2000), Effects of cybersex addiction on the family: Results of a survey, *Sexual Addiction & Compulsivity, 7,* 31–58; R. M. Bergner and A. J. Bridges (2002), The significance of heavy pornography involvement for romantic partners: research and clinical implications, *Journal of Sex & Marital Therapy, 28,* 103–206.
3. A. Cooper, D. L. Delmonico, and R. Burg (2000), Cybersex users, abusers, and compulsives: New findings and implications, *Sexual Addiction & Compulsivity, 7,* 25.
4. P. J. Birch (2002, September), Pornography use: Consequences and cures, *Marriage & Families,* 20; available at www.marriageandfamilies.byu.edu
5. Ibid.
6. Gordon B. Hinckley (2003, November), An ensign to the nations, a light to the world, *Ensign, 33*(11), 83, 84.
7. First Presidency and Council of Twelve Apostles (1995, November), The family: A proclamation to the world, *Ensign, 25*(11), 102.
8. K. J. Mitchell, D. Finkelhor, and J. Wolak (2003), The exposure of youth to unwanted sexual material on the Internet: A national survey of risk, impact, and prevention, *Youth & Society, 34*(3), 330–358. Many clients who struggle with pornography problems report beginning their habit between the ages of 7 and 12.
9. M. Russell Ballard (1999, May), Like a flame unquenchable, *Ensign, 29*(5), 86.
10. J. P. Schneider, R. R. Irons, and M. D. Corley (1999), Disclosure of extramarital sexual activities by sexually exploitative professionals and other persons with addictive or compulsive

sexual disorders, *Journal of Sex Education and Therapy, 24*, 277–287; Bergner and Bridges (2002).

11. Spencer W. Kimball (1977), Marriage and divorce, *1976 Devotional Speeches of the Year: BYU Bicentennial Devotional and Fireside Addresses* (Provo, UT: Young House), 146.

12. Richard G. Scott (2000, May), The sanctity of womanhood, *Ensign, 30*(5), 37.

13. See, for example, Schneider, Irons, and Corley (1999).

14. E. L. Thayne and J. G. Meredith (1985), Where can I turn for peace? *Hymns* (Salt Lake City: The Church of Jesus Christ of Latter-day Saints), 129.

15. Boyd K. Packer (2004, May), Do not fear, *Ensign, 34*(5), 79.

16. Elder Robert D. Hales stated: "Sometimes the Spirit prompts us . . . to seek special help beyond ourselves through such resources as doctors and qualified counselors. The Spirit will direct when and how such help should be obtained." In Robert D. Hales (2004, May), With all the feeling of a tender parent: A message of hope to families, *Ensign, 34*(5), 90.

17. Neal A. Maxwell (1976, November), Notwithstanding my weakness, *Ensign, 6*(11), 12–14.

18. J. A. Spring (1996), *After the Affair: Healing the Pain and Rebuilding Trust When a Partner Has Been Unfaithful* (New York: Perennial).

19. Spring (1996), 240, 242.

20. S. Lieblum and N. Döring (2002), Internet sexuality: Known risks and fresh chances for women; in A. Cooper, ed., *Sex and the Internet: A Guidebook for Clinicians* (New York: Brunner-Routledge), 20.

21. J. P. Schneider (2000), A qualitative study of cybersex participants: Gender differences, recovery issues, and implications for therapists, *Sexual Addiction & Compulsivity, 7*, 249–278.

HEALING WOUNDS OF INFIDELITY

MARK BUTLER AND SHELLY BUTLER

Children are entitled to birth within the bonds of matrimony, and to be reared by a father
and a mother who honor marital vows with complete fidelity.[1]
—"The Family: A Proclamation to the World"

Marital infidelity may be emotional and psychological, or sexual. While infidelity does not have to lead to the end of a marriage, the consecration required to redeem a marriage from infidelity is Christlike in its scope and sacrifice.

EMULATING CHRIST'S CONSECRATION

Infidelity is an intimate betrayal of such a magnitude that the healing ordeal a betrayed spouse may willingly yield her or his heart to represents an emulation of the Savior's own consecrated self-sacrifice. Offered with the simple words, "Here am I, send me" (Abraham 3:27), no more poignant consecration of self exists than His. We are moved as we contemplate the magnitude of His infinite love and atoning sacrifice and consider the emotional, physical, and spiritual challenges that we will face as we follow in His footsteps.

Sacred covenants invite us to embrace such self-sacrificing consecration. In spite of this evident invitation, no other can judge the inspiration of the husband or wife for the marriage. All are called upon by the Lord to emulate and enact His mercy and to extend the invitation for repentance and redemption (see D&C 64:9–11); but whether relationship reconciliation will also occur is a matter of inspiration. No other can judge the comparative preparation of individuals to take this yoke upon themselves. No other

can judge the heart of the "infidel"[2] and the merit in her or his plea for reconciliation. No other can know the mind of the Lord. (President James E. Faust offered prophetic counsel regarding choosing reconciliation or divorce.[3])

PLEADING AND PREPARING FOR MERCY

The serious sin of infidelity requires life-changing repentance. Time alone does not cancel sin.[4] President Spencer W. Kimball said:

> The plaster must be as wide as the sore. The fasting, the prayers, the humility must be equal to . . . the sin. There must be a broken heart and a contrite spirit. . . . There must be tears and genuine change of heart. There must be conviction of the sin, abandonment of the evil, confession of the error. . . . There must be restitution and a confirmed, determined change of pace, direction and destination. Conditions must be controlled and companionship corrected or changed. There must be . . . a new consecration and devotion to living all of the laws of God.[5]

For those so prompted and inspired, this chapter describes this process of healing from infidelity. The hope we hold dear is for repentance, redemption, and renewal in and through Christ, trusting that "with God nothing shall be impossible" (Luke 1:37), "after all we can do" (2 Nephi 25:23).

UNDERSTANDING INFIDELITY

Marriage is the primary attachment or trust relationship for adults.[6] In the same way we looked to our parents for safety and security as children, we look to our spouse to faithfully "be for us" as adults. Marriage covenants signify our mutual consecration to each others' well-being. In its broadest sense, marital fidelity is the fulfilling of our covenants and provides secure attachment with its abiding trust. Given the centrality of the marriage relationship to adults' emotional and spiritual well-being and their generativity in life, the consequences of marital betrayal are severe. Marital infidelity inflicts severe attachment trauma. Such trauma does not result from ordinary, everyday selfishness of which all of us are guilty. Rather, it springs from egregious self-preoccupation leading to profound betrayal. While most equate infidelity with sexual relations outside marriage, emotional and psychological infidelity can be equally destructive, often lead to sexual infidelity, and also violate covenant commitment to one's spouse. Infidelity can be experienced in any intimacy one cleaves to outside of marriage (see essay C5). However, in this chapter we describe the path to healing for couples who have experienced sexual infidelity.

THE HEALING ORDEAL

As one couple related, healing is a wrenching ordeal that drained them emotionally and relationally and demanded every ounce of strength and stamina, fortitude, and commitment they could muster. Their eternal reward is a renewal of sacred union, unspeakable joy, and renewed trust.

Infidelity may develop in many different ways. The subsequent pathway of repentance and healing also varies for different types of infidelity. Professional consultation or therapy can benefit a couple as they map out their personal path for healing. Healing from infidelity can be organized into four phases: confessing and forsaking infidelity, stabilizing the relationship, preparing the relationship, and healing the relationship.

Confessing and Forsaking Infidelity

Confession is the first, and often the hardest, hurdle in healing. Inspired guidance from the Brethren to priesthood leaders holding keys of judgment and repentance guides them in their counsel to members concerning confession. Individuals can find peace, as

well as inspired ways and means for healing confession, as they counsel with their bishop and stake president.

Similarly asked to weigh the issue of confession to one's spouse, marriage therapists and other helping professionals are guided by relationship ethics, which are informed by training, experience, professional codes of ethics, and their own reasoned and seasoned judgment. The counsel for confession to one's spouse offered below reflects the latter, professional perspective, anchored to considerations of relationship ethics and healing.

An unfaithful spouse may be quite reluctant to confess, for fear the marriage will end. Facing up to consequences is harrowing, but turns to advantage as it spurs repentance. Further, after the initial trauma, most covenant spouses support and participate in the healing process, whether or not they will ultimately remain in the marriage. Initially, many think they will not stay in the marriage, but statistics indicate that most couples ultimately renew their commitment to each other. Priesthood and professional counseling provides a scaffolding for the marriage, supporting and stabilizing it while repentance and repair are underway. Spouses should be encouraged to avoid life-changing decisions during the traumatic period following confession.

Confession to one's spouse and to priesthood leaders is an act of contrition, submission, and humility and a key to the blessings of heaven and to unforeseen relationship blessings as well. Indeed, paradoxically, while the prospect of confession to one's spouse is foreboding, professional experience recommends it as the path to complete personal and relationship healing, as well as spiritual redemption. We deem confession to all parties to the covenant to be essential. Persons promoting repentance and healing are appropriately cautious of counsel to forego confession. Avoiding confession to one's spouse may seem convenient to all concerned, but it places repentance at risk and usually leaves marital healing unsatisfyingly incomplete. Individually, a restless spirit, nagging conscience, and heart still not at peace is the common legacy; and in the marriage, marital attachment and intimacy may never quite measure up without confession to one's spouse followed by healing labor.

To be sure, confession is initially a seismic cataclysm. It harrows the souls of both spouses. Yet passage through this dark valley with the shadow of death upon it helps ensure complete reliance upon the Atonement and a real rebirth—individually and as a couple—through the repentance process (see Alma 36:16–18; also verses 12–24). Christ's Atonement is the only power that will completely heal, redeem, and sanctify both us and our covenant relationships. Neither repentance nor healing will be as complete without confession; true intimacy is only fully realized when both spouses live in truth. Anything less creates an enduring barrier to intimacy.

In consideration of the rights, interests, and welfare of each spouse and the relationship, I (first author) consistently counsel for and seek to prepare for and assist healing confession to one's spouse, which includes significant labor and support following confession. If a choice not to confess is made, one must bear in mind that all parties to an infidelity secret thereby bring some jeopardy to their ongoing relationship of trust with the (presently) unwitting spouse. As a marriage therapist, I do not judge that I can ethically take it upon myself to counsel against spousal confession. Additionally, I am sensitive to the host of ethical dilemmas that ensue if I become—even unwittingly—party to one spouse's infidelity secret Therefore, at the outset of marital therapy I share with couples the importance of honesty in their marriage, and I request written "consent to disclose" from both spouses. Thereby, I prevent confidentiality from making me an unwilling party to damaging deception or lies.

In truth, the burden of repentance and healing is probably heaviest, and most unrelenting, where confession does not take place and forgiveness is not explicitly pleaded for, earned, and received. Further, spousal confession is necessary to honor the moral agency of one's spouse in the marriage—their right to truthfully know and then choose. Clearly, there is no "easy way out," nor any way to guarantee desired outcomes following infidelity. After committing to confession, one must carefully prepare beforehand for essential support afterward. Priesthood and professional assistance can help to scaffold the relationship during this difficult time. Those who help will encourage both spouses to avoid immediate, life-changing decisions.

One must know that while infidelity may seem secret, in fact it is never hidden—especially from one's spouse. Not uncommonly, spouses have reported spiritual discernment or promptings concerning their partner's infidelity, which, for some, helped them spiritually and emotionally encourage and prepare for the time when their partner would confess to them and

marital healing could begin. Further, consequences—personal and marital reverberations—cannot be avoided and will eventually expose transgression (see D&C 1:3). Lying and withholding grossly magnify the devastation to marital trust and attachment when infidelity is finally exposed. Lying complicates and confounds healing, sometimes putting it out of reach. Clearly, the futility and the devastation of an attempt to keep infidelity secret—whatever the motive may be—should be evident and recommends caution concerning choosing counseling for, or participating in, keeping infidelity secret

To spouses experiencing the confusion and anxiety of knowing something is wrong, confession brings relief by naming the wrong and allowing the journey of repentance and healing to begin for both spouses. For the offending spouse, absolute humility leading to complete submission, manifest in one's willingness to confess and accept whatever consequences may ensue, will begin the repentance and healing process. Blessings come from confessing promptly, without delay. Heartfelt prayers for the willingness to humble oneself for confession, and for that confession to lead to choices for healing, will surely be answered with divine influence for good.

Next, know that any ongoing involvement, ties, or encounters with the extramarital accomplice will continue to create and exacerbate cycles of fear and anxiety, anger and apathy, pursuit and withdrawal, and emotional and psychological volatility, together with other symptoms of attachment trauma. Neither spouse can fairly consider the marriage or her or his own feelings amidst that kind of confusion, tension, and "insanity." For repentance or healing to have a chance, one must choose her or his spouse and forsake all others.

We conclude by reaffirming that confession opens the door to divine blessings. Even as it was declared that it isn't good for man to be alone (Genesis 2:18; Moses 3:18; Abraham 5:14), so also is it not good for man or woman to "go it alone," in life or repentance. God has designed and given us marriage and family life for the express purpose that we might have the joy He has and that we might have consecrated, covenant help—even marriages and families—for times of need. Additionally, God has placed His authority upon the earth for our guidance and direction. Priesthood leaders hold keys and authority to counsel in the name of the Lord and to set forth the path of repentance. Therefore, all would do well to seek inspired and authorized priesthood counsel concerning confession.

Stabilizing the Relationship

Infidelity is a marital earthquake. The covenant relationship and intimacy one supposed were rock solid beneath one's feet now heave like an unpredictable wave on the sea. Some liken the betrayed spouse's profound psychological, emotional, relationship, and spiritual disruption following infidelity to post-traumatic stress. Confusion, disorientation, fearfulness, anxiety, panic attacks, despair, and anger or rage are common. Associated behaviors include obsessive rumination or mental imaging of the betrayal, hypervigilance, crying, and retributive actions. For some, the experience can put them at risk for self-destructive or relationship-destructive behavior.

The offending spouse may also experience anxiety, panic attacks, a crushing weight of guilt, and self-loathing. She or he may seek to escape these feelings through addictive behavior, quick separation or divorce, or fleeing to the affair accomplice. But only repentance will restore peace to one's soul and joy to one's life.

Given these conditions and vulnerabilities, an obvious first response to infidelity is stabilizing each spouse and the marriage. Priesthood blessings are a first resort for spiritual comfort, safety, and reassurance. The Lord is especially mindful of our needs, and His blessings can make a miraculous difference. Reaching out to family members and counseling with priesthood leaders can help to steady one's emotions and experience. The offending partner cannot rightfully insist that the spouse protect her or him from shame by foregoing essential support from caring family members committed to each partner and the relationship.[7] Neither can the offender expect the spouse to shield her or him from the chastening consequences of infidelity. Professional counseling can also help stabilize each spouse. Simply understanding that this painful and disorienting crisis following infidelity is both normal and temporary is helpful.

As the couple together seeks support during their healing ordeal, they should look to trusted persons whose commitment to each of them and to the marriage is unquestioned. Both should avoid significant decisions, especially marital decisions, and take precautions against maladaptive coping (e.g., addictive escape). The betrayed spouse should avoid seeking graphic details of the infidelity and needs to be discerning of her or his motives regarding any disclosure of the affair outside the marriage, since any vengeful feelings or actions will forestall healing.

Preparing the Relationship

In consequence of infidelity, distancing by the offending spouse is common and represents an attempt to avoid pain and shame. For the betrayed partner, similar distancing can be protective, but it is also isolating. Preparing the relationship for change requires bridging this chasm and includes softening and shared perspective.

Softening. Hearts hardened by sin—whether one's own, or another's—cannot be "knit together in unity and in love" (Mosiah 18:21). Softening toward one another is an essential prelude to healing. A softened heart is an open heart and a willing heart. The alienation and isolation that follow infidelity stem from the pain of betrayal and the loss of trust, safety, and security. To begin healing, a husband and wife risk being emotionally vulnerable—being available, receptive, and responsive to one another—but some basis for hope is needed to make this possible.[8]

Common approaches to softening include remembering the good times and remembering redeeming virtues. Hearts can soften, hope can be renewed, and reservoirs of good will can be refreshed as couples remember their once-known happiness and strong basis of their marriage. Even amidst infidelity's heartache, there typically remains much good and goodness, here and now. Listing one another's redeeming virtues can help couples soften as they see more in one another and in their relationship than their present pain.

Choosing to see redeeming virtues and cultivate compassion in the midst of heartache and agony requires Christlike charity and consecration (see Luke 22:42–44). Prayer opens the windows of heaven, endowing us with "a portion of his Spirit to soften our hearts" (Alma 24:8), engendering meekness, willing hearts, and perspective that lead to softening.[9]

Softening encourages communication no longer full of blame and hostility, but full of love and compassion and entreaty, even when chastening (see Proverbs 15:1). Softening is a stepping stone to accepting shared perspective, which fosters repentance and healing.

Shared perspective. Shared perspective helps move the husband and wife away from blaming and hostility and toward embracing their healing as a couple. As husband and wife gently but honestly share the story of how their marriage came to this tragic place, a shared sensitivity to mutual neglect and indifference, or harshness and callousness, or other lapses and failures, can unfold. Responsibility for a weakened, ill relationship and its restoration can be shared. However, accountability for the destructive choice of infidelity *must be* individually owned by the offender.

Softening and shared perspective help couples reach out to again be emotionally receptive, available, and responsive to one another. This is the bridge across which they will reach as they next stretch their souls in the poignant, bittersweet ordeal of healing. However, we must caution that though spouses may be emotionally softened and receptive, they may not be ready for sexual intimacy at this point. Trust, safety, and love need to be sufficiently restored to sanction and sustain healthy marital intimacy following infidelity. To otherwise compromise risks self-abnegation and degradation that is destructive to both the individual and the relationship. Intimacy must be approached with respect, sensitivity, and willing hearts. Sufficient healing must have taken place to assure that physical intimacy will help rather than hinder healing. In this there must be complete consent.

Healing the Relationship

Healing the relationship wounded by infidelity includes a time of mourning, boundary work, restoration of trust, strengthening the marriage, forgiving and receiving forgiveness, and renewing hearts and hope. Notably, the couple's labor toward healing the relationship strengthens the offending spouse's repentance as well. The steps are roughly sequential, but also overlap and work together.

A time of mourning. Bereavement for the loss of intimacy and trust leads to a predictable "protest-despair-detachment" sequence of grief behaviors—anger and enmity (protest), followed by hopelessness and apathy (despair), culminating in alienation and isolation (detachment)—which are only resolved as one passes through the healing process.[10] Healing involves experiencing, accepting, and working through shared grief for tragic losses associated with infidelity. There will be shock and numbing of feelings, desperate searching and mournful longing, anger and protest, sadness and despair.[11] But anguish

and torment can eventually dissipate as the couple becomes ready to let go of what once was and strive for the glorious relationship that *through Christ* can yet be. Faith in Christ and the healing possible through His Atonement becomes critical to assuaging grief and enabling forgiveness.

The acceptance stage of healing grief is represented by mournful acknowledgement that in a fallen world there is no perfect marriage—each "come[s] short of the glory of God" (Romans 3:23)—but personal and relationship redemption is possible through Christ. Through the grace and goodness of God, with firm reliance on the Atonement, marriage can be raised to a "newness of life" (Romans 6:4).

Boundary work. Mourning is followed by boundary work. Absolutely and completely forsaking infidelity is followed by further boundary work that provides protection against even gateway temptations, first-step behaviors, or any other equivocation in thought or action. Effective, complete boundary work provides reassurance to the betrayed spouse. Some general rules provide essential protection: husbands and wives should be completely open and honest with one another; and there should be no non-shared relationships or intimate conversations for married couples. For example, if one is uncomfortable having the spouse know completely about certain relationships or be privy to certain conversations, that is a red flag. Nor should conversations with others touching upon intimate aspects of one's own marriage be permitted.

Beyond these general rules, couples should negotiate other specific limits and rules they deem appropriate for relationships outside the marriage. The betrayed partner's safety and security is the overriding consideration; hence, she or he sets the boundaries. Rules that may seem unnecessarily restrictive to the offending spouse, but which are not punitive in their intent, should be accepted. The offending spouse's willing acceptance of reassuring boundaries is part of the burden of repentance, restitution, and healing.

Restoration of trust. To be trusted is more than to be loved[12]—more gratifying to the soul, more assuring to loved ones, more essential to eternal relationships. This truth is learned tragically in the aftermath of betrayal. Restoration of trust is imperative and decisive in healing and renewing the marriage.

Practical strategies for restoring trust include (1) ending all contact with the affair partner; (2) carefully honoring negotiated relationship boundaries; (3) investing oneself completely in the marriage, including resolving problems; (4) being completely honest: ceasing all deception, whether lying, withholding, or misleading; (5) renewing and emphasizing virtuous behavior (see Articles of Faith 1:13) that sustains and protects the relationship and spirituality (e.g., family activities, service, and spiritual activities such as attention to scripture study and prayer), and keeping one's spouse informed of these positive, protective activities; (6) immediately disclosing any mental, emotional, or behavioral lapse and promptly seeking support, help, or blessings as needed; (7) completely opening one's life to inspection and accountability to one's partner and to the Lord. Restoration of trust follows recognition of real rebirth.

A changed heart, witnessed in part by genuine, godly suffering for sin, also helps rebuild trust. When the Spirit helps the offending spouse comprehend the devastation of intimate betrayal as Christ does (see Alma 7:12–13), and feel the love Christ feels, then the offending spouse will suffer exquisite anguish for her or his infidelity (see Mosiah 3:7). For most, this is not a momentous, Alma-like awakening (Alma 36:13–14), but a gradual awakening to truth and love. As one accepts the tutoring of ensuing suffering and acts upon that experience for repentance, restitution, and restoration, she or he provides evidence of a change of heart. All in all, a broken heart and contrite spirit, a repentant and softened soul, represent a worthy sacrifice (3 Nephi 9:20; D&C 59:8) that the Lord will acknowledge and endow with power for healing, including the restoration of trust.

The offending spouse should be willing, therefore, to share with the betrayed spouse sincere suffering, remorse, and contrition—in intimate conversation, by letter, by journaling. Spiritual renewal, together with reaffirmation of covenant consecration, will in time restore trust and all the blessings of godly intimacy.

STRENGTHENING THE MARRIAGE

Alongside the reassurance conveyed by one's sincere repentance will be the confidence inspired by complete investment in the marriage. Strengthen the marriage through shared effort in overcoming problems and challenges. Broaden repentance to include marital renewal and revitalization. The assistance of family members, priesthood leaders, or a trusted professional may be important to gain needed insight and receive helpful counsel and coaching.

Forgiving and Receiving Forgiveness

Forgiveness is essential to healing. The path to forgiving is eased by understanding what forgiveness is and what it is not[13] and by knowing what the process of forgiving entails. Forgiveness is neither condoning nor simply pardoning transgression. Nor is it a foreclosure on appropriate consequences, although it certainly excludes retribution. Forgiveness is a voluntary offering of compassion and mercy to a transgressor, a gift of love to self and other, unlocking hearts and inviting repentance and healing. Forgiveness is, therefore, essential (see D&C 64:10). Living in forgiveness arises from our experience of love—God's love for us manifest in our own forgiveness, and our subsequent love for our fellow beings (see 1 John 4:10–11).[14] Forgiving intimate betrayal requires tremendous spiritual strength and psychological resilience. Therefore, "pray unto the Father with all the energy of heart" (Moroni 7:48) for Christlike love, which brings the will and strength to forgive—for your own healing, and for the person you hope to forgive.

Righteous indignation. The path to forgiving is also eased by understanding the process it entails, which includes the experience of righteous indignation followed by a spirit of forgiving and finally by renewed hope. Because of the close connection of love and forgiveness, some believe that anger inherently opposes a spirit of forgiveness. However, righteous indignation is not hostile anger and is not opposed to love, but an expression of it, promoting action for personal and relationship change and healing. Thus, righteous indignation is actually a prelude to forgiving and part of the healing process.

Indignation resolutely yet meekly affirms that "What you did was wrong! I did not deserve this." Once this truth is validated, and by implication the inherent worth and sanctity of the self also, then the door to forgiveness is actually more readily opened. It is important for an offending spouse to accept that the other spouse's heartache and indignation are part of the offender's burden in healing. Righteous indignation will wax and wane and can then eventually transform to forgiving.

Forgiveness typically includes specific additional dimensions: (1) praying for the will and strength to forgive; (2) softening toward the offender through seeing the offense in context; (3) softening toward the offender through remembering her or his redeeming virtues and divine worth; (4) fortifying one's faith that through Christ nothing of eternal worth is forever lost; (5) seeking succor through prayer and priesthood blessings; and (6) where possible, working with the offender toward forgiveness.[15]

Renewing Hearts and Hope

Renewing hearts and hope are final milestones of healing from the betrayal of infidelity. This renewal is a spiritual miracle, which comes through faith in Christ, our Redeemer. How fitting, therefore, that couples whose lives and relationships were marred by infidelity, but who have gained redemption and restoration through meek submission to the healing ordeal we have described, often poignantly signify their renewal in the temple when they are worthy of these sacred blessings. Reaffirming the marriage through meaningful ritual sets a certifying seal upon the ordeal of repentance, growth, and healing.

Couples may further signify their renewal through symbolic ceremonies. Ceremonies may include a public expression—such as an exchange of wedding rings within the embracing witness of the family circle. Ceremonies may also include an intimate, private expression—such as a kneeling plea for forgiveness combined with reaffirmation of resolve to fulfill to "the uttermost farthing" (Matthew 5:26) the work of healing and to keep sacred forevermore one's marriage covenants and relationship.

Given the bright prospect of such a day of renewal, and the bereavement of present losses, it is not surprising that some couples try to push the timeline for healing and, in some instances, for a restoration of blessings. There is a natural order and a significant season to healing from infidelity. One must persevere until the merciful judgment of the Lord's servants concurs with one's own witness of renewed hearts and relationship, hope and faith. A couple must persist in patience until they can confidently sing the song of redeeming love.

THE SONG OF REDEEMING LOVE

Among couples who seek professional counseling following infidelity, the majority of marriages are preserved.[16]

Still, an intact marriage is only a crude indicator of marginal reconciliation; it is not necessarily a healed marriage.

Renewal and redemption result only from soul-deep repentance, redemption, and sanctification—a change of heart perfected through Christ's Atonement,

"after all we can do" (2 Nephi 25:23). Complete restoration requires complete transformation. The offending spouse must not stop short of full repentance or settle for "getting by" with little more than stopping the affair, "letting it go," and "trying harder." Complete repentance and healing is worth the price. The soul-satisfying witness of complete repentance and healing transformation will be when the offending spouse looks into the eyes of the betrayed spouse and once again sees unreserved trust and intimate affection. Then both will know and cherish that to be trusted is more than to be loved.

ABOUT THE AUTHORS

Mark Butler, Ph.D., teaches in BYU's School of Family Life and is a marriage and family therapist.

Shelly Butler, BA, obtained her degree in family living from Brigham Young University. Mark and Shelly head the Spiritual Exodus Foundation, Inc., a nonprofit entity producing LDS-oriented curriculum for recovery from pornography, sexual, substance, and alcohol addictions. Mark and Shelly are the parents of five children.

ADDITIONAL READING

James E. Faust (2004, August), Fathers, mothers, marriage, *Ensign, 34*(8), 3–7.

James M. Harper and Mark H. Butler (2000), Repentance, forgiveness, and progression in marriages and families; in David C. Dollahite, ed., *Strengthening Our Families: An In-Depth Look at the Proclamation on the Family* (Salt Lake City: Bookcraft), 154–166.

Spencer W. Kimball (1969), *The Miracle of Forgiveness* (Salt Lake City: Bookcraft).

Terrance D. Olson (2000), Chastity and fidelity in marriage and family relationships; in David C. Dollahite, ed., *Strengthening Our Families: An In-Depth Look at the Proclamation on the Family* (Salt Lake City: Bookcraft), 50–59.

NOTES

1. First Presidency and Council of Twelve Apostles (1995, November), The family: A proclamation to the world, *Ensign, 25*(11), 102.

2. F. Pittman (1989), *Private Lies: Infidelity and the Betrayal of Intimacy* (New York: W. W. Norton), 23.

3. James E. Faust (2004, August), Fathers, mothers, marriage, *Ensign, 34*(8), 3–7.

4. C. S. Lewis (1944), *The Problem of Pain* (New York: Macmillan), see 49.

5. Spencer W. Kimball (1982, March), God will forgive, *Ensign, 12*(3), 6.

6. C. Hazan and D. Zeifman (1999), Pair bonds as attachments: Evaluating the evidence, in J. Cassidy and P. R. Shaver, eds., *Handbook of Attachment: Theory, Research, and Clinical Applications* (New York: Guilford), 336–354; R. Kobak (1999), The emotional dynamics of disruptions in attachment

relationships: Implications for theory, research, and clinical intervention, in Cassidy and Shaver (1999) 21–43.

7. M. E. Kerr and M. Bowen (1988), *Family Evaluation* (New York: W. W. Norton).

8. Cassidy and Shaver, eds. (1999).

9. M. H. Butler, B. C. Gardner, and M. H. Bird (1998), Not just a time-out: Change dynamics of prayer for religious couples in conflict situations, *Family Process, 37,* 451–478; M. H. Butler, J. A. Stout, and B. C. Gardner (2002), Prayer as a conflict resolution ritual: Clinical implications of religious couples' report of relationship softening, healing perspective, and change responsibility, *American Journal of Family Therapy, 30,* 19–37.

10. Hazan and Zeifman (1999), 343. Resolution of grief brings acceptance and capacity for reattachment.

11. J. Bowlby (1973), *Attachment and Loss, Volume 2: Separation Anxiety and Anger* (New York: Basic Books); M. H. Butler and R. S. Seedall (2004), Grief process as a normative approach to family life cycle transitions, manuscript submitted for publication; E. Lindemann (1944), Symptomatology and management of acute grief, *American Journal of Psychiatry, 101,* 141–148.

12. L. R. McKay, comp. (1966), *True to the Faith: From the Sermons and Discourses of David O. McKay* (Salt Lake City: Bookcraft), 272; LeGrand Richards (1976, June), A constructive life, *New Era, 6*(6), 7.

13. M. H. Butler, S. K. Dahlin, and S. T. Fife (2002), "Languaging" factors affecting clients' acceptance of forgiveness intervention in marital therapy, *Journal of Marital and Family Therapy, 28,* 285–298.

14. J. M. Harper and M. H. Butler (2000), Repentance, forgiveness, and progression in marriages and families; in D. C. Dollahite, ed., *Strengthening Our Families: An In-Depth Look at the Proclamation on the Family* (Salt Lake City: Bookcraft), 154–166.

15. See Harper and Butler (2000); S. R. Freedman and R. D. Enright (1996), Forgiveness as an intervention goal with incest survivors, *Journal of Consulting and Clinical Psychology, 64,* 983–992; Spencer W. Kimball (1969), *The Miracle of Forgiveness* (Salt Lake City: Bookcraft); M. E. McCullough, S. J. Sandage, and E. L. Worthington Jr. (1997), *To Forgive Is Human: How to Put Your Past in the Past* (Downers Grove, IL: InterVarsity Press); Richard G. Scott (1992, November), Healing your damaged life, *Ensign, 22*(11), 60–62; J. N. Sells and T. D. Hargrave (1998), Forgiveness: A review of the theoretical and empirical literature, *Journal of Family Therapy, 20,* 21–36; E. L. Worthington Jr. (1998), An empathy-humility-commitment model of forgiveness applied within family dyads, *Journal of Family Therapy, 20,* 59–76; E. L. Worthington Jr., and F. A. DiBlasio (1990), Promoting mutual forgiveness within the fractured relationship, *Psychotherapy, 27,* 219–223.

16. S. Glass (2000), Prevalence and impact of extramarital involvement, *AAMFT Clinical Update, 2*(1) (Washington, D.C.: The American Association for Marriage and Family Therapy), 1–8.

Infidelity and Betrayal: Finding Hope and Healing

Name Withheld

I often ponder that nearly forty years of my life, my second estate, have been spent in a marriage that ended in divorce. Is it really possible that one can work so long and give one's all and still fail? That was not how it was supposed to be: I always believed that once I discovered the right formula and dedicated my life to righteousness, I would succeed. Even now, seven years after the divorce, I still sometimes wonder, did I fail? Yes, the marriage ended. But I would be wrong to say that the effort, the struggles, the determination, and certainly the sacrifice, were in truth years of failure. They were years filled with good people, choice experiences, and beautiful children. I know now that all I endured transformed me into a woman of faith.

The years were not without intense loneliness, anguish, and heartbreak; sometimes I was afraid. But the tears led me to my knees, as I had no other avenue but to lay my burdens at God's feet It took many months, even years of pain before I realized I could turn completely to the Lord. Then I experienced peace amidst conflict.

Oh, I tried all the marriage classes, read the books, attended seminars, and rededicated my will. I tried to alter my personality, for I felt that I needed to be more: more desirable, more assertive, more submissive, more domestic, more progressive, more beautiful, and more interesting. Year after year I tried every possible change or technique to increase my husband's interest and become someone he would love. Slowly I came to know, however, that his were shallow wishes that I could never satisfy. He had an insatiable need for success, position, possessions—and mostly his own space, his own time, and secretive living that took him away from me and us. He wanted his family and his freedom; his home, but mostly his business; his church, with his own type of dedication; his moments with children, yet hours with business associates; and time with others who were not business associates.

Looking back, I know that the marriage decision was made too young. I was idealistic and innocently optimistic about life. I just knew the flaws and differences I saw would change with enough love and patience. We were married in the temple, but it didn't take long before I realized how unequally yoked we really were in our commitment to righteousness. Still, I had a reservoir of hope and a belief in a bright future. I did want to walk this life with him. He was smart, capable, strong, and hard working. However, I came to understand that he did not want me; he did not want to walk this part of eternity with me, and so the next eternal steps would never be taken together. When I realized that my reservoir of hope was empty and knew that my dream for us would never be, I felt despair.

Our life began as so many young couples' lives begin, my husband in school and me fulfilling the words of the prophets to have children and nurture them in the home. I was thrilled at the prospect of motherhood. I believe with all my heart that blessed is a woman who has her "quiver full" of children (see Psalm 127:5). My heart was full of love for every baby placed in my arms, but my heart was empty of the love I longed to receive from my husband. Many, many times, my feelings of gratitude for these precious children kept me willing to try again to keep the family, the sacred institution, together. There were times of recommitment and admissions of indiscretions and new promises of direction, but they were short lived. And so again I would sorrow and look into the faces of my children and pray that we could hang on. I felt impressed that I needed to preserve the marriage until the children were mature and firm in their testimonies. I know this is not the answer for every couple experiencing infidelity, but it was the answer for our family at that time. "O Lord give me the strength to do this," I would pray. "O Lord, please take me through another day." "Dear Father," I would pray, "please direct my path. So many little lives are at risk." "O God, please let me know Thou art mindful of my pain and my desire." "Please, dear Lord, give me Thy strength through this hour."

How did such praying increase my resolve? Sometimes the direction seemed clear; other times I was so demanding that I had to repent and wait for the feelings that would come. Scriptures and lonely temple sessions brought new insights and I came to know that Christ knew betrayal as I never could, betrayal directed toward an innocence that I could not comprehend. He did know me and I needed to know Him. My scriptures became my seminar, my submissiveness was redirected toward Him, and my change this time began with repentance.

Pride, I knew, was to be addressed first. How did I know? It was simple. I asked in prayer and I knew! I listened to the messages in church, for some were expressly for me. I was profoundly moved by the classes I was called to teach. The hymns fed me truths. They gave me the strength to put one foot in front of the other, one sorrowful Sunday after another. I came to know that the Lord could heal me. Certainly He could heal my pain, but by now I desired that He heal my soul. I recognized my own unworthiness. I began to understand why "he descended below all things, in that he comprehended all things, that he might be in all and through all things, the light of truth" (D&C 88:6). I sorrowed for His suffering and, at the same time, I was grateful for His suffering. I began to feel the meaning of His atoning sacrifice. I began to remember His body bruised and His blood shed for me. The bread and water of the sacrament each Sunday stirred me deeply as I remembered Him, the "bread of life" (John 6:35).

Through the years I found my prayers were redirected away from my many wants as I began to consider the needs of others. I had discovered the formula: "Please, Lord, let me see all people as Thou seest them." How differently I looked into the faces of those around me, and how precious most people were to me. I have always loved people, but now I felt a new feeling of love for them. How far could I extend this love? As a Relief Society president I would pray before I entered a home and silently ask how I could love the people inside when I didn't know them. But then I acknowledged, "I go into their homes because I love Thee," and I came out sweetly filled with love for them. I had awakened to what had always been there:

the love of the Lord that is so freely given in spite of our imperfections. Soon I knew I really could forget myself, and the by-product of forgetting myself was finding my worth in Christ. I discovered that faith swallowed up fear. Like Peter (see Matthew 14:24–33), as we walk on the water in faith, if for a moment we begin to sink, we may look to Christ, call out "Lord, save me," and He will reach out His hand. He will walk with us back into the ship. The winds will cease. This I know.

How then can I ever say these forty years of my life have been a failure, when I know they have been a gift? No matter where the rest of my life takes me, I have partaken of much because I needed much; and now my reservoir of hope is filled in Him, and with that assurance I have much to give.

My thoughts go back to a sacred time, a particularly difficult year. It seemed a divorce was imminent. What was I to do? I had asked the Lord so many times to let me know what was right, and no direction was forthcoming. One of our sons was on a mission; the divorce would be devastating for him and certainly would affect his work. We had so many young ones at home and teenagers just beginning their long-anticipated high school experience. Was I to gather them up and take them away? Almost every day my husband asked for a divorce. I was blind to the fact that he was in another relationship, and when that was confirmed to me I was weak to the point of letting go. However, I begged him to stay with the family until our son returned, so we made an agreement: an uncomplicated divorce if he consented to wait. Again, the choices that I felt were best for our family might not be the right choices for another family in similar circumstances. The months were long and my resolve waned. How could I stay, and how could I leave? I felt humiliated, rejected, betrayed.

While driving one morning in a rare moment of privacy, I was praying, pleading out loud. Then I had a holy experience. My whole being filled with love, and I knew immediately what I was supposed to do. I also felt a glorious truth: I knew that in spite of any love I felt I was denied, the Lord had love enough for me, and His love was more glorious than I could ever have supposed. It was love so exactly as the scriptures said: It was so pure that I felt it was surely the sweetest of all gifts, something I had never known, and more filling and more fulfilling than I could ever dream (see 1 Nephi 8:11–12; 11:22–23; 15:36). This love is available to all: "Pray unto the Father with all the energy of heart, that ye may be filled with this love, which he hath bestowed upon all who are true followers of his Son, Jesus Christ" (Moroni 7:48). For "charity is the pure love of Christ, and it endureth forever" (Moroni 7:47).

After that moment I was able to rededicate myself and continue in the marriage for 13 more years. I found I could suffer long; I was kinder and not so easily provoked. I rejoiced in truth. I was able to bear more things, to believe in God's goodness (see Moroni 7:45). My hope returned. That sweetness and joy helped me to see the worth of every soul, even the one that had betrayed me. The hope of living with such love eternally sustained me then and sustains me now. I am lacking no more!

By the time my son returned, my husband had moved on to other things. His new relationship was over, and I steadfastly held onto the family once again. This time I did so because I knew it was right for us and for no other reason. Despite my husband's unwillingness to change, and the knowledge I had that our marriage would end, we sent three other missionaries into the field. Father in Heaven had given me stewardship over wonderful children, and I was able to give them back in service to His Son. When the marriage ended I also knew it was time. I had done enough.

I have since walked a new walk, not the one I had expected to walk with my husband, but a walk that is founded in Jesus Christ. His gospel is the walk of faith; it is the walk with hope; and it is walking with charity. No longer are these just words to me. They are the answer. This is my testimony to those who are in pain: There is a better way, a way of healing, and a way of forgiving, a way of light, and a way of love. To all who are walking through betrayal and loneliness, I add my witness that Christ is the way. He is the only way.

THE ADVANTAGES OF MARRIAGE AND DISADVANTAGES OF DIVORCE

BRENT A. BARLOW

There are two scriptural passages of particular significance to Latter-day Saint students of contemporary marriage and family trends. First, the Prophet Joseph Smith received the 49th section of the Doctrine and Covenants in 1831, regarding the teachings of the Shakers. This sect believed that a person became closer to God by remaining single or by abandoning marriage and living a celibate life.[1] The Lord declared through the Prophet Joseph Smith that just the opposite was true. "And again, verily I say unto you, that whoso forbiddeth to marry is not ordained of God, for marriage is ordained of God unto man," and marriage was instigated "before the world was made" (D&C 49:15, 17).[2] Second, during ancient times, the Lord condemned the men of Israel for abandoning spouses through divorce. The prophet Malachi declared:

Yet ye say, Wherefore? Because the Lord hath been witness between thee and the wife of thy youth, against whom thou hast dealt treacherously: yet is she thy companion, and the wife of thy covenant. . . . Therefore take heed to your spirit, and let none deal treacherously against the wife of his youth.

Then comes this insight and warning: "For the Lord, the God of Israel, saith that he hateth putting away [or divorce]" (Malachi 2:14–16).[3]

Divorce is warranted in some instances. During His mortal ministry, Jesus Christ acknowledged this when He gave Peter the sealing powers of the priesthood: "And I will give unto thee the keys of the kingdom of heaven: and whatsoever thou shalt bind on earth shall be bound in heaven: and whatsoever thou shalt loose on earth shall be loosed in heaven" (Matthew 16:19; see Matthew 18:18). Elsewhere He noted that divorce was warranted when sexual unfaithfulness, including adultery and fornication, had occurred (see Matthew 19:9), although divorce is not necessarily best even in cases of sexual infidelity (see chapter 14). President Gordon B. Hinckley has said:

> There may be now and again a legitimate cause for divorce. I am not one to say that it is never justified. But I say without hesitation that this plague among us, which seems to be growing everywhere, is not of God, but rather is the work of the adversary of righteousness and peace and truth.[4]

President James E. Faust has similarly observed:

> What, then, might be "just cause" for breaking the covenants of marriage? . . . In my opinion, "just cause" should be nothing less serious than a prolonged and apparently irredeemable relationship which is destructive of a person's dignity as a human being.[5]

In her book, *The Case Against Divorce,* Diane Medved includes a chapter on exceptional situations that may warrant divorce. Among other reasons, she lists chronic addiction or substance abuse, psychosis or extreme mental illness, and physical or mental abuse as reasons to divorce.[6] Although, again, these conditions do not necessarily or always justify divorce.

Circumstances that lead to divorce can exist even before a marriage occurs but may be unacknowledged or ignored by the couple. Even when one is wise in choosing a marriage partner, events occur or circumstances evolve after the marriage that may make it best for some not to stay married. President Faust observed, "Only the parties to the marriage can determine [when to divorce]. They must bear the responsibility for the train of consequences which inevitably follow."[7]

DISADVANTAGES OF DIVORCE

In summarizing the effects of divorce on America, researchers observed:

> Each year, over 1 million American children suffer the divorce of their parents; moreover, half of the children born this year to parents who are married will see their parents divorce before they turn 18. Mounting evidence in social science journals demonstrates that the devastating physical, emotional, and financial effects that divorce is having on many children will last well into adulthood and affect future generations. Among these broad and damaging effects are the following:
>
> Children whose parents have divorced are increasingly the victims of abuse. They exhibit more health, behavioral, and emotional problems, are involved

---

WHY MARRIAGE MATTERS

Summary of the pamphlet by the Institute for American Values (New York: 2002), "Why Marriage Matters: Twenty-One Conclusions from the Social Sciences"

Family: (1) Marriage increases the likelihood that fathers have good relationships with their children; (2) Cohabitation [or living together] is not the functional equivalent of marriage; (3) Growing up outside an intact marriage increases the likelihood that children will themselves divorce or become unwed parents; (4) Marriage is a virtually universal human institution.

Economics: (5) Divorce and unmarried childbearing increase poverty for both children and mothers; (6) Married couples seem to build more wealth on average than singles or cohabiting couples; (7) Married men earn more money than do single men with similar education and job histories; (8) Parental divorce (or failure to marry) appears to increase children's risk of school failure; (9) Parental divorce reduces the likelihood that children will graduate from college and achieve high-status jobs.

Physical Health and Longevity: (10) Children who live with their own two married parents enjoy better physical health, on average, than do children in other family forms; (11) Parental marriage is associated with a sharply lower risk of infant mortality; (12) Marriage is associated with reduced rates of alcohol and substance abuse for both adults and teens; (13) Married people, especially married men, have longer life expectancies than do otherwise similiar singles; (14) Marriage is associated with better health and lower rates of injury, illness, and disability for both men and women.

Mental Health and Emotional Well-Being: (15) Children whose parents divorce have higher rates of psychological distress and mental illness; (16) Divorce appears significantly to increase the risk of suicide; (17) Married mothers have lower rates of depression than do single or cohabiting mothers.

Crime and Domestic Violence: (18) Boys raised in single-parent families are more likely to engage in delinquent and criminal behavior; (19) Marriage appears to reduce the risk that adults will be either perpetrators or victims of crime; (20) Married women appear to have a lower risk of experiencing domestic violence than do cohabiting or dating women; and (21) A child who is not living with his or her own two married parents is at greater risk of child abuse.[8]

Box C 2.1

more frequently in crime and drug abuse, and have higher rates of suicide.

Children of divorced parents often perform more poorly in reading, spelling, and math. They are also more likely to repeat a grade and to have higher drop-out rates and lower rates of college graduation.

Families with children that were not poor before the divorce see their income drop as much as 50 percent. Almost 50 percent of the parents with children that are going through a divorce move into poverty after the divorce.

Religious worship, which has been linked to better health, longer marriages, and better family life, drops after the parents divorce.

The divorce of parents, even if it is amicable, tears apart the fundamental unit of American society.[9]

So while it is true that a large number of children of divorced parents survive the experience and later become capable and stable adults,[10] it is also becoming increasingly evident that many children of divorce are at risk for developing detrimental behaviors, personality disorders, and disruptive lifestyles. Some of the variables in adjustment of children to divorce are: (1) age of child at divorce, (2) amount of conflict in the marriage, (3) access to both parents after the divorce, (4) adjustment to a stepparent, if there is one, and (5) access to other nurturing adults during the childhood years.

THE BIG BOUNCE BACK

Besides the disadvantages of divorce and the "train of consequences" of which President Faust speaks, there are other good reasons for married couples to work through troubled times in their marriage. It has been estimated that about 30 percent of contemporary marriages in the United States are ended because of physical and mental abuse or excessive conflict or other serious events.[11] What about the other 70 percent of marriages—especially in light of the documented evidence indicating that many married couples recover from marital distress? Researchers Linda J. Waite and Maggie Gallagher stated:

How many unhappy couples turn their marriages around? The truth is shocking: 86 percent of unhappily married people who stick it out find that, five years later, their marriages are happier. . . . In fact, nearly three-fifths of those who said their marriage was unhappy in the late '80s and who stayed married, rated this same marriage as either "very happy" or "quite happy" when reinterviewed in the early 1990s. . . . The very worst marriages showed the most dramatic turnarounds: 77 percent of the stably married

people who rated their marriage as very unhappy (a one on a scale of one to seven) in the late eighties said that the same marriage was either "very happy" or "quite happy" five years later.

They conclude: "Permanent marital unhappiness is surprisingly rare among couples who stick it out. Five years later, just 15 percent of those who initially said they were very unhappily married (and who stayed married) ranked their marriage as not unhappy at all."[12]

ADVANTAGES OF MARRIAGE

One researcher articulated the benefits of marriage as follows:

What would you say if someone told you that a particular social bond could add years to your life and ensure your children a better education and economic livelihood? Furthermore, what would you say if you also found out that breaking this social bond was only slightly less harmful to your health than smoking a pack or more of cigarettes per day and could significantly increase your risk of depression, alcohol abuse, and committing suicide? And, what would you say if you found out that this social bond that was potentially so beneficial to you and your children's health and personal well-being was *marriage?*[13]

Truly, the research on marriage is striking. For decades, studies have shown that the married live longer and have a lower risk of a variety of physical and psychological illness than the unmarried.[14]

In 2002, the Institute for American Values published a pamphlet titled "Why Marriage Matters: Twenty-One Conclusions from the Social Sciences."[15] The report summarized the findings of more than a dozen family scholars in the nation and included more than 93 citations from research and published articles. Their fundamental conclusion was: "Marriage is . . . a social good."[16] (See Box C2.1 for a summary of these outcomes.)

This report affirms that marriage is important for men, women, and children. It provides additional insights about why "marriage is ordained of God" (D&C 49:15) and helps us further understand why God dislikes and even hates what divorce often does to those involved (Malachi 2:16).

Latter-day Saint couples and others contemplating divorce should seriously consider the advantages of a stable marital relationship and the possible consequences of terminating their relationship.

Therapist and lecturer Michele Weiner Davis has written:

> The decision to divorce or remain together to work things out is one of the most important decisions you will ever make. It is crucial for those considering divorce to anticipate what lies ahead in order to make informed decisions. Too often the fallout from divorce is far more devastating than many people realize when contemplating the move.[17]

With the light of the gospel, prayer, pondering, and the assistance of wise ecclesiastical leaders and other appropriate support, couples considering divorce can make an "informed decision"—and where possible, decide to stay together.[18]

ABOUT THE AUTHOR

Brent A. Barlow, Ph.D., teaches in the School of Family Life at Brigham Young University. He and his wife, Susan, have seven children and thirteen grandchildren.

ADDITIONAL READING

Catherine C. Lundell (2000), Helping couples in counseling remain committed to their marriage; in David C. Dollahite, ed., *Strengthening Our Families: An In-Depth Look at the Proclamation on the Family* (Salt Lake City: Bookcraft), 48–49.

Glenn T. Stanton (1997), *Why Marriage Matters: Reasons to Believe in Marriage in Postmodern Society* (Colorado Springs, CO: Pinon Press).

Elizabeth VanDenBerghe (2000), The enduring, happy marriage: Findings and implications from research; in David C. Dollahite, ed., *Strengthening Our Families: An In-Depth Look at the Proclamation on the Family* (Salt Lake City: Bookcraft), 16–28.

Judith S. Wallerstein, Julia M. Lewis, and Sandra Blakeslee (2000), *The Unexpected Legacy of Divorce* (New York: Hyperion).

NOTES

1. See E. D. Andrews (1953), *The People Called Shakers* (New York: Oxford University Press); M. F. Melcher (1941), *The Shaker Adventure* (Princeton, New Jersey: University Press); C. Nordhoff (1875), *The Communistic Societies of the United States* (reprint, New York: Schocken Books, 1965).

2. See Brent A. Barlow (1999, October 12), Marriage is ordained of God; BYU Devotional Address; available at http://speeches.byu.edu

3. Translations of Malachi 2:16: "For I hate divorce, says the LORD the God of Israel," *Revised Standard Version* (2003); "For I hate divorce, says the LORD, the God of Israel," *New American Bible* (1990); "'For I hate divorce!' says the LORD, the God of Israel," *New Living Translation* (1996); "'I hate divorce,' says the LORD God of Israel," *New International Version* (1990).

4. Gordon B. Hinckley (1991, May), What God hath joined together, *Ensign, 21*(5), 74.

5. James E. Faust (1993, May), Father, come home, *Ensign, 23*(5), 37.

6. D. Medved (1989), Chapter 8: Exceptional situations: When you should divorce; in *The Case Against Divorce: Discover the Lures, the Lies, and the Emotional Traps of Divorce—Plus the Seven Vital Reasons to Stay Together* (New York: Donald I. Fine), 103–130.

7. Faust (1993), 36.

8. See Institute for American Values (2002).

9. P. Fagan and R. Rector (2000), The effects of divorce on America (on-line: The Heritage Foundation); available at http://www.smartmarriages.com, click on "marriage reports."

10. D. B. Larson, J. P. Swyers, and S. S. Larson (1995), *The Costly Consequences of Divorce: Assessing the Clinical, Economic, and Public Health Impact of Marital Disruption in the United States* (Rockville, MD: National Institute for Healthcare Research), 136.

11. P. R. Amato and A. Booth (1997), *A Generation at Risk: Growing Up in an Era of Family Upheaval* (Cambridge, MA: Harvard University Press), 220.

12. L. Waite and M. Gallagher (2000), *The Case for Marriage: Why Married People Are Happier, Healthier, and Better Off Financially* (New York: Doubleday), 148–149.

13. Larson, Swyers, and Larson (1995).

14. For a detailed summary of the benefits of marriage, see Elizabeth VanDenBerghe (2000), The enduring, happy marriage: Findings and implications from research; in D. C. Dollahite, ed., *Strengthening Our Families: An In-Depth Look at the Proclamation on the Family* (Salt Lake City: Bookcraft), 16–28.

15. Institute for American Values (2002), *A Report from Family Scholars—Why Marriage Matters: Twenty-one Conclusions from the Social Sciences*, pamphlet (New York: Institute for American Values); available at http://www.americanvalues.org

16. Ibid., 6.

17. Michele Weiner Davis (1989), *Divorce-Busting: A Step-by-Step Approach to Making Your Marriage Loving Again* (New York: Simon and Schuster), 21–28.

18. See also Brent A. Barlow (2003, January), Marriage crossroads: Why divorce is often not the best option: Rationale, resources, and references, *Marriage & Families*, 21–28.

RECOVERING FROM PORNOGRAPHY ADDICTION

SARAH JANE WEAVER

The lie survived months, then years and decades. He carried it on his mission and into his temple marriage. It drove a wedge between him and his family and robbed his wife of trust and security. It jeopardized his relationship with God and controlled, then ultimately ended, his career as a Church employee.

For years he justified his lifestyle; he wasn't hurting anyone but himself. But it is hard to live a lie—to carry the persona of a perfect family man and Church member on the outside while fighting a sexual addiction on the inside, that of indulging in the silent sin of pornography.

This Latter-day Saint couple agreed to share with readers their battle with a sexual addiction that he traces back to his youth. Through counseling, recovery programs, and the power of the Atonement, he was finally able to overcome his addiction, and his wife was finally able to let go of her feelings of betrayal and hurt that accompanied their temple marriage from the beginning. They hope others will learn from their decades-long trial and know help and healing are available. "We are so grateful for what has happened in our life [since finding help]," he said. "We are trying to help others. It is not something we feel like we have to hide—we did that already."

A lifelong Church member and the son of a stake president, his troubles began as a teenager at a sleepover. By his late teens, he knew that if he needed an escape he could find it by looking at "the female body." But at 19, he went through a sincere repentance process. He believed he had been cured. He served an honorable and worthy mission and returned to Brigham Young University.

In Provo, he found a spiritual bubble that seemed to protect him from the troubles of his teens. He taught at the Missionary Training Center and met a young woman whom he married a short time later in the Salt Lake Temple. They left Provo and he began a challenging job working as a salesman, paid only on commission. They had a son and the pressure to support the young family became a constant concern.

He found relief in pornographic movies and by calling phone sex lines. "I could escape through sexual arousal," he said. "I could feel a rush of self-medication. It became a drug inside my body."

Two years into their marriage, his young wife caught him in a lie, and he confessed his transgressions. "That was like a kick in the stomach," she recalled. "I really felt like we had a near-perfect marriage. To realize he was lying shattered the dream."

That started a cycle of addiction that the couple has fought ever since. He would undergo sincere repentance, always with the help of supportive bishops who did not understand the cycle. But "every time the addiction cycle came around, there was something always worse."

Absent serious Church discipline (he was usually placed on probation), she became the moral enforcer in their marriage. At first she didn't mind; she blamed herself for the problem. "It was very easy to rationalize," she said. "I never told my parents. I was embarrassed and ashamed. I figured if I was not overweight, if I was prettier, if I was a better mom he wouldn't be doing this." Not until years later did she realize that his pornography addiction had very little to do with her.

For years he searched for help. "I became a world-class repenter," he said. "I felt like I was the only person out there. I felt totally and completely alone." He read Church books. He memorized the scriptures. After slipping he became "intensely religious." And he forced his family into another cycle. After Church leaders learned of his transgressions and his repentance process was complete, he moved his family to a new ward where no one was aware of his problems. He served as a counselor in the bishopric, as elders quorum president, as a gospel doctrine teacher, and as ward choir director.

On the outside people viewed the family, which now included four children, as "perfect." But inside the home, things were far from perfect.

The couple's children witnessed intense fights between their parents; she yelled, he made promises. The children, not knowing about their father's problems, blamed their mother, believing she had "anger issues."

"The image I was selling was dishonest to myself," he said. He begged his wife to "cut him some slack." After all, he was so good at so many things, why couldn't she allow him some leniency in this one area? "He felt like this is a victimless crime," she said. "He told me that he didn't feel like he was hurting anyone but himself."

His life came crashing down around him four years ago. He was working for the Church in his dream job. He was respected in his ward and community. Things were so good he "transgressed in the face of consequences, sincerely believing I was above the consequences." Frequently testing and navigating his Internet filter at home, he began to test the system in the Church Office Building. He spent hours trying to outwit the Church's system, unaware his actions were being tracked.

When faced with the evidence, his boss defended him. "Someone else is using his computer," his boss insisted. But it was too late; it was too hard to keep living the lie. He submitted his letter of resignation and went home. Days later he found the strength to tell his wife.

"That time he could tell a difference in me," she said. "I didn't have anything else to say. I was done." While she contemplated divorce, she secretly wished he would die. "I wanted him gone where he couldn't hurt me anymore." She couldn't face friends or neighbors; she went to sacrament meeting in a different ward from her own and sat in the foyer, praying no one would ask how she was.

Their bishop worked diligently to find answers to their problems. He "called and called and called and called. He knew there was something out there that could help." The bishop found that help in a support group for those fighting pornography.

For the first time in his life, he knew the root of his problem: He was fighting more than moral inadequacies—he was fighting an addiction.

For years he didn't receive a birthday, anniversary, or Christmas card from his wife. She couldn't stand the sappy messages inside; none seemed to convey the way she felt about him, about the love she had for him and the hate she had for what he did.

After he lost his job with the Church, he was disfellowshipped. She couldn't find the emotional energy to even attend his Church disciplinary council. Yet after that night—with the help of gospel-based counseling, a community recovery program, and a support group for Church members with sexual addictions—"we started along a path of recovery, a path of redemption," she said. (See chapter 13 on overcoming the destructive influences of pornography and chapter 12 on overcoming addictions.)

He learned to apply the Savior's Atonement in his own life. He and his wife also began to understand the problem and its triggers. They spoke to their children. For the first time, they didn't move; instead they faced their friends and neighbors. He went to work in sales; friends paid their mortgage until they could again scrape by financially.

As he sat outside the temple when their son received his endowment before missionary service, and again when his daughter was married, she began to understand his grief.

As he looked back on his life, he learned his addiction had nothing to do with her, but instead was something he brought to the marriage. "It is hard to fall off a pedestal," he said, noting his life today feels honest but not comfortable.

And last June, he received an anniversary card from his wife. "It talked about being glad to walk this path together," he said. "I cherish that. That meant a lot. That is hope." Hope—and healing that accompanies it—has made the Atonement real in their lives, he said. "My heart was softened, my heart was changed."

ABOUT THE AUTHOR

Sarah Jane Weaver is a staff writer for *LDS Church News*. This story was adapted from her article, The silent sin: The enslavement of pornography (2003, November 29), *LDS Church News*, Z04–Z05, Z07, and is printed here by permission of *LDS Church News* and the couple.

A JOURNEY THROUGH A SPIRITUAL CRISIS

GERRY AND MARGO DYE

Gerry: A number of years ago I felt as if, after a long downward spiral, I had come close to hitting bottom. I felt that very little was right with my life.

I didn't carry many of the obvious scars of life. I was still given positions of leadership in the Church and other organizations. I was still generally respected, from a distance, by most of my family, friends, and associates. I say from a distance because I had become proficient at keeping people well away from me, my feelings, and my perceived failures. Those failures appeared to me to be many. I felt that my professional life had dead ended. The financial future looked bleak. My self-esteem was shattered. My testimony had ceased growing. One by one, I felt my dreams crumble.

My relationship with my dear wife, Margo, was particularly devastated. An absence of relationship honesty on my part had driven us far apart. I was physically faithful, but was not true to my promise to cherish my wife and our relationship as an eternal blessing.

Margo: I knew something was terribly wrong. I have always believed that nothing in a relationship is one-sided and that each individual shares in the successes and the challenges of the relationship. Like every human being I was carrying my own baggage and feeling my own fears. But I felt that if Gerry and I could just connect again, look each other in the eye and share our feelings, we could help one another overcome our fears and the distance that separated us. But Gerry was so elusive, it was like trying to embrace smoke.

Gerry: We all possess a long list of fixed beliefs about ourselves, others, God, and the world around us. Many of those beliefs are positive and nourishing to us. But destructive beliefs tend to keep us trapped in fear and unfulfilled expectations. In my prison of self-imposed loneliness, I believed that people would despise or pity me if they really knew me. I had a terrible fear, not of failure itself, but of being perceived as a failure.

Then, in the darkness, beams of light reached me and brought a hint of half-remembered warmth. My bishop met with me. While I admitted that I was going through some difficult times, I hedged his efforts to learn more. The bishop realized he was hitting a brick wall and did something extraordinary by sharing his own time of sorrow. Though I admired this man as someone who had his life in order and his priorities straight, he told me of a time when life seemed to lose meaning. He had questioned his own value and wondered if his contribution had any worth. He described struggling with a melancholy in his soul that influenced every area of his life.

He shared with me the extraordinary joy he felt in his life now. He expressed his gratitude for the experiences of those dark times that had helped lead him to the brightness of today. He did not go into detail about how he turned his beliefs around. But it was clear to me that during that difficult time, he had discovered something important about himself and his relationship with God and others. I left the interview with a tiny flicker of hope.

By following the promptings of the Spirit, he had shown me that in overcoming our weaknesses, there is strength. Rather than feeling shame for our weaknesses, we can rejoice as they lead us to true humility and a greater dependence on God (see Ether 12:27).

Was my travail over? Hardly. But never underestimate the power of one tiny candle lit in the midst of the great darkness. Its light appears all the brighter for the darkness that surrounds it.

The other beam of light came from my wife. That particular light had always shone upon me but was obscured by my own destructive beliefs. Margo had suffered and was confused by my behavior. Her inability to connect with me was leading her to question her own value. She worked hard to keep lines of communication open, even as I set up roadblocks. She was steady in her efforts to make certain that family was a priority through regular family home evening and family prayer. Without my realizing it at the time, those and other family traditions helped provide an anchor when I had very little else I could cling to.

Margo sometimes felt she was fighting a losing battle. At length, her tears of desperation turned my eyes from my own selfish beliefs. I glimpsed how close to the precipice I had come. I saw Margo's hand extended to me, inviting me to come and find safety and refuge. I took her hand.

Margo: Over the months, I had internalized the struggles of our relationship. I questioned my own value and obscured Gerry's inherent goodness under a cloud of fear and despair. The Lord encourages us not to fear. Where there is fear, there can be no love (1 John 4:18). Through prayer and time spent in the temple, I found within myself a willingness to forgive myself and Gerry. All desire to blame or punish melted away, leaving the simple desire for Gerry and me to lay our burdens down and start anew.

Gerry: The active part of healing my life and relationships began with writing a letter to my wife detailing my experiences and sharing my regret for the pain I had caused. I now realize that the letter was full of inaccuracies, erroneous beliefs, and self-pity. But it was the best I had to offer at the moment. And it was just enough. I hadn't felt "just enough" in a long time. I felt beaten up and bedraggled when I wrote that letter, but I stretched as far as I knew how, shook off the self-induced lethargy, and rubbed the scales from my eyes. Through the Spirit of a loving God, the power of the Atonement, and the forgiveness of a loving wife, another candle was lit.

The process of my recovery included a willingness on my part to surrender—a willingness to lay down my masks, change my beliefs, drop my wooden sword and paper shield, spread my arms, and say to God and my family, "Here I am. I cannot do this on my own." The change of heart had begun.

This change of heart illuminated to me the messages of hope and peace that had always been there in the scriptures and the words of the prophets. I read the words of Joseph Fielding Smith: "[Perfection] will not come all at once, but line upon line . . . and even then not as long as we live in this mortal life, for we will have to go even beyond the grave before we reach that perfection and shall be like God."[1]

Elder Marvin J. Ashton added: "I am also convinced of the fact that the speed with which we head along the straight and narrow path isn't as important as the direction in which we are traveling. That direction, if it is leading toward eternal goals, is the all-important factor."[2]

Somebody once said to me regarding slow progress, "We are not growing radishes here; we are growing oak trees." And so it is. As I study the rings of my small but growing oak tree, I note that the rings representing my times of greatest sorrow and struggle have not weakened me but now lend a strength and beauty to the grain of my character.

Ultimately, two very personal truths emerged. First, faith is understanding that everything that happens to us is for our good (D&C 122:7). Second, in this life and in this place, progress toward perfection is our goal.

Margo: It is truly remarkable to realize the Lord's promise in our lives that weaknesses can turn to strengths. As Gerry and I humbled ourselves and forgave one another, paths previously obscured opened to our view. We have been led to knowledge and experiences that have allowed us to build a foundation from which we can reach for joy and happiness every day. We still encounter minor bumps in our relationship and make course corrections, but we have the confidence that we can find love and peace in our relationship.

Gerry: Many good members of the Church feel inadequate and lost. They are often past feeling the Spirit or the love of God, and they do not perceive the messages of hope contained in the scriptures and the gospel. We have the duty and the privilege, particularly within our own homes, to help others once again see the light. In my case it was two people who extended hope and forgiveness and light to me, one a leader willing to magnify his stewardship, the other my wife, determined to honor her covenants. I trust that their joy shall be great in the kingdom of God, for the one that was lost is found again.

ABOUT THE AUTHORS

Gerry and Margo Dye will celebrate their 28th wedding anniversary in 2005. Margo is an alumna of Southern Utah University, and both Margo and Gerry are alumni of BYU. Outside their home duties, Margo is a nurse and Gerry works for a large company in the computer industry. They are the parents of five children and grandparents of two.

ADDITIONAL READING

Neal A. Maxwell (1979), *All These Things Shall Give Thee Experience* (Salt Lake City: Deseret Book).

M. Scott Peck (1978), *The Road Less Traveled* (New York: Touchstone).

B. L. Top (2005, April), A balanced life, *Ensign, 35*(4), 26–29.

NOTES

1. Joseph Fielding Smith (1954–1956), *Doctrines of Salvation*, 3 vols. (Salt Lake City: Bookcraft), 2:18.

2. Marvin J. Ashton (1989, May), On being worthy, *Ensign, 19*(5), 20–21.

E s s a y   C 5

Dealing with Emotional Infidelity

James M. Harper

I sat in my professional office listening to an all-too-familiar story. Jill was telling me that she had become emotionally involved with another man. "You don't understand," she said. "I didn't intend for this to happen. It was innocent. He really listened to me. I felt I could share things with him that my husband doesn't care about. He seemed to care more about my feelings. I could tell him how I feel, and he would understand without judging me or being upset by how I felt."

When I asked her if she had told her husband, she shouted at me, "I didn't do anything sexual. He probably won't even care that I have feelings for someone else." Yet, she was in my office because of the internal emotional struggle created by becoming emotionally involved with someone other than her husband. Even though she had committed no sexual transgression, she still felt like the betrayer.

As a professional marriage and family therapist, I have often been called upon to help both husbands and wives work through issues created by inappropriate emotional involvement with someone outside the marriage (not sexual, and sometimes not even involving romantic behavior such as kissing or hugging). In each case I am asked the same questions: Should I tell my husband or wife? If I do tell my spouse, how will he or she react? Do I need to talk to my bishop, rabbi, minister, or priest even though I didn't do anything sexual? What do I do with all the feelings that this has created? Why was I so vulnerable? This made me feel alive again. Can't I just keep this relationship and have my marriage too?

The relationship we call marriage is unique among all relationships. Scriptures reserve the word "cleave" for only two types of relationships, between God and man and between husband and wife. The admonition for a man to leave his father and mother and cleave unto his wife appears early in the Old Testament (Genesis 2:24), the New Testament (Matthew 19:5, Mark 10:7), the Doctrine and Covenants (D&C 42:22), and the Pearl of Great Price (Moses 3:24, Abraham 5:18). To "cleave" is to adhere firmly and closely or loyally and unwaveringly.[1]

How does one cleave? I like to think of this in therapy terms like boundaries around the marriage, appropriate flow of information within and without that boundary, and personal disclosure with the right person in the right place at the right time. First, the boundary around a marriage is created by both partners' willingness to deeply share all aspects of themselves—spiritual, emotional, physical, and mental—with each other and to contain that information within the boundary of the marriage. In other words, they do not share with outsiders in the same way they share with their spouse—not with children, not with parents, not with friends, and not with anyone else.

Deep personal disclosure in this sense is meant to be exclusive and only shared with one's spouse within the boundary of marriage. The boundary of a marriage is maintained in part by both partners' willingness to spend time with each other to the exclusion of outsiders. While married couples also need mutual couple friends, they must have some time just for the two of them. Such cleaving between spouses not only involves devotion of time to each other, but deep sharing of emotion, dreams, and goals; sexual union; and commitment to sustain and protect the marital boundary even in the face of struggle and crises. Doing these things creates the heart, the spirit, the trust that marriage alone so profoundly provides. It has been useful to me as a professional to think that when a husband and wife cleave, they are creating a "marital heart."

In the case of Jill, she not only felt like a betrayer, she had betrayed the heart and spirit of her marriage. While her situation was not complicated by sexual transgression, she had much work to do. In terms of marital dynamics, the consequences of an emotional affair are very similar to the consequences of a sexual affair. However, an emotional affair does not usually have the complications of sexual transgression and the complexities of the repentance process that are consequences of a sexual affair (see chapter 14 on healing from infidelity).

The heart, the spirit, of marriage is always damaged by affairs, even emotional ones. The Lord warned, "whosoever looketh on a woman to lust after her hath committed adultery with her already in his heart" (Matthew 5:28). Elder James E. Faust stated:

> Loyalty to our companion should not be merely physical but mental and spiritual as well. Flirtations are never harmless, and jealousy has no place in a marriage. Marriage partners must avoid the very appearance of evil by shunning any questionable contact with any person to whom they are not married. Virtue is the strong glue that holds marriage together.[2]

When the boundary around a marriage is strong, husband and wife look out at the world as through a window. They face the world together. When that marital boundary is broken by inappropriate disclosure and emotional entanglement with someone other than the spouse, the husband or wife joins together with someone else. This frequently turns the window on their marriage, and sometimes on the marriage of the other person involved, as well. This violation of marital boundary makes it impossible to continue an emotional affair and maintain the marriage.

Let me describe this in the words of a man who had an emotional affair:

> She listened to me as I described all the things that bother me. When I found myself talking about the things about my wife that bother me, I found her even more accepting and solicitous. When she talked about how her husband didn't meet her needs, I felt sorry for her and became more empathetic for her circumstance. Slowly we discussed each other's marriage so much we had left no room for our spouses. They were under "our" looking glass. Our spouses, the people who had power to change in response to our com-plaints, were slowly closed out while we found solace in each other and gazed ever more intensely at our marriages, almost as if we had become outsiders.

Because even emotional infidelity violates the heart of a marriage, it may be helpful to seek the support of your bishop, priest, rabbi, or minister. They can serve as a confidential sounding board to help you gain perspective and sort through what to do. While emotional infidelity does not require confession to ecclesiastical leaders in the way that sexual infidelity does, an ecclesiastical leader offers a confidential setting in which personal issues such as this can be discussed. While secrets are generally viewed as damaging to marriage, spiritual leaders can help one work through issues of if, when, and how to tell a spouse.

Researchers have discovered that emotional infidelity causes greater hurt feelings for both genders than sexual infidelity and that sexual infidelity causes greater anger and blame.[3] The emotional upheaval and impact of emotional infidelity is equal to and, in some cases, stronger than the distress resulting from sexual infidelity. The disclosure of emotional infidelity leads to a similar "roller coaster" of emotions as does disclosure of sexual infidelity. Both violate the marriage heart, the marriage spirit, and turn the protective boundary of marriage inside out. Both situations lead to intense traumatization and a sense of major interpersonal betrayal.

Researchers have also investigated why men and women get involved in emotional infidelity.[4] Women are more likely than men to be involved emotionally with someone other than their spouse, and they cite emotional and romantic reasons as the primary cause. It is much easier to find someone who might listen well and be empathetic when conversation is the only situation in which you are involved with him or her. It would be much harder for the individual to always be that way when having to engage with you in the daily tasks of living such as paying bills, doing household chores, taking care of children, making major decisions together, and so on. If you as a reader are already caught up emotionally with someone other than your spouse, it may be helpful to remember that the comparison you make between the situation of your marriage and the situation of your emotional dependency on someone other than your spouse is not a fair comparison. The demands in each situation are strikingly different.

The feelings involved in emotional infidelity are

often intense. Such intensity in emotion should be a signal to examine why one is so vulnerable. It is a time to introspect, not to act on feelings. Whenever I am asked to counsel professionally with an individual in a case involving an emotional affair, I point out that the individual's vulnerability to the offered empathy and professed care is a signal about him or her—about what the individual needs to do to care for self and what the couple needs to do in their marriage.

Emotional infidelity often starts in situations in which someone listens well and encourages further disclosure. The setting is often innocent, in an office with a coworker, or after a meeting related to Church assignments. Each shows too much empathy for the other's disclosures that are violations of a marital boundary and marriage heart. Men who have grown up being taught to care for women are particularly vulnerable in these circumstances because they desire to help. Too much listening leads to emotional dependency, and marital boundaries are eventually bent or broken by the nature of the disclosures that occur. A search for personal answers to the question, "Why was I so vulnerable to an empathetic heart and a listening ear?" allows people to take charge of caring for themselves and seeking from their spouse what they think they may need.

Married couples heal every day from marital hearts broken by emotional infidelity. Through commitment, deep sharing of selves, and renewed promises, marriages recover and the marital heart beats even stronger because of what both have learned and suffered together.

ABOUT THE AUTHOR

James M. Harper is director of the BYU School of Family Life, associate dean in the College of Family, Home, and Social Sciences, a Zina Young Williams Card Endowed University Professor, and a marriage and family therapist. He is a former president of the BYU 21st Stake and of the Korea Pusan Mission, and he currently serves as Gospel Doctrine teacher in the Timpanogos Park Second Ward.

ADDITIONAL READING

Gordon B. Hinckley (1991, May), What God hath joined together, *Ensign, 21*(5), 71–74.

Spencer W. Kimball (1972, July), Keep the lines of communication strong, *Ensign, 2*(7), 37–39.

Spencer W. Kimball (1976, September 7), Marriage and divorce; BYU Devotional Address; available at http://speeches.byu.edu

M. D. Richardson (2005, April), Three principles of marriage, *Ensign, 35*(4), 20–24.

Lynn G. Robbins (2000, October) Agency and love in marriage, *Ensign, 30*(10), 16–22.

Wendy L. Watson (2000), Personal purity and marital intimacy; in David C. Dollahite, ed., *Strengthening Our Families: An In-Depth Look at the Proclamation on the Family* (Salt Lake City: Bookcraft), 60–62.

NOTES

1. *Oxford English Dictionary,* 2d ed. (1989), s.v. "cleave."

2. James E. Faust (2004, January 10), Challenges facing the family; address delivered in the Worldwide Leadership Training Meeting (Salt Lake City: The Church of Jesus Christ of Latter-day Saints), 2.

3. S. Banfield and M. P. McCabe (2001), Extra relationship involvement among women: Are they different from men? *Archives of Sexual Behavior, 30,* 119–142.

4. J. Sabini and M. C. Green (2004), Emotional responses to sexual and emotional infidelity: Constants and differences across genders, samples, and methods, *Personality and Social Psychology Bulletin, 30,* 1375–1388.

CHAPTER 15

CHILDREN ARE AN HERITAGE OF THE LORD

SYDNEY S. AND NOEL B. REYNOLDS

*The first commandment that God gave to Adam and Eve pertained to their potential for parenthood
as husband and wife. We declare that God's commandment for His children to multiply and replenish the earth
remains in force. "Children are an heritage of the Lord" (Psalm 127:3).[1]*
—"The Family: A Proclamation to the World"

What does it mean to say that children are "an heritage of the Lord" (Psalm 127:3)? Most people understand as they read this scripture that children are a "gift" from a loving God and that there is something long-lasting, even eternal, about the nature of this gift. The children we receive from God are not only "our" children, they are the offspring of God—His literal spirit children—and so doubly a gift from Him.

In ancient Israel children were seen as a mark of God's favor. Sarah, Hannah, and Elisabeth each rejoiced at her son's long-awaited birth (Genesis 21:1–8; 1 Samuel 1:2–2:21; Luke 1:5–60). Remember the admonishment to the daughter-in-law of Eli as she herself lay dying and those surrounding her cried out, "Fear not; for thou hast born a son" (1 Samuel 4:20)—in other words, her place in history was assured even if she died in the same hour. The Psalmist wrote, "As arrows are in the hand of a mighty man; so are children of the youth. Happy is the man that hath his quiver full of them" (Psalm 127:4–5).

When the Savior was on the earth He reinforced the importance of children and His own love for them as He bid the disciples to "Suffer little children, and forbid them not, to come unto me: for of such is the kingdom of heaven" (Matthew 19:14). "And Jesus called a little child unto him, and set him in the midst of them, And said, Verily I say unto you, Except ye be converted, and become as little children, ye shall not

enter into the kingdom of heaven. Whosoever therefore shall humble himself as this little child, the same is greatest in the kingdom of heaven. And whoso shall receive one such little child in my name receiveth me" (Matthew 18:2–5). There are few examples in scripture more touching than the experience of the Savior blessing the children recounted in 3 Nephi 17. There are few things more firmly attested to in the scriptures and our own experience than that the Lord loves little children.

As the Lord loves little children, He also loves those who receive them and love them in His name. When He sends children to us, He expects us to love and care for them and teach them as He would. Latter-day Saint understanding of eternal life is that it will be a life such as God has. Elder Henry B. Eyring said:

> Eternal life means to become like the Father and to live in families in happiness and joy forever. . . . What we want is eternal life in families. We don't just want it if that is what happens to work out, nor do we want something that might seem to be only approaching eternal life. We want eternal life, whatever its cost in effort, pain, and sacrifice. . . . Family life here is the schoolroom in which we prepare for family life there. . . . The proclamation describes our schooling here for family life.[2]

Those who achieve an exaltation in the celestial

kingdom will have the blessing of eternal lives; that is, eternal increase (D&C 131:1–4; D&C 132:19, 30, 63). Where are we going to learn how to be eternal parents? Life in a family unit is like a laboratory school to help us prepare for eternal life.

The idea that children are sent to us by the Lord implies both that they are a great blessing to their parents, and that the parents are responsible to the Lord for the nurture and instruction of their children. On reflection, we will see that these dual implications are closely connected through love—our love for our children, and the Lord's love for us.

IS A COUPLE HAPPY WHO HAVE THEIR "QUIVER FULL" OF CHILDREN?

We might reasonably ask ourselves if the perspective of the ancient psalmist might not be out of date or no longer applicable in the global economy of the twenty-first century. Children are no longer regarded as economic assets, but rather as expensive luxuries, or even as burdens to be avoided, especially now that medical science makes them so easily avoidable. Consequently, the average size of families is falling everywhere, and in highly developed countries has fallen below the replacement rate in many cases.[3] Lamentably, as parents become more educated and financially able to nurture children effectively, statistics show they are less likely to welcome more offspring into their homes.[4] One child takes twenty-four hours a day to rear and so do several children. Most parents have learned that love expands infinitely and resources stretch when children are welcomed in faith. Elder Dallin H. Oaks counseled:

> When married couples postpone childbearing until after they have satisfied their material goals, the mere passage of time assures that they seriously reduce their potential to participate in furthering our Heavenly Father's plan for all of his spirit children. Faithful Latter-day Saints cannot afford to look upon children as an interference with what the world calls "self-fulfillment." Our covenants with God and the ultimate purpose of life are tied up in those little ones who reach for our time, our love, and our sacrifices.

How many children should a couple have? All they can care for! Of course, to care for children means more than simply giving them life. Children must be loved, nurtured, taught, fed, clothed, housed, and well started in their capacities to be good parents themselves. Exercising faith in God's promises to bless them when they are keeping his commandments, many LDS parents have large families. Others seek but are not blessed with children or with the number of children they desire. In a matter as intimate as this, we should not judge one another.[5]

Few would contest the value for children of being reared in a stable and loving home environment. It is also true that the parents in such a family reap important benefits. Each of us who has benefited from a strong family background owes a great deal to parents who were willing to suffer and sacrifice for us. In turn, children provide parents with opportunities for growth and a way to make a contribution to the raising of a righteous generation that will serve the Lord and do His work. As President James E. Faust has said:

> To be a good father and mother requires that the parents defer many of their own needs and desires in favor of the needs of their children. As a consequence of this sacrifice, conscientious parents develop a nobility of character and learn to put into practice the selfless truths taught by the Savior Himself.[6]

President Spencer W. Kimball taught that married couples who "refuse to have children when they are able to do so" are acting selfishly and against their own best interests.[7] As parents make choices about family size, it is helpful to consider that the family they bring into the world will provide the primary context in which these great commandments and life opportunities will be fulfilled for them. Perhaps one reason the prophets have encouraged us not to be influenced by current fashions in family lifestyle[8] is that those who follow those fashions are choosing to invest in other things of less importance than children. When we reach the end of our lives, we will be able to judge better whether we have made the right choices as young parents. But we will not be able to change those choices.

PARABLE OF THE TALENTS AND INVESTING IN CHILDREN

The Savior's parable of the talents applies to our responsibility to welcome and nurture children (Matthew 25:14–30). Each of the three servants received a different amount of silver, with the expectation that he would invest and magnify it prior to his lord's return. The two faithful servants obeyed—in each case doubling the value of the original amount. But the third did not and found his lord displeased when he attempted to return exactly what he had received. When we interpret this parable in terms of the children our Lord has given us, we should note that what we do with our children is more important than the number we have. We also recognize that we cannot give them back in the form in which they were received. For good or for ill, children change. If they are not growing and improving in their physical, moral, and spiritual lives, they will stagnate, atrophy, and degenerate. But they do not stand still, suspended in time, like buried treasure. If they are not magnified during childhood, their adult opportunities will be limited—and the responsibility may lie with the parents. Many modern prophets have taught that parents have a responsibility to teach their children to have faith in the Lord and to serve others (see, for example, D&C 68:25). If we, who have been blessed with the light of the gospel, do not teach our children these things, who will? Our sacrifices to invest in the lives of our children will bring earthly and eternal blessings.

The distinguished Chicago economist Theodore W. Schultz chose to focus his Nobel lecture on the importance of investing in people, particularly during their younger years. Schultz noted that we ordinarily think of money spent on education and health care as consumption expenditures (like buying food or clothing), rather than as investments (like savings or purchases of land or stocks and bonds). He argued vigorously that money and effort devoted to the development of people's minds and bodies is a sound investment in the full sense of the term. He reported that the returns on money spent for health programs in poor countries have increased the average life expectancy more than 40 percent in a few decades. Investments in education provide a much greater total return in increased life expectancy. And the education helps people to be far more productive and to live much fuller lives.[9]

Although Schultz limited his discussion to the economic aspects of investment in people, his insights have great importance for all who accept Christ's injunction to love their neighbors as themselves. There are many ways in which we can show love to our neighbors. But it would not seem unreasonable to add to our understanding of this an analog of Schultz's insight. For what could be better evidence of love than accepting responsibility for a new life and willingly investing in the future quality of that life?

First Lady Barbara Bush shared with graduates of Wellesley College the importance of investing in children:

Whatever the era, whatever the times, one thing will never change: Fathers and mothers, if you have children, they must come first. You must read to your children and you must hug your children and you must love your children. Your success as a family, our success as a society, depends not on what happens in the White House but on what happens inside your house.[10]

President Boyd K. Packer added this insight:

The center core of the Church is not the stake house; it is not the chapel; that is not the center of Mormonism. And, strangely enough, the most sacred place on earth may not be the temple, necessarily. The chapel, the stake house, and the temple are sacred as they contribute to the building of the most sacred institution in the Church—the home—and to the blessing of the most sacred relationships in the Church, the family.[11]

Parents who invest in their children will find joy in family relationships and in their children's development. As President Gordon B. Hinckley has taught:

Of all the joys of life, none other equals that of happy parenthood. Of all the responsibilities with which we struggle, none other is so serious. To rear children in an atmosphere of love, security, and faith is the most rewarding of all challenges. The good result from such efforts becomes life's most satisfying compensation.[12]

Parents, however, are not the only ones with an opportunity to share in the work and glory of God by investing in His children. There are countless opportunities for childless couples and single adults, as well as experienced parents, to provide this kind of support for the children of others. Sister Ardeth Kapp personally struggled with the issue of childlessness and defined this choice: "We who do not have children can wallow in self-pity—or we can experience 'birth pains' as we struggle to open the passageway to eternal life for ourselves and others. . . . Instead of wrapping your empty and aching arms around yourself, you can reach out to others."[13]

INVESTING IN CHILDREN'S MORAL AND SPIRITUAL FOUNDATIONS

A few years ago social scientist Jennifer Roback Morse demonstrated the necessity of healthy families to the institutions of free government and free markets. Her argument started with a review of the psychosocial disorders that result when infants and children are deprived of the human love that ordinarily comes from parents and family. Scientists have long known that children need to be held and caressed to mature successfully. What they have not investigated, but which may be just as true, is the possibility that adults benefit as they hold and lovingly care for children. It is through the loving care of adults that young children learn to trust others and to value the esteem of others who monitor their conduct. It is through loving care for children that adults learn the value of patience and the importance of a child's developing his own inner strength and character. Children who do not experience the loving investment of parents were found to be far less likely to contribute positively to their communities, and far more likely to cause willful injury to others as they matured. This author concluded that trust and regard for the good opinion of others are essential elements of a free market and a free society—which could never ensure that people without these attributes would follow the rules or act in cooperative ways when they had opportunities to benefit themselves by acting otherwise.[14]

The kingdom of God requires the ability to trust to be raised another level. The first principle of the gospel is faith, or trust, in the Lord Jesus Christ. Parents teach their children, by their own actions, a tendency either to trust in the Lord or to trust in the arm of flesh. For all of us, worthiness to stand in the presence of God will finally be determined by our own trustworthiness. Will we have proved to the Lord that He can trust us in whatsoever thing He might command us? The desire we develop as lovingly nurtured children to enjoy the high regard of our parents must also move up another level, to a transcendent desire to enjoy the approbation of the Lord Himself— even to the exclusion of all other desires, as our love for Him and our gratitude for His Atonement grow to a fullness.

The importance of parental investment in children turns out, then, to be essential for the development of strong citizens of a free society, and also the principal means by which new generations will be prepared for citizenship in the kingdom of God. Further, as families live the gospel across generations, with the kind of parental nurturing that implies, they can rise to successively higher levels of effective citizenship in His kingdom, making the work of that kingdom increasingly effective in the pursuit of its mission to take the gospel to all the world.

Jesus Christ As Our Exemplar

It should be obvious now that the great investor in people, in His children, is our Father in Heaven. And that is how He characterized His entire purpose and effort to Moses when He spoke to him on the mount. "For behold, this is my work and my glory— to bring to pass the immortality and eternal life of man" (Moses 1:39).

The supreme example of one individual giving all that he has to enrich the life opportunities of others is seen in Jesus Christ. We are often so impressed with the magnitude of His contribution to us that we fail to recognize that we also have endless opportunities to bring enrichment and opportunity to the lives of others. Our service to others will also have eternal consequences. Would it be unreasonable to infer that this is precisely what He expects of us when He commands, "Love one another; as I have loved you" (John 13:34)? And is there any clearer opportunity for us to do just that than in the love and nurture of our own children?

Conclusion

Through our own experience, we have learned over and over again the truth of the Psalmist's observation that "children are an heritage of the Lord." And it becomes clearer to us every day that the Lord sends us children with the expectation that we are to build them in ways that bless them and serve His purposes. Recognizing that the work and glory of God is "to bring to pass the immortality and eternal life of man," we can also see that the Lord has invited parents and others to join Him in that work by loving and investing in His children, preparing them for immortality and eternal life. This is a great work, and it will consume the whole of our lives. It requires us to lose our own lives in its pursuit. The self-promotional assumptions of our culture are challenged radically when we understand life in terms of the Father's plan for exalting His children. The Lord's system is not of this world, but it works, day in and day out, to the salvation of His children—even in a world that rarely recognizes the great work that He is performing.

The covenants we have made with the Lord bind us to His work. And as we pursue that work with full purpose of heart, He delights to bless us. He always magnifies our efforts and makes us effective far beyond any abilities of our own in the great work of the salvation of His children. And in the process, we too will inevitably become more and more like Him.

ABOUT THE AUTHORS

Sydney S. Reynolds, BA, is a full-time homemaker, sometime writer, and former first counselor in the Primary general presidency. She and her husband, Noel, are the parents of eleven children and, at this writing, grandparents of twenty.

Noel B. Reynolds, Ph.D., is a professor of political science and director of the BYU Institute for the Study and Preservation of Ancient Religious Texts (including FARMS). His professional interests include research on the rule of law, the Book of Mormon, and authorship studies. He is currently serving as president of the Florida Fort Lauderdale Mission.

ADDITIONAL READING

Spencer W. Kimball (1979, May), Fortify your homes against evil, *Ensign, 9*(5), 4–7.

Dallin H. Oaks (1993, November), The great plan of happiness, *Ensign, 23*(11), 72–75.

Shirley S. Ricks (1995), Eternal lives, eternal increase; in *Encyclopedia of Mormonism,* Daniel H. Ludlow, ed. (New York: Macmillan), 2:465.

Strengthening the family: Multiply and replenish the earth (2005, April), *Ensign, 35*(4), 18–19.

NOTES

1. First Presidency and Council of Twelve Apostles (1995, November), The family: A proclamation to the world, *Ensign, 25*(11), 102.

2. Henry B. Eyring (1998, February), The family, *Ensign, 28*(2), 10.

3. B. Crossette (1996, November 17), World is less crowded than expected, the U.N. reports, *New York Times,* Section 1, p. 3, col. 1.

4. T. J. Matthews and S. J. Ventura (1997, April 24), Birth and fertility rates by educational attainment: United States, 1994, *Monthly Vital Statistics Report, 45*(10), Supplement.

5. Dallin H. Oaks (1993, November), The great plan of happiness, *Ensign, 23*(11), 72.

6. James E. Faust (1990, November), The greatest challenge in the world—Good parenting, *Ensign, 20*(11), 32.

7. Spencer W. Kimball (1979, May), Fortify your homes against evil, *Ensign, 9*(5), 4.

8. See Boyd K. Packer (2004, November), The least of these, *Ensign, 34*(11), 88. Elder Packer said, "Generation after generation of youth come forward. They are given in marriage. They keep the covenants made in the house of the Lord. They have children and do not let society set limits upon family life."

9. See T. W. Schultz (1981), *Investing in People: The Economics of Population Quality* (Berkeley: Univ. of California Press).

10. Barbara Bush, wowing Wellesley (1990, June 2), *Washington Post,* C01.

11. Boyd K. Packer (1982), *That All May Be Edified* (Salt Lake City: Bookcraft), 234–235.

12. Gordon B. Hinckley (1997), *Teachings of Gordon B. Hinckley* (Salt Lake City: Deseret Book), 421.

13. Ardeth Kapp (1989, February), Just the two of us—for now, *Ensign, 19*(2), 21.

14. J. R. Morse (1999), No families, no freedom: Human flourishing in a free society, *Social Philosophy and Policy, 16*(1), 290–314.

CHAPTER 16

PARENTING THAT STRENGTHENS EACH FAMILY MEMBER

CHRIS L. PORTER AND NANCY B. ROLLINS

I have tremendous respect for fathers and mothers who are nurturing their children in
light and truth, who have prayer in their homes, who spare the rod and govern with love, who look upon
their little ones as their most valued assets to be protected, trained, and blessed.[1]
—President Gordon B. Hinckley

The Apostle Paul taught that we are each the "offspring of God" (Acts 17:29). We were, in fact, born as spirit children of heavenly parents in our pre-earth life. As such, we have, as the Apostle Peter proclaimed, "divine power . . . given unto us" that we might be "partakers of the divine nature" (2 Peter 1:3–4). That divine power includes access to spiritual gifts given to each of us to help us develop our divine natures more fully and return to Heavenly Father (see D&C 46:11–26). As every parent knows, our children come to us with differing inclinations, capacities, abilities, and traits, but they are all children of God and as such have "something of divinity" within each of them[2] and the capacity to develop spiritual gifts.

President Brigham Young, speaking on the topic of individual differences, stated that "there is the same variety [of individuals] in the spirit world that you behold here, yet [we] are of the same parentage, of one Father, one God."[3] More recently, Elder Dallin H. Oaks stated that "in ways that have not been revealed, our actions in the spirit world influence us in mortality."[4] While each of us brings individual qualities to this earth, we share a common divine heritage, and, to some degree, a common pattern of growth and development.[5] Understanding this, we can find ways to appropriately strengthen each family member. This chapter will address four primary ways to strengthen each family member: (1) understand children's devel-

opment, (2) understand and support children's individual talents and intelligences, (3) understand and support each child's temperament, and (4) adapt parenting to the individual and changing needs of our children.

UNDERSTANDING CHILDREN'S DEVELOPMENT

Understanding normal developmental processes in children is an important part of learning to strengthen each family member. Many resources are available on what to expect of children's physical, social, emotional, moral, language, and intellectual development. While much of this information can be helpful, some may conflict with gospel principles. We have been counseled to "seek learning, even by study and also by faith" (D&C 88:118). Such learning increases our understanding of human development. Parents may obtain a wealth of information from Church websites, including www.mormon.org, the new Home and Family section at www.lds.org, and from Church publications, such as *A Parent's Guide*.[6] These resources provide information in general terms about what to expect of children's and teens' abilities, needs, and behaviors at different stages. Studying material on human development can help parents recognize normal development and when development departs from a normal path. In addition, information about typical developmental processes can guide parents in judging what might be appropriate expectations for their children of different ages.

A good understanding of children's changing abilities can help parents tailor strategies for guidance that support each child's talents and abilities. Child psychologist Jean Piaget researched the way children's thinking about the world changes during the course of childhood and adolescence.[7] He found, for instance, that young children often make faulty assumptions about the way the world works, given their limited capacity to think beyond themselves (e.g., "The moon is following me while I am traveling in a car"). He also showed that children at a young age have a strong need to test things out in order to better understand the way the world operates. Such needs often lead to behaviors parents perceive as mischievous, such as pulling out pots and pans to test the various sounds or dumping out a cup of milk to observe the way liquid flows. A creatively inclined child may draw on walls or make creative "messes." All of these behaviors are commonly motivated by children's need to explore and may reflect their own predispositions. Understanding these motivations, parents can choose an appropriate response, such as kindly giving the child a towel to clean up spilled milk or providing a wooden spoon to help the child discover new ways to bang on pots and pans, or placing butcher paper outside for painting murals. Fortunately for parents, these behaviors change as children mature and start to work things out in their minds. When parents recognize a change, they can adjust their responses to align with the child's new level of understanding.

In addition to studying scholarly knowledge of children's development, we should counsel with a loving Heavenly Father regarding the needs and abilities of each family member. President Hinckley reminded us that we should "never forget that these little ones are the sons and daughters of God and that [ours] is a custodial relationship to them, that He was a parent before [we] were parents and that He has not relinquished His parental rights or interest in these His little ones."[8] Our Heavenly Father stands ready to assist us in our parenting endeavors. We should turn to Him often in prayer to seek His will in guiding children's growth.

UNDERSTANDING DIFFERENCES IN CHILDREN'S TALENTS AND INTELLIGENCE

Another key for parents desiring to strengthen their children lies in understanding the qualities of children's various talents and intelligences. While many parents think of intelligence as a description of their child's ability to do well in school (being "smart"), some scholars have offered more comprehensive descriptions. For example, Robert Sternberg suggested that intelligence can be described in three ways: *analytical intelligence* (the kind most often assessed in school tests), *creative intelligence* (having insight, creative answers, and observations), and *practical intelligence* (having good social skills and common sense).[9] Children with each of these types of intelligence can be successful and can contribute to their families and communities. Parents can learn to notice and value these differing gifts of intelligence in their children.

Scholar Howard Gardner went beyond Sternberg by proposing eight different types of intelligence or "frames of mind." These include *verbal* (use of language), *mathematical* (use of mathematical and logical concepts), *spatial* (the ability to understand spaces, as an architect or artist does), *bodily-kinesthetic* (being physically skilled, as in dance or athletics), *musical* (skill and ability in musical endeavors), *interpersonal* (understanding others), *intrapersonal* (understanding oneself), and *naturalist* (understanding nature).[10] Only a few of Gardner's types of intelligence are typically assessed or valued in today's school systems. But attentive family members can notice and encourage talents in each of these areas.

Many parents become discouraged if their child's grades in math, language arts, or science are not high, and feel that the child is not "smart" or talented. However, learning about the many other types of intelligence can help parents to focus on their child's other gifts and talents. Elder Marvin J. Ashton listed "less-conspicuous gifts: the gift of asking; the gift of listening; the gift of hearing and using a still, small voice; the gift of being able to weep; the gift of avoiding contention; the gift of being agreeable; the gift of avoiding vain repetition; the gift of seeking that which is righteous; the gift of not passing judgment; . . . the gift of caring for others; the gift of being able to ponder," and many others.[11] Indeed, psychologist Robert Emmons suggests another type of intelligence:

spiritual intelligence, the ability to be sensitive to spiritual realities and influences.[12]

Reducing Sibling Rivalry

Parents should help each child understand and appreciate his own gifts and should avoid making inappropriate comparisons between children (e.g., "Why can't you be more responsible with your school work like your sister?"). Such practices encourage sibling rivalry, which leads to disharmony and conflict in the home. Instead, learn to celebrate the unique qualities and abilities that each child possesses and find ways to appropriately strengthen those abilities. This may be accomplished by consciously giving focused attention, accompanied by prayers for discernment, to help parents more easily recognize each child's God-given gifts and intelligences and avoid favoritism. Priesthood blessings can help reveal to parents, as well as children, a child's individual spiritual preparations and abilities.

If each child's gifts and talents are valued in the family, there is more likely to be little occasion for sibling rivalry engendered by the inevitable differences. Jealousy or rivalry usually stem from a child's fear of losing a parent's affection or recognition and from wanting to be equally recognized.[13] These feelings may stem from legitimate unmet needs. In speaking of a scriptural example of sibling jealousy, the return of the prodigal son, Elder Jeffrey R. Holland noted that "the father in this story does not . . . compare [his children] with each other. His gestures of compassion toward one do not require a withdrawal or denial of love for the other. He is divinely generous to both of these sons."[14] Parents may prevent jealousy and rivalry by helping to foster feelings of self-worth in each child. They can be sure to emphasize each child's individual positive contributions to the family and wider community. A child's self-worth, according to educator Lillian Katz, "is most likely to be fostered when children have challenging opportunities to build self-confidence and esteem through effort, persistence, and the gradual accrual of skills, knowledge, and appropriate behavior."[15] (See essay G1 on reducing contention among siblings.)

Safeguarding Childhood and Finding Balance

While helping to build self-confidence and individual gifts and talents, parents should at the same time work to safeguard the family from being overrun by these efforts. We should learn to appreciate and support one another's talents without allowing those talents to take over the family. All too often parents feel an urge to push their children harder at increasingly younger ages to develop their abilities. In our rush to offer our children a "better life," we often forget that at the core of our energies and efforts is a child. David Elkind argued in his book, *The Hurried Child,* that "the concept of childhood . . . is threatened with extinction in the society we have created. Today's child has become the unwilling, unintended victim of overwhelming stress—the stress borne of rapid, bewildering social change and constantly rising expectations."[16] He admonished parents to avoid pushing children so hard that they are deprived of an essential need, namely, their childhood.

Families today often feel consumed by the sheer number of their activities. Children experience life that is fast-paced and highly structured, going from school to soccer games to dance lessons to piano practice, and then home to tackle chores and homework and myriad other activities that leave little time for childhood. Childhood should be a time for self-paced discovery, being with friends, learning to negotiate social relationships, and exploring the world through the process of fantasy and physical play. Instead, the breakneck speed of school and family life is leaving children and parents feeling stressed, burned-out, and disconnected.[17]

Children, just like adults, need downtime, time to relax and unwind. Parents should take care to safeguard the home and to avoid the temptation of "doing it all." Instead, find ways to shield children as best you can from unrealistic and heavy demands. Remember the counsel of Elder Richard G. Scott, who said that "Satan has a powerful tool to use against good people. It is distraction. He would have good people fill life with 'good things' so there is no room for the essential ones."[18] Be sure not to neglect the essential need to strengthen the home with faith. Do not allow one child's talents to overtake parents' essential responsibilities to all family members. (See chapter 31 on protecting and balancing family time.)

UNDERSTANDING DIFFERENCES IN TEMPERAMENT

Almost a century ahead of modern child development research, President Brigham Young offered this insight to parents: "Bring up your children in the love and fear of the Lord; study their dispositions and their temperaments, and deal with them accordingly."[19] Scholars today recognize that each child is born into this world with an individual temperament.[20] *Temperament* is thought to be a set of traits that are observable early in life and remain fairly stable across situations and time. While there is still some disagreement about the specific dimensions of temperament, most scholars agree that children vary in terms of their *activity level* (how much a child moves about), *emotionality* (how the child typically responds emotionally to moment-to-moment events), *adaptability* (how flexible the child is to changes in routines), *sociability* (how outgoing or shy the child is), and *self-regulation* (how well the child is able to calm down or stay in control of his or her emotions and behaviors).[21]

Each child, even those in the same family, commonly differs along these dimensions of temperament. One child may be more irritable and become easily upset, another may be more active and have a greater need to constantly move about, and still another may be more shy or withdrawn and have difficulty adjusting to new people and experiences. A combination of these various traits may make some children more challenging to parents. However, studying and then recognizing your child's disposition, as President Young counseled, can go a long way in determining the best way to approach each child and to structure guidance that fits each child's disposition. Alexander Thomas and Stella Chess, scholars of child temperament, refer to this idea as developing "goodness-of-fit."[22] A good fit is achieved when a child's temperament meshes well with parents' demands and expectations and the structure of the home environment.

Adapting Parenting

Because of the innate quality of temperament, some characteristics in children may be difficult to change or may never change. Instead of trying to force their child to change, parents may need to change their own expectations and demands. This idea was reinforced by Elder James E. Faust: "Child rearing is so individualistic. Every child is different and unique. What works with one may not work with another. . . . It is a matter of prayerful discernment for the parents."[23] This approach to child rearing necessitates careful attention to children's qualities and recognizing and learning over time what works best for each child.

Elder Faust further explained that our parenting actions should be governed by the "overarching and undergirding" principle of love.[24] Love serves as the foundation upon which a parent learns to adapt to each child, especially as the child grows, changes, and matures toward adulthood. Sara Ruddick noted that "attentive love" is foundational to a parent's ability to serve the needs of children in appropriate ways. Citing the work of Iris Murdoch, Ruddick wrote:

> Attention to real children, children seen by the "patient eye of love, . . . teaches us how real things [real children] can be looked at and loved without being seized and used, without being appropriated into the greedy organism of the self." . . . The love of children is not only the most intense of attachments, but it is also a detachment, a giving up, a letting grow. . . . [It is seeing] the child's reality with the patient, loving eye of attention.[25]

As parents, it is important to invest the time to really come to know our children. It is also important that parents allow themselves to experience the joy that comes with parenting and to convey that joy to their children. Too often we see children only through our adult eyes, forgetting that our children and teens often see and experience their immediate world differently. Parents can spend quantity and quality one-on-one time with each child and learn about his or her hopes, fears, desires, qualities, and abilities. At the same time, we should be willing to allow our children to come to know us on these same terms in this process. Doing so can bring greater insight and greater wisdom in determining how best to approach each of our children and care for their varying needs.

Conclusion

In this chapter we have briefly touched on the proclamation concept that "each is a beloved spirit son or daughter of heavenly parents, and, as such, each has a divine nature and destiny."[26] Understanding our divine nature should strengthen our commitment to each family member. At the same time, while each of us shares a common divine lineage, we come with great variety in our individual characteristics, talents, and intelligence. Understanding these individual features helps us approach each of our children with a "loving eye of attention." In doing so, we can tailor our attempts at guidance to suit the needs of each child. Understanding common and individual patterns of human growth can help parents determine how best to "let grow."

Sister Patricia Holland related an experience that is illustrative. A musician herself, Sister Holland was anxious that her musically talented daughter, Mary, develop to her fullest potential. She noted: "I was convinced that Mary's talent would not be developed unless I lurked over her at the piano and, like Simon Legree, insistently supervised her practice."[27] As Mary moved into her teenage years, Sister Holland began to realize that this once useful motherly practice was placing an increasing strain on their relationship. She realized that there needed to be a change. So she "poured out [her] soul in prayer, seeking wisdom that could help [her] keep communication open with [her] daughter."[28] This heartfelt prayer resulted in the spiritual discernment and parental wisdom she needed to respond appropriately to her daughter. Sister Holland then left an apron on Mary's bed, with the strings cut off, and the following note tucked into a pocket:

> Dear Mary,
>
> I'm sorry for the conflict I have caused by acting like a federal marshal at the piano. I must have looked foolish there—just you and me and my six-shooter. Forgive me. You are becoming a young woman in your own right. I have only worried that you would not feel as fully confident and fulfilled as a woman if you left your talent unfinished.
>
> I love you.—Mom[29]

From this experience, Sister Holland learned to feel confident in her daughter's personal determination to continue developing her musical skill. She also learned that just as our Father in Heaven had to "let us go" to experience mortality and grow here on earth, each of us as parents must recognize those times when it is best to adapt our parenting and cut restraining apron strings. With these adaptations comes the realization that each child has power to choose his or her own destination. Our responsibility as parents is to strengthen children for their journey and to do our best, given our own abilities, talents, and characteristics, to set their feet upon the path that will return them to our Father in Heaven and fulfill their divine destinies.

ABOUT THE AUTHORS

Chris L. Porter received his Ph.D. in child development and family studies at Purdue University. He is currently an associate professor of marriage, family, and human development in the School of Family Life at Brigham Young University. He is married to the former Julie Ann McNeal and together they are the parents of three wonderful children.

Nancy B. Rollins received her Ph.D. in family studies from Brigham Young University. She teaches at Brigham Young University–Idaho in the Department of Child and Family Studies. She is the mother of seven amazing children, all of whom are married. They have blessed her with thirteen grandchildren (so far!).

ADDITIONAL READING

William B. Carey, with Martha M. Jablow (1997), *Understanding Your Child's Temperament* (New York: Macmillan).

H. Wallace Goddard and Larry C. Jensen (2000), Understanding and applying proclamation principles of parenting; in David C. Dollahite, ed., *Strengthening Our Families: An In-Depth Look at the Proclamation on the Family* (Salt Lake City: Bookcraft), 124–134.

Kathy Hirsh-Pasek, Roberta Michnick Golinkoff, and Diane Eyer (2003), *Einstein Never Used Flash Cards: How Our Children Really Learn—And Why They Need to Play More and Memorize Less* (New York: Rodale).

Mary Sheedy Kurcinka (1991), *Raising Your Spirited Child: A Guide for Parents Whose Child is More Intense, Perceptive, Persistent, Energetic* (New York: HarperCollins).

Robert J. Sternberg (1996), *Successful Intelligence: How Practical and Creative Intelligence Determine Success in Life* (New York: Simon & Schuster).

NOTES

1. Gordon B. Hinckley (1995, May), This is the work of the Master, *Ensign*, 25(5), 70.

2. Gordon B. Hinckley (1995, May), The light within you, *Ensign*, 25(5), 99.

3. John A. Widtsoe, sel. and arr. (1925), *Discourses of Brigham Young* (Salt Lake City: Deseret Book; reprint, Salt Lake City: Deseret Book, 1971), 391; page number is to the reprint.

4. Dallin H. Oaks (1993, November), The great plan of happiness, *Ensign*, 23(11), 72.

5. L. E. Berk, *Child Development*, 6th ed. (Boston: Pearson Education).

6. The Church of Jesus Christ of Latter-day Saints (1985), *A Parent's Guide* (Salt Lake City: The Church of Jesus Christ of Latter-day Saints); available at http://ldscatalog.com, no. 31123000.

7. Piaget's theory; in P. H. Mussen (Series Ed.) and W. Kessen (Vol. Ed.), *Handbook of Child Psychology: Formerly Carmichael's Manual of Child Psychology*, 4th ed. (1983), Vol. 1: *History, Theory, and Methods* (New York: Wiley), 103–108.

8. Gordon B. Hinckley (1997, July), Excerpts from recent addresses of President Gordon B. Hinckley, *Ensign*, 27(7), 73.

9. R. J. Sternberg (1997), *Thinking Styles* (New York: Cambridge University Press).

10. H. Gardner (1999), *Intelligence Reframed: Multiple Intelligences for the 21st Century* (New York: Basic Books).

11. Marvin J. Ashton (1987, November), There are many gifts, *Ensign*, 17(11), 20.

12. R. A. Emmons (1999), *The Psychology of Ultimate Concerns: Motivation and Spirituality in Personality* (New York: Guilford Press).

13. D. Zollinger (1975, February), When sibling rivalry strikes: How parents can diminish jealousy between their children, *Ensign, 5*(2), 53–56.

14. Jeffrey R. Holland (2002, May), The other prodigal, *Ensign, 32*(5), 63.

15. L. G. Katz (1993, summer), All about me, *American Educator,* 21.

16. D. Elkind (2001), *The Hurried Child: Growing Up Too Fast Too Soon,* 3rd ed. (Cambridge, MA: Perseus), 3.

17. C. H. Hart, et al. (1998), Stress behaviors and activity type participation of preschoolers in more and less developmentally appropriate classrooms: SES and sex differences, *Journal of Research in Childhood Education, 12,* 176–196.

18. Richard G. Scott (2001, May), First things first, *Ensign, 31*(5), 7.

19. Quoted in Widtsoe, sel. and arr. ([1925] 1971), 207.

20. M. K. Rothbart and J. E. Bates (1998), Temperament; in N. Eisenberg, ed., *Handbook of Child Psychology, volume 3: Social, Emotional, and Personality Development,* 5th ed. (New York: Wiley), 105–176.

21. T. D. Wachs (1999), The what, why, and how of temperament: A piece of the action; in L. Balter and C. S. Tamis-LeMonda, eds., *Child Psychology: A Handbook of Contemporary Issues* (Philadelphia: Psychology Press), 23–44.

22. A. Thomas and S. Chess (1977), *Temperament and Development* (New York: Bruner/Mazel); A. Thomas, S. Chess, H. G. Birch, M. E. Hertzig, and S. Korn (1963), *Behavioral Individuality in Early Childhood* (New York: New York University Press).

23. James E. Faust (1990, November), The greatest challenge in the world—Good parenting, *Ensign, 20*(11), 34.

24. Ibid.

25. S. Ruddick (1984), Maternal thinking, in J. Trebilcot, ed., *Mothering: Essays in Feminist Theory* (Totowa, NJ: Rowman & Allanheld), 223–224; internal quote from I. Murdoch (1971), *The Sovereignty of Good* (New York: Shocken Books), 65.

26. First Presidency and Council of Twelve Apostles (1995, November), The family: A proclamation to the world, *Ensign, 25*(11), 102.

27. Patricia Holland and Mary Holland (1985, November), Cutting the apron strings, *New Era,* Young Women Special Issue, *15*(11), 11.

28. Ibid., 12.

29. Ibid., 11.

CHAPTER 17

REARING CHILDREN IN LOVE AND RIGHTEOUSNESS

JULIE H. HAUPT, CRAIG H. HART, AND LLOYD D. NEWELL

*Parents have a sacred duty to rear their children in love and righteousness, to provide for
their physical and spiritual needs, to teach them to love and serve one another, [and] to observe the
commandments of God. . . . Husbands and wives—mothers and fathers—will be held
accountable before God for the discharge of these obligations.[1]*
—"The Family: A Proclamation to the World"

The Book of Mormon records a tender moment in the Savior's ministry among the Nephites: "And he took their little children, one by one, and blessed them, and prayed unto the Father for them. . . . And he spake unto the multitude, and said unto them: Behold your little ones. . . . And they saw the heavens open, and they saw angels descending out of heaven . . . and the angels did minister unto them" (3 Nephi 17:21, 23, 24). This account conveys the depth of the Savior's love for children, His kindness toward them, and His desire to bless them. As we seek to fulfill our sacred duty as parents to "rear [our] children in love and righteousness,"[2] this passage of scripture can provide a pattern.[3] In this chapter, we will consider practical ways to individualize childrearing and minimize parenting difficulties. We emphasize prophetic teachings that can help parents fulfill their sacred responsibilities.

In the Book of Mormon account, the Savior called each child to come to Him, one by one. He considered their needs, bestowed blessings, and offered prayers for them. Earlier, He had ministered to the sick and afflicted, "and he did heal them every one as they were brought forth unto him" (3 Nephi 17:9). While principles and covenants were introduced to the multitude as He spoke to those assembled at Bountiful, His ministering in the Americas and in the Old World was characteristically bestowed on individuals—one by one. Likewise, our ministry as

parents among our children will best be accomplished as we consider their individual needs, pray to the Father for help, and welcome the assistance of many who will act as angels in our children's lives.

Our Heavenly Father's plan for families includes the education and sanctification of parents as well as children through the parenting process. Parents and children must learn to be "submissive, meek, humble, patient, full of love, [and] willing to submit to all things which the Lord seeth fit to inflict upon [them]" (Mosiah 3:19). Rearing our children in love and righteousness, nurturing our children's strengths, and helping them overcome their weaknesses require steadfast commitment, often in the face of trying circumstances. Lest we be discouraged, we can pray for inspiration in developing a long-term vision that allows us to "behold [our] little ones" (3 Nephi 17:23) and chart a steady course, moving forward with a "brightness of hope" (2 Nephi 31:20).

No greater joy in life can come to parents than to see their children grow up in light and truth (see 3 John 1:4), hold firm to the iron rod, learn from triumphs as well as disappointments, and become responsible adults as well as loving parents. But things may not always work out the way that parents hope. Ultimately, the person a child becomes is not entirely up to the parents. Children's choices may or may not reflect the teachings and guidance they received in their youth (see chapter 26). Instead of saving all the joy for a hoped-for outcome (for the moment when children marry well, serve a mission, or graduate from college), parents who enjoy the journey have many rewards. One mother will never forget the time her kindergartner asked if he could take a picture of her to school with him—just in case he might feel lonely. A couple will cherish the Saturday mornings when all of the kids piled into the parents' bed and read stories together. A father will smile whenever he hears the song that played while he danced with his sixth grader at the school Valentine's dance. Parents will cry a little when they re-read the note they found stuffed in their scriptures one morning. They'll laugh a little inside as they watch their teenaged son fumble for the right words when trying to impress a young woman. While parenting surely has its heartache and sorrow, its anxiety and disquieting moments, it can also be full of fun, lightheartedness, and happiness. Truly, it can be one of our greatest blessings and a source of some of our deepest joys.

MINISTERING ONE BY ONE

As each new child joins the family unit, parents discover and are often amazed by the differences in the personalities, interests, talents, and dispositions of their children. President Brigham Young encouraged parents to "study [children's] dispositions and their temperaments, and deal with them accordingly."[4] While family rules and gospel principles can be taught and applied in the home generally, each child will require encouragement, guidance, and interactions that are uniquely fitted to his or her needs. (Chapter 16 provides suggestions for parenting that strengthens each family member.)

Children come from our Heavenly Father "trailing clouds of glory"[5]; they also come with unique purposes and missions to perform. One conscientious mother spoke of coming to appreciate her daughter's potential and unique personality. She said that during adolescence the daughter surprised her by going in a different direction than she had anticipated. "It's much like preparing and placing an apple pie into the oven, only to find when taking it out that it's actually a chocolate cake. It's not that I don't like chocolate cake, it's just that it took some getting used to." Since parents can't place orders, it's no wonder that the complexities of each child's makeup provide opportunities for discovery of new and surprising characteristics at different times across development.

Researchers have described children's behavioral styles as *temperaments*. Parents notice these kinds of differences from the child's earliest days. Some babies are active, some easy to comfort, some very impulsive, and some easily irritated. While the dimensions of temperament appear to be inborn characteristics of the child,[6] they are by no means unchangeable.[7] For example, one father noted the tendency of his 3-year-old to cling to the familiar, desire lots of affection and playful interaction with her parents, and yet act shyly in the presence of those not in her immediate family. As the father took time each night to check his business volume periodically on the computer, he held his daughter on his lap. During the hour before her bedtime when she was tired and settling down from a busy 3-year-old day, he provided this quiet time for her to be cuddled in the context of a relaxed, nonthreatening activity. This consistent, no-pressure, daddy-daughter time was suited to her needs. Building upon those secure moments, she later began to venture out more confidently. As in this example, children's temperaments can provide valuable clues to parents about their desired modes of interaction.[8] Parents' reading of a child's cues and responding sensitively to the child's temperament is what researchers refer to as "goodness of fit."[9]

While a good fit between a child's temperament and a parent's practices is not always easy to achieve, research indicates that a good fit is an important part of promoting healthy growth and development.[10] Parents may find that frustration is reduced and parent-child relationships are more rewarding when they give themselves permission to adapt parenting interactions to their children's individual needs.[11] It takes courage to face parenting challenges and make adjustments for children's personalities and needs. More free-spirited teens, for example, may require careful monitoring and parental limits in potentially dangerous aspects of their lives, while allowing for growth that comes through expressing their individuality in "safer" domains of adolescent experience. Alternatively, more naturally compliant siblings may require less oversight, but perhaps more reassurance, emotional support, and encouragement. As Brigham Young taught, this study of children's temperaments and dispositions is an important guide in properly teaching and relating to our children. In pursuing such a course, we can let go of unrealistic expectations, find joy in the personality of each child, and enjoy mutually beneficial interactions. In short, we will find ways to minister as the Savior did, one by one.

CONSIDERING EACH CHILD'S NEEDS AND RESOLVING DIFFICULTIES

Through latter-day revelation, God has provided wisdom that can guide us in parenting. "The Family: A Proclamation to the World" lists nine key principles that can help parents strengthen their families and resolve difficulties. These include "faith, prayer, repentance, forgiveness, respect, love, compassion, work, and wholesome recreational activities."[12] Parents can trust that parenting approaches clearly built on proclamation principles will ultimately help in resolving challenges with individual children. Elder Francisco J. Vinas said:

> These principles, once applied, will act as a light that will illuminate each member of the family and, in a progressive way, will lead us to integrate other related values and principles which will strengthen family relationships.[13]

In desperate moments when we are at a loss for what to do to help a struggling child, the inspiration of the Holy Ghost can guide us in applying these principles to individual situations. Being open to this guidance will help things turn out better than had we relied solely on our own judgment and wisdom.

Even when we are doing our best, there are times when parenting challenges increase—taxing our strength, testing our faith, helping us grow, and requiring more sacrifice than we had imagined would be required. Some children place heavy demands on emotional, financial, psychological, and spiritual family resources (essays F1, F2, and H4 address some of these challenges). Rather than simply wringing our hands and giving up, we can take "fresh courage"[14] as we prayerfully seek the guidance of the Lord.

A healthy style of parenting forms the basis for day-to-day interactions with children and for working through these challenging situations. In researching the effects of parenting style, social scientists have found that both the "permissive" and "coercive" styles of parenting are less effective than "authoritative" (sometimes called "democratic") parenting.[15] Authoritative parenting emphasizes three interdependent elements: (1) a strong connection or parent-child relationship, (2) the appropriate use of regulation or limit setting to help children develop self-control and establish socially acceptable behavior, and (3) the granting of autonomy to the degree to which the child is prepared for such responsibility by respecting agency and teaching choice and accountability.[16]

GOSPEL RESOURCES FOR PARENTING

In the challenges of parenting, the Lord has not left families without direction. The words of apostles and prophets will guide parents as they seek to build homes in which each family member is valued, loved, and taught. Readers may find much of value at www.mormon.org under "parenting tips." A BYU website, foreverfamilies.byu.edu, also provides excellent resources. The following general conference addresses and many others related to parenting can be accessed on-line at www.lds.org.

Gordon B. Hinckley (1993, November), Bring up a child in the way he should go, *Ensign, 23*(11), 54–60.

Jeffrey R. Holland (2003, May), A prayer for the children, *Ensign, 33*(5), 85–87.

Coleen K. Menlove (2005, May), All thy children shall be taught, *Ensign, 35*(5), 13–15.

Boyd K. Packer (1983, May), Agency and control, *Ensign, 13*(5), 66–68.

Boyd K. Packer (2002, May), Children, *Ensign, 32*(5), 7–10.

Boyd K. Packer (1998, November), Parents in Zion, *Ensign, 28*(11), 22–24.

Box 17.1

Imagine for a moment that children have inside them their own "music" to make. As they begin to perform, a skilled mentor-musician (parent) is prepared to assist. The mentor introduces new instruments and sounds to add to the repertoire, then stands at the sound mixer to help control volume and achieve proper balance. The music lifts and edifies the parent and the children. Together, they create something better than either could have anticipated. This analogy emphasizes that parent–child relationships are dyadic. In other words, while parents will have a significant effect upon their child, the child will also affect the way parents choose to interact with him or her.[17] Each learns from the other.

As mentors, parents are not responsible for composing the music, but for enhancing it. Allowing for individualization and encouraging the unique elements of our children's personalities can be a joyful process. We may find that one child's creative need is met by building things, another is fulfilled by drawing, and still another enjoys sports and keeping track of team and player standings. Watching for those moments when a child is enlivened by what he or she is doing is truly fulfilling for parents. One father who struggled to assemble things found that his son had a real knack for it. A mother who had difficulty decorating noticed that her daughter was energized by the process. Another family found that riding horses brought great joy to their child and helped the entire family more fully appreciate the wonders of creation. When we help our children develop their God-given abilities, our children feel more appreciated and are less likely to be suffocated by comparisons with siblings. Effectively assisting our children will depend upon our abilities to build connections, set limits, and promote appropriate levels of autonomy.

Build Connections

Imagine on the "parenting mixer board" three dials that represent the three components of authoritative parenting. Authoritative parenting would dial high on connection (a loving and strong parent–child relationship). Our children will always need our unconditional love. President Brigham Young said, "Kind looks, kind actions, kind words, and a lovely, holy deportment towards them will bind our children to us with bands that cannot easily be broken; while abuse and unkindness will drive them from us."[18]

Children in the same family will have different preferences for support and affection. While one may prefer sitting with a parent's arm around him, another may prefer a roughhousing kind of physical affection. Support is also evidenced as parents attend children's extracurricular events and take an interest in their talent areas. While all children need similar types of support, some children require more of a listening ear, while others may find greater satisfaction in seeing a parent in the stands, cheering.

Our children will benefit from our time, interest, and support throughout their developing years. President Ezra Taft Benson provided this counsel: "Take time to be a real friend to your children. Listen to your children, really listen. Talk with them, laugh and joke with them, sing with them, play with them, cry with them, hug them, honestly praise them. Yes, regularly spend unrushed one-on-one time with each child. Be a real friend to your children."[19] President Gordon B. Hinckley encouraged, "Fathers, be kind to your children. Be companionable with them."[20] All this takes significant time and energy. Elder M. Russell Ballard, speaking to mothers, advised: "Mothers must not fall into the trap of believing that 'quality' time can replace 'quantity' time. Quality is a

direct function of quantity—and mothers, to nurture their children properly, must provide both. To do so requires constant vigilance and a constant juggling of competing demands. It is hard work, no doubt about it."[21]

The research literature clearly warns parents not to use the parent–child connection "against" the child by engaging in "love withdrawal" and other harmful forms of psychological manipulation.[22] As parent–child connection forms the foundation for the relationship, threatening to take it away, even for a time, puts the relationship on unstable footing. Like our Heavenly Father, we need to be the kind of parent who can convey unconditional love to a child despite his or her choices, always and forever. Elder Robert D. Hales counseled parents to remember that when their teenagers begin testing family values and make poor choices, "this is the time for added love and support and to reinforce your teachings on how to make choices"[23] (see essay F1 on guiding teens).

Set Limits

A strong connection between parent and child forms the foundation for effective correction, or the second "dial," which is limit-setting. Attempting to correct a child's behavior without a warm, loving relationship is like making heavy withdrawals on a bank account with few deposits. President Brigham Young counseled, "I will here say to parents, that kind words and loving actions towards children will subdue their uneducated nature a great deal better than the rod, or, in other words, than physical punishment."[24] Elder Ballard further counseled: "Parents need to set limits in accordance with the importance of the matter involved and the child's disposition and maturity. . . . Help children understand the reasons for rules, and always follow through with appropriate discipline when rules are broken."[25]

Authoritative parents find that learning to set the "limits dial" to its appropriate moderate level is a challenge. Surely, high expectations motivate children to succeed. However, when parental expectations are based upon parents' own unfulfilled dreams, a desire to keep up with the neighbors' children, or as a basis for parents' own self-worth, the dial is likely to be set inappropriately.

It is helpful to recognize that children will often outgrow some of the behaviors associated with their age that may be annoying, disturbing, or inconvenient. The Lord taught the prophet Mormon that "little children are whole, for they are not capable of committing sin" (Moroni 8:8). Children's errors during the early childhood period are their experiments in the laboratory of life. Our response can emphasize teaching, guiding, explaining, helping, and perhaps gently removing children physically from a problem situation.[26]

Encourage Independence

Finally, parents will need to properly set the third "dial," autonomy, which refers to appropriate levels of independence. As children grow and demonstrate their ability to handle new challenges and new situations, parents will do well to allow and encourage the development of their autonomy. Elder M. Russell Ballard taught:

> Helping children learn how to make decisions requires that parents give them a measure of autonomy, dependent on the age and maturity of the child and the situation at hand. Parents need to give children choices and should be prepared to appropriately adjust some rules, thus preparing children for real-world situations.[27]

Strengthening children's autonomy can be done in a variety of ways, such as providing children choices within limits and allowing them to make their own decisions whenever reasonable and possible.[28] A daughter of Sister Marjorie Pay Hinckley remarked: "My mother taught me some basic philosophies of rearing children. One is that you have to trust children. I tried hard never to say 'no' if I could possibly say 'yes.' I think that worked well because it gave my children the feeling that I trusted them and they were responsible to do the best they could."[29]

A daughter of President Heber J. Grant explained the way his parenting approach encouraged responsibility:

> In matters of small importance, father seldom said "No" to us. Consequently, when he did say "No," we knew he meant it. His training allowed us to make our own decisions whenever possible. He always explained very patiently just why he thought a certain procedure was unwise and then he would say, "That's the way I feel about it; but of course, you must decide for yourself." As a result, our decision was usually the same as his. He was able somehow to motivate us to want to do the right thing rather than to be *forced* to do it.[30] (See Box 17.2, "Respecting Agency.")

An "autonomy dial" set too high can result in overly permissive parenting. Research indicates that while children of permissive parents feel love, they may not develop the self-control and socially acceptable behaviors that allow them to function most productively in society.[31] As Elder Joe J. Christensen warned: "We should avoid spoiling children by giving them too much. In our day, many children grow up with distorted values because we as parents overindulge them. . . . One of the most important things we can teach our children is to deny themselves. Instant gratification generally makes for weak people."[32]

A dial set too low in this dimension can also result in a kind of overprotectiveness that may "protect" children from the very experiences they need for growth. Such parenting often results in childhood withdrawal from peers, problems in decision making, and not being accountable for one's behavior.[33] In a child's younger years, parents will need to make many decisions about the level of responsibility a child can handle. Later, during important discussions with an older child, parents will undoubtedly emphasize the wise use of agency and accountability for choices. Parents may need to dial back and make adjustments when children prove untrustworthy for a time. As they are able, children can regain privileges and become deserving of new ones. Parents can learn to guide behavior in ways that allow their children to develop independence, learn to make good choices, and express their own personalities and talents.

Sister Hinckley told about a call she received from one of her daughters about her son's swimming lessons. "All the mothers were tossing their reluctant, screaming children into the teacher's outstretched arms in the pool," she explained to her mother. She just couldn't bring herself to do the same. When she asked for her mother's advice, Sister Hinckley's statement was classic: "Just save the relationship." The daughter later reflected, "I believe those words are the most simple and powerful parenting principle I have ever learned."[34] As we consider and respect each child's needs, we will save relationships and build a firm footing from which all of our other parenting decisions can spring, especially when parenting gets tough.

PARENTING PARTNERSHIPS

The proclamation designates two parents as the ideal model for rearing children. While many must make adaptations to individual circumstances, families

RESPECTING AGENCY

Sherrie Mills Johnson

Moral agency is the ability to choose between good and evil. This principle is so fundamental to the plan of happiness that God Himself will not interfere with the use of it. As Brigham Young explained, "The volition of the creature is free; this is a law of their existence, and the Lord cannot violate his own law; were he to do that he would cease to be God."[35] As parents, we disregard basic laws of the gospel when we try to force our children (D&C 121:36–39). While coercive tactics may bring about immediate compliance, they may create long term problems caused by the negative emotions they produce in our children. Research shows that children and teens are more likely to exercise their agency by voluntarily conforming to righteous parental expectations when a kind, patient, persuasive, and long-suffering approach is taken (D&C 121:41–43).[36]

How do we help our children to use their agency to make wise choices? One of the best things we can do is to educate their consciences so that they can govern themselves. President Boyd K. Packer referred to this as doing "what we are commissioned to do, to foster the Light of Christ, which is within every soul we meet."[37] To help do this, we can teach our children the following:

- What agency is, its importance to their salvation, and how best to use it (John 6:38; 7:17; 2 Nephi 2:27; D&C 19:24; 29:35).
- That there are eternal consequences to every moral decision (Mosiah 2:24; D&C 130:20–21).
- That it is through making correct choices that they gain faith. Elder Bruce R. McConkie wrote: "Faith is a gift of God bestowed as a reward for personal righteousness. It is always given when righteousness is present, and the greater the measure of obedience to God's laws, the greater will be the endowment of faith."[38]
- To take responsibility for their own actions. For example, when a toddler runs into a chair, it is a mistake to comfort the child by blaming the chair; or when a teenager fails a test, to blame the teacher for making the test too hard.
- To pay attention to their own consciences and follow promptings when making a decision. When children are capable, don't make decisions for them. (Helaman 14:30–31; Moroni 7:16).
- To think through alternatives. You can practice this by asking "What if?" questions. "What if someone offered you drugs?" or, "What if someone wanted you to skip Sunday School?"
- That all actions have consequences. You help them to recognize this when you follow though with consequences you establish (D&C 121:43).

One mother struggled with an exceptionally stubborn 5-year-old daughter. One day when the daughter lied about having eaten her lunch, the mother, instead of accusing, lecturing, and contending with the child as she usually did, merely said, "You know what is right and you know what is wrong." She was surprised a few minutes later to find that instead of the usual tantrum, the daughter retrieved the hidden sandwich and ate it. The daughter's conscience led her in ways the mother could not.

The conscience is a powerful tool. It will correctly guide children of all ages to use their agency wisely. Parents may focus their energies on educating the conscience and teaching gospel principles rather than attempting to force children's compliance.

Box 17.2

with two parents in the home can benefit from the power of an effective parenting partnership.[39] (See chapter 21 on parenting issues related specifically to single parents.) Partnering can be helpful when one parent's level of frustration is reaching the boiling point. Signaling that it is time for a break, the frustrated parent can take a walk around the block, while the other parent, who has been less involved in the situation, can take over. Parents in strong partnerships will avoid "keeping score" and will seek to find ways to serve the needs of the family by leading and supporting as needed.

Research shows that when parents work together, they combine complementary strengths in ways that help children best meet their potential.[40] President James E. Faust said: "It is useless to debate which parent is most important. . . . Both fathers and mothers do many intrinsically different things for their children. Both are equipped to nurture children, but their approaches are different. . . . Parents in any marital situation have a duty to set aside personal differences and encourage each other's righteous influence in the lives of their children."[41]

Homes run more smoothly when parents work together to support rather than criticize one another's childrearing efforts. For example, a bedtime routine with one parent might consist of a story, a song, a prayer, and a kiss. The other parent might let a younger child ride on his or her back to the bedroom and offer a hug.

Within the authoritative parenting style, there is plenty of room for different parenting personalities. For example, while the consistency of both parents' taking an authoritative approach to parenting is important, differences in this approach can be complementary and helpful in a family setting. For example, North American research shows that fathers are typically more physically playful with children and more likely to encourage risk taking (e.g., promoting higher climbs on jungle gyms), while mothers are more protective and involved in caretaking and nurturing activities.[42] Some cases may not be so gender specific. One parent may be a stickler about bedtimes and no food outside the kitchen, while another parent puts a foot down on certain safety issues, schoolwork, or expectations for quality completion of family chores. One parent takes the lead in teaching children to garden, while another shares his or her love of camping with the family. Indeed, spouses need not have, nor may they want to have the same approach; their differences can ultimately enhance their children's opportunities to learn from two different people. While serious differences in philosophy and parenting style may need to be discussed, differences within the same style can be supported and celebrated. (See essay B2 and essay B3 on the topic of marital differences.)

CROSSING THE LINE

One of the greatest challenges of parenting is discerning on a daily basis, from situation to situation, when parents are being too hard on a child (coercive) and when parents are being too soft (permissive). As President Faust counseled:

> Every child is different and unique. What works with one may not work with another. I do not know who is wise enough to say what discipline is too harsh or what is too lenient except the parents of the children themselves, who love them most. It is a matter of prayerful discernment for the parents. Certainly the overarching and undergirding principle is that the discipline of children must be motivated more by love than by punishment.[43]

When reasonable family rules are established and expectations are set, some behaviors can obviously be considered as "crossing the line." Yet, all parents know that extenuating circumstances arise. Sometimes, the "rules committee" has not actually taken a stance on a newly introduced issue. At times, a rule infraction may be due to an unfortunate set of circumstances rather than a defiant, disobedient child. Sometimes, a minor infraction can properly be ignored, if it proves to be a one-time offense or is to be expected under the circumstances. On occasion, holding the child at fault may be counterproductive and even unfair. For example, expecting a bored, tired 10-year-old to be on his best behavior for the last 15 minutes of a long drive may be an unrealistic expectation. A teenager may get a poor grade due to unrealistic teaching demands relative to the teen's developmental level rather than for lack of effort. Justifiably, parents may feel they are often walking a tightrope.

The spirit of discernment is needed to determine which kinds of behavior cross the line. The promptings of the Spirit, coupled with the study of credible resources on child and adolescent development, can help parents address problems early on, understand what behaviors are normal and expected, and remain patient rather than resorting to extreme reactions when children "cross the line." Like weeds, problems are easier to uproot when they are still developing a presence in the garden and have not had time to rob resources and space.

One parent came to rely upon an internal alert system (i.e., "red flags flying") to help her decide when she or her child crossed the line into unacceptable behavior and needed to be held responsible. Patience and a willingness to explain expectations and guide behavior were generally the norm in her home and the children were generally well behaved. However, red flags flew, for example, when the 3-year-old child in a burst of anger began to kick her, or when her 8-year-old child became increasingly unwilling to participate in Saturday morning chores, or when her teenager refused to go to church. These "red flag" realizations helped her to recognize when the patient, tolerant, understanding approach needed to be exchanged for "putting her foot down." For example, she chose to physically restrain the kicking 3-year-old; provided the 8-year-old with a clear consequence of no friends until the work was done; and discovered over lunch with her daughter that lack of church attendance was associated with being excluded by girls in her class. In the latter case, rather than imposing consequences or incentives, the mother worked with youth leaders to help ensure that church was a more inviting place to be.

Red flags can also fly when parents feel frustrated and resort to such practices as yelling, threatening, withdrawing love, and excessive lecturing. With increased self-awareness and practice, parents can learn to notice and control the angry thoughts and feelings that precede these ineffective parenting behaviors. Research suggests that parents who maintain at least a 5- or 6-to-1 ratio of positive to negative interactions with their children and teens have more stable and adaptive relationships with them.[44] When parents have made mistakes, sincere apologies can open doors and strengthen, rather than weaken, the parents' authority and the children's respect for their parents.

In handling parenting challenges, knowledge of typical developmental characteristics and a keen eye of observation toward other children of the same age group can be useful. Carefully studying troubling patterns can help parents to determine whether behaviors fit into normal, expected patterns. In some cases, minor infractions and annoying behaviors may need to be tolerated until the child grows out of these developmental tendencies.

The common fallacy that behavioral issues evident with children at one age will only get worse at another can cause parents unnecessary distress. This idea reflects a belief that development is a simple linear trajectory rather than a complex, divinely ordained progression through various ages that are each associated with a set of typical characteristics. These normal, expected behaviors do not constitute a "crossing of the line." They will require some teaching, some forbearance, some intervention, and much patience.

If the troubling behavior is common to the age but is highly pronounced and begins interfering with healthy development, parents may need to take additional steps to educate themselves in addressing this behavior pattern. For example, parental action is needed when a child becomes so picky and demanding that mealtimes are unpleasant and adequate nutrition is impossible, or when a teen spends so much time with friends that school grades are steadily declining and household chores are not getting

done.[45] Research shows that the developmental forces that tug at older children and teens will require some compromise to create patterns of interaction that both parent and child can live with.[46] For example, a schedule for getting homework done may need to be negotiated with the teen, while allowing time for friends. Perhaps the schedule for accomplishing chores can also be negotiated to better meet his other needs, while still allowing him to accomplish the required tasks. Allowing teens to exercise their autonomy at this age by providing input in the decision-making process increases the likelihood of compliance to parental expectations.

PUNITIVE PARENTING

It is common but misguided thinking that if all the other compassionate, helpful, good-hearted parenting practices don't work with a child, then authoritarian or coercive parenting, including the use of physical punishment, is an acceptable last resort. Parents may feel social pressure in more difficult situations with their children to try these short-term, quick fixes to incite immediate reaction and even newfound compliance. However, moving to extremes in parenting practices tends to upset balances that have taken many months, even years, to set in place. Some research suggests that for younger children in a warm, supportive parent–child relationship, an occasional nonabusive swat on the behind may help capture their attention so that the inappropriateness of a misdeed can be better taught. Other research suggests that such punishment can produce resentment and more misbehavior.[47] However, any type of physical coercion with older children and teens has consistently been shown to increase oppositional behavior.

Parents should keep in mind that the gospel teaches us that coercive tactics are not the ultimate answer to difficulties with children. Coercion may damage the parent–child relationship, prevent the opportunity to find mutual resolution to the problem, and interfere with long-term solutions that would ultimately prove more effective.[48] President Hinckley counseled: "Of course, there is need for discipline with families. But discipline with severity, discipline with cruelty inevitably leads not to correction but rather to resentment and bitterness. It cures nothing and only aggravates the problem. It is self-defeating."[49] President Joseph F. Smith also spoke to this theme: "Use no lash and no violence, but . . . approach them with reason, with persuasion and love unfeigned. . . .

The man that will be angry at his boy, and try to correct him while he is in anger, is in the greatest fault. . . . You can only correct your children by love, in kindness, by love unfeigned, by persuasion, and reason."[50]

Paradoxically, times of correcting misbehavior offer some of our best opportunities to demonstrate concern, strengthen relationships, and show forth an increase of love (see D&C 121:43–44). Correcting "betimes" (D&C 121:43), or in a well-timed way, can prove crucial to our children's safety and optimal development. One mother recalls taking her own children and some neighbor children for a walk to the park. The neighbor's 6-year-old son became upset and began running away. To this mother's horror, he ran into a busy street and began weaving back and forth on the road as he ran. She left the other children with strict instructions to stay where they were and ran as fast as she could. She was relieved that there were no cars on the road at the time, but was desperate to get to him before the inevitable wave of traffic came. As soon as she caught up with him, she grabbed him by the collar, swept him up into her arms, and then held him as they panted on the sidewalk. He defiantly commented, "You pinched my neck!" Tearfully, this mother replied, "I pinched your neck to save your life!"

Often our children and teens resent the consequences we may impose for misbehavior. They may moan, murmur, rationalize, or disagree. However, we can remember in those times of necessary correction that we may be "pinching their necks" now in order to save their lives later. Kind feelings toward the disobedient child are often possible when parents have maintained their cool during the incident. This requires separating feelings about the behavior from loving feelings toward the child. Over time, working through these moments of strain and difficulty can prove to children that our overriding love for them and concern for their welfare is what motivates us to be firm and consistent in our parenting role (see D&C 121:44).

CONCLUSION

As we face daily parenting challenges, we can call upon our Heavenly Father through prayer. We can seek to individualize our parenting and provide the environment and counsel that each child needs. We can grow through the demanding moments and difficult challenges we face as we teach our children "to walk uprightly before the Lord" (D&C 68:28). As we do this, we will find joy and wisdom beyond our own and our hearts will draw near to our children. We may not be able to solve all problems, but we and our children will be strengthened to face those problems.

Our opportunity to bless our children may come in unexpected and important ways, turning seemingly transitory moments into memorable experiences. One night after basketball practice, a 10-year-old boy was more quiet than usual. His mother sensed that he needed to talk. She invited her husband to come away from the other children to sit alone with their son. It didn't take more than a minute before the son started to cry. Pouring out feelings of rejection, the boy explained that some boys had been unkind to him. The father carefully listened with his arm around his son. He didn't try to solve the problem. He asked questions that would help his son to sort through his feelings. The wise father didn't hurry the son. He listened and listened and then said, "I wish I could take away the pain you're feeling." Then in a moment of intense bonding, the son hugged his father and said, "It feels like you already have." That's what good parenting is about: strengthening our children to navigate the storms of life and learning, with them, to follow the pattern provided by our Savior, Jesus Christ.

ABOUT THE AUTHORS

Julie H. Haupt is a part-time faculty member in Marriage, Family, and Human Development at Brigham Young University and the managing editor of this volume. She and her husband, Bob, have three children.

Craig H. Hart is recent chair of Marriage, Family, and Human Development at BYU and a Zina Young Williams Card Endowed University Professor. His cross-cultural research focuses on parenting and children's social adjustment. His Church service has included callings as a bishop in Louisiana and a counselor in a Springville, Utah, stake presidency. Craig and his wife, Kerstine, are parents of four children.

Lloyd D. Newell has a Ph.D. from BYU, where he is on the faculties of Religious Education and the School of Family Life. He has spoken to organizations in 45 states and a dozen countries and is the author of numerous books. Karmel and Lloyd are the parents of Hayley, McKay, Abigail, and Jacob.

ADDITIONAL READING

Marjorie V. Fields and Debby Q. Fields (2006, in press), *Constructive Guidance and Discipline for Early Childhood Education*, 4th ed. (Upper Saddle River, NJ: Merrill Prentice Hall).
John Gottman with Joan DeClaire (1997), *The Heart of Parenting: How to Raise an Emotionally Intelligent Child* (New York: Simon & Schuster).

Craig H. Hart (2004, Spring and Summer issues), What children need from parents, *Marriage & Families*, 12–18 and 16–23; available on-line at http://marriageandfamilies.byu.edu

Craig H. Hart, Lloyd D. Newell, and Lisa L. Sine (2000), Proclamation-based principles of parenting and supportive scholarship; in David C. Dollahite, ed., *Strengthening Our Families: An In-Depth Look at the Proclamation on the Family* (Salt Lake City: Bookcraft), 100–123.

Jane Nelsen, Lynn Lott, and H. Stephen Glenn (1999), *Positive Discipline—A to Z* (Rocklin, CA: Prima Publishing).

NOTES

1. First Presidency and Council of Twelve Apostles (1995, November), The family: A proclamation to the world, *Ensign,* 25(11), 102.

2. Ibid.

3. Many of the practical parenting applications presented in this chapter stem from C. H. Hart, L. D. Newell, and L. L. Sine (2000), Proclamation-based principles of parenting and supportive scholarship; in D. C. Dollahite, ed., *Strengthening Our Families: An In-Depth Look at the Proclamation on the Family* (Salt Lake City: Bookcraft), 100–123.

4. John A. Widtsoe, ed. (1978), *Discourses of Brigham Young* (Salt Lake City: Deseret Book), 207.

5. William Wordsworth (1807), *Ode: Intimations of Immortality from Recollections of Early Childhood,* 4.62–66; reprint, M. H. Abrams, ed. (1993) *Norton Anthology of English Literature,* 7th ed. (New York: W. W. Norton), 2:189–193. Wordsworth wrote, "Not in entire forgetfulness, / And not in utter nakedness, / But trailing clouds of glory do we come / From God, who is our home: / Heaven lies about us in our infancy!"

6. See Hart, Newell, and Sine (2000).

7. Neal A. Maxwell (1996, November), According to the desire of [our] hearts, *Ensign,* 26(11), 21–23; Hart, Newell, and Sine (2000); see also C. H. Hart, L. D. Newell, and S. F. Olsen (2003), Parenting skills and social-communicative competence in childhood, in J. O. Greene and B. R. Burleson, eds., *Handbook of Communication and Social Interaction Skills* (Mahwah, NJ: Lawrence Erlbaum Associates), 753–797.

8. A. Russell, C. H. Hart, C. C. Robinson, and S. F. Olsen (2003), Children's sociable and aggressive behavior with peers: A comparison of the U.S. and Australia, and contributions of temperament and parenting styles, *International Journal of Behavioral Development, 27,* 74–86; C. L. Porter, C. H. Hart, C. Yang, C. C. Robinson, S. F. Olsen, Q. Zeng (in press), A comparative study of child temperament and parenting in Beijing, China, and the Western United States, *International Journal of Behavioral Development.*

9. A. Thomas and S. Chess (1977), *Temperament and Development* (New York: Brunner/Mazel); A. Thomas, S. Chess, H. G. Birch, M. E. Hertzig, and S. Korn (1963), *Behavioral Individuality in Early Childhood* (New York: New York University Press).

10. Hart, Newell, and Olsen (2003).

11. For practical examples, see C. H. Hart (2004, Spring and Summer issues), What children need from parents, *Marriage & Families,* 12–18 and 16–23; available at http://marriageandfamilies.byu.edu

12. First Presidency and Council of Twelve Apostles (1995), 102.

13. Francisco J. Viñas (2004, May), Applying the simple and plain gospel principles in the family, *Ensign, 34*(5), 38.

14. W. Clayton (1985), Come, come, ye saints; in *Hymns of The Church of Jesus Christ of Latter-day Saints* (Salt Lake City: The Church of Jesus Christ of Latter-day Saints), 30.

15. See Hart, Newell, and Sine (2000); see also Hart, Newell, and Olsen (2003).

16. For additional practical application of these elements, see C. H. Hart (2003, Spring), Three essential parenting principles, *BYU Magazine,* available at http://magazine.byu.edu. Elder M. Russell Ballard noted: "Parents need to be consistent and loving, taking into account each child's unique nature and disposition; setting appropriate limits to acceptable behavior, including modest dress, clean language, and dignified appearance; and then allowing each child his or her needed autonomy." M. Russell Ballard (in press), The sacred responsibilities of parenthood, *Ensign;* Brigham Young University Education Week Devotional Address, (2003, August 19); available at http://speeches.byu.edu

17. This is often referred to as *co-regulation* in the research literature. The dynamics of this bidirectional process change significantly across childhood and adolescence. See W. A. Collins and S. D. Madsen (2003), Developmental change in parenting interactions; in L. Kuczynski, ed., (2003) *Handbook of Dynamics in Parent-Child Relations* (Thousand Oaks, CA: Sage), 49–61.

18. Brigham Young (1864, December 7), *Deseret News,* 2.

19. Ezra Taft Benson (1987, February 22), To the mothers in Zion; in Ezra Taft Benson (1990), *Come Listen to a Prophet's Voice* (Salt Lake City: Deseret Book), 32. President Gordon B. Hinckley stated, "Mothers, take good care of your daughters. Be close to them. Listen to them. Talk with them. Lead them from doing foolish things. Guide them into doing the right thing. See that they dress in a comely and modest fashion. Safeguard them from the terrible evils that are all about them. Nurture your sons with love and counsel. Teach them the importance of personal cleanliness, of neatness in their dress. Sloppy ways lead to sloppy lives. Instill in them a sense of discipline. Keep them worthy of service to the Church as missionaries. Give them things to do that they may learn to work. . . . Teach them that nothing really good happens after 11 o'clock at night. And do not spoil them." Gordon B. Hinckley (2003, November), To the women of the Church, *Ensign, 33*(11), 115.

20. Gordon B. Hinckley (1997, November), Some thoughts on temples, retention of converts, and missionary service, *Ensign,* 27(11), 52.

21. Ballard (2003).

22. C. H. Hart, D. A. Nelson, C. C. Robinson, S. F. Olsen, and M. K. McNeilly-Choque (1998), Overt and relational aggression in Russian nursery-school-age children: Parenting style and marital linkages, *Developmental Psychology, 34*(4), 687–697; B. K. Barber (2002), *Intrusive Parenting: How Psychological Control Affects Children and Adolescents* (Washington, D.C.: American Psychological Association).

23. Robert D. Hales (1999, May), Strengthening families: Our sacred duty, *Ensign, 29*(5), 34.

24. Brigham Young (1864), 2.

25. Ballard (in press).

26. See parenting practices discussed in Hart, Newell, and Sine (2000).

27. Elder Ballard continued: "Parents, let's listen and know what is important in the lives of our children. If we fail to listen, if we don't try to understand their point of view, how can we expect them to come to us for guidance in making important decisions?" Ballard (in press).

28. For additional practical application of this concept, see Hart (2004, Spring).

29. Virginia H. Pearce, ed. (1999), *Glimpses into the Life and Heart of Marjorie Pay Hinckley* (Salt Lake City: Deseret Book), 55.

30. Quoted in *Teachings of the Presidents of the Church: Heber J. Grant* (2002), (Salt Lake City: The Church of Jesus Christ of Latter Day Saints), 200.

31. Hart, Newell, and Olsen (2003).

32. Joe J. Christensen (1999, May), Greed, selfishness, and overindulgence, *Ensign, 29*(5), 9.

33. L. J. Nelson, C. H. Hart, B. Wu, C. Yang, and S. F. Olsen (in press), Relations between Chinese mother's parenting practices and social withdrawal in early childhood, *International Journal of Behavioral Development.*

34. Pearce, ed. (1999), 56.

35. Brigham Young (1866, August 19) *Journal of Discourses* (London: Latter-day Saints' Book Depot), 11:272.

36. L. Kuczynski, ed. (2003).

37. Boyd K. Packer (2005, April), The Light of Christ, *Ensign, 35*(4), 13.

38. Bruce R. McConkie (1966), *Mormon Doctrine,* 2d ed. (Salt Lake City: Bookcraft), 264.

39. C. H. Hart (2000, August), Parents do matter: Combating the myth that parents don't matter, *Marriage & Families;* available at http://marriageandfamilies.byu.edu

40. Hart (2000, August).

41. James E. Faust (2004, August), Fathers, mothers, marriage, *Ensign, 34*(8), 3–4.

42. R. D. Parke (2002), Fathers and families; in M. H. Bornstein, ed., *Handbook of Parenting, Vol. 3: Being and Becoming a Parent* (Mahwah, NJ: Lawrence Erlbaum Associates), 27–73.

43. James E. Faust (1990, November), The greatest challenge in the world—Good parenting, *Ensign, 20*(11), 34. Also, in terms of motivating more by love than by punishment, Brigham Young taught, "Parents should never drive their children, but lead them along, giving them knowledge as their minds are prepared to receive it. Chastening may be necessary betimes, but parents should govern their children by faith rather than by the rod, leading them kindly by good example into all truth and holiness." Quoted in Widtsoe, ed. (1998), 208.

44. T. A. Cavell and P. S. Strand (2003), Parent-based interventions for aggressive children; in L. Kuczynski, ed., (2003), 395–415. See pages 408–409 for reviews of research on positive to negative parent–child interaction ratios.

45. Some excellent, practical advice on dealing with these issues is offered by H. W. Goddard (2005), First comes charity, then comes teaching, *Meridian Magazine;* available at http://www.meridianmagazine.com

46. E. M. Cummings and A. C. Schermerhorn (2003), A developmental perspective on children as agents in the family, in L. Kuczynski, ed., (2003), 91–107; T. Dix and S. H. Branca (2003), Parenting as a goal-regulation process, in L. Kuczynski, ed., (2003), 167–185.

47. See Hart, Newell, and Sine (2000) for alternatives to physical punishment and related research and prophetic statements. Note that research is not entirely conclusive on the topic. Compare the following two articles: E. T. Gershoff (2002), Corporal punishment by parents and associated child behaviors and experiences: A meta-analytic and theoretical review, *Psychological Bulletin, 128*(4), 539–579; and R. E. Larzelere, B. R. Kuhn, and B. Johnson (2004), The intervention selection bias: an underrecognized confound in intervention research, *Psychological Bulletin, 130*(2), 289–303.

48. Dix and Branca (2003).

49. Gordon B. Hinckley (2001, June), Behold your little ones, *Ensign, 31*(6), 4. In another address, President Hinckley noted: "In terms of physical abuse, I have never accepted the principle of 'spare the rod and spoil the child.' . . . Children don't need beating. They need love and encouragement." Gordon B. Hinckley (1994, November), Save the children, *Ensign, 24*(11), 53.

50. Joseph F. Smith (1977), *Gospel Doctrine* (Salt Lake City: Deseret Book), 316–317.

CHAPTER 18

BUILDING SPIRITUAL PATTERNS IN THE HOME

KARMEL AND LLOYD D. NEWELL

The greatest job in this world is to build a home. I don't mean the physical structure,
I mean the spiritual environment of a good home.[1]
—President Gordon B. Hinckley

The day began as most do. A mother helped her young daughter get ready for school. She prepared breakfast, combed her hair, reminded her to brush her teeth, put a warm coat over her shoulders, and kissed her good-bye. Then the mother began her day's work. While the mother was on the telephone, fiery darts were assaulting her child just outside their front door. The little girl collapsed from their blows and lay motionless on the sidewalk. And then another dream began. In the second dream, a mother was again getting her daughter ready for school. The only difference was that she took a few minutes and opened the scriptures with her daughter. They read together and knelt and prayed. Again the mother sent her daughter out the front door. Again the fiery darts started flying. But this time, they did not penetrate. The little girl kept walking. The lesson from these consecutive dreams was so clear to the mother that she woke up with a feeling of resolution: she would be more intentional about establishing a climate of spirituality in the home.[2]

DEFINING SPIRITUAL PATTERNS

Family scripture reading, prayer, family home evening, family councils, father's interviews and blessings, church and temple attendance, sacred music, family history work, dressing modestly, observing the Sabbath, and paying tithing are all examples of spiritual patterns Church members have been counseled to weave into the fabric of family life. The list is not all-inclusive, but provides a sampling of what is meant by *spiritual patterns*. When well established and maintained, spiritual patterns fortify family members during times of trial, give them strength against temptation, and help them to withstand "the fiery darts of the adversary" (1 Nephi 15:24). President Gordon B. Hinckley outlined some basic spiritual patterns when he counseled parents:

> Rear your children in light and truth. Teach them to pray while they are young. Read to them from the scriptures even though they may not understand all that you read. Teach them to pay their tithes and offerings on the first money they ever receive. Let this practice become a habit in their lives. Teach your sons to honor womanhood. Teach your daughters to walk in virtue. Accept responsibility in the Church. . . . Your example will set a pattern for your children. . . . That will mean more than all the teaching you can give them.[3]

Most often, spiritual patterns are not established in a single moment. They evolve over time, are shaped by everyday circumstances, and are often passed from one generation to the next. We influence our families not so much by flashes of spirituality during journal-worthy events, but more by the day-to-day spiritual habits for which we make time.

Spiritual patterns help to define who we are; they help us see past mortality's blind spots and give us a glimpse into the real joy and fulfillment of eternal family life.

As Latter-day Saints, we have been counseled by prophets to establish and maintain spiritual patterns in our homes. A First Presidency letter counseled families to make spiritual patterns the priority of family life:

> We counsel parents and children to give highest priority to family prayer, family home evening, gospel study and instruction, and wholesome family activities. However worthy and appropriate other demands or activities may be, they must not be permitted to displace the divinely appointed duties that only parents and families can adequately perform.[4]

Spiritual patterns in the family are to be our "highest priority." Pausing to evaluate what we do or don't do for our family's spiritual health is vital. President Gordon B. Hinckley taught: "It is not enough simply to provide food and shelter for the physical being. There is an equal responsibility to provide nourishment and direction to the spirit and the mind and the heart."[5]

Though some days of spiritual patterning may seem lackluster, parents who persist will discover why those patterns are worth establishing and how deeply meaningful they can be. Spiritual patterns can unite family members and give them a strong sense of stability, identity, and cohesion. Spiritual patterns need not be burdensome. They can be a great source of joy, fun, and gratification in the home. Nothing quite compares with marching around the kitchen table singing "We Are All Enlisted"[6] after family prayer, or sipping hot chocolate together during scripture study, or watching your children act out an especially adventurous scripture story. When done with an attitude of shared purpose, spiritual patterns can blur the lines between devotion and wholesome family recreation.

BARRIERS TO SPIRITUAL PATTERNS

Perhaps the most common obstacle to establishing and maintaining spiritual patterns is the lack of immediate compensation or reward. When children resist, parents often don't persist. Parents may wonder if their children are really benefiting from their efforts—especially when the family experiences recurrent problems like quarreling, complaining, boredom, nonparticipation, or other disruptions. Oftentimes, it's not until much later that children really appreciate their parents' dedication.

A 19-year-old BYU student tells of a morning ritual her parents enacted that she sometimes thought was meaningless. She describes how her parents put imaginary armor on her and her siblings before they left for school each day: "This way, we would be spiritually prepared to combat whatever came our way that day. I never really appreciated this until I was older. . . . I am just now realizing the significance of this ritual they created. . . . Even if it was something I thought was stupid, I know it had an impact on the way I lived my life. I even felt shielded from mean or criticizing kids. . . . I really felt like it worked."[7]

Everyone encounters resistance to establishing spiritual patterns. The obstacles aren't so daunting if we expect to have them. Often, opposition comes in the form of unrealistic expectations, simply forgetting, or being busy. These difficulties often attend processes of spiritual growth. Sister Marjorie Pay Hinckley put this in perspective when she wrote to one of her daughters: "I have a new project, one chapter a day from each of the standard works. I have been on it for four days and am only three days behind. Better to have tried and failed than never to have tried."[8]

Unfortunately, too many families feel paralyzed by a picture of perfection that they've never seen but somehow think is happening in other families: "Other families never get stuck in 1 Nephi like we do"; "Other families don't have contention during family night"; "Other families don't forget to say prayers. What's wrong with us?" No family is perfect. Otherwise, we wouldn't need spiritual patterns to help us through mortality. We wouldn't need the weekly sacrament on the Sabbath if that were the case. We wouldn't need family prayer or scripture study. Too many keep from trying because they are discouraged by previous failed attempts. Other families rationalize that an occasional dose of spirituality is enough. But our Father in Heaven knew we would need continual nurturing of our spirits. He commanded, "Thou shalt teach [the commandments] diligently unto thy children, and shalt talk of them when thou sittest in thine house, and when thou walkest by the way, and when thou liest down, and when thou risest up" (Deuteronomy 6:7). Persistence is key, especially at first, and so are (1) gaining a testimony of the spiritual pattern, (2) working ahead of distractions, and (3) making a specific plan as a guide or reference.

Gain a testimony of the spiritual pattern. Our efforts

to establish a spiritual pattern will be strengthened as we become convinced of the worth of that pattern. If we have had family home evenings, but not consistently, we can pray for wisdom and strength to establish family home evening as a reliable source of spiritual strength in our family. If we've never held family home evenings, we can begin to have them. We send a powerful message to our children as we meekly commit to follow the prophet No matter the spiritual pattern, no matter how many previous attempts have faltered, a sincere effort to start anew is a meaningful and worthwhile step in the right direction. We can't expect to gain a testimony of a commandment we have not yet obeyed. President Hinckley tells how his parents began and continued the spiritual pattern of family night:

> In the beginning, we would laugh and make cute remarks about one another's performance. But our parents persisted. We sang together. We prayed together. We listened quietly while Mother read Bible and Book of Mormon stories. Father told us stories out of his memory. Out of those simple little meetings, held in the parlor of our old home, came something indescribable and wonderful. Our love for our parents was strengthened. Our love for brothers and sisters was enhanced. Our love for the Lord was increased. An appreciation for simple goodness grew in our hearts. These wonderful things came about because our parents followed the counsel of the President of the Church. I have learned something tremendously significant out of that.[9]

President Hinckley's testimony was twofold: the power of following prophetic counsel and the value of family home evening. Seeking a testimony of the gospel principle is a vital first step.

Work ahead of distractions. An informal survey of more than 100 BYU students revealed that competing "good" commitments were the biggest obstacle to establishing spiritual patterns in the families in which they grew up. The disruptions to spiritual patterns included athletics, time with friends, Church callings, school activities, homework, work schedules, social activities, television shows, and computer games. Far fewer students listed more serious family challenges (i.e., contention, divorce, abusive behavior) as the reason spiritual patterns were either disrupted or discontinued. Busy lives were the main reason that spiritual patterns faltered.

Methods for working ahead of distractions are as varied as the distractions. Each family is entitled to inspiration for successfully integrating a spiritual pattern into their busy lives. Creativity and flexibility, coupled with consistency, is at the heart of every spiritual pattern. Adapt the spiritual pattern to the ages and stages of family members. What works for young children will be quite different from what works for older children—or for a wide range of ages. Realistic expectations for the duration of a spiritual pattern are vital. Scripture study for small children may last a few minutes each day. Family home evening lessons for teenage children with demanding homework loads may be a well-planned 15 minutes. The length of time is not as important as the consistent bonding that spiritual patterns provide when they are given priority and regularly held.

Some other ideas for avoiding distractions include deciding not to answer the phone during family home evening, designating a time to begin and end family scripture study, rotating discussion leaders during scripture study, placing a basket full of scriptures as the centerpiece on the kitchen table, gathering in a family council on Sunday to plan the upcoming week, and preparing a chart with family home evening assignments.

Make a specific plan. Spiritual patterns won't just happen. They have to be intentionally established and maintained. Parents begin by counseling together and presenting a plan. In council, they make adjustments as needed to accommodate family members' needs and desires. An important element of this intentionality is establishing a regular time and place for the spiritual pattern. For example, many families have found that by scheduling a time for scripture study, or marking a day on the calendar for temple attendance, or holding father's interviews every fast Sunday, or consistently gathering as a family for morning and evening prayers, the spiritual pattern takes priority over the other good activities that compete for family members' time and energy. When expectations regarding the spiritual pattern are clearly outlined, family members more readily embrace the habit.

For example, one family reasoned that if they gathered around the kitchen table for scripture study, there would be less contention. At the kitchen table, everyone has an assigned spot and could pay better attention because it's more difficult to fall asleep there. This simple clarification reduced contention and improved interaction. Another family arrived at several ways to bring greater meaning to their fast. They decided to remind each other of the fast one day in advance, to consider special needs for which they could fast, and to begin their fast with a prayer. They agreed on a time to gather on Sunday to share feelings of gratitude. The mother concluded: "We feel the Spirit of the Lord more in our home, and we are more grateful. Making fast Sunday more meaningful to our family has drawn us closer to each other and to the Lord."[10]

Involving all family members in the process of establishing a plan can allay problems that disrupt spiritual patterns. When a disturbance or lapse does occur, family members can more easily get back on track because (1) they decided together to follow the prophet and determined how they could do this; and (2) they've already experienced the sweetness of a spiritual pattern, the greatest motivation to work through the rough spots toward their shared goals. As President Thomas S. Monson reassured: "Learning the gospel, bearing a testimony, leading a family are rarely if ever simple processes. Life's journey is characterized by bumps in the road, swells in the sea—even the turbulence of our times."[11]

A DAY TO REMEMBER

A family was gathered for scripture study when the phone rang. The children had been taught not to answer the phone during scripture study, but the mother sensed something unusual about the early-morning call. When she checked caller ID and saw that it was her husband's sister from New Jersey, she picked up the phone. "Hurry! Turn on the news," her sister-in-law said instead of hello. "I'm just going to check my kids out of school. You won't believe what's happened."

The day was September 11, 2001. The news was incomprehensible. The children were shaken. Going to school, going anywhere, seemed a little scary now. Were their cousins, so close to New York City, all right? Was everything going to be okay? The parents turned off the TV and turned back to the scriptures. The children were more subdued than usual. No one seemed to know whose turn it was to read. Instead of reading, they knelt to pray. After the prayer, the mother wiped away her tears and looked up at her children. Her 8-year-old daughter was the first to speak. She simply said, "It's going to be all right. I think it's just like the Gadianton robbers. We don't need to be afraid of them." Peace started to replace the fear. As the children left for school, the mother and father turned to each other and said, "That's why we do this every morning."

Certainly, not every morning is so memorable or meaningful, but because a spiritual pattern was in place, this family was fortified during a time of great distress. Similarly, a 21-year-old BYU student explained how already having a spiritual pattern in place helped during a family crisis: "After my parents' divorce, night prayer became more consistent, and again it was a testimony-builder to see answers to those prayers."[12] Research indicates that Latter-day Saint youth view spiritual patterns in the family as an important source of security and strength (see chapter 29). When youth are not only attending Church, seminary, and youth activities but also making time for private religiosity (i.e., personal prayer and scripture study), the effects are even more substantial.[13]

EFFORT NOT OUTCOME

No matter the outcome of our sincere efforts, the Lord blesses us for trying. He is aware of our offerings of time and energy in behalf of our families. To all who make earnest effort, the Lord said: "[your] sacrifice shall be more sacred unto me than [your] increase" (D&C 117:13). In the Lord's sight, effort is sacred.

Sincerity and love are the greatest motivators. Elder Robert D. Hales counseled against using anything less than love and sincere concern to involve our children in spiritual patterns: "Act with faith; don't react with fear. When our teenagers begin testing family values, parents need to go to the Lord for guidance on the specific needs of each family member. This is the time for added love and support and to reinforce your teachings on how to make choices. . . . The Lord's way of love and acceptance is better than Satan's way of force and coercion, especially in rearing teenagers."[14] A 23-year-old BYU student bore testimony of the power of love: "There was a time of decision early in my life where . . . I tried to separate myself from any situation where I might be reminded of my wrong choices. Yet, my angel mother kept extending herself, even in the face of my blatant rejection. She constantly invited me to come to prayer and scriptures, even when I refused to come. It was her consistency that helped me to repent."[15]

If, by intentionally trying to establish spiritual patterns, we can make our homes places of peace and joy, sanctuaries from the world, our families will be armed with spiritual power and enjoy the protection of the "whole armour of God" (Ephesians 6:11). President Boyd K. Packer taught: "[The] shield of faith is not produced in a factory but at home. . . . It takes the steady strength of a father to hammer out the metal of it and the tender hands of a mother to polish and fit it on. Sometimes one parent is left to do it alone. It is difficult, but it can be done. . . . The actual making of and fitting on of the shield of faith belongs in the family circle. Otherwise it may loosen and come off in a crisis."[16]

In the home, in our families, we build and preserve spiritual patterns that protect us against the fiery darts of the adversary and prepare us to live in peace together eternally.

ABOUT THE AUTHORS

Karmel Newell holds bachelor's and master's degrees in English from the University of Utah. She is an author, has worked as an editor, and served on a general writing committee for the Church.

Lloyd D. Newell has a Ph.D. from BYU, where he is on the faculties of Religious Education and the School of Family Life. He has spoken to organizations in 45 states and a dozen countries and is the author of numerous books. Karmel and Lloyd are the parents of Hayley, McKay, Abigail, and Jacob.

ADDITIONAL READING

Gene R. Cook (1993), *Raising Up a Family to the Lord* (Salt Lake City: Deseret Book).

Henry B. Eyring (1996, May), A legacy of testimony, *Ensign, 26*(5), 62–64.

Thomas S. Monson (2001, October), Hallmarks of a happy home, *Ensign, 31*(10), 3–8.

Lloyd D. Newell (2000), Research on the benefits of family traditions; in David C. Dollahite, ed., *Strengthening Our Families: An In-Depth Look at the Proclamation on the Family* (Salt Lake City: Bookcraft), 328–330.

Joseph B. Wirthlin (1993, May), Spiritually strong homes and families, *Ensign, 23*(5), 68–71.

NOTES

1. Gordon B. Hinckley (1997), *Teachings of Gordon B. Hinckley* (Salt Lake City: Deseret Book), 613–614.

2. Lana Jardine, personal communication to authors, 2004.

3. Gordon B. Hinckley (1995, November), Stand strong against the wiles of the world, *Ensign, 25*(11), 98.

4. First Presidency Letter, 11 February 1999.

5. Gordon B. Hinckley (1993, November), Bring up a child in the way he should go, *Ensign, 23*(11), 54.

6. W. B. Bradbury and Anonymous (1985), We are all enlisted, *Hymns* (Salt Lake City: The Church of Jesus Christ of Latter-day Saints), 250.

7. Name withheld, first-person account, female, age 19; data gathered Spring 2004.

8. V. H. Pearce, ed. (1999), *Glimpses into the Life and Heart of Marjorie Pay Hinckley* (Salt Lake City: Deseret Book), 79.

9. Gordon B. Hinckley (1993, May), Some lessons I learned as a boy, *Ensign, 23*(5), 54.

10. S. S. Brook (2004, March), Making more of our fast Sunday, *Ensign, 34*(3), 73.

11. Thomas S. Monson (2004, November), If ye are prepared ye shall not fear, *Ensign, 34*(11), 115.

12. Name withheld, first-person account, male, age 21; data gathered Spring 2004.

13. B. L. Top and B. A. Chadwick (1998, Summer), Raising righteous children in a wicked world, *BYU Magazine, 15*(3), available at http://magazine.byu.edu

14. Robert D. Hales (1999, May), Strengthening families: Our sacred duty, *Ensign, 29*(5), 32.

15. Name withheld, first-person account, female, age 23; data gathered Spring 2004.

16. Boyd K. Packer (1995, May), The shield of faith, *Ensign, 25*(5), 8.

SHORT SHORTS AND OTHER TEENAGE IDENTITY CRISES

RACHEL DOLLAHITE

As I look back on the significant milestones in my growing-up years that have led up to my being a relatively confident, independent young adult, I find, somewhat ironically, that my journey to a definite sense of personal identity has been formed not when I was off by myself or with my friends but mostly during experiences with my parents. I have collected here a few of the most vivid memories that helped define me as myself—and as a child of God.

Allow your children to make (at least some of) their own mistakes. Your children will not forget the principles you have taught, and they will learn by making their own decisions. My large, noisy family moved temporarily out of our safe, predictable part of Orem, Utah, into a politically and morally turbulent area in western Massachusetts. While my dad researched families of different faiths, my siblings and I attended public school and early-morning seminary. I had not expected to make friends during our short time in Massachusetts, but I was blessed with two friends, Molly and Amanda. I remember one particular day at school in early spring. I wore a pair of shorts (of which my mom did not approve) that I had picked up at the Salvation Army. I obstinately wore them anyway.

My new friends stopped me in the hall and Amanda looked me up and down, then said, "Rachel, your shorts are too short." The rest of the day I kept pulling the legs as far down as they could go. I was embarrassed and devastated that I had not been the "example" I was supposed to be. Then I realized that I could change my personal standard of modesty by following the example of my friend Amanda in speaking the truth—even to myself. I'm grateful that after teaching me principles of modesty and encouraging my obedience, my mom allowed me this opportunity to make my own choice and to learn.

Listen to the Spirit and follow its promptings during conversations with your children. In Amherst, Massachusetts, I took an honors constitutional law class that was more academically strenuous than any university-level course I have yet taken. Being one of two admitted "conservatives" in the class, I felt my viewpoint ought to be heard, if not acknowledged. The students and teacher thought I was told what to think by my parents. I commented to my mom one evening that I felt I was becoming even more conservative in response to the intense and consuming liberalism. She was quiet for a moment then said, "Rachel, I think you're just finding your own boundaries." This response struck me powerfully. I recognized this was exactly what was happening in all my life, not only in the situation of my political views being questioned and clarified. I realize, in hindsight, that the Spirit was present during that conversation, making me receptive and helping my mom know what I needed to hear.

Instill the idea that, while a unique entity, a child is a fundamental part of the family—nuclear and extended. My sister and I had our wisdom teeth removed on the same day. I was still feeling the effects of the operation and subsequent medication (and my horrible reaction to both) a week later when I began the semester. My dad drove me home after my plodding through eleven hours on campus. The day had gone by in a hazy blur and I was fatigued. One portion of the day stood out vividly, however. My professor in the first class of the day (when I was not yet completely senseless) shook my hand sincerely and asked my name. I told her "Rachel Dollahite." She inquired, "Is your dad David?" I replied yes. She explained she had worked with him in her chapter for his book. Then she praised my mom's essay in the same book, saying it was her favorite. Later in class she spoke of my great-grandfather and told how much she loved and respected him. I related this to my dad in the car and, overwhelmed by exhaustion and the stress of the new semester, exclaimed, "I know how wonderful you and Mom and Great-grandpa are, but I don't know who I am!" My dad calmly returned, "Oh, Rachel, you do know who you are."

Yes, I realized, I did know who I was. What felt the best right then was that my dad knew it. Later I recognized that while it is important that I know myself, it is also crucial that I understand where I come from. As you allow your children to become acquainted with themselves, also teach them about their ancestors—immediate and distant. Children can be inspired by the qualities of their extended family members, including ancestors, and cultivate those in themselves. Ancestors are an inherent, precious part of me that I am coming to value, even as I grow in appreciation for my own identity.

Help your children see how they belong to a bigger sphere than just themselves or their nuclear family. In Amherst, we became acquainted with the mothers of my friends Amanda and Molly through Pony Club, a national organization devoted to helping children learn respect and love for horses. We shared several polite exchanges over the size of my family, the habit of avoiding activities such as horse competitions on the Sabbath, and other of our unusual customs. One day as we were driving home from the barn, I remarked, "We really are a peculiar people, as President Hinckley says, aren't we?" My mom smiled at me. I felt proud to belong to a group of people around the world who were peculiar, too.

Affirm your children's hard work in becoming an adult. Growing up takes effort. Children need to hear they are doing a good job—from their parents especially! Never let the chance pass to boost your children. My dad makes a point of periodically telling each of his children that he is proud of us. He takes the opportunity in father's blessings to say how much he loves us and to mention the love Father in Heaven has for us. In conversations with me, he specifically names my role as the oldest child and thanks me for living a good life, which my siblings observe. He is proud of the choices for education that I've made, and he has confidence in my making future decisions with the help of the Lord. His confidence in me lifts me up immeasurably, giving me assurance of my own worth.

Support your children as they reach for their dreams. Guide them on the way up and comfort them when they fall. Let them discover for themselves that sometimes it is necessary to take one step backward in order to proceed two steps forward. Big dreams have always been an active part of my imagination. My parents often say I need three lifetimes—or at least eternity—to do all the things I want to do. Still, they encourage my ambition and help me succeed.

Many young girls go through a "horse-crazy" stage. I hit mine around eleven, when a horse-crazy friend came to visit. Soon books and movies, posters and models were not enough. I proved my willingness to work by mucking stalls. From there it was a long road through all my teenage years to acquire the necessary mental skills, muscles, and trained emotions that are essential when teaching a 1200-pound animal some manners.

Much of my character, and thus my identity, has been formed while working with horses. The concepts of stewardship, communication without words, far-reaching consequences of a simple action, building trust and love, and hard, grimy work have shaped me and changed me, finally becoming part of me. I try to bring these concepts with me into other aspects of my life. I soon abandoned the big dream of becoming an Olympic rider. But quickly the dream was replaced with another dream—that of truly loving and trusting one of God's creations and having the animal love and trust me in return. I appreciate the sacrifices of time and money that my parents made to help me follow this dream.

Don't discourage quirky character traits. As a keen reader and a very verbal person, I have many times embarrassed myself by speaking a word I have only read and never heard spoken. To this day I often blurt out a word—perfectly apt in context and meaning, but off in pronunciation. However awful my pronunciation is, and however much my family laughs, I know that they appreciate my courage.

It takes many years—time and experiences—to shape a person. Have patience and enjoy your children! Children must become familiar and comfortable with themselves, which happens through making choices and experiencing consequences. With love, parents can guide and support their children in the process of discovering their eternal identities. Love your children. They will grow to love themselves as children of God and in turn will serve and love others, knowing that others, too, are sons and daughters of God.

ABOUT THE AUTHOR

Rachel Dollahite is a nineteen-year-old Brigham Young University student studying classical civilization and art history. She is the oldest of seven, a confirmed vegetarian, and a thrift store shopaholic—and she is still looking for "Mr. Darcy."

SAVORING INFORMAL TEACHING MOMENTS

JENNIFER Y. THATCHER AND BRENTON G. YORGASON

Often, the most effective teaching occurs not during scheduled, formal lessons, but during daily interactions. Parents discern what works best for each child through trial and error, inspiration and prayer. Children remember the experiences that shaped their character, faith, and testimony. In this essay, we present a daughter's and father's perspective of parent–child teaching moments from our family. Although we realize that all parents and children make mistakes, we have purposely focused on positive teaching moments to provide ideas and hope.

LEARNING MOMENTS THROUGH THE EYES OF A DAUGHTER

Looking back over my childhood, the greatest learning moments with my parents were during our special talks. Most of these conversations were spontaneous, occurring when *I* needed to talk. Others transpired because my parents created opportunities for personal conversations. Because we had a daily dose of positive, meaningful interaction, we were comfortable going to each other to discuss more difficult issues. The following are ways that my parents made time for us to talk.

Mom made a special effort to be there at the "crossroads" of our day.[1] She always had a snack prepared when we returned from school. We talked about our day and then got started on homework, knowing Mom was available for us through the evening. On days when I needed a friend, I knew I had one waiting at home.

Dad also made himself available when I needed him. When I entered his office, he would stop midsentence on the computer to talk. If I accidentally interrupted him in a counseling session, he would introduce me to his guests, then give me the few minutes I needed to schedule a time when we could talk.

I appreciate the effort my parents made to create and maintain an intimate relationship with each of

their children. I now see how intentional they needed to be to establish regular one-on-one moments with each of us. One of these moments was at the end of the day. If we hurried to bed, we'd be rewarded with exclusive time with mom. She would rub our back, resolve our concerns, tell us stories of our ancestors, then pray with us individually.

Dad initiated informal talks with us when he became our family barber. Having a captive audience allowed him to listen closely to our problems and then whisper words of counsel into our ears. He also conducted priesthood interviews with each of us. He would ask us questions, then listen intently to hear wisdom "out of the mouth of babes" (Psalm 8:2). One time, Dad asked me why Heavenly Father sent me to our home. I replied, "Because we fit together like a puzzle." Responses like these were recorded in our journals and remembered through the years.

Mom and Dad looked for reasons to celebrate a special event with each of us. Following family tradition, our sixteenth birthday meant a "first date" with Mom and Dad.

Like most moms, ours spent many hours a week driving us to and from our various activities. Instead of just being a chauffeur, she was deliberate in making each shuttle a special time for the two of us to visit and enjoy each other's company.

Because my parents were "there" for me throughout my childhood, I didn't have to go to my friends for answers. Instead, I went to them. This close relationship continues in my adult years.

TEACHING MOMENTS THROUGH THE EYES OF A FATHER

Teach children to repent when they make a mistake. The consequence of a child's misbehavior should never be the withdrawal of a parent's love. When Jordan was a deacon, he and a friend adventured to the store. They found the skateboard section and started skating up and down the aisle. The manager caught them. "You boys pick up your skateboards and get out of here," he scolded. The boys looked at each other with dismay; then, avoiding further confrontation, they left the store with the skateboards under their arms. When they got home, Jordan confessed the misdeed. We thanked him for not intentionally stealing, then taught him to never take anything from a store that didn't belong to him.

We then showed him how he could fully repent. The three of us knelt together and offered prayer. We explained to Jordan that he needed to pay for the board, and asked him to empty his savings. I then offered to pay the balance until he could repay me. We returned to the store with the skateboard. Jordan confessed what he had done, then paid the manager the skateboard's retail price. Jordan worked hard to pay back the money I had loaned him. As parents, we used this moment to teach all of our children of the Savior's mercy "after all we can do" (2 Nephi 25:23).

Seize the moment to reinforce gospel truths. When our children were young, 3-year-old Jeremy was invited to offer family prayer. He whispered his words in his usual fashion. Aaron, age 4, became frustrated halfway through the prayer. He hit Jeremy and exclaimed, "Don't whisper when you pray! Heavenly Father can't hear you when you whisper!" Five-year-old Jason quietly arose from his knees and placed his arms around both younger brothers. "Aaron, it's okay if Jeremy whispers because Heavenly Father has bionic ears!"

I could have used this opportunity to discipline Aaron for hitting. Instead, I reinforced what Jason taught. We spent the next several moments bearing witness that Heavenly Father does, indeed, hear our prayers.

Help children resolve conflicts through love. One day, when Jennifer was 8 and David was 4, they began teasing each other to the point of tears. After stopping the fray, I invited them to face each other. Then, encircling them in my arms, I helped them embrace each other. Their mutually-shared pain must have been excruciating. I then said, "Hug each other until you can each say 'I love you.'"

Tears stopped, protestations ceased, and they broke into laughter. They begrudgingly repeated the words. Although at that moment they didn't feel love, my display of love for them was a reminder that they should love each other. I was teaching them a principle that the Savior taught when he said, "As I have loved you . . . love one another" (John 13:34). This way of resolving a "fight" was repeated many times over the years, and the result came to be expected.

Create alternatives that allow the child to make a "correct" decision. One Sunday morning 15-year-old Aaron came upstairs and announced that he was not feeling well and that he was going to stay home from church. "Besides," he moaned, "Sunday School is boring."

Thinking beyond my initial inclination to disagree with him, I paused. "I understand. I'll call and get a substitute teacher for my class and we can stay home together. We'll enjoy three of the greatest hours any father and son could experience studying the Book of Mormon."

Aaron was startled, then he slowly disappeared back down the stairs. Five minutes passed. Suddenly, he bounded up the stairs while putting on his tie. When I asked where he was going, he said, "I'm feeling better and I've got to help prepare the sacrament."

My response had worked! I had resisted the impulse to show disapproval, to lecture, or to threaten a rebellious son. Instead, my response was spontaneous and positive and allowed him to change his own mind.

Provide reinforcement when a child has made a righteous decision. It is easy to find a reason to discipline when children misbehave. However, it is much more effective to accentuate their good behavior. When Josh was 14, he announced that he wanted to spend Friday evening with two new friends. They were a year older and were struggling to keep various commandments.

We were concerned; but we also wanted to show Josh our trust. When he assured us that the friend's parents would be there, and that no girls were invited, we consented. "Josh," I cautioned, "have a fun time and be a good example. If something happens that causes you to become uncomfortable, give us a call. One of us will come and pick you up. Just tell us that you aren't feeling well—and we'll know it means that you're not feeling well *spiritually.*"

At 9:15 P.M., the phone rang. When I answered, it was Josh. "I'm not feeling well," he complained. "Could you come and pick me up?" Soon Josh was sitting in our room explaining what had happened. "When my friend's parents left the house and three girls showed up, I knew I shouldn't be there so I called home."

We could have said, "We knew it sounded like a bad idea!" Or, we could have restricted Josh from those friends. Instead, we expressed our trust and thanked him for obeying our request.

CONCLUSION

As father and daughter, we often reflect on our positive family experiences. We cherish the trust and mutual respect that developed over the years. We took time for each other then, which created an environment of love that motivates us to spend time with each other now. This relationship of trust built across the years binds us together in ways that bless our lives every day.

ABOUT THE AUTHORS

Jennifer Y. Thatcher, BS, is currently a master's student in marriage, family, and human development at Brigham Young University. She is the fifth of nine children. She was recently married in July 2005.

Brenton G. Yorgason, Ph.D., is a part-time instructor at Brigham Young University's Salt Lake Center. An author and former marriage and family therapist, he is married to Margaret Yates. They have nine children and ten grandchildren.

ADDITIONAL READING

James Dobson (1987), *Parenting Isn't for Cowards: Dealing Confidently with the Frustrations of Child-Rearing* (Dallas, TX: Word Publishing).
John Gottman (1997), *The Heart of Parenting: Raising an Emotionally Intelligent Child* (New York: Fireside).

NOTE

1. Ezra Taft Benson (1987, February 22), To the mothers in Zion; address given at a fireside for parents; published as a pamphlet (Salt Lake City: The Church of Jesus Christ of Latter-day Saints), 8.

E S S A Y   D 3

MODESTY: A ROYAL BIRTHRIGHT

DENNIS G. MARTIN, WITH MARY J. THOMPSON AND DENISE MARTIN RICHARDS

My life as a professor was drastically altered when my daughter Denise Richards dropped by my office at Brigham Young University. "Dad, I need a small favor. Would you help me do a study on modesty?" This was more than two years ago, and we're just now finishing up the research. Perhaps even more exciting, we created what may be the first film on modesty for Latter-day Saints, titled *A Modest Revolution*.[1] Denise recruited another mentor, Dr. Mary Thompson, a professor in the School of Family Life. Together we raised more than $80,000 in grants and traveled thousands of miles, videotaping hundreds of young men and women. Denise interviewed all of them on camera—Mormons, Jews (including three rabbis), Muslims, Catholics, Protestants, and a Hindu nun.

It's impossible to grow up in a culture and not be affected by all the images portrayed in toys, video games, movies, and sitcoms—what I call tidal waves of mass media that wash over us daily. Denise and her family were not immune; we were all affected. Fortunately, because of her life experiences and expo-

sure to a liberal arts education, Denise was now curious about the world she had grown up in—a world that could barely define the word *modesty*, let alone dress modestly. She was troubled by the paradox of a fashion world making more and more money with less and less fabric. This was the moment when she began to claim her birthright to modesty, both intellectually and spiritually.

Good research demands a razor-sharp definition of the problem; it took a month for us to condense our study into a single question: "How is modesty interpreted and defined by women of different faiths, and how do they talk about modesty?"

Modesty also had to be grounded in its religious roots, so we turned to the Old Testament: "And the eyes of them both were opened, and they knew that they were naked; and they sewed fig leaves together, and made themselves aprons" (Genesis 3:7).

The Bible includes other examples of modesty, like the story of Isaac and Rebekah. Consistent with Jewish culture, Abraham's servant assumed the role of matchmaker. After traveling to the city of Nahor, the servant stood by a well and he prayed for the Lord to guide him to a worthy virgin for Abraham's son, Isaac, to take for a wife. Immediately "Rebekah came out," and she "was very fair to look upon, a virgin, . . . and she went down to the well, and filled her pitcher" (Genesis 24:10–16). Rebekah gave him drink and drew water for all his camels. Because of her thoughtfulness and her kind heart, the servant knew Rebekah was the answer to his prayers. He made the proper arrangements, and we join the story where Rebekah sees Isaac for the first time and asks, "What man is this that walketh in the field to meet us? And the servant had said, It is my master: therefore she took a vail, and covered herself" (Genesis 24:65).

Rebekah is a compelling example of modesty in action. When Wendy Shalit, best-selling author of *A Return to Modesty,*[2] accepted my invitation to visit BYU, she talked with students about the symbolism in this story: "We dress modestly not because we are ashamed, but because we want others to value us for who we are on the inside. When Rebekah saw Isaac, it was an instinctive, cultural reflex for her to cover herself. As long as we've been human, we cover up the physical. Not because it's ugly or that we're ashamed, but because it's beautiful, sacred, and mysterious."[3] Shalit framed the conflict as a battle that began thousands of years ago:

> The world battles between the Greek and Judeo-Christian philosophies. Greek philosophy says, if you've got it, flaunt it. While the Judeo-Christian belief says, if something is precious, you protect it for someone special. Postmodern society has turned everything upside down. Popular culture teaches us that women are valued mostly for their bodies. We all know instinctively that if you see yourself only as a body, you're not going to be happy. Everyone has a body; it's the soul that makes us special.[4]

The soul—body and spirit together—are the essence of our eternal identity (see D&C 88:15). Quoting Apostle James E. Talmage on this doctrinal point, BYU President Jeffrey R. Holland told students: "We have been taught . . . to look upon these bodies of ours as gifts from God. We Latter-day Saints do not regard the body as something to be condemned, something to be abhorred. . . . We regard [the body] as the sign of our royal birthright."[5] (See chapter 24.)

Many faiths teach that we should esteem our bodies as sacred and that we will be happier in marriage if we choose *sexual modesty*[6] as a lifestyle. Shalit suggested that sexual modesty is really much more rewarding than promiscuity: "The more we pursue sex without emotion, the less satisfaction we get; there's no moral perspective. We're actually finding that in order to protect sexuality in its right context, and to preserve it, that you really need modesty—so if we act like animals, we just don't have as much fun."[7]

When Denise interviewed Hana Shihab, a young Indonesian woman, Hana told her the honor code was one of the main reasons she felt comfortable at BYU. "In Islam," she explained, "we are taught to regard the body as sacred; we should not display ourselves by wearing clothes or perfume that define us in ways that cry out for attention from the opposite sex."

When we visited a Jewish school for girls in Hollywood, Tali Gordon defined modesty as "being attractive, not attracting. It's encompassing dignity into every aspect of your life."

Daisy Castro, a senior at Mary Mount, a Catholic girls' school in Beverly Hills, was disappointed by the lack of modesty in popular culture: "The whole point that sex sells is really a huge thing. . . . It brings a lot of publicity and a lot of attention."

Daisy was talking about an important concept that resonates throughout our study: far too often women are taught by the secular culture that their principal role in life is to objectify themselves. Objectification happens when women are treated as sexual objects instead of complete persons. When Denise interviewed Elsa Metchek, director of the California Fashion Association, Metchek lamented, "I think women want to be objectified. I'm sorry, but a young girl sees herself in the mirror as she looks. She does not see her brain power."

Lindsay Sockcheski, a senior at Yula, a Jewish girls' school in Hollywood, is also out to destroy this myth: "That's a big lie. Women don't want to be objectified. We want to be treated as people. I want to be seen as who I am; I don't want to be seen as an object. I want to be me."

Brittany Lemire, a Latter-day Saint teenager from La Mesa, California, was equally firm: "I used to dress immodestly. I used to wear the short sleeves and the short little shorts. . . . I was just trying to get attention from guys. Now I know I don't have to show off my body for them to like me. I don't want a guy that likes me just for that." Brittany grasps the deeper meaning of modesty—fundamentally it's about defining self-worth. She understands that her body is half of her soul, and she shows respect for herself as a daughter of God by choosing to dress modestly.

Although our interviews included more young

women, we also talked with young men because they share an equal responsibility for modesty in dress, language, and behavior. President Holland put the weight for sexual modesty "squarely on the shoulders of young men." He stated: "I have heard all my life that it is the young woman who has to assume the responsibility for controlling the limits of intimacy in courtship because a young man cannot. What an unacceptable response to such a serious issue!"[8] Our research findings resonate with President Holland's point. The way we think and talk about the opposite sex cannot be separated from modesty. For both men and women, dress, attitudes, and behavior are forever linked because sexual modesty is at the center of our eternal identity. According to Jewish law, the root of modesty is holiness. It is respect for self and others that separates us as children of God. Tali Gordon, a senior at Yula High, summed up the essence of our two-year study:

> Modesty is a lifestyle; it's not just a dress code. Modesty is really [about] self-respect and confidence. It's taking all of your abilities and everything you have and showing them in the proper way so people look at you, and they don't see a body, and they don't see nice clothing or lack thereof, but they see an intelligent, a capable, a talented human being, a product essentially of God.

Young women like Tali Gordon give us reason to be optimistic about her generation. Whether Mormons, Jews, Muslims, Catholics, or Protestants, our youth are speaking up for modesty. And, despite the tidal wave of mass media that washes over them daily, they don't soak it all up like mindless sponges. Most are aware of the cultural sea they swim in, and they know how to think and talk about it critically. Evidence presented here strongly suggests our youth are intelligent, talented children of God, worthy heirs to a royal birthright grounded in modest thoughts and deeds.

ABOUT THE AUTHORS

Dennis G. Martin, Ph.D., is a professor of communications at Brigham Young University, an author and developer of dozens of books and creative works, films and scholarly articles, and is also CEO of his own national software company. His primary interests include cultural and human studies in mass communication. He and his wife, Gayle Maze Martin, met in southern California and have six children and six grandchildren.

Mary J. Thompson, Ph.D., is assistant professor of home and family living at Brigham Young University with an emphasis in clothing and women's issues. She and her husband, John, are parents of four children, Bryan, Karyn, Diana, and Christopher.

Denise Martin Richards is a graduate of the Department of Communications at Brigham Young University. Codeveloper of the film, *A Modest Revolution,* her primary interests include fashion and interior design. She is married to Stephen R. Richards and they have a son, Paul Stephen.

ADDITIONAL READING

Michele Thompson-Holbrook (1992), Modesty in dress; in Daniel H. Ludlow, ed., *Encyclopedia of Mormonism* (New York: Macmillan), 2:932.

Wendy Shalit (1999), *A Return to Modesty: Discovering the Lost Virtue* (New York: Simon & Schuster).

NOTES

1. D. G. Martin, M. J. Thompson, and D. A. Richards (2005), *A Modest Revolution,* film (Covenant Communications).

2. W. Shalit (1999), *A Return to Modesty: Discovering the Last Virtue* (New York: Simon & Schuster).

3. W. Shalit (2003, January 15), Modesty: Virtue or hang-up; address delivered in the Joseph Smith Building, Brigham Young University; sponsored by BYU Student Honor Association; recorded in Martin/Thompson transcript, "Fashion Talk: Hoochie to Gucci," 24.

4. Shalit (2003), 25.

5. Jeffrey R. Holland (1988, January 12), Of souls, symbols, and sacraments; BYU Devotional Address; in K. Seely, ed., *Brigham Young University 1987–1988 Devotional and Fireside Speeches* (Provo, Utah: University Publications), 78; also available at http://speeches.byu.edu

6. "Sexual modesty" is an expression encountered in both Islam and Judaism. It recognizes that modesty, at its core, is about limiting the sexual signs exchanged between men and women. For example, flirting to attract the opposite sex in the workplace would be considered a form of sexual immodesty. Dress or costume may or may not be part of the flirt; the point is that sexual signals, however communicated, are at the root of immodest behavior. When I greeted author Wendy Shalit at the Salt Lake City International Airport, I noticed she was carrying something in both arms and I offered to help. With a gentle smile, Wendy gave me a lesson in sexual modesty: "Keeping both hands busy is a strategy I employ to avoid embarrassing men who might offer to shake hands." As a sign of sexual modesty, some Jewish women do not shake hands with single or married men. Sexual modesty recognizes both the physical and the symbolic, like Rebekah's covering herself with a veil. Touching is a form of communication and, among Orthodox Jews, touching the opposite sex is reserved for the bonds of marriage.

7. Martin, Thompson, and Richards (2005), DVD time code: 18:36.

8. Holland (1988), 81.

E S S A Y   D 4

RAISING THE BAR FOR PARENTS IN PREPARING YOUNG MISSIONARIES

JOHN P. LIVINGSTONE

As a mission president I learned that the best missionaries seem to wear their religion like a comfortable, well-fitting coat. For some missionaries that spiritual confidence grew naturally with careful nurturing from parents who radiated the love of the Lord. For others it came with deliberate, often painful decisions and struggles against societal norms. Still others achieved that comfort only after profound soul searching and sincere repentance. Regardless of the pathway to missionary success, the standard is the same: an unwavering testimony, unequivocal worthiness, and an unflagging commitment as a representative of Jesus Christ.

Church leaders have indicated that missionaries must now qualify at higher standards to be called on missions. Elder M. Russell Ballard said:

> As an Apostle of the Lord Jesus Christ, I call upon you to begin right now—tonight—to be fully and completely worthy. Resolve and commit to yourselves and to God that from this moment forward you will strive diligently to keep your hearts, hands, and minds pure and unsullied from any kind of moral transgression. Resolve to avoid pornography as you would avoid the most insidious disease, for that is precisely what it is. Resolve to completely abstain from tobacco, alcohol, and illegal drugs. Resolve to be honest. Resolve to be good citizens and to abide by the laws of the land in which you live. Resolve that from this night forward you will never defile your body or use language that is vulgar and unbecoming to a bearer of the priesthood.[1]

President Gordon B. Hinckley gave full endorsement when he said:

> Elder Ballard has spoken to you concerning missionaries. I wish to endorse what he said. I hope that our young men, and our young women, will rise to the challenge he has set forth. We must *raise the bar* on the worthiness and qualifications of those who go into the world as ambassadors of the Lord Jesus Christ.[2]

Effective missionaries are open and honest and fun to be around. They know how to work hard and they are resilient in the face of challenges and temptations. Mission life is hard work. Waking at 6:30 A.M., getting showered and groomed by 7:30, having companion, personal, and language study (not to mention breakfast), and hitting the road by 10:00 or 11:00 means being organized and efficient. Missionaries are to be in for the night by 9:00 P.M. with lights out at 10:30. Sometimes, senior companions will suggest something like, "Let's run from door to door today, so we can get twice as much done." A young missionary may swallow a little harder when he or she hears something like that!

The mission that I presided over required missionaries to ride bicycles when they served in densely populated urban areas. They could ride through troubled neighborhoods safely and quickly. New missionaries struggled initially to keep up with a seasoned companion who seemed to have legs of iron. They rode in summer and in winter, sometimes in the snow. Sister missionaries rode bikes in dresses. All were required to wear helmets, and "helmet hair" was the bane of both the elders and sisters. Sometimes they would ride for miles to keep an appointment. A Midwestern downpour could drench them in seconds, and this always seemed to happen when they were miles from home. Yet they continued tracting, checking out media referrals, stopping to talk to people on the street who were willing to speak to them. Proselyting activity could take from sixty-five to eighty hours each week. The workload and their hearty performance were amazing. I would like to focus on ways I have observed parents promote the necessary spirituality, gospel knowledge, attitudes, and social skills that provide the foundation for successful missionary service.

FOSTERING SPIRITUALITY

Good missionaries enjoy the constant companionship of the Holy Ghost, which provides a kind of "spiritual radar" that guides them around social potholes and spiritual landmines. Good missionaries know how to behave appropriately in the apartment and on the street, on the doorstep as well as in the living room. Quick to smile and willing to listen, they attract all kinds of people with their ready wit and strong spirits. There is nothing quite like a missionary for The Church of Jesus Christ of Latter-day Saints who is fired with gospel enthusiasm but tempered by good spiritual judgment.

Parents who present spirituality in practical ways, making faith part of everyday living, raise children who are comfortable with their religion. When religion seems forced and out of character for the parents, children see little value in going through the motions. They have a hard time putting faith into any kind of meaningful context. Seminary and institute classes, personal study of the scriptures and the approved missionary library,[3] experience in serving others, and good role models will help prospective missionaries develop their spirituality. It is important to keep in mind that many missionaries come from nonmember families or less-than-ideal families. Nevertheless, friendships with other young people who are planning to serve missions or have returned from honorable missionary service can give support and encouragement.

FOSTERING GOSPEL KNOWLEDGE

Helping children adopt gospel perspectives requires teaching. Latter-day Saint parents can use family home evening as an opportunity to teach children about Heavenly Father, Jesus Christ, and the Holy Ghost. Principles of love, honesty, and kindness can be taught by example and practiced during home evenings, mealtime, and daily family interactions. As children get older, parents may teach directly from the scriptures, present the plan of salvation and the Atonement, talk about the power of procreation and the law of chastity, and ask questions that can help children see beyond unrighteous influences. The formal teaching opportunities parents take augment the learning that takes place in the home by example (see

essay D2 and chapter 29 for more ideas on nurturing children's faith). Teaching children practical ways to live the gospel, in an atmosphere of love and trust, helps them choose the right without feigned motives or competitive attitudes.

Preparing good future missionaries means teaching them to recognize various forms of temptation and transgression. This prepares them against the adversary and arms them with reasons to follow Heavenly Father's plan of happiness. For example, parents might discuss the real-life negative consequences of yielding to a temptation that may not have been portrayed in a TV show, film, or play. Role-playing difficult situations can also help children learn what to say and how to handle troubling questions or comments from others. Children who are thus prepared usually know what to say (or at least the right direction to take) when faced with temptation or ridicule outside the home.

FOSTERING APPROPRIATE ATTITUDES

Sharing honest, forthright testimony with young children allows them to hear gospel conviction from a loved one and feel the Spirit in a private setting. This builds faith beyond that which is learned in more public situations. While Church meetings and programs augment and confirm what children learn at home, learning at home allows for tailoring of gospel principles to the lives of family members. (Chapter 18 provides ideas for improving family worship and gospel study.) When children have not been taught spiritual things at home, they are more susceptible to attitudes that value public presentation and the appearance of gospel living over personal covenants and obedience. Recognizing and feeling the Spirit regularly will go far in helping youth not only internalize gospel principles, but to live gospel standards for the right reasons.[4]

A manifestation of an outward appearance orientation is seen on occasion when missionaries unwittingly develop a false "missionary persona" throughout their missionary service, which is often dropped soon after they return home. Wise parents will spend the time and effort to see that gospel principles and church activity are appropriately encouraged in their children, starting from a young age. They realize that pushing children too hard to conform to appropriate appearance and proper public deportment can encourage rebellion or create a kind of allergy to authority that may result in sneaky disobedience to parents and leaders, rather than heartfelt willingness to follow wise counsel.[5]

Some children are more free spirited, less likely to conform easily, but make great missionaries once they catch the vision. When parents notice a troubling attitude or inclination, it would be appropriate to talk about it in kind and sensitive ways at opportune moments. Ward youth leaders, home teachers, and members of extended family who have developed a rapport with a struggling young man or woman can also make a tremendous difference during times when teens are less open to parental input.

FOSTERING SOCIAL SKILLS

Inviting nonmember friends and neighbors into our homes can be helpful as well. When parents try to create an open, friendly atmosphere at home, children see the importance of sociability and become good neighbors themselves without feeling they have to compromise gospel standards to make friends. They can learn from parental modeling how to be good hosts and not to be defensive about their religion as they develop the ability to share their beliefs without causing undue social or personal pressure.

As we do our best to teach correct principles and let our children learn to govern themselves,[6] we will maximize the probability that children and teens will make gospel-centered choices during their formative years. These good choices will help prepare missionaries who are resilient, happy, and prepared to meet whatever levels of faith and performance are required by inspired Church leaders.

ABOUT THE AUTHOR

John P. Livingstone, Ed.D., is an associate professor of Church history and doctrine at Brigham Young University and is chartered as a psychologist in Canada.

ADDITIONAL READING

Church Educational System (2005), *Missionary Preparation: Religion 130 Student Readings* (Salt Lake City: Intellectual Reserve). This book is available at ldscatalog.org, item 36913.

Ed J. Pinegar (2001), *Ultimate Missionary Companion* (American Fork, UT: Covenant).

S. Brent Scharman (2004, October), Preparing your future missionary, *Ensign, 34*(10), 17–21.

Richard G. Scott (2005, May), The power of *Preach My Gospel, Ensign, 35*(5), 29–31.

NOTES

1. M. Russell Ballard (2002, November), The greatest generation of missionaries, *Ensign, 32*(11), 47.

2. Gordon B. Hinckley (2002, November), To men of the priesthood, *Ensign, 32*(11), 57; emphasis added.

3. Missionaries are encouraged to study the standard works and the approved missionary library, which consists of the following four books: James E. Talmage, *Jesus the Christ* (item 80352000, available at ldscatalog.com); M. Russell Ballard, *Our Search for Happiness* (item 80870000); *True to the Faith* (item 36863000); and *Our Heritage* (item 35448000). See *Preach My Gospel* (item 36617000), page viii.

4. B. L. Top and B. A. Chadwick (1998, Summer), Raising righteous children in a wicked world, *BYU Magazine, 52*(3), 41–51.

5. C. H. Hart, L. D. Newell, and L. L. Sine (2000), Proclamation-based principles of parenting and supportive scholarship; in David C. Dollahite, ed., *Strengthening Our Families: An In-Depth Look at the Proclamation on the Family* (Salt Lake City: Bookcraft), 100–123.

6. The Prophet Joseph Smith said of the Latter-day Saints, "I teach them correct principles, and they govern themselves." See George Q. Cannon (1888), *Life of Joseph Smith, the Prophet* (Salt Lake City: Juvenile Instructor Office; reprint, Salt Lake City: Deseret Book, 1958), 529.

CHAPTER 19

FAITHFUL FATHERING

E. JEFFREY HILL AND DAVID C. DOLLAHITE

By divine design, fathers are to preside over their families in love and righteousness and are
responsible to provide the necessities of life and protection for their families. . . . In these sacred responsibilities,
fathers and mothers are obligated to help one another as equal partners.[1]
—"The Family: A Proclamation to the World"

Becoming a faithful father is a noble mission. Of the myriad titles that He could have chosen, God has asked us to call Him Father. President Gordon B. Hinckley taught, "What greater thing in all this world can there be than to become the father of a precious child, a son or daughter of God, our Father in Heaven?"[2] President Ezra Taft Benson emphasized, "Remember your sacred calling as a father in Israel—your most important calling in time and eternity—a calling from which you will never be released."[3] Respected researchers recognize that fathers serve essential roles in the home as "companions, care providers, spouses, protectors, models, moral guides, teachers, [and] breadwinners."[4]

When a man becomes a new father, this weighty responsibility can seem overwhelming. The purpose of this chapter is to explore the sacred stewardship of being a faithful father as outlined in the proclamation and to share an optimistic vision that, with the help of the Lord, most fathers can successfully fulfill these responsibilities. Being an excellent father may be hard. But, with the help of the Lord, faithful men can do hard things (see Philippians 4:13). Our perspective is that being a successful father is not so much about doing grand and glorious things. It is more about persevering in doing many faithful things, each of which can be done. As Alma taught, "by small and simple things are great things brought to pass" (Alma 37:6). We are convinced that being a faithful father is

within the grasp of all faithful men as they persist doing these small, simple, yet great things.

In this chapter we explore the four key stewardships of faithful fathering mentioned in the seventh paragraph of the proclamation: presiding, providing, protecting, and partnering. By magnifying these four sacred stewardships, fathers learn what they need to know, do what they need to do, and become who they need to become in order to bless their children and become heirs of eternal life together.

PRESIDING

The stewardship to preside in love and righteousness rests squarely on the shoulders of a faithful father. President Howard W. Hunter taught, "Your leadership of the family is your most important and sacred responsibility."[5] Elder L. Tom Perry explained: "Fathers, by divine decree, you are to preside over your family. . . . You place the family in its proper priority. It's the part of your life that will endure beyond the grave."[6]

Presiding in love requires faithful fathers to follow the example of their Heavenly Father. Almost every time Heavenly Father's voice was heard, the Father referred to His Son as "my beloved Son" and said that He was "well pleased" with Him (Matthew 3:16–17; 17:5; 3 Nephi 11:7; see also Joseph Smith— History 1:17). This is a divine pattern that all faithful fathers can follow. Unfortunately, some children rarely hear the words "I love you" and "I am pleased with you" from their fathers. Faithful fathers will frequently communicate sincere and uplifting messages, both verbally and in writing, to show that they love their children and are pleased with them. This can be difficult, especially for those without role models. It's difficult, but it can be done.

To preside in righteousness, faithful fathers must lead out in family worship within the home. Presiding involves extending the blessings of the priesthood to children through father's blessings and leading the family in prayer, scripture study, family home evening, Sabbath day activities, and other family devotional activities. Recent research shows that highly religious fathers are more likely to be both highly involved and more affectionate with their children.[7]

As one who presides, a faithful father helps his children capture a vision of what the Lord expects for them. One of the best ways to do this is to give fathers' blessings on a regular basis. Some fathers have the tradition of blessing their children before each school year or before other special occasions. One father shared this example:

> On the Saturday before the first fast Sunday after the birthday, I take the birthday child out on a one-on-one date. We eat wherever she chooses and we talk about the highlights of the year just past. Then we converse about the upcoming year and consider special hopes, needs, and wants. After returning home from the meal, we start our fast, kneeling with the rest of the family in prayer and asking for the Lord's Spirit to be with us. The next day (fast Sunday), before breaking our fast, I give that child a blessing for the coming year.

As part of their stewardship to preside, fathers are responsible to organize the everyday activities of the home so that family members are brought together frequently to be nourished physically and spiritually. Elder L. Tom Perry taught, "You preside at the meal table, at family prayer. You preside at family home evening; and as guided by the Spirit of the Lord, you see that your children are taught correct principles."[8] Author Robert Bellah wrote, "The family meal . . . is the chief family celebration, even a family sacrament."[9]

Faithful fathers who serve as righteous priesthood holders are often called to preside in places besides the home. These fathers may find it difficult to find adequate time to fulfill their priesthood and family responsibilities. While Church callings are important and should be a high priority, the work of a father is the greatest calling any man can have. The scriptures provide an important lesson. The only time the Lord used the word *rebuke* to chasten the Prophet Joseph Smith was when Joseph failed to teach his children at a time of compelling Church responsibilities (see D&C 93:47–48). If the head of the dispensation of the fulness of times (D&C 112:30) was expected to make time for his fathering, fathers now ought to do the same.

Author George Durrant provides a perspective that serving one's family is Church work:

> While I was mission president, I would quite often resolve that it was again time for some more high-priority Church work. Then [our family] would all go to an amusement park. . . . I just walked around the park with a smile on my face, holding hands with my children, eating all the cotton candy I could stand. Once in a while, a thought would enter my mind: "Hey, you're the mission president. You'd better get back to the office." But then I'd smile again and say to myself, "Well, I'm doing my Church work here. I'm with my children and my wife. We're having a fun day and tonight I'll be able to write in my journal that I did six hours of glorious Church work today.[10]

As a faithful father learns to harmonize Church and paternal responsibilities, he can also reach out and assume a fathering role for others among God's children. The Lord has said, "Wherefore, be faithful; . . . succor the weak, lift up the hands which hang down, and strengthen the feeble knees" (D&C 81:5). Home teaching is a wonderful way to be a caring father figure, and men may act as surrogate fathers in informal settings, as well. These fathers enrich the lives of others while teaching their own children important lessons of service.

PROVIDING

Faithful fathers are responsible to provide the necessities of life for their families. President Gordon B. Hinckley emphasized the importance of providing adequately: "It is your primary obligation to provide for your family."[11] President Howard W. Hunter taught, "You [fathers] have the responsibility, unless disabled, to provide temporal support for your wife and children."[12]

Faithful fathers are not only responsible for providing an income, but also for establishing sound financial management at home. President Hinckley taught: "I urge you to be modest in your expenditures; discipline yourselves in your purchases to avoid debt to the extent possible. Pay off debt as quickly as you can, and free yourselves from bondage."[13]

Fathers should work as partners with their wives in tending to financial matters. In this joint responsibility, husbands and wives should be respectful to one another, even when disagreements may arise. (Chapter 8 includes suggestions for making financial decisions together.) Fathers must teach their children principles of providing. President Benson said, "Teach your children to work. . . . Establishing mission funds and education funds for your children shows them what Dad considers to be important."[14]

Providing the necessities of life, however, should not be used as justification for spending too much time and energy at work simply to provide a high standard of living. Sometimes hopes of achieving greater success, a higher salary, or a more powerful title lure men to spend more time in the workplace, rather than in the home. One of the most important aspects of providing for one's children is to bestow upon them enough paternal time and enthusiastic involvement.

George Durrant captured the relative importance of work and family:

> At your place of work, you are needed. But, sad as it may seem, there has never been a man who, when he leaves his daily job . . . or when he retires, is not adequately replaced. . . . As one man said, "I felt that if I left the company, it would take a month or so and then I'd be replaced and they wouldn't even miss me. But," he said, "I was wrong. It only took a week." . . . But there is a place where a man has no substitute. Not after a month or a year or a generation. That is the place where they call him "Father." When he leaves home [for work], he's missed. And until he returns, there will be an empty, unfilled space in the hearts of his family.[15]

PROTECTING

President Howard W. Hunter taught, "A righteous father protects his children with his time and presence in their social, educational, and spiritual activities and responsibilities."[16] Elder L. Tom Perry said: "We need to make our homes a place of refuge from the storm, which is increasing in intensity all about us. Even if the smallest openings are left unattended, negative influences can penetrate the very walls of our homes."[17] We live in a world in which moral dangers confront children at earlier and earlier ages. Faithful

fathers should actively protect their children by helping them make wise choices about the literature they read, the movies they see, the television programs they watch, the Internet sites they visit, and the friendships they establish. President Gordon B. Hinckley wrote: "Guard your homes. How foolish it seems to install bars and bolts and electronic devices against thieves and molesters while more insidious intruders stealthily enter and despoil."[18]

Faithful fathers protect their children by setting clear boundaries about what is and is not allowed in the home. It is especially important that fathers are good examples in this respect. As the father of the home shuns evil and keeps his thoughts, words, and actions pure, his children will learn to do the same. It is helpful for parents to watch media with their children and turn it off with an explanation when it violates the standards of the home. Faithful fathers can also provide both spiritual and physical protection by surveying the environment and preparing their children ahead of time to meet known dangers.

Physical protection is important. A faithful father protects his family by wisely selecting with his wife a safe neighborhood in which to locate their home. The father can also take the lead in providing physical protection by insisting upon seat belt use, installing smoke alarms, locking up dangerous chemicals, and seeing that bike helmets are worn. Appropriate physical affection between fathers and children helps them feel secure. Hugging, holding hands, and sitting close give children a tangible sense of security that words alone cannot provide. Research confirms the emotional and psychological benefits to children of meaningful physical affection, from parents in particular.[19]

While appropriate touch is important for healthy emotional and psychological development, the effects of inappropriate touch can be devastating. Abuse is harmful to the development of the heart, mind, and relationship. The Lord condemns any man who would abuse his children. President Hinckley taught, "No man who abuses his wife or children is worthy to be a member in good standing in this Church"[20] (see also D&C 121:37). A faithful father knows how to control his temper and never threatens his wife or children with actions, words, or thoughts. Where destructive abuse has occurred, there is a difficult, but achievable road to repentance, forgiveness, and eventual healing (see chapter 35 for more on abuse).

One way for a faithful father to offer protection is to formally dedicate his home as a place of safety. Some fathers have recorded and transcribed the dedicatory prayer and then displayed it in a prominent place as a reminder that the home is the Lord's. We are counseled:

> Church members may dedicate their homes as sacred edifices where the Holy Spirit can reside and where family members can worship, find safety from the world, grow spiritually, and prepare for eternal family relationships. Homes need not be free of debt to be dedicated. Unlike Church buildings, homes are not consecrated to the Lord. To dedicate a home, a family might gather and offer a prayer that includes the elements mentioned above and other words as the Spirit directs.[21]

PARTNERING

In studying proclamation-based principles of faithful fathering, we most often limit our study to the three P's: preside, provide, and protect. However, the stewardship to partner with one's eternal companion is equally important. As President Boyd K. Packer stated: "However much priesthood power and authority the men may possess—however much wisdom and experience they may accumulate—the safety of the family, the integrity of the doctrine, the ordinances, the covenants, indeed the future of the Church, rests equally on the women. . . . No man achieves the supernal exalting status of worthy fatherhood except as a gift from his wife."[22]

For a man acting alone, the responsibility to be a faithful father may seem difficult, burdensome, even overwhelming. "Fortunately, you are not required to preside and judge and act without counsel, without assistance. You have a wife—a companion, a counselor, a partner, a helpmeet, a friend."[23] With a helpmeet to help bear this burden, the stewardship of being a faithful father may become light (see Mosiah 18:8).

Faithful fathers seek help from their wives in their own stewardships to preside over their families in love and righteousness. President Howard W. Hunter wrote: "Presiding in righteousness necessitates a shared responsibility between husband and wife; together you act with knowledge and participation in all family matters. For a man to operate independent of or without regard to the feelings and counsel of his wife in governing the family is to exercise unrighteous dominion."[24] The assistance of a faithful wife can make a large difference in all family dynamics. (Chapter 7 discusses other aspects of partnering and presiding.)

Faithful fathers assist their wives in nurturing and caring for their children, as well as in the daily main-tenance of the home. President Ezra Taft Benson wrote: "Remember, brethren . . . to help with the dishes, change diapers, get up with a crying child in the night, and leave the television or the newspaper to help with the dinner. Those are the quiet ways we say 'I love you' with our actions. They bring rich dividends."[25] Scholarly research reveals that when the father is more involved in housework and childcare, both husbands and wives rate their intimate relationship as more satisfying.[26]

Faithful fathers are also sacred partners in procreation. President Benson wrote: "Husbands and wives, as co-creators, should eagerly and prayerfully invite children into their homes. Then, as each child joins their family circle, they can gratefully exclaim, as did Hannah, 'For this child I prayed; and the Lord hath given me my petition which I asked of him.'"[27]

Fathers must join with their partners in teaching their children the proper principles of procreation. President Hinckley wrote, "Let parents teach their children the sanctity of sex, that the gift of creating life is sacred, that the impulses that burn within us can be and must be disciplined and restrained if there is to be happiness, peace, and goodness."[28]

A father can show his love for his wife by expressing appreciation to her, supporting her in her individual endeavors, and assisting her in every way possible. President Hunter taught, "One of the greatest things a father can do for his children is to love their mother."[29]

While the assistance of a helpmeet is invaluable, there are circumstances in which a father is required to take on both the roles of nurturing and providing. Whether through death, disability, divorce, or other circumstances, a rapidly growing number of men are single parents. While they may feel overwhelmed, with the Lord's help, single fathers are fully capable of raising a righteous family. (Chapter 21 discusses single parenting.)

CONCLUSION

Year in and year out, faithful fathers do the everyday tasks, founded upon the gospel of Jesus Christ, that are necessary to establish, maintain, and strengthen their families. They endure to the end of their paternal stewardship in mortality and are then crowned with the glory of an eternal posterity. A faithful father does his best to fulfill his stewardships of presiding, providing, protecting, and partnering. Becoming a faithful father is of transcendent importance. President Gordon B. Hinckley taught: "When life is over and you look back, you will not take any money with you. The only thing that will give you satisfaction is what you see in the lives of your children, and you will have an understanding that comes of the gospel that these children are also our Father in Heaven's children."[30]

The process of becoming a faithful father is, in essence, the process of becoming like God. It is an apprenticeship. As a man seeks God's help to preside, provide, protect, and partner in righteousness, he receives divine direction. Just as an apprentice learns line upon line from his master, so faithful fathers can look to God for guidance and they too will learn. We believe that becoming a faithful father is within the grasp of every faithful man. Remember, "the most important of the Lord's work you and I will ever do will be within the walls of our own homes."[31]

ABOUT THE AUTHORS

E. Jeffrey Hill, MOB, Ph.D., CFLE, is an associate professor of home and family living in the School of Family Life at Brigham Young University. He and his wife, Juanita, have nine children and three grandchildren.

David C. Dollahite, Ph.D., is a professor of family life and associate director for outreach education in the School of Family Life at Brigham Young University, where he teaches and conducts research on faith and family life. He and his wife, Mary, have seven terrific kids.

ADDITIONAL READING

Alan J. Hawkins, et al. (2000), Equal partnership and the sacred responsibilities of mothers and fathers; in David C. Dollahite, ed., *Strengthening Our Families: An In-Depth Look at the Proclamation on the Family* (Salt Lake City: Bookcraft), 63–82.

E. Jeffrey Hill (2000), Balancing family and work; in David C. Dollahite, ed., *Strengthening Our Families: An In-Depth Look at the Proclamation on the Family* (Salt Lake City: Bookcraft), 202–205.

Jeffrey R. Holland (1999, May), The hands of the fathers, *Ensign*, 29(5), 14–17.

Boyd K. Packer (1998, November), Parents in Zion, *Ensign*, 28(11), 22–24.

L. Tom Perry (2004, May), Fatherhood: An eternal calling, *Ensign*, 34(5), 69–72.

Quorum of the Twelve Apostles (2002, June), Father, consider your ways, *Ensign*, 32(6), 12. Originally printed as "A message from The Church of Jesus Christ of Latter-day Saints" pamphlet, December 1973.

NOTES

1. First Presidency and Council of Twelve Apostles (1995, November), The family: A proclamation to the world, *Ensign*, 25(11), 102.

2. Gordon B. Hinckley (1998, May), Living worthy of the girl you will someday marry, *Ensign*, 28(5), 49–51.

3. Ezra Taft Benson (1987, November), To the fathers in Israel, *Ensign*, 17(5), 48–51.

4. M. E. Lamb (1997), Fathers and child development: An introductory overview and guide; in M. E. Lamb, ed., *The Role of the Father in Child Development*, 3rd ed. (New York: Wiley), 1–18.

5. Howard W. Hunter (1994, November), Being a righteous husband and father, *Ensign*, 24(11), 49–51.

6. L. Tom Perry (2004, May), Fatherhood, an eternal calling, *Ensign*, 34(5), 69–72.

7. W. B. Wilcox (2002), Religion, convention, and paternal involvement, *Journal of Marriage and the Family*, 64, 780–792.

8. Perry (2004), 71.

9. R. N. Bellah, R. Madsen, W. M. Sullivan, A. Swidler, and S. M. Tipton (1991), *The Good Society* (New York: Harper & Row), 260.

10. George D. Durrant (1976), *Love at Home Starring Father* (Salt Lake City: Bookcraft), 29.

11. Hinckley (1998), 50.

12. Hunter (1994), 51.

13. Gordon B. Hinckley (1998, November), To the boys and to the men, *Ensign*, 28(11), 51–54.

14. Benson (1987), 51.

15. Durrant (1976), 15.

16. Hunter (1994), 51.

17. L. Tom Perry (2003, May), The importance of the family, *Ensign*, 33(5), 40.

18. Gordon B. Hinckley (2002, January), Overpowering the Goliaths in our lives, *Ensign*, 32(1), 2–6.

19. P. L. Blackwell (2000), The influence of touch on child development: implications for intervention, *Infants and Young Children*, 13, 25–39.

20. Gordon B. Hinckley (1998, November), What are people asking about us? *Ensign*, 28(11), 70–72.

21. *Church Handbook of Instructions, Book 2: Priesthood and Auxiliary Leaders* (1998), 174.

22. Boyd K. Packer (1998, May), The Relief Society, *Ensign*, 28(5), 72–74.

23. Quorum of the Twelve Apostles (2002, June), Father, consider your ways, *Ensign*, 32(6), 12–16.

24. Hunter (1994), 51.

25. Benson (1987), 50.

26. S. Coltrane (2003), Fathering: paradoxes, contradictions, and dilemmas; paper presented at the Second Annual Work and Family Conference, Boston, Massachusetts; available at http://www.bcfwp.org/Conference_papers/Coltrane2003.ppt

27. Ezra Taft Benson (1987, February 27), To the mothers in Zion; fireside for parents; available at http://www.byu.edu/fc/ee/w_etb87.htm

28. Gordon B. Hinckley (1996, September), Four simple things to help our families and our nations, *Ensign*, 26(9), 2–8.

29. Hunter (1994), 51.

30. Gordon B. Hinckley (2002, September 10), What President Hinckley told the Russian Saints; available at http://www.meridianmagazine.com/prophettour/gbhtalkprint.html

31. Harold B. Lee (1974), *Stand Ye in Holy Places* (Salt Lake City: Deseret Book), 255.

CHAPTER 20

FAITHFUL MOTHERING

LILI DE HOYOS ANDERSON AND CAMILLE S. WILLIAMS

By divine design, . . . mothers are primarily responsible for the nurture of their children.
In these sacred responsibilities, fathers and mothers are obligated to help one another as equal partners.[1]
—"The Family: A Proclamation to the World"

The proclamation boldly states that the primary responsibility of mothers is to nurture their children. Although Latter-day Saint women also fill a variety of other roles—as equal partners in marriage relationships, as teachers and officers in the Church, as neighbors and members of communities—they have also been counseled that "our youth need steadfast, courageous mothers" to guide them in this age when "gender is being confused, and gender roles are being repudiated."[2]

Because we live in a society with shifting values, it is essential that women understand their callings and responsibilities and then pursue a steady course to fulfill them. Sister Sheri L. Dew noted: "There is not a man or woman in this Church who doesn't have a specific mission to perform in helping build up the kingdom of God. And the more we come to *really believe* that, the more immune we become to the world's distractions."[3] "Some [gospel teachings]," President Gordon B. Hinckley said, "may appear a little out-of-date in our society, but this does not detract from their validity nor diminish the virtue of their application."[4] As women follow prophetic counsel to nurture their children and seek God's help in this stewardship, the pull of worldly influences will be diminished.

President Ezra Taft Benson asked women to consider the eternal consequences of their call to serve in the home: "Mothers in Zion, your God-given roles are so vital to your own exaltation and to the salvation and exaltation of your family."[5] President David O. McKay also reminded us:

Th[e] ability and willingness properly to rear children, the gift to love, and eagerness, yes, longing to express it in soul development, make motherhood the noblest office or calling in the world. . . . In her high duty and service to humanity, endowing with immortality eternal spirits, [a mother] is co-partner with the Creator himself.[6]

THE RESPONSIBILITY TO NURTURE CHILDREN

The proclamation affirms that "mothers are primarily responsible for the nurture of their children."[7] Their nurturing blesses the lives of their children and blesses their own lives. The day-to-day work of rearing children invites mothers to develop kindness and longsuffering, to teach wisely, and to be sensitive to each child's individual needs. Elder M. Russell Ballard assured mothers that they have the ability to nurture:

Nurturing refers to parenting behaviors such as warmth, support, bonding, attachment, recognizing each child's unique needs and abilities, and attending to children's needs. Nurturing in and of itself is more important in the development of a child than is any particular method or technique of child rearing. It hardly needs saying that nurturing is best carried out in a stable, safe, family context.[8]

Scholarly literature similarly identifies the aspects of nurturing as "attachment, warmth, support, recognizing the individuality of each child, and attending to children's needs."[9] Research supports the important links between the quality of mother–child interactions and children's developmental outcomes, as well as the skills and personal qualities they later develop.[10] Research also indicates that a critical component of these interactions is the ability of the mother and child to adapt to one another.[11]

Unfortunately, much of the research on mothering tends to reduce it to a set of tasks connected to the care of children and the home.[12] Similarly, contemporary discourse describes these family responsibilities as a set of mundane chores that undermine the dignity and intelligence of women. As a result, it may appear to some that mothering consists simply of a set of chores that could be performed by anyone equally well. Church leaders, however, have repeatedly recognized the gifts and the calling of mothers and have emphasized the importance of the unique relationship that connects a mother to each of her children.

Currently, there is growing recognition in the scholarly community that some sex differences are real and should be taken seriously in our individual lives and in the public policy arena.[13] (Chapter 3 discusses sex differences and the development of gender identity.) The nurturing of fathers is an important and complementary influence for children (see chapter 19). Family circumstances sometimes require a mother to enter the workforce, which may limit her time with her children. Whatever her circumstances, however, her children benefit greatly from her enduring, watchful, and inspired care.

While the nurturing role of mothers is a divine and noble calling, mothering may not feel noble on a daily basis. One mother explained to Elder Jeffrey R. Holland that "whenever she heard talks on LDS motherhood, she worried because she felt she didn't measure up." She felt that the world expected her to produce a child prodigy, and "she often felt people were sometimes patronizing, almost always without meaning to be, because the advice she got or even the compliments she received seemed to reflect nothing of the mental investment, the spiritual and emotional exertion, the long-night, long-day, stretched-to-the-limit demands that sometimes are required in trying to be and wanting to be the mother God hopes she

will be." But one thing, she said, kept her going: "'Through the thick and thin of this, and through the occasional tears of it all, *I know deep down inside I am doing God's work.*'"[14] This mother found peace of mind in giving mothering her best efforts by partnering with God in the nurture of her children.

Whether single, married, or divorced, with children or without, the doctrine of the kingdom teaches us that each woman who qualifies for the matchless gift of eternal life will be exalted in the highest level of the celestial kingdom; that is, she will be a mother.[15] Every woman is invited, even admonished, to develop the qualities of righteous mothers. All around us are neighbors, ward members, family members, friends, coworkers; young, middle-aged, and older people who are "desperate for [the] love and leadership" our mothering can provide.[16]

GIVING MOTHERING OUR BEST EFFORTS

In a society that has devalued mothering and homemaking,[17] women need to have confidence that the Lord will help them find ways of understanding and succeeding in their call to nurture children. Nurturing children demands intellectual, physical, and spiritual effort, in addition to large quantities of time, love, and preparation. President Hinckley counseled:

> I think the nurture and upbringing of children is more than a part-time responsibility. I recognize that some women must work, but I fear that there are far too many who do so only to get the means for a little more luxury and a few fancier toys.
>
> If you must work, you have an increased load to bear. You cannot afford to neglect your children. They need your supervision in studying, in working inside and outside the home, in the nurturing that only you can adequately give—the love, the blessing, the encouragement, and the closeness of a mother.[18]

Especially challenging for women in our time is the influence of a post-feminist world. While we can rejoice in the expansion of opportunities for women in the last 150 years, some people promote the idea that freedom from oppression requires that women be free of marriage and children. Less extreme, but more pervasive in our society is the belief that to feel fulfilled, a woman needs a career outside of home and family. The counsel of the prophets, however, remains unchanged. Accepting a full-time mothering role when there may be full-time work opportunities beckoning from outside the home requires trusting that God loves us, that He wants us to have joy here on earth as well as in the next life, and that as with any calling, in motherhood we are entitled to His help and will receive joy in our service. The proverb "Trust in the Lord with all thine heart; and lean not unto thine own understanding" (Proverbs 3:5) provides an inspired framework for setting aside the things of the world (see D&C 25:10) to better serve our children.

Deliberately delaying marriage, motherhood, or both to first establish a career can be costly in unforeseen ways.[19] Because female fertility drops at age 30 and more dramatically at 35, taking time to establish a career prior to beginning a family affects how easily a woman can have children and the number of children she can have.[20] In speaking to the young women of the Church, President James E. Faust suggested that it may, in fact, be possible to "have it all," just not all at the same time.[21] Children—despite our feelings on those long, challenging days—do grow up and move on, generally when mothers still have many productive adult years ahead of them. A second career is available to most women who have the interest or inclination.

While some daily demands on mothers are reduced when the last child goes to school, it is a mistake to conclude that school-aged children and adolescents don't benefit profoundly from maternal engagement and monitoring.[22] Parental supervision is crucial to teens' emotional, scholastic, and moral development.[23] The lack of parental monitoring is "a risk factor in children's development of delinquent, antisocial behavior problems."[24] "Be at the crossroads," President Ezra Taft Benson advised mothers, "when your children are either coming or going—when they leave and return from school, when they leave and return from dates, when they bring friends home. Be there at the crossroads whether your children are six or sixteen."[25]

A further consideration for the dual-income couple is that the work pressures on parents affect "adolescents' psychological well-being indirectly via [their] effect on [parents] . . . and on parent-adolescent conflict."[26] Also, recent large-scale research found that for young children, more time spent in out-of-home child care arrangements (regardless of quality) is associated with elevated risk for oppositional, disobedient, and aggressive childhood behavior.[27] These are factors to prayerfully consider when making decisions about employment and other pursuits that affect family life.

NURTURING CHILDREN IS DOING GOD'S WORK

With fathers usually working away from the home, with schools usually educating children, and with families more often consuming than producing goods and services, some women feel that mothers' roles have become mostly ornamental: creating a beautiful home and garden, beautiful children, and a beautiful self. Child-rearing can even become a competitive endeavor, with a mother's feelings of worth and success based on how close she comes to being a "super-mom" with "super-kids," while looking like a supermodel. Such misplaced expectations, with their largely superficial focus, may ultimately undermine our ability to succeed in nurturing God's children as He would have us do. One woman suggested a better focus for mothers:

> The great strength of a good woman—a Saint, if you will—is her personal testimony of the Savior and her faith in his spokesmen, the prophet and the Apostles of Jesus Christ. If she follows them, she will have the countenance of Christ for her beauty, the peace of Christ to support her emotionally, the Savior's example as a means to solve her problems and to strengthen her, and the love of Christ as the source of love for herself, her family, and those about her. She can be sure of herself as a wife and mother and find joy and fulfillment in her role in the home.[28]

Our society often promotes the idea that the measure of our worth is our ability to generate income, succeed at a career, and to acquire worldly goods. The gospel invites us instead to fulfill the measure of our creation and to recognize marriage and family as the primary context in which this can happen. We can view each other, whether full-time in the home with children or in the workforce, neither with envy nor with condemnation. As women, we ought to be able to give each other the benefit of the doubt, always recognizing that we don't fully know the heart, the motivations, or the circumstances in which each mother decides how she can best serve her family. We can love, help, appreciate, and learn from each other whatever our familial, economic, or employment situations may be.

Single mothers face the tremendous challenges of both providing for and nurturing their children, too often without the consistent support of the children's father or of the larger community. President Hinckley recognized the particular needs of mothers raising children alone:

> For you who are single parents, I say that many hands stand ready to help you. The Lord is not unmindful of you. Neither is His Church.
>
> May He bless you, my beloved sisters who find yourselves in the situation of single parenthood. May you have health, strength, vitality to carry the heavy burden that is yours. May you have loving friends and associates to bear you up in your times of trial. You know the power of prayer as perhaps few others do. Many of you spend much time on your knees speaking with your Father in Heaven, with tears running down your cheeks. Please know that we also pray for you.[29]

Single mothers can seek support from family, friends, and Church members (see chapter 21) and can trust that God will strengthen them in their difficult responsibilities.

PARTNER WITH GOD IN NURTURING CHILDREN

As we partner with God in nurturing His children, it may be helpful to consider the following suggestions. They reflect practical knowledge gained through mothering, as well as the advice of prophets; they are also consistent with contemporary research on the family.

Nurture self and children in the doctrines of the kingdom. Study the scriptures and the words of the prophets. Study the great plan of happiness so that you can teach it to your children "when thou walkest by the way, and when thou liest down, and when thou risest up" (Deuteronomy 6:7). Study what has been specifically written or spoken by prophets and other inspired leaders about marriage, family, and motherhood. Elder Holland reminded mothers: "Remember, remember all the days of your motherhood: 'Ye have not come thus far save it were by the word of Christ with unshaken faith in him, relying wholly upon the merits of him who is mighty to save' [2 Ne. 31:19]. Rely on Him. Rely on Him heavily."[30]

Nurture children through a positive attitude. Teaching and correction are certainly called for regularly, but a parent's pervasive criticism damages children and the parent–child relationship.[31] One study associated satisfaction in marriage relationships with a ratio of at least five positive messages to every nega-

tive message.[32] Similarly, as we teach, correct, and direct children, our voice tone, language choice, and facial expression should be positive as often as possible.

Nurture genuine connections with your children. It is important to take time to play with our children, go on walks, learn together, read together, do something fun every day. Enjoying our children together and individually allows us to become better aware of what is unique and precious about each child. This kind of "quality time" should not be confused with the trend some years ago to justify spending less time with children by planning shorter, "higher quality" interactions. Elder Ballard reminded parents, "Quality is a direct function of quantity—and mothers, to nurture their children properly, must provide both."[33] In addition, each child will have her own opinion about what is valuable.[34] Neither is quantity time sufficient by itself. Just being in the home or even in the room with children does not make for effective mothering. Of course, a mother's every minute need not be focused on children, but being full-time at home, or working only part-time, or running a home business may not guarantee connectedness with children. Television, e-mail, shopping, scrapbooking, going to the gym, cleaning, cooking, scripture study, Church callings, or any activity can become our focus to such an extent that we ultimately are not truly engaged with our children, involved in their lives, and listening carefully to their concerns.

Being aware of how we use our time and making conscious decisions to regulate the unending distractions of daily life can help us develop an "active involvement in and connection to the lives of [our] children, even during the middle years of adolescence," a potent protector of children.[35] Prayerful attention to priorities and direction from priesthood blessings can be particularly helpful when demanding Church callings, children with special needs, or other circumstances stretch a mother's ability to connect with her children.

Be patient in nurturing. Motherhood is an exercise in delayed gratification. Infants are demanding, toddlers are exhausting, and teens can be intensely focused on themselves. Many of the results of mothers' efforts appear in children's lives years later, as they mature and choose to live worthily. (Essay E3 discusses finding joy in the early years of motherhood and as children mature.) Sometimes those results don't happen in a timely manner, despite much service and sacrifice. (Chapter 26 provides helps for parents whose children choose a different path.)

Nurture children's understanding of the importance of work in the home. Often mothers must find a livable compromise between desires for a clean, orderly home and a home that is functional, comfortable, and welcoming to every family member, including the youngest.[36] Take the time and make the effort to teach children to complete household chores that are age-appropriate, and to understand that work within the home is necessary and honorable.[37] It is sometimes hard to remember that children act their ages and that they are not like small adults. Help them to understand that work in the home is vital for keeping the family functioning and is a genuine labor of love. (Chapter 27 and essay A1 describe the blessings of family work.)

Recognize that nurturing children is physically, emotionally, and spiritually demanding.[38] In mothering, fatigue is common.[39] Perhaps one of the greatest challenges of mothering is to remain pleasant and attentive to children when exhaustion is a day-to-day reality. "And let us not be weary in well doing: for in due season we shall reap, if we faint not" (Galatians 6:9). It is also vital for women to find ways to replenish their reserves of energy and patience and to restore their vision and perspective. Prayerfully seeking to find and work towards appropriate expectations, rather than seeking to keep up an image, also liberates mothers from unnecessary stress. Play groups, baby-sitting co-ops, or trading child care can give mothers a break from the energy drain of being on constant call, and can provide good friendships for adults and children. Helping others and being willing to accept help when needed can provide the rejuvenation that comes through service as well as through having one's own needs met

Nurture other mothers. It is important that we express gratitude and support for those who "mother" our children at school, at church, in our neighborhood, and in the extended family. Extend fellowship to all mothers, whether or not they are in the same life stage or circumstances. Let us lend helping hands, restraining criticism or gossip.

CONCLUSION

President Hinckley identified mothers as "one bright shining hope in a world that is marching toward self-destruction."[40] Ultimately, mothering is about helping to save souls in a God-given steward-

ship. Jesus Christ is the Teacher from whom we will learn what we need to know to succeed as mothers. Elder Ballard asked women to consider whether they, like the Savior Himself, may have "stepped forward" to accept their stewardships: "If you are wondering if you make a difference to the Lord, imagine the impact when you make commitments such as the following: 'Father, if you need a woman to rear children in righteousness, here am I, send me. . . . If you need a woman of faithful steadiness, here am I, send me.'"[41] If we joyfully press forward, blessing and nurturing the rising generation, each mother can be part of that brightness of hope that will bless us, our families, and the world.

ABOUT THE AUTHORS

Lili De Hoyos Anderson, MSW, Ph.D., full-time wife and mother of eight for almost 20 years, now has a private practice in individual, marriage, and family therapy and teaches part time for the BYU School of Family Life. She and her husband, Christian, are grandparents of seven.

Camille S. Williams, JD, MA, BA, administrative director of the Marriage and Family Law Research Grant at the J. Reuben Clark Law School, is an assistant Provo City attorney and has taught and practiced family law. She and her husband, Richard, are parents of five children and grandparents of six.

ADDITIONAL READING

Alan J. Hawkins, et al. (2000), Equal partnership and the sacred responsibilities of mothers and fathers; in David C. Dollahite, ed., *Strengthening Our Families: An In-Depth Look at the Proclamation on the Family* (Salt Lake City: Bookcraft), 63–82.

Gordon B. Hinckley (2000, November). Your greatest challenge, mother, *Ensign*, 30(11), 97–100.

Jeffrey R. Holland (1997, May), Because she is a mother, *Ensign*, 27(5), 35–37.

NOTES

1. First Presidency and Council of Twelve Apostles (1995, November), The family: A proclamation to the world, *Ensign*, 25(11), 102.

2. M. Russell Ballard (in press), The sacred responsibilities of parenthood, *Ensign*; Brigham Young University Education Week Devotional Address, 19 August 2003.

3. Sheri Dew (2004), *No One Can Take Your Place* (Salt Lake City: Deseret Book), 21.

4. Gordon B. Hinckley (2005, January), Pursue the steady course, *Ensign*, 35(1), 5.

5. Ezra Taft Benson (1987, February 22), To the mothers in Zion; address given at a fireside for parents; published as a pamphlet (Salt Lake City: The Church of Jesus Christ of Latter-day Saints), 8.

6. David O. McKay (1953), *Gospel Ideals* (Salt Lake City: Improvement Era), 453–454.

7. First Presidency and Council of Twelve Apostles (1995), 102.

8. Ballard (in press).

9. A. J. Hawkins, et al. (2000), Equal partnership and the sacred responsibilities of mothers and fathers; in D. C. Dollahite, ed., *Strengthening Our Families: An In-Depth Look at the Proclamation on the Family* (Salt Lake City: Bookcraft), 70. For an excellent discussion of various aspects of nurturing, see pages 70–74 in that volume.

10. K. E. Barnard and J. E. Solchany (2002), Mothering; in M. H. Bornstein, ed., *Handbook of Parenting, 2d ed., Volume 3: Being and Becoming a Parent* (Mahwah, NJ: Lawrence Erlbaum), 3–25 (especially page 17).

11. Barnard and Solchany (2002), 16.

12. T. Arendell (2000), Conceiving and investigating motherhood: The decade's scholarship, *Journal of Marriage and Family, 62*, 1192–1207; see also R. M. Beckwith (2003), *Ambivalence: Comparing Findings with Two Opposing Paradigms of Intent;* master's thesis, Brigham Young University, Provo, UT, 55–61.

13. S. E. Rhoads (2004), *Taking Sex Differences Seriously* (San Francisco: Encounter Books).

14. Jeffrey R. Holland (1997, May), Because she is a mother, *Ensign, 27*(5), 36.

15. Sheri L. Dew (2001, November), Are we not all mothers? *Ensign, 31*(11), 96–98.

16. Ibid., 97.

17. See Beckwith (2003).

18. Gordon B. Hinckley (1998, November), Walking in the light of the Lord, *Ensign, 28*(11), 99.

19. See Russell M. Nelson (2005, February 6), Faith and families; CES Fireside Address; available at http://speeches.byu.edu

20. S. A. Hewlett (2002), *Creating a Life: Professional Women and the Quest for Children* (New York: Talk Miramax Books).

21. James E. Faust (1986, September), A message to my granddaughters: Becoming "great women," *Ensign, 16*(9), 19.

22. M. Eberstadt (2001, June and July), Home-Alone America, *Policy Review*, 18.

23. S. A. Newman (2000), America's after-school choice: The prime time for juvenile crime or youth enrichment and achievement (Washington, D.C.: Fight Crime: Invest in Kids), 2–3; available at http://www.fightcrime.org/reports/as2000.pdf; G. S. Pettit, R. D. Laird, K. A. Dodge, J. E. Bates, and M. M. Criss (2001), Antecedents and behavior-problem outcomes of parental monitoring and psychological control in early adolescence, *Child Development, 72*, 596.

24. Pettit, et al. (2001), 596.

25. Benson (1987), 8. President Benson ended this address with "Ten Ways to Spend Time with Children." They are as follows: (1) Be at the crossroads, (2) Be a real friend, (3) Read to your children, (4) Pray with your children, (5) Have weekly home evenings, (6) Be together at mealtimes, (7) Read scriptures daily, (8) Do things as a family, (9) Teach your children, (10) Truly love your children.

26. A. C. Crouter, M. F. Bumpus, M. C. Maguire, S. M. McHale (1999), Linking parents' work pressure and adolescents' well-being: Insights into dynamics in dual-earner families, *Developmental Psychology, 35*, 1460.

27. National Institute of Child Health and Human Development Early Child Care Research Network (2003), Does amount of time spent in child care predict socioemotional adjustment during the transition to kindergarten? *Child Development, 74*, 976–1005.

28. Quoted in Ezra Taft Benson (1981, November), The honored place of woman, *Ensign, 11*(11), 107.

29. Gordon B. Hinckley (1996, November), Women of the Church, *Ensign, 26*(11), 69.

30. Holland (1997), 37.

31. C. H. Hart, L. D. Newell, and L. L. Sine (2000), Proclamation-based principles of parenting and supportive scholarship; in D. C. Dollahite, ed., *Strengthening Our Families: An In-Depth Look at the Proclamation on the Family* (Salt Lake City: Bookcraft), 100–123.

32. J. Gottman, with N. Silver (1994), *Why Marriages Succeed or Fail: What You Can Learn from the Breakthrough Research to Make Your Marriage Last* (New York: Simon & Schuster), 56–61.

33. Ballard (in press).

34. P. H. Christensen (2002), Why more "quality time" is not on the top of children's lists: The "qualities of time" for children, *Children & Society, 16*(2002), 77–88. Children particularly valued family time as ordinariness and routine, and as someone being there for them; Christensen's study also refutes and refines the findings of Ellen Galinsky (1999), *Ask the Children: What America's Children Really Think About Working Parents* (New York: William Morrow).

35. K. Bogenschneider, M. Wu, M. Raffaelli, J. C. Tsay (1998), "Other teens drink, but not my kid": Does parental awareness of adolescent alcohol use protect adolescents from risky consequences? *Journal of Marriage and the Family, 60*, 368.

36. See Beckwith (2003).

37. N. R. Ahlander and K. S. Bahr (1995), Beyond drudgery, power, and equity: Toward an expanded discourse on the moral dimensions of housework in families, *Journal of Marriage and the Family, 57*, 54–68.

38. See Beckwith (2003).

39. Ibid.

40. Gordon B. Hinckley (2004, January 10), Standing strong and immoveable; address delivered at the Worldwide Leadership Training Meeting: The Priesthood and the Auxiliaries of the Relief Society, Young Women, and Primary (Salt Lake City: The Church of Jesus Christ of Latter-day Saints), 20.

41. M. Russell Ballard (2001, March 13), Here am I, send me; BYU Devotional Address; available at http://speeches.byu.edu

CHAPTER 21

TOWARD SUCCESSFUL SINGLE PARENTING

ELAINE WALTON AND GARY BURLINGAME

Disability, death, or other circumstances may necessitate individual adaptation.
Extended families should lend support when needed.[1]
—"The Family: A Proclamation to the World"

The proclamation has special application to families who fall outside of the traditional two-parent model. As we consider single-parent families, it is important to keep in mind that no uniform template exists. These homes emerge from a variety of special circumstances. Some are created when a parent dies; others from abandonment, divorce, or from out-of-wedlock pregnancies. Single-parent families are also created when a grandparent or other relative assumes the parenting responsibilities from biological parents. While the number of variations leading to these special homes seems infinite, a common theme found with many single parents and their children is their struggle with the proclamation's statement: "Children are entitled to birth within the bonds of matrimony, and to be reared by a father and a mother who honor marital vows with complete fidelity."[2]

Latter-day Saints subscribe to an ideal family model and are counseled by Church leaders not to lower their standards. How then do the ideals of the proclamation apply to single-parent homes? In our view, the proclamation describes an ideal and establishes principles that can be used to strengthen all families, regardless of their structure. While a married, two-parent family unit is clearly the ideal, it is equally clear that Heavenly Father has a special interest and concern for single-parent homes. "For the Lord your God . . . doth execute the judgment of the fatherless and widow" (deals justly with them) (Deuteronomy 10:17–18; cf. Isaiah 1:17). Religion that God accepts as pure is "to visit the fatherless and widows in their affliction" (James 1:27). This same special concern must be kept in mind as we view the ever-increasing number of single-parent homes. Our loving God, who knows all things, surely understands the difficulty of single parenting and has commanded the religious community to pay special attention to single parents' needs, just as He asks us to pay attention to the poor. In doing so, He acknowledges there are special blessings for those who attend to the poor, fatherless, and widows—and for those who are the recipients of this care. An understanding of God's special concern emerges as one considers the challenges that often arise for single parents.

CHALLENGES OF SINGLE PARENTING

In some cases, children may be better off in single-parent homes, particularly when divorce marks the end of domestic violence. However, the majority of studies clearly demonstrate the benefits of two married parents for children. Children of divorce are more likely than children from two-parent families to suffer economically, academically, and psychologically, and they are at greater risk for physical or sexual abuse.[3] Children may respond to the pressures of a single-parent family with disruptive behaviors,[4] and daughters without a father in the home may be at risk for early sexual activity and teenage pregnancy.[5] The findings from these studies are sobering, but conclusions should be made with caution. The challenges faced by children from single-parent families are typical for most children who grow up in any conditions that put pressure on the family structure.

DIFFERENT CHALLENGES FOR DIFFERENT FAMILIES

Widow or widower. Despite Latter-day Saints' understanding that death is not a permanent separation, feelings of grief associated with the death of a parent or spouse are profound. The grief of the surviving spouse is compounded by the children's grief. The grieving parent may be torn between wanting to protect the children from the painful realities of the loss and wanting to protect herself or himself from the realities of parenting. Grieving is a lengthy, complex process and cannot be rushed (see chapter 32). But life cannot be suspended while family members grieve, especially when there are children to feed and care for. Mourners adjust to the fact that with each anniversary or important family event, the process will be experienced anew. In time the grief becomes increasingly manageable and growth-promoting rather than simply painful.

Divorced. In the United States, divorce is the most common reason for parents' being single. "More than one million children experience parental divorce every year, and about 40% of all children will experience parental divorce before reaching adulthood."[6] (Chapter 4 provides statistics on marriage and divorce among Latter-day Saints.) Compared to married individuals, divorced persons suffer more psychological and physical problems, experience greater social isolation, and have a lower standard of living.[7] Children of divorce are also at risk for a number of psychological, medical, and social problems, including difficulty with school.[8] According to family scholar Judith Wallerstein, the major impact of divorce is evidenced only after the children are grown. "The absence of a good image negatively influences their search for love, intimacy, and commitment. Anxiety leads many into making bad choices in relationships, giving up hastily when problems arise, or avoiding relationships altogether."[9]

There is disagreement among scholars regarding the consequences of divorce. Despite the bleak statistics, researchers have demonstrated that many children of divorce are stronger for their struggles. "They understand the importance of economic independence and hard work. They do not take relationships lightly. Most maintain a reverence for good family life."[10] However, this independence may contribute to postponing marriage to delay interdependence. Depending upon the circumstances, divorce may be viewed as either a departure from the stability of a two-parent family or escape from a dysfunctional home environment. There is consensus, however, regarding the resulting stress for both parents and children.[11]

Never married. Almost half of children in single-parent homes live with never-married mothers,[12] although this rate is not nearly as high in Latter-day Saint homes. It is hard to conceptualize as a loss something the family never had—two parents. Nevertheless, children of a never-married parent may feel that loss as they compare their situation with that of friends and classmates. Unwed teenage mothers may grieve lost adolescence and resent children who represent lost opportunities. For these mothers, the adjustment to parenthood will be aggravated by the fact that they must parent alone or with the help of their own parents—help that teenage mothers may simultaneously want and resent.

Single fathers. Single parenting varies by role (fathers versus mothers) and by the circumstances that created single parenthood, which in turn lead to a wide range of single-parent experiences for fathers. Fathers who do not share ongoing custodial privileges with a divorced spouse, yet embrace the ideals espoused by the proclamation, may feel disenfranchised in their ability to guide their children's lives. This often leads to disillusionment and a tendency to withdraw, further exacerbating father–child relationship strain. This "no-win" dynamic can create a cycle that estranges fathers from their children and generates additional turmoil between custodial mothers and noncustodial fathers, particularly in cases where there is failure to pay child support.

Custodial fathers face a different set of challenges. Although decreases in financial resources are less pronounced for them than for custodial mothers, uncharted territory for many fathers includes home-based tasks and responsibilities as well as child care. Simple domestic chores such as curling a daughter's hair, ironing clothes, or dealing with the school system can lead to feelings of inadequacy and frustration. Many single dads are poorly equipped to handle the overwhelming emotions associated with their newfound role. This can lead to a premature retreat into a new romantic relationship as a survival strategy for both themselves and their children. (Essay E4 includes ideas for keeping parent-child relationships strong while the parent works toward remarriage in healthy ways.)

SIMILAR CHALLENGES

Regardless of the family structure or history, all single-parent families experience some of the same challenges. In short, it is difficult for one parent to do the job of two.

Double duty. Double duty as a parent might work if it came with double resources. Instead, single parents often have twice the responsibility with half the resources. One mother commented that during the five years she was single, she received eight traffic tickets for speeding, having previously received only one—and that a warning. She explained that being single didn't make her more reckless or less law-abiding. She was just perpetually harried.[13]

Single parents are likely to be in survival mode. They give up hobbies as well as basic homemaking tasks they used to enjoy. There is never enough time or money, and they feel there is no backup when things go wrong. Some single-parent families cannot afford adequate health insurance, making preventative healthcare difficult to obtain. Single parents pray they won't get sick and that their children won't be sick or injured when the parent is unavailable. Ironically, stress makes both the parent and the children more at risk for illness.

Quality time. The time single parents have for their children may not be less but is certainly different than it would be for a two-parent family. Traditionally, fathers' interactions with children tend to be predominately task oriented or playful and mothers' interactions tend to be nurturing, although many fathers are involved with their children in various other ways, including nurturing activities.[14] However, in single-parent families where the mother is the custodial parent, the pattern is reversed. Single mothers may spend as much time with their children as mothers in two-parent families, but the time is more likely consumed in maintenance interactions, such as household chores or homework.[15] There is less time for nurture. The nurturing interactions (e.g., eating, socializing, and active leisure) are more likely to be the noncustodial father's role. This role reversal can be uncomfortable for both parents.

Noncustodial fathers can experience a similar imbalance. The so-called "Disneyland Dad" syndrome can emerge from the absence of the maintenance interactions that would naturally characterize family exchanges. Noncustodial parenting eliminates natural maintenance opportunities (e.g., mowing the lawn, taking out the garbage), while also putting a premium on the limited time fathers have with their children. Noncustodial fathers' task-oriented opportunities are limited, leading them to engage in more nurturing and entertaining activities.

Of course, more fathers are taking on the role of custodial parent, making the aforementioned examples somewhat stereotyped. In short, the custodial parent is consumed with the demands of organizing and managing, reminding and reprimanding, teaching and preaching. Quality time for enjoyable activities or meaningful sharing usually gets short shrift. One mother commented:

> I remember one day when I felt particularly energized. . . . I made a list of seventeen things we would do better as a family. Then I presented this list to the children at family home evening. I couldn't wait for their little faces to light up with enthusiasm as we launched this new program. But it didn't happen. Instead, they just sat quietly and looked at me. They didn't say anything, but I got the message. They were overwhelmed and discouraged.
>
> A few weeks later I tried a different approach for family home evening. . . . I brought into the living room a bottle of hand lotion. After our song and prayer, I announced to the children that for family home evening that night we would rub each other's feet Suddenly giggles were heard, and the evening was a time for unwinding and loosening instead of tightening the pressure on an already stressed family.[16]

Single parents will never be able to do everything they want to with their children, but they will learn that the most important things can be accomplished. God has promised that even out of bad, good can emerge: "All things work together for good to them that love God" (Romans 8:28). Even out of horrible divorces growth can occur. Many parents report that they grew closer to their children after becoming single parents, and this closeness came from dealing with difficulties.

SUCCESSFUL SINGLE PARENTING

For the most part, successful single-parent families have the same characteristics as successful two-parent families, but there are notable differences. For example, parenting, rather than the marital relationship, takes top priority. And, in the absence of marital support, single parents must be particularly diligent in taking care of themselves.

Parenting as a Priority

A successful family is often the byproduct of a successful marriage. By contrast, a single parent may devote more time to studying parenting patterns and monitoring the home environment. A family structure, rules, and norms should be carefully thought out and implemented in a consistent, meaningful way.

In reflecting on the lessons learned as a single parent, one mother commented:

> [If I had it to do over again,] I would attempt to be more consistent. Instead of feeling sorry for my children, I would recognize that they have to do some suffering, too. I cannot protect them as much as I might like. They need to be allowed to experience their own frustration and to go through their own grieving in their own way. In the meantime, the best way I can support them is to give them the benefit of a family that is relatively stable and predictable. I would prioritize goals and pick my battles carefully, but my children would learn that "no" means "no."[17]

Many single parents agonize over the time they must spend away from their children at work. President Gordon B. Hinckley joined with previous prophets in encouraging women to be at home with their children. Then he stated:

> Nevertheless, I recognize, as [President Ezra Taft Benson] recognized, that there are some women (it has become very many in fact) who have to work to provide for the needs of their families. To you I say, do the very best you can. . . . I know how some of you struggle with decisions concerning this matter. I repeat, do the very best you can. You know your circumstances, and I know that you are deeply concerned for the welfare of your children.[18]

He went on to reaffirm the importance of making parenting a priority:

> As the years pass, you will become increasingly grateful for that which you did in molding the lives of your children in the direction of righteousness and goodness, integrity and faith. That is most likely to happen if you can spend adequate time with them.[19]

Successful single parents have dealt with the demands of employment in many different ways. One mother became skilled as a medical transcriptionist—work she could do at home. Others have developed a variety of cottage industries in order to stay at home or organized co-ops exchanging child care services with other parents. Trusted friends or extended family members have tended children when employment out of the home was necessary, and some parents have successfully relied on professional child care services. In accepting their limitations, successful single parents become more creative in exploring possible resources and expanding their supportive networks. Particularly relevant for these families is the statement from the proclamation: "Extended families should lend support when needed."[20]

Take Care of Your Own Needs

Single parents who, by necessity or choice, focus on sacrificing and enduring, can deprive their children of the most valuable gift they can give—a happy parent. With the absence of marital support, successful single parents recognize the need to take care of themselves. They engage in a variety of strategies for self-care, such as developing meaningful friendships, maintaining supportive relationships with extended family members, engaging in physical exercise, obtaining professional counseling, going to single-parent support groups, and maintaining religious affiliation.

As with every other aspect of single parenting, self-care requires planning and creativity. One mother thought of her physical and emotional reserves as a bank account: "If I wanted to make withdrawals, I had to also make deposits." She chose walking and hiking as valuable deposits because "I could visit with a friend and exercise at the same time." This mother learned later to include benefits for her children in these social and recreational experiences by fostering friendships with parents who had children roughly the same ages as hers.[21]

Custodial fathers face similar challenges and run the risk of eliminating activities that energize and rejuvenate them. Guilt emerges for some if they attempt to maintain their interest in sports or exercise routines. Often fathers discontinue such activities to avoid the perception that Dad is still out playing with his friends and neglecting his parenting responsibilities. However, activity-based experiences are more likely to be the self-care strategies relied upon by fathers, and these should not be eliminated because of distorted perceptions. One custodial father maintained his workout routine at the gym and brought his children with him in the early morning. Eventually his kids began to run the track with him—an additional bonding activity.

HELP IS AVAILABLE

President Ezra Taft Benson urged single parents to "counsel with your priesthood leaders. Let them know of your needs and wants."[22] Pride often keeps single parents from speaking up, even in desperate circumstances. One mother commented:

> In retrospect, I had more flexibility than I realized. I had a tremendous support system as a single parent. In fact, if I had been injured in an accident or had a disabling disease, many people from my extended family and from my ward family would have come to my aid. I had a veritable army of people ready to take care of me . . . [who] had specifically covenanted to be part of my support system. But I was proud and determined to survive on my own.[23]

Most bishops, home teachers, youth leaders, Relief Society presidents, and visiting teachers, although happy to provide help, may not be sensitive to the specific needs of single-parent families. Rather than feeling neglected or annoyed, single parents can help teach, inform, and sensitize their Church leaders. Help them do their jobs better by sharing in detail the needs of each member of the family and of the family in general. This is an ongoing process of sharing, requesting, reminding, reassessing, reassuring, repenting, and forgiving.

CONCLUSION

The authors of this chapter write from our personal experiences as single parents. We know what it is to feel lonely, discouraged, exhausted, and worried about our children. We have experienced despair but have also reached out and claimed the special promises and blessings found in the scriptures for single parents. At times, our discouragement drove us to these scriptures, resulting in a deeper relationship with God. In our loneliness, we found new resources from within as well as without. In our suffering we learned patience. In surrendering our pride and relying upon a spiritual solution, we found a new sense of freedom and renewed energy. We are different today because of our experiences as single parents. We are better; we have grown. That is our hope for all single parents.

ABOUT THE AUTHORS

Elaine Walton, Ph.D., is a professor of social work and associate dean in the College of Family, Home, and Social Sciences at Brigham Young University. She and her husband, Wendel, have a blended family of ten children and twenty-four grandchildren.

Gary Burlingame, Ph.D., is a professor of psychology at Brigham Young University. He and his wife, Camille, have a blended family of four children who continue to learn from each other about the importance of flexibility and personal growth in life's journey.

ADDITIONAL READING

Linda Hunter Adams (2000), Moving forward after divorce; in David C. Dollahite, ed., *Strengthening Our Families: An In-Depth Look at the Proclamation on the Family* (Salt Lake City: Bookcraft), 239–241.

A. Dean Byrd (1997), *Finding Wholeness and Happiness after Divorce* (Salt Lake City: Deseret Book).

Cynthia Doxey, et al. (2000), Single adults and family life; in David C. Dollahite, ed., *Strengthening Our Families: An In-Depth Look at the Proclamation on the Family* (Salt Lake City: Bookcraft), 227–238.

The gospel and the single parent (2004, January), *Ensign, 34*(1), 63.

Frances E. Warden (2000, July), Time and the single parent, *Ensign, 30*(7), 30.

NOTES

1. First Presidency and Council of Twelve Apostles (1995, November), The family: A proclamation to the world, *Ensign, 25*(11), 102.

2. Ibid.

3. B. Maher (2004), *The Family Portrait: A Compilation of Data, Research and Public Opinion on the Family,* 2d ed. (Washington, D.C.: Family Research Council), 127–129.

4. J. M. Hilton and S. Desrochers (2002), Children's behavior problems in single-parent and married-parent families: Development of a predictive model, *Journal of Divorce and Remarriage, 37*(1/2), 13–36.

5. B. J. Ellis, et al. (2003), Does father absence place daughters at special risk for early sexual activity and teenage pregnancy? *Child Development, 74,* 801–821.

6. P. R. Amato (2001), The consequences of divorce for adults and children; in R. M. Milardo, ed., *Understanding Families into the New Millennium: A Decade in Review* (Minneapolis, MN: National Council on Family Relations), 488.

7. Ibid., 493.

8. Ibid., 496.

9. J. S. Wallerstein (2000), *The Unexpected Legacy of Divorce: A 25 Year Landmark Study* (New York: Hyperion), xxix.

10. Ibid., xx.

11. Amato (2001), 489–490.

12. See Maher (2004), 123.

13. E. Walton (1997), Single parenting after divorce; in A. D. Byrd, *Finding Wholeness and Happiness after Divorce* (Salt Lake City: Deseret Book), 137.

14. A. J. Hawkins and D. C. Dollahite, eds. (1997), *Generative Fathering: Beyond Deficit Perspectives* (Thousand Oaks, CA: Sage).

15. Walton (1997), 141.

16. Ibid., 142.

17. Ibid., 158.

18. Gordon B. Hinckley (1996, November), Women of the Church, *Ensign, 26*(11), 69.

19. Ibid.

20. First Presidency and Council of Twelve Apostles (1995), 102.

21. Walton (1997), 155.

22. Ezra Taft Benson (1988, November), To the single adult sisters of the Church, *Ensign, 18*(11), 96–97.

23. Walton (1997), 155.

CHAPTER 22

BLENDED FAMILIES

S. BRENT AND JANET S. SCHARMAN

*There are no perfect families, either in the world or in the Church, but there are many
good families . . . who are righteously and "anxiously engaged" in nurturing and providing for
their families, often against such heavy odds.[1]*
—Elder Neal A. Maxwell

Alex and Terri were two individuals whose lives took some unexpected turns. Alex served a successful mission, went to college where he met Terri, and was married at 23. In a 15-year marriage, Alex and Terri had three children and held a variety of Church callings, but developed an escalating pattern of bickering that progressed to explosive confrontations and divorce.

Barbara met Kyle in an institute class at the community college, and it was love at first sight. They had two children in their 10-year marriage and their love seemed to grow each day. Barbara's life fell apart when she received a telephone call informing her that Kyle had been seriously hurt in an automobile accident. He died before she arrived at the hospital.

Approximately three years after Alex's divorce and five years after Barbara was widowed, Alex and Barbara met, fell in love, and were married. None of their childhood dreams included a wedding reception with five children at their sides. They definitely had never pictured a wedding where the family of Barbara's late husband was in attendance and expressing genuine feelings of love and best wishes.

Every blended family has its own story.[2] Most parents of blended families freely acknowledge that their marriage and family circumstances vary, sometimes dramatically, from what they had anticipated as younger people. Their family experiences are a mixture of good times and tremendous demands. When difficulties arise, some quickly assume the problems are associated with and maybe even caused by the complexity of being in a remarriage.

Unfortunately, like all families who focus on what they don't have instead of what they do have, blended families may actually create unnecessary problems for themselves. It is true that blended families tend to be more complicated than two-parent biological families, but research supports the notion that the same ingredients vital to developing healthy first-marriage families are also essential in remarriages.[3]

SUCCESSFUL FAMILIES

From earliest years, members of the Church have been taught the significance of marriage and of providing a healthy and righteous atmosphere for raising children. For a variety of reasons, people find themselves trying to fulfill this important responsibility in a blended family. Because their families are different in some ways from two-parent biological families, they sometimes wonder if they have the tools or if they can even access the blessings of our Heavenly Father to help their family progress eternally.

"The Family: A Proclamation to the World" is a powerful statement given to us by our prophetic leaders to guide our efforts as we desire to raise good families. Sometimes "disability, death, or other circumstances may necessitate individual adaptation."[4] To those who worry that required adaptations for their family's set of life's complications may be too challenging, President Gordon B. Hinckley has offered this reassurance: "Every home," he said, "can provide an environment of love which will be an environment of salvation."[5]

Elder Bruce C. Hafen of the Seventy reminded us that "family life is by its nature a continual struggle between the ideal and the real. But if your home often knows warm feelings of love and laughter, if your family is trying—even most of the time—to have family prayer, home evening, and honestly shared gospel experiences, you are learning the pattern for happiness."[6] And it is "devotion to God in the home," President Faust said, that "seems to forge the spiritual moorings and stability that can help the family cope."[7]

FACTORS INCREASING THE LIKELIHOOD OF SUCCESS

Every blended-family story is a complicated mix of sadness and disappointment combined with optimism. Two hundred years ago, Samuel Johnson said that remarriage "represents the triumph of hope over experience."[8] Half of all recent marriages in the United States are remarriages for either the husband, wife, or both.[9] This is a remarkable figure given that all remarriages are born out of loss, either the death of a spouse or divorce. In spite of these painful experiences, most people desire to remarry if given an opportunity. About 75 percent of divorced people, even after a difficult first marriage, remarry,[10] with 30 percent remarrying within a year after their divorce.[11] The impact of this on children is tremendous. About one-third of children living in the United States today will live in a blended or stepfamily situation before they become adults.[12]

As blended family and stepfamily life is becoming more prevalent, researchers are trying to understand the complex dynamics of this family structure. In a search of the professional literature, three scholars found that stepfamily research published in the 1990s exceeded the entire output of the previous 90 years of the century.[13]

The good news is that today we know a lot about what is needed to help these families thrive. Elizabeth Einstein, a family therapist and also a member of a blended family, said of her earlier experiences: "My stepparenting mistakes were not so much misdeeds as misinformation."[14] With good information and the motivation to build on proven principles, all families

can be optimistic about their chances to be productive and happy with those who matter most to them. The following are factors that have been shown to help blended families move forward in constructive ways.

Losses are acknowledged and mourned. All family members will have experienced significant losses prior to the organization of the new family, and each may need the opportunity to work through individual concerns on his or her own timetable.[15] Losses will vary but may include relationships, money, prestige, security, and dreams. Divorced members of the Church may feel they are off course, stunted in their eternal progression without a way of redeeming themselves. Adjusting to divorce is sometimes more difficult than adjusting to the death of a spouse because of guilt, worries about failure, unresolved issues, and continued interactions with the former spouse concerning children.[16] It can be helpful for individuals to take some extended time for healing or to seek help in overcoming old injuries.

During these times the power of the Atonement can be called upon and its comfort felt. In addition to hard work and perseverance, success in family life also requires hope, faith, and trust in our Heavenly Father. The Lord has promised each one of us, in our unique set of circumstances, that He will make up for our shortcomings both during and "after all we can do" (2 Nephi 25:23).

Children may be dealing with issues that are quite different from those the adults are experiencing. They may see a remarriage as an end to their hopes of parents' reconciling at the very time when the adults are full of optimism for a new beginning.[17] Children often need to be invited to talk about concerns, and they may prefer to talk with someone other than a parent.

Expectations are realistic. It is important to remember that remarriage is not a replacement for a first marriage or a second chance to get a first marriage right. Remarriage is an entirely new, potentially rewarding opportunity. Being open to fresh possibilities and new ways of doing things, while keeping long-term, eternal goals in focus can help families let go of the past and move forward.

Many children experience what Judith Wallerstein calls "reconciliation fantasies."[18] Even if children were young when their parents divorced and both biological parents are now happily remarried, some children hang on to the hope that past issues can be resolved and their biological (or adoptive) parents will get back together. Understanding this particular dynamic can help parents to proceed carefully, making it possible for each individual to determine to what degree they will bond on an emotional level, be best buddies, or settle for a relationship that is less close. Openly acknowledging that the integration required for a group of people to feel like a family typically takes years, not weeks or months,[19] can allow individual members the time and space they need to become comfortable with each other.

Loyalty conflicts can be common in blended families.[20] Steprelatives do not have to love each other. At the same time, an unexpected side effect of developing feelings of love for a steprelative is a feeling that one is abandoning biological relatives. A young child, for example, may feel guilt at loving a stepfather as though it is a betrayal of his biological father. Such feelings, while they may sound illogical to an outsider who would point out that love is not exclusive or restrictive, may be surprisingly powerful and persistent.

The couple is unified. The Lord said, "If ye are not one ye are not mine" (D&C 38:27). Elder Robert E. Wells of the Seventy was raised in a stepfamily and then was a parent in his own stepfamily after the death of his first wife. Based on firsthand experience, he offered this wise observation: "Familial unity starts with the parents. Solidarity and love between couples help generate solidarity and love among siblings. That is why the primary relationship in a strong, unified family is the relationship between husband and wife."[21]

In remarriage, couples sometimes choose to put their relationship on hold while they work on the many complexities of their family, including forming good connections with stepchildren. While this is understandable, it is critical that couples view time together as a necessity rather than a luxury. Spending time together is not only desirable for the couple; it provides good modeling and reassures the children about the stability of the relationship.

Both partners need to decide together how they will deal with major issues. Generally, it is a good idea to phase slowly into parenting one another's children, allowing the biological parent to handle most of the disciplining of his or her own children initially. As time passes, parents of healthy families come to clearer agreement of how children should be reared.

Satisfactory relationships are formed. Gordon B. Hinckley was 20 years old when his mother Ada, his father's second wife, died. "Gordon had never felt such emptiness or hurt," his biography states.[22] Less than a year and a half later, Gordon's father announced to his children his intention to remarry. "The resulting silence was deafening."[23] "In our wildest dreams," Gordon's sister Ramona said, "I don't think we imagined Father would remarry. We just couldn't imagine him with anyone but Mother."[24] After the normal silences and awkward family interactions, Gordon's father, Bryant, spent the time necessary to talk through the issues with his son; he reassured Gordon of his continued love of Ada but also of his desire not to be alone for the rest of his days on earth. From the first, May, the new stepmother, made it clear that she had no intentions of replacing Ada; she just wanted to find a place of her own in the family. It took time, but "Aunt May," as they came to call her, was patient and loving and eventually earned the respect of all the family.[25]

Whether a person comes into the new family because there has been a death or a divorce, stepparents who at least initially define their role with their stepchildren as that of a friend are usually most satisfied.[26] No matter how open, caring, sincere, or unselfish a person is, step-relationships may never feel exactly like biological or adoptive relationships, and that's okay. Many report that, given time and opportunity, their interactions have progressed to a place where they are extremely meaningful and rewarding.

Often under-considered in discussions about remarriage adjustment are the multitude of individuals who do not live under the family roof. Forty percent of all families include step-grandparents, for example.[27] Other relatives—uncles, aunts, nieces, nephews, cousins, and even friends—are forced to adjust to the new family. One of the factors that make this particularly difficult is that, while a remarriage may significantly influence their lives, they may have had little or no input into the decision. Successful stepfamilies are inclusive and make an effort to identify and reach out to concerned family members.

Families are informed. Successful families read enough relevant literature to have a basic awareness of what other blended families say has worked for them. Some individuals have found it beneficial to develop their own support system with one or two other successful, similar families.

It can be helpful to have some understanding of the typical stages of blended or stepfamily development.[28] Patricia Papernow offers one model with these typical stages:

- *Fantasy.* This is a time filled with complex, hopeful wishes and expectations.
- *Immersion.* The family structure begins to appear and the stepparent may feel somewhat like an outsider.

- *Awareness.* Family members make more sense out of the confusion.
- *Mobilization.* During this sometimes chaotic, confusing time, differences are openly expressed as individuals are more aware of their feelings and are more comfortable in sharing them.
- *Action.* Enough time has passed that new negotiations are made about how the family will function and new boundaries are drawn.
- *Contact.* The family now functions without constant attention to "step" issues and more authentic one-on-one relationships are formed.
- *Resolution.* The family now has solid and reliable relationships and a new history is being created.

Most families go through these stages, although the timing and smoothness of progression may vary significantly from one family to another, and different life crises may cause the same family to cycle through some phases more than once. The important point is that families understand there are predictable phases their family is likely to experience. A difficult period of time should not signal to the family that life will always be hard or chaotic. In fact, over time, families naturally adjust and adapt. People tend to do best when they understand that the challenges they are experiencing are normal and most often temporary.

Constructive rituals are developed. Remarriage changes everything, both important and less significant things. Soon after a remarriage takes place the new family will have to decide how to celebrate a birthday, Christmas, the Fourth of July, or how to handle a summer vacation. If the children are older, traditions will have been formed. Traditions are good for families and most people reflect pleasantly as adults on the patterns they lived out in their childhood. In a blended family there may be four different parents and many opinionated extended family members who have a bias about who should be where for specific occasions.

As complicated as these realities can be, they are solvable. Part of the fun of remarriage can be the forming of new traditions. Families where divorced parents have agreed to alternate spending Christmas Eve with children find it works well. Developing new rituals like celebrating the remarriage date as a family, honoring birthdays on the first Sunday of the month, or spending a weekend away together every six months can be satisfying.[29] Of course, maintaining previous rituals such as having regular family prayer,

scripture study, family home evenings, and father's blessings, when possible, offer the stability and continuity that strengthens everyone.

LATTER-DAY SAINT BLENDED FAMILIES

Jennie's mother woke up in the middle of the night to the sound of crying down the hall. She went into Jennie's room to comfort the 10-year-old, who seemed almost inconsolable. As Jennie began to calm down, she was willing to tell her mother what was bothering her. "I don't know who I'm going to be with in heaven," she blurted out. "I want to be with you and dad, but how can that work now that you're divorced? Now that you're married in the temple to somebody else, what will happen to me? I wish this would all go away and things could go back to being the way they used to be."

A frequent question raised by Latter-day Saint blended families is how sealings will work in the eternities. How does divorce affect the promises of the sealing covenant when one marriage partner has been true to the gospel and one has not? How does remarriage to a second wife, following the death of a first wife, affect what the family dynamic will be like in the celestial kingdom? What happens when a wife, previously sealed in the temple to a man killed on their honeymoon, civilly marries another man and they live happily together for fifty years? These are difficult but common questions.

Although of prime concern to Latter-day Saint remarried families, these questions are among many others for which we will likely not receive a neatly defined answer during this existence. Elder Robert E. Wells, drawing from his experience, offered this advice: "Family members need not worry about the sealing situation of blended families as it might be in the next life. Our concern is to live the gospel now and to love others, especially those in our family. If we live the gospel to the best of our ability, the Lord in His love and mercy will bless us in the next life and all things will be right."[30] There is additional counsel from Elder Neal A. Maxwell: "Of course we cannot know the meaning of all things *right now.* But we can know, *right now,* that God knows us and loves us individually!"[31]

CONCLUDING THOUGHTS

The family is the basic structure the Lord devised to help train and protect His children so that they might return to His presence. Families are entitled to all the supports and all the blessings needed to fulfill the Lord's great purpose. Elder Henry B. Eyring said: "The test a loving God has set before us is not to see if we can endure difficulty. It is to see if we can endure it well. . . . To endure well is to keep those commandments whatever the opposition, whatever the temptation and whatever the tumult around us."[32] In the midst of the tumult many feel at times, it is important to remember that God wants us to be happy and successful. He will bless our righteous efforts in our families as we endeavor to expand loving networks, develop new and creative traditions, learn from mistakes, and refine the qualities that create maturity and enable us to live "after the manner of happiness" (2 Nephi 5:27).

ABOUT THE AUTHORS

S. Brent Scharman is a licensed psychologist who works as director of Evaluation and Training for LDS Family Services and chairs the Missionary Mental Health Committee for the Church.

Janet S. Scharman is also a licensed psychologist and is currently vice president of Student Life at Brigham Young University. They have a blended family of nine daughters, one son, and seventeen grandchildren.

ADDITIONAL READING

Francine Christensen (1981, June), Blending family styles: Making a second marriage work, *Ensign, 11*(6), 28–31.

S. Brent Scharman (2002, April), When you don't have custody, *Ensign, 32*(4), 58–63.

Robert E. Wells (1997, August), Uniting blended families, *Ensign, 27*(8), 24–29.

NOTES

1. Neal A. Maxwell (1994, May), Take especial care of your family, *Ensign, 24*(5), 89.

2. The term *blended family* is used where there are children of more than one union. *Stepfamily* is used where all the children are of one union. As information in this chapter applies to both situations, these terms are used interchangeably and are not differentiated in the chapter.

3. E. M. Hetherington and W. G. Clingempeel (1992), Coping with marital transitions: A family systems perspective, *Monographs of the Society for Research in Child Development, 57*(2–3), Serial No. 227; M. A. Fine and L. A. Kurdek (1992), The adjustment of adolescents in stepfather and stepmother families, *Journal of Marriage and the Family, 54*, 725–736.

4. First Presidency and Council of Twelve Apostles (1995, November), The family: A proclamation to the world, *Ensign, 25*(11), 102.

5. Gordon B. Hinckley (1994, November), Save the children, *Ensign, 24*(11), 54.

6. Bruce C. Hafen (2003, October), Your longing for family joy, *Ensign, 33*(10), 30–31.

7. James E. Faust (1983, May), Enriching family life, *Ensign, 13*(5), 40.

8. Samuel Johnson (c. 1780), as quoted in E. B. Visher and J. S. Visher (1988), *Old Loyalties, New Ties: Therapeutic Strategies with Stepfamilies* (New York: Brunner/Mazel), vii.

9. L. Bumpass, J. Sweet, and T. C. Martin (1990), Changing patterns of remarriage, *Journal of Marriage and the Family, 52*, 747–756.

10. R. M. Kreider and J. M. Fields (2002, February), Number, timing, and duration of marriages and divorces: 1996, *Current Population Reports* (Washington, D.C.: U.S. Census Bureau); available at http://www.census.gov/prod/2002pubs/p70–80.pdf

11. B. F. Wilson and S. C. Clarke (1992), Remarriages: A demographic profile, *Journal of Family Issues, 13*, 131.

12. L. L. Bumpass, R. K. Raley, and J. A. Sweet (1994), The changing character of stepfamilies: Implications of cohabitation and nonmarital childbearing, *NSFH working paper 63*; available at http://www.ssc.wisc.edu/cde/nsfhwp/nsfh63.pdf

13. M. Coleman, L. Ganong, and M. Fine (2000), Reinvestigating remarriage: Another decade of progress, *Journal of Marriage and the Family, 62*, 1288.

14. E. Einstein (1982), *The Stepfamily: Living, Loving, and Learning* (New York: Macmillan; reprint Ithaca, NY: E. A. Einstein, 1994), 124; page number is in reprint.

15. J. Bray (1995), Interventions that work for stepfamilies, *Family and Relationships: Get the Facts* (American Psychological Association); available at http://helping.apa.org/family/step.html (accessed April 15, 2004). Now available, slightly modified, as J. Bray, Making stepfamilies work (American Psychological Association); available at http://helping.apa.org

16. J. H. Larson (1987, February), How to unite a stepfamily, *Ensign, 17*(2), 46.

17. J. S. Wallerstein and S. Blakeslee (1989), *Second Chances: Men, Women, and Children a Decade After Divorce* (New York: Ticknor & Fields), 14.

18. Ibid., xvii.

19. P. L. Papernow (1993), *Becoming a Stepfamily: Patterns of Development in Remarried Families* (San Francisco: Jossey-Bass), 323.

20. Larson (1987), 46.

21. Robert E. Wells (1997, August), Uniting blended families, *Ensign, 27*(8), 27.

22. S. L. Dew (1996), *Go Forward With Faith: The Biography of Gordon B. Hinckley* (Salt Lake City: Deseret Book), 51.

23. Ibid., 53.

24. Ibid.

25. Ibid., 54.

26. Bray (1995).

27. M. E. Szinovacz (1998), Grandparents today: A demographic profile, *The Gerontologist, 38*(1), 47.

28. Papernow (1993), 311–370.

29. Ibid., 353.

30. Wells (1997), 28.

31. Neal A. Maxwell (2002, November), Encircled in the arms of His love, *Ensign, 32*(11), 18.

32. Henry B. Eyring (2004, May), In the strength of the Lord, *Ensign, 34*(5), 17.

CHAPTER 23

SUPPORTING FAMILIES OF CHILDREN WITH SPECIAL NEEDS

TINA TAYLOR DYCHES AND KAREN W. HAHNE

Spirits which are beautiful and innocent may be temporally restrained by physical impediments. If healing does not come in mortal life, it will come thereafter. Just as the gorgeous monarch butterfly emerges from a chrysalis, so will spirits emerge.[1]
—Elder Boyd K. Packer

Throughout the pregnancy, Rose and Joshua prayed daily for a healthy child. They did not care if their baby was a boy or a girl; their greatest prayer was that their child would have "ten fingers and ten toes." They anticipated that their first baby would be perfect, and it seemed that this was to be so. The pregnancy was uneventful, the delivery routine, and their baby developed normally for the first two years of his life. Then Rose and Joshua became concerned that some aspects of their son's development did not seem to be following the normal course and they began searching for answers. Their hopes crumbled when their son was diagnosed with autism.

Meanwhile, other ward members, Clara and Jim, both retired professionals, were trying to come to grips with the news just delivered to them by their son, Kevin. Kevin and his wife, Linda, were heartsick because medical tests indicated that their sixth child would be born with Down syndrome. Clara and Jim wondered how they could help this family to accept and cope with all the issues surrounding the birth of a child who will have a lifelong disability.

Another ward member, Bill, was dealing with the news that his 17-year-old son, LaMont, the center of Bill's life since his wife died, received such massive head injuries when he wrecked his motorcycle that his abilities will never be fully restored. LaMont will likely be paralyzed for the rest of his life.

No family is exempt from the trials of disabling conditions, whether the disabilities are present at birth or arise through accidents, illnesses, aging, or other circumstances. Disabilities include mental, emotional, cognitive, physical, or other conditions that hinder adequate or normal function of the mind or body, resulting in the need for specialized care and attention. People with disabilities are a large group in any community, and anyone may become part of this group at any time.

While the birth of a child is usually a happy and exciting time, when the child has a disability, family members may experience a wide range of feelings, including sadness, anger, despair, discouragement, loneliness, and guilt. These are normal and may occur with varying intensity at different times. With the passing of time, these feelings may be juxtaposed with those of great joy, anticipation, and spiritual comfort that come through the understanding of God's love for all of His children and the purposes of mortal life.

When Rose and Joshua learned that their child had a disability, they experienced strong reactions. They felt sad, angry, alone, and afraid. They also had many questions: "Why did this happen to us?" "What sin did we commit to deserve a child who cannot talk and tantrums incessantly?" "Is it fate that we must suffer through this life with a child who may make no valuable contributions to society, or is it just bad

189

luck?" "If he will never be able to care for himself, how will this affect the adult lives of our other children?" Clara and Jim asked similar questions and, "Why is this happening to our children?" Bill felt guilty because even though he loves his son, sometimes he wondered, "Does LaMont's life have meaning; is his life worth living?"

These questions are normal for families who raise children with disabilities. However, they are based on a paradigm that regards individuals with disabilities as burdens to society—a concept that is not consistent with the gospel. An alternate view is that "disability is a natural part of the human experience"[2] and that people with disabilities are children of God who have many characteristics, some of which may or may not include a disability.

All children need love, respect, nurturing, and opportunities for growth and development. However, because information regarding the child's disability often emphasizes possible limitations, ways in which this child is like other children may not be readily considered. When the child's strengths and abilities are emphasized, positive outcomes are more likely to be realized.

PRINCIPLES FROM THE PROCLAMATION REGARDING DISABILITY

The proclamation provides spiritual insight for understanding the divinity in all of God's children, including those with disabilities. First, the proclamation affirms that all human beings are created in the image of God (see Moses 2:27) and have a divine nature. Latter-day prophets have made it clear that this includes children with disabilities. Elder Boyd K. Packer bore witness of the divinity of God's special children when he spoke of their restoration:

> Each body and mind will be restored in perfect frame. However long and unfair mortality may seem, however long the suffering and the waiting may be, he [Jesus Christ] has said: "After that cometh the day of my power; then shall the poor, the lame, and the blind, and the deaf, come in unto the marriage of the Lamb, and partake of the supper of the Lord, prepared for the great day to come. Behold, I, the Lord, have spoken it" (D&C 58:11–12).[3]

The proclamation also states that in our premortal existence, God's children accepted His plan to obtain a physical body and gain earthly experiences. Many people experience physical, mental, social, or emotional challenges. Many of these earthly challenges are not accidental, but are a part of God's divine plan. God does not punish his children by giving them disabilities. Elder Packer reiterated this concept, stating that such notions have "been taught since ancient times. It is false doctrine."[4] The proclamation also teaches that all of God's children can realize their divine destiny as heirs to eternal life. God's work and glory is "to bring to pass the immortality and eternal life of man" (Moses 1:39), and this applies to all of His children.

Further, the proclamation affirms the sanctity of life. As God sees all of His children as spiritual beings having a physical experience,[5] we too, can view our brothers and sisters with spiritual eyes. Looking at the divine history and potential of each person, we can know, as God knows, that the worth of all souls is great (D&C 18:10). Speaking about the sanctity of life, Elder James E. Faust stated: "Some justify abortions because the unborn may have been exposed to drugs or disease and may have birth defects. Where in all the world is the physically or mentally perfect man or woman? Is life not worth living unless it is free of handicaps?"[6]

The proclamation admonishes parents to take upon themselves sacred responsibilities to raise their children in love and righteousness, and those with disabilities are not excepted. All children need to have their physical and spiritual needs met, to be taught to love and serve others, to keep the commandments, and to be good citizens. Naturally, the degree to which any child will mortally progress varies. Parents who are guided by the Spirit will provide appropriate learning experiences for all of their children at home, school, and in the community. The balance between the parents' responsibility for teaching and children's responsibility for learning was discussed by Elder Packer. He taught that those with disabilities "have responsibility to work out their own salvation. The nearer the normal patterns of conduct and discipline apply to [those with disabilities], the happier they will be. Every quarter of an inch of physical and mental improvement is worth striving for."[7] Further, the Prophet Joseph Smith said that "all the minds and spirits that God ever sent into the world are susceptible of enlargement."[8] It is the privilege and responsibility of parents to help their child grow within the constraints of his or her specific situation, not excusing low performance or unacceptable behavior merely because of the child's disability.

Finally, the proclamation teaches that fathers have primary responsibility to provide and mothers to nurture their children, but that "disability . . . may necessitate individual adaptation."[9] Raising a child with a disability often requires greater financial, physical, and emotional resources than does raising other children. Therefore, each family member, including ex-

tended family, may need to adapt to new roles and responsibilities.

BLESSINGS OF RAISING A CHILD WITH DISABILITIES

Teachings from the restored gospel help families realize that many blessings come when they are faced with experiences that tax their faith and understanding, such as raising a child with a disability. A few examples include spiritual insight, acceptance of others, and character development.

Families who raise children with disabilities may gain greater spiritual insights about God's plan of salvation. With an eternal perspective on life, families understand gospel principles that help them get through the daily difficulties associated with raising a child with disabilities.[10] Such families are blessed by knowing that children who are not accountable will inherit eternal glory, as they "are redeemed without baptism and will go to the celestial kingdom of God, there, we believe, to have their faculties or other deficiencies restored according to the Father's mercy and justice."[11]

Also, when families raise a child with disabilities, there are opportunities to become more accepting of others who are different. By protecting, defending, and advocating for individuals with disabilities, family members serve as role models for community members regarding the treatment of those who may not be typically valued in popular culture.

Raising a child with disabilities may help all family members develop strength and character. Siblings may develop cooperative attitudes and greater self-control than if they did not have this family experience.[12] Parents, in retrospect, often say that they were prepared for the birth of their child through patriarchal blessings, other blessings, or experiences in life. They appreciate the courage of their child and the opportunity to learn that afflictions are truly blessings of God (see 1 Nephi 1:1). As Paul noted, "Tribulation worketh patience; and patience, experience; and experience, hope" (Romans 5:3–4). In other words, the Lord allows us to have experiences that enable us to become like Him. Parents who have felt profound despair and sorrow have later recognized God's great love for them and their child. Some say, in effect, "I would not have chosen this particular trial. I would have wished my child had not suffered so, but I am a changed person because of what I have learned through all of the experiences with this child. I would not go back to what I was before. And what my child has become as a person is, in part, a result of her struggles with her limitations." They may say with assurance that they have felt the truth of these scriptural verses: "[I] know . . . that all these things shall give [me] experience, and shall be for [my] good" (D&C 122:7) and "all things work together for good to them that love God" (Romans 8:28).

CHALLENGES OF REARING A CHILD WITH DISABILITIES

Even when parents value the eternal nature of each of their children, life may be difficult for families raising a child with disabilities. Often parents struggle with many issues directly relating to their child, the siblings, extended family, and the community.

Some parents experience stress with circumstances directly related to their child with disabilities, which may include obtaining a correct diagnosis, monitoring ongoing medical procedures and emergencies, seeking appropriate services, paying for medical expenses, and advocating for their child. When the survival of an infant is questionable, parents may, consciously or unconsciously, be afraid to bond with their child. Further, many parents of children with disabilities are challenged with daily caretaking chores such as feeding, dressing, grooming, and transporting their no longer young or small child. The more assistance the child needs for a longer duration of time, the greater the stress on parents. Such stressors affect families physically, socially, emotionally, financially, and even spiritually.[13]

Siblings of a child with disabilities are often challenged by the family's circumstances. They may feel neglected because their parents spend much energy attending to the child with disabilities. They may also feel isolated from the broader community, due to embarrassment or the inability of the family to engage in community activities such as eating at restaurants, going to movies, or going on family vacations. They may also feel burdened by the extra caretaking responsibilities required of them. Some siblings feel guilty about being "normal," or feel that they may have caused the disability. Also, some siblings may be concerned about their future (e.g., "Who will take care of my sister when mom and dad die?" "What if I have a child with the same condition?").[14]

Interactions with extended family members may pose problems for families raising children with disabilities. Some may dismiss parents' concerns for their child, saying, "She'll grow out of it," or, "Boys develop later than girls—don't worry." On the other hand, parents may be blamed for their child's behavior or development. Extended family members may not be willing or may be afraid to provide respite care to parents, creating further isolation from other extended family and community members.

Negative attitudes and unrealistic expectations of community members may also challenge families. Some families may hesitate to attend church on a regular basis because their child is disruptive in meetings, they feel unwelcome, they feel that their parenting skills are being judged, or they think the leaders or teachers are not equipped with the skills or attitudes to include their child in the life of the Church. This may make church attendance for these families neither spiritually uplifting nor socially comfortable. Yet there are strategies for meeting these challenges with hope. As people develop skills and attitudes founded on the principles of the gospel, they are more likely to have joyful experiences accepting and interacting with children with disabilities.

MEETING THE CHALLENGES OF REARING A CHILD WITH DISABILITIES

Parents who rely on inspiration from the Holy Spirit will be guided when they receive conflicting advice regarding diagnosis, treatment, or other issues. With so much information available, parents need to prayerfully analyze which treatments, therapies, or programs will best meet the needs of their child and family. Relying on the Spirit may help parents make informed decisions for their child, which may differ from decisions of other families. However, parents must be cautious of those who give advice that may not be trustworthy. They can avoid those who charge inordinate amounts of money for treatment, promise miraculous cures, tout treatments that may have adverse effects on the child and the family, and promote unquestionable acceptance for treatments that have not been scientifically validated.

Mothers and fathers may deal with the child's condition differently. These differences are normal, expected, and even healthy. Following promptings of the Spirit, parents will support each other in rearing all of their children. They will recognize that they may need to adapt their traditional roles to help the family function more fully. For example, in a family council, a family may decide that an important goal is to ensure that the kitchen is cleaned after each meal.

sitive to the needs of families, bonds of love will be formed. Home and visiting teachers should be particularly sensitive while fulfilling their stewardships to families rearing a child with disabilities. Although many families wish to be self-reliant, at times they may struggle financially, socially, emotionally, and spiritually, and will require support. Almost all families will respond to genuine love (see Box 23.1 for ways to support families of children with disabilities).

A helpful perspective to increase sensitivity is to ask oneself, "If I had a disability, how would I want to be treated by others?" Most of us would not want to be defined solely by our disabilities, but by our personalities, interests, heritage, associations, and other characteristics that make us whole. For example, one might say, "Jans is a young man who does a beautiful job of blessing the sacrament, and he has cerebral palsy," rather than "the handicapped priest." If we use the word *disabled* to mean that someone is broken, not working, or a problem, then we limit our ability to help families and their children. In contrast, when we say that someone "has a disability," we are describing just one trait of that person. In fact, the only labels people really need are their names.

CHURCH RESOURCES

Church leaders have shown sensitivity to members with disabilities by establishing a Special Curriculum unit for the Church. Special Curriculum materials include information regarding how Church members, teachers, and leaders can increase awareness and understanding of those with disabilities, help each member feel loved and accepted, help each member learn about the Savior and His gospel, help each member participate successfully in religious life, and help members with disabilities serve, lead, and teach. Many materials are available for members with disabilities via the LDS catalog and distribution centers (i.e., Braille, American Sign Language videotapes and CDs, large-print books and manuals, and half- or standard-speed cassette tapes). Further, the Boy Scouts of America has materials for serving Scouts with disabilities (see Box 23.2 for information on these materials).

The principles of the gospel of Jesus Christ guide and comfort parents of children with disabilities. They also assist members of the community in supporting all families. The message is clear: all of God's children have a divine nature and it is a privilege and responsibility of families to raise them in love and

However, Johnny, who has spina bifida, needs physical assistance in order to eat with the family, a process that takes him longer than the rest. The family then divides responsibilities according to the needs and skills of each person. Prior to Johnny's birth, the mother assumed all of the kitchen responsibilities; after his birth, the family had to assume different responsibilities to allow the family to function smoothly.

When parents, including single parents, realize that they do not need to accept life's challenges alone, they give others opportunities for service and growth. Friends and family can be supportive by listening to the parents without judgment, providing advice when asked to do so, and helping with daily caretaking chores. Further, financial support from extended family members may be helpful when a child's disability creates added expenses.

The most important community for Latter-day Saint families raising children with disabilities may be the ward or branch. When Church members are sen-

righteousness. Extended family play an important role in providing this support, as does the broader community, including members of the Church.

ABOUT THE AUTHORS

Tina Taylor Dyches, Ed.D., is an associate professor and director of special education programs at Brigham Young University. She lives in Mt. Pleasant, Utah, with her husband, David, and son, Logan.

Karen W. Hahne is the mother of six children and grandmother of eight. She founded Kids on the Move to serve families of children with disabilities. Her life has been enriched through experiencing the courage of families.

ADDITIONAL READING

Joseph M. Lucyshyn, Glen Dunlap, and Richard W. Albin (2002), *Families and Positive Behavior Support: Addressing Problem Behavior in Family Contexts* (Baltimore: Brookes).

Ann P. Turnbull and H. Rutherford Turnbull III (2001), *Families, Professionals, and Exceptionality: Collaborating for Empowerment,* 4th ed. (Upper Saddle River, NJ: Merrill, Prentice Hall).

Marleen S. Williams (2000), Raising a child with a mental disability: A personal story; in David C. Dollahite, ed., *Strengthening Our Families: An In-Depth Look at the Proclamation on the Family* (Salt Lake City: Bookcraft), 293–294.

NOTES

1. Boyd K. Packer (1991, May), The moving of the water, *Ensign,* 21(5), 7.

2. Developmental Disabilities Assistance and Bill of Rights Act of 2000, § 1(a)1, 42 U.S.C. § 15001.

3. Packer (1991), 7.

4. Ibid.

5. Steven R. Covey (1989), *The Seven Habits of Highly Effective People* (New York: Fireside), 319.

6. James E. Faust (1975, May), The sanctity of life, *Ensign,* 5(5), 27.

7. Packer (1991), 7.

8. Quoted in *Teachings of the Prophet Joseph Smith* (2002), Joseph Fielding Smith, ed. (American Fork, UT: Covenant Communications), 354.

9. First Presidency and Council of Twelve Apostles (1995, November), The family: A proclamation to the world, *Ensign,* 25(11), 102.

10. E. S. Marshall, S. F. Olsen, B. L. Mandleco, T. T. Dyches, K. W. Allred, and N. Sansom (2003), "This is a spiritual experience": Perspectives of Latter-day Saint families living with a child with disabilities, *Qualitative Health Research, 13*(1), 57–76.

11. Joseph Fielding Smith (1966), *Answers to Gospel Questions* (Salt Lake City: Deseret Book), 3:20–21.

12. B. Mandleco, S. F. Olsen, E. S. Marshall, and T. T. Dyches (2003), The relationship between family and sibling functioning in families raising a child with a disability, *Journal of Family Nursing, 9,* 365–396.

13. M. McCubbin and H. McCubbin (1993), Families coping with illness: The resiliency model of family stress, adjustment, and adaptation; in C. Danielson, B. Hamel-Bissel, and P. Winstead-Fry, eds., *Families, Health, & Illness: Perspectives on Coping and Intervention* (St. Louis, MO: Mosby), 21–63.

14. D. J. Meyer (1994), *Sibshops: Workshops for Siblings of Children with Special Needs* (Baltimore: Brookes).

THE RIGHTEOUS DESIRE TO HAVE A CHILD: COPING WITH INFERTILITY

HELEN W. AND ROSS FLOM

Most couples desire to have a child. For many reasons, however, this is not always possible. Couples who cannot have children may feel they are being punished, may experience moments of frustration toward their Heavenly Father, and may even feel that their prayers have gone not only unanswered but unheard. These feelings are not uncommon. Over the past ten years we have experienced each of these.

In our professional lives each of us works with children, either assisting them in learning how to communicate or studying basic processes of development. Unfortunately we are not able to have children. According to the American Society for Reproductive Medicine, approximately 10 percent of the reproductive-age population is infertile.[1] While no two couples share an identical path of infertility, we believe that many of the experiences and emotional reactions that we encountered are common to other couples who are also infertile. In this essay we share some of the experiences we encountered and describe how we negotiated our path of infertility.

We were married in our mid-twenties. Like most couples, we led rather busy lives and had begun to plan for our future. We initiated retirement plans, started saving for a house, and, like most couples, we planned on having children. Yet after eighteen months of "well-timed intercourse" we were not pregnant. By this time most of our friends were pregnant and were in the process of organizing nurseries and buying baby and maternity clothes. They exhibited an understandable level of joyful nervousness. While we were certainly happy for our friends, we were disappointed with our own lack of success.

During this 18-month period of trying to conceive a child, we received questions such as, "When are you and Ross going to start a family?" "Well, haven't you tried . . . ?" or "I wouldn't worry about it,

just try again next month." Friends and family meant well by their comments but they did not understand that we had tried everything and we could not help but worry. In seeking the advice of several physicians who specialized in infertility, we were told we had less than a 3 percent chance of getting pregnant. We remained hopeful. We had heard a number of stories of couples who had been told they could never have children, but went on to have several children. After a year of various medical procedures to improve our "chances," including surgery, artificial inseminations, and fertility medications, we still could not conceive. By this point we had become frustrated and it seemed our options were dwindling away.

Throughout this time, each month brought an emotional roller coaster. Each month began by hoping and wondering and looking for possible pregnancy symptoms; then at the end of the month feeling foolish for thinking that we could be pregnant. This was, and is still, the most difficult part of our infertility. With each month of not being pregnant and each procedure's failing to result in a pregnancy, we began to question our personal worthiness. Our marriage was strained. We had emotionally and physically drifted apart and we were financially unable to pursue more aggressive forms of infertility treatment. At this point we stopped trying. It was too emotionally difficult. This "break" lasted the better part of three years.

While we were not actively trying to conceive a child in terms of fertility medications or any other form of assisted reproductive technology, we still experienced the emotional roller coaster each month in terms of wondering "what if?" This season of not trying, while difficult, was important for us because it allowed us the opportunity to examine whether our desire to have children was in accordance with Heavenly Father's plan. We believed, based on blessings, counsel with our ecclesiastical leaders, and the doctrine of the Church, that it was in fact a righteous desire to want and to seek after children. However, we learned that we needed, for whatever reason, to pass through this trial. This realization did not come easily or quickly, but it did come. Still, we knew we needed to do all that we could in order to move through this trial.

After the three-year break we prayerfully considered our options and realized that, being in our early thirties, we were not too old to start a family, that having children was something we really wanted, and that we felt comfortable with planning for and pursuing in-vitro fertilization (IVF). While the cost associated with IVF is left to the couple, and the procedure relatively expensive, we felt a confirmation about going forward. Given that we thought it unwise to go into debt for such a procedure, we took the time necessary to save for it. For us that meant some sacrifice and diligent savings, but we knew this was something we needed and wanted to do. We both felt a spiritual confirmation that going through IVF is what Heavenly Father wanted us to do. This was a trial designed for us, and we needed to face this trial head-on.

The roller coaster again commenced.

The procedure yielded two eggs that were fertilized. At this point all that was required was for at least one of the fertilized eggs to implant within the uterine wall. Two weeks later the roller coaster hit another valley; the pregnancy test was negative. There was, however, a striking occurrence that happened a few days prior to the pregnancy test: we both received independent spiritual promptings that we were not pregnant. In this way, the negative result came less as a surprise and more as the usual disappointment. Nonetheless, that was a difficult day for us and it took several weeks to work through the different emotions. We were comforted, however, in the fact that we knew we had done all that we could, we had done what we believed God wanted us to do, and that He knew of our desire.

Today as we look back, we see and understand how we needed to go through each step along the way. Each failed attempt to have a child has brought us closure and comfort knowing that we are doing all that we can and the rest is in the hands of our Heavenly Father. We have both developed an increased patience for the Lord's timetable and we have received an increase in faith in the Lord's plan for our family. In one sense each failure has brought us disappointment, but it has equally strengthened us. Quoting from the fifteenth-century author Thomas à Kempis:

> It is good for us that we sometimes have sorrows and adversities, for they often make a man lay to heart that he is only a stranger and sojourner, and may not put his trust in any worldly thing.[2]

à Kempis recommended a positive approach to life's setbacks. Instead of complaining over them, he advised discovering their use. Every trouble has some use for the person who is willing to seek diligently with help from the Holy Spirit. This, of course, is the twist. In other words, we may not see the spiritual benefit of the trial during its presence, yet we must realize that while each trial is temporary, its spiritual benefits can last throughout all eternity. In addition, our trials serve to remind us that we cannot look to ourselves for our own salvation. Infertility has taught us humility and reminded us of where we should turn for refuge.

Infertility does not preclude a couple from becoming parents. At this point in our own journey we realize that conceiving, carrying, and giving birth to a child is a miraculous process that comes to many but not all. Giving birth is the first step involved in being a parent. Most parents would attest that the day their child entered this world was truly special, but so was the child's first day of school, his or her day of graduation, and the day that child was sealed to a spouse in the temple of the Lord. We have reached a level of peace in terms of our infertility. We don't perceive our infertility to be a punishment, curse, or an indication of our faith. We see it as a part of us and, more important, we see it as a part of the larger path our Father in Heaven knows we need to walk. Just as the Savior's moment on the cross was turned into a glorious resurrection, we, too, need to convert each of life's disappointing setbacks into experiences that spiritually move us forward. We continue to press forward and we have now begun the process of adoption. Whether or not this new vista in our path brings a child into our family, we will continue onward because we believe it is in accordance with God's will and it is, after all, a righteous desire.

ABOUT THE AUTHORS

Helen W. Flom received her B.A. in audiology and speech-language pathology in 1991 and an M.S. in speech-language pathology in 1993. Currently Helen is a speech-language pathologist for a local school district and for Brigham Young University. Helen is originally from Maine.

Ross Flom received both his B.A. and Ph.D. from the University of Minnesota and is currently a professor of psychology at Brigham Young University. Ross is originally from Minnesota.

ADDITIONAL READING

Jason S. Carroll, et al. (2000), The family crucibles of illness, disability, death, and other losses; in David C. Dollahite, ed., *Strengthening Our Families: An In-Depth Look at the Proclamation on the Family* (Salt Lake City: Bookcraft), 278–292.

Tamara A. Ilich (2000, August), I longed to be a mother, *Ensign, 30*(8), 59–61.

Ardeth G. Kapp (1989, August), Unable to have children, *Tambuli,* 9–11.

Ana N. Shaw (2000, August), Being sensitive to couples without children, *Ensign, 30*(8), 61.

NOTES

1. American Society for Reproductive Medicine, Quick facts about infertility, at http://www.asrm.org/Patients/faqs.html. "Infertility affects about 6.1 million women and their partners in the U.S.—about ten percent of the reproductive-age population (*Source: National Survey of Family Growth, CDC 1995*)."

2. T. à. Kempis (c. 1395), *The Imitation of Christ: Four Books,* translated from the Latin by W. Benham in 1874 (reprint London: Macmillan), 28.

ESSAY E 2

ADOPTING A CHILD

DENNIS AND JOYCE ASHTON

Newly married couples rarely question their ability to conceive and bear children. But as time passes and efforts to become pregnant are unsuccessful, some couples discover that they must deal with the challenging problem of infertility. In spite of faith, prayers, and righteousness, pregnancy may still elude them. Couples may look to adoption as they anticipate bringing a child into the family. The majority of non-relative adoptions occur with married couples who are unable to bear children on their own.[1] Six in every 10 Americans have had some experience with adoption. Either they or a family member or close friend were adopted, were placed for adoption, or have adopted a child.[2]

Many milestones mark the road to adoption. One woman shared the tender feelings she experienced during the adoption process:

Although we filled out all the papers and went through all the adoption procedures, I still hoped each month I would conceive. After a year or so we got a call from the adoption agency. A newborn was available. We had requested a male that matched our blonde hair and blue eyes. This was a brown-eyed female. We said, "No." We felt so guilty for not accepting this child. My grief was particularly complicated and intense. A week or so went by and the agency

called again with the same request. We felt impressed to say "yes" this time. I cried and cried because I realized I really had failed to conceive my own child. This really was the end of a dream I had and I felt I was giving up. Of course once this beautiful baby was put in my arms I felt a witness and peace that she was mine and I have never regretted our decision.

Many families find meaning and resolution as they come to accept their infertility and realize that they, like many others, can have an eternal posterity through the adoption process and temple sealing. One temple sealer explained to an adoptive couple: "Adam and Eve were commanded to multiply and replenish the earth. As you bear, or carry, this child back to his Heavenly Father, you are being obedient to that commandment." The burden of infertility lightens as couples experience the spiritual stretching and blessings that occur when birth parents lovingly choose adoption.

Most successful adoptions occur through licensed private adoption agencies like LDS Family Services.[3] These full-service adoption agencies provide adoption education classes designed to address the personal challenges of adoptive applicants, while sensitizing them to the unique needs of birth parents. For example, most couples and their extended families are

LEGAL ASPECTS OF ADOPTION

Adoption laws in different states and countries, though similar, often differ on significant points. Some states require that all adoptions be handled through state-licensed private or public agencies; others allow private adoptions. Federal laws regulate the placement of children from one state to another as well as international placements. The Indian Child Welfare Act limits in some instances the placement of children with American Indian blood into non-American Indian families.

Traditionally the rights of birth fathers were often ignored. Today all states have laws governing the voluntary and involuntary termination of birth fathers' rights. The legal procedures required to terminate birth fathers' rights to children being considered for adoption can vary significantly from state to state. Prior to the finalization of an adoptive placement with a prospective couple, all parental rights must be terminated in a court of law. A birth mother is not allowed to sign papers terminating her parental rights until after the child is born and she has had sufficient time to consider all her options and make a decision without duress, coercion, misrepresentation, or overpromising.

Painful and disappointing adoption disruptions can almost always be avoided by carefully following state and federal laws and seeking competent legal counsel. Adoption attorneys working with licensed public and private adoption agencies provide the best protection to all parties associated with the adoption.

Following placement, most couples will receive six or more months of supervision from a licensed adoption agency or state-appointed adoption specialist. Most adoptive couples can have their adopted child sealed to them immediately following the judge's signing of the final adoption decree. Contact your local temple for specific instructions.

Box E 2.1

not completely familiar with the increased involvement of the birth parents in screening and meeting the adoptive family.

Licensed adoption agencies also offer a home study process designed to educate and prepare adoptive couples for the unique opportunities and challenges associated with adoption. Adoption interviews that are part of the adoption study process prepare each participant in adoption to better understand, support, and communicate with one another. Adoptive families who are successfully prepared for place-

ment opportunities are more likely to be chosen by birth parents and less likely to have their adoption disrupted by birth parents' changing their minds following the birth of the child.

Birth mothers often exert significant and sincere efforts as they consider and pray about a potential eternal family for their unborn child. Adoptive families who are willing to meet and communicate with the biological parents who have selected them experience mutual healing. Anticipating face-to-face visits prior to placement with biological parents of a yet-to-be-born child can be difficult and threatening. Adoptive couples, already vulnerable with their own infertility, struggle when they realize that a young, single birth mother has so much control over their future parenting opportunities. This personal involvement of the adoptive couple is often helpful as the birth mother and maternal grandmother search for meaning in their anticipatory loss.

Communication and mutual support also provide a forum through which the birth mother grants permission to the adoptive couple to claim and begin bonding with the new baby. The transition of parenting opportunities between birth and adoptive mother—from "your" baby, to "our" baby, and finally to "my" baby—is difficult and rewarding.

A few adoptive couples wonder if they will love their adopted child like their own biological child. Research and thirty years of personal observation confirms that the vast majority of adoptive parents report feeling very satisfied with their adoption and report that their relationships with their child have made positive contributions to their lives.[4] Additional findings reveal that both birth parents and adoptive parents report satisfaction with their decision two years after placement.[5]

Adopting older children and those with special needs is significantly more difficult than adopting newborn infants; disruptions during the first year are not uncommon. This is especially true in situations where a child has been exposed to any form of abuse or raised by multiple caretakers prior to the adoptive placement. Most states have specialized classes, made available through government-sponsored child welfare agencies, designed to prepare families for the opportunities and challenges available through foster parenting and adopting older children and those with special needs. Counsel from Church leaders has been clear for nearly thirty years concerning the importance and spiritual blessings inherent in adoption (see essay F4).

The First Presidency has released five letters to Church leaders supporting, clarifying, and encouraging adoption. The most recent letter states that "Adoption is an unselfish loving decision that blesses both parents and the child in this life and in eternity. . . . Unmarried parents should give prayerful consideration to the best interests of the child and the blessings that can come to an infant who is sealed to a mother and father."[6]

Many couples feel that divine guidance has led them to the children they adopt. One adoptive parent related the following:

After 13 years of marriage, we were parents of four children, one by birth and three by adoption. Both my husband and I felt that we should fill out an application for another adoption. We marked on our application that we were willing to consider adopting a child with a physical impairment, but not with a mental impairment. We were specifically looking for a preschooler who would be just younger than our youngest child. Then we waited.

Our social worker called us often about possible children. Some of the children even stayed with us for a while, but always some legal issue would interfere with the placement or another family was selected. While waiting, I learned of a baby boy who would soon be born with Down syndrome and who would be adopted by another couple. I realized to my surprise that I would be willing to mother a child in that situation—if I knew that the child was meant to be in our family. With that realization, a great peace filled my heart. I began to have many impressions about a Chinese infant daughter.

One Friday afternoon our caseworker called. "I have some information about a baby. She is 3 weeks old. She is Chinese. She has Down syndrome and a small hole in her heart. The birth parents want a letter from you and Gary explaining why you would want to adopt a child with Down syndrome."

I quickly replied, "Down syndrome? I'll call Gary, but I don't think we are interested."

When Gary and I talked, our first impressions were that this was not the situation for us, but that we should ask the Lord. That evening I joined our ward in the Dallas Texas Temple. My thoughts were filled with concerns about this child when, suddenly, peace filled my heart and words were placed there. "Walk in confidence with the Lord. Do not be afraid." I left the temple not knowing whether this child was to come to us, but knowing that we wouldn't do anything to prevent her coming. We would walk in faith and trust in the Lord.

Two weeks later we flew home with our new little daughter, Jena Marie Mei-Ling Hall. I didn't know what life with her would mean, but I knew that it was the life that we were meant to travel together. . . . I received a witness that this spirit in this mortal body was sent to be with us by our loving Heavenly Father.[7]

Young couples seeking to adopt generally seek a healthy infant matched to their physical characteristics. They are generally most comfortable with biological parents who have similar economic, cultural, racial, and spiritual backgrounds. Not everyone has the emotional, physical, or financial resources to accept a disabled child.

The decision to adopt a specific child always makes an eternal impact on all those involved. Lives are redirected, family dynamics are adjusted, and even posterity is affected. Feelings of assurance through the Holy Ghost guide couples as they welcome adopted children and cope with challenges of the adoption process. Almost without exception, adoptive couples and birthparents acknowledge the involvement of our Heavenly Father in this sacred process of creating eternal family relationships through adoption.

ABOUT THE AUTHORS

Dennis Ashton, LCSW, APA, is a former assistant commissioner of LDS Family Services and current agency director. Dennis has made over five hundred adoptive placements and supervised many more in his thirty-year career with LDS Family Services.

Joyce Ashton, RN, is a spiritual and bereavement advisor for hospice. She and Dennis have authored two books on loss: *Jesus Wept* and *Loss and Grief Recovery*. Joyce and Dennis are the parents of six children, four of whom are living, and several grandchildren.

ADDITIONAL READING

Carole W. Hankal (1989, October), Who will adopt a dying child? *Ensign, 19*(10), 62–67.
LDS Family Services (2002, February), Adoption and the unwed mother, *Ensign, 32*(2), 63.
Other excellent articles can be found at www.lds.org. Click on "Provident Living," then "Social and Emotional Strength," then "LDS Family Services."

NOTES

1. Evan B. Donaldson Adoption Institute (1997, October), *Benchmark Adoption Survey: Report on the Findings*, pamphlet (Washington, D.C.: Princeton Survey Research Associates).
2. W. D. Mosher and C. A. Bachrach (1996), Understanding U.S. fertility: Continuity and change in the National Survey of Family Growth, *Family Planning Perspectives, 28*, 4–12.
3. M. Berry, R. P. Barth, and B. Needell (1996), Preparation, support, and satisfaction of adoptive families in agency and independent adoptions, *Child and Adolescent Social Work Journal, 13*, 157–183.

4. Ibid.

5. B. W. Donnelly, and P. Voydanoff (1996), Parenting versus placing for adoption, *Family Relations, 45,* 427–434.

6. First Presidency letter dated June 26, 2002.

7. Judy Hall, personal communication to authors.

E S S A Y   E 3

The Joys and Struggles of Mothering

Emily Watts

When I learned I was expecting our first baby, I was ecstatic. I had wanted to be a mother for as long as I could remember, and I had always thought I would be a good one—right up to the moment we brought that baby home from the hospital. That day, the realization of all I didn't know swept over me like a tidal wave, and I seriously thought I might drown in the sea of my conflicting emotions. I was elated; I was terrified. I already loved this little person more than I could ever imagine loving anyone, and I was sick at heart at her utter dependence on a flawed being like me.

Fortunately, Heavenly Father in His wisdom sent a calm, mature, patient spirit to be our eldest child, and she gave us the confidence to keep at it until we completed our family at five children—two girls and three boys. We adore them all. We wanted them all. And sometimes we have wondered what we were thinking when we imagined we could handle them all.

I'd like to be able to say that I have loved every minute of being a mom, but that wouldn't be strictly true. There have been days when I thought if I heard the word *Mommy* one more time I would implode. There have been stretches of time, months in duration, when I thought I might be truly happy if I could just take a shower unaccompanied. I have dragged myself and my offspring through innumerable science projects and book reports, multiplication tables and state capitals, school band concerts and dance recitals and Primary talks and Cub Scout badges—an unending stream of worthwhile projects whose worth is sometimes not apparent for years. I have giggled and mourned and prayed—and I have learned. If I could

pick three ideas from my own observations to pass along to those who find themselves now in the trenches of motherhood, they would be these:

1. Remember the role of mistakes. One of the fears that gripped my heart as a young mother was that I would make some kind of terrible mistake that would scar my child for life. Determined to do everything perfectly, I soon made life miserable for myself and my children with the dark specter of my unfulfilled expectations. The fact is, socks get lost—especially tiny ones of the sort worn by 2-year-olds. Babies cry in church sometimes and have to be carried out in front of the whole congregation. Toddlers escape in church sometimes and have to be chased down the aisle in front of the whole congregation. Deacons forget to behave sometimes and embarrass their mothers in front of the whole congregation.

And, despite my best efforts, sometimes I respond to such events in a less-than-charitable fashion. I vow not to, but it still happens on occasion. I've learned in such instances to put myself in time-out and then, when I have cooled off, to apologize to my children for having messed up. They're usually pretty forgiving.

I used to think that if the kids found out I wasn't perfect, the game would be up and they would never respect me or obey me again. Now I recognize that they can learn from their experience with me that it's possible to keep loving a person who makes mistakes sometimes. That translates in reverse, too: they know I'll keep loving them in spite of their mistakes as well.

2. Treasure the glimmers of hope. Every now and then you'll get a hint that something you're doing as a mother is working. When this happens, write it down quickly. In the tough times, you can turn to this evidence that the struggles are going to be worth it.

Because I have five children, I estimate that I have spent roughly 12.5 years of my life at church in the foyer, or in the kitchen sitting on a cold, metal chair nursing a baby, or in the bathroom changing a diaper. There have been many times as I have bounced a screaming infant outside yet another missed sacrament meeting that I have thought, "What is the point? We could be home, the baby could be having a lovely nap, and I could be reading my scriptures and getting some spiritual nourishment, which I'm certainly not getting here."

Then one Sunday, our son came dragging up the stairs from his bedroom with a whine in his voice, saying, "Mom, do I have to go to. . . ." Suddenly he stopped, right in mid-sentence, shook his head, and said resignedly, "I know, I know: This family goes to church on Sunday." Well, where does a 7-year-old get the idea that "this family goes to church on Sunday"? Because he sees his mom pack up the diaper bag week after week and go over there even if it's just to sit on a metal chair or walk the foyer or stand over the changing table in the bathroom. When you're doing your best to be where you're supposed to be, the Lord compensates you for what you might be missing.

It might take years and years of begging the children to clear their plates off the kitchen table before you come home late one night, tired and hopeless as you consider the state you left the house in, to find that the 12-year-old has cleaned the entire place by herself. This has happened to me—honest! I suppose there are children's picture books I've read a thousand times aloud (I can still quote most of them) but I didn't really know the impact this was having until I got a letter from our daughter who was serving a mission in Africa. She and her companion were helping unload some books for an orphanage there, and she wrote: "Mom, they had *Madeline!* And *Harold and the Purple Crayon!* I could hardly make myself put them on the shelf, I was so excited!" That's a glimmer. You just never know how the little things you do and do and do are going to end up blessing your children's lives when they need it the most. Those glimmers are the things that keep you going as a mother.

3. Trust the Lord that there's a blessing in there somewhere. Every stage of mothering is like a coin that has two sides—a blessing side and a trial side. Because we're constantly trying to work through our trials, we have a tendency to focus on that side of the coin. We need to stop and take time to contemplate the blessing side.

For example, is there anything sweeter than a brand-new baby? Here's this little spirit, fresh from heaven, every bit a perfect miniature person. It's a genuine miracle, as vivid the fifth time as it was the first time.

On the flip side of that coin is the sheer exhaustion that comes with the sleep deprivation, the constant attendance to the baby's needs, and the inability of the child to explain why he or she is crying (if indeed there is a reason). It's easy to feel trapped, which is just a heartbeat away from feeling resentment. Don't succumb to it. Instead, feel the joy of committing yourself deeply and completely to something wonderful. Treasure the opportunity to sacrifice, which lifts you out of yourself and teaches you to draw upon the resources you possess in the deepest reservoirs of your soul. And get a sitter once in a while so you can get your perspective back!

I remember the little walks we used to take when we had just two children, a toddler and a baby. The toddler always wanted to ride her "bike," but she rarely made it all the way, and we usually ended up carrying the bike and the baby and pushing the toddler in the stroller. One evening as we set out I explained in perfect plainness to the 3-year-old that she could bring her bike only if she promised to be responsible for it the entire way. Of course, she did—and of course, about halfway home she started to fuss and just couldn't push the pedals any longer. We were standing on the sidewalk arguing about this when our neighbor pulled into her driveway next door to where we had stopped. She got out of the car and rushed over to see the children, exclaiming, "Oh, aren't they beautiful! You need to treasure every moment; the years just fly by!" I thought she was crazy. How could the years fly by when every day seemed to drag on so interminably?

But you know what? Now that erstwhile 3-year-old is a newlywed, and her baby brother is a returned missionary, and their youngest sibling is in junior high. We haven't had a diaper in the house for a decade. Everyone ties his or her own shoes. When we read scriptures as a family, the children can all participate without having to sound out the words. We find ourselves thinking about the things we always knew we would do someday, astonished to see that "someday" is suddenly here.

Every day has struggles, and every day has joys. Every season has mistakes, and every season has glimmers of hope. With the Lord's help, you can focus on the joys and the hope and know that the struggles are worth it and the mistakes can be overcome. Someday—maybe even today—you'll be glad you chose to be a mother.

ABOUT THE AUTHOR

Emily Watts is a senior editor at Deseret Book Company. A graduate of the University of Utah, she is the author of two published books. She and her husband, Larry, are the parents of two girls and three boys.

ADDITIONAL READING

Janene W. Baadsgaard (2003), *The LDS Mother's Almanac* (Salt Lake City: Deseret Book).

Emily Watts (2002), *Being the Mom: 10 Coping Strategies I Learned by Accident Because I Had Children on Purpose* (Salt Lake City: Bookcraft).

E S S A Y   E 4

SINGLE-PARENT DATING AND REMARRIAGE

KERRI L. AND BRENT W. ROBINSON

I looked up, Brent's arm around me, as we watched a football game. His 12-year-old daughter, whom I had not met, and who was supposed to be gone, was standing at the doorway of the dimmed room. Her dark, wide eyes were staring intently. I instinctively waved and smiled. Brent said, "Sweetheart, this is my friend Kerri." She said, "Mind if I turn on some more lights?" The lights quickly brightened and she disappeared. Brent and I looked at each other and awkwardly laughed.

Later, she said, "I was coming home to grab a sleeping bag. My dad was snuggly with a strange lady with blonde hair. My dad said, 'This is my friend.' Yeah, right, just a friend. That's why I kind of had a freak out. I wasn't going to stay there for 25 minutes to talk to my dad's so-called 'friend.'"

This "freak out" reaction, our feelings of helplessness, and the sensitivity of this experience are not uncommon to single parents who date. Brent had told his daughter that he was dating and she had heard him talking with someone on the phone. But she wasn't ready to actually see her daddy with that person. And she wasn't sure that she liked it. She emotionally needed space after setting some boundaries (turning on more lights). She was certainly not interested in getting to know me that night. My heart ached for what I imagined this daughter's confusion to be. That night we realized the need to choreograph our developing relationship with the emotional needs of nine children. We had been caught off guard in spite of careful planning.

Dating as a single parent is complicated and often hard. Sometimes it's a struggle to just survive, with little time, money, or energy to even think about dating. The most carefully laid plans are inevitably unraveled by unpredictable children. There are myriad individual circumstances and questions. When should I start dating? How can I find time to date with all of the heavy demands? Is it okay not to date? How do I balance my needs and the needs of my children? Am I being selfish? When and what do I tell my kids as a relationship develops? What are the messages and values that I am communicating to my children?

As parents, nurturing our children and teaching them values is our stewardship from the Lord, no matter our circumstances. Sometimes when caught up in a new romantic relationship, single parents unknowingly may lose perspective. When dating Brent, there were moments I caught myself feeling off balance. My 11-year-old daughter said, "I was in your bathroom and you were all nervous getting ready and you asked, 'What should I wear?' Just like a teenager." She noticed much more than I realized. Though my feelings were normal, it was important to evaluate the messages I sent and to be consistent and available. How Brent and I spent time and what we chose to do clearly communicated our priorities, values, and commitment to our kids, each other, and the Lord.

We found answers concerning dating and our relationship in frequent, honest discussions with each other; in counseling with bishops and professionals; in books; and especially through tutoring from the Holy Spirit. The things we learned were simple in concept but sometimes difficult to implement. First, choose actions that communicate that each child is a precious gift. Second, identify and address your own physical, social, emotional, and spiritual needs, modeling healthy living and relationships. Third, allow your romantic relationship and new relationships among prospective family members to grow at the appropriate time, in natural ways, and at a natural pace.

CHILDREN ARE A PRECIOUS GIFT

"Children are an heritage of the Lord" (Psalm 127:3). As children feel how precious they are to their parent and understand their valued place in the family—especially in single-parent homes, where there has been some trauma or loss—they feel more secure and have the resources physically and emotionally to grow and develop. In single-parent homes there can be harmful role reversals that are confusing to children. Sometimes, because parents are in pain, they may look to children to fill emotional needs in ways that are inappropriate. For example, it took conscious effort for me not to put too much responsibility on my oldest son and to avoid interacting with him as a peer or confidant. Parents need to clearly communicate, "I am the parent. It is my job to be the parent. You do not need to worry about taking care of me."

A parent can communicate how precious an individual child is by being involved in the seemingly small but important events of his or her life. When Brent and I began dating, I told him immediately that I didn't go out on Friday nights because of my son's football games. In return he told me he would not date on the nights when his children were with him. As our relationship became more serious, we continually assessed the circumstances, responses, and needs of each child, searching for how to best communicate our interest, love, and commitment.

MODEL HEALTHY LIVING

Our children's health and healing mirrored our own. We tried to be examples of physical and emotional health by paying attention to our own well-being. Healthy people attract others who are healthy, and they have healthier relationships. It's perfectly acceptable not to date because of individual or family circumstances. Brent and I both devoted a lot of time, before we met, in working individually to make sure we were ready for dating and a romantic relationship.

After my divorce, there were several things that helped me to heal and meet my individual needs. (Chapter 21 provides suggestions for meeting one's needs as a single parent.) Through inspiration, my path included exercising with friends, working with a competent counselor, and completing graduate studies while trying to balance the demands of my schooling with the needs of my five young children. I would occasionally date, but it was just too hard and not a priority. It was my season to fulfill my responsibilities as a mother. When I was introduced to Brent, I had been divorced ten years. I was content in my life, but the Spirit was nudging me to grow in new directions.

After his divorce, Brent focused on his children's needs and worked extensively with a trusted counselor to heal and to prepare for a new life. We each realized our dependence on the Lord and gained strength and direction through searching the scriptures and attending the temple regularly.

NATURAL PROGRESSION AND PACE

Though we knew that we were really interested in and attracted to one another, we consciously limited the involvement of our children (beyond just meeting briefly at the door or when we were in transit). It was important to us to protect them. Children should not be exposed too early in relationships because they may become emotionally involved, only to potentially experience additional heartache and loss. After considerable time, there came a point when our relationship had deepened and it spiritually felt natural to involve the children in the process.

We carefully worked together to plan more formal introductions and experiences for our children. We often asked, "What is the message that we should be communicating to our children now?" Those messages varied according to the individual needs and developmental stage of each child. When we introduced our two daughters, ages 11 and 12, we planned a "safe" activity of noncompetitive fun and lots of laughing. The older teenagers needed more casual interactions that felt unplanned and like "hanging out."

We talked with the children about our growing feelings for each other. We allowed them to ask questions: "What does this mean to me?" "Do I have to move? Change schools?" We found it most effective to support the children as they found answers and observed and accepted our relationship and resulting changes on their own terms and in their own time.

Shortly after our wedding, one son commented, "Your getting married was kind of expected. We saw it coming and could be ready." When Brent told his once-startled daughter that he was in love with me and that he was going to ask me to marry him, her response was, "Duh, do ya think?" We considered these comments wonderful compliments.

Conclusion

Our experiences are not uncommon to single parents who are devoted to their family and the Lord. A valuable tool for us is found in Proverbs: "Trust in the Lord with all thine heart; and lean not unto thine own understanding" (3:5). Just as we tried to learn what to do for each of our children at particular times, we found that the Lord knew what we needed and when. There are still many things to figure out, but Brent and I have been given the gift of each other and want to share that joy with our children.

ABOUT THE AUTHORS

Kerri L. Robinson, LCSW, MSW, is a licensed clinical social worker, most-of-the-time mom, and part-time therapist with the Family Support and Treatment Center.

Brent W. Robinson, MBA, is a dad and principal in the Durian Group, an information technology consulting company. They are blending a family of nine children and one grandchild.

ADDITIONAL READING

A. Dean Byrd (1997), *Finding Wholeness and Happiness After Divorce* (Salt Lake City: Deseret Book).

Frances E. Warden (2000, July), Time and the single parent, *Ensign, 30*(7), 30–34.

Robert E. Wells (1997, August), Uniting blended families, *Ensign, 27*(8), 24–29.

E S S A Y   E 5

Dispelling the Myths of Mormon Womanhood

Sherrie Mills Johnson

A friend related a discussion in a Relief Society meeting in which a sister made the comment, "It's common knowledge Mormon women are more depressed than other women." The remark distressed my friend. "I realize some LDS women get depressed just like others get broken legs or have cancer. Depression is one of the trials of mortal experience. But it seems to me we would have less—not more. Are we really more depressed?"

The answer to her question is a resounding no! Recently a religiosity and life satisfaction study[1] using nationally representative samples compared depression levels between LDS and non-LDS women. The study showed that on a scale of zero to seven with seven meaning that the respondent felt symptoms of depression seven days during the last week, the average level of depression among LDS women is 1.11 while the average for non-LDS women is 1.39.[2] One of the reasons the "depressed Mormon woman" myth has been perpetuated in Utah is that reports show more Prozac is sold in Utah than in other states and that sales of antidepressants in general are also higher than national averages.[3] Since Utah is predominantly LDS, the false assumption has then been made that LDS women are more depressed than women in other states.

There are several problems inherent in this

assumption. One is that non-LDS people often self-medicate for depression with alcohol and stimulants. Therefore, they don't obtain antidepressant prescriptions. In addition, LDS women are better educated than non-LDS women. The religiosity and life satisfaction study showed that 36 percent of LDS women between the ages of 24 and 44 have college degrees while only 15 percent of the women from the national sample do.[4] While studies have not been done to corroborate the following explanation, some people speculate that better-educated people are more open to psychological intervention and more apt to identify when they need help and seek it. If this is the case, as one psychologist pointed out, LDS women should be praised (rather than stereotyped) for getting help and taking care of the problem.[5] In short, before anyone can make assumptions about antidepressant sales among LDS people, further studies need to be done.

Besides the depression levels, the religiosity and life satisfaction study showed other factors that indicate LDS women are doing well. LDS women reported being happier. On a scale of 1 to 5 with 1 being "very unhappy" and 5 being "very happy," the average for the LDS women was 4.08, while the average for the non-LDS women was 3.84. The difference in these two averages is statistically significant, but more interesting was the fact that 33 percent of LDS women reported being "very happy" while only 18 percent of the non-LDS women did so.[6]

When asked why she felt LDS women were happier, one woman said, "Because we have an eternal perspective. We believe in a plan. We know who we are, where we are going, and why." Another LDS woman added, "It also helps that we have such an amazing support system. Family, ward members, friends . . . there's always someone to pick us up when we fall."

As to why the myth has persisted, a woman said, "We meet together so much that we are comfortable expressing ourselves. LDS women are freer with our comments and sharing our lives. Other women aren't as free. We talk more about depression when others hide it." My own research has confirmed this. While the media has occasionally presented a bleak picture of LDS women, we have perpetuated the myth by assuming it to be true and feeding it with our own stories. It is important to note that everyone feels sorrow, disappointment, and depression at times (see 2 Nephi 4:15–35 for an example). Since the gospel includes high goals and expectations, we sometimes want immediate perfection and forget that gospel living is a lifetime process, not a momentary accom-

plishment. We need to recognize the difference between clinical depression and having a down day. Those with long-term, serious depression or conditions such as post-partum depression should be encouraged to seek reliable counseling and medication; others may need to prayerfully seek new ways to deal with the ups and downs of life.

Another myth that has evolved concerning LDS women is that a majority of LDS women with children work outside the home. According to the religiosity and life satisfaction study, 56 percent of LDS women between the ages of 24 and 44 are employed.[7] This compares to the national average of 57 percent. However, when we break the LDS figures down, we discover that of the married women who have children in the home (all ages), only 23 percent work full-time. Another 22 percent work part-time, and 1 percent are working full- or part-time while attending school. The other 10 percent are single mothers or have not yet married.[8]

One of these part-time workers is a nurse who explains that she only works one shift a week and does it on Saturday when her husband is home with the children. He is self-employed and by working she is able to obtain much needed health insurance for the family. Many other LDS women run part-time businesses out of their homes. This allows them to bring in needed income while still being with their children. While we can't know the stories of all the women in the survey, what the statistics and interviews with women tell us is that most LDS mothers are taking seriously the prophet's counsel to be at home with their children and to make children their priority.

When explaining why she is grateful she can be a stay-at-home mom, a woman explained, "It isn't just better for my children. It's better for me. There are lessons you can't learn any other way. For one thing, I've learned not to be judgmental. Because I'm there in the trenches with my children, I see what they are going through and why. I see life through their eyes, not my own, and realize that my view is not the only one."

Another woman expressed this sentiment: "Being a stay-at-home mom has taught me godly sorrow. My greatest sorrowings have come because of my children. I don't mean that in a bad way. It is beautiful. Loving my children so much that I feel their sorrow makes me closer to God. My quest for happiness is greater because I've felt that sorrow."

More and more women, not just LDS women, are realizing the importance of being mothers in the home.[9] One sister related the story of a conversation she had at her husband's company social. The woman who is the company CFO said to this sister, "You always look so put together and confident and your children are always so nice and well mannered. You always seem so happy."

In an effort to be cordial, the sister tried to return the woman's compliment. "But you are so accomplished. You have this incredible career and accounting skills and—"

Before she could say more, the woman interrupted. "Forget the math! I'd rather have what you have."

Another woman reported a similar experience. "An older woman who worked with my husband looked at me with tears in her eyes and said, 'If I could do anything differently in my life, I would not work while my kids were young. Now that they are all grown and gone I can't take that back. No matter how fulfilling the job is, it just cannot replace the fact that you need to be with your kids. I admire you for the choice you've made, and I know it's something you will never regret.'"

Now is a wonderful time to be an LDS woman. While so much of the world is searching for answers, we have been taught the truths that bring happiness. After introducing the proclamation on the family to the Relief Society in 1995, President Hinckley said: "The strength of any nation is rooted within the walls of its homes. We urge our people everywhere to strengthen their families in conformity with these time-honored values."[10] While there is often little we can do about the attacks against us from outside the Church, there is much we can do within our Church community to curb misinformation that may demoralize and mislead us.

Because we are struggling mortals, we will always have adversity. It is important to help those who suffer in any way we can. But we should realize that for the most part, active LDS women are strong, obedient, and striving to help bring forth the kingdom of God. They understand that being women of God is a noble calling. Most of all, they understand what President Hinckley meant when he said, "He who is our Eternal Father has blessed [the sisters of the Church] with miraculous powers of mind and body. He never intended that you should be less than the crowning glory of His creations."[11]

ABOUT THE AUTHOR

Sherrie Mills Johnson, wife of Carl M. Johnson, went back to school after raising nine children (eight daughters and one son), earned a Ph.D. in sociology, and now teaches in the Religious Education Department at BYU. Most of all, she enjoys her twenty grandchildren (seventeen grandsons and three granddaughters).

ADDITIONAL READING

The Best of Women's Conference: Selected Talks from 25 Years of BYU Women's Conference (2000) (Salt Lake City: Bookcraft).
Women of Destiny: Reflections on the Relief Society Declaration (2002), Jennie J. Ford, comp. (Salt Lake City: Eagle Gate).

NOTES

1. Sherrie Mills Johnson (2003), *Religiosity and Life Satisfaction of LDS Women,* doctoral dissertation, Brigham Young University.
2. The instrument used for evaluation in both of the surveys was the Center for Epidemiologic Studies Depression Scale [CES-D], created by L. S. Radloff (1977); described in APA Task Force for the Handbook of Psychiatric Measures (2000), *Handbook of Psychiatric Measures* (Washington, D.C.: American Psychiatric Association), 523–526.
3. C. Crosby (1994, March 27), The ups and downs of Prozac—Utah's favorite drug, *The Salt Lake Tribune,* A1, A4. In preparing this news article, Crosby did her own investigation. She used drug company reports of sales and then interviewed pharmacists, doctors, and patients.
4. Johnson (2003), 138.
5. N. C. Gardner (1994, April 15), Prozac is effective in treating depression, *The Salt Lake Tribune,* A19.
6. Johnson (2003), 141.
7. Ibid., 119.
8. Ibid. Statistics generated by author from data presented in A. Sweet and L. L. Bumpass (1996), The national survey of families and households (waves land 2): Data description and documentation (Madison: University of Wisconsin Center for Demography); available at http://www.ssc.wisc.edu/nsfh/home.htm
9. See Staying at home (2004, October 10), report on *60 Minutes;* available at http://cbsnews.com
10. Gordon B. Hinckley (1995, November), Stand strong against the wiles of the world, *Ensign, 25*(11), 101.
11. Ibid., 98.

CHAPTER 24

TEACHING PRINCIPLES OF MODESTY AND CHASTITY

LILI DE HOYOS AND CHRISTIAN ANDERSON

*Our physical bodies indeed are temples of God. Consequently . . . you and I must
carefully consider what we take into our temple, what we put on our temple, what we
do to our temple, and what we do with our temple.[1]*
—*Elder David A. Bednar*

Helping our children and youth learn to obey the commandments of God includes teaching them to observe God's standards concerning modesty and chastity. Jesus Christ made it clear that His followers are not "of the world" (John 15:19). He refers to His people as "peculiar" (Deuteronomy 14:2; 1 Peter 2:9) and admonishes us, "come ye out from the wicked, and be ye separate" (Alma 5:57). We can help our youth feel joy and confidence as they adhere to the Lord's standards rather than adopting the popular standards of dress, media, and chastity that are becoming increasingly inconsistent with Church standards. While president of Ricks College (now BYU–Idaho), Elder David A. Bednar taught: "Just as the Church's temples portray light and an inner beauty through their outward appearance, so we must be thoughtful and careful about how we dress."[2] Members of the Church can be a "light to the world" through modest dress and demeanor. President Harold B. Lee advised: "Do not underestimate the important symbolic and actual effect of appearance. Persons who are well groomed and modestly dressed invite the companionship of the Spirit of our Father in Heaven and are able to exercise a wholesome influence upon those around them."[3]

Observing the Lord's standards as outlined in *For the Strength of Youth* is a matter of both mind and heart and, as such, has a profound significance on who we are and how we behave. This counsel from the First Presidency reads: "Through your dress and appearance, you can show the Lord that you know how precious your body is. . . . Never lower your dress standards for any occasion. . . . Do not disfigure yourself with tattoos or body piercings."[4] Thus, showing respect for God and oneself goes beyond the way that we dress. As defined in *True to the Faith:* "Modesty is an attitude of humility and decency in dress, grooming, language, and behavior. If you are modest, you do not draw undue attention to yourself. Instead, you seek to 'glorify God in your body, and in your spirit' (1 Corinthians 6:20; see also verse 19)."[5]

In our stewardships as parents and leaders, we can help children and youth learn to choose wholesome media to avoid the negative influences of immodest dress and behavior commonly depicted and encourage them to be modest and chaste in thought and action.

MEDIA INFLUENCES

Unfortunately, in our day, the media's depiction of immodesty and unchastity can make these destructive practices seem acceptable and normal. The content of movies, music, music videos, books, magazines, television, video games, and Internet sites can damage the spirit. (Chapter 13 discusses pornography addiction and ways to protect families from pornography; chapter 25 provides guidelines for selecting appropriate media.) Almost always, unmarried sexual encounters are presented in the media as spontaneous, uncommitted, immediately satisfying, and without negative emotional and physical consequences, including adjustments needed between the parties. Though a growing number of studies demonstrate the media's influence on adolescent sexual attitudes, values, and beliefs, sex between unmarried partners is shown on television 24 times more often than sex between married adults.[6] Rarely is there any mention of sexually transmitted disease or unwanted pregnancy. One study demonstrated that teens who watch a lot of television with sexual content are twice as likely to engage in sexual activity as those who watch few such programs.[7] We need to discuss media depictions of relationships with our youth and help them understand that these are false presentations of human sexuality.

The authors, both clinical social workers and parents of eight, suggest another detrimental effect of television on family interaction. We have noticed that even the "safe" family situation comedies offered on television are generally inundated with insults, put-downs, and "zingers," all accompanied by a laugh track to convince us that this is the cleverest way to talk to others. To add to the deceptive message, the friends and families depicted on the show are loving, loyal, and happy, in spite of the adversarial way they communicate with each other.[8] Both parents and children may benefit tremendously by becoming aware of how often family communication mirrors the negative kind of speech heard on television shows and by making deliberate efforts to speak with more kindness and respect. This kindness and respect is often overlooked as another facet of modesty. Demonstrations of courtesy, love, tolerance, and consideration for others' feelings lift us above the coarseness, contempt, incivility, and lack of respect for others so common in today's media.

ENCOURAGING MODEST PRACTICES

Modesty is a way of living and behaving, as well as of choosing clothing. Our choices reflect what we worship and what our hearts are set upon. The Lord, through the prophet Isaiah, said, "For my thoughts are not your thoughts, neither are your ways my ways. . . . For as the heavens are higher than the earth, so are my ways higher than your ways, and my thoughts than your thoughts" (Isaiah 55:8–9). This is an invitation to lift our vision and our ways to His. If

we accept that God's view of beauty—including its connection to modesty and righteousness—is more correct than the world's view, we can avoid the world's obsession with the perfect body, hair, face, and clothes and take appropriate measures to be well-groomed and develop a pleasing appearance. When mothers and fathers are overly focused or preoccupied with "perfect body" goals, children may adopt that orientation, as well. Mothers and fathers who spend time, energy, and money on looking "just right" to their peers may not see the connection when their children want to look "just right" to their peers, as well.

UNDERSTANDING THE CONCEPT OF BEAUTY

In order to be a modest people, acceptable to the Lord, it is helpful to understand the concept of beauty as spoken of in the scriptures. Beauty is pleasing to God and always includes modesty of dress, speech, and behavior. When God speaks of beauty it is usually coupled with strength, virtue, or righteousness (see Isaiah 52:1 and Articles of Faith 1:13). For example, beauty is found in the freshness and vibrancy of youth—where it is coupled with cleanliness, innocence, and purity. It is found in the tired young mother, not always perfectly manicured, often without makeup, and perhaps still hoping to lose a few pounds left over from her last pregnancy, who desires to bear children and rear them in love. Beauty is in the single sister who builds a meaningful life, reaching out to nurture others in a world hungry for love.

There is beauty in the middle-aged parents, starting to collect wrinkles, who have worked long and hard together to prepare their children for missions, advanced schooling, and marriage, and who continue to support them in these endeavors. Truly, there is beauty in the deep lines and creases, thickening ankles and waistlines, and the white or thinning hair of the elderly who are nearing the end of a righteous life, completing family histories, serving missions, working in temples, extending love and support to children and grandchildren. Isaiah, describing the Savior, wrote, "there is no [worldly] beauty that we should desire him" (Isaiah 53:2). Yet, surely there was no more beautiful being to ever walk the earth than He who gives us "beauty for ashes" (Isaiah 61:3).

By contrast, popular culture has a much narrower definition of beauty. This definition is reflected in magazine covers, television shows, movies, and commercials. The mainstream societal view of beauty often has little to do with modesty and chastity, focusing instead on perfection of form and feature. Consider that several entire industries are oriented around doomed-to-fail efforts to avoid the aging process and achieve physical perfection. While it is good for us to take care of ourselves, we can balance our stewardship over our bodies with an equivalent effort to progress spiritually, emotionally, and intellectually, rather than fretting too much about appearance or aging.[9]

OVERCOMING MISUNDERSTANDINGS ABOUT MODESTY

When teaching youth, care must be taken to avoid conveying misunderstandings about modesty. For example, one common misunderstanding was expressed by a Young Women president who, reviewing the standards of modesty with girls in her ward, concluded: "I know it's really hard to dress modestly. I know you look darling in those [immodest] clothes." Her misguided message: "If you wear immodest clothes, you look darling, but let's be homely because this is what is expected." Other mixed messages include thumbing through fashion magazines or browsing through racks of immodest clothing, lamenting that it's "too bad I can't wear that," or encouraging youth to wear revealing clothing before they go to the temple and can no longer "look that cute."

Others may misunderstand what constitutes modesty in dress. For example, when confronted about their clothing, young women often protest, "This IS modest!" They consider covered flesh to be modestly clothed. But tight-fitting clothes are not modest.[10] A similar error is made when women wear skirts that seem to be of modest length or shirts that seem to have a modest neckline, but fail to consider that when they bend, sit, or lean over, this choice in clothing is too revealing.[11] Parents should provide specific guidance in clothing choices and modest posture, beginning when children are young.

Parents can also help their girls become more aware of the strength of reaction that immodest clothing can generate in boys. One Young Women president conducted a survey of the 30 young men in her ward. She asked what they considered to be immodest clothing and how certain items of clothing—tight tops, low-cut tops, midriff-revealing clothes—affected their thinking and their opinions about the girls wearing those clothes. Most of the boys said that they really didn't want to focus on those clothes, but that it was difficult not to. Further, the vast majority of boys indicated that these clothes lowered their opinion of the young women wearing them. The Young Women president read the responses to the young women of the ward and reported that in the weeks following, there was a noticeable increase in the girls' level of modest dress.

Of course, not only young women should make righteous clothing choices. Women of any age can be an example to others by demonstrating that fashionable clothes can also be modest. Men and boys also should consider their clothing choices to avoid revealing or inappropriate clothing.[12] All Latter-day Saints can take care to avoid the use of immodest clothing when dressing for yard work and recreation. Modest clothing (or modifications that make the clothing modest) can be used for athletic teams, ballroom or modern dance, costume parties, beauty pageants, theatrical costumes, formal dances, proms, and weddings. When activities call for a uniform that allows for strenuous movement, most uniforms can be selected or altered so they do not reveal backs and midriffs.[13]

The First Presidency taught that

Endowed members of the Church wear the garment as a reminder of the sacred covenants they have made with the Lord and also as a protection against temptation and evil. How it is worn is an outward expression of an inward commitment to follow the Savior.[14]

Specifically, the First Presidency mentioned that endowed members of the Church

should not remove either all or part of the garment to work in the yard or to lounge around the home in swimwear or immodest clothing. Nor should they remove it to participate in recreational activities that can reasonably be done with the garment worn properly beneath regular clothing.[15]

Just as endowed members should not "[seek] occasions to remove" the garment and should "[restore it] as soon as possible" when it is necessarily removed, members of the Church at all life stages should not seek occasion to wear clothes that are immodest.

The scriptures remind us to carefully examine ourselves for personal consistency between our testimony and our choices (see Luke 6:46), including choices of modest dress and behavior. Sister Susan Bednar encouraged such consistency: "If we love the Savior, we will follow the counsel of his leaders to dress modestly. If we desire a temple marriage, we will dress so as to qualify for that blessing."[16]

When counseling with those in our families who are having difficulty making choices that reflect standards of modesty, we need to have the courage to discuss these choices clearly, in a spirit of love and understanding. Parents will naturally have more success encouraging obedience to family standards if they agree on family standards. When parents disagree, however, one parent can still teach and testify of correct standards, referencing scriptures, the prophets, and other authoritative sources. This can be accomplished respectfully and without becoming adversarial. At home, the foundation of a warm, loving relationship between parents and youth allows for better communication on these sometimes delicate issues (see chapter 17 for more ideas on parenting children in love and righteousness). In all settings, we can demonstrate kindness and tolerance, teaching principles by word and example within appropriate stewardship responsibilities. Those who are less grounded in faith are likely to respond positively as they feel accepted and loved.

What Parents Can Do

Examine your own attitudes and beliefs concerning beauty and modesty and make adjustments as necessary to show your commitment to being among God's "peculiar people." Teach principles of beauty and modesty in the context of a commitment to care more about God's opinion than about the world's opinion.

Recognize that permissiveness is ineffective in promoting standards of modesty. While children, especially teens, can and should make many of their own decisions, they have a responsibility to honor parental standards. Even children who are earning their own money can be regulated in their expenditures.

Teach sons principles of beauty and modesty. Teach them to honor womanhood and to seek the companionship of modest young women. Teach both sons and daughters that modest dress and behavior includes moderation in hairstyles and makeup as well as in gestures, speech, movement, and dance.

Share President Gordon B. Hinckley's counsel about avoiding multiple body piercings (except one earring in each ear for girls) and tattoos.[17] Follow and teach the standards outlined in *For the Strength of Youth* and the counsel of latter-day prophets.

Identify stores that sell modest clothing and shop there. Generally the "Misses" departments of large department stores offer many modest choices. "Juniors" departments and youth clothing shops in malls may have few modest offerings.

Be creative. Many young women have learned to wear long tank tops underneath tops that may expose midriffs with movement. Learn to alter clothing as necessary or to sew modest clothing. President James E. Faust said: "You young ladies may have a hard time buying a modest prom dress. May I suggest that you make your own? You may need some help, but plenty of help is available."[18]

Although standards of modest dress change across cultures and time, they are not arbitrary. Modesty, because it precludes drawing inappropriate attention to oneself, is always conservative—whether that means covering one's ankles in one time period or not exposing midriffs in another. Elder Bednar stated: "It is interesting to me that [the] fashions and trends of the world frequently promote a false individuality that is nothing more than a shallow, superficial, and curious outward conformity. True individuality is the product of spirituality and is not a function of trinkets or ornaments."[19] Start early to teach principles of modesty. Help girls and boys to grow up with "a style of their own."[20] (See essay D3 for more on modesty.)

Teaching About Chastity

Obedience to the standards of modesty set forth by latter-day prophets can help youth remain close to the Spirit and choose chastity in thought and action. Elder Bruce R. McConkie wrote that modesty "is an aid in preserving chastity. . . . [I]mmodesty . . . excites passions and lusts . . . and frequently encourages and invites . . . immoral practices."[21] As we teach our children to dress and behave modestly, we need to clearly connect modesty with chastity, and chastity with happiness. President Hinckley taught that "[we] must recognize, that both experience and divine wisdom dictate virtue and moral cleanliness as the way that leads to strength of character, peace in the heart, and happiness in life."[22]

As we teach our youth and children, it is essential to frame teachings of chastity in the context of the plan of salvation. "God gave unto them commandments, after having made known unto them the plan of redemption" (Alma 12:32). Elder Boyd K. Packer emphasized the importance of teaching youth about Heavenly Father's plan: "Young people wonder 'why?'—Why are we commanded to do some things, and why are we commanded not to do other things? A knowledge of the plan of happiness, even in outline form, can give young minds a 'why.'"[23] In addition, we can use many available resources. *A Parent's Guide*[24] was prepared to help parents teach about physical intimacy in the context of the gospel, with specific suggestions for communicating these subjects to children at different stages of development. Other resources include family home evening materials, conference talks, and Church magazines.

In addressing this sensitive topic, it is important to be positive and careful not to teach chastity by making sexual intimacy or natural desires seem bad or evil. We can help our children understand that human intimacy is an important, wonderful, and even holy part of the marriage relationship, with the power to bind and unite a husband and wife when kept within proper bounds. Watch for teaching moments when children become aware of good and bad choices made in the lives of friends, neighbors, relatives, or schoolmates. We can—and should—model righteous judgment, often as simple as judging behaviors, not people.[25]

Monitoring teen activity and building strong relationships between parents and their teens are also crucial. For example, a national study indicated that the most common place for teens to lose their virginity was in their home. Evening hours are becoming more common as compared with previous surveys that showed that most teens had sexual involvement during the afternoon hours when parents were less likely to be home.[26] Father absence in the home has also been strongly associated with elevated risk for early sexual activity and adolescent pregnancy for daughters.[27] However, mothers who convey strong moral values to their children can help make a difference. Another recent study showed that maternal disapproval of premarital sex and a connected relationship with their teens was associated with girls' avoiding or delaying sexual involvement.[28]

Peers have also been shown to have a powerful influence on teen choices and preferences in many areas. An interesting connection between media choices and peer influence was reported by one study done in Sweden that found teens to be less influenced by parents and more influenced by peers when they developed an early interest in hard rock music.[29] However, when parents develop warm and trusting relationships with teens through which strong moral values are regularly taught, negative peer influence is more likely to be diminished. In fact, research in adolescence and young adulthood indicates that parents can influence deep and enduring personality traits and core values in areas such as religiosity.[30] Additionally, research indicates that it is the quality of the parent–child relationship that often seems to determine the type of peers that teenagers choose.[31]

In many positive ways, we can protect our homes from the threats, help our children avoid temptation, and assist them as they grow in virtue and moral strength. The following suggestions can help to encourage chaste thought and behavior.

What Parents Can Do

Develop and nurture a warm and responsive relationship with each child. Recognize that no parent should exercise coercive control over children, and that coercion is ultimately neither lasting nor successful (D&C 121:41). However, where there is an appropriate and loving relationship, parents can have significant influence.[32]

Help children understand that the body and spirit are the soul of man and that unlawful use of the body, our own or someone else's, "desecrates the Atonement of Christ, which saved that soul and which makes possible the gift of eternal life."[33]

Emphasize that the purpose of commandments concerning morality is not to "spoil our fun" or cause us to "miss out" on life, but to fulfill life's purposes by helping us become pure as the Savior is pure. Help children understand the difference between focusing on obeying "just enough" to think we have avoided serious transgression and, in contrast, making choices from the heart that help us become more like Jesus Christ, keeping us far away from sin.[34]

Observe appropriate boundaries. This should include appropriate privacy between brothers and sisters, between parents and children, and between children and friends or extended family members. Be mindful of states of dress around the home, of closing doors, and so on. Help protect your children from uncomfortable and unsafe situations by teaching them what is appropriate interaction with others.

Prepare your children to use the law of the fast, when baptized, to gain mastery over the natural man. Many families encourage newly baptized children to begin by fasting for one meal, then gradually increase the length of their fast. Help children understand that fasting is a monthly opportunity to strengthen "spiritual muscle." Teach them that their spirits can conquer their flesh, and that they do not need to fulfill every appetite and desire. Help them see that as they learn to fast correctly, they are preparing to keep all appetites under appropriate control and that as they gain this mastery, the Lord can endow them with power.

Teach young men to honor womanhood and to treat women respectfully, beginning with their mother and sisters. Help them understand the responsibility God has given men to protect women,[35] and make it a practice for men in the family to speak and act respectfully toward all women.

Teach young men that Satan has devised numerous temptations for men, specifically seeking to exploit and corrupt natural feelings and desires, but that preparing for priesthood responsibilities and then honoring the priesthood can be a harness for those desires. Teach them that appropriately harnessing masculinity produces men such as Captain Moroni and the sons of Helaman who bless the lives of women and children. But unbridled appetites lead to injurious and exploitative behaviors that destroy individuals and families.

CONCLUSION

Elder Robert D. Hales taught: "It used to be that the Church and the world weren't very far apart. Now the world is accelerating downward fast. . . . But wherever the world goes, however deviant it becomes, the Church will remain constant. Once you understand that, you understand that you can't do something just because it's popular. You don't base everything on where the world is. You decide who and what you are."[36] We can take a stand and live by moral standards. We can teach others to do so. The commandments of God are instituted to protect and bless us. As we live modest and chaste lives, we, our children, and those we lead can receive the blessings promised to the faithful (Mosiah 2:41).

ABOUT THE AUTHORS

Lili De Hoyos Anderson, MSW, Ph.D., full-time wife and mother of eight for almost 20 years, now has a private practice in individual, marriage, and family therapy and teaches part time for the BYU School of Family Life. She and her husband, Christian, are grandparents of seven.

Christian Anderson, MSW, is a licensed clinical social worker who has provided individual, marriage, and family therapy in agency and private practice for 25 years. He and his wife, Lili, have eight children and seven grandchildren.

ADDITIONAL READING

A Parent's Guide (1985), (Salt Lake City: The Church of Jesus Christ of Latter-day Saints); available at http://ldscatalog.org, item number 31123000.

Carlos E. Asay (1997, August), The temple garment: An outward expression of an inward commitment, *Ensign, 27*(8), 18–23.

David A. Bednar (2000, January 11), Ye are the temple of God; Ricks College Devotional; available at http://www.byui.edu/alumni/summit/summit2/devotional.htm

Terrance D. Olson (2000), Chastity and fidelity in marriage and family relationships; in David C. Dollahite, ed., *Strengthening Our Families: An In-Depth Look at the Proclamation on the Family* (Salt Lake City: Bookcraft), 50–59.

NOTES

1. David A. Bednar (2000, January 11), Ye are the temple of God; Ricks College Devotional; available at http://www.byui.edu/alumni/summit/summit2/devotional.htm

2. Ibid., 5.

3. C. J. Williams, ed. (1998), *The Teachings of Harold B. Lee* (Salt Lake City: Bookcraft), 219–220.

4. First Presidency (2001), *For the Strength of Youth: Fulfilling Our Duty to God,* pamphlet (Salt Lake City: The Church of Jesus Christ of Latter-day Saints), 14–16.

5. *True to the Faith: A Gospel Reference* (2004), (Salt Lake City: The Church of Jesus Christ of Latter-day Saints), 106; available at http://ldscatalog.org, item number 36863000.

6. Impact of media use on children and youth (2003), Canadian Paediatric Society position statement: Psychosocial Paediatrics Committee, *Paediatrics & Child Health, 8*(5), 301–306 (Reference No. PP 2003–01).

7. R. L. Collins, et al. (2004), Watching sex on television predicts adolescent initiation of sexual behavior, *Pediatrics, 114,* 280–289.

8. Marvin J. Ashton (1992, May), The tongue can be a sharp sword, *Ensign, 22*(5).

9. Of course, we are not suggesting that youthful beauty is not pleasing to the eye, mind, and other senses. One of the amazingly generous—and unconditional—aspects of the great plan of happiness is the resurrection, through which each mortal soul will be restored to a perfect, young, and undoubtedly beautiful immortal body. What we are suggesting, however, is that the emphasis on youth and beauty, particularly as separate from substantive individual character, is a worldly trap.

10. Ezra T. Benson, ed. (1998), *The Teachings of Ezra Taft Benson* (Salt Lake City: Bookcraft), 562.

11. Susan A. Bednar (2001, September 16), Reverencing womanhood; BYU–Idaho Six-Stake Fireside; available at http://www.byui.edu/Presentations/Transcripts/Devotionals/2001_09_16_Bednarsusan.htm

12. The BYU Honor Code provides guidelines that can be used as a worthy standard. The section for men includes the following: "Clothing is inappropriate when it is sleeveless, revealing,

or form fitting. Shorts must be knee length or longer." See http://campuslife.byu.edu/HONORCODE and click "Honor Code" then "Dress and Grooming Standards."

13. The BYU Honor Code provides guidelines that can be used as a worthy standard. The section for women includes the following: "Clothing is inappropriate when it is sleeveless, strapless, backless, or revealing; has slits above the knee; or is form fitting. Dresses, skirts, and shorts must be knee length or longer." See http://campuslife.byu.edu/HONORCODE and click "Honor Code" then "Dress and Grooming Standards."

14. Quoted in Carlos E. Asay (1997, August), The temple garment: "An outward expression of an inward commitment," *Ensign, 27*(8), 22.

15. Ibid., 22.

16. Susan A. Bednar (2001), 5–6.

17. Gordon B. Hinckley (2001, January), A prophet's counsel and prayer for youth, *Ensign, 31*(1), 2; see also David A. Bednar (2000).

18. James E. Faust (2000, May), Womanhood: The highest place of honor, *Ensign, 20*(5), 95.

19. David A. Bednar (2000), 6.

20. For examples of ways that youth are exemplifying a "style of their own," see the following articles published in the *New Era:* J. Benson, M. L. Call, and E. O. Jennings (2005, January), Cute *and* modest, *New Era, 35*(1), 36–39; N. Miner (2003, May), Dressed up! *New Era, 33*(5), 45–46; and C. H. Benzley (2002, January), Evaluate your style, *New Era, 32*(1), 28–33.

21. Bruce R. McConkie (1966), *Mormon Doctrine,* 2d ed. (Salt Lake City: Bookcraft), s.v. "modesty," 510–511.

22. Gordon B. Hinckley (1987, May), Reverence and morality, *Ensign, 17*(5), 47–48.

23. Boyd K. Packer (1993, August 10), The great plan of happiness; address given at the Seventeenth Annual CES Religious Educators' Symposium, Brigham Young University; quoted in Robert L. Millet (1998), Divine deterrent to creeping relativism; in *LDS Marriage and Family Relations: Student Manual* (Dubuque, IA: Kendall/Hunt), 30–31.

24. *A Parent's Guide* (1985), (Salt Lake City: The Church of Jesus Christ of Latter-day Saints); available at http://ldscatalog.org, item number 31123000.

25. See Dallin H. Oaks (1998, March 1), Judge not and judging; BYU Devotional Address; available at http://speeches.byu.edu

26. N. Harrison (2002, September 26), Teens report having first sex in homes: The encounters have shifted to later hours; see also A. R. Papillo, et al., comp. (2002, September), *Facts at a Glance* (Washington, D.C.: Child Trends), 1.

27. B. J. Ellis, et al. (May/June 2003), Does father absence place daughters at special risk for early sexual activity and teenage pregnancy? *Child Development, 74*(3), 801–821.

28. C. McNeely, et al. (2002), Mothers' influence on timing of first sex among 14- and 15-year-olds, *Journal of Adolescent Health, 31*(3), 256–265; see also R. Sieving, C. S. McNeely, R. W. Blum (2000), Maternal expectations, mother-child connectedness, and adolescent sexual debut, *Archives of Pediatric and Adolescent Medicine, 154,* 809–816.

29. Reported in Children, violence, and the media: A report for parents and policy makers (1999, September 14), Senate Judiciary Committee Media Violence Report; prepared by Majority Staff, Senate Committee on the Judiciary.

30. W. A. Collins, et al. (2000), Contemporary research on parenting: The case for nature and nurture, *American Psychologist, 55,* 218–232.

31. J. E. Kim, E. M. Hetherington, and D. Reiss (1999), Associations among family relationships, antisocial peers, and adolescents' externalizing behaviors: Gender and family type differences, *Child Development, 70,* 1209–1230.

32. B. L. Top and B. A. Chadwick (1998, Summer), Raising righteous children in a wicked world, *BYU Magazine, 52*(2), 40–51.

33. Jeffrey R. Holland (1998, November), Personal purity, *Ensign, 28*(11), 75; see also Jeffrey R. Holland (1988, January 12), Of souls, symbols, and sacraments, BYU Devotional Address, available at http://speeches.byu.edu

34. For an excellent treatment of this point, see Hartman Rector Jr. (1973, January), Live above the law to be free, *Ensign, 3*(1), 130.

35. See First Presidency and Council of Twelve Apostles (1995, November), The family: A proclamation to the world, *Ensign, 25*(11), 102.

36. Integrity and values: A discussion with Elder Robert D. Hales (2005, April), *Ensign, 35*(4), 49.

CHAPTER 25

MEDIA AND VIOLENCE

BRAD J. BUSHMAN

*Good entertainment will help you to have good thoughts and make righteous
choices. . . . Do not attend, view, or participate in entertainment that is . . . violent . . . in any way.[1]*
—For the Strength of Youth

More than two thousand years ago, Socrates was concerned about the stories told to impressionable young children. He asked, "Then shall we carelessly and without more ado allow our children to hear any casual stories told by casual persons, and so to receive into their souls views of life for the most part at variance with those which we think they ought to hold when they come to man's estate?"[2] In the past, parents, teachers, and religious leaders told most of the stories to children. Today, the mass media tell most of the stories. The average child in America spends about 40 hours per week consuming media—it's a full-time job.[3] Adults spend more time consuming media than they spend at any other activity except sleeping and working.[4]

What kinds of stories are the mass media telling? Violence dominates each of the three major visual entertainment industries (television, movies, video games), including products aimed at children. The National Television Violence Study is an analysis of almost 10,000 hours of programming that revealed that about 60 percent of programs contained violence.[5] By the time the average American child graduates from elementary school, he or she will have seen more than 8,000 murders and more than 100,000 other assorted acts of violence on broadcast television.[6] The numbers are higher if the child has access to cable television, a VCR player, or a DVD player, as most do. Violence dominates the big screen as well as the small screen. Typically two-thirds of movies receive an R rating, and 5 percent or fewer receive a G rating.[7] The ratings are becoming more lenient over time.[8] Even G-rated films contain more violence now than ever before.[9] The overwhelming majority of video games contain violence as a central theme.[10]

IT'S ONLY VIOLENCE

I once conducted an informal (and unscientific) survey among several Church members about movies and TV programs. I asked Church members what makes a show bad or evil. By far the most common response was sex, followed by profanity. Nobody mentioned violence. When I asked Church members about specific movies, a common response was "That movie only had one bad scene." I asked, "What happened? Did someone get killed?" The answer was always the same—"No. It was a sex scene." Sex in marriage is a private act not meant for public viewing. Sex outside of marriage is a serious sin. In fact, Alma ranked it second on his list of serious sins (Alma 39:3–5). What did Alma rank first? Shedding innocent blood and denying the Holy Ghost—the unpardonable sin (Alma 39:5). Profanity, though bad, was not on Alma's list. I was puzzled that many Church members considered profane shows to be more evil than violent shows.

Aggression is defined as any behavior that

intentionally harms another person.[11] *Violence* is an extreme act of physical aggression, such as murder, assault, rape, and robbery.[12] Often violence only works in the short run—violent people get what they want right away. In the long run, however, there are many negative side-effects and unintended consequences of violence (e.g., it damages relationships). Elder Dallin H. Oaks said, "There is no happiness in violence, only pain and sorrow."[13] Ironically, many people regard violence in the mass media as a form of entertainment.

Violence hurts our bodies and our spirits. Consuming violent media makes it more difficult to keep ourselves "unspotted from the world" (James 1:27). If we fill our minds and hearts with violent images, the guidance of the Spirit may scarcely be heard through the turmoil. Elder M. Russell Ballard warned: "Far too much programming is not wholesome and uplifting but is violent, degrading, and destructive to moral values. This kind of television offends the Spirit of the Lord; therefore, I express a word of warning and caution about such programming."[14]

Of course, some forms of violence are more offensive than others. Sometimes violence can be justified, such as in protecting personal and religious freedoms. For example, the scriptures describe some wars and other acts of justified violence. On the other hand, much of the violence in the media is unjustified (e.g., the victims of media violence appear to "deserve it"). As with all things, Church members must rely on the Spirit as their guide. If the comfort of the Holy Ghost leaves when we watch a show, play a video game, listen to a song, or read a book, then we should leave, too.[15] Allowing ourselves to get caught up in the emotionality of violent acts can limit our ability to yield to the enticings of the Spirit (see Mosiah 3:19).

VIOLENT MEDIA EFFECTS

For more than 50 years, social scientists have conducted research on the effects of violent media, including TV programs, films, comic books, and video games. Researchers have identified four different effects of media violence: the aggressor effect, the victim effect, the bystander effect, and the appetite effect. Each type of effect is described below.

Aggressor effect. One effect of violent media is that it increases aggressive behavior. Apostles have not said much about the aggressor effect specifically, but the impact of media has been acknowledged. Elder

M. Russell Ballard said: "Volumes of research data show the detrimental effects of television, but I just say that television and videocassette viewing by youngsters has a significant impact on their behavior."[16]

Social scientists have said a lot about the aggressor effect. About 300 studies involving more than 50,000 subjects have shown that violent media increase aggression. In fact, the U.S. Surgeon General came to this conclusion over 30 years ago. In March 1972, Jesse Steinfeld, former U.S. Surgeon General, said: "It is clear to me that the causal relationship between televised violence and antisocial behavior is sufficient to warrant appropriate and immediate remedial action. . . . There comes a time when the data are sufficient to justify action. That time has come."[17]

The effect of violent media on aggression is not trivial. Yet many people do not believe that violent media cause aggression. There are at least two possible reasons for this. First, people may think, "I watch violent shows and play violent video games and I've never killed anyone." But murders are rare (less than 6 per 100,000 people annually in the United States), and it is difficult to predict rare events.[18] One can, however, predict more frequent violent behaviors. For example, in a 15-year longitudinal study[19] involving 329 children, heavy viewers of violent TV shows in first and third grade were three times more likely to be convicted of criminal behavior by the time they were in their twenties. They were also more likely to abuse their spouse and to have assaulted other people at least once in the past year. Researchers have also found that people believe the media have a much stronger effect on others than on themselves.[20] This false belief, called the *third-person effect*,[21] is pervasive.

A second possible reason people do not think violent media affect them is that most people use the popular press as a source of information, and the popular press frequently denies any harm done by violent media.[22] Although scientific studies find that violent media effects are becoming stronger over time, an analysis of more than 600 news reports showed that over time news stories have softened their position on the harmful effects of violent media. The simplest explanation for this apparently irresponsible reporting pattern is that the print news media industry has a vested interest in denying a link between media violence and aggression. Many print news media companies are part of larger conglomerates that directly profit from the sale of violent media such as television and movies. Many print news media companies also get a lot of their advertising revenue from companies that produce and sell violent media (e.g., almost all newspapers advertise movies).

Regardless of the reason, the entertainment industry is reluctant to admit that it is marketing a harmful product, much as the tobacco industry was reluctant to admit that cigarettes were addicting. For example, Jack Valenti, past president of the Motion Picture Association of America, said, "If you cut the wires of all TV sets today, there would still be no less violence on the streets in two years."[23] Here is the paradox: On the one hand, the TV industry claims that a few minutes of advertising can sell soap, salsa, cereal, and even political candidates to viewers. On the other hand, the TV industry claims that the hours of programming surrounding the few minutes of advertising have no effect on viewers.

The scriptures indicate that thoughts are just a short step away from behaviors. In Proverbs 23:7 we read, "For as he thinketh in his heart, so is he." King Benjamin warned, "If ye do not watch . . . your thoughts . . . ye must perish" (Mosiah 4:30). The Lord said, "Look unto me in every thought" (D&C 6:36) and counseled us to "let virtue garnish [our] thoughts unceasingly" (D&C 121:45). Violent thoughts are not virtuous thoughts. Elder M. Russell Ballard said, "I believe the entertainment industry cannot portray on film people gunned down in cold blood, in living color, and not have it affect the attitudes and thoughts of some of the people who see it."[24] The research evidence indicates that violent media increase aggressive thoughts.[25]

The Lord and His Apostles have warned us of the dangers of becoming angry (e.g., see Matthew 5:21–22). Numerous studies have shown that violent media increase angry feelings.[26] These studies directly contradict the *catharsis hypothesis,* which proposes that behaving aggressively or even viewing aggression is an effective way to reduce angry and aggressive impulses. There isn't a shred of scientific evidence to support the catharsis hypothesis.[27]

Victim effect. People who consume a lot of violent media are also more fearful of becoming victims of violence themselves. In comparison to light TV viewers, heavy TV viewers are more fearful about becoming victims of violence, are more distrustful of others, and are more likely to perceive the world as a dangerous, mean, and hostile place.[28] Heavy TV viewers may also be more likely to misinterpret others' actions

as hostile and to behave aggressively in retaliation. The Lord does not want us to be afraid. He said: "Look unto me in every thought; doubt not, fear not" (D&C 6:36). The Apostle Paul also wrote, "For God hath not given us the spirit of fear; but of power, and of love, and of a sound mind" (2 Timothy 1:7). For many viewers, violent media may increase the spirit of fear.

Bystander effect. People who consume a lot of violent media become desensitized to it over time and less sympathetic to victims of violence. Apostles have warned us about the desensitizing effect of violent media. Elder Marvin J. Ashton said of individuals who consume violent media, "Soon the person is desensitized and is unable to react in a sensitive, caring, responsible manner, especially to those in his own home and family."[29] In *For the Strength of Youth,* the First Presidency states: "Depictions of violence often glamorize vicious behavior. They offend the Spirit and make you less able to respond to others in a sensitive, caring way. They contradict the Savior's message of love for one another."[30] Elder M. Russell Ballard said, "I believe that the desensitizing effect of [violent] media abuses on the hearts and souls of those who are exposed to them results in a partial fulfillment of the Savior's statement that 'because iniquity shall abound, the love of many shall wax cold.'"[31]

The scientific evidence is consistent with the words of apostles and prophets. For example, research has shown that after watching filmed Hollywood violence, people are less physiologically aroused by real depictions of violence.[32] Research has also shown that people who have watched a violent show or played a violent video game are less likely to help a victim of violence in the real world.[33] In a recent study conducted in our lab,[34] college students were randomly assigned to play a violent or nonviolent video game for 20 minutes. Next, they were given a lengthy questionnaire to complete. While working on the questionnaire, they heard a staged fight just outside their door, where one person was injured and fell to the ground groaning in pain. The aggressor left, so it was a safe situation to help the victim. People who played a violent video game were less likely to help the victim, took longer to help the victim if they did offer help, and reported that the fight was less serious than did those who played a nonviolent game.[35]

Appetite effect. Finally, the more violent media people consume, the more they want. Elder Marvin J. Ashton said: "A diet of violence or pornography dulls the senses, and future exposures need to be rougher and more extreme. . . . Good people can become infested with this material and it can have terrifying, destructive consequences."[36] There is also some research evidence on this topic, although not as much as for the other media effects described above. Research has shown that people can become addicted to violent media, as they can to tobacco, alcohol, and other drugs.[37]

WHAT TYPES OF VIOLENT MEDIA ARE MOST HARMFUL?

What types of media are most likely to increase aggression? In general, realistic violence is more likely to increase aggression than fantasy violence (e.g., cartoons). But in young children under about 7 years old the effects of realistic and fantasy violence are about the same because young children have a difficult time telling the difference between reality and fantasy. News programs and aggressive sports (e.g., hockey, football) also can increase aggression, but not as much as violent drama, probably because people can see the harmful consequences of violence in the news and in sports.[38] Media violence is less likely to increase aggression when the negative consequences of violence are depicted.[39] Justified violence is more likely to increase aggression than unjustified violence.[40] People generally have strong inhibitions against behaving aggressively, but when they see others use aggression in a justified manner, their inhibitions are reduced and they are more likely to think their own aggression is also justified.

Violent video games. Research has shown that violent video games are more likely to increase aggression than are violent TV programs and films.[41] There are at least three reasons why. The first is involvement level. TV viewing is a relatively passive activity, whereas video game playing is highly active. Viewers of violent TV programs and films watch other characters behave aggressively. Players of video games control the actions of aggressive characters. Research has shown that learning is enhanced when people are actively involved.[42] The second reason is identification with violent characters. Viewers of violent films might identify with the characters they see, and, if they do, they are more likely to be affected by the violence.[43] In contrast, players of violent video games are required to take on the identity of a violent game character. In first-person games, the player controls the actions of the violent game character and sees the game environment from the character's visual perspective. In third-person games, the player can "become" one of an array of characters that differ in gender, appearance, and special fighting skills. In some games, the player can apply scanned images (e.g., a photo of themselves) to characters in the game (called "skins").

Research has shown that identifying with a violent character increases the media violence effect.[44] The third reason is the reinforcement of violent acts. In the mass media, aggression often pays (e.g., the aggressor gets what he or she wants). When people watch a TV program or film, this reinforcing effect is indirect. When people play a video game, this reinforcing effect is direct. The player of the violent video game is directly reinforced for behaving aggressively by receiving points, advancing to the next level of the game, seeing stimulating visual effects, hearing sound effects (e.g., groans of pain from the enemy), or hearing verbal praise (e.g., the computer says "nice shot" after killing a character). A large body of literature indicates that aggressive behavior increases when it is reinforced.[45] The reinforcement characteristics of violent video games may make them addictive to players.[46]

What about violence in the scriptures? So what is the difference between violence in the scriptures and violence in the mass media? From the scriptures we learn that aggression and violence can be justified, but only when God commands it. For example, God commanded the Israelites, "thou shalt not kill" (Exodus 20:13), but He commanded Nephi to kill Laban (1 Nephi 4:10–13). It is worth noting that Nephi was not eager to kill Laban, even though Laban had tried to kill him and had stolen his property. Nephi said, "Never at any time have I shed the blood of man. And I shrunk and would that I might not slay him" (1 Nephi 4:10).

Captain Moroni, who led an army of Nephites against an army of Lamanites and Nephite dissenters, provides another scriptural example of justified violence. Captain Moroni, like Nephi, did not want to use violence: "Yea, and in fine, their wars never did cease for the space of many years with the Lamanites, notwithstanding their much reluctance. Now, they were sorry to take up arms against the Lamanites, because they did not delight in the shedding of blood; yea, and this was not all—they were sorry to be the means of sending so many of their brethren out of this world into an eternal world, unprepared to meet their God. Nevertheless, they could not suffer to lay down their lives, that their wives and their children should be massacred by the barbarous cruelty of those who were once their brethren, yea, and had dissented from their church, and had left them and had gone to destroy them by joining the Lamanites" (Alma 48:22–24).

Still, violence is rarely justified by the Lord, inside or outside the home. (See D&C 98 for the Lord's guidelines in dealing with enemies.) Jesus raised the standards for the use of violence when he replaced the Mosaic law with the higher law: "whosoever shall smite thee on thy right cheek, turn to him the other also" (Matthew 5:39). And the scriptures do not glorify violence. Instead, they describe the spiritual and temporal consequences of violent behavior.

The mass media do tend to glorify violence. In fact, violence is often portrayed as humorous in the mass media. The National Television Violence Study found that even though more than half (53 percent) of the violent scenes on television were lethal, more than 40 percent of the violent scenes were portrayed as humorous. Media characters are quick to use violence and are reluctant to use nonviolent solutions to problems. For example, the National Television Violence Study found that less than 4 percent of the violent programs contained an anti-violence theme.

The mass media rarely depict the harmful consequences of violence, either short-term or long-term. The National Television Violence study found that more than half (55 percent) of the violence victims showed no pain or suffering, more than one-third (36 percent) of the victims experienced unrealistically low levels of harm, and only 15 percent of the violent programs showed the long-term consequences of the violence to the victim's family, friends, and community.

In summary, the scriptures can teach us much about when violence is justified and when it is not. The scriptures teach us about the harmful consequences of unjustified violence. We rarely learn these lessons from the mass media.

WHO IS MOST AFFECTED BY VIOLENT MEDIA?

Several factors influence the effect violent media may have on an individual. Parents should consider these factors as they establish media guidelines for their families.

Age. Research shows that although people of all ages are affected by media violence, children are more affected than adults.[47] Compared to adults, children are more impressionable, have a more difficult time distinguishing reality from fantasy, and have a more difficult time understanding motives for aggression (e.g., revenge, self-protection). Before about age seven, most children don't know what is real and what is not.[48]

Gender. In studies conducted in the 1970s and 1980s, researchers found that violent TV programs had a stronger effect on males than on females.[49] However, a more recent 15-year longitudinal study reported that both boys and girls who had watched more TV violence in grade school were more aggressive 15 years later as young adults. In the study, TV violence was most closely related to physical aggression for males, but related to both physical and relational aggression for females.[50] Two possible explanations for lessening gender differences are: (1) aggressive female role models have become much more prevalent in the mass media, and (2) it has become more socially acceptable for females to behave aggressively.

Intellectual ability. Several studies have shown that children with lower intellectual ability watch more television in general and watch more violent television in particular than do children with higher intellectual functioning.[51] Children with low intellectual ability are also more at risk for growing up to behave aggressively and violently.[52] But the research evidence indicates that media violence affects children of all intellectual abilities.[53]

Socioeconomic class. As with intellectual functioning, several studies have shown that children from lower socioeconomic classes watch more television in general and more violent television in particular than do children from middle or upper socioeconomic classes.[54] It is also well established that children from lower socioeconomic classes are more at risk to become violent young adults.[55] But the research evidence indicates that media violence affects people of all socioeconomic classes.[56]

Aggressiveness. Research has also shown that people who are characteristically aggressive are more affected by violent media than are less aggressive people.[57] Media violence and aggression also seem to feed on each other. Not only do violent media increase aggression, but aggressive people are attracted to violent media.[58] This reciprocal relationship between media violence and aggression can create a vicious cycle. People consume violent media and behave more aggressively afterwards. Then they turn back to media violence because it makes them feel better about having behaved aggressively, and the cycle continues. But the research indicates that media violence affects both aggressive and nonaggressive people.[59]

COUNTERACTING THE HARMFUL EFFECTS OF VIOLENT MEDIA

Church leaders and social scientists offer many ideas for reducing the negative impact of violent media. Several ideas are described below:

Become educated on this issue. Do not rely on the mass media for valid information about media violence effects.[60] Instead rely on scriptural sources, the teachings of the prophets, and reliable scholarly and scientific research.

Hold family councils and decide what your media standards are going to be. The thirteenth article of faith helps us decide: "If there is anything virtuous, lovely, or of good report or praiseworthy, we seek after these things." The First Presidency's counsel to youth of the Church applies to all of us: "Have the courage to walk out of a movie or video party, turn off a computer or television, [or] change a radio station . . . if what is being presented does not meet Heavenly Father's standards."[61] Internet filters and TV programming locks can be used to reduce the likelihood of family members' chancing upon things they should not see.

View programs selectively. Avoid turning on the TV just to see what's on. Put excellent TV programs on the calendar and watch them together as a family. Consult a television schedule and reviews that can help you choose excellent programs. TV programs contain content codes, such as V for violence, S for sex, and L for coarse language. Don't depend upon media ratings, however, because they are self-assigned and parents often disagree with ratings.[62] Even video games rated by the industry as appropriate for "everyone" are dominated by violence.[63]

Spend enough time with your children to ensure that you, rather than the mass media, are consistently the main influence in their lives.[64] More often than not, there are better family-time choices than media entertainment.

Make good media choices and set good examples for your children. If parents and older siblings have a heavy diet of TV violence, then younger children will be exposed to more TV violence as well. Elder Joe J. Christensen said, "Remember that anything that is not good for children is rarely good for adults."[65]

Limit the amount of time children watch TV, play video games, or use the Internet each day. Many child psychologists and the American Academy of Pediatrics suggest that exposure should be limited to no more than one or two hours per day.[66] One mom and dad bought a big roll of carnival tickets and gave each child a fixed number of TV tickets per week.[67] Each ticket was worth 30 minutes of TV viewing, and when the tickets were gone, the TV time was also gone. The youth in the Penasquitos First Ward in San Diego, California, went on a television "fast" for a month. "This was a hard thing for me to do, but I feel that not watching TV has helped me be nicer to other people," said 13-year-old Tiffany Clark.[68]

Have TVs and computers in a public place such as a much-used common room in the home, not in a bedroom or a private place.[69]

Parents can watch and discuss media with their children.[70] If a character behaves in a violent way, parents can talk about it with their child. Co-viewing allows parents to discuss with their child how unrealistic the scene really was, what motivated the characters to use violence, what a better response could have been, how the character might have solved the problem differently, and what the painful consequences of violence are. Parents can also be reassuring if something on TV seems frightening to the child.[71]

Tell the people who produce and sponsor violent media that you object to violent media. If advertisers did not sponsor violent TV programs, the programs would cease to exist. Elder Ballard said: "Brothers and sisters, we can write to local radio and television stations and to cable and national networks to express our concerns. The sponsors and advertisers who pay for programs and advertising that are offensive would most likely appreciate hearing from us also."[72] In another address, Elder Ballard stated, "The time has come when members of the Church need to speak out and join with the many other concerned people in opposition to the offensive, destructive, and mean-spirited media influence that is sweeping over the earth."[73]

CONCLUSION

The mass media are tools that can be used for good or ill. We are free to choose how to use these tools (see 2 Nephi 2:26–27). When watching violent media, we surrender ourselves to that influence and the positive influence of the Holy Ghost may be diminished in our lives. With the Holy Ghost as our guide, we will know what choices are good and what choices are bad.[74] In the case of violent media, the message from apostles and prophets and from social scientists is the same: Violent media harm both the individual and the society.

ABOUT THE AUTHOR

Brad J. Bushman, Ph.D., is a professor of psychology and of communication studies at the University of Michigan. He is also a faculty associate at the Institute for Social Research. He and his wife, Tammy Stafford, have three children.

ADDITIONAL READING

American Psychological Association (2005), Violence on television: What do children learn? What can parents do? available at www.apa.org/pi/pii/vio&tv.html

Craig A. Anderson and Brad J. Bushman (2002), The effects of media violence on society, *Science, 295,* 2377, 2379.

M. Russell Ballard (2003, November), Let our voices be heard, *Ensign, 33*(11), 16–19.

Brad J. Bushman (2003, June), It's "only" violence, *Ensign, 33*(6), 62–67.

NOTES

1. First Presidency (2001), *For the Strength of Youth: Fulfilling Our Duty to God,* pamphlet (Salt Lake City: The Church of Jesus Christ of Latter-day Saints), 17.

2. Quoted in Plato (c. 380 B.C.), *The Republic,* book 2, section 377b, A. D. Lindsay, trans. (reprint, London: Dent), 55.

3. Kaiser Family Foundation study (2000), in Kids spend almost 40 hours using media; available at http://www.momsrefuge.com/news/9911

4. A. C. Huston, E. Donnerstein, H. Fairchild, N. D. Feshbach, P. A. Katz, J. P. Murray, et al. (1992), *Big World, Small Screen: The Role of Television in American Society* (Lincoln, NE: University of Nebraska Press).

5. National Television Violence Study, vol. 1 (1996), (Thousand Oaks, CA: Sage); National Television Violence Study, vol. 2 (1997), (Thousand Oaks, CA: Sage); National Television Violence Study, vol. 3 (1998), (Thousand Oaks, CA: Sage).

6. Huston, et al. (1992).

7. J. Cantor (1998), Ratings for program content: The role of research findings, *Annals of the American Academy of Political and Social Science, 557,* 54–69; see also Federal Trade Commission (2000), Appendix B: Children as consumers of entertainment media: media usage, marketing behavior and influences, and rating effects; in Marketing violent entertainment to children: A review of self-regulation and industry practices in the motion picture, music recording and electronic game industries; available at http://ftc.gov/oa/2000/09/youthviol.htm

8. S. Waxman (2004, July 14), Study finds film ratings are growing more lenient, *New York Times;* available at http://www.nytimes.com

9. F. Yokota and K. M. Thompson (2000, May 24), Violence in G-rated animated films, *Journal of the American Medical Association, 283,* 2716–2720.

10. See J. B. Funk (2000), The impact of interactive violence on children, testimony before the U.S. Senate Commerce Committee; available at http://brownback.senate.gov/FinishedDocs/MediaViolence/000321fun.pdf

11. B. J. Bushman and C. A. Anderson (2001a), Is it time to pull the plug on the hostile versus instrumental aggression dichotomy? *Psychological Review, 108,* 273–279.

12. See ibid.

13. Dallin H. Oaks (1991, November), Joy and mercy, *Ensign, 21*(11), 75.

14. M. Russell Ballard (1989, May), The effects of television, *Ensign, 19*(5), 78.

15. The First Presidency provides these guidelines for media selection: "Good entertainment . . . will allow you to enjoy yourself without losing the Spirit of the Lord. . . . Don't [participate in media] that drives away the Spirit." First Presidency (2001), 17, 20.

16. Ballard (1989), 79.

17. Quoted in Parents Television Council (2003), TV bloodbath: Violence on prime time broadcast TV; available at http://www.parentstv.org/PTC/publications/reports/stateindustryviolence/reportonviolence.pdf

18. Federal Bureau of Investigation (2002), Crime in the United States 2002: Uniform crime reports (Washington, D.C.: U.S. Government Printing Office), available at http://www.fbi.gov/ucr/cius_02/x1/021b1101.xls

19. L. R. Huesmann, J. Moise-Titus, C. L. Podolski, and L. D. Eron (2003), Longitudinal relations between children's exposure to TV violence and their aggressive and violent behavior in young adulthood: 1977–1992, *Developmental Psychology, 39,* 201–221.

20. J. M. Innes and H. Zeitz (1988), The public's view of the impact of the mass media: A test of the "third person" effect, *European Journal of Social Psychology, 18,* 457–463.

21. W. P. Davison (1983), The third-person effect in communication, *Public Opinion Quarterly, 47,* 1–15.

22. B. J. Bushman and C. A. Anderson (2001b), Media violence and the American public: Scientific facts versus media misinformation, *American Psychologist, 56,* 477–489.

23. Quoted in W. J. Moore (1993, December 18), Lights! Camera! It's gun control time, *National Journal,* 3007.

24. M. Russell Ballard (1996, December), When shall these things be? *Ensign, 26*(12), 58.

25. C. A. Anderson and B. J. Bushman (2001), Effects of violent video games on aggressive behavior, aggressive cognition, aggressive affect, physiological arousal, and prosocial behavior: A meta-analytic review of the scientific literature, *Psychological Science, 12,* 353–359; H. Paik and G. Comstock (1994), The effects of television violence on antisocial behavior: A meta-analysis, *Communication Research, 21,* 516–546.

26. C. A. Anderson (1997), Effects of violent movies and trait hostility on hostile feelings and aggressive thoughts, *Aggressive Behavior, 23,* 161–178; B. J. Bushman (1995), Moderating role of trait aggressiveness in the effects of violent media on aggression, *Journal of Personality and Social Psychology, 69,* 950–960; B. J. Bushman and R. G. Geen (1990), Role of cognitive-emotional mediators and individual differences in the effects of media violence on aggression, *Journal of Personality and*

Social Psychology, 58, 156–163; C. H. Hansen and R. D. Hansen (1990), The influence of sex and violence on the appeal of rock music videos, *Communication Research, 17,* 212–234.

27. B. J. Bushman (2002), Does venting anger feed or extinguish the flame? Catharsis, rumination, distraction, anger, and aggressive responding, *Personality and Social Psychology Bulletin, 28,* 724–731; B. J. Bushman, R. F. Baumeister, and A. D. Stack (1999), Catharsis, aggression, and persuasive influence: Self-fulfilling or self-defeating prophecies? *Journal of Personality and Social Psychology, 76,* 367–376; R. G. Geen and M. B. Quanty (1977), The catharsis of aggression: An evaluation of a hypothesis, in L. Berkowitz, ed., *Advances in Experimental Social Psychology* (New York: Academic Press), 10:1–37.

28. G. Gerbner and L. Gross (1976), Living with television: The violence profile, *Journal of Communication, 26*(2), 173–199.

29. Marvin J. Ashton (1977, November), Rated A, *Ensign,* 7(11), 71.

30. First Presidency (2001), 19.

31. Ballard (1996), 58; see Matthew 24:12.

32. M. H. Thomas (1982), Physiological arousal, exposure to a relatively lengthy aggressive film, and aggressive behavior, *Journal of Research in Personality, 16,* 72–81.

33. R. S. Drabman and M. H. Thomas (1974), Does media violence increase children's toleration of real-life aggression? *Developmental Psychology, 10,* 418–421; R. S. Drabman and M. H. Thomas (1976), Does watching violence on television cause apathy? *Pediatrics, 57,* 329–331; M. H. Thomas and R. S. Drabman (1975), Toleration of real life aggression as a function of exposure to televised violence and age of subject, *Merrill-Palmer Quarterly, 21,* 227–232.

34. N. L. Carnegey, B. J. Bushman, and C. A. Anderson (in press), Video game violence desensitizes players to real world violence, *Personality and Social Psychology Bulletin.*

35. Ibid.

36. Ashton (1977), 71.

37. M. D. Griffiths and N. Hunt (1998), Dependence on computer games by adolescents, *Psychological Reports, 82,* 475–480.

38. Paik and Comstock (1994), 516–546.

39. Ibid.

40. Ibid.

41. Meta-analytic studies have found an average correlation of .20 between violent media exposure in general and aggression, and an average correlation of .26 between violent video game exposure and aggression. See C. A. Anderson (2003), An update on the effects of playing violent video games, *Journal of Adolescence, 27,* 113–122; Bushman and Anderson (2001b), 477–489.

42. For example, R. Atlas, L. Cornett, D. M. Lane, and H. A. Napier (1997), The use of animation in software training: Pitfalls and benefits; in M. A. Quiñones and A. Ehrenstein, eds., *Training for a Rapidly Changing Workplace: Applications of Psychological Research* (Washington, D.C.: American Psychological Association), 281–302; see also R. G. Geen (2001), *Human Aggression: Theories, Research, and Implications for Social Policy* (San Diego: Academic Press).

43. L. R. Huesmann and L. D. Eron (1986), *Television and the Aggressive Child: A Cross-National Comparison* (Hillsdale, NJ: Erlbaum); Huesmann, Moise-Titus, Podolski, and Eron (2003), 201–221.

44. J. P. Leyens and S. Picus (1973), Identification with the winner of a fight and name mediation: Their differential effects upon subsequent aggressive behavior, *British Journal of Social and Clinical Psychology, 12,* 374–377; D. G. Perry and L. C. Perry (1976), Identification with film characters, covert aggressive verbalization, and reactions to film violence, *Journal of Research in Personality, 10,* 399–409.

45. A. Bandura (1973), *Aggression: A Social Learning Analysis* (Englewood Cliffs, NJ: Prentice-Hall); A. Bandura (1983), Psychological mechanisms of aggression, in R. G. Geen and E. I. Donnerstein, eds., *Aggression: Theoretical and Empirical Reviews* (New York: Academic Press), 1:1–40.

46. C. M. J. Braun and J. Giroux (1989), Arcade video games: Proxemic, cognitive and content analyses, *Journal of Leisure Research, 21,* 92–105; K. E. Dill and J. C. Dill (1998), Video game violence: A review of the empirical literature, *Aggression and Violent Behavior, 3,* 407–428.; M. H. Klein (1984), The bite of Pac-Man, *The Journal of Psychohistory, 11,* 395–401.

47. Paik and Comstock (1994).

48. M. M. Davies (1997), *Fake, Fact, and Fantasy: Children's Interpretations of Television Reality* (Mahwah, NJ: Erlbaum); M. W. McKenna and E. P. Ossoff (1998), Age differences in children's comprehension of a popular television program, *Child Study Journal, 28,* 53–68.

49. L. D. Eron, L. R. Huesmann, M. M. Lefkowitz, and L. O. Walder (1972), Does television violence cause aggression? *American Psychologist, 27,* 253–263; L. R. Huesmann (1986), Psychological processes promoting the relation between exposure to media violence and aggressive behavior by the viewer, *Journal of Social Issues, 42,* 125–139.

50. L. R. Huesmann, J. Moise-Titus, C. Poldoski, and L. D. Eron (2003), Longitudinal relations between children's exposure to TV violence and their aggressive and violent behavior in young adulthood: 1977–1992, *Developmental Psychology, 39,* 201–221.

51. For example, S. H. Chaffee and J. M. McLeod (1972), Adolescent television use in the family context, in G. A. Comstock and E. A. Rubinstein, eds., *Television and social behavior: Reports and Papers, Volume 3, Television and Adolescent Aggressiveness,* 149–172 (Washington, D.C.: U.S. Government Printing Office); J. Sprafkin and K. D. Gadow (1986), Television viewing habits of emotionally disturbed, learning disabled, and mentally retarded children, *Journal of Applied Developmental Psychology, 7,* 45–59; A. H. Stein and L. K. Friedrich, with F. Vondracek (1972), Television content and young children's behavior, in J. P. Murray, E. A. Rubinstein, and G. A. Comstock, eds., *Television and Social Behavior: Reports and Papers, Volume 2: Television and Social Learning,* 202–317 (Washington, D.C.: U.S. Government Printing Office); O. Wiegman, M. Kuttschreuter, and B. Baarda (1986), Television viewing related to aggressive and prosocial behaviour (Enschede, Netherlands: University of Twente).

52. L. R. Huesmann, L. D. Eron, and P. W. Yarmel (1987), Intellectual functioning and aggression, *Journal of Personality and Social Psychology, 52,* 232–240; J. Q. Wilson and R. J. Herrnstein (1985), *Crime and Human Nature* (New York: Simon & Schuster).

53. B. J. Bushman and L. R. Huesmann (2001), Effects of televised violence on aggression; in D. G. Singer and J. L. Singer, eds., *Handbook of children and the media* (Thousand Oaks, CA: Sage), 223–254.

54. Chaffee and McLeod (1972), 149–172.

55. L. R. Huesmann, K. Lagerspetz, and L. D. Eron (1984),

Intervening variables in the television violence–aggression relation: Evidence from two countries, *Developmental Psychology, 20,* 746–775; Wilson and Herrnstein (1985).

56. Bushman and Huesmann (2001).

57. Bushman (1995); Bushman and Geen (1990); L. K. Friedrich and A. H. Stein (1973), Aggressive and prosocial television programs and the natural behavior of preschool children, *Monographs of the Society for Research in Child Development, 38*(4), (Serial No. 151, pp. 1–63); W. L. Josephson (1987), Television violence and children's aggression: Testing the priming, social script, and disinhibition predictions, *Journal of Personality and Social Psychology, 53,* 882–890; G. W. Russell (1992), Response of the macho male to viewing a combatant sport, *Journal of Social Behavior and Personality, 7,* 631–638.

58. Bushman (1995); A. Fenigstein (1979), Does aggression cause a preference for viewing media violence? *Journal of Personality and Social Psychology, 37,* 2307–2317; B. Gunter (1983), Do aggressive people prefer violent television? *Bulletin of the British Psychological Society, 36,* 166–168; E. C. O'Neal and S. L. Taylor (1989) Status of the provoker, opportunity to retaliate, and interest in video violence, *Aggressive Behavior, 15,* 171–180.

59. Bushman and Huesmann (2001).

60. Bushman and Anderson (2001b).

61. First Presidency (2001), 19.

62. B. J. Bushman and J. Cantor (2003), Media ratings for violence and sex: Implications for policymakers and parents, *American Psychologist, 58,* 130–141.

63. K. M. Thompson and K. Haninger (2001), Violence in E-rated video games, *Journal of the American Medical Association, 286,* 591–598.

64. Ballard (2003), 19.

65. Joe J. Christensen (1993, November), Rearing children in a polluted environment, *Ensign, 23*(11), 11.

66. American Academy of Pediatrics (2001), Children, adolescents, and television, *Pediatrics, 107,* 424.

67. Lisa Ray Turner (1999, July), Taming TV, *Ensign, 29*(7), 70–71.

68. Lisa M. Grover (1997, May), Fine tuning, *Liahona, 21*(5), 32–34.

69. Ballard (2003), 19.

70. American Academy of Pediatrics (2001), 424.

71. J. Cantor (1998), *"Mommy, I'm Scared." How TV and Movies Frighten Children and What We Can Do to Protect Them* (New York: Harcourt Brace).

72. Ballard (1989), 81.

73. Ballard (2003), 17.

74. *For the Strength of Youth* states, "You have the gift of the Holy Ghost, which will give you strength and help you make good choices." First Presidency (2001), 19.

CHAPTER 26

WHEN CHILDREN CHOOSE A DIFFERENT PATH

ELAINE WALTON AND ROBERT L. MILLET

*To those brokenhearted parents who have been righteous, diligent, and prayerful in the
teaching of their disobedient children, we say to you, the Good Shepherd is watching over them.
God knows and understands your deep sorrow. There is hope.[1]*
—*President James E. Faust*

All parents have hopes and dreams for their children. Latter-day Saint parents imagine missions, temple marriages, and generations of descendants, all faithful members of the Church. But life rarely turns out as we wish. Many Latter-day Saints experience the heartache of seeing loved ones violate covenants and turn away from what they have been taught.

DIMINISHED HOPES

If the greatest joys in life are family joys, then surely the greatest sorrows in life are family sorrows. As President James E. Faust expressed: "The depth of the love of parents for their children cannot be measured. It is like no other relationship. It exceeds concern for life itself. . . . [Therefore,] the grief of a parent over a rebellious child is almost inconsolable."[2] The joy associated with our understanding of the eternal nature of the family makes disappointment in a wayward child even more poignant.

DEALING WITH LOSS

When a child seems to be lost, the parents' grief, no matter how profound, has the potential to create miraculous personal growth. Grief has been explained as a five-stage process: denial, anger, guilt and bargaining, depression, and finally acceptance and reso-

lution.[3] Initially, it is natural for grieving parents to say to themselves: "This can't be happening to my child. Surely this is misinformation, a misunderstanding, or a passing phase"—denial. When evidence mounts, denial is replaced with anger. "Not me" is replaced by "Why me?" Anger may be aimed at the wayward child, a person who influenced the child, the messenger who delivered the evidence, or even God. Although a natural part of the grieving process, anger is seldom rational and often ugly. Latter-day Saints usually try to move quickly through that stage, turning blame inward. The third stage, guilt and bargaining, is sometimes referred to as the "if only" stage: "If only I had read the scriptures and prayed more regularly with Johnny." "If only I had been firmer in enforcing the family rules." "If only I had noticed his disobedience earlier." There is no end to the "if only" list. Self-blame is natural. When we take responsibility for an event not of our doing, we deceive ourselves into thinking we have the power to change it. Or we tend to bargain with ourselves or the Lord, giving up hope in one area in order to retain it in another: "I can accept Susan's smoking if she will at least attend family home evening." "I can accept Rick's not being active in the Church as long as he doesn't engage in illegal activities." When parents have exhausted themselves with guilt and fruitless bargaining, they may give up completely. This is the fourth stage, depression. Feelings of hopelessness sap energy and life seems dark. Not only is the child lost, but the parent, too. At some point in this process, parents become aware of what they have, not just what was lost, and they move to the fifth stage, resolution and acceptance. That accomplishment is linked to a deeper perspective. Previous feelings of a miserable finality are replaced with eternal hope in Christ and His gospel and an ongoing commitment to love the wayward child.

THE JOY AND AGONY OF AGENCY

Agency is to be enjoyed, even relished, but the consequences of misuse are often devastating. In response to a priesthood lesson highlighting the importance of agency, a brother volunteered: "To be honest, as far as my family is concerned, sometimes I wish there were no agency. . . . I assure you that nothing hurts more than watching your children self-destruct through poor choices."[4] Most parents in the Church empathize at times with the feelings of that brother.

Valuing agency means accepting children's failings along with their successes—not forcing children to conform. Yet, we are a part of a Church that has high ideals. We take seriously the Master's commandment to strive to be perfect (Matthew 5:48), even though we all fall short. Despite the distress over failures in the home and family, we do not lower our vision or dilute our ideals to compromise with a decaying society. The challenge is to maintain our goals while becoming more sensitive to and solicitous of those who come up short, including ourselves.

In speaking of the decaying society, President Boyd K. Packer suggested it may be that the power of evil in these last days is so oppressive that it chokes or restrains the proper exercise of moral agency. One day that will change.[5] Although this statement is reassuring to parents whose children have wandered away from gospel ideals, it does not change parents' immediate heartache—or their responsibility.

WHEN IS PARENTING GOOD ENOUGH?

The responsibility of parents is unequivocal: "And again, inasmuch as parents have children in Zion, or in any of her stakes which are organized, that teach them not to understand the doctrine of repentance, faith in Christ the Son of the living God, and of baptism and the gift of the Holy Ghost by the laying on of the hands, when eight years old, the sin be upon the heads of the parents" (D&C 68:25). The instruction continues: "And they shall also teach their children to pray, and to walk uprightly before the Lord" (D&C 68:28).

Numerous prophets, ancient and modern, have taught us about the importance of wise parenting. But when is parenting wise enough or good enough? President Faust defined successful parents as "those who have sacrificed and struggled to do the best they can in their own family circumstances."[6] There is no absolute measure for good parenting. In the words of President Howard W. Hunter, "[some children] would challenge any set of parents under any set of circumstances."[7] Rather than fixating on the past, parents can pray for assurance that their sincere efforts are pleasing to the Lord. (Chapter 18 discusses the importance of measuring success by effort, rather than outcome.)

FINDING WAYS TO HEAL AND DEMONSTRATE GENUINE LOVE

Judge not. Harsh reactions don't help. President Joseph F. Smith gave the following advice: "Fathers, if you wish your children to be taught in the principles of the gospel, if you wish them to love the truth and understand it, if you wish them to be obedient to and united with you, love them! . . . However wayward they might be, . . . when you speak or talk to them, do it not in anger, do it not harshly, in a condemning spirit. Speak to them kindly. . . . You can't drive them; they won't be driven."[8] Elder Dallin H. Oaks explained that "the world's way is to judge competitively between winners and losers. The Lord's way of final judgment will be to apply His perfect knowledge of the law a person has received and to judge on the basis of that person's circumstances, motives, and actions throughout his or her entire life."[9] Joseph Smith called upon us to repent of littleness of soul and broaden our horizons. "Our heavenly Father is more liberal in His views, and boundless in His mercies and blessings, than we are ready to believe or receive."[10] We don't know all that God knows about our children.[11] Withholding judgment provides freedom to truly love those whose actions we cannot love.

We must also refrain from judging other parents. We can rejoice with mothers and fathers whose children excel and obey. We can feel deep gratitude for the young ones who are not our own but whose lives bless the lives of their parents and grandparents. On the other hand, we must, as a part of our Christian covenant, "bear one another's burdens, that they may be light; yea, . . . mourn with those that mourn . . . and comfort those that stand in need of comfort" (Mosiah 18:8–9). Parents whose children have gone astray need our friendship, not our judging. In a spirit of mourning with parents of wayward children, we may in public settings sensitively limit our expressions of thanks for our own children's faithfulness.

SOME PRACTICAL SUGGESTIONS

Take care of yourself. Don't let the chaos of your children's lives overwhelm or consume you. Pay attention to your physical and emotional health, and continue with your own appropriate activities insofar as possible.[12]

Seek help. Although family is the primary influence, there are many outside sources for support. Parents might consult with a Relief Society president, home teacher, quorum leader, bishop, or branch president. Also, they should investigate resources that might be available, such as professional counseling, substance abuse treatment, and school or community programs. Through professional help, parents may be in a better position to bring organization and structure to the household with appropriate rules and reasonable expectations. The children must understand that they are accountable for their behavior, and disobedient children must not sap the energy and productivity of the entire family.

Evaluate your expectations. Children's desires and aspirations differ from their parents' hopes and dreams. Elder John K. Carmack counseled: "Too much emphasis on parental expectations may place undue pressure and stress on their children."[13] However, accepting a child's decisions does not obligate the parents or family to change their goals and standards. At some point parents must make decisions focused on the well-being of the family, not just the child who has chosen a different path. In some cases, a different path might mean a different place to live for the child whose behavior jeopardizes the safety of family members. (Essay F2 offers ideas for minimizing the negative influence of a wayward teenager on siblings.)

Don't let pride—yours or theirs—get in the way. It is difficult to admit that a child has chosen to leave the Church or to participate in illegal or harmful activities. But do not make excuses for your children. Feelings of self-pity and shame may drive a wedge between parent and child and make it difficult to maintain a loving relationship.[14] One mother explained her feelings this way: "[Following my divorce,] I was embarrassed when people found out that my 14-year-old daughter had chosen to live with her . . . father instead of me. It was even more embarrassing to admit that [she] had chosen an alternative lifestyle. . . . I trusted that my friends and family would support me and not judge me." Later, through exercising faith, the mother found that "[her] broken heart became a broken heart and a contrite spirit. Not a crushed heart, but a heart broken open to receive help, guidance, wisdom." With guidance from the Lord, she was able to maintain a positive and loving relationship with her wayward daughter.[15]

Seek the Lord. Parents who are struggling with wayward children find themselves increasingly on their knees in prayer, studying the scriptures, and in the temple. Because the Lord cannot take away a child's moral agency, parents may feel their prayers go unanswered. The Apostle Paul reminds us, "we know not what we should pray for as we ought" (Romans 8:26). Prayers are most commonly answered not through a dramatic event but rather through an enlightening of our minds (D&C 11:13). As we grow in our ability to listen to the Spirit, we are tutored in specific ways, and our faith is deepened. One mother recounted that deepening process as follows: "I used to try to exercise faith by saying, 'Heavenly Father, please help my children to change. Help them to become aware of the harmful effects of alcohol or being sexually active. Help them to recognize the truth of the gospel.' Now I'm more likely to exercise faith in the Lord Jesus Christ by saying, 'Heavenly Father, I know you love my children. Help me to feel about them the same way that you do. Help me to love them more. Help me to understand your plan for them. And help me to be patient.'"[16]

REMEMBER THE WORTH OF SOULS

Children's reasons for choosing a different path vary. Some children drift away because of distraction and inattention. As in the Savior's parable of the lost sheep (Luke 15:3–7), they simply wander off in search of food. Other children may be like the silver coin that was lost because of neglect (Luke 15:8–10). Most troubling are children who choose a different path because of willful disobedience, as in the parable of the prodigal son (Luke 15:11–32).

The common ending of the parables is rejoicing in finding or restoring what was lost. The parables teach that God loves His children—all of them. "Remember the worth of souls is great in the sight of God; . . . And how great is his joy in the soul that repenteth!" (D&C 18:10, 13). By praying for the gift of charity, we may experience joy for the worth of our children's souls that can exceed any sorrow brought by their poor choices.

All of us, at one time or another, may play each of the roles described in the parable of the prodigal son. In reflecting on that parable, President Gordon B. Hinckley said: "Every parent ought to read it again and again. It is large enough to encompass every household, and enough larger than that to encompass all mankind, for are we not all prodigal sons and daughters who need to repent and partake of the forgiving mercy of our Heavenly Father and then follow his example?"[17] Parents' concern reaches troubled children much more effectively than parents' harsh words or punishments.[18] And parents who feel their own dependence on the Savior's Atonement are more likely to respond to their wayward children with forgiveness and love.

THE SPIRIT OF ELIJAH

Among the remarkable visions experienced by Joseph Smith and Oliver Cowdery in the Kirtland Temple was the visit of Elijah, who was "sent, before the great and dreadful day of the Lord . . . to turn the hearts of the fathers to the children, and the children to the fathers, lest the whole earth be smitten with a curse" (D&C 110:14–15). President Harold B. Lee explained that Elijah's mission "applies just as much on this side of the veil as it does on the other side of the veil."[19] Parents of wayward children qualify for unifying blessings as they pray for the spirit of Elijah to be alive in their hearts as they reach out to their children.

CHILDREN OF THE COVENANT

In the midst of disappointments and challenges, Latter-day Saints find comfort in covenants. Many prophets have reminded us of promises inherent in the temple covenant. President Boyd K. Packer reiterated one promise as follows: "When parents keep the covenants they have made at the altar of the temple, their children will be forever bound to them."[20]

Elder Orson F. Whitney counseled: "You parents of the wilful and the wayward! Don't give them up. Don't cast them off. They are not utterly lost. The Shepherd will find his sheep. They were his before they were yours—long before he entrusted them to your care; and you cannot begin to love them as he loves them. . . . Our Heavenly Father is far more merciful, infinitely more charitable, than even the best of his servants, and the Everlasting Gospel is mightier in power to save than our narrow finite minds can comprehend."[21] Referring to the words of the Prophet Joseph Smith, he continued:

> The eternal sealings of faithful parents and the divine promises made to them for valiant service in the Cause of Truth, would save not only themselves, but likewise their posterity. Though some of the sheep may wander, the eye of the Shepherd is upon them, and sooner or later they will feel the tentacles of Divine Providence reaching out after them and drawing them back to the fold. Either in this life or in the life to come, they will return. They will have to pay their debt to justice; they will suffer for their sins; and may tread a thorny path; but if it leads them at last, like the penitent Prodigal, to a loving and forgiving father's heart and home, the painful experience will not have been in vain. Pray for your careless and disobedient children; hold on to them with your faith. Hope on, trust on, till you see the salvation of God."[22]

The sealing power is more profound than our ability to comprehend. Trying to answer questions such as "who will be sealed to whom?" or "who will be in which kingdom?" is not productive. The Lord loves all his children and will, within the constraints imposed by human agency and divine justice and mercy, work out these eternal relationships to the fullest blessing possible of all involved.

NEVER GIVE UP

In addressing the Saints in Great Britain, President Hinckley said: "May there be . . . a sense of security and peace and love among your children, precious children every one of them, even those who may have strayed. I hope you don't lose patience with them; I hope you go on praying for them, and I don't hesitate to promise that if you do so, the Lord will touch their hearts and bring them back to you with love and respect and appreciation."[23]

God will never stop loving His children, and neither must we, regardless of their mistakes. In our prayers for our children, we should pray to understand the love that Jesus has for them. "Can a woman forget her sucking child, that she should not have compassion on the son of her womb?" Isaiah recorded the Savior's question. "Yea, they may forget, yet will I not forget thee. Behold, I have graven thee upon the palms of my hands; thy walls are continually before me" (Isaiah 49:15–16).

We trust in the power of Christ, the Mediator of the covenant, to forgive, to repair, to renew, and to rekindle the gospel light within the hearts of those who stray for a season. If we never give up; if we seek the Lord's help to become more like Him in loving all our children, He will comfort and bless us, as He promised: "Be faithful and diligent in keeping the commandments of God, and I will encircle thee in the arms of my love" (D&C 6:20).

ABOUT THE AUTHORS

Elaine Walton, Ph.D., is a professor of social work and associate dean in the College of Family, Home, and Social Sciences at Brigham Young University. She and her husband, Wendel, have a blended family of ten children and twenty-four grandchildren.

Robert L. Millet is Richard L. Evans Professor of Religious Understanding and former dean of Religious Education at Brigham Young University. He and his wife, Shauna, are the parents of six children and the grandparents of five.

ADDITIONAL READING

John K. Carmack (1997, February), When our children go astray, *Ensign, 27*(2), 13.

James E. Faust (2003, May), Dear are the sheep that have wandered, *Ensign, 33*(5), 61.

Robert Millet (1996), *When a Child Wanders* (Salt Lake City: Deseret Book).

Kyle L. Pehrson, Jacqueline S. Thursby, and Terrance D. Olson (2000), Gospel ideals and adversity in family life; in David C. Dollahite, ed., *Strengthening Our Families: An In-Depth Look at the Proclamation on the Family* (Salt Lake City: Deseret Book), 242–250.

NOTES

1. James E. Faust (2003, May), Dear are the sheep that have wandered, *Ensign, 33*(5), 68.

2. Ibid., 61.

3. Elisabeth Kübler-Ross (1969), *On Death and Dying: What the Dying Have to Teach Doctors, Nurses, Clergy, and Their Own Families* (New York: Macmillan).

4. Robert L. Millet (1996), *When a Child Wanders* (Salt Lake City: Deseret Book), 34–35.

5. Boyd K. Packer (1992, May), Our moral environment, *Ensign, 22*(5), 66–68.

6. Faust (2003), 61.

7. Howard W. Hunter (1983, November), Parents' concern for children, *Ensign, 13*(11), 63.

8. Joseph F. Smith (1939), *Gospel Doctrine,* 5th ed. (Salt Lake City: Deseret Book), 316.

9. Dallin H. Oaks (1999, August), "Judge not" and judging, *Ensign, 29*(8), 7.

10. Joseph Smith (1938), *Teachings of the Prophet Joseph Smith,* Joseph F. Smith, ed. (Salt Lake City: Deseret News Press), 257.

11. See Stephen E. Robinson (1995), *Following Christ: The Parable of the Divers and Other Good News* (Salt Lake City: Deseret Book), 146.

12. John K. Carmack (1997, February), When our children go astray, *Ensign, 27*(6), 13.

13. Ibid., 6–13.

14. Ibid.

15. Elaine Walton (2003), I know my sheep, and they are numbered; in *The Rock of our Redeemer: Talks from the 2002 BYU Women's Conference* (Salt Lake City: Deseret Book), 233, 235.

16. Ibid., 235.

17. Gordon B. Hinckley (1980, November), Of you it is required to forgive, *Ensign 10*(11), 61–63.

18. K. L. Pehrson, J. S. Thursby, and T. D. Olson (2000), Gospel ideals and adversity in family life; in D. C. Dollahite, ed., *Strengthening Our Families: An In-Depth Look at the Proclamation on the Family* (Salt Lake City: Bookcraft), 245–246.

19. Harold B. Lee (1996), *Teachings of Harold B. Lee,* C. J. Williams, ed. (Salt Lake City: Bookcraft), 280.

20. Packer (1992), 68.

21. Orson F. Whitney (1929, April), in Conference Report, 110; cited in Millet (1996), 114–116.

22. Whitney (1929), 116.

23. Gordon B. Hinckley (1995, September 2), Prophet returns to beloved England, *Church News,* 4.

GUIDING TROUBLED ADOLESCENTS THROUGH LOVE AND LIMITS

DAVID R. HILLSTEAD

In today's tough social environment, many adolescents face the challenge of putting off the cares of the world and holding true to the standards of the gospel. President Gordon B. Hinckley encouraged the youth of the Church: "You face tremendous temptation. . . . Peer pressure may be almost overpowering. But, my dear young friends, you must not give in. You must be strong."[1]

As a therapist, I have worked almost exclusively with adolescents and their families. In the hundreds of encounters that I have had with young people, I continue to recognize the great challenge they face as they enter a world that emphasizes "being cool." The "great and spacious building" (1 Nephi 8:24–28) is a constant threat to the hearts and minds of our youth; many teens wish to feel the love of the Lord and of their parents but disobey commandments and family rules to be accepted and praised by their peers, or to cope with deep-seated pain.

In my work as a wilderness therapist, my challenge is to understand the intent of an adolescent's behavior; in other words, how does this adolescent's behavior provide function for him, yet cause his parents distress? I have discovered that difficult behaviors are ways that teens find immediate insulation from uncomfortable emotion. The behavior provides short-term relief from pressing problems that the teen may feel powerless to deal with in any other way.

For example, 16-year-old Kody was into hard rock music, was a good fighter, and was quite a "cool cat" with the girls. He wanted me to see his masculinity, his toughness. But I saw something different. I saw a boy who was caring and friendly. A young man who suppressed a ready smile, a smile he hid with aloofness. I could see sensitivity and strong emotions at work inside him. The more I worked with Kody, the more I noticed that he struggled with peer acceptance and that he had experienced much pain

with peer rejection. Some of this rejection appeared to relate to multiple moves and having to find new friends, and some of the rejection related to his social style. In any event, when Kody stumbled across his new identity as the tough guy, he discovered that acceptance became available.

Many Latter-day Saint parents struggle to comprehend why their son or daughter has rebelled against the light of the gospel. Although every adolescent is different, parents can be certain that their son or daughter is fulfilling some kind of emotional need through these choices. An adolescent must develop the skills of recognizing his or her emotions, developing a tolerance for those emotions, and choosing effective behaviors to manage the emotions. The journey of adolescence involves developing a sense of reality. Just as the wilderness has stunning vistas, beautiful sunsets, and breathtaking peace, it is also fierce, rugged, and merciless at times. Similarly, life has many beautiful moments and times of joy along with many difficult and painful experiences. Parents can help an adolescent learn to walk the road of life, just as a guide might lead an explorer through a wilderness experience. Veteran guides teach their clients to recognize and effectively use resources and to respect the powerful forces of nature; guides also share with clients a true concept of natural consequences. This process provides both the guide and the explorer with a rewarding and enriching experience that is based on challenge and fulfillment.

Limits involve setting clear boundaries for the adolescent to grow within. President Spencer W. Kimball said, "Setting limits to what a child can do means to that child that you love him and respect him."[2] Some teens naturally accept limits, trusting the experience of their parents, while other children more often test the boundaries for themselves. When an inquisitive or willful teen tests limits, it is important that parents (1) allow natural consequences to occur, and (2) actively provide logical consequences that give the son or daughter an undistorted perspective of reality.

It is difficult for parents to watch a child struggle through the consequences of a poor choice. However, if these natural consequences are replaced with angry lectures or the child is rescued, discipline becomes ineffective. Angry lectures are not an effective tool for limit setting and they often strain or damage the parent-child relationship. With a fractured relationship, the parent is unable to help the teen back to a true path where she may live gospel principles and thus learn to rely on the Lord for comfort, security, and help through life's challenges. Elder Robert D. Hales wisely counseled:

> Act with faith; don't react with fear. When our teenagers begin testing family values, parents need to go to the Lord for guidance on the specific needs of each family member. This is the time for added love and support and to reinforce your teachings on how to make choices. It is frightening to allow our children to learn from the mistakes they may make, but their willingness to choose the Lord's way and family values is greater when the choice comes from within than when we attempt to force those values upon them. The Lord's way of love and acceptance is better than Satan's way of force and coercion, especially in rearing teenagers.[3]

For example, a teen may feel popular and accepted during his late-night drinking escapades, but problems will eventually mount and natural consequences will occur as he disregards curfew and his grades in school drop. Shame-based comments from parents (i.e., "I can't believe you don't think about your Mom and me as we sit up worried sick each Friday night") may have early effectiveness, but experience shows that adolescents soon become immune to such comments. Allowing consequences to occur provides better evidence for the adolescent of the ineffectiveness of his or her choices. For example, the parents of this teenager might ask themselves, what would a good employer do in this situation? When an employee arrives late and is unable to function effectively, an employer might withdraw privileges or cut hours or pay.

Similarly, providing logical or related consequences by setting limits requires that when adolescents have broken rules, these indiscretions result in a loss of some parent-controlled privileges (restrictions on going out with friends, earlier curfews) and an eventual cut in pay (no more use of the car). For a healthy life, the teenager must connect choices with positive or negative consequences. Many teenagers require strong boundaries to help them prepare for the future. Parents must also recognize that when an adolescent has become involved in addictive behaviors (such as drugs or alcohol), they may need to use strong interventions to break their child away from the tenacious grasp of addiction.

The second key to effective parenting is love. Parents who are effective in relationship development are more likely to be especially effective in setting limits. These parents manifest ability to "emotionally bond" with their child. They take time to truly talk to their adolescent about his or her life. An emotionally connected parent focuses on listening and understanding. He or she enters an interaction with a difficult adolescent with a gentle heart, a heart that is full of empathy. The "real" conversations that result are the metaphorical cement that links a parent and child to one another. The Prophet Joseph Smith stated:

> Our heavenly Father is more liberal in His views, and boundless in His mercies and blessings, than we are ready to believe or receive. . . . God does not look on sin with [the least degree of] allowance, but . . . the nearer we get to our heavenly Father, the more we are disposed to look with compassion on perishing souls; we feel that we want to take them upon our shoulders, and cast their sins behind our backs.[4]

This decision to work towards an emotional bonding, along with the ability to "cast their sins behind our backs," requires great insight, often developed through many hours of fasting and prayer. Parents may also find that this process requires them to reevaluate and overcome their own prejudices. Some may worry so much about how their child will affect their image or the reputation of their family that they may forget to nurture the child and focus on the parent-child relationship. One teen from a highly successful family came to treatment as a result of the many poor choices that he had made. This young man was despondent and difficult to reach. He was the second son of a well-respected father who had always placed high expectations upon family members. This young man's older brother had excellent grades and great skill on the playing field. The younger brother deeply believed that to merit his father's love, he would need to achieve. However, his brother had already done well in school ("that's taken," he reasoned) and in athletics ("that's also taken"). Because his father was unskilled in his ability to convey his love to his sons except through praise for their achievements, the boy despaired in ever meriting his father's love. He was deeply pained that he could never feel valued as a worthwhile individual. M. Scott Peck wrote:

> The feeling of being valuable—"I am a valuable person"—is essential to mental health and is a cornerstone of self-discipline. It is a direct product of parental love. . . . When children have learned through the love of their parents to feel valuable, it is almost impossible for the vicissitudes of adulthood to destroy their spirit.[5]

It is not through mechanical expressions of love that this can be accomplished, rather through the amount and quality of time devoted to the children, which indicate in a real way the degree to which children are valued.[6] Effective conversations with youth require adults to lay aside many layers and speak from an emotional perspective with an honest, genuine heart. Parents help their teen feel valued, lovable, and precious, regardless of the choices he or she is making. Parents can learn to separate their unconditional love for the child from their approval or disapproval of his or her behavior, just as our Father in Heaven provides each of His children with unconditional love (see Luke 15:21–24).

Parental love and clear limits work together to assist adolescents who are moving through difficult places in their lives, experiencing pain, encountering disappointment, and needing so desperately to belong and to be loved. Resources are available to help parents as they negotiate the process of learning to blend love and limits in ways that will help their children plant themselves more firmly in the gospel soil and learn to make wise choices. Like the guide and the explorer in the wilderness, parents and adolescent together can each be strengthened by the climb as they learn to live fully and well.

ABOUT THE AUTHOR

David R. Hillstead, Ph.D., and his wife, Kara, are the parents of four boys. He has treated adolescents in both a private practice and wilderness setting for approximately eight years. He is currently the clinical director of Second Nature Wilderness Program.

ADDITIONAL READING

Foster W. Cline and Jim Fay (1992), *Parenting Teens with Love and Logic: Preparing Adolescents for Responsible Adulthood* (Colorado Springs: Piñon Press). For excellent suggestions on how to reason with your teenager, visit www.loveandlogic.com, then click "About Love and Logic" on the right sidebar.

Glenn I. Latham (1999), *Christlike Parenting: Taking the Pain out of Parenting* (Seattle: Gold Leaf Press).

Glenn I. Latham (1997), *What's a Parent to Do? Solving Family Problems in a Christlike Way* (Salt Lake City: Deseret Book).

Scott P. Sells (1998), *Treating the Tough Adolescent: A Family-Based, Step-by-Step Guide* (New York: Guilford Press).

C. Ross Clement (2005, June), Talking with teens, *Ensign, 35*(6), 32–37.

NOTES

1. Gordon B. Hinckley (2003, November), An ensign to the nations, a light to the world, *Ensign, 33*(11), 83.

2. E. L. Kimball, ed. (1982), *The Teachings of Spencer W. Kimball* (Salt Lake City: Bookcraft), 341.

3. Robert D. Hales (1999, May), Strengthening families: Our sacred duty, *Ensign, 29*(5), 34.

4. Joseph Fielding Smith, sel. and arr. (1976), *Teachings of the Prophet Joseph Smith* (Salt Lake City: Deseret Book; reprint, Salt Lake City: Deseret Book, 1977), 257, 240–41; see D&C 1:31.

5. M. Scott Peck (1978), *The Road Less Traveled: A New Psychology of Love, Traditional Values, and Spiritual Growth* (New York: Simon & Schuster), 24.

6. Ibid., 23.

E S S A Y   F 2

ANSWERS FOR PARENTS OF STRUGGLING ADOLESCENTS

MONICA L. BLUME

Latter-day Saint parents grieve when children use agency to make choices that are destructive and lead to unhappiness and spiritual deterioration. Whether the children are choosing to be involved in alcohol or drug use, to participate in out-of-wedlock sexual behavior, to act abusively towards siblings or parents, or to engage in any other harmful and unhealthy behavior, there are serious questions for parents to consider. Below are several commonly asked questions with responses that can help provide perspective and strategies.

1. What do we do when a teen makes dangerous and harmful decisions? To begin with, it is helpful to apply basic problem-solving principles. Try to remain calm, assess what the problem is, and identify where it came from. Maintain hope that all is not lost and prayerfully consider solutions. Seek counsel from appropriate and able sources, such as ecclesiastical leaders and professionals. While studying the options, avoid making rash or uneducated decisions. Expect and allow the teen to be involved in the decisions, address the problem, and take responsibility for her actions. Recognizing the consequences of her actions may help her see the need for change (see essay F1). Express and demonstrate that you believe the teen is capable of change. This may help her to believe it is possible as well.

It is crucial to communicate the message, "We love you, and we want your happiness more than you can possibly imagine."[1] Sometimes, however, teens equate love with trust. Parents may hear the teen say, "Don't you trust me?" While trust may wane after multiple infractions, conversations at opportune moments can enable parents to calmly convey how, from their perspective, love does not always imply trust.

2. How can we show acceptance for our teen without showing tolerance for his behavior? Following Christ's example can be helpful as we struggle to express love to our teens when we cannot and should not condone their behaviors. Although this approach may not pay immediate dividends in resolving the problem, it is more likely to pay off over time if parents are willing to take the charitable, patient, longsuffering, and long-term approach (see D&C 121:41–43). In His chastisement of Simon Peter, for example, the Lord showed His sadness for Peter's choices while still clearly expressing His love for him (see Matthew 16:17–19, 22–28). Charity can help you accept your teenager without accepting his behaviors.

Remember that your teenager is a good person struggling with difficult problems. Also, it is helpful to carefully pick your battles. Some teen choices may conflict with gospel principles and others with parental preferences. Perhaps a modest, but faddish kind of clothing is chosen by a teen struggling to establish an identity. If the behavior doesn't compromise principles (i.e., modesty), the choice can help the teen learn to make decisions and see the consequences of certain choices. When parents respect their teen's preferences within the bounds of principles, the parent–teen relationship can flourish. This parent–teen relationship forms a foundation for working through more difficult challenges that may arise. However, if teens make choices that compromise principles, a loving stand must be taken.

3. What do we do if our teen comes under the influence of someone who does not have her best interests at heart? We cannot entirely protect our children from coming into contact with people who may be unwholesome influences. However, we can help them recognize when they are making poor choices about friends or are involved in unhealthy relationships. President Gordon B. Hinckley warned:

> Be careful of your friends. They can make you or break you. Be generous in helping the unfortunate and

those in distress. But bind to you friends of your own kind, friends who will encourage you, stand with you, live as you desire to live; who will enjoy the same kind of entertainment; and who will resist the evil that you determine to resist.[2]

If you are concerned about the friends your teen spends time with, remain close to the situation and offer guidance. Try to determine the extent to which the person is influencing your teen. If the teen can be guided to end the relationship on her own by seeing the effects of poor choices, it is best to help her make the choice. If it is a friend who steals, does drugs, leads your teen to participate in pornography, or encourages sexual relationships, it is best to remove the teen from those associations. Since this is neither a simple nor an easy thing to accomplish, it generally involves enlisting the help and support of others, such as a professional therapist, a trusted ecclesiastical leader, family members, or even the child's peers. For example, one young woman, Meghan, described the support she felt as she worked to leave behind an abusive boyfriend. She eventually designated the ecclesiastical leaders, home teachers, counselors, parents, and friends who rallied around her as "Team Meghan." While, in the beginning, Meghan was not entirely willing to leave this boyfriend, as her mother gathered support in sensitive, confidential ways, Meghan came to feel safe enough to make the break herself.

Do not shy away from setting firm boundaries out of fear that those boundaries will be ignored. Talk with your teen about what part of the friendship is benefiting her (i.e., having someone to eat lunch or hang out with). Together, determine positive ways to reap those same benefits without staying in a compromising or dangerous relationship. Let your teen know that while you will not allow her to remain in harm's way, you will be supportive of her efforts while she builds new relationships.

Remember that being alone socially is a difficult scenario for teenagers to imagine. If you expect your child to walk away from her social support group without somewhere to go, you may be thinking unrealistically. I have heard teen clients express relief when their parents helped them out of unhealthy friendships that they were unable to get out of themselves.

4. How do I provide effective consequences for a series of poor choices? Remember, you enforce the rules because you love your child. If you find yourself weak in allowing consequences to occur, consider this question: Do I want my child to be happy with me right now, or do I want him to be happy with himself later? Struggling teens need to be able to see the results of their actions (see essay F1). When those consequences are severe, such as facing criminal charges for breaking the law or losing the privilege of living at home for behaviors that harm other family members or disrespect certain family rules, it is all the more painful for parents to allow or impose consequences. But parents who wish to bring their child safely back must allow the child's bad decisions to result in bad consequences rather than good ones. As in Church disciplinary action, the consequences that result from transgression are imposed as a loving invitation to come back into the fold once certain standards can be lived. Even in the darkest of circumstances, teens need to see hope. In order to make it through, they need to recognize that same hope in those who are guiding them.

5. How can we keep an oppositional teen from disrupting and damaging other family members? Family members will be affected by a troubled sibling's behavior and choices. In these family situations, it is important that parents take the leadership role in helping each family member to see and believe that their family is one that pulls together. Siblings will feel more secure when they understand that despite difficulties, the family will face problems as they arise and rally in support of one another. Parents can be clear and candid with all family members about values and expectations in ways that allow other family members to continue to progress positively when a sibling is struggling. As these children become older and face problems of their own, they will more likely trust that parents and family are a source of help available to them.

Families that help support struggling teens may begin by recognizing and drawing on strengths that exist in the nuclear and extended family. For example, one child may have a great sense of humor that releases tension. Perhaps one of the parents shares a common interest that strengthens connection with the struggling child. Or a younger child in the family offers heartfelt prayers that lift everyone's spirits. Speaking of extended family support, President James E. Faust said, "I know of a close-knit family that is wonderfully successful in keeping everyone together. When the parents feel they are losing influence with teenagers, the help of cousins is enlisted to exert some counter peer pressure. I would urge members of extended families—grandparents, uncles, aunts, nephews, nieces, cousins—to reach out in concern, to succor."³ Ward family members such as youth leaders and bishops can also have a tremendous positive influence on a difficult teen. (Essay H5 provides ideas for reaching toward those who are less active in the Church).

In age-appropriate ways, involve family members in the effort, while taking care to adequately protect them. For instance, if a teen is struggling with drug abuse, other family members can be taught to show love for the sibling without enabling him to manipulate or indoctrinate them. Protective measures such as limiting unsupervised interaction with impressionable siblings can help. In ways that do not compromise safety, join together as family members to seek after the sheep who has wandered (see Matthew 18:12–13). Remember to humbly acknowledge that, like sheep, we have all gone astray (see Isaiah 53:6) and require the redeeming love of the Savior to bring us back.

While families may be disrupted temporarily, they need not be permanently damaged. During these difficult times, the need for steady adherence to gospel principles has never been more important. Make time for scripture study; family, personal, and couple prayer; temple attendance; and family home evening. Follow the principles outlined by Church leaders and "remember that it is upon the rock of our Redeemer, who is Christ, the Son of God, that ye must build your foundation" (Helaman 5:12). Remaining strong and united as a couple is possibly the single best thing you can do for the wayward child and for your other children as well. Be humble. Be open to your spouse's concerns, suggestions, and impressions. It is not unusual for parents to have different approaches when dealing with teen challenges. Calmly and respectfully counsel together when you disagree on how to handle a child's misbehavior, and don't be afraid to seek couple counseling when resolutions can't be reached. (Essay B3 includes information on resolving marital differences.)

Even after extensive counseling and readjustment of family dynamics, some teens may continue to heap extreme emotional abuse upon family members, willfully disregard basic family rules, and engage in serious delinquent behavior (e.g., drug addictions or alcohol abuse). Harming another family member in serious ways emotionally or physically is never acceptable. There should be a "no-tolerance" policy in these cases, and for behaviors such as hostile physical aggression, any type of sexual abuse, drug use, and so on (see additional readings for ideas). Like victims of

abuse, the innocent family members need to be protected first and foremost. The home needs to be a safe and secure place for all family members.

In these more severe cases, it is important to counsel with a trusted therapist as well as ecclesiastical leaders before making serious long-term decisions about handling the teen's continuing disruptive influence. In some few cases, more dramatic steps may need to be taken. Those decisions, such as removal of the teen from the home to a safe environment in order to provide space and healing for all family members, should be based upon good counsel, solid information, and much fasting and prayer.

6. *What do we do if nothing seems to work?* First, never give up. President James E. Faust related the following story:

> An anonymous Church member wrote about the continuous heartache her brother caused her parents. He got involved in drugs. He resisted all efforts at control and discipline. He was deceitful and defiant. Unlike the prodigal, this errant son did not come home of his own accord. Instead he got caught by the police and was forced to face the consequences of his actions. For two years his parents supported Bill's treatment program, which brought about his eventual recovery from drugs. In summary, Bill's sister observed: "I think my parents are extraordinary. They never wavered in their love for Bill, though they disagreed with and even hated what he was doing to himself and to their family life. But they were committed enough to their family to support Bill in any way necessary to get him through the tough times and onto more solid ground. They practiced the deeper, more sensitive, and extensive gospel of Christ by loving one who had gone astray."⁴

Practicing "the deeper, more sensitive, and extensive gospel of Christ" may require developing better listening skills and coming ready to hear, prepared to value the teen's reality and listen without a lecture waiting in the wings. It may require that parents analyze ways to improve themselves⁵ and their ability to reason with their children (see essay F1).

Resolving these complex issues with teens will require skillful parenting practices. The Book of Mormon prophet Lehi repeatedly counseled his errant sons, Laman and Lemuel (see, for example, 1 Nephi 8:37). His interactions provide a model for families as he continued to teach, admonish, and love his sons through all the struggles they faced. Answers to difficult family questions will be worked out a day at a time, perhaps an hour at a time, as we prayerfully seek to bring our children back to safety. We can find the spiritual reserve to watch for that day when, like the father of the prodigal son, we will see them return: "But when he was yet a great way off, his father saw him, and had compassion, and ran, and fell on his neck, and kissed him" (Luke 15:20).

ABOUT THE AUTHOR

Monica L. Blume is a licensed clinical social worker who has worked with unwed mothers and their families for more than ten years. She has been a featured speaker and has coauthored a book on adoption. She and her husband are the parents of six children.

ADDITIONAL READING

Sue Bergin (1988, March), When a teenager uses drugs or alcohol: How to cope . . . *Ensign, 18*(3), 15–20.

Glenn I. Latham (1997), *What's a Parent to Do? Solving Family Problems in a Christlike Way* (Salt Lake City: Deseret Book).

C. L. Player (2005, January), When a loved one struggles with addiction, *Ensign, 35*(1), 62–66.

Scott P. Sells (1998), *Treating the Tough Adolescent: A Family-Based, Step-by-Step Guide* (New York: Guilford Press).

NOTES

1. Richard G. Scott (1986, May), We love you—Please come back, *Ensign, 16*(5), 10.

2. Gordon B. Hinckley (2004, May), Stay on the high road, *Ensign, 34*(5), 113–114.

3. James E. Faust (2005, March 1), Where is the Church?; BYU Devotional Address; available at http://speeches.byu.edu

4. James E. Faust (2003, May), Dear are the sheep that have wandered, *Ensign, 33*(5), 67–68; story originally printed in Name withheld (1991, June) With love—from the prodigal's sister, *Ensign, 21*(6), 17–19. See also chapter 26 in this volume.

5. Elder Boyd K. Packer (1982) noted in this regard: "Parents, can we first consider the most painful part of your problem? If you want to reclaim your son or daughter, why don't you leave off trying to alter your child just for a little while and concentrate on yourself. The changes must begin with you, not with your children. You can't continue to do what you have been doing (even though you thought it was right) and expect to unproduce some behavior in your child, when your conduct was one of the things that produced it. . . . And parents, if you seek for a cure that ignores faith and religious doctrine, you look for a cure where it never will be found." *That All May be Edified* (Salt Lake City: Bookcraft), 139.

E S S A Y   F 3

THE EARLY-RETURNING MISSIONARY

RICHARD FERRE

Elder Michael Snow[1] appeared exhausted and yet nervous. He made little eye contact as he shared with the doctor his mission experience and the reason for his early return home. Elder Snow's recollections began with his excitement and nervousness in preparing for a mission—a mission he had been planning since he was a young boy. Soon after he entered the Missionary Training Center, he felt increased nervousness gradually crippling his ability to cope with this new challenge. Learning a foreign language was not only difficult, but he felt that he was making far less progress than the other missionaries in his district. He was sleep-deprived as a result of his attempt to continue studying at night. Within a month his concentration had begun to fail and he could not initiate sleep nor sleep soundly. Tired during the day, he realized that anxiety was dictating his thoughts, filling his mind with unwanted worries. He spoke to no one about his distress, believing that things would be better once he was in the mission field.

A proselyting mission has its own unforeseen perils. Missions demand consistent high levels of energy. The pace is relentless and weekends collapse into a busy preparation day. The structure of mission rules often leaves little choice about how to find effective relaxation and rejuvenation. A missionary prone to anxiety may make demoralizing comparisons to other missionaries about his or her own performance. The physical, emotional, and mental demands on a missionary can be stressful. In addition, some missionaries must work hard to overcome predispositions toward anxiety disorders, depression, obsessive thinking, and other emotional and psychological difficulties. For most missionaries, the challenges of the mission, along with the joys of missionary service, provide significant opportunities for spiritual and emotional growth. In some cases, when a susceptible missionary experiences high levels of stress, a deteriorating capacity to work, and the added loss of self-esteem, emotional illness may escalate or emerge.

The mission president discovered some of Elder Snow's symptoms in an interview. The president made helpful suggestions and then involved the Church Missionary Department in finding ways to keep him in the field. Several phone calls from an experienced social worker were of some benefit in helping him reframe his thinking. Nonetheless, Elder Snow could not reverse the panic that he was falling into a black hole, and he frequently wrestled with thoughts of suicide. After nine months in the mission field, Elder Snow was sent home to obtain appropriate psychological and medical treatment.

Serious questions arise when traumatic events of this nature are experienced. For example, how will the missionary be received when he or she returns home? Will it be a reunion of compassion and safety? Will there be the presence of a "secure base" in the home and the ward where the early-returning missionary can feel safe while recovering from this overwhelming experience? Some of the greatest needs of early-returning missionaries are to feel protected from repeated trauma and to be embraced by the support of significant relationships.

In discussing Elder Snow's condition with the family, the psychiatrist found that the parents' greatest desire was to have their son return to the mission field as soon as possible. Surely, they thought, with some brief treatment he would recover and could resume his mission. Grief over failed expectations was evident as, tearfully, Sister Snow spoke about all the years of hope she had placed in her son's mission. Patiently, the doctor explained the gravity of Elder Snow's illness. His parents began to understand that their son's desire to serve was accepted of the Lord and by inspiration he had been sent home to heal. They accepted the stewardship to protect their son. They determined that their home would become a haven of safety for him as he received treatment and developed the ability to manage his illness.

The unexpected early release of a missionary is traumatic for everyone. Parents rarely have previous experiences that prepare them to cope with such a situation. After the missionary's arrival home, it is helpful for parents to respond with love, compassion, and willingness to understand their missionary's tragedy. A nonjudgmental attitude leads to the greatest healing.

The missionaries themselves are sometimes confused and distressed about the cause and necessity of the release. A return to a familiar routine can help an emotionally traumatized missionary to feel secure. The patterns before the mission that supported the son's or daughter's ability to cope are the best routines to reinstitute. Missionaries heal best when they have adequate opportunity to rest. Healthy sleep cycles should be encouraged and good nutrition should be provided. As recovery permits, exercise is also helpful.

Although early-returning missionaries need this kind of structure, there should initially be few expectations for performance tasks like job seeking, schooling, or returning to the mission field. Finding ways to encourage this balance between needed structure and the ideal of moving from fewer to greater expectations as healing occurs, without arousing animosity, is sometimes challenging, particularly when dealing with less-cooperative and more "free spirited" personalities. Along with seeking divine guidance, parents can often utilize the support of bishops, professional counselors, and individuals the missionary is close to in providing proper encouragement in these more difficult situations.

Reduction of stress is essential. Beyond encouraging healthy sleep cycles and exercise, and lowering performance expectations while healing occurs, stress is also reduced when the family allows the missionary to express his or her thoughts and feelings as he or she feels comfortable, particularly feelings about the missionary experience and the symptoms that led to the illness. Discussions of returning to the mission field should wait until the missionary has had a few weeks to improve. In cases of emotional illness, missionaries are generally not allowed to return to the mission field until six months of recovery time and stability have transpired. Parents should honor this policy.

It is essential that friends and ward communities also provide safe havens for early-returning missionaries after their arrival home. Finding fault and blaming the missionary or the family is not helpful. Although reasons for an early return are to be kept confidential by ecclesiastical leaders, bishops and ward leaders can do all in their power to encourage ward members to provide the compassion, friendship, and support that helps the missionary heal. It is vitally important that ward members and friends not subject early-returning missionaries to questions about their release or spread gossip that would inflict additional trauma.

Another missionary, Elder Brown, found himself in a compromising situation with a young woman of the ward in which he was serving. After a few weeks of writing to her and talking with her on the phone, they began secretly meeting in late-night rendezvous that eventually lead to sexual transgression. When his parents were informed about his release and his Church disciplinary status, they felt shamed. They expressed to each other that they would never have suspected this from their son and did not know how they would respond to him when they saw him.

Indeed, the shame and trauma of early release for moral transgression is devastating to the missionary and the missionary's family. Often parents unjustly blame themselves for what they didn't do to prevent such a tragedy. Thoughts that perhaps they could have been more faithful, developed better parenting skills, or attended the temple more regularly are not helpful. In the end, the transgression was due to the missionary's own choices. A more productive approach is for the family and the missionary's local ecclesiastical leaders to create a plan and "close a circle" around the missionary with the commitment that they will not abandon the missionary through this trial. The willingness to suffer with those who suffer and "mourn with those that mourn" (Mosiah 18:9) is the first principle on which to build. It is the principle of love.

While not condoning poor choices, family members do well not to condemn the missionary for his actions. Rather they can help the missionary get a new start and move past this traumatic event in his or her life. Ideally, an increase of love should follow Church disciplinary action and the accompanying release from missionary service. Although initial feelings of disappointment and devastation will likely be expressed to the missionary, it does little good to continually bring up past mistakes, unless the missionary does so in an effort to talk things through and seek counsel. Parents should be open to these opportunities when initiated by the missionary. Recollections of guilt must be minimized if they promote self-loathing and do not direct a path to change. Bishops and stake presidents can also meet with parents and other family members as needed to counsel with them, help them cope with grief, and suggest strategies for demonstrating a charitable attitude toward the transgressor. (Chapter 26 has more suggestions for parents of children who stray.) Ecclesiastical leaders should meet regularly with the missionary to provide coun-

sel on the path to repentance and to help him or her get on with life.

Another important part of the healing process is to assist the sufferer to find peace and forgiveness through the teachings of the gospel and the Atonement of Jesus Christ. Alma's conversion story records his discovery of God's grace. He stated, "After wading through much tribulation . . . I am born of God" (Mosiah 27:28). Later, Alma's trials also included counseling his son Corianton, who was guilty of sexual transgression during his missionary service (see Alma 39:2–16). This father's tender teachings to his errant son provide a pattern for counseling our children through the repentance process (see Alma 39–42). Alma teaches his son about basic doctrines, addresses the specific concerns his son feels, and uses the scriptures to help his son avoid rationalizing his behavior.[2] After repenting, Corianton became valiant in the service of the Lord (see Alma 43:1–2; 49:30).

In summary, each early-returning missionary has a different story and a unique experience. The missionary, family, and ecclesiastical leaders should all be united in a common plan to assist the missionary. Supportive relationships are critical to recovery in such cases. Professional counseling such as that provided by LDS Family Services can be especially beneficial in these circumstances. Ward members can reach out with hearts full of charity as the trauma of illness or transgression is best healed in the safety of a supportive ward community. Perhaps most of all, missionaries need an understanding family who will provide a safe haven and will nurture them with compassion back to emotional or spiritual health. Through the atoning power of Jesus Christ, healing can begin and hope can be restored.

ABOUT THE AUTHOR

Richard Ferre is a child and adolescent staff psychiatrist at Primary Children's Medical Center. He serves as a member of the emotional illness committee of the Church's Missionary Department and as a psychiatrist in the LDS Family Services clinic that treats early-returning missionaries.

ADDITIONAL READING

Richard G. Scott (2003, November), Realize your full potential, *Ensign, 23*(11), 41–43.

NOTES

1. Names have been changed.
2. See D. L. Largey, ed. (2003), *Book of Mormon Reference Companion* (Salt Lake City: Deseret Book), 214–215.

E S S A Y F 4

UNWED PREGNANCY AND ADOPTION

MONICA L. BLUME

The experience of adoption is amazing. As I have witnessed the miracle of babies being placed from the arms of one loving mother into the arms of another, I have been humbled and deeply moved. Few actions exemplify greater unselfishness and more complete faith than that of young parents who choose, for the sake of the child they love deeply, to allow that child to be placed into another family who can give him all he will need to return to his Father in Heaven. And I have rarely seen, even in my own life, the hand of God so clearly and lovingly directing an experience.

The realization that an out-of-wedlock pregnancy has occurred can be cause for great sadness and loss. There is pain for the young people involved, and there is pain for all those who love them and care about the decisions they will make. The decision to place a child for adoption is a choice wrought with heartache, driven by unselfishness, and guided by love. Coming to a determination that adoption is in the child's best interest is painful, and following through with that decision is one of the most difficult things ever done. At points in adoption there is sorrow; at other times happiness and peace. I have had the opportunity to meet some amazing people who became happy and peaceful through the process of placing a child for adoption. Ellen was one of them.

Ellen had fallen from strong activity in the Church. She was raised by parents who honored their responsibilities and taught her about the gospel, parents who felt sadness and disappointment in her decisions to become closely involved with a boyfriend who did not share her beliefs. As she became more distant from her parents and the Church, she found she cared less and less about the consequences of her actions. When Ellen learned she was pregnant, she felt that her entire world was falling apart.

She said, "I thought I had my life under control, that I was doing what I wanted to do and being who I wanted to be. When I found myself suddenly having

to care for someone else's life as well, I realized that I couldn't do anything without my family and the foundation of the gospel." Ellen was learning a painful but important lesson, a lesson of humility and, ultimately, faith: "I knew early on that I would place my baby for adoption. I loved her from the first day I knew I was pregnant and I wanted her to have a good life. Suddenly all of the things I had learned in my childhood became so much more important to me, like the importance of eternal families and the desire to marry in the temple."

But even though what she wanted for herself and her child was so much clearer, the faith to trust in her Heavenly Father and the personal strength to follow through with her decision were qualities Ellen had to acquire. Throughout the following months, months spent in counsel with her parents and ecclesiastical leaders and hours of humble prayer, she came to believe that her Heavenly Father was not only deeply concerned about the life of her unborn child but about her own life as well. As she developed a relationship with the Savior, she realized that she could not only be forgiven for her past serious mistakes, she could become the person she was to Him, someone who was strong enough to work towards all she believed was right and good. Ellen grew not only to trust in her Heavenly Father but also to believe in herself. She explained, "I loved my baby more than anyone I've ever loved in my life. And I knew, when I held her in the hospital and looked into those piercing eyes, that I would do what I had to for her." Ellen was one of so many who have had the courage to overcome their mistakes and allow precious children to be placed for adoption. Ellen had gained perspective and personal strength through her experience, qualities that helped her as she went on to meet a worthy young man and marry in the temple. As stated in "The Family: A Proclamation to the World," "Children are entitled to birth within the bonds of matrimony, and to be reared by a father and a mother."[1] Choosing adoption allows the child a life with two parents who are prepared and desirous to raise her in righteousness.

THE CHOICES

Adoption is not the only choice; there are other options. Some choices are less desirable than others, and all of them have eternal consequences. President Gordon B. Hinckley has given counsel to those who are unmarried and are dealing with an unplanned pregnancy: "Marriage is the more honorable thing. . . . When marriage is not possible, experience has shown that adoption, difficult though this may be for the young mother, may afford a greater opportunity for the child to live a life of happiness."[2] The choices of marriage, adoption, and single parenting are all considerations. Of the possibility of abortion, President Hinckley wrote: "Abortion is not the answer. This only compounds the problem. It is an evil and repulsive escape that will someday bring regret and remorse."[3]

The counsel to marry is given to those who are willing and able "to establish an eternal family relationship."[4] In order to make a successful marriage work, there needs to be humble willingness by both the young mother and the young father to work prayerfully towards an eternal family. This means that the couple has the maturity, the means, and the shared direction to pursue a temple sealing and to provide a secure and happy life for the child, themselves, and their future children.

The First Presidency taught, "When the probability of a successful marriage is unlikely due to age or other circumstances, unwed parents should be counseled to place the child for adoption through LDS Family Services to ensure that the baby will be sealed to temple-worthy parents."[5]

There are a number of reasons why those dealing with unplanned pregnancies choose to place their babies for adoption. Andrea, a 22-year-old college student, described her decision this way: "If I were going to single parent my baby, all of my reasons would be for me: because I want to raise him, because I can afford to pay for his basic needs, because I love babies. But all of my reasons for placing him for adoption are for him: because he needs a mother *and* a father, because he deserves more than just the basics, because I love him." Andrea wanted him to have a full-time mother, not one who would be in school and at work all the time. She wanted him to

have a father who was always in his life, not in and out. She wanted him to have the best possible chances for returning to live with his Heavenly Father, and the blessings of the sealing covenant. And Andrea wanted those things for herself, as well.

Single parenting can have difficult consequences for the child and the mother. President Hinckley said: "The burdens that fall upon a young woman who alone must rear her child are unbelievably heavy and consuming. . . . The obstacles facing children born and reared in such circumstances are formidable."[6] We are counseled to consider the following: "[Unwed parents] are generally unable to provide a stable, nurturing environment which is so essential for the baby's well-being."[7]

MAKING GOOD DECISIONS

As with other important life decisions, there are many who can guide unwed parents-to-be as they seek direction. Counseling with ecclesiastical leaders can provide knowledge and guidance as well as great peace. Counseling with loving parents and professional counselors can allow for further understanding of the choices and an awareness of the potential outcomes of each choice. Ultimately, the decision to place a baby for adoption is one that should be made through personal prayer and diligent study, guidance and support from others, and inspiration from the Lord.

Those in positions of supporting an unwed loved one who is expecting a baby need to realize that while they can make a great difference through support and understanding, the decision to be made is the decision of the unwed parent, and pressuring him or her towards one decision or another is not often helpful. Patience and gentle guidance, keeping in mind the counsel given by the Brethren to those faced with an unwed pregnancy,[8] can be far more effective in helping unwed parents-to-be understand the choices available and make good decisions regarding the child.

Adoption can be a blessing in the lives of many people, not the least of which is the child to be adopted and those adoptive parents who have built their family through the unselfish sacrifice of a young man and young woman (see essay E2). But adoption also allows for hope in the lives of those unwed parents. As the First Presidency so powerfully stated, "Adoption is an unselfish, loving decision that blesses both birth parents and the child in this life and in eternity."[9]

ABOUT THE AUTHOR

Monica L. Blume is a licensed clinical social worker who has worked with unwed mothers and their families for more than ten years. She has been a featured speaker and has coauthored a book on adoption. She and her husband are the parents of six children.

ADDITIONAL READING

Monica L. Blume and Gideon O. Burton (2005), *For the Love of a Child: The Journey of Adoption* (Salt Lake City: Deseret Book).

Monte J. Brough (1994, September), Guidance for unwed parents, *Ensign*, 24(9), 19.

Joy F. Evans, (1985, September), From tragedy to hope: Helping unwed parents, *Ensign 15*(9), 41.

NOTES

1. First Presidency and Council of Twelve Apostles (1995, November), The family: A proclamation to the world, *Ensign*, 25(11), 102.

2. Gordon B. Hinckley (1994, November) Save the children, *Ensign*, 24(11), 53.

3. Ibid.

4. Gordon B. Hinckley, Thomas S. Monson, and James E. Faust (1998, June 15), Adoption and unwed parents; letter to ecclesiastical leaders.

5. Gordon B. Hinckley, Thomas S. Monson, and James E. Faust (2002, July 19), Adoption and unwed parents; letter to ecclesiastical leaders.

6. Hinckley (1994), 53.

7. Hinckley, et al. (2002, July 19).

8. Ibid.

9. Ibid.

E s s a y   F 5

COPING WITH SUICIDE

STEVEN C. YAMADA

The day Devon died I thought the world should stop spinning," recalled one mother. "How could life go on when our beautiful son had died? No prior life experience had prepared any of us for the searing pain we would experience from Devon's suicide. I had to keep reminding myself to breathe—slowly, in and out—and eventually, I thought, we could make sense of this surreal tragedy." Seventeen-year-old Devon, the oldest of five children, had committed suicide on a beautiful spring day. His mother wrote:

Devon's death reverberated through our family like a stone through a glass window; we were shattered. I have come to believe that one of the greatest pains a family can experience is a self-inflicted wound from one of its own members. Suicide, addiction, or any choices family members make that ultimately bring harm to them and hurt to you are synonymous with cutting out your own heart: "How could he do this to himself and to us?" I wondered. "How can life possibly go on without him?"

But life does go on. Rather than give in to my instincts to curl into a fetal position and weep, I simply had to look into the faces of our four children and my husband to know that I was not alone in the abyss of my grief. My children needed parents to comfort them. My husband needed a wife to hold him, and I needed a family to need me. Being needed gave me a desperate directive to navigate through the pain. The children's own pain was palpable evidence of the love they had for their older brother. It could be seen in their faces, in their tears, heard in their prayers, and felt even in the silence that permeated our home.

As much as we were defined by Devon's death, Russ and I were determined not to let this destroy our family; rather, we hoped to let this experience strengthen us. Our wounded souls bound together and shored each other up. For instance, our family prayers became incredible moments of shared testimony and tears. As parents, our nightly routines became wonderful opportunities to sit and talk with our children, to listen to them, and to express our testimony and love. Older sisters encouraged younger brothers to spend time with them, just to drive around or to talk. We watched out for each other's moods and needs and were tender toward the ache that each was feeling.

SURVIVING SUICIDE

Two families who survived the loss of a loved one to suicide shared what has helped them.

The first family suggested the following:
- Seek priesthood blessings for comfort and understanding.
- Rely on the power of personal prayer.
- Study the scriptures for comfort and doctrinal understanding.
- Listen to music that has special meaning and brings comfort.
- Let time pass without the need to do anything. It is especially important not to make major life decisions too quickly.
- Let family members and friends serve. Small, seemingly insignificant gifts (like plates of cookies) can be meaningful and remembered in trying times. Friends and family can pray to Heavenly Father for inspiration in knowing how to provide comfort.[1]

The second family made these observations:
- We still did family traditions, even though they were incredibly painful at first. We continued with our Lake Powell trips, carving pumpkins, and putting out our son's Christmas stocking. We felt that this really helped the kids to see that although our son was dead, our family wasn't.
- At first, as parents, we were guilt-ridden over our parenting and relived every discussion or event we had experienced with him. This took our energy from effectively parenting our other children. When we came to terms with his suicide and were able to put our part of it into perspective, we were able to be better parents. Kids need parents who are neither afraid to parent nor consumed with guilt for past events.
- We talked about our son and kept his pictures around the home. We would say, "I wish your brother were here to see you play ball. He would have been so proud of you." This helped to open discussions of him and keep him alive in our hearts.
- We consciously tried not to make our son out to be better (or worse) than he really was. Parents have a tendency for selective memory. Our oldest daughter caught us on this a few times and helped us to keep our son real—funny, sarcastic, good-looking, intense, but real.
- One thing that was never allowed was to implicate any guilt to another family member over his death. The guilt from a suicide or any fatal accident can act like poison in a home, destroying everyone it touches.
- Through constant prayer and pleading for understanding and peace, we were directed to each other's needs and to the needs of each child. Our oldest daughter refused to visit her brother's grave and was uncomfortable talking about him. Our young sons had to sleep on the floor of our bedroom for months, just needing their parents close. We each had our own way of expressing our grief, and with time and patience, we learned to accept and allow our differences.[2]

Box F 5.1

My husband and I lost a son and experienced the requisite grief and unimaginable guilt that a suicide demands. Our children lost their older brother and each felt guilt and grief differently, unique to the child's age and relationship with Devon. As parents, we gained an appreciation of just how deep the love we have for each other and the hurt we can cause one another can be as we watched the children try to regain their footing and continue on with life.[3]

UNANSWERED QUESTIONS

The survivors of the tragedy of suicide may ask: "Why did this happen? How can I cope? Will I ever find peace?" The feelings survivors experience are frightening, often leaving them barely able to function. Survivors do not have parting time with the individual, the opportunity to tie up loose ends and prepare for the tragedy. They are left behind with *what ifs* and *whys* that often turn to anger, blame, denial, and guilt.

Elder M. Russell Ballard stated: "The act of taking one's life is truly a tragedy because this single act leaves so many victims: first the one who dies, then the dozens of others—family and friends—who are left behind, some to face years of deep pain and confusion."[4] While statements from latter-day prophets emphasize the seriousness of suicide, Elder Bruce R. McConkie shared this insight:

> Persons subject to great stresses may lose control of themselves and become mentally clouded to the point that they are no longer accountable for their acts. Such are not to be condemned for taking their own lives. It should also be remembered that judgment is the Lord's; he knows the thoughts, intents, and abilities of men; and he in his infinite wisdom will make all things right in due course."[5]

WHY DID THIS HAPPEN?

The reasons for suicide are often complex. Many medical, psychological, and social factors such as depression, substance abuse, and personal crisis can put a person at risk. There typically is no single cause or reason for committing suicide; however, several factors or a combination of factors may trigger it. People considering suicide feel such intense pain; they would do anything to stop that pain, even taking their own lives.

There are some warning signs, listed by Hyde and Forsyth, that should be acknowledged with appropriate help:

- Preoccupation with thoughts of death. Verbal clues can be faint. Discussions of heaven and hell can be hints about thoughts of death, even when talked about "objectively."
- Statements of worthlessness. Events that trigger a loss of faith in oneself can range from a bad grade on an exam, to losing a job, to an argument with a friend, the loss of a loved one, a broken engagement, or a change in lifestyle.
- A settling of affairs. Concerns about life insurance, will, or other documents may signal that an individual is considering suicide.
- Giving away prized possessions. People of all ages may be signaling their suicide mentally when they give away, for no apparent reason, prized possessions.
- Suicidal threats. The false belief that "people who say they are going to kill themselves never do" has long been disproved. Every suicide threat should be taken seriously.
- Possession of suicidal plans. Question a person who appears suicidal to determine if any detailed plans have been made. At any hint of such a plan, call for help.
- A sudden apparent peace of mind. Unex-

plained comments such as "all is going to be fine" can be a warning.[6]

What should you do when you notice these signs? Believe it, listen to the individual, and get help. Elder Alexander B. Morrison suggested: "Parents of teenagers who are at risk for suicidal behavior should enlist the help of Church leaders. There is no substitute for the counsel of a wise bishop, who also may encourage the young person involved to seek professional help."[7]

HOW CAN I COPE?

In a way, one never fully recovers from the suicide of a loved one and may always feel the loss. It is like riding the waves of the ocean. There are times when the ocean is calm, and we feel that we have mastered the waves. We swim with confidence toward the beach, then suddenly we are confronted with a series of waves that pummel us, and we find ourselves fighting to stay afloat. We must learn to ride the waves and not fight against them, just as we must learn to deal with the waves of emotion that come following the loss of a loved one. Do not put a timetable on your grief. No two people grieve in the same way. Grief usually lasts longer than one would expect. To nurture healing as a survivor, you should consider the following:

- Let others help you. When offers of help come, accept them. Loved ones appreciate being able to express their love by doing something.
- On days when you are feeling down and need to get your feelings out, talk with someone who is a good listener. Share your feelings with a friend or your religious leader.
- Keep busy with purposeful activities but avoid frantic activity.
- Take care of yourself. One of the best gifts you can give the deceased loved one is to truly take good care of yourself.
- Remember it's okay to begin to laugh and enjoy life again. You don't have to remember the loved one by lingering in grief. Your sorrow is one way of honoring your loved one; carrying on with your life is another.

Consider seeking professional help if symptoms are extreme or persist beyond what you feel is healthy.[8] (Chapter 32 describes common aspects of the grieving process.)

WILL I EVER FIND PEACE?

In mortality you may never find out why a loved one chose to take his or her life, but the ability to overcome the fear and uncertainty brought on by this tragic event will come as you seek peace and comfort from the ultimate source: our Savior, Jesus Christ. He knows and understands the circumstances that your loved one was experiencing. He also understands the pain you are feeling. Approach Him in prayer and in faith for His healing and comfort, for He said, "Blessed are all they that mourn, for they shall be comforted" (3 Nephi 12:4). "Peace I leave with you, my peace I give unto you: not as the world giveth, give I unto you. Let not your heart be troubled, neither let it be afraid" (John 14:27).

Devon's mother described her family's path to peace this way:

> We have healed a great deal. We have learned the incredible power of love through the devastation of our loss. Devon will always be a vital part of our family. We talk about him, pray for him, and think of him every day. The hole that was left in our family from Devon's death has been, in time, filled with love from extended family and friends and from wonderful family experiences. I will always ache from the loss of my son, but I have felt such a tremendous love from my Heavenly Father, and gained such a strong testimony of the power of the Atonement, that I can live with the hurt. I keep breathing, and with every breath am aware of how dependent I am on those whom I love, need, and who, thankfully, need me.

ABOUT THE AUTHOR

Steven C. Yamada is the director of Behavioral Medicine at Mountain View Hospital in Payson, Utah, and directs the Crisis Teams at Mountain View and Timpanogos Regional Medical Center in Orem, Utah. He and his wife, Teriann, live in Provo, Utah, and are parents of four children.

The editors wish to thank Russ and Jolene Jones for their contributions to this essay.

ADDITIONAL READING

M. Russell Ballard (1987, October), Suicide: Some things we know, and some we do not, *Ensign, 17*(10), 6–9.

Julie Dockstader Heaps (2004, March 13), Surviving the loss of a loved one to suicide: Finding peace, coping with the heartache, *LDS Church News,* Z10; available on-line at http://www.desnews.com/cn

NOTES

1. Name withheld, personal communication to Elaine Walton, 19 March 2005.

2. Russ and Jolene Jones, personal communication to Lloyd Newell, 19 March 2005.

3. Ibid.

4. M. Russell Ballard (1987, October), Suicide: Some things we know, and some we do not, *Ensign, 17*(10), 7.

5. Bruce R. McConkie (1966), *Mormon Doctrine,* 2d ed. (Salt Lake City: Bookcraft), 771.

6. M. O. Hyde and E. H. Forsyth (1986), *Suicide: The Hidden Epidemic* (Minneapolis: CompCare), 93–95.

7. Alexander B. Morrison (2003), *Valley of Sorrow: A Layman's Guide to Understanding Mental Illness* (Salt Lake City: Deseret Book); quoted in J. D. Heaps (2004, March 13), Surviving the loss of a loved one to suicide: Finding peace, coping with the heartache, *LDS Church News,* Z10; available on-line at http://www.desnews.com/cn

8. *About Suicide: From Depression to Hope* (1998), (San Bruno, CA: Krames Communications).

CHAPTER 27

MAGNIFYING THE SANCTITY OF OUR HOMES

SHIRLEY R. KLEIN AND E. JEFFREY HILL

Successful marriages and families are established and maintained on principles of faith,
prayer, repentance, forgiveness, respect, love, compassion, work, and wholesome recreational activities.[1]
—"The Family: A Proclamation to the World"

The counsel from prophets, past and current, leaves little doubt about the importance of creating a home that is the sacred center of family life. The advice is clear and steady: "No other success [in life] can compensate for failure in the home."[2] A First Presidency statement also reminds us, "The home is the basis of a righteous life, and no other instrumentality can take its place or fulfill its essential functions."[3] Homes are laboratories for life, yet they are so embedded in our being and thinking that it is difficult to appreciate their importance to the routines and activities repeated day by day, year to year.

Through daily family routines in our homes we make meaning of our lives as we connect with each other. Rich and satisfying experiences in daily home life facilitate healthy family relationships and help to avoid the feelings of rootlessness and isolation that plague modern life.[4] Our homes also need to be places of safety and security for all family members. As Elder L. Tom Perry reminded us, home is the last defense and should be "a place of refuge from the storm, which is increasing in intensity all about us."[5]

Most families find it surprisingly difficult to establish homes of order and peace. Comparing circumstances of today's Latter-day Saints with circumstances of earlier eras, President Harold B. Lee said, "Today we are being tested and tried by another kind of test that I might call the 'test of gold'—the test of plenty, affluence, ease—more than perhaps the youth of any

generation have passed through, at least in this Church."[6] That "test of gold" often threatens our families as it tempts us to discard family routines such as children's chores, family meals, and time together. Family needs and interests are often preempted by activities away from home; sometimes by individual tastes and wants; sometimes by greed, selfishness, and overindulgence.[7]

Negative rhetoric about home life and homemaking has provided a context for devaluing and discarding aspects of everyday work in the home. Other voices encourage family members to promote home life and respect family work. In her best-seller, *Home Comforts,* Cheryl Mendelson wrote: "Housekeeping creates cleanliness, order, regularity, beauty . . . makes your home alive [and] turns it into a small society in its own right, a vital place with its own ways and rhythms."[8] Everyone needs a home and, no matter who lives in it, the value of domesticity is the same: "to offer sanctuary and shelter, to give comfort and creative satisfaction and the assurance of connection."[9]

Home life offers abundant opportunities for development. Children learn the lessons of life at home. They can learn how to work, how to govern themselves; they learn manners and morals; they learn how to become self-reliant. Children can be smart, educated, and successful; but at the same time, they can also be selfish, self-centered, and uncaring—

unable to live in a spirit of community.[10] Elder Russell M. Nelson said that in the home it is possible that the "raw chemicals of selfishness and greed are melded in the crucible of cooperation to yield compassionate concern and love one for another."[11] In the simple and ordinary routines of family life are often found the character-building and family-bonding activities that hold family members together and prepare children effectively for the future.

INFLUENCES THAT AFFECT THE HOME

Each home is affected by a variety of influences both from without and from within. As families apply proclamation principles, they can be better prepared to magnify the sanctity of the home. A family who lives providently provides adequately for present and future needs. Here are four suggestions to consider:

Evaluate external influences. External influences may include culture, ethnic and religious practices, expectations based on gender or social status, and economic, political, and geographic realities. In very real ways, these factors influence families as they meet needs for food, clothing, shelter, and monetary exchange. When family members recognize the influence of external influences on everyday acts of providing, they are better able to choose helpful influences and eliminate harmful influences.

For example, one father found that after discussing with his daughter the various pressures calling for a certain clothing brand that would stretch the family budget beyond its limits, the daughter made prudent decisions about clothing purchases. A couple who discussed the external influences tempting them to purchase a home they could not afford were then able to base their home selection on what they valued more—financial security.

Strengthen positive family influences. Families are also influenced by forces within the family system. These can include family life stages, generational patterns, interaction patterns, the family climate, the family's belief system, cohesiveness, strength, wellness, and the ability of the family to connect to people and entities outside the family. As family members recognize the influence of these factors on everyday routines, they can build on family strengths and overcome family weaknesses. (Chapter 28 describes family interaction patterns and their influence on family well-being.) Though family members have been affected differently by generational patterns of home living, they can choose to accept healthy patterns and change or discard unhealthy ones.

All families have strengths that can be assets in everyday routines. Families who have established healthy communication patterns, a strong value system, and other hallmarks of effective families will be better able to guide choices in many areas.[12] For example, one family that regularly engages in wholesome family recreational activities finds that these settings give them good opportunities to talk with the teenaged children and discuss family values in an open and positive way. The rich communication that happens around the campfire might not be possible for their family in a more formal setting. Another family has a strong work ethic, grows a large garden each year, and engages in home canning projects at harvest time. As they include children of all ages in these work projects, they find that family members are learning to work together and respect each other's needs and differences.

Use personal knowledge and skills. When personal knowledge and skills are developed to provide for the temporal needs of the family, family members increase the likelihood that they can make adequate provisions for the family. Providing for the temporal needs of the family involves skills in cooking, budgeting, and car, home, and yard maintenance. Individuals can make contributions to the family as they learn new skills, develop greater knowledge, adjust standards, and learn to recognize personality traits that help or hinder homemaking efforts. Parents can actively teach children the skills that they have acquired, preparing them to create a home of their own in the future.

The acquisition of new skills and the use of existing skills add to the beauty and function of the home. For example, one young mother who wanted to decorate a room for her second baby found drapery panels through an on-line second-hand market and found a friend to help her convert some of them to a quilt for the crib. She saved money by making the quilt herself, achieved the look she wanted, and gained confidence in her ability to create the physical environment in her home. She also plans to increase her sewing skills to create things for her home by enrolling in a class at a local fabric store.

Maintain the Spirit in the home. When the Spirit of God is an influence in the home, all other influences are likely to be managed positively. Spiritual influence is evident in the home when parents and children try to live proclamation principles. "Faith, prayer, repentance, forgiveness, respect, love, compassion, work, and wholesome recreational activities"[13] are practices that make everyday living more enjoyable and promote growth. The Spirit is invited into the home when parents lead together in family worship. Consistent, well-functioning religious activities in the home lighten and improve daily routines. (Chapter 18 provides ideas for establishing and strengthening these spiritual patterns.)

The influence of the Spirit also mitigates other difficult familial and external influences. For example, if a father is unemployed or other economic or political conditions make everyday life challenging, the influence of the Spirit in the home can provide peace, comfort, and direction. As Elder Dennis B. Neuenschwander said: "Our homes . . . are holy places filled with sacred space. Though not always tranquil, our homes can be filled with the Spirit of the Lord."[14] The basics of prayer, scripture study, and family home evening invite the Spirit of the Lord and help create homes that are sacred centers.

The basics helped when one family struggled with a daughter's choice to dress immodestly. In response, the parents looked for ways to improve the spiritual climate of their home through family and personal worship. Over a period of time, their daughter's heart was touched and she chose clothing that coincided more with her role as God's beloved daughter.[15] In our families, we can access God's great power to help us provide optimally for temporal needs and at the same time develop spiritually.

HOME AS A LABORATORY

"Our homes are the laboratories of our lives," wrote President Thomas S. Monson.[16] A *laboratory* is a place equipped for experimental study, testing, or analysis.[17] In this sense, any home can be a laboratory that allows family members to develop characteristics that will prepare them for eternity. These characteristics include those spoken of in the Doctrine and Covenants: "Remember faith, virtue, knowledge, temperance, patience, brotherly kindness, godliness, charity, humility, diligence" (4:6).

The work of the home is not a casual responsibility but an opportunity to contribute to one another's eternal progression in partnership with God. Our perspective matters. Tasks can be approached as unwelcome drudgery or as opportunities for growth and connection. Parents can teach children valuable lessons in the context of participating in family chores

and work projects, as well as by performing acts of service in the neighborhood. Keep in mind that

> it is in the small, ordinary, unglamorous, and sometimes tedious experiences of everyday family life that our children become anchored, learn who they are, and discover what is truly important in life, and what is expected of them. . . . Someone must take responsibility for protecting and defending the physical, emotional, and spiritual spaces in which our children can be grounded morally and grow spiritually.[18]

By design, these tasks of mortality often constitute the bulk of daily living for most families.[19] The vision of those leading the family makes a difference. Adam and Eve were clothed and admonished to till the earth, and they labored together. They taught their children as they participated together in the tasks and tests of mortality while "eat[ing their] bread by the sweat of [their] brow" (Moses 5:1). In His great wisdom, God gave Adam and Eve the very thing that would bring them the most happiness and unite them as a couple—the opportunity to work together and rear their family in love and righteousness. Modern revelation expands our understanding that the temporal work we do has great spiritual importance. The Lord said: "Wherefore, verily I say unto you that all things unto me are spiritual, and not at any time have I given unto you a law which was temporal" (D&C 29:34, see also verse 35).

BE INTENTIONAL ABOUT CREATING YOUR HOME

Creating a home that is truly a sacred center requires effort and planning. In other words, it requires intentionality. Scholar William Doherty coined the phrase "intentional family."[20] In this chapter we extend this idea to an "intentional home." The opposite of the intentional home is the entropic home. Entropy is the tendency of a physical system to lose energy and coherence over time. Think of your own living space—what happens when you don't spend your energy to keep up with the daily tasks of living? It quickly descends into chaos. Of course, many factors create additional stress despite our best efforts, such as a sick child, an unexpected financial commitment, care for an aged parent, or other important interruptions to the routine. At times when caring for the needs of our families, the "ideal" home will seem a distant dream. It helps to remember that an intentional home is more than clean dishes and empty laundry baskets—it's family members who feel comfortable and loved.

The decision about how to use time in the home is difficult. The crucial choices between reading a book to a toddler and mopping the floor are constant challenges of balance that can tax even the most organized and intentional parent. However, with persistence and thoughtfulness a parent can find peace and joy in these everyday choices. Consistent effort to balance our priorities will help us create an overall positive environment. Below are some examples of ways families can create an intentional home:

Make plans for adequate housing. Follow the advice that was given to President Gordon B. Hinckley: "When I was a young man, my father counseled me to build a modest home, sufficient for the needs of my family, and make it beautiful and attractive and pleasant and secure. He counseled me to pay off the mortgage as quickly as I could so that, come what may, there would be a roof over the heads of my wife and children."[21] Consider what is too much or too little given your family circumstances. Once you have obtained housing, make plans to beautify, organize, and maintain it. Develop and practice organizational skills to establish an orderly environment.

Make plans for managing food, nutrition, and wellness in the home. Elder Robert D. Hales counseled that to strengthen our families we should "Eat together . . . and have meaningful mealtime discussions."[22] Sister Susan W. Tanner counseled young women to learn cooking and budgeting skills.[23] Successful mealtimes require the ability to plan healthy menus, select fresh produce and meats, use storage techniques to prevent spoilage or illness, prepare attractive and delicious foods, and shop and budget effectively. In addition, mealtime requires leadership and planning to divide up the tasks and help family members make appropriate contributions. (Essay A1 describes one family's strategy for cleaning up after meals).

Author Jean Zimmerman cites many advantages of home-cooked meals: Mealtimes can be a time of anticipation as familiar and loved aromas fill the air. Problems of life can seem easier to manage when seen in the perspective of ordinary tasks like baking a cake. Children can learn important lessons for later life through simple problems now, like how to recover from a disaster when they make a cooking mistake. A culture of caring can be developed as family members prepare food in partnership with people they love.[24]

One family reported success in delegating the responsibility for evening meals to different children each night of the week. This helped the older children to learn responsibility and gain many meal-preparation skills. In addition, they were able to contribute meaningfully to family well-being, feel satisfaction, and develop talents, self-reliance, and self-confidence. While families may encounter ups and downs as they actively plan for a meaningful mealtime, the benefits of these family times together will outweigh the challenges.

Make plans for selecting, obtaining, and maintaining clothing. Clothing choices reflect and help form a sense of being and belonging for all family members. (Chapter 24 discusses modesty in behavior and dress and provides ideas for selecting modest clothing.) Maintenance of clothing offers opportunities for developing an ethic of care. Develop skills, then intentionally set aside regular time for the tasks. At developmentally appropriate ages, children can be involved in caring for clothing. Small children can learn to sort laundry, match socks, and fold clothing; teens can learn laundry and mending skills.

Make plans for adequate financial management in the home. A couple must be intentional about managing their financial resources. And they must teach principles of self-reliance to their children. Elder Joe J. Christensen taught: "All too many enter marriage who have never learned to cook, sew, or develop other important life skills. Ignorance of these needed skills, along with the lack of understanding of the management of money, sows the seeds for many failures in our children's marriages."[25] Parents in one home set up a family bank to teach the principle of compound interest to their offspring. Their family bank paid a whopping 10 percent interest per month. The bank also made loans at the same rate of interest. The children internalized quickly how much better it is to save than to borrow. (Chapter 8 discusses wise management of financial stewardships.)

CONCLUSION

Retain the good examples from your past; change what needs to be changed. Be intentional about making good use of the laboratory in your home to develop those qualities that will enable you and your family members to live in the presence of Heavenly Father again. Decide to magnify the sanctity of your home by following advice of prophets and others who emphasize the value of home life. Create your plans for an intentional home and follow through. Experience the joy of everyday living.

ABOUT THE AUTHORS

Shirley R. Klein, Ph.D., CFLE, is an associate professor and chair of the Home and Family Living Program in the School of Family Life at Brigham Young University. She and her husband, Michael, are the parents of eight children and ten grandchildren.

E. Jeffrey Hill, MOB, Ph.D., CFLE, is an associate professor of home and family living in the School of Family Life at Brigham Young University. He and his wife, Juanita, have nine children and three grandchildren.

ADDITIONAL READING

William J. Doherty (1997), *The Intentional Family* (Reading, MA, and Menlo Park, CA: Addison-Wesley).

Maribeth C. Clarke, et al. (2000), Home as a sacred center of family life; in David C. Dollahite, ed., *Strengthening Our Families: An In-Depth Look at the Proclamation on the Family* (Salt Lake City: Bookcraft), 83–93.

Kristine Manwaring (2000), My home as a temple; in David C. Dollahite, ed., *Strengthening Our Families: An In-Depth Look at the Proclamation on the Family* (Salt Lake City: Bookcraft), 94–96.

Dennis B. Neuenschwander (2003, May), Holy place, sacred space, *Ensign, 33*(5), 71.

Francisco J. Viñas (2004, May), Applying the simple and plain gospel principles in the family, *Ensign, 34*(5), 38–40.

NOTES

1. First Presidency and Council of Twelve Apostles (1995, November), The family: A proclamation to the world, *Ensign, 25*(11), 102.

2. Originally quoted by President David O. McKay from J. E. McCulloch (1924), *Home: The Savior of Civilization* (Washington, D.C.: The Southern Co-operative League), 42; in Conference Report (1935, April), 116.

3. Keeping children close to the Church (1999, June), News of the Church, *Ensign, 29*(6), 80.

4. J. Zimmerman (2003), *Made from Scratch* (New York: Free Press), 29–30.

5. L. Tom Perry (2003, May), The importance of the family, *Ensign, 33*(5), 40.

6. Harold B. Lee (1962, February 7), Sweet are the uses of adversity; BYU Devotional Address; *Speeches of the Year* (Provo, UT: BYU Press), 3.

7. Joe J. Christensen (1999, May), Greed, selfishness, and overindulgence, *Ensign, 29*(5), 9.

8. C. Mendelson (1999), *Home Comforts: The Art and Science of Keeping House* (New York: Scribner), 7.

9. Zimmerman (2003), xiii.

10. E. G. Aird (2002), On rekindling a spirit of "home training": A mother's notes from the front; in S. A. Hewlett, N. Rankin, and C. West, eds., *Taking Parenting Public: The Case for a New Social Movement* (Lanham, MD: Rowman and Littlefield Publishers), 13–28.

11. Russell M. Nelson (1999, May), Our sacred duty to honor women, *Ensign, 29*(5), 38.

12. N. Stinnett and J. DeFrain (1989), The healthy family: Is it possible? in M. J. Fine, ed., *The Second Handbook on Parent Education: Contemporary Perspectives* (San Diego: Academic Press), 53–74.

13. First Presidency and Council of Twelve Apostles (1995), 102.

14. Dennis B. Neuenschwander (2003, May), Holy place, sacred space, *Ensign, 33*(5), 71.

15. J. Walker (1992, February), More than hemlines and haircuts, *Ensign, 22*(2), 22.

16. Thomas S. Monson (2000, June), Precious children, a gift from God, *Ensign, 30*(6), 2.

17. *Merriam-Webster's Collegiate Dictionary* (1993), 10th ed., s.v. "laboratory."

18. Aird (2002), 19–20, 27.

19. K. S. Bahr, C. A. Loveless, K. Manwaring, M. Rice, and V. E. Worthen (2000), The meaning and blessings of family work; in D. C. Dollahite, ed., *Strengthening Our Families: An In-Depth Look at the Proclamation on the Family* (Salt Lake City: Bookcraft), 177–189.

20. William J. Doherty (1997), *The Intentional Family: How to Build Family Ties in Our Modern World* (Reading, MA, and Menlo Park, CA: Addison-Wesley).

21. Gordon B. Hinckley (2001, November), The times in which we live, *Ensign, 31*(11), 72.

22. Robert D. Hales (1999, May), Strengthening families: Our sacred duty, *Ensign, 29*(5), 32.

23. Susan W. Tanner (2003, May), Did I tell you . . . ? *Ensign, 33*(5), 73.

24. Zimmerman (2003), 148, 154.

25. Christensen (1999, May), 10.

CHAPTER 28

HEALTHY FAMILY PROCESSES

JAMES M. FACER, RANDAL D. DAY, AND SUZANNE L. DASTRUP

Happiness in family life is most likely to be achieved when founded upon the teachings of the Lord Jesus Christ.[1]
—"The Family: A Proclamation to the World"

The purpose of this chapter is to show how healthy family processes, or the ways families do things, can help families create, sustain, and maintain important family goals. Families are, for the most part, goal-seeking entities. That is, the family is a group of individuals, linked together by generational connections (such as mothers and fathers, children, grandparents), who share common goals, ambitions, aspirations, and purpose. Families marshal resources, make decisions, solve problems, and organize assets in a collective effort to attain the goals they select. In most cases, those common goals are rather implicit and sometimes families don't find success in achieving what they set out to do. But most families do the best they know how in making progress toward the goals they have in mind.

Popular culture teaches family members that they should pay less attention to the common goals of family life and more attention to personal goals and desires. Of this cultural shift away from focusing on the common good of the family and the larger community, Elder Neal A. Maxwell stated: "Healthy, traditional families are becoming an endangered species! Perhaps, one day, families may even rank with the threatened spotted owl in effective attention given! . . . A few regard the family as an institution to be drastically redefined or even to be rid of. There are no perfect families, either in the world or in the Church, but there are many good families. My spiritual applause also goes to those heroic parents—left alone by death or divorce—who are righteously and 'anxiously engaged' in nurturing and providing for their families, often against such heavy odds."[2] The "heavy odds" with which we as families contend as we raise our children in the time foreseen by prophets of old (see 2 Timothy 3:1–7) can be improved as we begin to understand the family as a system and enhance the processes we use to meet our family goals.

THE FAMILY AS A SYSTEM

Family scientists sometimes view families as a system, or complex whole, in which the goals and purposes of the family itself, rather than those of its individual members, takes center stage. These researchers treat the family as an entity that goes beyond a simple combination of the wishes of each individual.[3] The approach assumes that all of the family members are connected and interrelated to form a collective group. From this perspective, parenting is not seen as a one-way process in which parents influence children. Instead, it is a multidimensional or bi-directional process,[4] in which parents influence children, children influence parents, parents influence each other, and children influence one another. To be successful, a parent nurtures each child within the family, but must also nurture the relationships the children have with one another because each relationship is part of the family system as a whole. Changes in the relationship between a parent and one child, for example, may affect the characteristics and behavior of the family system and thus affect other family members as well.

When Adam and Eve were placed in the Garden of Eden, they were two individuals, yet connected. When Eve partook of the fruit of the Tree of Life, her relationship with God changed, which change caused a change in her relationship with Adam. Adam was now faced with a choice with various outcomes for himself and others (see Moses 5:10). Eve's statement demonstrates that she chose to view her choice through a systemic or relational lens: "Were it not for *our* transgression we never should have had seed" (Moses 5:11, emphasis added). Another example is teenaged siblings who constantly argue about the wearing of each other's clothes. The one who borrows the clothes can't understand "the big deal." Yet the constant arguing influences the family in a negative way. The choices of Laman and Lemuel brought distress to their family, at one point bringing Lehi and Sariah "near to be[ing] cast with sorrow into a watery grave" and causing Jacob and Joseph to grieve (see 1 Nephi 18:17–19). Examining the family as a system will help youth and their parents understand the impact of conflict and look for solutions to resolve it.

MAINTAINING HEALTHY FAMILY BOUNDARIES

"Family boundaries—the rules defining who participates how—function to protect the differentiation of the system. . . . The parental subsystem . . . must establish generational boundaries to maintain its own psychosocial territory and protection from interference by demands of children and extended family."[5] It is imperative for parents to establish righteous, kind, charitable boundaries that establish clear rules to govern power and status in the family. Boundaries are similar to fences or screen doors that protect and separate entities from one another. Boundaries help each family member develop a sense of self. Clear boundaries also validate each person, value the eternal soul and worth of the individual, and at the same time correct or reprimand unacceptable behavior.

For example, a father who is the sole provider for his family has been asked by his employer to accept a promotion that will require him to move out of state. The family has several children, some in high school and some in grade school. Healthy family communication processes will allow the family to engage in productive decision making. Prior to the family's being made aware of the pending move, husband and wife will have shared their feelings, concerns, and ideas with each other. They come to the family council as a unified subsystem to hear the feelings, concerns, and ideas of the children. From those exchanges, the family can choose the option that is in the best interest of the family. Elder Marvin J. Ashton said: "To be effective, family communication must be an exchange of feelings and information. Doors of communication will swing open in the home if members will realize time and participation on the part of all are necessary ingredients."[6]

Boundary problems are most evident, however, when family members attempt to control the thoughts and feelings of others. In this same example, the feelings of a teenaged son who expresses displeasure at the news might be told to "Be quiet" or be asked, "Don't you care about your father's career?" Such comments leave no room for flexibility or feelings and are identified with family boundaries that are too rigid. Elder Richard G. Scott explained: "A fundamental purpose of earth life is personal growth and attainment. Consequently, there must be times of trial and quandary to provide opportunity for that development. What child could ever grow to be self-supporting in maturity were all the critical decisions made by parents?"[7] Families with healthy family processes are highly flexible and use a large repertoire of behaviors to make decisions and solve family problems, while families with unhealthy patterns are rigid and inflexible.

As another example, a mother is highly concerned about the influences of media in the home. She sees no need for any television or video games. The father, on the other hand, enjoys watching sports and occasionally relaxing in front of the television. The children enjoy playing video games and watching DVDs. Solving this family's problem will require flexibility, charity, and creativity. A healthy family process might include the mother and father consulting together and then inviting their children to share their feelings and thoughts about media and to suggest solutions that fit their needs. On the other hand, the process may become dysfunctional if the father simply agrees with his wife when she brings up the concern (to stop her from pestering him about it), leaves the television alone for a few days to please her, and then promptly returns to old habits. Actions such as this may lead to contention in the family, one of the major barriers to healthy family processes.

CONTENTION

Elder Marvin J. Ashton described the effects of contention: "The family as an institution today is beset on all sides. Conflicts within the family are critical and often damaging. Contention puts heavy strain on stability, strength, peace, and unity in the home. There is certainly not time for contention in building a strong family."[8] It is likely to be more difficult for parents in marriages characterized by conflicted exchanges to maintain their respect and value for each other as parents, and accordingly to develop and maintain a strong parenting alliance. Parents' preoccupation with their marital conflict impairs most dimensions of their child-rearing practices, particularly in the areas of discipline and acceptance.[9] Parents engaged in conflict administer harsher punishments and find it difficult to be accepting of their children. Fathers are more likely than mothers to emotionally withdraw from their children.[10] Marital interaction patterns in which both spouses engage in hostile behavior are associated with low levels of marital satisfaction and with marital dissolution.[11] (Resolving marital conflict is discussed in chapter 7 and essay B3.) When marriages are plagued with conflict, there is a possibility for husbands and wives to form triangulation alliances with their children. Triangulation is another major barrier to healthy family processes.

Triangulation

Triangulation is an imbalance in a relationship between three members of a family. "A triangle exists in which two members are close and a third is distanced; and once a family has evolved such a pattern, it tends to stick."[12] In these relationships, "there is a stated closeness without a real sense of warmth—a pseudo-closeness," concluded three researchers.[13] (Chapter 37 discusses triangulation among extended family.)

For example, a couple married twenty years is experiencing marital difficulty. Neither spouse feels comfortable facing their issues directly. In response to contention and strain in the home, their son has begun to engage in problem behaviors. Their unhappiness with each other is then redirected toward their son, whom they come to believe (or tell others) is the primary source of difficulties in their marriage. The son becomes the scapegoat, the person on whom dissatisfaction in a relationship is displaced.

In another example, a wife feels that her husband is too harsh in his discipline of the children. Instead of communicating and resolving their differences, she forms an alliance with her misbehaving daughter to justify her feelings of contention toward her husband. In turn, the daughter plays Mom against Dad, thus increasing the stress and anxiety in the home. Siblings can also engage in triangulation. For example, when a brother and sister are in conflict, they might involve a third sibling through such statements as, "I cannot believe how rude Susan is!"

Though family members create triangles to spread stress and anxiety across a greater number of people, this is a dysfunctional way to avoid dealing with unhealthy marital and other relationship issues; bringing a child or third party into the subsystem results in a breach in healthy family boundaries. As a result, the child and the marriage suffer. The Savior taught us to "go thy way unto thy brother, and first be reconciled to thy brother," even if it is "thy brother [that] hath aught [feelings of contention] against thee," and to "agree with thine adversary quickly while thou art in the way with him" (3 Nephi 12:23–25).

STRENGTHENING FAMILY PROCESSES

Research suggests that children can flourish when family processes are strengthened. "The Family: A Proclamation to the World" makes a bold statement about family process: "Happiness in family is most likely to be achieved when founded upon the teachings of the Lord Jesus Christ."[14] President Gordon B. Hinckley has stated: "The family is divine. It was instituted by our Heavenly Father. It encompasses the most sacred of all relationships. Only through its organization can the purposes of the Lord be fulfilled."[15] Actions relating to the teachings of Jesus Christ are expressed in the words of a favorite Primary song: "Love one another as Jesus loves you. Try to show kindness in all that you do. Be gentle and loving in deed and in thought, For these are the things Jesus taught."[16] Elder Francisco J. Viñas of the Seventy reminded us that "The old and sacred values . . . are the plain and simple principles of the gospel of Jesus Christ. These should be firmly established in our homes to ensure happiness in family life."[17] By studying their own family processes, families can evaluate how their approach to living the gospel of Jesus

Christ helps or hinders their progress toward family happiness.

Content and Processes

We as Latter-day Saints have been taught *what* Latter-day Saints should be doing, but when strengthening family processes we also must focus on the *how*, or content, of family interactions and routines. The content of a family routine refers to what the family does when they are having meals together, assigning chores, reading scriptures and praying, organizing efforts to get people to church, deciding on family vacation destinations, or determining how to resolve conflict. The important aspect of family processes is the examination of *how* family members enact these activities. It is possible to complete an entire checklist of gospel-oriented tasks, or to completely follow prophetic counsel regarding family tasks, and yet be empty or incomplete in righteous family processes. In other words, no matter how diligent we are in completing a religious activities checklist, we may be quite unrighteous in the process used to complete the checklist.

The process of family home evening provides one example. Many families employ a righteous approach or process in their teaching, with genuine compassion, tolerance, and charity. Others, however, might be faithful to the assignment, but fail to be Christlike in their approach. Their process might include arrogance, judgment, and criticism. President James E. Faust declared, "Family home evening is a time for patience and mutual respect. Let there be no ill will or anger between parents and children, husbands and wives, brothers and sisters, and kinsmen."[18] (Essay G1 includes ideas on handling contention among siblings). The First Presidency stated in 1976: "Regular participation in family home evening will develop increased personal worth, family unity, love for our fellowmen, and trust in our Father in heaven."[19] Healthy or righteous family process refers to the feeling of charity and acceptance within the home. Such homes are characterized by an atmosphere of equality and honesty, trust and belonging, agency and independence.

Elder Neal A. Maxwell warned, "When parents fail to transmit testimony and theology along with decency, those families are only one generation from serious spiritual decline, having lost their savor."[20] The First Presidency wrote to Church members: "We [call] on parents to devote their best efforts to the teaching and rearing of their children in gospel principles which will keep them close to the Church. We also [counsel] parents and children to give highest priority to family prayer, family home evening, gospel study and instruction, and wholesome family activities."[21] Research has shown that family worship practices predict parental marital satisfaction,[22] are associated with better youth psychological adjustment and lower substance abuse,[23] and have healing effects.[24]

Ask Questions

The type of approach, or process, used for family worship (e.g., family home evening, family prayer and scripture reading, family decision making) can influence youth outcomes. Elder Henry B. Eyring suggested that asking and answering questions is at the heart of all learning and all teaching. The most important questions are the ones that invite inspiration.[25] Using open-ended questions in family scripture reading and family home evening will invite family members to apply gospel learning to their own situations. Family scholars Chris Boyatzis and Denise Janicki demonstrated that conversations between parents and children, identified as having open-ended questions and minimal correction from parents, help youth to recognize and value their own religious feelings.[26] A study by Douglas Flor and Nancy Flanagan Knapp demonstrated that for both boys and girls, frequent interaction with parents was more effective than lecturing in determining religious behavior and the importance adolescents attach to religion.[27] These researchers found that when children are viewed as active participants in family religious activities, children initiate a major percentage of religious conversations.

Involve All Family Members

Children are taught religious truth through words and action. Jerry Lee and his colleagues found that "youth involvement and participation in worship is much more important than the mere presence of worship in the family experience" and that active faith is highest among youths whose families have a worship pattern that involves the youth.[28] Thus, family worship activities that do little to actively involve the children will not optimally nurture the child's faith. The seven patterns of family worship in Lee's study were shared worship, rotated worship, father-led, mother-led, infrequent mother- or youth-led, infrequent father-led, and no worship. The youth with the highest active faith were located in the shared-worship category. Some may wonder: Why was shared worship more effective than father-led worship? Scholarly research shows that when fathers permanently lead, as opposed to preside, the amount of time children and mothers talk decreases 50 percent. President Gordon B. Hinckley pled with fathers to preside, not dominate: "Yours is the basic and inescapable responsibility to stand as head of the family. That does not carry with it any implication of dictatorship or unrighteous dominion. . . . Yours is the power and the responsibility to preside in a home where there is peace and security, love and harmony."[29] (Chapter 7 and chapter 19 provide more information on leadership in the home.)

Elder Robert D. Hales offered this message of comfort to parents who feel they fall short: "No parent on earth is perfect. In fact, children are very understanding when they sense and feel that parents truly care and are attempting to be the best they can be. . . . Certainly parents will make mistakes in their parenting process, but through humility, faith, prayer, and study, each person can learn a better way."[30] Elder Hales encouraged parents to model positive patterns of interaction, even when they disagree: "It helps children to see that good parents can have differing opinions, and that these differences can be worked out without striking, yelling, or throwing things. They need to see and feel calm communication with respect for each other's viewpoints so they themselves will know how to work through differences in their own lives."[31]

Charity in Communication

Charity has been defined as the "pure love of Christ, and it endureth forever. . . . if ye have not charity, ye are nothing, for charity never faileth" (Moroni 7:47, 46). Elder Jeffery R. Holland taught that "it is Christ's love for us that 'suffereth long, and is kind, and envieth not.' . . . it is as demonstrated in Christ that 'charity never faileth.'"[32] Because Christ's love will never fail, we can expect to be forgiven of our sins, be resurrected, and enter into the presence of our Father in Heaven. Mormon admonishes us to pray for the gift of charity (Moroni 7:48). When we sense Christ's love, when we are charitable, we are better able to extend that love in our interactions with family members. Charity will never fail as an approach to communication, solving differences of opinion, holding family home evening, decision making, and all other family processes.

CONCLUSION

President Gordon B. Hinckley declared: "There is too much selfishness. There is too much of worldliness in our homes. We need to get back to the basics of respect one for another and concern one for another, love and appreciation for one another, working together, worshiping together, and living together as families who love the Lord and look to Him for light and strength and comfort. We need to rear our families in the nurture and admonition of the Lord, as He instructs us to do."[33] Understanding our family as a system and endeavoring to strengthen family processes will enable families to answer this call of President Hinckley. Barriers to healthy family processes can be removed through our diligent and prayerful efforts. Barriers will crumble at "the touch of the Master's hand"[34] and with the charity of each family member.

ABOUT THE AUTHORS

James M. Facer received advanced degrees in health care administration from the University of Colorado. He is finishing his Ph.D. in marriage, family, and human development at BYU. Prior to teaching full time for CES, James directed adult and adolescent programs.

Randal D. Day is a professor in the School of Family Life at Brigham Young University. His research interests include father involvement and parent-child interaction. He teaches courses about families in crisis, family systems, and family research.

Suzanne L. Dastrup is a native of Champaign, Illinois. She moved to Utah more than thirty years ago, raising three children (David, Kimberly, and Benson) and receiving her Ph.D. from Brigham Young University. She is currently a family therapist.

ADDITIONAL READING

Randal D. Day (2003), *Introduction to Family Processes*, 4th ed. (Mahwah, NJ: Lawrence Erlbaum).

Brent D. Slife, Melinda J. Petersen, and Daniel K Judd (2000), Faith and prayer in a Christ-centered family; in David C. Dollahite, ed., *Strengthening Our Families: An In-Depth Look at the Proclamation on the Family* (Salt Lake City: Bookcraft), 142–151.

C. Terry Warner (2001), *Bonds That Make Us Free: Healing Our Relationships, Coming to Ourselves* (Salt Lake City: Shadow Mountain).

NOTES

1. First Presidency and Council of Twelve Apostles (1995, November), The family: A proclamation to the world, *Ensign*, 25(11), 102.

2. Neal A. Maxwell (1994, May), Take especial care of your family, *Ensign*, 24(5), 89.

3. J. M. White and D. M. Klein (2002), *Family Theories*, 2d ed. (Thousand Oaks, CA: Sage), 122–127.

4. R. Q. Bell (1968), A reinterpretation of the direction of effects in studies of socialization, *Psychological Review, 75,* 81–95.

5. F. Walsh, ed. (1993), *Normal Family Processes,* 2d ed. (New York: Guilford Press), 28.

6. Marvin J. Ashton (1976, May), Family communications, *Ensign, 6*(5), 52.

7. Richard G. Scott (2003, May), The sustaining power of faith in times of uncertainty and testing, *Ensign, 33*(5), 75.

8. Marvin J. Ashton (1978, May), No time for contention, *Ensign, 8*(5), 8.

9. A. Krishnakumar and C. Buehler (2000), Interparental conflict and parenting behaviors: A meta-analytic review, *Family Relations, 49,* 25–44.

10. J. H. Grych and F. D. Fincham (1990), Marital conflict and children's adjustment: A cognitive-contextual framework, *Psychological Bulletin, 108,* 267–290.

11. L. F. Katz and J. M. Gottman (1993), Patterns of marital conflict predict children's internalizing and externalizing behaviors, *Developmental Psychology, 29,* 940–950.

12. L. G. Bell, D. C. Bell, and Y. Nakata (2001), Triangulation and adolescent development in the U.S. and Japan, *Family Process, 40,* 176.

13. Ibid.

14. First Presidency and Council of Twelve Apostles (1995), 102.

15. Gordon B. Hinckley (1994, January), Pillars of truth, *Ensign, 24*(1), 5.

16. J. K. Perry (1989), I'm trying to be like Jesus, *Children's Songbook* (Salt Lake City: The Church of Jesus Christ of Latter-day Saints), 78–79.

17. Francisco J. Viñas (2004, May), Applying the simple and plain gospel principles in the family, *Ensign, 34*(5), 38.

18. James E. Faust (2003, June), Enriching our lives through family home evening, *Ensign, 33*(6), 6.

19. Family Home Evening Manual (1976), (Salt Lake City: The Church of Jesus Christ of Latter-day Saints), 3.

20. Maxwell (1994), 90.

21. Monday nights reaffirmed as family home evening (1999, October 23), *LDS Church News,* Z05.

22. M. G. Dudley and F. A. Kosinski Jr. (1990), Religiosity and marital satisfaction: A research note, *Review of Religious Research, 32,* 78–86.

23. C. Smith, with M. L. Denton (2005), *Soul Searching: The Religious and Spiritual Lives of American Teenagers* (Oxford: Oxford University Press).

24. E. D. Stover and M. Stover (1994), Biblical storytelling as a form of child therapy, *Journal of Psychology and Christianity, 13,* 28–36.

25. Henry B. Eyring (1998, February 6), The Lord will multiply the harvest; an address to CES religious educators; available at http://ldsces.org under employee login.

26. C. J. Boyatzis and D. L. Janicki (2003), Parent–child communication about religion: Survey and diary data on unilateral transmission and bi-directional reciprocity styles, *Review of Religious Research, 44,* 252–270.

27. D. L. Flor and N. F. Knapp (2001), Transmission and transaction: Predicting adolescents' internalization of parental religious values, *Journal of Family Psychology, 15,* 627–645.

28. J. W. Lee, G. T. Rice, and V. B. Gillespie (1997), Family worship patterns and their correlation with adolescent behavior and beliefs, *Journal for the Scientific Study of Religion, 36,* 379.

29. Gordon B. Hinckley (1993, November), Bring up a child in the way he should go, *Ensign, 23*(11), 60.

30. Robert D. Hales (1993, November), How will our children remember us? *Ensign, 23*(11), 9, 10.

31. Hales (1993), 9.

32. Jeffrey R. Holland (1997), *Christ and the New Covenant: The Messianic Message of the Book of Mormon* (Salt Lake City: Deseret Book), 336.

33. Gordon B. Hinckley (1997), *Teachings of Gordon B. Hinckley* (Salt Lake City: Deseret Book), 208.

34. Myra Brooks Welch, The touch of the Master's hand; quoted in Boyd K. Packer, (2001, May), The touch of the Master's hand, *Ensign, 31*(5), 24.

CHAPTER 29

NURTURING PERSONAL RELIGIOUS EXPERIENCES IN CHILDREN AND YOUTH

BRUCE A. CHADWICK AND SUSAN L. WARNER

With all of our doing, with all of our leading, with all of our teaching, the most important
thing we can do for those whom we lead is to cultivate in their hearts a living, vital, vibrant testimony and
knowledge of the Son of God, Jesus Christ, the Redeemer of the world.[1]
—President Gordon B. Hinckley

The seeds of testimony are planted in the hearts of children at home by parents who teach them to pray, read the scriptures, obey the commandments, and attend Church meetings. To be prepared to make their way safely among the evils of the world, children must develop their own testimonies and private, inward religiosity as they grow into adolescence and young adulthood. Manifestations of this religiosity include personal prayer, individual scripture reading, Church attendance, and personal spiritual experiences.

A recent study of youth and religion concluded that teenaged members of The Church of Jesus Christ of Latter-day Saints are the most engaged in practicing their faith compared with teens in other denominations. Researchers concluded that "devout teens hold more traditional sexual and other values than their nonreligious counterparts and are better off in emotional health, academic success, community involvement, concern for others, trust of adults and avoidance of risky behavior."[2] Research with Latter-day Saint high school students has disclosed that attendance at meetings, religious belief, and private religiosity are all related to lower delinquency, enhanced feelings of self-worth, and strong academic achievement.[3] Importantly, private religiosity (i.e., personal religious experiences) has greater influence than other dimensions of religiosity. While it is important for parents to get their children to church, it is much more important for

youth to internalize a conviction of Jesus Christ and to live rich inward spiritual lives.

NURTURING RELIGIOSITY IN YOUNG CHILDREN

Our children come "trailing clouds of glory . . . From God, who is our home."[4] President Gordon B. Hinckley has reminded us, "Never forget that these little ones are the sons and daughters of God and that yours is a custodial relationship to them, that He was a parent before you were parents and that He has not relinquished His parental rights or interest in these His little ones."[5]

Children come into the world with a natural spiritual sensitivity. As parents, our sacred responsibility is to nurture that sensitivity in an atmosphere at home that keeps their spiritual awareness alive and growing. Contention, unkindness, selfishness, and disobedience in the home drive away the Spirit and offend the tender feelings of every family member, especially the children.[6] Inappropriate sibling relationships can also discourage religiosity and impede a child's spiritual growth (see essay G1 on curbing contentious tendencies). But in homes where children experience peace, kindness, and love, which are fruits of the Spirit (Galatians 5:22), they feel inwardly secure; when they later encounter evil influences, they respond uncomfortably and want to return to that security. The atmosphere in the home, set by the parents, plays a critical role in fostering children's religiosity.

From the time they are very young, children can feel the loving and forgiving nature of Heavenly Father and His Son, Jesus Christ. They can recognize a picture of Jesus and feel the warmth of the Spirit as they do. One couple assembled a picture album of Jesus, and His face became as familiar to their children as the faces of family members. The parents seek to "talk of [and] rejoice in Christ" in their home, so "that [their] children may know to what source they may look for a remission of their sins" (2 Nephi 25:26). Children who grow up in a home where they are reminded of Christ's love for them, even when they have made mistakes, have a much easier time understanding the personal nature of the Savior's Atonement.

Teaching children to choose right over wrong provides significant opportunities to help them become aware of their spiritual feelings. Even though children younger than eight years old are not considered accountable by God (see Moroni 8:10–11; D&C 20:71, 68:27), they feel unrest and sadness following misbehavior, and peace and joy when they do right. When parents help a child recognize these feelings, they are nurturing their child's awareness of his spiritual nature and divine heritage. If we desire to nurture the private religiosity of our children, we will faithfully follow the prophets' repeated counsel about exemplifying and teaching the gospel in our homes.

Prayer

Young children want to do the things they see their parents and other family members doing. They learn to pray by watching others fold their arms and bow their heads before a meal. The language of prayer is readily absorbed when children are young and they learn to pray by hearing others pray. They learn that family prayer is a time when all the family kneels together. They listen to hear their own names, and they learn that Heavenly Father cares for them just as their family members do. A small child delights to find that there is a special time each night before she goes to sleep when mother or father kneel with her alone to talk to Heavenly Father and review her day. She feels loved and cherished when she kneels next to a parent with a warm arm around her shoulder.

Before long a child wants to give voice to his own thoughts in the pattern that he has learned by the side of his parent. As the child grows he is taught in family home evening and Primary that prayers can be said anytime, anywhere. A foundation of prayer, established when a child is young, prepares him to go to a loving Heavenly Father for comfort when disappointment, loneliness, sadness, and hurt inevitably enter his experience.

Parents also play an important role in helping a child recognize that personal prayers are answered. Parents can talk with the child about the ways her previous prayers have been answered. They can help her identify blessings that have come in direct response to her seeking. Then, when a child is faced with difficult temptations and problems in later years, she is fortified by the knowledge that Heavenly Father has heard and answered her prayers in the past. And she is more inclined to ask for help, protection, and knowledge when confronting challenges in her teens.

Scripture Study

Research on the development of the brain helps us understand how and when a child learns. From birth, the brain continues to exhibit dramatic changes, making connections that can be important for later experience. These developments can be facilitated during the early years by warm and nurturing parent–child relationships. Mutually enjoyable activities appropriate to the child's age and maturity level that are not overly stimulating can go far in fostering brain development. Although there is no solid scientific evidence indicating that children who miss out on these types of experiences will never catch up,[7] language and literacy development flourishes during the early years[8] and can be facilitated by parents' reading to their children.[9]

Reading and discussing stories and principles from the scriptures are among the parent–child activities that can contribute to the child's brain development and at the same time nurture his spiritual development. Many parents can attest to the spiritual feelings and sacred experiences that accompany the reading of scriptures with their children. As children learn patterns of scriptural language, they develop a vocabulary to describe their own spiritual feelings and experiences. They discover that God speaks to them through the scriptures and that there are answers to their personal questions and problems in the instructions and counsel found there.

As parents assess the use of the scriptures in their home, they might answer these questions: Do our children see their parents privately reading and studying the scriptures? When questions arise in our family, do we look in the scriptures for direction and answers?

Planning Regular Family Home Evenings

Mothers and fathers should regularly counsel together about helping each child develop a personal testimony of Jesus Christ. One couple has this meeting on Sunday evening in preparation for Monday night's activities. They review with each other what they have observed in the family and the concerns they have for each child. Together they prayerfully consider how to address children's present challenges. They plan family home evening lessons or activities that address specific concerns by teaching relevant gospel principles. Helping children understand how to use gospel principles to find solutions to their challenges is a way of "fitting the armor"[10] on each child at home (see Ephesians 6:11). When parents seek the guidance of the Holy Ghost in planning and preparing family home evening lessons and activities, they are preparing the soil for planting the seeds of testimony.

Helping Children Feel the Spirit[11]

Personal and family prayer, scripture study, and family home evening are all settings where parents can help children feel and recognize the Spirit. It is also important to create other opportunities within the sacred family circle to talk about our observations, experiences, and feelings. When children talk about school, Church activities, and social interactions, parents can help them see how the Spirit might have been present to prompt, teach, comfort, or strengthen them. In thus speaking of the children's inward experiences, parents can increase the children's sensitivity to the Spirit and nurture their personal religious experiences.

One family creates an opportunity for sharing personal experiences each week after their Sunday meal. To keep the family from dispersing, a few family members clear the dishes while the rest of the family remain at the table. Each person then shares a time during the week when he or she felt the Spirit. As the parents listen to the children tell of their experiences, they can make comments that help their children recognize and identify feelings of the Spirit. The children look forward to this simple but meaningful activity. Sharing such experiences draws the family closer to each other and to Heavenly Father. Every week this discussion reinforces each child's identity as a son or daughter of God who is loved, watched over, and remembered by Him. When family members share their experiences, the Spirit confirms in their hearts the truths of testimony that they speak.

NURTURING RELIGIOSITY IN TEENS

Many parents have had the experience of helping a child learn to ride a bike. In a similar pattern, parents can assist teens to develop a personal testimony. For example, a parent begins by holding the bike upright as the child tries to pedal and steer. Loving parents comfort the child when she falls, as surely she will in learning to ride. But neither the child nor the parents would be content with mom or dad forever jogging along, holding up the bike. Parents must reduce their support, so that the child becomes self-sufficient to experience the joy of riding a bike. Similarly, parents teach, love, and support their teen as she seeks her own testimony, which will enable her to stand firm in a wicked world. There are a growing number of social science studies documenting the role of parents in the religiosity of their teenaged children.[12]

The activities used to foster spiritual feelings in young children should be continued with teenagers. As teens mature into young adults, parents shift to them more responsibility for developing spiritually. Teens become responsible for their personal prayer and scripture reading. They have the opportunity to choose the right in activities independent of their parents. These and similar opportunities that they initiate themselves will bring the Spirit into their lives.

Teach the Gospel

Too many parents are content to leave gospel training to Sunday School teachers, priesthood and Young Women advisers, sacrament meeting speakers, and seminary teachers. These parents fail to realize that the loving bond parents and teenagers share has the potential to enhance not only learning of gospel principles, but also their application. Elder A. Theodore Tuttle challenged parents to assess "how much of the gospel would your children know, if all they knew is what they had been taught at home?"[13] He then encouraged parents to take seriously their responsibility to teach the gospel to their children.

Family home evening is an excellent time to teach the gospel in an organized manner, but daily life experiences offer opportunities to demonstrate gospel principles and their application. Teens encounter myriad challenges each day at school or with their friends. Discussing these situations together allows parents to explain how righteous principles provide guidance for daily life. Another method is for parents to discuss their own challenges. For example, a BYU student reported that his dad would ask family members during their evening meal to help him deal with "the problem of the day." They would discuss a Christlike way for the father to react to an event at his office. Years later, the young man realized that his dad may not have always needed the children's help. Rather, he used "the problem of the day" to teach gospel principles and how they can guide our daily lives. Parents should seek opportunities to teach the gospel, to apply its principles, and to bear testimony.

Be Good Examples

Elder Jeffrey R. Holland wisely counseled parents to make sure their children see them living and loving the gospel. He asked, "Do our children know that we love the scriptures? Do they see us reading them and marking them and clinging to them in daily life? Have our children ever opened a closed door and found us on our knees in prayer?"[14] We are not suggesting that parents engage in ostentatious public displays of religious behavior, but parents can let their children see them living the gospel throughout the day.

Teenagers are lightning-quick to spot hypocrisy in their parents—and the consequences can be devastating. Parents simply cannot teach a principle and then disregard it in their own behavior. Teens are quick to note that what is important to parents is demonstrated in how they live. Of course parents will make mistakes, but they must not try to hide their sins behind a cloak of righteousness. In making an honest effort to live the gospel, parents influence their children to internalize gospel principles.

Encourage Personal Prayer

The most important activity in helping teenagers to internalize gospel principles, gain a testimony, and develop personal spirituality is personal prayer. Some teenagers believe that with all the family and mealtime prayers offered in their home, they may skip their personal prayer. What a mistake! Parents should emphasize that youth must talk one-on-one with their Heavenly Father if they desire to feel His Spirit daily. Regular personal prayer, combined with regular family prayer, becomes doubly powerful.

President Ezra Taft Benson promised the youth of the Church: "If you will earnestly seek guidance from your Heavenly Father, morning and evening, you will be given the strength to shun any temptation."[15] Latter-day Saint youth who consistently petition the Lord have significantly lower levels of inappropriate behavior, including sexual immorality and drug and alcohol use.[16] "Pray always," the Lord instructed the Prophet Joseph Smith, "that you may conquer Satan" (D&C 10:5). Parents need to teach both by personal example and by explicit counsel that personal prayer is one of the most important protections against temptation.

Provide Opportunities for Spiritual Experiences

In order for teenagers to develop their own testimonies, they need to feel the Spirit in their lives. Parents can provide youth with opportunities for spiritual experiences but cannot provide the actual experiences. These come from the Lord, according to His timing and when teens are ready. The influence of the Spirit cannot be manipulated, but parents may hope that it will be manifest at times and in places to which they have lovingly guided their children. Teens themselves can facilitate the Spirit in their lives by approaching religious activities with a humble and teachable attitude. On appropriate occasions, youth may fast to petition the Father for spiritual awakenings.

A father of teenagers complained to his wife about the Young Women leaders' failure to provide activities designed for spiritual development or service. His wife replied, "Why do we have to wait for the Young Women? Why don't we do spiritual activities as a family?" Parents can and should sponsor family activities that foster spiritual experiences. Trips to the temple grounds, baptisms for the dead, singing hymns around the piano, fasting for a sick family member, service to a neighbor, attendance at general conference, and many other activities can expose teenagers to spiritual feelings.

Parents should encourage their teenaged children to seek a testimony of gospel truths and principles. This may be as simple as encouraging teens to ask in their personal prayers whether verses the family read in the Book of Mormon are true. Again, parents cannot control the timing of spiritual witnesses, but they may trust the Lord's promise: "If ye will not harden your hearts, and ask me in faith, believing that ye shall receive, with diligence in keeping my commandments, surely these things shall be made known unto you" (1 Nephi 15:11).

HOPE

There are times when a parent's efforts seem to have been in vain, when a son or daughter abandons the Church and chooses a worldly lifestyle. The gospel offers great hope to parents that wayward youth will some day find their way back into activity in the kingdom.[17] Parents should remember that there is help from beyond the veil in leading their children to the tree of life (see chapter 26). President Hinckley summarized this promise of hope: "Rear your children in love, in the nurture and admonition of the Lord. Take care of your little ones, welcome them into your homes, and nurture and love them with all of your hearts. They may do, in the years that come, some things you would not want them to do, but be patient, be patient. . . . You have not failed as long as you have tried. Never forget that."[18] Even though children have married and have families of their own, parents and grandparents must keep at it; that is, continue to love and encourage them.

Raising righteous children is a work in progress. At all phases of children's development, parents can find formal and informal opportunities to demonstrate how gospel principles apply to daily life. Young children can be helped to develop a spiritual vocabulary and to recognize the love of the Savior. Older children can be encouraged to share spiritual experiences and to study scriptures and pray meaningfully on their own. A loving, peaceful atmosphere in the home will help family members of all ages feel the influence of the Spirit. Private religiosity, nurtured in the home, provides a foundation from which children may resist temptation as they grow in testimony and commitment to the gospel of Jesus Christ.

ABOUT THE AUTHORS

Bruce A. Chadwick is a professor of sociology at Brigham Young University and has published numerous books and articles. He is a past recipient of the Karl G. Maeser Distinguished Research Award at BYU and holds the Maeser Professorship in General Education. He and his wife, Carolyn, are the parents of three sons and grandparents of seven.

Susan L. Warner has a B.S. from Brigham Young University and has taught elementary school. She and her husband, C. Terry Warner, are the parents of ten children and grandparents of twenty-seven. She served on the Primary General Board and in the Primary General Presidency (1994–1999).

ADDITIONAL READING

R. Wayne and Leslee S. Boss (2003), *Arming Your Children with the Gospel: Creating Opportunities for Spiritual Experiences* (Salt Lake City: Deseret Book).

Brent L. Top and Bruce A. Chadwick (1999, March), Helping teens stay strong, *Ensign, 29*(3), 27–34.

Brent L. Top and Bruce A. Chadwick (2004), *10 Secrets Wise Parents Know* (Salt Lake City: Deseret Book).

NOTES

1. Gordon B. Hinckley (1997), *Teachings of Gordon B. Hinckley* (Salt Lake City: Deseret Book), 648.

2. R. N. Ostling (2005, February 24), Most teens believe in God, poll finds, but knowledge is lacking; LDS tops in practicing faith, *Deseret Morning News*, AO2. See also the volume documenting results of the research: C. Smith with M. L. Denton (2005), *Soul Searching: The Religious and Spiritual Lives of American Teenagers* (Oxford University Press).

3. B. A. Chadwick and B. L. Top (1993), Religiosity and delinquency among LDS adolescents, *Journal for the Scientific Study of Religion, 32*(1), 51–67; B. L. Top and B. A. Chadwick (1998), Raising righteous children in a wicked world, *BYU Magazine, 52*(2), 40–51; B. L. Top and B. A. Chadwick (2003), Protecting purity, *BYU Magazine, 57*(3), 46–54.

4. William Wordsworth (1807), *Ode: Intimations of immortality*, 5.64–65.

5. Excerpts from recent addresses of President Gordon B. Hinckley (1997, July), *Ensign, 27*(7), 74.

6. L. Okagaki, K. A. Hammond, and L. Seamon (1999), Socialization of religious beliefs, *Journal of Applied Developmental Psychology, 20*(2), 273–294.

7. J. T. Bruer (1999), *The Myth of the First Three Years: A New Understanding of Early Brain Development and Lifelong Learning* (New York: Free Press); H. R. Shaffer (2000), The early experience assumption: Past, present, and future, *International Journal of Behavioral Development, 24*(1), 5–14.

8. R. A. Thompson and C. A. Nelson (2001), Developmental science and the media: Early brain development, *American Psychologist, 56*(1), 5–15.

9. B. Hart and T. R. Risley (1995), *Meaningful Differences in the Everyday Experience of Young American Children* (Baltimore: Paul H. Brookes).

10. See Boyd K. Packer (1995, May), The shield of faith, *Ensign, 25*(5), 8.

11. See C. T. Warner and S. L. Warner (1994), Helping children hear the still, small voice, *Ensign, 24*(3), 19–22.

12. C. Smith (2003), Religious participation and parental moral expectations and supervision of American youth, *Reviews of Religious Research, 44*(4), 414–424; C. Smith and P. Kim (2003), Family religious involvement and the quality of family relationships for early adolescents, *Research Report of the National Study of Youth and Religion, Number 4*; L. Okagaki and C. Bevis (1999), Transmission of religious values: Relations between parents' and daughters' beliefs, *The Journal of Genetic Psychology, 160*(3), 303–318.

13. A. Theodore Tuttle (1979, October), Therefore I was taught, in Conference Report, 28.

14. Jeffrey R. Holland (2003, May), A prayer for the children, *Ensign, 33*(5), 87.

15. Ezra Taft Benson (1977), A message to the rising generation, *Ensign, 7*(11), 32.

16. B. L. Top and B. A. Chadwick (1998), Raising righteous children in a wicked world, *Brigham Young Magazine, 52*(2), 40–51.

17. James E. Faust (2003, May), Dear are the sheep that have wandered, *Ensign, 33*(5), 61–62, 67–68.

18. Hinckley (1997), 422.

CHAPTER 30

FAMILY WORSHIP IN CHRISTIAN, JEWISH, AND MUSLIM HOMES

LOREN D. MARKS AND DAVID C. DOLLAHITE

We must never forget that we live in a world of great diversity. The people of the earth are
all our Father's children and are of many and varied religious persuasions. We must cultivate tolerance
and appreciation and respect one another. We have differences of doctrine. This need not bring
about animosity or any kind of holier-than-thou attitude.[1]
—President Gordon B. Hinckley

Latter-day Saint scholars have highlighted important similarities between the beliefs of other faiths and Latter-day Saint doctrine on the family as articulated in the proclamation on the family.[2] This chapter builds on that work by showing some ways that our brothers and sisters of other faiths strive to live their religions in their homes.

LDS families are joined by many families of other faiths in the effort to live a God-centered family life while surrounded by a secular, individualistic society and challenges of contemporary culture that are often hostile to the sacred ideals of home and family.[3] Our faith offers a wealth of wisdom and guidance, but we can also learn from our friends and neighbors as we better understand their efforts to live their faith in their families. Learning about how our friends of other faiths strive to live and worship can provide ideas and motivation for our own families. This chapter presents a variety of examples drawn from our experience of interviewing highly religious families in their homes.

A BRIEF OVERVIEW OF RELIGION AND FAMILIES

Religious faith is a measurable influence in American families. Husbands and wives who are actively involved in the same faith are significantly less likely to divorce than other couples and tend to report higher levels of marital satisfaction and quality, although research tells us little about why this is the case.[4] Additionally, religious fathers tend to be more involved and have higher quality relationships with their children than other fathers, but again research offers few explanations.[5] Given the applied "helping and healing" focus of this volume, we draw upon in-depth interviews that we have conducted with over one hundred Christian, Jewish, LDS, and Muslim families from around the United States. These families illuminate why and how faith influences marriages and families.

In this chapter, we present portions of interviews that show how a variety of families strive to translate faith into sacred, home-based practices. Specifically, we will address family scripture study, sacred family ritual, and family prayer.

HEARING THE WORD TOGETHER: FAMILY SCRIPTURE STUDY

For several of the families we interviewed, family scripture study was a meaningful religious practice. One of the more striking and long-term examples of studying the word together was offered by a Jehovah's Witness family.

> *Jennifer*[6] (Mother): When the kids were younger, . . . our family study was reading through the Bible.

Each kid read out loud through the entire Bible. It took about three years. . . . We used all different Bible translations.

Mark (Father): And . . . we discussed it.

Jennifer: And then when Nick did it, then Erica started doing it. . . . And we did it as a whole family. So the whole family, we have listened [to] both of our kids read the Bible out loud from beginning to end.

Note how Mark and Jennifer added their own variation of studying a sacred text by comparing various translations and discussing the texts with their children as they read.

A Muslim mother, Asalah, similarly explained her family's approach to studying sacred texts together:

[After] saying prayers together as an entire family, most evenings . . . we read from the religious books [the Qur'an and teachings of Mohammed] and talk about Islam and the values, which in your daily life you can sometimes forget [It serves as] a reminder to everyone again [and it] is done as a family.

For many Jewish families, the most poignant family scripture reading or recitation takes place as part of sacred rituals, such as the Passover Seder, where the Lord's sparing of the children of Israel and their liberation from slavery is revisited. A Jewish mother, Rachel, related:

A Seder is telling a story. . . . You tell the story and you remember. . . . Mostly, at our family we take turns reading through the *Haggadah,* [then] we say [scripture-based] blessings together.

For Jasmine, a Methodist teen, and her family, Christmas sparked a family scripture study that in many ways parallels Rachel's family's reading of the *Haggadah:*

[There is a] ritualistic nature of the things that kind of bring us together, like every Christmas, before I get to open any presents, we always read the Christmas story; and it's not because we don't know the Christmas story. We can all recite it from memory . . . but it's just being together and reliving that story every year. And it's not even necessarily [just] the religious aspect of it. I think it's just because we're all together . . . and we can appreciate each other in that way.

Elise, an LDS mother, reflected on the value of scripture study in her family:

One of the most important [sacred practices] for me is [reading] scripture verses. . . . Each night we gather together and we study from the scriptures, and each

child who can read [will] take turns reading verses from the scriptures and when the kids don't understand something they'll stop us . . . and it's a wonderful opportunity for us every day to teach them a little bit more, and to find out what they know. We never cease to be surprised at how much they are already picking up and how much they understand. And doing that every day is something that I hope will continue to instill . . . what we believe.

In families where scripture study is important, an underlying theme is that what is taking place is bigger than the book. It is a time for motivation, discussion, learning, and worship; but perhaps above all, it is a time for hearing the sacred word together.

FINDING MEANING IN A HURRY-UP WORLD: SACRED FAMILY RITUALS

Although scripture study was important to some families, other families mentioned rituals that held sacred meaning for them. The focus, however, is the unifying and coming together of the family. A Muslim father, Ibrahim, explained:

In addition to prayer and scripture, . . . we cherish the month of Ramadan, 'cause we do so many things together as a family. We wake up in the middle of the night. We sit together, we eat together, we pray together. . . . It's a very, very good experience for us. . . . The month of Ramadan has been prescribed to us where every Muslim is supposed to . . . fast from dawn to sunset So what we do is we get up early, very early in the morning [and] . . . we have a meal together, and then after the meal, we read Qur'an, our scripture. And after we do that, it's time for prayer. We pray together. . . . [I]n the evening during breaking of the fast, again, the same thing happens as during the morning. We all come together as a family, and we eat together and we thank God together, we pray together, [then] we break the fast. . . . So the whole month of Ramadan is a . . . unique experience. We do a lot less of the worldly things and a lot more of godly things than we normally do. . . . And especially when you do those kinds of things together every day . . . it tends to bring people together and it strengthens our beliefs and family.

Brian, a Catholic father, recalled a memorable enactment of their Christmas ritual that held particular meaning for him many years later:

Mary initiated this [Christmas ritual that's] taken on a life of its own. The kids come down [and], before they rip open the presents, kneel down and say [a] prayer and thank Him for Jesus being born and saving us, and we'll pray [as a family]. And one [Christmas] morning I was . . . grumbling about getting up early. [I said], "Don't get up until it's light." . . . But no, they'd got up early. [But] the kids were just waiting; they were all kneeling down and waiting right under the tree. I'm like, "Wow!" And they did it . . . on their own.

Several Jewish mothers explained how the Jewish ritual of welcoming in the Sabbath (on Friday evening) with the lighting of the candles and the Sabbath meal has added depth to their family relationships. One mother, Sarah, said:

When we take the time out, when we light the candles Friday night, that's a time that I feel really close to [my children]. . . . I always say a prayer of thanks for my children. . . . When we sit across the table from each other, my husband and I, and the Sabbath candles are lit, and I see the kids, there is something I get from that that is so deep. It's just a feeling that [all is right in the world,] . . . it doesn't matter what else is going on. Right in that circle . . . it's awe-inspiring.

Daniel, Sarah's husband, summarized, "I don't know that the Sabbath meal is a religious experience for most people, but for me it's the heart of religion." Aida, an LDS mother, similarly discussed and described her family's sacred weekly practice of family home evening:

We have [family home evening] every week. We sing a hymn and we have a prayer. My husband or I will prepare a short lesson or teaching from the gospel and then our daughter Maria will retell the lesson in her words. This has tremendous impact on her [and on her younger sister].

Sacred family rituals varied in frequency, including the daily, weekly, and yearly examples offered here. However, a central commonality was that whether through discussion of beliefs, Sabbath meals, or special annual traditions, families felt that sacred rituals brought them together and connected them more closely with each other and with God.

CONNECTING WITH THE CREATOR: THE POWER OF FAMILY PRAYER

Family scripture study or sacred family rituals like those just mentioned were central to many families we interviewed. Even so, neither scripture study nor sacred ritual compared with family prayer in terms of reported prevalence or importance. For many of the families we interviewed, prayer was a time to feel a sacred closeness to God, as well as a connection with each other. Khalid, a Muslim father, described evening prayer with his children:

We have five prayers a day [in Islam] . . . and once a day I get the kids to pray with me, in the evening time. . . . This is the central activity for our daily life. We start our day in the morning with a prayer, we pray all during the day, and there's one in the evening time. . . . [At prayer time, we say to] the kids, "Let's quit the TV, and pray." . . . [So at] the end of the day I have my kids around me and [I] thank God that they are healthy and safe.

Bobby, a Jehovah's Witness teen, talked about the important effort he felt his father had made to pray daily with him and his sisters:

It tends to be difficult to get us together. Prayer has always been something that's central. [I] mean, we'll be here before school in the morning, before my sisters hop on the bus. . . . Dad still gets up early and prays with them, and prays with me, before I go off [to school].

An Episcopalian teen, Ben, similarly recalled:

When I was younger . . . we used to pray before I went to bed. And I always liked that, not necessarily because we were praying, but [because it was] just time when I was with my mom and with my dad just talking and being thankful. [Also,] every time we eat at home, we always sing . . . a prayer. And that's pretty cool [too].

As in Ben's family, the family dinner table was a sacred place for many of the families we interviewed. A Methodist father named Patrick told us:

[One meaningful practice is] grace before meals, and trying to have a moment in every day where we gather together as a family and start it with a blessing. It's really important to us. We have very busy children, and we're very busy. . . . So it is really a priority to us to keep that family time there and to start that family time with a blessing.

Mary, a Catholic mother, explained a dinner prayer ritual her family has:

A couple of years ago I started to take the Advent prayer and fold it up and put it under somebody's plate, [someone] different all the time. And it was one of those traditions I didn't remember the next year, but the kids [did]. And now, even our youngest . . . around Thanksgivingtime, she starts looking under plates before supper. And sometimes I forget how those very simple, but important things . . . connect faith and family.

Like Mary's, Muslim families seemed to take delight in seeing the practice of prayer passed on to their children. A Muslim named Aisha said:

> The baby even, she'll try to come in . . . and she'll try to put the prayer mats down. . . . It's a wonderful thing to see that this is something that they want, that you don't force them. . . . That's really the beauty of Islam.

Although family prayer was often meaningful for the families we interviewed, the above narratives do not capture the effort and hassle frequently involved. There were several references to resistance (e.g., "dragging kids," "pulling teeth") and failure to have anything resembling a spiritual experience (e.g., "just going through the motions"). The question arises, "Why is it worth it?" Responses to this question varied. For one Jewish father named Seth, a key answer to this question was that prayer was a legacy that linked the family not only with God and each other, but also with their late grandfather, who had inspired their family prayers through his faithful example:

> I looked at my grandfather and he was religious, I mean *very* religious. . . . He was one of the few people where I really did see a passion and a love for his God and his religion. When he prayed, you could see him well up with emotion, it really meant something to him. It broke through to a whole other level. . . . Now we say prayers before dinner every night, and that was actually a decision we made when my grandfather died. One of the memories I had of him was that he wouldn't sit down to a meal without saying a blessing, "Thanks for this bread." When he died, we decided, "Let's do that before each meal, that way we'll remember him for eternity," and it really stuck. We started doing it right away and we have been doing it every day since his passing.

For Jessica, a nondenominational Christian mother, an important purpose for prayer was that it offered a faith-based approach to conflict resolution in marriage:

> We have disagreements . . . and faith is a source of help. We can pray about things together and [I believe] the Lord can help us work things out. Sometimes one person has to give in and accept the other person's point of view [but] it helps to be able to pray about things. The Lord, He's the best counselor

you could ever have. I don't know how marriages can work without God. I'm sure that there are people who are so compatible that they can still get along, but [our faith] has been really helpful [for us].

Tina, an LDS mother, offered an additional reason for prayer in her family:

> [We want] to make sure [God] is a part of what we do all the time. . . . He's real. He's always there for you. He's part of who you are as a family. . . . We say family prayer and say thanks for the opportunities we've had, please help us to grow together, please help us. . . . I mean I just said family prayer tonight and . . . it's just, I want him to be there as a partner with us, and our family, and our [marriage] relationship.

Prayer seemed to influence persons ranging from Muslim toddlers to a Jewish grandfather. Family prayer was a way to express thanks, establish sacred traditions, connect with other family members, resolve conflict, and invite God to bless and be "part of who you are as a family."

WHAT CAN WE LEARN FROM THESE FAMILIES AND THEIR FAITHS?

The Prophet Joseph Smith emphasized, "We should gather up all the good and true principles in the world, and treasure them up, or we shall not come out true 'Mormons.'"[7] Certainly, some families implement and apply certain truths more effectively than others, and the various families we interviewed provide inspiring examples of how individuals and families can unite to draw closer to each other and to the God of us all.

In this chapter we have discussed scripture study, sacred family rituals (e.g., family home evening), and family prayer. Those familiar with Latter-day Saint culture might refer to these activities as familiar "Sunday School answers." Even so, these three important issues were mentioned repeatedly by these 107 families—not all LDS—who have avoided divorce and maintained a high level of commitment to their God, their spouses, and their children over a period that exceeds 3,000 total years of experience in marriage and family life.[8] We repeat the words of a Catholic mother named Mary, who reflected, "Sometimes I forget how those very simple but important things . . . connect faith and family." Perhaps we all do. Indeed, the words of Doctrine and Covenants 123:14–15 might be profitably applied to the practices of family scripture study, sacred family rituals, and family prayer: "These [things] should then be attended to with great earnestness. Let no man count them as small things; for there is much which lieth in futurity, . . . which depends upon these things."

ABOUT THE AUTHORS

Loren D. Marks, Ph.D., is an assistant professor of family, child, and consumer sciences at Louisiana State University, where he teaches and conducts research on faith and family life. He and his wife, Sandra (Martindale) Marks, have three boisterous but lovable children.

David C. Dollahite, Ph.D., is a professor of family life and associate director for outreach education in the School of Family Life at Brigham Young University, where he teaches and conducts research on faith and family life. He and his wife, Mary, have seven terrific kids.

ADDITIONAL READING

Henry B. Eyring (2001), The family; in *Eternal Marriage* (Salt Lake City: Intellectual Reserve), 104–110. (ldscatalog.org item no. 35311000.)

Gordon B. Hinckley (2001), Cornerstones for a happy home; in *Eternal Marriage* (Salt Lake City: Intellectual Reserve), 127–130. (ldscatalog.org item no. 35311000.)

Truman G. Madsen, Keith Lawrence, and Shawn L. Christiansen (2000), The centrality of family across world faiths; in David C. Dollahite, ed., *Strengthening Our Families: An In-Depth Look at the Proclamation on the Family* (Salt Lake City: Bookcraft), 370–381.

Spencer J. Palmer and Roger R. Keller (1993), *Religions of the World: A Latter-day Saint View* (Provo: Brigham Young University Press). (ldscatalog.org item no. 32508000.)

NOTES

1. Gordon B. Hinckley (1999, May), The work moves forward, *Ensign, 29*(5), 4.

2. First Presidency and Council of Twelve Apostles (1995, November), The family: A proclamation to the world, *Ensign, 25*(11), 102.

3. T. G. Madsen, K. Lawrence, and S. L. Christiansen (2000), The centrality of family across world faiths; in D. C. Dollahite, ed., *Strengthening Our Families: An In-Depth Look at the Proclamation on the Family* (Salt Lake City: Bookcraft), 370–381.

4. D. C. Dollahite, L. D. Marks, and M. Goodman (2004), Religiosity and families: Relational and spiritual linkages in a diverse and dynamic cultural context; in M. J. Coleman and L. H. Ganong, eds., *The Handbook of Contemporary Families: Considering the Past, Contemplating the Future* (Thousand Oaks, CA: Sage), 411–431.

5. V. King (2003), The influence of religion on fathers' relationships with their children, *Journal of Marriage and Family, 65,* 382–395; see also, W. B. Wilcox (2002), Religion, convention, and parental involvement, *Journal of Marriage and Family, 64,* 780–792.

6. All names have been changed.

7. T. G. Madsen (1989), *Joseph Smith the Prophet* (Salt Lake City: Bookcraft), 48. See diary of William Holmes Walker, p. 13.

8. The typical couple in our study had been married for more than fifteen years. Therefore, if one takes the wife's marital experience (15 years) and adds this to the husband's marital experience (15 years) and multiplies this experience by the number of families interviewed (107), we have the following equation: (15 years +15 years) x 107 = 3,210 years of marital experience. We gratefully acknowledge research support from Brigham Young University and Louisiana State University in conducting this study.

CHAPTER 31

PROTECTING AND BALANCING FAMILY TIME

STEPHEN F. DUNCAN AND PATTI FREEMAN

We must be better Latter-day Saints. We must be more neighborly. We cannot live a
cloistered existence in this world. We are a part of the whole of humanity. [1]
—President Gordon B. Hinckley

We live in an increasingly fast-paced society, with many demands placed on the time, energy, and means of families. Because of its benefits to both families and society, active involvement in community institutions has been strongly encouraged by Church leaders[2] and family scholars.[3] Research shows that extracurricular involvement benefits children and is associated with positive outcomes such as higher levels of academic achievement, higher standardized test scores, positive religious development, stronger sense of self, prosocial development, and lower levels of problem behavior.[4] Such involvement appears to benefit children of all ages, with benefits during younger years extending into young adulthood.[5] Thus, involvement in extracurricular activities is more than just child's play. It helps young people discover and share talents, develop character and competence, and often provides the added benefit of close relationships with caring, principled adults outside the home. This helps parents do their jobs more effectively.

Notwithstanding the benefits, for many families, these activities can lead to overscheduled children, overbooked and "over-taxied" adults, and underconnected families, seriously eroding the amount of time families spend together.[6] These outside activities, as helpful as they may be, may make it difficult for families to give highest priority to family activities, as counseled by the First Presidency.[7] Some family schol-

ars, noting the serious decline in the amount of time families spend together, are calling on us to "take back" our families from so many external pursuits.[8] Are there ways of finding harmony and synergy among these activities, including well-planned, wholesome recreational activities, to minimize stresses and detriments to families while preserving the benefits of community and extracurricular involvement?

HOW COMMUNITY CONTEXTS INFLUENCE FAMILIES

Families do not live in isolation. They are embedded in a lively community web of social institutions that influence how families allocate time, space, and energy—mental and physical. Many transactions between families and community systems occur each day, ranging from simple visits to the grocery store to parent-teacher conferences. Much of this community connectedness is health producing, both for families and the communities in which they live. For example, research demonstrates that strong families are closely involved with schools, churches, and local organizations that promote the well-being of individuals and communities.[9] In addition, three national studies found that a family's social connectedness is associated with less problem behavior among their children.[10]

Organizations originating outside the family can

help parents accomplish the sacred work of parenting, extending and supplementing their work. Elder Alexander B. Morrison observed:

As families nurture and strengthen individuals, so also communities nurture families, providing a setting within which they can become and stay strong. Families are both protected and assisted by strong communities. Strong community organizations, including schools, churches, councils, service clubs, and so on, supplement and complement the efforts of parents, not only making their work easier but often making the difference between success and failure. Without denying in any way the paramount importance of the family, the old African proverb that it takes a village to raise a child has much truth in it. . . . It is much easier to raise and maintain strong families if the community is strong.[11]

The reverse is also true. Elder Morrison added, "It is much more difficult for families to succeed if the community is divided, uncaring, rundown, crime-ridden, and unsafe."[12]

The most influential community contexts for each family will be those with whom the family interacts on the most frequent basis and that likely have the most direct and indirect effects on how they conduct family life. These include the school, the workplace, the church, and associations with friends and neighbors.

The school. For those who choose public schools as the agency for their children's education, schools become the primary partner with parents in affecting the academic success of children. The school schedule affects how families organize their time and attention (e.g., time for rising and retiring, the scheduling of after-school activities, and the timing of family recreation, particularly summer vacations).

Parental involvement in school activity of children is associated with positive educational outcomes.[13] According to research conducted by the U.S. Department of Education: "Three factors over which parents exercise authority—student absenteeism, variety of reading materials in the home, and excessive television watching—explain nearly 90 percent of the difference in eighth-grade mathematics test scores across 37 states."[14]

As beneficial as school activities are, school-related extracurricular events and heavy homework loads can encroach on sacred family time. President Gordon B. Hinckley, speaking of family home evening, observed "a growing tendency to schedule other events on Monday night. We respectfully request that our public school officials and others let us have this one evening a week to carry forward this important and traditional program."[15]

The workplace. Workplace contexts have the built-in potential to either conflict or harmonize with family life, resulting in either negative or positive spillover from work to family. For example, an important meeting at work may be scheduled on the same night as your child's school play. On the other hand, your work environment may be "family friendly" enough to allow you the flexibility to attend family events. In addition, parents can become so psychologically absorbed in or stressed by their employment that they withdraw from active family involvement or have difficulty enjoying family time even when they do take it.

Unfortunately, time with family is often the first area of compromise, since evidence of our neglect of family isn't always immediately apparent, but a neglected project is. Such neglect, however, negatively affects child and adolescent psychological well-being.[16] Elder James E. Faust, while serving as a member of the Quorum of the Twelve, emphasized the importance of family time: "Time together is precious time—time needed to talk, to listen, to encourage, and to show how to do things. Less time together can result in loneliness, which may produce inner feelings of being unsupported, untreasured, and inadequate."[17]

Friends and neighbors. Strong families are not only connected to community institutions, but are connected to friends and neighbors on whom they depend for emotional and practical support.[18] Support of one's social network, including close friends, has a buffering effect during "crucibles" families may face, such as illness, death of loved ones, disability, and other circumstances.[19]

As children mature, the influence of peer networks becomes increasingly important. Research on Latter-day Saint youth shows that, next to parents, peers and friends provide the strongest influence either to follow or not follow gospel standards.[20] Thus parents are wise to encourage their children to select friends whose values support those reflected in their home.

The Church. If families are open to the Church's influence, they can be strengthened by having a strong spiritual and religious orientation. Families derive meaning from their religious beliefs in connection with religious organizations. Strongly religious families believe in something greater than themselves and agree more frequently about what is right and wrong. Religious commitment and religious practices such as prayer help protect youth from a variety of negative behaviors, such as substance use and sexual activity.[21] Researchers have found that religiosity, independent of peer influences, has a significant effect on youth behavior.[22] (Chapter 29 offers ways to nurture religious commitment in children.)

USING WHOLESOME RECREATIONAL ACTIVITIES TO STRENGTHEN FAMILIES

The proclamation on the family states, "Successful marriages and families are established . . . on principles of . . . wholesome recreational activities."[23] President Ezra Taft Benson emphasized the power of these simple activities in the lives of children: "Build traditions of family vacations and trips and outings. These memories will never be forgotten by your children."[24] Brigham Young said, "Life is best enjoyed when time periods are evenly divided between labour, sleep and recreation. . . . All people should spend one-third of their time in recreation which is rebuilding, voluntary activity—never idleness."[25] Likewise, President Benson counseled, "Successful families do things together: family projects, work, vacations, recreation, and reunions."[26] How can we use wholesome recreational activities to strengthen our families?

A family leisure researcher concluded that there is a direct relationship between how families spend their leisure time and their families' cohesion and adaptability, two important indicators of family strength.[27] *Cohesion* refers to the level of emotional closeness in a family, while *adaptability* refers to a family's ability to handle everyday and unexpected stresses and strains.

Two basic categories or patterns of family leisure can be used to meet families' goals of cohesion and adaptability. One type of activity called "core" activities consists of informal activities such as watching television and videos together, playing board games, shooting baskets in the driveway, doing activities in the yard, gardening, or having a water fight while washing the car. The other kind, or "balance" family activities, are more formal and require more planning, such as family vacations, most outdoor recreation such as fishing or boating, special events, and trips to a theme park, sporting event, or bowling alley. Families who have an appropriate balance of both core and balance activities are likely to function better than those who participate in extremely high or low amounts in either category.

According to Susan Shaw, a noted family leisure researcher, high-quality family leisure experiences usually don't just happen, they are planned and are purposeful.[28] Knowing the need for both core and balance activities, families should counsel together in order to use leisure time not only for entertainment but for the purpose of strengthening their family.

FAMILY-FRIENDLY IDEAS

Recognizing that being purposeful in family extracurricular and leisure activities requires some planning, here are some suggestions for involvement in community, extracurricular, and leisure activities that can benefit the family. The ideas demonstrate ways that families can solve "time together" dilemmas while maintaining family involvement in activities outside the home.

Limit participation in extracurricular activities. Consider how much time is spent in extracurricular activities by both parents and children and how such involvement may actually distract from family time together. Be choosy in your involvement. How do you solve this dilemma when there is so much to choose from? Many families have chosen to limit family members to two outside activities at a time (say, music lessons and playing on the soccer team) to free up family together time. If children want to add another activity, they need to subtract one from the existing group. They can rotate activities in and out depending on the season of the year, but not add to the list without subtracting something.

Get involved in community issues as a family. Church leaders encourage the Saints to be involved in strengthening communities. As a family, one possibility is to attend a community meeting such as a school board meeting or community planning board meeting to combine participation in community affairs with time together.

One family was troubled when they learned that many teachers at the local high school showed R-rated movies in their classes. The father was also a bishop and had heard many of his youth complain about it. The parents contacted the school superintendent, who investigated, discovered the seriousness of the problem, and agreed to discuss it at the next school board meeting. The school board received a letter from the parents outlining their concerns and proposed changes. Public discussion during and subsequent to the meeting led to important modifications in school policy regarding the use of movies.

Establish strong school connections. Find ways to stay involved in your child's education from kindergarten through graduation. Possibilities could include sharing a talent in the classroom, attending parent-teacher conferences, supporting school events, and participating in school policymaking. Make your home a learning place. Show your children you love to learn. Children can benefit by writing down their academic goals and by discussing and agreeing on rules about homework.

One family has a "homework table" in their basement where family members congregate to do their homework. Family togetherness is fostered as school assignments are met Older children often help tutor the younger ones. Another family has a "homework before friends" rule, unless homework involves inviting friends over for group study.

Neighbor to neighbor. Strengthen ties you have with neighbors by being neighborly. Find ways to be helpful, such as shoveling snow, installing fencing, or looking after children. Maybe participate together as neighbors in a humanitarian project. Get permission from authorities to close off a section of the neighborhood and have a block party. Two sons and their father aided a neighbor who had recently suffered a heart attack; they split all the wood the neighbor's family would need for the winter. As they reached out to a neighbor, they built bonds among themselves.

Address an issue. Parents can teach their children to become involved citizens. Consider looking for a local, state, or national issue in the news that you can favor or oppose. Perhaps write a letter on one issue to a city commissioner, school board member, a legislator, or even the President. Let each family member, even younger ones, compose his or her own original letter. When the replies arrive, discuss them as a family and place the letters in a scrapbook. During a citizenship lesson for family home evening, an 11-year-old girl wrote a letter to a senator, criticizing his position on abortion, with only minor edits from her parents. She thought nothing would come of it. How surprised she was to receive a letter from the senator, thanking her for her letter and explaining more clearly his position.

Other ideas include visiting the city council, a county commissioner's meeting, traffic court, the state legislature, or the U.S. Congress as a family. This provides opportunities for watching regulations and laws being made. Interview a lawmaker. Learn the process

for making policies and laws. These and other Scouting merit badge requirements can be used to experience community processes together. (See chapter 40 for additional suggestions.)

Restrict television viewing and use it to strengthen your family. Recognize the impact of the TV on your perception of free time for family leisure. Maybe consider turning the TV off during designated days or times and choose an activity that the family can do together. During the 2004 Summer Olympics, one family took a break from watching the events together and held their own mini-summer Olympics in their backyard, running races, doing long jumps, and other events.

Instead of watching television alone, schedule TV or movie time together. Talk about what you watch. One son and father watched a TV episode where a teen girl was pressured by friends to steal doughnuts from the faculty lounge at school and smoke in the girls' restroom. The young girl successfully resisted and won friends at the same time. The program provided a context for father and son to talk about standing up for the right even when it's not popular.

Keep it simple. Don't underestimate the value of simple activities that all or part of the family can do together. Taking time to design a building block city with the preschooler, taking a walk on a Sunday afternoon, taking a plate of cookies to a new neighbor, or using time in the car to spark meaningful conversations are all simple. Many of these informal core activities can come about spontaneously and have lasting value in the lives of family members.

Serve in the community as a family. Volunteering together as a family at a community facility or event (e.g., food bank, library, adopt-a-highway, prison, homeless shelter, fund-raisers, road races) provides some excellent service possibilities. Many families enjoy planning a vacation that is not only fun but incorporates volunteering to help others in need. During Christmas holidays, one family volunteered to stock shelves at the community food pantry. Another family visited the Church humanitarian center and packaged hygiene kits.

Unite and recreate, keeping the whole family together. Consider seeing movies together as a whole family rather than dividing up to see different shows. Try making a train on a water slide rather than merely having the individualized experience. Maybe take a vacation in the car so family members can balance opportunities to interact, play games, and share stories. Spending time together using your library and visiting local museums, city and state parks, and recreation centers are other valuable experiences that can become central to your family's core leisure activities.

Take back Monday night. Consider reclaiming Monday evenings as a time to be together to hold family home evening. While some Latter-day Saint families have responded to increased time pressures from school and work by holding family home evening on Sundays, Church leaders continue to reemphasize Monday evenings. President Hinckley stated, "We urge, in the strongest terms possible, that fathers and mothers regard most seriously this opportunity and challenge to make of Monday evening a time sacred to the family."[29] How can we follow this counsel?

Deciding that Monday evening is nonnegotiable time is one approach. One family was surprised when they found that schools in their predominantly Latter-day Saint community were regularly holding rehearsals and various so-called "family" activities on Monday night. This family told the teachers in charge that their young people would not be available for rehearsals or activities on Monday evening. The rehearsals and activities went on without these students without reprisal, but also without change of schedule. However, soon after President Hinckley's talk, the school rescheduled these activities.

Another family established Monday evening, all evening, as a time when everyone in the family is expected to be at home. They all participate in the formal family home evening lesson. Conducting responsibility is rotated, giving all the children the opportunity to fulfill Duty to God, Faith in God, or Personal Progress program goals. After the lesson and treats, family members may share an informal activity together. When excessive homework necessitates extra sensitivity to overstressed teens preparing for college, the family activity portion is moved to Saturday afternoon. Every family can find their own ways to make Monday evenings at home a traditional pattern in their lives.

Conclusion

As parents prayerfully seek ways to improve family life, encourage their children's talents and worthy involvement, and find ways to follow counsel, solutions can be found that will strengthen family and limit the pull of other worthy, but less important activities. Wise families will continue to find ways to

creatively integrate and harmonize a variety of activities to ensure that family strengthening retains its critical and primary focus.

ABOUT THE AUTHORS

Stephen F. Duncan, Ph.D., is a professor in the School of Family Life at Brigham Young University. He and his wife, Barbara, have five children.

Patti Freeman, Ph.D., is an associate professor in the Department of Recreation Management and Youth Leadership at Brigham Young University and is the coordinator of the youth and family recreation graduate program. She and her husband, Eric Andersen, have twin boys.

ADDITIONAL READING

William J. Doherty and Barbara Z. Carlson (2002), *Putting Family First: Successful Strategies for Reclaiming Family Life in a Hurry-up World* (New York: Henry Holt).
Putting Family First, http://www.puttingfamilyfirst.org
Take Back Your Time, http://www.timeday.org
B. L. Top (2005, April), A balanced life, *Ensign, 35*(4), 26–29.
Mark A. Widmer, et al. (2000), Wholesome family recreation; in David C. Dollahite, ed., *Strengthening Our Families: An In-Depth Look at the Proclamation on the Family* (Salt Lake City: Bookcraft), 190–201.

NOTES

1. Gordon B. Hinckley (1997, November), Look to the future, *Ensign, 27*(11), 67.
2. L. Tom Perry (1980, November), For whatsoever a man soweth, that shall he reap, *Ensign, 10*(11), 7; Robert D. Hales (1999, May), Strengthening families: Our sacred duty, *Ensign, 29*(5), 32.
3. M. Krysan, K. A. Moore, and N. Zill (1990), Identifying successful families: An overview of constructs and selected measures (Washington, D.C.: Child Trends).
4. M. Kerestes, J. Youniss, and E. Metz (2004), Longitudinal patterns of religious perspective and civic integration, *Applied Developmental Science, 8*(1), 39–46; National Institute of Child Health and Human Development Early Child Care Research Network (2004), Are child developmental outcomes related to before- and after-school care arrangements? Results from the NICHD study of early child care, *Child Development, 75*(1), 280–295; P. S. Braverman (2003), Self concept, life satisfaction, and academic performance in adolescents, *Dissertation Abstracts International, 64* (1-A), 66; J. Zaff, K. A. Moore, A. R. Papillo, and S. Williams (2003), Implications of extracurricular activity participation during adolescence on positive outcomes, *Journal of Adolescent Research, 18*(6), 599–630.
5. Zaff, Moore, Papillo, and Williams (2003).
6. W. J. Doherty and B. Z. Carlson (2002), *Putting Family First: Successful Strategies for Reclaiming Family Life in a Hurry-up World* (New York: Henry Holt).
7. First Presidency letter, 11 February 1999, cited in Robert D. Hales (1999), 33.
8. Doherty and Carlson (2002).

9. Krysan, et al. (1990).

10. B. V. Brown (1993), Family functioning and adolescent behavior problems: An analysis of the National Survey of Families and Households (Washington, D.C.: Child Trends); B. W. Sugland (1993), The effect of family strengths on youth behavior: An analysis of the national survey of children (Washington, D.C.: Child Trends); D. R. Morrison and D. Glei (1993), Assessing family strengths in the National Longitudinal Survey of Youth—Child Supplement, (Washington, D.C.: Child Trends).

11. Alexander B. Morrison (1999, February), A caring community: Goodness in action, *Ensign, 29*(2), 13.

12. Ibid., 15.

13. U.S. Department of Education (1994, September), *Strong Families, Strong Schools: Building Community Partnerships for Learning* (Washington, D.C.: U.S. Department of Education).

14. Ibid., iii.

15. Gordon B. Hinckley (2002, November), To men of the priesthood, *Ensign, 32*(11), 56.

16. A. C. Crouter and M. F. Bumpus (2001), Linking parents' work stress to children's and adolescents' psychological adjustment, *Current Directions in Psychological Science, 10,* 156–159.

17. James E. Faust (1983, May), Enriching family life, *Ensign, 13*(5), 40.

18. Krysan, et al. (1990).

19. J. S. Carroll, W. D. Robinson, E. S. Marshall, L. C. Callister, S. F. Olsen, T. T. Dyches, and B. Mandleco (2001), The family crucibles of illness, disability, death, and other losses; in D. C. Dollahite, ed., *Strengthening Our Families: An In-Depth Look at the Proclamation on the Family* (Salt Lake City: Bookcraft), 278–292.

20. B. L. Top and B. A. Chadwick (1998), *Rearing Righteous Youth of Zion* (Salt Lake City: Deseret Book).

21. M. D. Resnick, P. S. Bearman, R. W. Blum, K. E. Bauman, K. M. Harris, J. Jones, J. Tabor, et al. (1997), Protecting adolescents from harm: Findings from the National Longitudinal Study on Adolescent Health, *The Journal of the American Medical Association, 278,* 823–832.

22. Top and Chadwick (1998).

23. First Presidency and Council of Twelve Apostles (1995, November), The family: A proclamation to the world, *Ensign, 25*(11), 102.

24. Ezra Taft Benson (1987, November), To the fathers in Israel, *Ensign, 17*(11), 50.

25. S. Y. Gates and L. D. Widtsoe (1930), *The Life Story of Brigham Young* (New York: Macmillan), 251.

26. Ezra Taft Benson (1993, August), Counsel to the Saints, *Ensign, 23*(8), 2.

27. R. Zabriskie and B. McCormick (2001), The influences of family leisure patterns on perceptions of family functioning, *Family Relations, 50,* 281–289.

28. S. M. Shaw and D. Dawson (2001), Purposive leisure: Examining parental discourses on family activities, *Leisure Sciences, 23,* 217–231.

29. Hinckley (2002), 56.

CURBING CONTENTIOUS TENDENCIES

JULIE H. HAUPT

One Sunday morning we ran into a snag. Having refused the Saturday night bath offered by the baby-sitter, my beautiful 8-year-old was obstinately refusing her bath again. I tried to reason with her, but I was becoming increasingly agitated. Her older sister noticed the situation and came to my aid. With a hug, some patience, and a few gentle words, she enticed her younger sister to the bathroom. Over the course of nearly an hour, she lovingly filled the tub with water, watched over her sister as she played, washed her hair, chose appropriate Sunday attire, and did her hair as elegantly as a 10-year-old could. In those sweet moments, I saw Isaiah's prophecy fulfilled once again in our home: "and a little child shall lead them" (Isaiah 11:6). My daughters had reminded me that morning of the gospel principles that govern relationships and curb contentious tendencies.

As a youth, I carefully considered King Benjamin's directive: "And ye will not suffer your children that they . . . fight and quarrel one with another, and serve the devil, who is the master of sin, . . . but ye will teach them to walk in the ways of truth and soberness; ye will teach them to love one another, and to serve one another" (Mosiah 4:14–15). I long pondered this statement, wondering how I would deal with contentious tendencies in my home. In our homes, while our children are yet at tender ages, we have a unique opportunity to plant the seeds of love, respect, compassion, and forgiveness. These proclamation principles[1] ultimately combine to produce the love and unselfishness that is the Lord's answer to contention. As indicated in King Benjamin's address, the Lord asks us not to merely object to contention, but to actively teach our children a better way (see Mosiah 4:15).

Satan would have us believe that fighting and quarreling in the home is unavoidable, natural, and generally harmless. While the process of teaching our children to be loving and unselfish will be ongoing, and difficult moments will crop up, contention is not unavoidable. In describing the golden era of the Nephite civilization, Mormon wrote: "There was no contention in the land, because of the love of God which did dwell in the hearts of the people" (4 Nephi 1:15). It is natural for pre-baptismal children to be egocentric (that is, it is difficult for them to perceive or consider differing viewpoints in ways that older children and adults do);[2] however, they are also by nature "submissive, meek, humble, patient, full of love" and exemplars for the putting off of the natural man (see Mosiah 3:19). Finally, contention is not harmless, for it has the power to dismiss the Spirit from the home and is a common starting point for the unraveling of unity. Also, sibling aggression can increase the risk of aggression in other social contexts and create a sense of individual inadequacy and incompetence.[3] Elder Henry B. Eyring stated that it is Satan "who plants the seeds of discord in human hearts in the hope that we might be divided and separate."[4] The following experiences provide suggestions for fostering love at home.

"A soft answer turneth away wrath" (Proverbs 15:1). After several harried mornings in a row helping children get ready for school, I prayed in desperation for help. My answer was unexpected: "You are the problem." Assuming that my dawdling young ones just needed more focus on the business at hand, I had not noticed how my own emotional tone was disturbing their ability to focus and leading to an increased incidence of discord. When this tone was replaced by a few extra minutes of individual attention and many offers to help, our troubles dissipated. Of utmost importance in teaching our children to love and be unselfish is our own example. Indeed, if we are to exemplify the high standard that we would ask of them, we must learn to bridle our tongues, keep our emotions in check, and respond with a soft, patient voice. One author noted: "Controlling anger doesn't mean ignoring the emotion. Instead, it involves first

calming oneself so the emotion can be used to achieve constructive ends, such as solving problems and restoring emotional connections with others."[5]

Coming upon an argument in progress among siblings, it is easy to match the emotional tone and enter the fray. In doing so, we can be tempted to spiral with increasing intensity, with the accompanying risks of losing control, losing the Spirit, and losing our ability to reason clearly. If we can initially withhold judgment, remain neutral, and state clear expectations (rather than accusations) in kindly tones, we can often turn the unhappy encounter into a conversation focused on solutions. This approach models an appropriate problem-solving pattern for our children, who first observe and eventually begin to imitate.

"That ye love one another; as I have loved you" (John 13:34). Given the diversity of personalities with which each family is blessed, differences are bound to arise. This variety of strengths and weaknesses can divide or strengthen a family. Parents can work intentionally to engender appreciation for individual family members and their unique strengths. Statements that directly or indirectly compare one child to another should be avoided, even when the intention is to encourage good behavior. A better method is to verbally point out the positive in each child, frequently note the child's progress (even in small steps), and use words of encouragement when a child's early attempts fail.

Help children respect one another by taking time to listen to each side of a dispute. One mother designated a special spoon as the "talking spoon." When her young children were talking over one another in an attempt to clarify their own positions, the spoon designated whose turn it was to speak. The children learned to wait and listen until the talking spoon was in their hands.

Parents who are available and aware of their children's activities can anticipate trouble when strong emotions begin to take hold. They can respond quickly and respectfully in resolving small problems rather than allowing these situations to reach verbally or physically harmful proportions.

"But ye will teach them to . . . serve one another" (Mosiah 4:15). Learning to serve begins in small incremental steps. Service can be encouraged by the wise, loving parent who learns to use the smallest denominator possible in meeting the needs of the family. If the 5-year-old can tie the toddler's shoe, then he is frequently invited to do so. If the 8-year-old can read stories to the preschooler, she is liberally praised for

her 10-minute sacrifice. Inviting children often to serve one another and taking notice of those efforts resulted in the following statement by the previously mentioned 8-year-old: "If Daddy gets sick, I'm going to be his helper. I can bring him water and do whatever he needs."

"Observe all things whatsoever I have commanded you" (Matthew 28:20). Obedience to the commandments of God entitles us to the blessings of the Spirit in our home. Spiritual routines, such as family home evening, scripture study, family prayer and family councils, will build spiritual reserves that can be called upon in times of temptation and frustration. Often I have called spontaneous family councils when the spirit in our home begins to deteriorate. These councils allow our family to discuss problems, share concerns, and plan a new strategy. I had not fully appreciated the power of this family pattern until one day while dealing with a child's tantrum in my husband's absence. Quite unintentionally, my daughter kicked me in the mouth, compressing newly installed braces against an already distressed lip. As the blood began to flow, I tearfully called out, "Family council!" The other children came running, saw my distress, and began to hug me and provide words of comfort that I had often given to them. One child also provided support for the newly sobered child who had caused the injury. I was grateful for children who had learned over time how to comfort, serve, and provide encouragement.

Often I have reflected upon the Savior's perfect pattern for human relationships: "No power or influence can or ought to be maintained . . . , only by persuasion, by long-suffering, by gentleness and meekness, and by love unfeigned; by kindness, and pure knowledge" (D&C 121:41–42). When my impatience engendered increased agitation and thoughts of negative consequences on that Sunday morning, my daughter reminded me of the way in which the Lord's doctrine (see 3 Nephi 11:29–30) allows hard feelings to melt and warm memories to begin. As we pray diligently for the Lord to change our hearts and our natures, we can be inspired to sow the daily seeds of love and kindness that will bind our families together. In our humble pleadings for help, the Spirit will surely "teach [us] all things, and bring all things to [our] remembrance" (John 14:26). While our vigilant efforts to plant these seeds will require time and patience, we will find contention being shaken at its roots and new examples of love and service sprouting up, promising a growing sense of unity in our homes and families.

ABOUT THE AUTHOR

Julie H. Haupt is a part-time faculty member in Marriage, Family, and Human Development at Brigham Young University and the managing editor of this volume. She and her husband have three children.

ADDITIONAL READING

Stephen F. Duncan (2004, Spring), Family focus: Subduing the spirit of contention, *BYU Magazine,* 48–49.

Henry B. Eyring (1998, May), That we may be one, *Ensign, 28*(5), 66–68.

NOTES

1. First Presidency and Council of Twelve Apostles (1995, November), The family: A proclamation to the world, *Ensign, 25*(11), 102. The nine principles listed in paragraph 7 are "faith, prayer, repentance, forgiveness, respect, love, compassion, work, and wholesome recreational activities."

2. See J. Gnepp and J. Klayman (1992), Recognition of uncertainty in emotional inferences: Reasoning about emotionally equivocal situations, *Developmental Psychology, 28,* 145–158.

3. J. Dunn (2002), Sibling relationships; in P. K. Smith and C. H. Hart, eds., *Blackwell Handbook of Childhood Social Development* (Oxford: Blackwell), 223–237.

4. Henry B. Eyring (1998, May), That we may be one, *Ensign, 28*(5), 66.

5. S. F. Duncan (2004, Spring), Family focus: Subduing the spirit of contention, *BYU Magazine,* 48.

ESSAY G 2

LAUGHTER—THE PERFECT FAMILY MEDICINE

GARY K. PALMER

One Sunday in sacrament meeting, my 4-year-old son was making a major disturbance. He had a bad case of the wiggles. After several minutes of trying to calm him down, I abruptly picked him up, tucked him under my arm like a sack of potatoes, and marched down the aisle to the nearest exit. With his head bobbing, my son looked up at me and said, "Hey Dad, where we goin'?" He had no idea he was in trouble. My anger was defused instantly. Through the years, I have learned that one's ability to laugh at everyday family calamities keeps life in perspective.

If we learn to laugh and play more with our families, we will not only feel better but so will they. Studies show that humor and laughter help people live longer, happier lives, be more creative and productive, and have more energy with less physical discomfort.[1] Laughter reduces stress, fear, intimidation, embarrassment, and anger.[2] Laughter has extraordinary healing power.[3] When a person laughs, blood pressure decreases, heart rate and respiration increase, the body releases endorphins, and depression declines.[4] After the laughter subsides, that good feeling has a lasting effect, even until the next day.[5] There aren't many medicines that will do that. It's like "a spoonful of sugar helps the medicine go down."[6]

Children laugh four hundred times a day, while adults laugh fifteen.[7] Why the gap? Did we lose something? Have we forgotten the way we used to be? Why is it that children seem to cope with life's oddities better than adults? Perhaps it's simply because they laugh. As we grow older, we get way too serious. Watch children play. They don't need things. Everything is fun to them. They're spontaneous. It's only when we become adults that we start to get boring. Humor is the way we see things; it's the way we think; it's an attitude, not an event. Perhaps the key lies in becoming more childlike.

When I return home from work each day, I conscientiously think about what I'm going to say the moment I enter the door. I usually shout some outlandish remark to get my family's attention. A typical loud entrance for me is "Hello, all you lucky people; I'm home!" Visitors to our home may have a few questions, but for the rest of the family, they know that it's just Dad. I find that it helps set the tone for a fun home and instantly puts everyone at ease. I'm sure that it occasionally embarrasses my children, but the good outweighs the bad. It also helps me to make the change mentally from work to home. I do not want to come home tired, ornery, or dull. Most of us can make ourselves be our best at work. Doesn't our family deserve at least that? "A little craziness once in a while perpetuates sanity."[8]

I think laughter is more important than a family vacation, because it's always available, it can happen every day, and it's free. Happy families are those living together every day and making the most of it. Laughter is like getting away without going away. It gives you a break. "A merry heart doeth good like a medicine" (Proverbs 17:22).

Play and laughter are closely related. Does this mean we should play with our kids? Absolutely. Laugh more, play more, swing out of familiar places. Play puts everyone on an equal footing, first, by the nature of play itself and second, because you can change the rules to fit the situation. Play brings families together. It is a subtle tool for interaction and talk. It builds confidence. Inhibitions are minimized while our real personalities emerge.

Years ago, I saw through my kitchen window a man playing with his children in a park sandpile. He was right down there on his hands and knees in the sand, building a small imaginary town with streets, cars, trucks, trees, houses, stores, and schools. I watched him push a wooden block like a bulldozer, pretending to build a road and including the sound effects. I remember thinking, now there is an example of a great dad who knows how to play with his children. He was seen by every passing car. Was he embarrassed or ruffled? Not at all. Such enthusiasm for play encourages growth in children, relieves stress, and builds friendships among family members. Laughter and play become a calming influence in the home environment.

Laughter also improves communication and builds relationships because everyone laughs in the same language. Your children will remember your humor much longer than they will the things you buy them. Children are more receptive when they are having fun. Laughter helps us remember. Humor creates an unforgettable learning experience because it makes us laugh and feel good. And we remember what we feel.

Early in our marriage, my wife said, "Let's make our home more fun for our kids than any other place our children could be." Laughter and play are the best ingredients for that. We cannot duplicate Disneyland, nor should we. A family firmly rooted in love and wholesome recreation is far better than any commercial entertainment. In other words, home should be a fun place to hang out with family and friends.

Laughter builds friendships. Families that laugh together are inseparable. Laughter makes us approachable. It removes barriers. If you want to talk to your children about a serious matter, try a lighter approach. Family meetings and interviews would be far more effective if play, laughter, and refreshments were added.

Humor, used with sensitivity, can unite spouses. While serving as a bishop of a singles ward, one engaged couple asked me if they could have their wedding reception at our house. I quickly replied, "Of course you can." I forgot to tell my wife. When my wife received the wedding invitation a few days before the big event, she happened to notice that the reception location was the same address as our house. When I got home from work, she asked me if I had forgotten to tell her something important. After considerable thought, I said, "Not that I can think of." "Are we having a wedding reception at our house?" she asked. I knew I was in trouble. "Oooooh, you mean *that* reception," I replied. I quickly volunteered to prepare our home for the reception—under her able direction, of course. We laughed together and went to work.

Humor disarms most family tension. Once while talking to my children about some family issues, one of our teenagers crouched over, wrinkled up his nose, and with a tone of disapproval, blurted out some outlandish comment about what I had said. I found myself taken aback by his behavior when suddenly I crouched over, wrinkled up my nose, and with a tone of disapproval, blurted out some outlandish reply, perfectly mimicking his behavior. The entire family burst into laughter and the tension vanished.

Of course humor will vary depending on our personalities. While some people seem to have a natural sense of humor, most of us must work to develop it. Some of us will tell stories, while others will share jokes and one-liners. Still others will use art, humorous clippings, and e-mails. For some of us, smiling will be our humor. Smiling is something we can all do, and smiling leads to laughter. As Sister Marjorie Pay Hinckley said: "The only way to get through life is to laugh your way through it. You either have to laugh or cry. I prefer to laugh. Crying gives me a headache."[9]

There are some cautions with humor. Family members must be careful not to offend, intimidate, or embarrass. We should laugh with rather than at someone. No one likes to be teased. No one likes to be the brunt of a joke. By learning to laugh at ourselves, we usually become safe from offending. As Sister Hinckley said about her husband, "He didn't take himself very seriously and was often the first to poke fun at his own quirks."[10]

Most family calamities, given enough time, provide humor. Like the time I took my misbehaving 2-year-old son, Tyler, home from sacrament meeting. After turning on cartoons for my son, I fell asleep. I didn't wake up when my 5-year-old showed up to take Tyler back to Primary. Trouble was, Tyler had stripped down to moon boots and training pants and picked up his popgun rifle on the way out the door. Sacrament meeting was not quite out, and the bishop was pouring out his soul to the congregation. It was whisper quiet when Tyler, wearing moon boots and training pants, marched up the aisle with his rifle, took aim, and shot the bishop. It woke up the congregation. Of course, it wasn't funny then. Time helps humor emerge gradually. The trick is finding the humor in the event now.

So does this mean we go around laughing all the time? Of course not. But we certainly could laugh a lot more.

ABOUT THE AUTHOR

Gary K. Palmer, Ed.D., is a teaching professor in the Department

of Recreation Management and Youth Leadership at BYU. He and his wife, Shirley, have six children and fourteen grandchildren.

ADDITIONAL READING

Jack Canfield (1998), *Chicken Soup for the Kid's Soul: 101 Stories of Courage, Hope and Laughter* (Deerfield Beach, FL: Health Communications).

George D. Durrant (1976), *Love at Home, Starring Father* (Salt Lake City: Bookcraft).

Bruce Lansky (1999), *Laugh Twice and Call Me in the Morning* (Minnetonka, MN: Meadowbrook Press).

NOTES

1. R. Robinson, D. N. Khansari, A. J. Murgo, and R. E. Faith (1990), How laughter affects your health: Effects of stress on the immune system, *Immunology Today, 11*(5), 170–175.

2. W. S. Hamerslough (1995, June 22), Laughter and wellness; paper presented to the Southwest District of AAHPERD; Kahuku, Hawaii.

3. N. Cousins (1979), *Anatomy of an Illness* (New York: W. W. Norton).

4. L. S. Berk (1989), Neuroendocrine and stress hormone changes during mirthful laughter, *The American Journal of the Medical Sciences, 296*(7), 390–396.

5. K. S. Peterson (1996, October 31), A chuckle a day does indeed help keep ills at bay, *USA Today,* 10D; Berk (1989), 390–396.

6. R. M. Sherman and R. B. Sherman (1964), Just a spoonful of sugar helps the medicine go down, *Mary Poppins* (Walt Disney Pictures).

7. Robinson (1990).

8. Anonymous.

9. Quoted in Virginia H. Pearce, ed. (1999), *Glimpses into the Life and Heart of Marjorie Pay Hinckley* (Salt Lake City: Deseret Book), 107.

10. Sheri L. Dew (1996), *Go Forward with Faith: The Biography of Gordon B. Hinckley* (Salt Lake City: Deseret Book), 106.

ESSAY   G 3

ENRICHING FAMILY LIFE THROUGH MUSIC

ANDREW H. DABCZYNSKI AND SUSAN HOBSON KENNEY

As president of Brigham Young University, Jeffrey R. Holland recounted the story of a boy who left southern Utah to travel to the East many years ago. At age 18, he had never traveled much and certainly never by train. The prospect of changing trains in Chicago with a one-night layover terrified him despite his sister's carefully written directions. Bidding him good-bye, his father put the name of a Chicago bishop into his shirt pocket To allay the boy's concerns, the bishop's wife in Chicago invited him to join with her family and others at a park the morning of his layover. "We will make sure you get safely on your way," she promised. But when the boy arrived at the park, he couldn't find the group. President Holland said:

> Suddenly he felt more alone and overwhelmed than he had at any moment in his life. As the tears welled up in his eyes, . . . he thought he heard something hauntingly familiar in the distance. . . . Then he started to smile. . . .
>
> *Though hard to you this journey may appear,*
> *Grace shall be as your day.*
>
> The sounds were crystal clear, and he was weeping newer, different tears. For there over a little rise huddled around a few picnic tables and bundles of food were the bishop and his wife and their children and most of the families of that little ward. The date: July 24, 1934. The sound: a slightly off-key a cappella rendition of lines that even a boy from Southern Utah could recognize. . . . Knowing that it was about time for the boy to arrive, the ward [had decided] to sing a verse or two of "Come, Come, Ye Saints"[1] to let him know their location.[2]

Music can be a powerful influence in our lives and in our homes and families. It can anchor our souls, soothe our fears, calm our hearts, inspire our thoughts, motivate us to act for good, heal our hearts, strengthen traditions, and bind us together. When family members come together through musical experiences, music can lift and heal in remarkable ways.

Music has the capacity to unify and motivate (imagine the crowd response to a national anthem or a college fight song), to define a social occasion (think of the purpose of a bridal march or "Hail to the Chief"), and to enhance play, recreation, or work (as with children's jump rope songs, music played at a dance, and FM-radio "office music"). Music also serves to assist in teaching (singing A-B-Cs or Primary songs), to send a message (as in radio and TV jingles or protest songs of the 1960s), to express feelings that cannot be captured in words alone (reflected in most classical music compositions and country music love songs), and of course, to enhance religious worship (as with sacrament hymns, chants of the Catholic mass, or the trance music of various African shaman-based religions). When music is central to family life, not only do individual family members benefit, but the family as a unit finds harmony and often a closeness to the Spirit than can be found in no other way. How can families place music at the heart of family life?

Enriching family life with musical experiences can be done in a variety of ways and most often begins with the parents. If parents love music and show that love

by listening to quality music, by singing, or by playing instruments, the children will love it too, merely because children tend to love what their parents love. Parents need not feel self-conscious about their own voices, for children benefit not from a perfect musical performance but rather from hearing songs presented in a loving, caring way. A child's early experiences with a singing parent will remain for a lifetime. Lullabies, children's songs, Primary songs, hymns, and other songs loved by the parents will enrich the child's world and provide a foundation for musical growth.

This love of music also can be communicated by playing a variety of recorded music including classics, jazz, show tunes, folk music, and music from a variety of cultures. As the family provides a rich musical environment during the early years of life, the child will develop a sense of rhythm, pitch, and musical forms. The child's musical tastes are often shaped at an early age, though they may change over the life course. At a young age, the child likes best what he has heard the most. Well-known musicians—such as Wolfgang Amadeus Mozart; the "Father of Bluegrass," Bill Monroe; and the "Queen of Soul," Aretha Franklin—developed their love of music because of the influence of parents and musical families.

If as a parent you don't play an instrument, consider inviting the neighbors or extended family into the home occasionally to perform together or to sing a few hymns. Invite the extended family or friends over for periodic "music nights." Sing together, or play instruments together, or share your favorite recorded music. When neighbors gather together, the community is strengthened through music making.

If your children take music lessons, there is no substitute for being with them when they are with the teacher and when they practice. It is not easy to always give that kind of time, but the children who continue lessons until they master an instrument usually have a parent who practices with them frequently. Encourage your children to join school choirs and instrumental groups, and then be sure to share in these musical experiences as a family.

When traveling, plan to sing together in the car. Consider keeping track of how many songs you know, then be prepared to add a new song at the end of the list. Let each family member take a turn choosing their favorite song. In Wales, a small country known for its singing, families used to sing whenever they went anywhere together. The streets were filled with families singing. Often, a whole neighborhood sang when they went to church, or to school, or to community meetings. Cars have changed the sounds in the streets, but the singing tradition still goes on for the Welsh, inside their homes and cars.

Visit libraries and bookstores for copies of folk songs and recorded music. Search for folk songs that represent the ancestry of your family. Find recorded music that represents a variety of music types and styles, including classical, jazz, ethnic music, and popular music through the ages. The Internet has many resources in music. A search might lead you to folk songs, opera for children, interactive music games, and recorded music of all types.

Watch for public performances and attend them together as a family. Many communities offer "concerts in the park" where children of all ages are welcome. More formal concerts that require quiet behavior and a longer attention span should be attended only by children over age eight. Make it a special event for the older children. Younger ones will look forward to the time when they are old enough to attend.

As children enter adolescence, many prefer to listen to music that may not be as appreciated by the rest of the family. Invite the children to share whatever music they like with the family, explaining why they like it. Parents might help the family explore those elements that are in common with most music throughout the world (such as beat, melody, or harmony). Then together take notice of how these elements appear in Primary songs, folk songs, classical music, and other recorded types of music. By noticing the similarities in music, children learn that many different kinds of music can be powerful.

Perhaps the most important gift that arises from purposeful, family-oriented participation and education in music is the capacity to understand and convey feelings with one another that otherwise may go undetected, underdeveloped, or unexpressed. Developing the capacity to respond appropriately to the emotions captured in a performance of Beethoven's Ninth Symphony, or discovering the ability to participate in the energy found in dancing to folk or rock music, or uncovering sensitivity to the message arising in the quiet performance of a hymn, or developing the skills necessary to perform a musical nuance such that it elicits a smile or a tear from the listener—these may be seen as analogous to training the rational mind, both in adults and children, to recognize the prompting of the Spirit. When these experiences occur on a regular basis within the context of family life, they call us home. The family bond is strengthened and magnified in a manner that is tangible, fulfilling, motivating, and ultimately celestial.

ABOUT THE AUTHORS

Andrew H. Dabczynski, Ph.D., is a professor of music education at BYU. He is internationally recognized as a string orchestra educator, clinician, author, arranger, and composer. He has held a variety of Church leadership positions. Dr. Dabczynski, his wife Diane, and two musical daughters live in Provo, Utah.

Susan Hobson Kenney, MM, is a professor of music at BYU, specializing in music education for children from birth to age eight. She is former National Chair of the Society for General Music and has served on the Primary General Board and the Church Music Committee. Susan Kenney and her husband have two daughters and one grandson.

ADDITIONAL READING

Dallin H. Oaks (1994, November), Worship through music, *Ensign, 24*(11), 9–12.

Boyd K. Packer (1974, January), Inspiring music—Worthy thoughts, *Ensign, 4*(1), 25–28.

Jessica Baron Turner (2004), *Your Musical Child: Inspiring Kids to Play and Sing for Keeps* (Milwaukee: Hal Leonard).

NOTES

1. William Clayton (1985), Come, come, ye Saints, *Hymns* (Salt Lake City: The Church of Jesus Christ of Latter-day Saints), 30.

2. Jeffrey R. Holland (1980, March 18), For times of trouble; BYU Devotional Address; available at http://speeches.byu.edu

ESSAY G4

TEACHING CHILDREN TO SACRIFICE: MIRRORS TO WINDOWS

DUANE E. HIATT

Nothing in the universe is cuter than a baby. Self-absorbed, uninhibited, spontaneous, babies sit in the center of their own universe surrounded by mirrors that reflect their cuteness. They are irresistible to watch. Now let me tell you what is not fun to watch—a 15-year-old with the same outlook and attitude. Helping children turn those mirrors of self-importance, self-concern, and plain selfishness into windows to look out on and respond to the needs of others is a big part of parenting. So how do we do it? I asked our children.

"We just knew that Saturday was for working together at home; then we could play."

"We did it because our older brothers and sisters did. We followed the tradition."

"Fasting was really hard for me when I was little. But I knew that even though Dad was on tour with his music and comedy group, he would be fasting after his show and would be really hungry and thirsty."

"We love to be together, and that sometimes takes sacrificing."

"We never even thought of leaving a Church meeting without helping to put the chairs away."

From these responses and other comments, I gleaned the following principles:

Enjoy our successes. Along the way we get tantalizing glimpses of the people our children will one day be. An esteemed member of the Church and community told me once, "I was feeling down one gray winter morning, but then I drove past your place. I saw in the snow four little dwarfs with a bucket of water in each hand, joking with each other as they climbed up the trail behind your house to your goat barn. I said, 'With children like that, the world has a future.'"

People often told us, "I love to see your children in church sitting quietly with a younger brother or sister on their laps."

My friend Louise Baird calls such moments "parental payoffs." We all get some, not nearly enough

to satisfy our appetite, but sufficient to strengthen us as we push, drag, cajole, and encourage our children up the trail toward adulthood.

Cheer for our children. Honest compliments are easier to come up with when the children's sacrifices fill real needs and not parental make-work projects.

We often told our boys, "Thanks for bringing us this delicious milk. If it weren't for you, we wouldn't have it." The gratitude was particularly true for the members of our family who had allergic reactions to cows' milk but did better on our goats' milk.

We formalized our pouring on the praise with a weekly meeting we named "Brag Time." We still hold it, now including the grandchildren. Brag Time is a family gathering that is dedicated to cheering for ourselves and for each other. It sounds like this:

"I said an article of faith in Primary."

"Yea!"

"Desiree didn't want to go to seminary, but I invited her and she came."

"Yea!"

"I helped clean the patio."

"Yea!"

"Tom helped me learn to tie my shoes!"

"Yea!"

There is only one rule to Brag Time. When someone brags, the rest of us applaud and cheer. No sarcastic comments, no put-downs are allowed in Brag Time. When someone has a brag in which he or she reached out and sacrificed to help someone else, it is time for an extra burst of applause.

"Bend the twig"[1] (see Proverbs 22:6). Probably the earliest interchange our children remember with me happened every night after prayer and before the piggyback ride to their bedrooms. I asked them two questions: "What was your happiest thing today? What did you do to build the Lord's kingdom today?"

"Our Scout troop did stealth cleaning of the widows' yards."

"I let John wear my new shirt."

They each knew this report was due every day—from their earliest lisps until their high school graduation. By then we hoped the tree was inclined. The answers included much repetition, but more than rarely some sincere thinking. Sometimes we struck gold when the happiest thing and the building the kingdom activity were the same.

Build togetherness. Teaching sharing and sacrifice is probably easier if your family is blessed with limited means. But with a little ingenuity even the financially blessed need not be sacrificially impoverished. I know a well-to-do family who takes "service vacations." They hit the road in their motor home, and their only destination is to find people along the way whom they can help and serve. Their children love it.

But as a father it always strengthened my case when I could say such things as, "I had planned to get each of you a Ferrari on your sixteenth birthday so we wouldn't all be sharing the family van, but it looks like that won't quite fit into this month's budget."

With fifteen children in our family, there were a number of things that didn't quite fit into "this month's budget," but I am now told by our grown children that none of those things really mattered. What mattered to them, and still does, was to be together. What might seem to some people a sacrifice of privacy was and is to them a blessing of companionship. They still sacrifice to bring their families from all parts of the country for our annual family conference.

Build traditions. This closeness led to other kinds of sacrifices. Walking through the backyard once, I picked up this snatch of conversation. Danny's friend Cliff said, "Hey, Danny, let's go over to my house and play."

Danny replied, "Great. Hey, Bobby, let's go play at Cliff's place."

Cliff: "Not Bobby, just you and me."

A brief puzzled pause from Danny, and then, "See you later, Cliff. Have fun."

Perhaps Danny sacrificed a good time with a friend by including his younger brother, but it never occurred to him to do otherwise. That's just the way the Hiatt children did things. Invite one; expect some portion of the multitude to tag along. It was their tradition. I admit we planted the seed and nourished it.

Give for the fun of it. This led to such traditions as "no paybacks." When you do something for your brother or sister, if he or she pays you back, verily, you have your reward (see Matthew 6:1–4); if not, you get paid with blessings in heaven and warm feelings here.

Work together. We, like many families, feel that chores and housework should not be paid for. They are work that we all do because we all live in the house and eat the food. When they were small, our children accepted this and even enjoyed working around the house, sometimes for as long as four minutes. After that, it was other rewards like being with Mommy and Daddy; having Dad regale them with one of his signature stand-up comedy, storytelling routines; and knowing that after we all did the work, we would do something even more fun.

Our first six children were boys, and they were getting muscles while the later ones were getting permanent teeth. They needed more challenging and manly work to do. At least their parents thought so. We purchased, over what seemed interminable years, five acres of land on which we could grow animal feed, fruit trees, gardens, and a world-class crop of weeds.

"Dad, I want to get a paper route," Dan said a few weeks before his twelfth birthday. Thus began another tradition, hand-me-down paper routes. A quarter of a century later, Maren, our youngest, entered high school, and following the tradition declared paper-route emeritus status. We also did summer and after-school work. Good training, we thought, but what do we do with the money? My observation is that too much "walking around" money can be detrimental to young people. If they get into big-time recreation habits, costly clothes, car payments, and expensive vacations early, they may have a hard time scaling back later as missionaries, college students, or newlyweds. For these reasons and more—including the opportunity to learn to sacrifice—we decided to pool our resources every month, then determine what each person needed, and provide that. Generally the system worked well for us.

Did our efforts always work? Does the sun shine every day we plan a picnic? Does the stock market always go up right after we invest? This is a real world. We have a drawer full of plans that "coulda, shoulda, woulda" worked but didn't. Others didn't work at first, but later bore fruit. Some we thought withered, but found they grew as the children matured. Now we are seeing them blossoming in the hearts of our grandchildren. Traditions by definition take time to take hold. But gradually, with gentle, loving reinforcement from us as parents, they can strengthen from silken threads to iron rods.

Selfless sacrifice for the good of others because of our love for the Lord qualifies us for the kingdom. Helping our children transform their mirrors of self-absorption into windows of empathy with a view into heaven may be the most treasured inheritance we can give them.

ABOUT THE AUTHOR

Duane E. Hiatt was a Brigham Young University administrator, a writer of "The Spoken Word" for the Mormon Tabernacle Choir, author of the book *Overcoming Personal Loss*, composer of the Primary song "Follow the Prophet," member of The Three Ds music and comedy group, and twice a bishop. He and Diane

Robertson have fifteen children. Following Diane's death he married Sharon Lee Johnson.

NOTE

1. Alexander Pope (1731–35), *Moral Essays*, 1.149; quoted in *The International Thesaurus of Quotations* (1970), R. T. Tripp, comp. (New York: Thomas Y. Crowell), 646. "'Tis education forms the common mind / Just as the twig is bent the tree's inclined."

E s s a y   G 5

Surviving the Death of a Child: It Takes Courage to Believe

John Craig and LouAnn Newell Christensen

Carrie (16) and Sarah (14) Christensen, along with two friends, were killed in a car–train accident on March 3, 1987. Another daughter, Robin (16), died January 31, 1993, of Neisseria meningitidis. In this essay, parents Craig and LouAnn Christensen share their experience in grieving the loss of these children.

LouAnn's Experience

Carrie had naturally curly hair, a contagious laugh, and a happy-go-lucky personality. Sarah, a perfectionist, loved little children and planned someday to become a child psychiatrist. She was with her older sister that tragic evening. I really loved these daughters. How could the Lord need them more than we did?

I wondered, "Why pay your tithing, go to the temple, and try keeping the commandments if you're not going to be blessed?" When I prayed, I felt hopeless. Why ask for comfort when your heart is aching and you know the situation can't be fixed? Why pray for our surviving, struggling teenage children when you're afraid God will take them, too? I was angry at God. These were beautiful teenagers who were taken in their prime. Only a split second and they would have missed hitting the train and they would be here today, laughing about their close call. They would have experienced their junior proms, dates, college,

marriage, and had families of their own. How could a loving God do this to us?

Over the following weeks, I realized I was becoming bitter and full of hatred. I didn't like the ugliness I felt. My behavior was negatively impacting my children and my husband. I was miserable, they were miserable, and our home was not a pleasant place to be. I'll never forget one Sunday during fast and testimony meeting when a friend bore her testimony about the blessings she experienced as a result of having their precious 6-week-old baby pass away. I couldn't believe her words. Through her tears she spoke of the opportunity of having their baby in their home if only for a short time and the blessings this brought her family. She spoke of the love God has for each of us and the fact that He sent His Only Begotten Son to the earth to live and die for us so that one day we could live with Him again. She explained that having the knowledge of one day seeing her daughter again and being able to raise her was reassuring. Her countenance radiated peace and gratitude.

At that moment I realized that in order to find peace, I had to change. I challenged myself to have complete faith and trust in the Lord's ways. I promised God that if ever I was faced with the same reality, I would not become bitter and angry. I vowed to have faith in His omnipotence. I knew that my test was to have faith and know that God's ways are not man's ways.

Nine months after the girls were killed, our daughter Lauren was born to us just one week before Christmas. I cannot begin to express the joy she brought into our family as we struggled to pick up the pieces. Our five remaining teenagers grappled with the concept and finality of death and we tried to move on as best we could. I figured we had paid the highest price a family could pay and that somehow we were exempt from future trauma.

Six years after our daughters were killed, our 16-year-old daughter, Robin, was near death. Within 18 hours of becoming sick with a fever and a headache, she had lapsed into a coma, her brain swelling. We had no idea of the seriousness of the situation until we were in the hospital emergency room with doctors and nurses scurrying around her and urgently discussing the need to take her by ambulance to the University of Utah Medical Center in Salt Lake City. Surely she would pull through this, I believed.

Craig rode with Robin in the ambulance and I followed after making arrangements at home for our other six children. While driving to the hospital, I prayed that Robin's life would be spared. I will never forget the powerful, yet quiet voice that clearly stated, "No."

This wasn't fair! I pleaded with the Lord again and felt the sweet, loving arms of the Savior wrap around me and heard a tender yet firm, "No." After I arrived at the hospital, the doctors told my husband and me there was nothing they could do to save Robin's life.

We were with Robin throughout the night. I was grateful for this time. All five of our sons took turns talking to Robin, holding her hands, and saying their goodbyes. The next morning she was pronounced legally dead. We took her off the respirator several hours later and were there as she took her last breath. A deadly bacterial infection, Neisseria meningitidis, had taken her life.

The chapel was filled with many of Robin's friends the day of her funeral. These teenagers, including our own five sons, were struggling to understand this senseless loss. My brother touched all of us with his words of comfort when he spoke that day. He stated:

> Why try? Why believe in God, or in anything or anyone else? It hurts too much to care; it may even hurt too much to believe. In a very real way, belief and hope take courage. *Great courage.* . . . I believe and I affirm [that] God lives. He knows the beginning from

the end, and everything in between as well. It takes courage to believe.[1]

The day after we buried Robin, Lauren, then five years old, was struck with this same disease. I panicked. As I prayed to the Lord and asked for His help, I felt peace. We had several anxious hours where the doctors weren't sure, but eventually she came through. As I thought about the major loss we had just experienced, and the loss we didn't experience, my brother's words kept echoing through my mind: "It takes courage to believe."

Psalm 31:24 states, "Be of good courage, and he shall strengthen your heart, all ye that hope in the Lord." God knows the beginning and the end; our job is to have faith in His will. President Spencer W. Kimball said:

> Is there not wisdom in [God's] giving us trials that we might rise above them, responsibilities that we might achieve, work to harden our muscles, sorrows to try our souls? Are we not exposed to temptations to test our strength, sickness that we might learn patience, death that we might be immortalized and glorified?
>
> If all the sick for whom we pray were healed, if all the righteous were protected and the wicked destroyed, the whole program of the Father would be annulled and the basic principle of the gospel, free agency, would be ended. No man would have to live by faith.[2]

The scriptures instruct: "Trust in the Lord with all thine heart; and lean not unto thine own understanding" (Proverbs 3:5). I do not know why our daughters were taken. I do not understand why Lauren was allowed to live. I do have firsthand knowledge "that all these things shall give thee experience, and shall be for thy good" (D&C 122:7). I've learned about compassion and empathy for those who grieve. After Robin died, I truly did try hard not to become angry and bitter and to this day, I have a strong testimony that it was Robin's time to leave this earth. I believe that someday I'll understand why. In John 14:27 the Savior states: "Peace I leave with you, my peace I give unto you: not as the world giveth, give I unto you. Let not your heart be troubled, neither let it be afraid."

CRAIG'S EXPERIENCE

For me, the night our two daughters died changed everything. I would never be the same, feel the same, or be completely at ease again. And even more significantly, neither would the rest of my family.

My grief began with outrage. How could God or life be so contemptuous of me? What possible wrong could I have committed that would bring such ruthless destruction to my family? It hit me with a blunt force hard enough that even after eighteen years I still experience an ache that threatens to undo me, to expel me from among the faithful.

Yet I have not yet given in to the demons of discouragement or succumbed to spiritual death—not even when six years later that "awful monster" death (2 Nephi 9:10) came again to my home. This time it was my middle daughter taken in one day from the blush of health to the darkness of the grave. Outrage again temporarily replaced acceptance of the eternal plan. A sense of injustice and victimization took over my consciousness. "Why me?" But this time there was a "Why not me?"

Through yet another siege of overwhelming sadness, way beyond my ability to endure, I remained confused, disoriented, and perpetually dissatisfied with my life, but I didn't and haven't quit. Instead I reach for the Comforter; I pray for peace nightly and I take heart in the promises extended by the Savior of the world. I would like to say that I have found peace, but I only can embrace acceptance so far: acceptance of the Lord's will, and the comfort that my Father in Heaven holds my children in my stead. I cling to the knowledge that God has lovingly assigned each person a time to die (see D&C 42:48). My daughters' time has come and passed.

Some days I recognize that my life has gradually evolved into being a little easier, a little smoother, a little better. I still have dreams that our daughters magically come back, although even in the dreams I know it can't be. I hold as sacred the knowledge of the opportunity to be with them and have them again, but not through magic, or a dream, but rather through the Atonement of Jesus Christ. That is what I hold to. It is part of my iron rod. It stills my soul. It lifts me above the seemingly inconsolable torment of losses and replaces the torment with a vision, sometimes a fleeting vision, of a brighter day, reunion sweet It is enough for me so far.

As it happens, not by chance, I work as a family therapist with many who want to make sense of the loss of their child. I have crossed over the wilderness of grief before them. I know the way, not by sight, but by faith. I can no longer merely have faith that everything will be all right just because I am an active

Latter-day Saint. Rather, it is faith in Christ that is my Liahona that guides me around land mines of doubt and discouragement and fatigue of soul. During the many exchanges of stories and within my efforts as a healer to bring some sort of reconciliation, I have found inspiration from many who walk the same lonesome path that I have traveled these last eighteen years.

Some I have admired for the brilliance of their courage, such as my spouse, LouAnn, who used her darkest moments to create a support group for parents who have lost children, to organize an activist group to examine youth issues, and to form an organization for young unwed mothers. Her salvation from the recesses of the hell of loss came through service and support to others who were experiencing their own suffering. Even in her own low state, she reached out to others to lift them up—and lifted herself up as well.

In summary, to survive and even be strengthened through the death of a child we suggest the following:

Constantly work to strengthen your testimony of the gospel. We strengthen our testimony through going to Church (even though we sometimes don't feel like it), by continually saying our prayers (even though we may feel no one is listening to us), by striving to read the scriptures often (even when, or especially when, we don't want to), and by struggling to live the commandments (even though we often make mistakes). These behaviors build a spiritual resiliency that helps us face severe challenges, such as the death of a child. Through this process we'll gain strength to take each challenge one at a time, consistently striving to do better with every step forward, minute by minute, hour by hour, and day by day.

Reach out to others. Service to others is salve to the wounds of loss. For as the Savior promised, "He that loseth his life for my sake shall find it" (Matthew 10:39).

Have faith in God's plan. By having the courage and faith to believe that God is mindful of us and by trusting in His eternal plan, we are given the strength necessary to survive any trauma, even the death of a child. By understanding His unconditional love for us, we are assured of His care and concern. Putting forth positive words and actions demonstrates our complete faith in Him that brings healing to our souls.

ABOUT THE AUTHORS

John Craig Christensen, Ed.D., has been in private practice as a marriage and family therapist for the past thirty years.

LouAnn Newell Christensen earned her B.A. at Brigham Young University. She is currently the mayor of Brigham City, Utah. She has been involved in numerous volunteer community efforts. She and her husband, John, have nine children, six of whom are living.

ADDITIONAL READING

Merrill J. Bateman (1995, May), The power to heal from within, *Ensign, 25*(5), 13–14.

Robert D. Hales (1998, May), Behold, we count them happy which endure, *Ensign, 28*(5), 75–77.

Neal A. Maxwell (1997, April), Enduring well, *Ensign, 27*(4), 7–10.

Patricia P. Pinegar (1999, November), Peace, hope, and direction, *Ensign, 29*(11), 67–68.

NOTES

1. L. D. Newell (1993, February), address given at Robin Christensen's funeral.

2. Spencer W. Kimball (1972), *Faith Precedes the Miracle* (Salt Lake City: Deseret Book), 97.

CHRONIC ILLNESS, DEATH, AND GRIEVING: PATHWAYS TO HEALING

ELAINE S. MARSHALL AND D. RUSSELL CRANE

*Among all the facts of mortality, nothing is so certain as its deathly end. How tragic,
how poignant is the sorrow of those left behind . . . all of these can speak of the wounds of parting.
But thanks be to God for the wonder and the majesty of His eternal plan.[1]*
—*President Gordon B. Hinckley*

Illness and death are universal human experiences. Though common among all of humanity, such profound experiences vary for each family. The range of challenges, opportunities, and rewards is vast. Some families come together in resilience and grow in spiritual strength. Others are devastated. Individual and family responses to such significant experiences of mortality have implications for growth toward eternal life.

HOW DOES CHRONIC ILLNESS AFFECT FAMILIES?

Chronic illness or disability affects individuals and families in a variety of ways. Some illnesses have symptoms that are intermittent, as with many autoimmune conditions. Some illnesses are obvious to others, such as the effects of a stroke, but most are subtle, like diabetes or hypertension. Some conditions are mild and relatively easily accommodated, while others require constant treatment that takes energy and time from all family members and interrupts daily life. Financial costs of treatment and care can also drain family resources.[2]

Some chronic illnesses are physical; others are mental or emotional. Illness that affects cognitive functioning, such as Alzheimer's disease, can be particularly devastating to family members as the loved one they once knew fades away. All chronic illness requires some individual and family adjustment. When expected complete recovery to health is not possible, there is a sense of loss. Social scientists have referred to such loss as "ambiguous loss"[3] or "chronic sorrow."[4] Generally, this loss results in a kind of grief.[5] Sometimes family members experience "survivor guilt" for having good health when their loved one does not.[6]

Not all chronic illness is terminal. Improved medical treatment has allowed people to live with many chronic conditions with little life interruption. Some maladies, such as rheumatoid arthritis, typically have symptoms that come and go over time, with periods of no symptoms alternating with flare-ups. Others, such as some cancers, are life-threatening and gradually lead toward death.

HOW DO WE DEAL WITH DEATH AND BEREAVEMENT?

Grief, or mourning, follows any profound loss, which may come in many forms. Some losses ambush us in a sudden assault, as in a natural disaster or traumatic death. A sense of loss may also emerge slowly from unrelenting sorrow over time, as in caring for a family member with dementia, watching a wayward child, suffering debilitating illness, or facing a dream unfulfilled.[7] Death at the end of a long, productive life or after a lingering illness may be viewed as a relief from suffering. Or death may suddenly steal a family member in an unexpected and unfair surprise. Grief is a normal response to death. Grieving is how we come to own the sorrow of our loss in order to carry on with life. Healing does not automatically follow intense suffering or sorrow. Grieving requires effort. We must "work" toward healing.[8]

There are a number of predictable elements of the grieving process.[9] Although these components appear discrete, they do not usually follow a linear stage-to-stage progression. Most often, one flows back and forth from stage to stage, sometimes beginning again, sometimes jumping forward for a time. How we grieve is personal and individual. The grieving process takes time and should not be hurried. The duration of time is different for each individual and family situation. There is not a set timetable for "stages" to be reached, but it can be helpful to be aware of some indications of grief and to consider that intense emotions and swift mood swings are normal.

Denial is usually the first reaction to death or serious illness. We refuse to believe what has happened. Feeling emotionally numb is often a primary reaction to a loss, and may last for a few hours, days, or longer. In some ways, this numbness can help one get through the practical arrangements and family pressures that surround the funeral, but if this phase goes on for too long, problems may emerge in resolving the loss.

Anger sometimes accompanies denial, and can manifest itself in many ways. We may blame others for our loss. We may feel agitated and find it difficult to concentrate, relax, or sleep. We may also feel guilty, dwelling on arguments we had with the person, or on emotions and words we wish we had expressed. We may become angry with the lost loved one for leaving us. This period of strong emotion usually gives way to bouts of intense sadness, silence, and withdrawal from family and friends. During this time, we may be prone to sudden outbursts of tears, set off by reminders and memories of the lost loved one. We may even become angry with ourselves. It is important not to turn this anger inward. It may be helpful to talk about it with a trusted friend. Recognition of anger is important to cope with grief.

Attempts at bargaining are indicators of grief. We may try to bargain with ourselves or with God. We may offer something to try to take away the reality or pain of what has happened. We may try to make a deal to have our loved one back as he or she was before the tragic event occurred. For example, we may try to promise greater personal obedience in exchange for the recovery of a loved one from a terminal illness.

Depression can accompany loss. This is often a most difficult stage. There can be feelings of listlessness and fatigue, with periods of bursting into tears. Feelings of a lack of purpose to life may arise. Guilt feelings, or feelings of being punished, are common. Pleasure and joy can be gone for a time. Professional counseling may help persons with these feelings to preserve emotional health.

Acceptance or resolution is ultimately part of the work of grief. We realize that life goes on, and the pain of the loss of the loved one becomes more manageable and less intense. Ultimately, grief is a process of sorting.[10] One author gave this description:

> Grieving is bits of many things—memories, regrets, reminders. . . . And each bit has to be gone through, patiently, silently, painfully, as one goes through old papers in a long-forgotten trunk, considering each one separately, remembering, assigning it to some new box within our hearts.
>
> Healing, too, is bits of many things—smiles which multiply as the days pass; chilling remembrances turned warm by the returning sun; new loves. A day will come when there will be more bits of healing than of grieving, and reasons for joy will begin to pile up in the freshly-swept rooms of our lives.[11]

During times of grief, it is important to ask for help from family, friends, or a support group. Try to recognize and express feelings of anger, guilt, or sadness. Accept that some things, like death, are beyond your control. Avoid making major decisions for a time, since judgment may change with the stress of grief. People need time and space to grieve. Over time, you may gradually "become one" with your loss. The loss does not disappear, but you accept it and learn to trust God and the reality of eternal life and reunion with your loved ones.

How we help others who are grieving is especially important. In general, the best thing to do is spend time with them and listen to them talk about their loss. Offer practical help, such as cooking dinner, shopping for food, or washing the car. For a grieving person, it is difficult to focus on everyday tasks. Finally, if the person is reacting in extreme ways for a prolonged period, encourage him or her to seek professional help.

Needs and responses of all family members, including children, need to be considered. Children feel loss when a loved one dies. They experience similar components of grief, though they may progress through them more quickly. Understandably, some people try to protect children from information about death and the grieving process. It is important that children be given simple, truthful explanations of a loss of a loved one according to their own perspective and developmental level. Information should be given in appropriate context for a child to understand. At the same time, children need assurance of their own emotional and physical safety. It is important to allow children to be appropriately included in family visiting, caregiving, and funerals. These are significant family experiences that can build strong, positive memories. It is helpful to be honest with children about your own grief and encourage them to talk about and work through their feelings of pain and distress. It may be therapeutic for children to express feelings through art or play. There may be times of developmental regression or sleep problems. These need to be simply supported. It is especially important to encourage children to express their own spiritual experiences. Helping children to recognize the Spirit in their lives during such tender times as death or illness can be a profound experience for all family members.

The experience of grieving the death of a loved one offers an exceptional and often bittersweet opportunity for families to come together to celebrate the life of the deceased person. Finding ways to memorialize the lost one can help to bring the family together in positive ways. These could include planting a tree, hanging a Christmas stocking, keeping photographs visible, and sharing stories about the loved one. Doing things for others, such as giving a book to a library or establishing a scholarship in the person's name, keeps memories alive and promotes healing.

The loss of a loved one always lingers. A healthy response is to learn to live beside the loss as an achy, bittersweet memory. Life never returns to how it was before, but some things can help a person come to a healthy resolution. Support of family and friends is important. It is also important to know that not all family members will work through grief in the same way or across the same time period. It is normal to experience a sense of "why me?" or "why wasn't it me?" Sometimes there is a sense of loss of the Comforter. However, though painful, as one works through grief, there can result a sweet sense of closeness to the Spirit.

How Can a Family Anticipate and Resolve Issues Associated with a Death?

It is impossible to fully prepare for a serious illness or death. Although death can strike at any age, it most commonly results from a process of aging and illness in adults. This implies that families can do some things to prepare for the change in the family situation.

The first step is to recognize that illness and death are likely to happen sometime. Even with the best health promotion and disease prevention practices, no one is entirely immune from illness or disability, especially in advancing age. Thus, some planning is possible and can be helpful. This issue is best addressed in open discussion by the entire family.

Extended family council and collective responsibility. Health and loss are best resolved when entire families work together in sharing caregiving responsibility and decision making. When the family council already functions well with appropriately designated roles and responsibilities of each member, it can be a helpful means to provide the most effective care for a family member in a time of need. (See chapter 36.)

Family councils should plan early for potential changes in the living environment, such as need for ramps or other physical adaptations or the need for professional care at home. Financial costs of long-term care can overwhelm families without advance planning in savings or insurance plans. In addition to financial planning, families need to explore options for care. Most communities have services to help families become informed on how to deal with difficult decisions of whether or how a loved one can receive care at home and how to evaluate resources for care outside the home, such as assisted living or extended care facilities. Families must consider their circumstances and needs and be able to accept new realities of family functioning. Family members are often required to assume new roles of communication and caregiving.

Families can prepare for the eventuality of death by deliberate and clear planning in some key areas. Legal documents, such as wills and advance directives, need to be thought out, discussed with an attorney, and made available to family members and health care providers. When a person makes decisions regarding end-of-life care or distribution of belongings after death while he or she has the capacity to do so, the outcomes are generally more positive for family members. The person's wishes are known, and there is less confusion and family conflict.

In addition to preparing a will, advance directives for health care are probably the most important way for adults to protect the desires and interests of loved ones regarding health care as death nears. Such documents may specify whether treatment procedures are desired to prolong life, and may designate a person responsible for such decisions. The legal terms for this may vary: "living will," "durable power of attorney," "surrogate," or "health care agent." In the United States, laws concerning advance directives and wills differ from state to state, although a local hospital or area agency on aging can provide information and forms available for advance directives. If the person making plans wishes to be an organ donor in the event of death, he or she should make that clear to spouse, adult children, and health care providers.

Funeral preparation. Advance planning of funeral arrangements and costs may reduce the burden on family members at the actual time of a death. Funerals can be a source of healing as families come together to consider the doctrines of the gospel in a meeting to comfort and inspire. Funerals should be planned with priesthood leaders in a manner that invites the Spirit and supports family members.[12]

When death is acknowledged as part of life, planning that decreases potential for family conflict or confusion may facilitate a peaceful passing. But families can do more by living each day. They can create lasting legacies of love and care for their posterity. Among the many means to achieve these eternal links are assuring a supportive living environment throughout the life span, creating family histories and personal journals (see chapter 38), and establishing family traditions that endure across generations.

Finally, although planning is important, the quality of lifelong relationships in one's family is most important. Are there unfinished emotional issues in family relationships that can be resolved with some effort? Are there past grievances that need to be discussed? Are there hurts that need to be forgiven? Are there conflicts that need to be resolved? Considering such questions not only facilitates a peaceful death and positive family response, but promotes family resilience and improves the quality of daily family life.

HOW DO ILLNESS AND DEATH FIT IN HEAVENLY FATHER'S PLAN?

Illness is a consequence of mortal life. Facing the challenges of physical or mental suffering in ourselves or family members teaches us valuable lessons that can be learned in no other way. Death is part of God's plan, required for our eternal progression. All families in all cultures, in all times and places experience illness and death.

Research has shown that individuals and families with strong religious beliefs adjust to illness and death better than those without a firm belief in God.[13] Those with such beliefs can look forward to the restoration of all things during the resurrection. The prophet Alma promised, "The soul shall be restored to the body, and the body to the soul; yea, and every limb and joint shall be restored to its body; yea, even a hair of the head shall not be lost; but all things shall be restored to their proper and perfect frame" (Alma 40:23). This promise has implications beyond the restoration of our physical bodies. As a gift of the Atonement, the Savior "Himself took our infirmities, and bare our sicknesses" (Matthew 8:17). The Atonement offers healing of physical, emotional, and spiritual grief. Through the Atonement, all illness, disability, and infirmity will be resolved and we will be restored to our divine and eternal state.[14] The sorrow of illness and death will be replaced with the joy of restored health and eternal reunion with those we love. Thus we may wait with joyful anticipation for the renewal of health and treasured relationships with family members.

ABOUT THE AUTHORS

Elaine S. Marshall, R.N., Ph.D., is dean and professor of the College of Nursing at Brigham Young University. She and her husband, John, are the parents of nine children and seventeen grandchildren.

D. Russell Crane, Ph.D., is a professor of marriage and family therapy, director of the Family Studies Center, and associate director for research in the School of Family Life at Brigham Young University. He and his wife, Eileen, are the parents of eight children and five grandchildren.

ADDITIONAL READING

Mitch Albom (1997), *Tuesdays with Morrie* (New York: Doubleday).

Jason S. Carroll, et al. (2000), The family crucibles of illness, disability, death, and other losses; in David C. Dollahite, ed., *Strengthening Our Families: An In-Depth Look at the Proclamation on the Family* (Salt Lake City: Bookcraft), 278–292.

Bruce C. Hafen (1989), *The Broken Heart: Applying the Atonement to Life's Experiences* (Salt Lake City: Deseret Book).

Neal A. Maxwell (1980), *All These Things Shall Give Thee Experience* (Salt Lake City: Deseret Book).

NOTES

1. Gordon B. Hinckley (1997, April), The victory over death, *Ensign, 27*(4), 2–5.

2. A. Corden, P. Sloper, and R. Sainsbury (2002), Financial effects for families after the death of a disabled or chronically ill child: A neglected dimension of bereavement, *Child: Care, Health, and Development, 28*(3), 199–204.

3. P. Boss and B. A. Couden (2002), Ambiguous loss from chronic physical illness: Clinical interventions with individuals, couples, and families, *Journal of Clinical Psychology, 58*(11), 1351–1360.

4. S. K. Drafft and L. J. Drafft (1998), Chronic sorrow: Parents' lived experience, *Holistic Nursing Practice, 13*(1), 59–67; L. Lowes and P. Lyne (2000), Chronic sorrow in parents of children with newly diagnosed diabetes: A review of the literature and discussion of the implications for nursing practice, *Journal of Advanced Nursing, 32*(1), 41–48.

5. P. Solomon and J. Draine (1996), Examination of grief among family members of individuals with serious and persistent mental illness, *Psychiatric Quarterly, 67*(3), 221–234.

6. M. Vamos (1997), Survivor guilt and chronic illness, *Australian and New Zealand Journal of Psychiatry, 31,* 592–596.

7. L. D. Newell (2003, November 9), A healing place called grieving, text from *Music and the Spoken Word,* copyright Bonneville Communications; available at http://musicandthespokenword.com

8. E. S. Marshall (2004, April), Lessons on healing, *Ensign, 34*(4), 56–61.

9. E. Kübler-Ross (1969), *On Death and Dying: What the Dying Have to Teach Doctors, Nurses, Clergy, and Their Own Families* (New York: Macmillan); E. Kübler-Ross (1981), *Living With Death and Dying* (New York: Macmillan).

10. Newell (2003); R. N. Remen (2000), *My Grandfather's Blessings: Stories of Strength, Refuge, and Belonging* (New York: Riverhead Books), 38.

11. M. Fumia (1992), *Safe Passage: Words to Help the Grieving Hold Fast and Let Go* (Berkeley, CA: Conari Press), 106.

12. Boyd K. Packer (1988, November), A time for reverence, *Ensign, 18*(11), 18.

13. C. G. Ellison and M. R. Benjamins (in press), Religion, health, and family life; in D. R. Crane and E. S. Marshall, eds., *Handbook of Families and Health: Interdisciplinary Perspectives* (Thousand Oaks, CA: Sage).

14. See Bruce C. Hafen (1989), *The Broken Heart: Applying the Atonement to Life's Experiences* (Salt Lake City: Deseret Book).

CHAPTER 33

MENTAL ILLNESS IN THE FAMILY

ELDER ALEXANDER B. MORRISON
EMERITUS MEMBER OF THE FIRST QUORUM OF THE SEVENTY

*From the bed of pain, from the pillow wet with tears, we are lifted heavenward
by that divine assurance and precious promise, "I will not fail thee, nor forsake thee" [Joshua 1:5].[1]*
—President Thomas S. Monson

Among the most painful and often protracted ordeals an individual or family can face is that of mental illness. One of the central characteristics of the cruel constellation of diseases grouped under the general rubric of mental illness is the suffering involved. Its intensity scarcely can even be described. Day follows dreary day in a long procession of gray emptiness, punctuated by flashes of acute torment.

The suffering not only colors every attempt to treat and hopefully to heal the victims of these devastating disorders, but extends outward to engulf others. Family members, caught up in the tsunami of suffering, the maelstrom of pain and despair, echo the anguish of the primary victims. Each longs for a day when solace will be provided, tears dried, hope rekindled, and torment ceased. And yet there is hope. Many mentally ill people find their suffering greatly reduced with proper treatment. Further, sufferers from mental illness commonly have times when they function normally, interspersed with bouts of illness. A case in point would be major depression, which typically involves episodes of severe, even debilitating depressive symptoms, usually over a period of several months, followed by remissions which may last for months or even years. Whatever the course of their illness, all involved can be assured that nothing should "be able to separate us from the love of God, which is in Christ Jesus our Lord" (Romans 8:39).

In this brief chapter, it is not possible to discuss all categories of mental illness. Some of the disorders include anxiety disorders (panic disorders, obsessive-compulsive disorder, and assorted phobias); mood disorders (depression and bipolar disorder); schizophrenia; and eating disorders (anorexia nervosa and bulimia, two disorders seen primarily, though not exclusively, in young women).[2]

The term "mental illness" does not describe the temporary social and emotional concerns associated with the normal wear and tear of life. Many people feel anxious when they start a new job, for example, and most of us are sad following the death of a friend. Those who act in those ways are not mentally ill. Their actions are normal. Nor should we include in the category of mental illness the secondary effects of physical disorders such as meningitis, high fevers, or brain tumors. Mental illness is something different. It lies at one end of a continuum linking the social and emotional concerns which are the transient accompaniments of daily living and mental diseases, many of which have their roots in human biology. Mental illness may be defined as a brain disorder that causes mild to severe disturbances in a person's understanding, thinking, and behavior. If such disturbances are sufficiently severe, and last long enough, they may seriously interfere with the victim's ability to function normally as an individual or productive member of society. The ability to cope with life's ordinary stresses and strains may significantly be impaired. Under severe circumstances, mental illnesses may threaten life. Significant numbers of patients with anorexia nervosa, for example, literally starve to death in the midst of plenty,[3] and approximately one of seven persons with severe depression dies by his or her own hand.[4]

A brief description of major categories of mental illness may help outline the devastating effects of these disorders. About one in four Americans will suffer from an anxiety disorder in his or her lifetime. Anxiety disorders may severely limit the ability of the sufferer to function effectively or get any enjoyment out of life. Up to one-third of anxiety sufferers essentially are disabled and unable to function effectively. Sufferers have increased likelihood of turning to alcohol or other mood-modifying drugs in vain attempts to deaden the physiologic and psychic pain they feel.[5]

It is estimated that more than 17 million Americans are severely depressed each year, and nearly two-thirds do not get the help they need. An estimated 2 percent of preadolescent children, aged 7–12, exhibit major depression. Severe depression is a malignant sadness, all-consuming, seemingly never-ending, not amenable to cheering up by an act of will or the actions of others. It may also be life-threatening. A high percentage of people who kill themselves are depressed, and anyone who is seriously depressed must be considered at risk for suicide.[6]

Schizophrenia causes bizarre and frightening symptoms in its victims, including hallucinations, most often involving the hearing of voices. Usually the voices are condemnatory and critical of the victim. Delusions—false, fixed, often paranoid ideas with no basis in reality—are common. Disorders of thought and behavior such that the patient speaks gibberish, or (for example) wears layers of heavy winter clothes on a hot summer's day, complete the triumvirate of psychotic symptoms seen in persons with schizophrenia. Social withdrawal, decreased intellectual abilities, apathy, and staring into space also are common.[7]

Victims of anorexia nervosa are most often young women. They are chronically unable to sustain minimally normal body weight; suffer intense, constant fear of becoming obese; and have distorted perceptions of their body weights or shapes. They become progressively more emaciated, fatigued, and depressed. Unless treated quickly, they die from starvation or heart failure.[8] Although no one knows with certainty what causes anorexia, many believe it represents an attempt, either conscious or unconscious, to control at least one part of life—body weight.[9]

Persons with bulimia are characterized by binge eating, followed by purging. Excessive physical exercising, in an attempt to balance out the episodic binge eating, is common. Like anorexics, bulimics see their bodies through a distorted perspective. They commonly suffer from intense self-hatred, guilt, depression, or anxiety. They also may die from heart failure and often have serious dental problems.[10] (Essay H2 discusses ways to help a family member who suffers from an eating disorder.)

Some of the heaviest burdens borne by sufferers from mental illness and their families are the prejudice, ignorance, misunderstanding, and social stigma which characterize the attitudes of many in society towards the mentally ill. Many victims and their families fear, for good reason, that they will be ridiculed, whispered about, even shunned if they seek help. They believe that their spouses, friends, children, or employers may abandon them and there will be no opportunities for marriage. Reports of treatment or hospitalization for mental disorders may result in decreased career opportunities. Some insurance companies limit their coverage of patients with mental illness, perhaps even refusing coverage.[11]

Misunderstanding and fear continue to surround mental illness. Silence, alienation, and prejudice concerning mental illness abound. Mental illness still is hidden, whispered about behind closed doors, denied, considered shameful. In this supposedly enlightened age, so many maintain irrational fears and wrong and hurtful ideas about mental illness. Many fail to see it for what it is, the mental analogue of physical disorders.

Overcoming Misconceptions

Myths and misconceptions about mental illness abound in our society. I wish I could say that Latter-day Saints are more enlightened than the general public on such matters, but many are not. Space permits only a brief description of three of the most prevalent of the myths with which sufferers from mental illness, and their families, must deal daily.

Myth 1: Mental Illness Is Caused by Sin

There is no doubt that sin—the deliberate breaking of God's commandments—is hurtful both to the individual concerned and to others. Perhaps nowhere in holy writ is the power of sin to torment and harrow up the soul more vividly exemplified than in the words of the repentant Alma: "But I was racked with eternal torment, for my soul was harrowed up to the greatest degree and racked with all my sins. . . . Oh, thought I, that I could be banished and become extinct both soul and body" (Alma 36:12, 15).

Sorrow and remorse during the repentance process—even feelings so galling and painful as those felt by Alma—are necessary prerequisites for true repentance. They are not, however, manifestations of mental illness. Those attempting to work through the pain, remorse, and depression associated with sin towards the goal of repentance will benefit greatly from confession to their bishops, followed by counseling from them. In this role, no mental health professional, regardless of his or her skills and training, can ever take the place of the faithful bishop, who receives spiritual gifts of discernment and wisdom as part of his calling. Guided by the Holy Ghost, the bishop can provide invaluable assistance to those suffering from sin and desirous of repentance.

That said, however, in many instances, aberrant, even bizarre thoughts, feelings, and actions result from mental illness and not from sin. Many faithful Latter-day Saints, who live the commandments and honor their covenants, experience profound personal struggles with mental illness. In common with those who suffer from physical ailments, such individuals are victims of *disease,* not sin. To assume that persons with mental illness have brought it upon themselves because they are sinners, that God is punishing them for their wickedness, is to my mind contrary to His very nature. I know He is not the source of sin, and I am of the firm view He does not give His children mental illness to punish them. Indeed, if the logic that He does so were carried to its logical conclusion, we would all be mentally ill, because "all have sinned, and come short of the glory of God" (Romans 3:23).

I believe that in His omniscience, God knows a trial is coming to us and declines to remove it, using it as a tutoring tool to help us to grow spiritually. He knows every detail of our DNA, and hence of our genetic predisposition to resist or acquire disease, including mental illness. He knows fully the myriad biological, social, and environmental factors to which we will be exposed in our lifetime and understands when genetic predisposition will converge with a stressful event or episode, whether environmental or emotional, to produce disorder, even serious disease.

A primary role of the bishop, then, is to ascertain whether a deeply distressed member of his congrega-

tion is suffering the effects of sin or of mental illness. He is able to do so as he is guided by the Holy Ghost, and if he knows the characteristics of mental illness. If the problem is sin, the bishop will know how to assist the member through the repentance process. If the bishop understands the nature and symptoms of mental illness, and discerns that the member's problems lie in that area, he should refer the individual to a properly qualified mental health professional for treatment.

Myth 2: The Only Thing All Mentally Ill Persons Need Is a Priesthood Blessing

I am a great advocate of priesthood blessings. Our beloved daughter, Mary, who has suffered from panic attacks and depression for more than half of her life, literally lives from blessing to blessing. I know from experience that priesthood blessings do inestimable good. I know, too, that Jesus Christ is the Great Physician, the unparalleled healer of both body and mind. He and He alone provides the healing balm of Gilead needed by all who suffer. In any and all circumstances, in good times and bad, in sickness and in health, our lives will become more peaceful and richer as we turn to Him. Only then can we find rest unto our souls, as He Himself has said (see Matthew 11:28–30).

That agreed, I suggest that priesthood leaders are ecclesiastical leaders and not mental health professionals. Almost all of them lack the professional skills and training needed to treat persons with mental illness effectively. They are well advised to seek competent professional assistance for those in their charge who are mentally ill and in need of skilled help.

When bishops, family members, or others refer mentally ill persons to mental health professionals, it is important that the individual chosen not only be professionally competent, but also that he or she follow practices and procedures compatible with gospel principles. Some mental health professionals are unwilling to work within the structure of a patient's faith system. A mental health professional need not be a Latter-day Saint to be effective, but should be willing to accept the way gospel principles are crucial to a patient's life and be respectful of them.

Myth 3: Someone Is to Blame for Mental Illness

It is common to blame others, or oneself, for whatever goes wrong in life. Many victims of mental illness work themselves into a frazzle and wear themselves out emotionally in futile, repetitive attempts to recall something they, their parents, siblings, or someone else might have done that resulted in the misery and despair they are forced to endure. Many blame themselves and are unable to rid themselves of the terrible, nagging conclusion that somehow, some way, even though they don't understand how or why, they are the cause of their own pain. They feel ashamed of themselves for being sick and think they are weak and defective. Parents, spouses, and other family members too often tear themselves apart emotionally trying in vain to determine where *they* went wrong. They may try to bargain with God, offering Him anything, even their own lives, if He will but cure their beloved family member.

Victims and their families may blame problems of mental health on demonic possession. Such has occurred, in very rare instances, but we should take care not to give the devil credit for everything that goes awry in the world! Generally speaking, mentally ill patients need treatment, love, and support, not exorcism.

Victims laboring under the false belief that they themselves are the cause of their problems because of something they did or didn't do are commonly wracked with false guilt. They may pray repeatedly for God to forgive them, even though there is no objective evidence they have anything of note to be forgiven of. In the false belief they have been deserted by God, they may become angry and bitter towards Him. They may turn to the false pleasures of the world to "get even" or to dull their pain. Nothing they do of this sort, whether it be blaming themselves, others, or even God, does any good. The reason is simple: in most instances, the thoughts and behaviors of people with mental illness result from disease processes, not the actions of others.

Ascribing blame for mental illness causes unnecessary suffering for victims and others alike. It takes time and energy that would better be used to get a complete and accurate diagnosis of the illness concerned; understand the biological processes involved, which often ultimately involve changes in the functioning of and communication between the cells of the brain; get proper medication to help reverse those changes; and learn cognitive and behavioral techniques that are crucial parts of the healing process. Family members and friends can best spend their time not in playing the "blame game," but in seeking understanding and enhanced compassion, empathy, forgiveness, and patience.

WHERE CAN WE TURN FOR HELP?

The community of professional caregivers in the mental health field, generally speaking, is divided between psychiatrists and psychotherapists—i.e., psychologists, social workers, and other licensed mental health professionals. Both groups provide invaluable assistance to sufferers from mental diseases.

Psychiatrists are physicians with specialized training in psychiatry and neurology. They also are trained to provide psychotherapy. Psychiatrists can prescribe medication, which psychologists cannot, and, because they are trained medical doctors, can determine if a patient is suffering from some other medical problem, such as brain cancer, which could cause symptoms of mental illness.

Psychologists are trained, often at the doctoral level, to provide cognitive and behavioral therapy to help patients with mental illness understand why they think and act as they do, and to assist them in developing behaviors which will aid in their healing. Many are excellent psychotherapists, as are other trained mental health professionals, such as clinical social workers.

Controversy about medication versus psychotherapy swirls and eddies through the community of mental health professionals. In my view, both have invaluable contributions to make. How the two sets of disciplines are used, and in what mix, will depend on the orientation and training of the practitioner involved and on the needs of a particular patient. My belief, supported by emerging research,[12] is that eventually we will find that medication and psychotherapy act in a common way, by altering brain chemistry and function, especially with respect to anxiety and mood disorders.

Much information on mental illness of value to the general public is available free from the National Institute of Mental Health (www.nimh.nih.gov). Information is available on a broad variety of topics, including anxiety disorders, depression, bipolar disorder, schizophrenia, and eating disorders.

Readers will find much of value at www .ldsmentalhealth.org. This website is not sponsored by The Church of Jesus Christ of Latter-day Saints, but it provides a great wealth of reliable, gospel-compatible information on a broad variety of mental illnesses. It is not intended to replace the spiritual direction of ecclesiastical leaders and does not provide information on medication or counseling of mentally ill persons.

LDS Family Services is an agency which serves Church members and others by providing information on a broad variety of family-related problems. Mental health concerns are dealt with through service and advice, consistent with gospel principles. Individuals usually are referred to Family Services by their bishops.

THE ROLE OF FAMILY MEMBERS

Family members are central to helping and healing those with mental illness. Some of the ways in which they can help include the following:

Get treatment promptly. It does no good, and may do a lot of harm, to delay getting appropriate treatment from a skilled mental health professional for a family member who, there is good reason to believe, is mentally ill. Psychotherapy given early in the course of a mental disease, before it becomes deep-seated and less easily treated, will yield quicker and better results. Medication administered by a skilled physician may reverse psychotic or other bizarre behavior, assist the brain to begin to heal, and improve the effectiveness of psychotherapy. Failure to provide needed treatment only increases the possibility that mentally ill persons may harm themselves or others. Those who need advice on where to go for treatment should discuss the matter with a trusted advisor—the bishop, other family members, the family doctor, or a knowledgeable friend.

Show forth additional love and compassion. If family members ridicule, demean, criticize, or abandon the victim involved; if they go on and on about supposed (and usually false) sin and blame; if they are judgmental and censorious, I guarantee the patient will not do well. But if they love and enfold, if they refuse to judge, if they are kind, compassionate, and empathetic, then therapy exerts its full beneficial effects. Provided patients are not a threat to themselves or others, and do not require intensive nursing care, a loving home may be the best place for healing to occur. There the patient feels safe, secure, and in the presence of those who really care in ways that professional detachment forbids. Psychiatric wards in hospitals remain necessary, but in my admittedly limited experience they are often frightening and foreboding places, which do little to calm and reassure many patients. They may provide little of the intensive treatment needed by seriously ill patients.

A word of caution is necessary. Home may not be the best place for mentally ill patients if there are small children there, who require constant care or may be frightened and influenced by a mentally ill family member. Further, the turmoil and hubbub in many busy homes may be excessively disturbing to some mentally ill persons.

Family members soon learn that developing and unfailingly demonstrating patience is a large part of love and compassion. Patience must be developed if one is to deal effectively with the seemingly endless ebb and flow of illness, the apparently never-ending routine of one step forward and another backward, the constant vigilance required of those who are caregivers for patients who may be in danger of suicide. Patience is needed to guard against the tendency to get out of sorts with the person who is sick, and whose sickness causes eddies of pain in the lives of others. Remember that no one with mental illness wants to be that way. People are not mentally ill because they lack willpower. They cannot, through any exercise of will, get out of the predicament they are in. To lose patience with them, to advise them to "just snap out of it" and "get a little backbone," is not only insensitive, but futile. Anyone who has ever witnessed the almost unbearable pain and uncontrollable weeping of a severe panic attack, or the indescribable sadness of a severely depressed person who cries all day and retreats into hopeless apathy, would never think for a moment that mental illness is just a matter of willpower.

At the same time that we must learn to be patient with ourselves and with the victim of mental illness, we also must learn to be patient with God. When prayers are not answered as we had hoped for so fervently, when our timetable is not that of the Almighty, when we are called upon to tread the winepress of affliction alone, it becomes seductively easy to grow angry with God, to feel He has abandoned us. Pain and patience are uneasy partners at best. But it is in learning to endure whatever mortality brings us—including the vicarious suffering we experience at the pain of loved ones—that we find the key which opens the door to celestial halls.

Family members must then learn to put their trust in God. No matter if our path be strewn with thorns, no matter how onerous our struggle through mists of darkness and torrents of tears, God will succor and sustain us. Learning that lesson is at best a stern struggle. It involves tutorial suffering and stretching. But it is the only path to peace, amidst the pain and suffering, the loneliness, depression, and despair of mental illness.

Those who suffer from mental illness, who are burdened with pain, depression, and confusion must, I believe, be especially on their guard against the devil and his agents. So too must the circle of loving family members and other caregivers.

Learn all you can about mental illness and how to deal with it. Family members of mentally ill persons will love better as they learn more about the causes of mental illness and the suffering it brings. Their compassion for the victim will increase, and they will be less judgmental and censorious. They will grow more patient and forbearing. They will begin to see mental illness for what it is—a disease of the brain, not of the spirit, a malady caused not by sin, but by problems in the working of the most complex structure in the body. They will grow thankful for medical and other therapeutic interventions which have revolutionized treatment of mental illness in the last four decades, and will look forward with hope to the rapidly approaching day when treatment will be more specific and more effective than ever.

As family members struggle to learn and understand mental illness, they will find that their insight will grow exponentially if they simultaneously succor the life of the spirit. As they do so, scriptures will become more meaningful, prayer sweeter, contemplation more attuned to the Divine. As they draw closer to God and put their lives, and that of their loved one, in His hands, they will find they are never alone. They will come to realize, as perhaps never before, the price which Christ paid that He may know more perfectly how to personally sustain us through the seasons of our trials.

Encourage the person who is ill. Persons with mental illness, who often are worn down and disheartened by pervasive feelings of hopelessness, need encouragement and hope for the future. This must be realistic: "Pie in the sky" advice will lead only to discouragement, a sense of betrayal, and increased cynicism. But there are solid grounds for optimism in nearly every instance. The victim can with total assurance be reminded often of God's love, of the unfailing love of family members, and of the reality of eternal family relationships. There is hope, too, that the therapeutic future will be brighter for sufferers from mental illnesses of all types.

Mentally ill persons should be encouraged to continue to pray, attend appropriate Church meetings, participate in sacred ordinances, and fulfill other religious obligations as they can. They will never benefit more from God's presence in their lives than now.

They should be encouraged to do the ordinary little things that provide meaning to life—to appreciate the beauties of nature, complete appropriate tasks, and exercise. Such encouragement may help the afflicted person decide to cooperate more fully with treatment, gain self-esteem, even to work harder in therapy and be more diligent in taking prescribed medication.

Maintain a life of your own. If family members are to be of the most help to a loved one afflicted with mental illness, they must maintain a life of their own. They owe that to themselves, to the sufferer, to those in their family who are not sick, to friends and business associates, even to God. And so, somehow, in the midst of turmoil and stress, constant worry, time and financial pressures, and all else that bears down upon them, they must find time, even if only for a few minutes daily, to recharge their own reservoirs of strength. They may be rejuvenated by reading a good book, practicing a hobby, or listening to uplifting music. Quiet discussions with trusted friends, a telephone call to a family member, or an hour of service to others in a setting away from the patient may be helpful. The selection of activities is endless. How and what is chosen is less important than the realization that nurturing personal well-being is essential to the health of all family members.

In conclusion, we can help those suffering from mental illness in many ways. Perhaps the most important involve love and patience, coupled with the understanding that mental illness is not the patient's fault, not the result of sin, and cannot be overcome by an act of will. Learning all we can about the illness will increase our compassion, enhance our abilities to respond appropriately to those who suffer, and help all to develop faith and hope for a brighter tomorrow. More than all else, victims and their loved ones can, with perfect assurance, turn to Him who in His infinite compassion has taken upon Himself "the pains and the sicknesses of his people" (Alma 7:11). He, "through his infinite goodness and grace, will keep [us] through the endurance of faith on his name to the end" (Moroni 8:3).

ABOUT THE AUTHOR

Elder Alexander B. Morrison, Ph.D., is an emeritus General Authority of The Church of Jesus Christ of Latter-day Saints. He spent most of his professional life as a senior officer in the Federal Health Department of the government of Canada.

ADDITIONAL READING

Sean E. Brotherson (2004, August), When your child is depressed, *Ensign, 34*(8), 53.

Jack M. Gorman (1996), *The Essential Guide to Mental Health: The Most Comprehensive Guide to the New Psychiatry for Popular Family Use* (New York: St. Martin's Griffin).

Alexander B. Morrison (2003), *Valley of Sorrow: A Layman's Guide to Understanding Mental Illness* (Salt Lake City: Deseret Book).

NOTES

1. Thomas S. Monson (1998, May), Look to God and live, *Ensign, 28*(5), 53.

2. American Psychiatric Association (1994), Diagnostic and Statistical Manual of Mental Disorders, 4th ed. (Washington, D.C.: American Psychiatric Association), 393–444; 317–391; 273–315; 539–550.

3. Ibid., 543.

4. Ibid., 340.

5. Ibid., 398.

6. Ibid., 340.

7. Ibid., 274–278.

8. Ibid., 543.

9. J. M. Gorman (1996), *The Essential Guide to Mental Health: The Most Comprehensive Guide to the New Psychiatry for Popular Family Use* (New York: St. Martin's Griffin), 303.

10. American Psychiatric Association (1994), 548.

11. Gorman (1996), 4.

12. J. M. Schwartz and B. Beyette (1996), *Brain Lock: Free Yourself from Obsessive-Compulsive Behavior* (New York: Regan Books), xix.

CHAPTER 34

SAME-SEX ATTRACTION

A. DEAN BYRD AND SHIRLEY E. COX

Our hearts reach out to those who struggle with feelings of affinity for the same gender. We remember you before the Lord, we sympathize with you, we regard you as our brothers and our sisters. However, we cannot condone immoral practices on your part any more than we can condone immoral practices on the part of others.[1]
—President Gordon B. Hinckley

Church leaders have consistently encouraged Latter-day Saints to demonstrate Christlike compassion for those who struggle with homosexual attraction and, at the same time, to adhere to the Lord's standards of morality. President Spencer W. Kimball emphasized forgiveness for those who seek it.[2] Elder Dallin H. Oaks wrote of kindness, compassion, and love, reminding us that "We should reach out lovingly to those who are struggling to resist temptation."[3] Elder Boyd K. Packer declared to those who have engaged in homosexual behavior: "We do not reject you, only immoral behavior. . . . We will not reject you, because we love you."[4] And President Gordon B. Hinckley expressed his desires for those who struggle with homosexual attraction: "We want to help these people, to strengthen them, to assist them with their problems and to help them with their difficulties."[5]

The clear message from Church leaders is that homosexual attractions can be diminished and that individuals can make changes in their lives. President Hinckley has spoken regarding those who have homosexual tendencies: "They may have certain inclinations which are powerful and which may be difficult to control. Most people have inclinations of one kind or another at various times. If they do not act upon these inclinations, then they can go forward as do all other members of the Church."[6] In understanding diverse susceptibilities that are part of the mortal experience, Elder Oaks said: "The feelings or other characteristics that increase susceptibility to certain behavior may have some relationship to inheritance. But the relationship is probably very complex. The inherited element may be nothing more than an increased likelihood that an individual will acquire certain feelings if he or she encounters particular influences during the developmental years. But regardless of our different susceptibilities or vulnerabilities . . . we remain responsible for the exercise of our agency in the thoughts we entertain and the behavior we choose."[7]

The Lord's perspective on homosexual behavior is clear as revealed through ancient and modern prophets. In a letter read to all congregations of the Church in 1991, the First Presidency reiterated:

> The Lord's law of moral conduct is abstinence outside of lawful marriage and fidelity within marriage. Sexual relations are proper only between husband and wife appropriately expressed within the bonds of marriage. Any other sexual contact, including fornication, adultery, and homosexual and lesbian behavior, is sinful. Those who persist in such practice or who influence others to do so are subject to Church discipline.[8]

Clinical observations and scientific research have not produced a clear picture of the origins of homosexuality.[9] Currently, most professionals believe the origins of same-sex attraction to be the result of a complex interaction among biological, developmental, and environmental events.[10]

ALTERING HOMOSEXUAL ORIENTATION

While research supports the idea that same-sex attraction evolves from a number of causes and is not generally chosen, it does not also imply that these attractions cannot be altered or diminished. Robert L. Spitzer, a Columbia University psychiatrist, conducted a survey of 200 persons and concluded that 66 percent of the men and 44 percent of the women, who had participated in therapy to change their homosexual attraction, had arrived at what he called good heterosexual functioning. Additionally, 89 percent of these men and 95 percent of these women reported that they were bothered slightly, or not at all, by unwanted feelings of same-sex attraction.[11] These percentages are in line with what we have seen in our combined clinical experience with this population. "Like most psychiatrists," says Dr. Spitzer, "I thought that homosexual behavior could be resisted, but sexual orientation could not be changed. I now believe that's untrue—some people can and do change." Spitzer concluded that the changes occurred not just in behavior but in core features of sexual orientation.[12] Christopher Rosik reviewed other studies that support this view and described factors that motivate such change.[13]

As with most complex challenges, there are differing outcomes for those attempting to alter unwanted homosexual attractions. However, the treatment of unwanted feelings of same-sex attraction has a rich history of successes, comparable to other therapeutic challenges.[14] While there are differing approaches to the treatment of unwanted homosexuality, the underlying theoretical framework is similar: social, emotional, developmental, and biological variables affect gender identity, which in turn determines sexual orientation. The work of the therapist is to help individuals understand their gender development. Subsequently, individuals are able to make choices consistent with their value systems. The focus of treatment is to help individuals fully develop their masculine or feminine gender identity.

IMPORTANT STEPS FOR THOSE WHO STRUGGLE WITH HOMOSEXUAL ATTRACTION

Individuals who experience feelings of homosexual attraction and yet maintain commitment to the Church face many difficult challenges. Often they struggle alone for long periods of time. Frequently, however, they feel a need for professional counseling. In such cases, it is important that individuals seek out therapists who not only have expertise in dealing with unwanted homosexual attraction but who also provide counseling consistent with gospel principles. Most commonly, individuals turn to family members and friends. Latter-day Saints who struggled with homosexual attraction reported that the following process helped them with the transitions in their lives.[15]

Developing intimacy through sharing with others. Although many individuals surveyed were fearful of rejection, disclosing to others was helpful. In spite of the risks and difficulties, disclosing one's struggle brought numerous positive results. Participants in therapy were surprised to learn that others would accept and love them even after learning that they were dealing with feelings of homosexual attraction.

Struggling individuals were more able to feel loved for who they truly are, rather than for the façade they had tried to present. Consider the following verbal reports: "The first person I told was a close friend. She didn't react at all the way I thought she would. I guess I was expecting rejection, but it didn't even faze her. She didn't think I was a bad person or anything! And we are still really close." Another participant reported, "I told my wife—my fiancée at the time. It was hard for her to hear. Eventually she asked, 'Well, what does it mean for us?' And I said, 'It doesn't change anything. I intend to marry you and to be faithful my whole life.' In the end she said, 'I can't believe you have gone through this for years and felt like you were alone. You won't ever have to go through this alone again. Now this is our problem and we will get through it together.' That made all the difference."

Some participants made a direct connection between disclosing their struggle to others and a notable decrease in the intensity of sexual urges. They discovered that the deep and compelling needs that initially drove them toward sexual involvement were replaced with positive, nonsexual, socially and emotionally connected relationships. One reported, "I can't believe how much it has helped to open up to my friends. It's not nearly as much of a problem as it was before." Another person noted, "When I talk about it, it's not as strong. Instead of being a secret I keep hidden, something I'm embarrassed about and never bring up, being open about it has made it less of a problem."

A great deal of courage is required to share such a difficult struggle, and individuals need to exercise judgment in confiding in others; however, many benefits resulted. As a result of sharing with others, many of their own perceptions had to be revised. Individuals found that others could still love them in spite of their homosexual attraction. Acceptance from others resulted in self-acceptance.

Acquiring increased understanding as an important foundation for transition. A greater understanding about their gender development in terms of psychological theories, as well as a better understanding of gospel truths, was tremendously valuable. One participant noted, "The real key was when I separated the feelings from the behavior and figured out, 'Okay, having those feelings doesn't mean you're evil. You are a good person.' Then I could give myself wholeness; I could say, 'I'm attracted to members of the same sex and I'm a good person. It doesn't have to be one or the other.' . . . You get a lot of your worth back because it allows you dignity."

Gaining increased knowledge, both of psychological theories of homosexuality and of gospel truths, helped participants gain perspective and understanding about what they were going through. Increased understanding led to less self-blame and a more realistic perception of what they could do to deal effectively with their struggle.

Developing a relationship with a loving God. A revolutionary change in one's perception of and relationship with God was a key factor for many individuals dealing with homosexual attraction. Rather than a harsh or distant figure, God came to be viewed as a loving Father on whom one could rely. One participant noted, "Ultimately, I think meeting those needs that I used to try to meet through sexual involvement has been a spiritual thing. Heavenly Father is the one who can change your heart and fill you up where you are lacking, so I tried hard to keep in close touch with Him all of the time." Another participant related, "The biggest secret is finding out for yourself that Heavenly Father values you; that gives you more strength than anything. You can get outside sources all the time but once it comes directly from Heavenly Father, it's powerful and it becomes a real teacher." (Essay H1 shares one individual's experience in overcoming same-sex attraction.)

FAMILIES AND FRIENDS: WHEN A LOVED ONE STRUGGLES WITH HOMOSEXUAL ATTRACTION

Most helpful for families and friends, when a loved one shares information about his or her struggles with same-sex attraction, is accurate information about homosexuality, coupled with the Lord's perspective. Helping a loved one understand and exercise agency can be empowering. Understanding the Lord's grace can be a valuable resource for those who struggle. The following guidelines may help.

1. Moderate your response to the news of your loved one's homosexual struggles. Keep in mind that this is the same person you have always known: a child of God. Be grateful that this individual is willing to share his or her burden with you. Let it be understood that you value him or her and that this difficult journey will not have to be traveled alone.

2. Become informed about what the Church teaches and study reliable information about homosexuality. Express your own feelings and testimony of change. Realize that your loved one may experience extreme pain because of the extensive changes required—often including changing one's thoughts and friendships. Freely share with him or her your testimony and the information you have gathered.

3. While maintaining a loving concern for the person, reiterate the Lord's position that sexual relations outside of heterosexual marriage are sinful, and don't lose sight of this gospel truth.

4. Kindly encourage the individual to seek counsel from his or her bishop. Real healing of wrong behavior comes from repentance and forgiveness; it comes from the Lord. A loving bishop can provide a needed bridge between the individual and the Lord. Remember that thoughts and feelings of same-sex attraction are not the same as behavior. Elder Boyd K. Packer said, "If you do not act on unworthy persuasions, you will neither be condemned nor be subjected to Church discipline."[16]

5. Help your friend or family member secure other necessary sources of support. Evergreen International is an organization that provides education, guidance, and support to those involved in the transition from homosexuality and serves as a resource to family and friends, professional counselors, religious leaders, and all others involved in assisting individuals along this pathway. When individuals need professional counseling, it is important to utilize only the services of therapists who are

skilled in the specific treatment for this issue and sub-scribe to moral standards consistent with your own. Evergreen International or LDS Family Services staff can be a valuable resource in this area.

6. Avoid the temptation to try to take control or fix the situation. Encourage. Be patient. Suffer long. Demonstrate love unfeigned. These actions and atti-tudes are more profoundly helpful than force. And they represent the Lord's way.

7. Keep the communication line open. Telephone calls, letters, and personal contacts remind the indi-vidual of your love. For example, one young man, Jon, left his family because they would not accept his lifestyle. Nevertheless, family members, particularly his parents, made phone calls and wrote letters, which Jon kept but never read. He reached a critical point one evening, when he was feeling particularly homesick. As he pondered his situation, he began, almost unknowingly, to open the letters. He reported experiencing such an outpouring of love that he called his parents and asked if he could come home. His parents were overjoyed to hear from him again. This was the beginning of his journey out of homo-sexual behavior and the impetus for his return home.

8. Pray trustingly. One mother told of her nightly conversations with Heavenly Father when she learned of her daughter's struggle with lesbianism. She prayed fervently that her daughter would be protected. Some time later, the daughter told of the many times she had felt a sense of protection and direction because of her mother's prayers. A mother's love and prayers made a tremendous difference.

9. Never give up on a loved one—never! Even when a loved one pursues a gay lifestyle for a time, the above counsel still has merit.

Conclusion

The prophets have declared that "Gender is an essential characteristic of individual premortal, mor-tal, and eternal identity and purpose."[17] Elder Oaks counseled, "[Homosexual] thoughts and feelings . . . should be resisted and redirected, . . . and homosex-ual and lesbian behavior" eliminated.[18] Such guidance should be clearly understood by family members and friends who reach out to those with homosexual dif-ficulties. Though homosexual attraction generally does not result from conscious choice, the divine gift of agency does provide choices in responding to such unwanted attraction. Gospel truths and ecclesiastical counsel combined with professional knowledge and

intervention can be a powerful resource in helping individuals who struggle with homosexual attraction and can form a foundation for hope.

ABOUT THE AUTHORS

A. Dean Byrd, Ph.D., MBA, MPH, is the president of Thrasher Research Fund and clinical professor, University of Utah School of Medicine (Family and Preventive Medicine and Psychiatry). He and his wife, Dr. Elaine Byrd, are the parents of five children.

Shirley E. Cox, DSW, LCSW, is a professor and the director of field education in the School of Social Work at Brigham Young University. She has four children and eight grandchildren.

ADDITIONAL READING

A. D. Byrd (2002), *Homosexuality and The Church of Jesus Christ* (Springville, UT: Bonneville Books).

A. D. Byrd (1999, September), When a loved one struggles with same-sex attraction, *Ensign* 29(9), 51–54.

Shirley E. Cox and Doris Dant (1999), *Developing Genuine Friendships: A Guide for Women Struggling with Same-Sex Attraction* (Salt Lake City: Evergreen International).

Fred Matis, Marilyn Matis, and Ty Mansfield (2004), *In Quiet Desperation: Understanding the Challenge of Same-Gender Attraction* (Salt Lake City: Deseret Book).

Spencer W. Kimball (1969), *The Miracle of Forgiveness* (Salt Lake City: Bookcraft).

Barbara Day Lockhart and Shirley E. Cox (2000), The divine nature of each individual; in David C. Dollahite, ed., *Strengthening Our Families: An In-Depth Look at the Proclamation on the Family* (Salt Lake City: Bookcraft), 217–226.

Peter Sprigg and Timothy Dailey, eds. (2004), *Getting It Straight: What the Research Shows about Homosexuality* (Washington, D.C.: Family Research Council).

NOTES

1. Gordon B. Hinckley (1995, November), Stand strong against the wiles of the world, *Ensign*, 25(11), 98.

2. Spencer W. Kimball (1969), *The Miracle of Forgiveness* (Salt Lake City: Bookcraft), 81–82.

3. Dallin H. Oaks (1995, October), Same-gender attraction, *Ensign*, 25(10), 7–14, 11.

4. Boyd K. Packer (2000, November), Ye are the temple of God, *Ensign*, 30(11), 72–74.

5. Gordon B. Hinckley (1998, November), What are people saying about us? *Ensign*, 28(11), 71.

6. Ibid.

7. Oaks (1995), 9.

8. First Presidency Letter (1991, November 14), Standards of morality and fidelity.

9. N. Mitchell (1995, April 30) Genetics, sexuality linked, study says, *Standard Examiner*, D. Nimmons (1994, March), Sex and the brain, *Discover, 15*(3), 64–71; R. Segelken (1996, August 29), Psychologist argues for new theory of how sexual orientation develops, *Cornell Chronicle*, 8; J. Nicolosi (1991), *Reparative Therapy of Male Homosexuality* (Northvale, NJ: Jason Aronson);

R. C. Friedman and J. I. Downey (2002), Sexual orientation and psychoanalysis (New York: Columbia University Press).

10. Friedman and Downey (2002).

11. R. L. Spitzer (2003), Can some gay men and lesbians change their sexual orientation? *Archives of Sexual Behavior, 32*(5), 403–417.

12. R. L. Spitzer (2001, May 23), Psychiatry and homosexuality, *Wall Street Journal.*

13. C. H. Rosik (2003), Motivational, ethical, and epistemological foundations in the treatment of unwanted homoerotic attraction, *Journal of Marital and Family Therapy, 29*(1), 13–21.

14. J. Satinover (1996), *Homosexuality and the Politics of Truth* (Grand Rapids, MI: Baker Books), 185–186; B. Murray (2000), Sexual identity is far from fixed in women who aren't exclusively heterosexual, *Monitor on Psychology, 31*(3), 15; W. Throckmorton (2002), Initial empirical and clinical findings concerning the change process for ex-gays, *Professional Psychology: Research and Practice, 33*(3), 242–248.

15. A. D. Byrd and Mark D. Chamberlain (1993), Dealing with issues of homosexuality: A qualitative study of six Mormons, *AMCAP Journal, 19*(1), 47–97.

16. Boyd K. Packer (2000).

17. First Presidency and Council of Twelve Apostles (1995, November), The family: A proclamation to the world, *Ensign, 25*(11), 102.

18. Oaks (1995), 9.

CHAPTER 35

AVOIDING ABUSE AND OVERCOMING ITS EFFECTS IN THE FAMILY

M. GAWAIN WELLS AND LESLIE FEINAUER

*We warn that individuals who violate covenants of chastity, who abuse spouse or
offspring, or who fail to fulfill family responsibilities will one day stand accountable before God.[1]*
—"The Family: A Proclamation to the World"

Abuse in the family is a complex and painful tragedy. Many factors contribute to such hurt, and the effects of abuse may influence family members even across generations. Modern prophets and the proclamation on the family decry the sin of abuse. In this chapter we consider some of the causes and effects of abuse, and we emphasize some of the elements that help to bring about healing in the family.

It is important to remember that the power of the gospel, coupled with appropriate care from compassionate leaders and professionals, can greatly help both the abuser and the abused, freeing them from the pain, sorrow, and captivity they may feel. We must let neither our anger at someone's abuse nor our fear of a difficult and painful situation keep us from overcoming the problem. For the sake of the entire family, we must get help quickly.

PROPHETIC WARNINGS AND PROMISES

Abuse is seen by the Lord as a great sin. Leaders of His Church are instructed to consider disciplinary councils wherein members guilty of abuse may be disfellowshipped or excommunicated from the Church in order to help them repent. The Savior warned, "But whoso shall offend one of these little ones which believe in me, it were better for him that a millstone were hanged about his neck, and that he

were drowned in the depth of the sea" (Matthew 18:6). And President Gordon B. Hinckley has spoken plainly on the subject: "Who can calculate the wounds inflicted, their depth and pain, by harsh and mean words spoken in anger? . . . A husband who domineers his wife, who demeans and humiliates her, and who makes officious demands upon her not only injures her, but he also belittles himself."[2]

Prophets of God do not just warn us away from sin, they attempt to help us prevent it by counseling us towards the behaviors and feelings that will protect our families. President Hinckley has often repeated his plea for family members to treat each other with greater kindness:

I hope that each one of us will be a better husband or wife, kinder to one another, more thoughtful, more restrained in criticism, and more generous with compliments. I hope that as fathers and mothers we will strive more fully to rear our children 'in the nurture and admonition of the Lord' (Ephesians 6:4), treating them with respect and love, giving encouragement at every opportunity and subduing our critical remarks.[3]

He counseled parents: "You need more than your own wisdom in rearing [your children]. You need the help of the Lord. Pray for that help and follow the inspiration which you receive."[4] He urged families: "Let us lower our voices in our homes. Let love abound and find expression in our actions."[5]

As we consider our behavior toward family members, the Lord's words in Matthew should give each of us solemn pause: "Verily I say unto you, Inasmuch as ye have done it unto one of the least of these my brethren, ye have done it unto me" (Matthew 25:40).

CAUSES AND EFFECTS OF ABUSE

Because abusive behavior ranges from extreme physical acts to verbal harshness, a general definition of abuse refers to a continuum. In terms of child abuse and neglect, the continuum describes aversive or inappropriate control strategies and/or failure to provide minimal standards of care and nurturance.[6] Although the following types of abuse sometimes occur together, varying causes may lead to separate effects.[7] Parenthetically, note that these definitions are legal definitions; many acts might not meet the letter-of-the-law definition while the intent—the spirit of the law—is clearly abusive. At its core, abuse is based on wrongful desires—a desire to hurt, a desire to control others or use them for one's own gratification, or even a lack of desire to care for someone else's needs.

Physical abuse represents an act in which a spouse, parent, or caretaker deliberately inflicts physical injury upon another. Slapping a person's face, pulling hair, or throwing someone against a wall is abusive. Similarly, objects used to inflict punishment such as belts, hairbrushes, or sticks are used to hurt someone, not to teach or correct a problem.

Neglect occurs when a child or elder is not given adequate love, supervision, or attention. Proper food, clothing, shelter, education, and medical care may be lacking. In contrast to physical abuse, the attitude of neglect is usually one of "Don't bother me. I don't care what you need. You're not getting it from me."

Sexual abuse refers to the involvement of a child or adolescent in sexual activities that they are developmentally too immature to understand or give consent to. It may also include forced sexual activities between married or unmarried adults. Sexual abuse ranges from exposing people against their will to sexual images, to fondling of sexual parts, to rape. The common denominator is treating someone else as though that person were an object to be used for sexual pleasure.

Verbal abuse refers to consistent emotional indifference, rejection, or verbal punishment. Verbal abuse may be particularly difficult to recognize and remediate because individuals often do not feel guilty when they hurt others with words. Name calling, demean-

ing comments, or cutting sarcasm may not seem like abuse, but the intent is the same as in physical abuse, and the victim's sense of being rejected, unloved, and unable to please can be profound.

Emotional abuse, like verbal abuse, represents an attempt to inflict emotional pain through humiliation, rejection, or psychological control.[8] It is usually present with all other forms of abuse and is potentially the most harmful, but the most difficult to identify and correct. Without any other action or even words, a withering look, the "silent treatment," avoiding eye contact, or turning away in disgust by a parent can be devastating to a child who desperately wants to please.

Spiritual abuse may not be found in any legal text, but it can apply to a believing people. This term refers to one's using Church doctrine or scriptures as a weapon for domination, a means to gratify one's pride, or to hurt another through creating inappropriate guilt and shame. For example, a husband may use Ephesians 5:22 ("Wives, submit yourselves unto your own husbands") as a means of demanding improper or unwanted sexual activity when the context of the scripture provides a virtually opposite meaning. President Spencer W. Kimball, commenting on Ephesians 5:25 ("Husbands, love your wives, even as Christ also loved the church, and gave himself for it") offered this counsel:

> Can you think of how [Christ] loved the church? Its every breath was important to him. Its every growth, its every individual, was precious to him. He gave to those people all his energy, all his power, all his interest. He gave his life—and what more could one give? . . . When the husband is ready to treat his household in that manner, not only his wife but also his children will respond to his loving and exemplary leadership. It will be automatic. He won't need to demand it.[9]

Consider again the common psychological themes in the several forms of abuse: a desire to hurt or inflict pain, a desire for total control of another, and a desire to gratify oneself without regard for another's feelings. Both women and men can be guilty of this desire for "unrighteous dominion" (D&C 121:39). A wife can demean her husband's efforts to provide for his family, can constantly repudiate his normal desires for affection and intimacy, or demand that a husband isolate himself from his family of origin, using as a weapon the scripture in Moses 3:24 ("Therefore shall a man leave his father and his mother, and shall cleave unto his wife; and they shall be one flesh"). Moreover, siblings can be abusive to one another in similar ways. Perhaps for that reason, King Benjamin declared that parents who have the Spirit of the Lord with them will not allow their children to fight and quarrel with one another but will teach them to love and serve one another (see Mosiah 4:14, 15).

CAUSES OF ABUSE

Turning briefly to causes, we recognize that some acts are simply evil, with no other explanation than that the abuser is gratified by his or her behaviors. Concerned only about themselves, these abusers have little desire to change their ways. They may justify their actions by blaming others for "making" them angry or "pushing" them into iniquity or abuse; some offenders view their acts as compensation for not having emotional or sexual needs met Yet even for these offenders, abuse may have grown out of a pattern of behavior which began as less damaging. Spankings may turn into beatings. The spiral of pornography that first trapped individuals by suggestive advertising may escalate into seeking pornography, followed by seeking harder and more and more explicit forms of pornography, and from there into behavioral acts of sexual abuse and violence.[10]

Personal and chronic stress is sometimes a factor in abuse, in the form of financial pressures, a poor job or none at all, health problems, or severe marital difficulties.[11] Mounting pressures, possibly of many kinds, stretch patience and tempt some to act out in a variety of ways, from blaming to vocal tirades to physical violence.[12] Physical and emotional isolation from relatives or other caring and supportive people also increases stress, leaving a person with a feeling of having no place to turn for relief.[13] Husbands, wives, or even the children in the family may themselves be experiencing emotional difficulties that distort their perceptions of their loved ones and their responsibilities toward them. The tension of obsessive-compulsive disorders, for instance, creates rigidity and anger when others are not helping to meet the demands for extreme order provoked by the illness. Women experiencing major depression may feel that they are unable even to get out of bed to care for their youngsters, let alone laugh and play with them.[14]

Some parents may feel overwhelmed and helpless to deal with a particular child and they may lash out in anger in moments when they feel inadequate. Children sometimes have physical or behavioral prob-lems that make them difficult to parent. When one form of behavioral control doesn't seem to work, many parents increase the severity of their attempts to control rather than consider other alternatives.[15] If spanking doesn't work, they angrily move to beating; if reprimands don't work, mounting frustration dictates more emotional punishment. Tired and under pressure, people act out in ways they might never have thought they would, damaging their relationships. Sadly, because the pressures continue, they may return to such behaviors with increasing regularity and force.

Abusive individuals may have been abused themselves as children or witnessed violence between their parents. They may not recognize that their ways of interpreting their children's or spouse's behaviors have been deeply influenced by their "training" as a child in their own family and that they have adopted their parents' means of handling conflict.[16] For example, one young husband, raised in a strict and physically punitive home, thought that his toddler should be quieter when he demanded it of her because he remembered the standard in his home. Needless to say, his scolding and then spanking did not work to get his daughter to be quiet The extremity required to frighten any child into silence is abusive. This does not mean, however, that a majority of parents who were abused as children will become abusers. Many parents have had to overcome such difficult beginnings and have done so with great courage. (Chapter 11 describes transitional people, individuals who break negative patterns of family interaction.) Some of these parents have testified to the healing power of the Atonement in relieving them of the burdens of their earlier experiences. However, considerable stress prompts some individuals to revert to patterns of behavior they learned as children. Thus, they may find themselves taking their anger, frustration, or desperation out on those closest and dearest to them—spouses and children.

Sadly, one's inability to control emotions may open the door to further abuse, creating a cyclic pattern. A husband may feel great remorse, plead for forgiveness, and be uncharacteristically loving following a violent argument. His wife, frightened but wanting to be reassured, forgives him and enjoys his special attentions, and neither takes steps to remediate the difficulties which occasioned the incident.[17] Without any other resolution, the stage may be set for another such occurrence.

Please note that the description of these "causes"

is not meant to excuse the acts but to provide a context for understanding how abusive behaviors can occur in the lives of otherwise normal and good people. It is important to add as well that people, particularly children, are resilient. With the help of the Savior, so much can be overcome. Parents should remember that there is a great deal of difference between an isolated incident of lost temper where harshness is used and the occurrence of repeated and frequent abuse. While not minimizing the effects of any abuse, we should realize that parents sometimes punish themselves unduly—even to the extent that they lose hope of changing their behavior.

EFFECTS OF ABUSE

Now let's consider how these experiences affect children and how the effects of abuse may be felt across generations. Any abusive event, experienced or observed, to some degree makes children insecure. Children must make meaning of both their experiences and their sense of themselves in relationship to their parents and other important people in their lives. Early in life most children accept what others say about them as accurate. Experiences in an abusive family may create for children a sense that they were not wanted, not protected, not good enough, or somehow "bad."[18]

Most mental health professionals agree that individuals who are neglected or abused physically or sexually will experience some difficulty with emotional intimacy and ability to relate to others.[19] These individuals experience the pain of feeling unacceptable, broken, defective, or damaged in some way. It is as though they feel that somehow something about them is so wrong that they can't fix it. Another name for this set of feelings is *shame*—not *ashamed,* which generally means that the individuals have done something that was inappropriate or questionable—but shame, which implies that the individuals see themselves as being disagreeable, disgusting, and offensive. Fears of rejection or abandonment are constant companions to shame. Because every person has a deep need to be accepted and loved, to feel shame is to fear that people who really know you will certainly not want to love you. Distressed individuals find ways to avoid their internal pain, their feelings of anxiety, sadness, alienation, and rejection.[20]

Many people who experience shame have tried to compensate for these feelings by trying to appear as "perfect" as possible. They try hard to present themselves as very capable people, keeping their inner sense of incompetence well hidden. Their inner turmoil is not exposed until well into a relationship.

Sometimes when these individuals become involved in intimate relationships with spouses and children, they are not able to contain their feelings of shame and "badness." Their fears of inadequacy and frustration seep out into the relationship; they attempt to gain more control over situations in order to avoid being rejected; and they may abuse others or engage in sexually inappropriate kinds of behaviors.

HEALING: INTERVENTION AND TREATMENT

Although the experience of abuse is devastating and its effects far reaching, much can be done to stop abuse and facilitate healing. Abused persons and their loved ones should consider the following steps.

Report the abuse and protect the victim. The best response to abuse is a clear message that it will not be tolerated. One of the most important acts we can perform for both parents and children is to report the abuse immediately to both ecclesiastical and legal authority. In many states it is a civil offense to be aware of abuse and not report it. Moreover, in spite of the family crisis that it occasions, calling attention to the problem is often the critical step in overcoming it. The victims must be protected against further abuse, and helping resources can then be mobilized on behalf of the entire family. In cases of spouse abuse, the spouse needs to seek protection from authorities or bring the abuse to the attention of someone who can prevent its happening again. Even though the offender will be remorseful and apologetic for the sinful act, the behavior is unlikely to stop unless there is intervention because nothing has changed in the pattern of interaction which provoked the abusive behavior. Church authorities, extended family members, police, and social services agencies can provide support and guidance.

Children are not powerful enough to stop the abuse but often approach someone they believe is trustworthy and might help them. The abuse needs to be investigated and the child needs to be safe, protected, and cared for in the meantime. If separation is required because of the nature of the abuse, the offender should be the one to be removed from the family rather than the child or spouse.[21]

It is also true that occasionally children may be prompted or "coached" to falsely report abuse. Angry or disturbed spouses or ex-spouses may misinterpret a child's report and in alarm use a vague story like a weapon to hurt the other. Similarly, adolescents may use "stories" as a dramatic way of getting back for supposed grievances against their fathers or step-fathers. Here it is important to use the bishop's counsel as well as his access to the Church's abuse hotline experts to reach appropriate decisions about when and how to report abuse. The key is to take the report seriously, although in some cases it may take some time to confirm whether to believe the report.

Help the victim accept that he or she is not at fault. When abuse is brought to the attention of someone, the victims are to be listened to carefully and not made to feel like they are at fault, and that reassurance must be repeated again and again.[22] In speaking to victims of abuse, Elder Richard G. Scott stated:

> I solemnly testify that when another's acts of violence, perversion, or incest hurt you terribly, against your will, you are not responsible and you must not feel guilty. You may be left scarred by abuse, but those scars need not be permanent. In the eternal plan, in the Lord's timetable, those injuries can be made right as you do your part.[23]

Especially in the case of sexual abuse, the perpetrator often tries to convince the victim either that no one will believe it if it is revealed or that the victim has actually encouraged it to happen. The guilt and shame that attends abuse is so heavy that many victims wrongly believe that they have brought it on themselves. Sometimes in an attempt to convey hope to the offender or simply because the revelation of abuse is so devastating, the victim of abuse is made to feel responsible, as though she or he were to blame for the terrible crisis now facing the entire family. However, the burden caused by carrying the awful secret without getting help has long-range consequences far more deleterious than the short-term embarrassment or difficulty facing the family.

Apart from the authorities mentioned, it is important to provide the child and family with as much confidentiality as possible. Knowledge throughout the school or neighborhood of a child's victimization can add to the confusion of the entire family, who may believe that somehow this problem makes each of them "less" than they were before the problem was discovered. One of the prominent struggles children have with sexual abuse is the feeling of being stigmatized for life as a result of the abuse.[24] They may need

---

RECOGNIZING EMOTIONAL ABUSE

Any time someone is berated, belittled, intimidated, or caused to feel less than another, the experience is emotionally abusive. Elder H. Burke Peterson provided a list of questions fathers could ask themselves to determine whether they are abusing family members emotionally.[25] The questions include the following, adapted to apply to both spouses:

1. Do I criticize family members more than I compliment them?
2. Do I insist that family members obey me because I am the parent or spouse?
3. Do I seek happiness more at work or somewhere other than home?
4. Do my children seem reluctant to talk to me about some of their feelings and concerns?
5. Do I attempt to guarantee my place of authority by physical discipline or punishment?
6. Do I find myself setting and enforcing numerous rules to control my family?
7. Do family members appear to be fearful of me?
8. Do I feel threatened by the notion of sharing with other family members the power and responsibility for decision making in the family?
9. Is my spouse highly dependent on me and unable to make decisions for himself or herself?
10. Does my spouse complain of insufficient funds to manage the household because I control all the money?
11. Do I insist on being the main source of inspiration for each family member rather than teaching each child to listen to the Spirit?
12. Do I often feel angry and critical toward family members?

Box 35.1

---

to hear over and over again that this is a problem they didn't cause, but it is one they can overcome.

Seek appropriate treatment. The experience of being abused as a child carries aftereffects long into adulthood. The ability to disentangle events, meanings, and abusive behaviors may require treatment from a trained therapist while individuals "wear out" the fear, anger, and shame or guilt surrounding the memories and find their way back to rebuilding their hope of a good life.[26] In couple and family therapy, the therapist helps to create a safe working relationship among the individuals involved as they explore not only what has happened but ways to understand what has happened and to restore healthy relationships. Often the better understanding helps resolve unhealthy feelings that attend such hurtful events.

Professional counseling for problems of sexual abuse is extremely important for a child, although he or she may act as if everything is all right. Research has shown that many victims, as children, denied their problems and tried to make them go away by pretending they weren't there. Instead, they experienced more serious and long-lasting difficulties later on, especially when faced with the challenges of intimacy in adult relationships and marriage.[27]

Counseling is never an easy process. Although there are many variations, generally treatment for trauma involves a careful and gentle "working through" of painful memories to gradually separate what happened from the terrible feelings that accompanied the events. The feelings associated with the experience keep the memories alive as though the events were still happening or are happening again. Gradually, through treatment, the memories truly become the past and the victims know that they have grown beyond those experiences. Throughout the counseling experience, the victim will need consistent encouragement and support from loving family, Church leaders, and the small circle of others who need to know. The victim will understandably dread being asked to revisit the traumatic circumstances and will often wonder if it isn't better just to never talk about it again. It isn't. Victims must be reassured again and again that what they are doing is, finally, the way out of the effects of the trauma.[28] Moreover, even though it may be very painful to face what one has done to another, getting the appropriate treatment is the greatest possible blessing in the life of the offender, helping that person face the problem, overcome it, and seek forgiveness from the victim and the Lord.

Provide support. Families recovering from abuse need the support of others. An understanding bishop and loving Church members can help by decreasing the sense of isolation, giving some respite with the children when extreme stress is felt, or bringing to bear the welfare resources of the Church for financial aid, employment, or professional counseling. The bishop, through his counsel and prayers, can help recovering individuals experience the healing that comes from the Savior. Like choosing to seek professional help, allowing other loved ones or Church leaders to participate is not easy, but it can be such a vital form of support. And the Savior, who is "mighty to save" (Alma 7:14), is our most important source of relief.

The calming presence of the Spirit of the Lord must be sought for all those involved. Priesthood blessings, loving counsel from priesthood leaders, earnest prayer, and striving to live the commandments will help create a sanctuary of protection from the buffetings of such a personal and family crisis.

Again it should be reiterated that, particularly when the victims are children, the knowledge of the situation must be kept to those trusted to both know about and protect the privacy of those hurt. It is helpful sometimes for family members to develop, memorize, and be prepared to repeat a "one-liner," a sentence or two they can use to explain the circumstance at an acceptable level to those who don't need to know.

Psychotherapy of necessity tends to be a short-term relationship. Appropriate social support not only significantly speeds the process of healing, but acts to prevent falling back into painful patterns of behavior. Sometimes the memories are specific and difficult for friends and family to handle. In those situations a support group may be helpful. It must be cautioned that inappropriate support groups may also exist. Groups that are "willing to mourn with those that mourn; yea, and comfort those that stand in need of comfort" (Mosiah 18:9) but encourage people back towards health can be most helpful. Groups that encourage anger, distrust of appropriate authority, or overwhelming dependence on either the group or the group leader can exacerbate problems.[29]

We can do much to establish a caring community where support acts as a great preventive measure against stress for the family, including those recovering from the trauma of abuse. Our Church programs, such as home teaching and visiting teaching, welfare resources, and priesthood quorums, exist to bless people's lives in ways that will prevent abuse. As mentioned earlier, as we are "willing to bear one another's burdens, that they may be light; yea, and are willing to mourn with those that mourn; yea, and comfort those that stand in need of comfort" (Mosiah 18:8–9), we will have done what we can best do to make abuse in any form unthinkable.

REPENTANCE AND FORGIVENESS

The offender, through the healing power of the Savior's Atonement, can truly be "born again," washed clean of the entrapping history and set free of the compulsive feelings that prompted the abuse. President Ezra Taft Benson spoke of this process in specific reference to child abuse:

> We must earnestly desire a righteous and virtuous life. . . . There are some . . . who must pray until they, too, have "a wicked spirit rooted" from them so they can find the same joy. Attaining a righteous and virtuous life is within the capability of any one of us if we will earnestly seek for it. If we do not have these character traits, the Lord has told us that we should "ask, and ye shall receive; knock, and it shall be opened unto you" (D&C 4:7).[30]

Finally, in answer to Jeremiah's question (see Jeremiah 8:22), we testify that there is a balm in Gilead; there is a Physician, and He is our Savior, Jesus Christ. He can heal us, and in the most fundamental way, only He can heal us, whether we are victims or perpetrators (Alma 7:11–12). It takes great courage and equally great humility to seek help or repentance, but "we know that it is by grace that we are saved, after all we can do" (2 Nephi 25:23).

ABOUT THE AUTHORS

M. Gawain Wells is a clinical child psychologist and professor and chair of the Psychology Department at Brigham Young University. Originally from St. George, Utah, he learned about kindness from his father's care of the cows and calves on the family's dairy farm.

Leslie Feinauer is a professor of marriage and family therapy at Brigham Young University, where she has taught since 1984. Prior to that time, she taught at Georgetown University and the University of Utah.

ADDITIONAL READING

Victor B. Cline (1993, July), Healing wounds in marriage, *Ensign*, 23(7), 16–20.

James S. and Jeanne N. Jardine (1990, September), Avoiding unrighteous dominion, *Ensign*, 20(9), 62–66.

Judy C. Olsen (1996, June), The invisible heartbreaker, *Ensign*, 26(6), 23–29.

Jini L. Roby, et al. (2000), Awareness of abuse in the family; in David C. Dollahite, ed., *Strengthening Our Families: An In-Depth Look at the Proclamation on the Family* (Salt Lake City: Bookcraft), 253–265.

Jini L. Roby, et al. (2000), Preventing and healing from abuse; in David C. Dollahite, ed., *Strengthening Our Families: An In-Depth Look at the Proclamation on the Family* (Salt Lake City: Bookcraft), 266–277.

NOTES

1. First Presidency and Council of Twelve Apostles (1995, November), The family: A proclamation to the world, *Ensign*, 25(11), 102.

2. Gordon B. Hinckley (1991, November), Our solemn responsibilities, *Ensign*, 21(11), 50, 51.

3. Gordon B. Hinckley (2000, May), A time of new beginnings, *Ensign*, 30(5), 87.

4. Gordon B. Hinckley (1995, November), The fabric of faith and testimony, *Ensign*, 25(11), 89.

5. Gordon B. Hinckley (2000, November), An humble and a contrite heart, *Ensign*, 30(11), 89.

6. D. A. Wolfe (1987), *Child Abuse: Implications for Child Development and Psychopathology* (Newbury Park, CA: Sage).

7. For a comprehensive review of types of abuse and definitions, see B. L. Bonner, M. B. Logue, K. L. Kaufman, and L. N. Niec (2001), Child maltreatment, in C. E. Walker and M. C. Roberts, eds., *Handbook of Clinical Child Psychology*, 3rd ed. (New York: Wiley), 989–1030; see also S. T. Azar and D. A. Wolfe (1989), Child abuse and neglect, in E. J. Mash and R. A. Barkley, eds., *Treatment of Childhood Disorders* (New York: Guilford Press), 451–489.

8. See B. K. Barber, ed. (2002), *Intrusive Parenting: How Psychological Control Affects Children and Adolescents* (Washington, D.C.: American Psychological Association).

9. Spencer W. Kimball (1975, September 12), *Men of Example*; address given to religious educators, published as a pamphlet (Salt Lake City: Church Educational System), 5.

10. Wolfe (1987).

11. D. J. Kolko (1996), Child physical abuse, in J. Briere, L. Berliner, J. A. Bulkley, C. Jenny, and T. Reid, eds., *The APSAC Handbook on Child Maltreatment* (Thousand Oaks, CA: Sage), 21–50; R. J. Gelles (1973), Child abuse as psychopathology: A sociological critique and reformulation, *American Journal of Orthopsychiatry*, 43, 611–621; D. G. Gil (1970), *Violence against Children: Physical Child Abuse in the United States* (Cambridge, MA: Harvard University Press).

12. C. H. Kempe and R. E. Helfer (1972), *Helping the Battered Child and His Family* (Philadelphia: J. B. Lippincott).

13. J. S. Milner (1998), Individual and family characteristics associated with intrafamilial child physical and sexual abuse; in P. K. Trickett and C. J. Shellenbach, eds., *Violence against Children in the Family and the Community* (Washington, D.C.: American Psychological Association), 141–170.

14. C. E. Walker, B. L. Bonner, and K. L. Kaufman (1988), *The Physically and Sexually Abused Child: Evaluation and Treatment* (New York: Pergamon Press).

15. S. Levine (1983), A psychobiological approach to the ontogeny of coping; in N. Garmezy and M. Rutter, eds., *Stress, Coping, and Development in Children* (New York: McGraw-Hill), 107–131.

16. R. M. Friedman, J. Sandler, M. Hernandez, and D. A. Wolfe (1981), Child abuse; in E. J. Mash and L. G. Terdal, eds., *Behavioral Assessment of Childhood Disorders* (New York: Guilford Press), 221–255.

17. N. S. Jacobson and A. Christensen (1996), *Integrative Couple Therapy: Promoting Acceptance and Change* (New York: Norton).

18. J. M. Harper and M. H. Hoopes (1990), *Uncovering Shame: An Approach Integrating Individuals and Their Family Systems* (New York: Norton).

19. Ibid.

20. Ibid.

21. Azar and Wolfe (1989).

22. C. S. Schroeder and B. N. Gordon (1991), *Assessment and Treatment of Childhood Problems* (New York: Guilford Press).

23. Richard G. Scott (1992, May), Healing the tragic scars of abuse, *Ensign, 22*(5), 32.

24. D. Finkelhor and A. Browne (1986), Initial and long-term effects: A conceptual framework; in D. Finkelhor, et al., eds., *A Sourcebook on Child Sexual Abuse* (Beverly Hills, CA: Sage), 180–198.

25. H. Burke Peterson (1989, July), Unrighteous dominion, *Ensign, 19*(7), 10–11, adapted to include both spouses.

26. K. S. Calhoun and P. A. Resick (1993), Post-traumatic stress disorder; in D. H. Barlow, ed., *Clinical Handbook of Psychological Disorders: A Step-by-Step Treatment Manual,* 2d ed. (New York: Guilford Press), 48–98.

27. L. L. Feinauer, J. Mitchell, J. M. Harper, and S. Dane (1996), The impact of hardiness and severity of childhood sexual abuse on adult adjustment, *The American Journal of Family Therapy, 24,* 206–214.

28. Calhoun and Resick (1993).

29. It may be wise to check with an ecclesiastical leader for assistance in selecting a program that meets Church-recommended guidelines.

30. Ezra Taft Benson (1983, November), What manner of men ought we to be? *Ensign, 13*(11), 43.

Overcoming Same-Sex Attraction

Erin Eldridge

I was Mia Maid president. I had a deep conviction of the truthfulness of the gospel. And I found myself attracted to other girls. I had no idea, at the time, of the turmoil those conflicting feelings would cause.

My attractions to girls created a flurry of emotions. I didn't welcome the attractions. I didn't understand them. And I certainly didn't choose them. Why would someone who has a strong testimony of the gospel choose to engage in a wrenching conflict with that testimony? After all, the terms "gay" and "Latter-day Saint" seem diametrically opposed. And when they clash within a faithful Saint, chaos results.

What was wrong with me? Was I a pervert? A misfit? I wanted desperately to choose the right. I even had a CTR ring to prove it. Scriptures said my faith would make me whole. Yet, in conflict with my emerging feelings, I felt torn apart. The Church said one thing. My heart said another.

I managed to subdue, or ignore, or disguise my homosexual feelings. I dated boys in high school, awkwardly, in a misguided attempt to somehow make it all work.

After I left home for college, I took a serious look at the Church. It seemed to offer no comfort, as far as living an alternative lifestyle. Whenever I attended, I felt worse about myself. Finally, I stopped attending altogether. I couldn't take the conflict anymore.

I started pursuing relationships with women and found I enjoyed their companionship. Feelings I'd kept buried for years soon surfaced. I felt as though I'd finally been set free—free to be the person I thought I wanted to be. At church I'd experienced a lack of understanding and a sense of rejection. But in same-sex relationships, I felt total acceptance. Something finally felt comfortable and good in my life. At least, it felt right and good as long as I ignored my testimony. And when my testimony resurfaced, I'd try to mold the gospel to fit my way of life. I'd insist that the Lord must approve of same-sex relationships since I

was "born that way." It was just a matter of time, I surmised, until a prophet would be savvy enough to pray for the revelation.

As time passed, I continued to struggle to make everything work. I'd step out of a relationship, start feeling cold and alone, then go back and start the cycle again.

In desperation, and out of ideas, I decided to meet with a bishop. He helped me start going to church again. But I didn't know anyone and felt so out of place. I'd sit in sacrament meeting and hope no one suspected what I struggled with and who I really was. Would I ever belong?

The struggle continued for years, off and on. What felt comfortable was wrong. Nothing made any sense, and I did not feel anyone had any answers. I abused drugs and alcohol in an attempt to ease the pain. I seriously considered committing suicide. Yet, even though I could not find rest then, I believed that someday I would. "Come unto me, all ye that labour and are heavy laden," the Savior had promised, "and I will give you rest" (Matthew 11:28).

It was by grace that I was saved—before, during, and after all I could do (see 2 Nephi 25:23). As I earnestly strived to live the gospel plan, I was helped in many ways: through the Savior, my bishop, a counselor, inspired friends, scriptures, prayer, and involvement in uplifting activities that took me outside of myself.[1]

I met with my bishop weekly, not just to be accountable but also to receive inspired counsel. He exercised priesthood influence "by persuasion, by long-suffering, by gentleness and meekness, and by love unfeigned" (D&C 121:41). I felt love in spite of my weakness. He gave me assignments—such as reading scriptural passages, talking with certain people, and participating in activities. He always praised me for small, significant successes.

A counselor helped me understand how experiences from my past, including sexual abuse and a poor relationship with my mother, may have contributed to same-sex attraction. Some past conditions and experiences didn't appear to contribute to my homosexual orientation, yet created weaknesses and unmet needs that affected my ability to overcome. I also learned to consider the conflict homosexual relationships caused me, not just the comfort they provided, and not use my past experiences as excuses to justify my behavior.

When I opened up to friends who were gospel centered, I felt a sense of belonging in the same Church that had once felt rejecting. Their acceptance of me helped me to accept myself. Their presence and their encouragement to serve others helped me cope with my unmet physical and emotional needs.

I learned to appreciate the scriptures, too. At first they were like an IV drip, providing just enough nourishment to keep me alive. I wanted to "feast upon the words of Christ" (2 Nephi 32:3) but was not accustomed to finding nourishment the Lord's way. So it came drip by drip, line upon line, here a little, and there a little.

Although the heavens seemed closed, my prayers began to break through. Heavenly Father really did know me and was willing to help as I poured my heart out to Him.

Throughout the process of overcoming, there were no life-altering events. There were just intermittent periods of light and darkness, strength and weakness, hope and hopelessness.

Today I have new challenges that are nothing like my battle between two opposing ways of life. Now my life is built upon a rock. I love the Savior's promise: "Therefore, fear not, little flock; do good; let earth and hell combine against you, for if ye are built upon my rock, they cannot prevail" (D&C 6:34).

I am now married to a man whom I deeply love. Together we are raising our children under the marriage covenant. However, whenever I talk about my struggle with same-sex attraction, I do not use marriage as an indicator of change. My change in orientation came long before I gained the desire to date men. Instead of being oriented toward homosexual relationships and a gay identity, I became oriented toward the Savior. That is the mighty change I have experienced. And a mighty change is what the Lord requires of all of us, regardless of our challenges.

Now, like King Benjamin's people, I believe the words spoken by the prophets and "know of their surety . . . which has wrought a mighty change in [me], or in [my heart], that [I] have no more disposi-

tion to do evil, but to do good continually." For I am "born of him and have become his [daughter]" (Mosiah 5:2, 7).

I don't know exactly when I went from being convinced I was a homosexual who could never find happiness outside of same-sex relationships to knowing I am a daughter of God who can only find happiness in righteous living. At some point, I decided I wanted a relationship with the Lord more than a same-sex relationship. I realized I couldn't have both. As Elder Neal A. Maxwell said, "Whatever we embrace instead of Jesus and His work will keep us from qualifying to enter His kingdom and therefore from being embraced by Him (see Mormon 6:17)."[2]

Some people who struggle with same-sex attraction fear they will have to spend the rest of their lives alone, without a close relationship with someone. But what alone feels like in the midst of the struggle is not what it feels like after the battle. I am no longer alone. I now have a close, personal relationship with the Lord Jesus Christ. And I greatly prefer a close relationship with the Savior over a homosexual relationship. It is impossible to maintain both.

During these last days, the adversary is trying to convince us that many trials and weaknesses cannot be overcome: "I am anorexic." "I'm an alcoholic." "I am weak." "I am gay." And all the while the Great I Am stands before us. He is calling us to something beyond our mortal condition and reminding us that we were with Him long before we were with the world. He is asking us to become "even as I am" (3 Nephi 27:27; see also D&C 29:1).

For years, truth was hidden from my view. Pain, anger, guilt, confusion, and doubt presented a false identity and smothered my true one. Sparks of divinity would flash, quickly doused by my mortal susceptibilities and temptations. Just as soon as I felt a call to something greater, I became painfully aware of something lesser.

Today, the constant awareness of my own divine potential far outweighs the fleeting awareness of my past. I don't feel that I am gay. I don't feel as though I'm denying myself or living a lie. I know that I am living the greatest truth of all. Deep within I have a sense of who I am and who I can become. Because of my past, some people may insist that I'm a latent homosexual. I lay claim to latent divinity.

ABOUT THE AUTHOR

Erin Eldridge is an author and speaker, with much of that work centered around her experiences with same-sex attraction. She and her husband are busy raising three children.

ADDITIONAL READING

A. Dean Byrd and Mark D. Chamberlain (1995), *Willpower Is Not Enough* (Salt Lake City: Deseret Book).

Erin Eldridge (1994), *Born That Way?* (Salt Lake City: Deseret Book).

Name withheld (2004, September), Compassion for those who struggle, *Ensign, 34*(9), 58.

NOTES

1. Many Latter-day Saints who struggle with same-sex attraction have been helped by participation in Evergreen International, an organization that provides education, guidance, and support to individuals and their families, friends, professional counselors, and religious leaders; visit http://www.evergreeninternational.org

2. Neal A. Maxwell (1992, November), Settle this in your hearts, *Ensign, 22*(11), 65.

E S S A Y   H 2

HELPING THOSE WITH EATING DISORDERS

MARLEEN S. WILLIAMS

Lucy[1] was the ideal daughter. Her parents basked in the sunshine of her many accomplishments. She worked hard and excelled in all she did. Everything about her life seemed perfect. When she began to lose weight and carefully restrict her eating, her parents initially saw it as part of her already ingrained habits of doing everything right. They became alarmed and confused when her weight dropped dangerously low and she adamantly refused to eat many of the foods prepared for the rest of the family. She became secretive about her eating and disappeared into the bathroom after meals. Her parents could not understand what was happening to their "perfect" daughter. They struggled to understand the tempest raging inside her that was ruining her health and causing her to withdraw emotionally from the family. Like many high-achieving, perfectionist women, Lucy had developed an eating disorder. This was her way of feeling "in control" as pressures in her life mounted.

Most individuals with eating disorders are women, but men are also at risk.[2] The prevalence for both men and women is rising sharply.[3] Although on the surface these disorders appear to be about food and eating, it is important to understand that they represent struggles with deeper problems. You might think of struggles with food, weight, and eating habits as the tip of a large iceberg. The tip is visible. Underneath the surface, however, is a larger mass of concerns that can be even more dangerous to the person's physical, emotional, and spiritual welfare.

Many individuals develop eating disorders as they attempt to master the skills necessary to live in the adult world. When these seem overwhelming, life may feel beyond their control. Some of these skills include learning how to have healthy relationships; becoming independent; understanding and regulating emotions; understanding new feelings and changes in their bodies as they enter puberty; managing social and cultural pressures to achieve; countering false media messages about thinness, beauty, and individual worth; and developing an adult identity. Difficulty in mastering these skills may flood young people with fear of not being "good enough."

Young people in today's world have more choices and opportunities than ever before in history. However, the expectation to do everything and do it all with excellence can create stress. Teens may not always have sufficient opportunity to learn important skills for managing stress, choosing between possible options, and setting priorities. They may also be required to perform beyond their current capabilities. When faced with these impossible situations, they frequently turn to the belief that keeping their eating and weight perfectly under control can provide a solution to their distress.

Mary's family moved when she was in the ninth grade. When she entered her new school, she felt lonely and frightened. She noticed that many of the more popular girls were very thin. Her body was naturally more rounded. She believed that her classmates would like her more if she could lose weight. She also began struggling to keep up in school.

Mary began to feel overwhelmed, left out, and under stress. She heard from some of the other girls that you could "eat whatever you wanted if you just throw it up after you eat." At first, she believed that this was the solution to her problems. She thought she could comfort her loneliness with food and still get thinner through purging (throwing up). This did not provide any real, lasting solutions to her problems, however. After a while, she found that she could not stop the cycle of bingeing and purging. What had been an attempt to control her life was now controlling her.

Eating disorders involve dynamics similar to other addictions. When skills are lacking to manage painful emotions, a person may turn to "quick-fix" solutions such as food, drugs, pornography, compulsive sex, alcohol, or compulsive shopping. These "quick-fix" solutions may temporarily soothe painful feelings but result in even more painful consequences (see chapter 12). In addition, the "quick fix" does not provide a real solution to the original problem. The person begins to feel helpless, inadequate, and out of control. This creates more emotional pain and even further reliance on the "quick-fix." Recovering from an addiction requires learning new skills, attitudes, and behaviors in addition to stopping the "quick-fix" behavior.

Mary had always trusted her parents. When she expressed her loneliness and fear of failing in school, her mother listened attentively without judging or punishing. She gently told Mary that she knew Mary had an eating disorder and that she wanted to help Mary. She reassured her that her health and happiness were more important than being a high achiever. She asked Mary what kind of support she needed to feel more confident at school. Her parents hired a tutor to help with her hardest classes. Her mother also agreed to prepare healthier meals and have healthy food available. This made it easier for Mary to manage her weight without bingeing and purging. Mary also agreed to see a counselor and a dietitian. Her parents took the counselor's suggestion to let Mary invite friends over to the house more often and even included a friend on some family outings.

Mary's father and brothers eliminated any negative comments about women's weight and body size.

They complimented Mary on her strengths and positive qualities. She began to appreciate her own unique beauty. As Mary began to feel more comfortable, she seldom resorted to bingeing and purging.

Many Latter-day Saints who struggle with eating disorders also struggle with spiritual concerns. They may misinterpret gospel concepts and see God as a demanding, punitive parent who is angry or withdraws love when they fail to perform well or struggle with weaknesses. They may not understand the difference between a frantic drive for a flawless performance and a healthy quest for wholeness, growth, and eternal perfection. Christ's admonition to be perfect (see Matthew 5:48) is not a command to immediately possess all possible skills and good qualities without ever making a mistake. It is a commandment to enter into a covenant process that involves repentance, change, and growth. This process is dependent upon Christ's Atonement and takes time, experience, and patience. Christ is the only one who ever lived a perfect life. However, even He "continued from grace to grace, until he received a fulness" (D&C 93:13). The Prophet Joseph Smith clarified the spiritual quest for perfection:

> When you climb up a ladder, you must begin at the bottom, and ascend step by step, until you arrive at the top; and so it is with the principles of the gospel—you must begin with the first, and go on until you learn all the principles of exaltation. But it will be a great while after you have passed through the veil before you will have learned them. It is not all to be comprehended in this world; it will be a great work to learn our salvation and exaltation even beyond the grave.[4]

People with perfectionist tendencies experience excessive shame over mistakes and struggles. They believe they are lovable and valued only if their lives are perfect. If young people have experienced abuse or other painful life events, they may interpret these traumatic events as evidence that God has abandoned them because they are unlovable. They may then turn to perfectionism and eating problems as a way to compensate for deep feelings of inadequacy and perceived unworthiness. Helping Latter-day Saints come to an accurate understanding of God's love, the Atonement, and the purposes of mortality can help them develop spiritual resources to combat the eating disorder.

How can parents and loved ones help to calm the emotional, psychological, and spiritual storm that accompanies an eating disorder? Do not try to control the person's eating for them. People with eating disorders often struggle with confusion about control of their own behavior. Tightening control by trying to force them to eat, forcing them on a diet, monitoring their eating, or other coercive measures usually backfires. It is important to understand, however, that eating disorders can be extremely dangerous. They contribute to serious health problems such as heart irregularities, osteoporosis, severe dental problems, infertility, gastrointestinal problems, and kidney failure and have a mortality rate as high as 20 percent.[5]

Warning signs that professional help is needed include rapid weight loss of 25 percent or more, or body mass index (BMI) below 19 (e.g., 5'7" and 121 lbs., 5'1" and 100 lbs.); prolonged exercise despite fatigue and weakness; intense fear of gaining weight; peculiar patterns of handling food; amenorrhea in women; episodes of bingeing and purging more than once a week for 3 months or longer; depression, suicidal thoughts, frequent insomnia, or extreme mood swings; insistence on dieting even though build/body is very slim; hair loss, fainting spells, gastrointestinal disturbances, frequent sore throats, and swollen glands or cheeks.

Suggestions for those who wish to help a loved one with an eating disorder[6] include the following:

- Reinforce definitions of success that focus on personal qualities rather than performance, achievement, and appearance. For example, being a good friend may be more important than winning a competition.
- Honor diversity of appearance and body build. Beauty is found in many sizes, shapes, and colors.
- Be aware of how competition and perfectionism can negatively affect relationships.
- Be inclusive rather than exclusive. A Zion community has a place of value and belonging for all of its members.
- Keep conversations about eating supportive and confidential rather than adversarial. Focus on concern for health rather than weight or appearance.
- Do not try to change the behavior yourself. Seek help from God and appropriate Church leaders. Seek competent professional help if necessary.
- Be supportive. Be available to listen with understanding. Show you care. Encourage the person to get help.

- Be yourself. Share your own struggles and challenges. Be open and real.
- Remember that a person with an eating disorder is just that—a person first and only secondarily a person who has problems with food.
- Provide positive reinforcement for strengths. This builds feelings of self-worth.
- Understand that recovery can be a slow process and may involve setbacks.
- Give nonjudgmental feedback. Use "I" statements such as, "I worry about you when you don't join us for dinner."
- Model healthy eating habits and attitudes.

A spiritual perspective can strengthen family relationships when a family member struggles with an eating disorder. Christ promised peace to those who have faith in him (see John 14:27; 16:33). That peace is not a promise of a "perfect" life without struggles, temptations, and challenges. It is not peace "as the world giveth," but the peace that comes from a correct understanding of the plan of salvation and from faith in Christ. He who calmed the tempest and stilled the sea can also calm the soul and bring peace to a troubled heart. This peace enables us to continue toward exaltation and eternal life with patience and hope.

ABOUT THE AUTHOR

Marleen S. Williams works as associate clinical professor of counseling psychology at Brigham Young University. Her Ph.D. is in clinical psychology and she specializes in women's mental health. She and her husband, Dr. Robert F. Williams, have nine children and sixteen grandchildren.

ADDITIONAL READING

Deborah Low (2002), *The Quest for Peace, Love and a 24" Waist* (Springville, UT: Bonneville Books).
Mary Pipher (1994), *Reviving Ophelia: Saving the Selves of Adolescent Girls* (New York: Random House).
Evelyn Tribole and Elyse Resch (1995), *Intuitive Eating* (New York: St. Martin's Press).

NOTES

   1. Names have been changed.
   2. Eating Disorders Coalition website, http://www.edauk.com
   3. Eating Disorders Coalition for Research website, http://www.eatingdisorderscoalition.org
   4. In L. E. Dahl and D. Q. Cannon (1997), *Encyclopedia of Joseph Smith's Teachings* (Salt Lake City: Bookcraft), 519.
   5. Eating Disorders Coalition website, http://www.eatingdisorderscoalition.org
   6. Gurze Books is an excellent resource for books on eating disorders; visit http://www.gurze.com

Effectively Coping with Moody or Angry Children and Teens

Kirk B. Thorn

Many times each year, despairing parents contact me, a clinical psychologist, with frustration and concern for their unhappy or difficult children and adolescents. Almost always they describe their son or daughter as demonstrating several of the following symptoms: irritable, impulsive, defiant, negative, stubborn, shy, unhappy, sad, withdrawn, aggressive, uncaring, hyperactive, argumentative, teary, unfocused, aimless, and angry. All of these characteristics can be expressed by normal children who are typically developing and learning the basics of self-control and social skills. Often, these behaviors can be properly viewed as difficulties or challenges that parents can address over time and in loving and patient ways.

In some cases, however, these same characteristics may be indicative of more serious disorders, particularly when these characteristics are also accompanied by additional symptoms. These symptoms may include increased or decreased appetite, increased or decreased sleep, fatigue, feelings of worthlessness or excessive worry or guilt, low self-worth, extreme grandiose ideas, excessive talking at a louder and faster pace than usual, jumping from topic to topic quickly without normal connections, agitation, and foolish or reckless behaviors. Also, in these serious cases, children or adolescents may have been behaving this way for years and nothing has seemed to help them. As a result, parents are often deeply concerned and may become increasingly fearful for their children and what the future holds. Problems with truancy, substance abuse, poor grades, and opposition or defiance, especially toward parents, intensify difficulties in home and family life.

As a clinical psychologist, I have had many opportunities to observe the interactions between parents and children or teens who struggle with these serious problems. As I counsel with parents, I find that clarifying for parents how these problems have come about gives them faith and hope in implementing solutions. In my initial interview, I ask parents what their discipline methods have been and how effective those methods have been with the child or teen. Moreover, I look for significant historical parent-child interaction patterns that may have contributed to the problem. Parents and adolescents can often point out ineffective interactive behaviors that have created frustration and stress in the parent-child relationship. As children grow into adolescence, they frequently choose impulsively to act out their anger, moods, and frustrations, reacting to their own problems and challenges. The longer these unresolved problems persist, the more likely it is that parents and their adolescent have fallen into a negative reciprocal pattern.

To correct a negative pattern requires that both parents and their teens consider their choices and interaction patterns. For example, parents may need to stop what they have been doing that has been ineffective, reevaluate the child or adolescent's behavior; and finally, implement effective changes in their own behavior. This process requires prayerful consideration, honest introspection, and observation of the results. The importance of prayerful consideration and subsequent introspective meditation cannot be overemphasized. In many cases when this is done, parents find ways, for example, to leave insecurities behind, create new patterns in the home that ease stressful communication and conflict, or shift the expectations they have for their children to more appropriate levels.

If positive changes in parenting interactions are made but the child continues to present the original symptoms, these children may have more serious issues that may require therapy and can be better identified, diagnosed, and differentiated as therapy progresses. It is not uncommon for children to exhibit more than one disorder or problem. It is also not unusual for one parent or both to display and suffer from symptoms of exactly the same disorder or problem from which the child is suffering. Mood disorders such as depression or bipolar disorder, many forms of anxiety (such as obsessive-compulsive disorder, panic disorder, separation anxiety, and generalized anxiety), thought and mood disorders, many phobias, and attention deficit hyperactivity disorder (ADHD) may have a strong genetic basis occurring in several members of the same family. Also, I have seen cases of children with mild autism or Asperger's (developmental disorders of sociality) go undiagnosed for years. Many of these disorders or traits may also have their roots in the environment, but when symptoms consistent with these problems exist, professional assistance is necessary. (See Essay H4 for more about learning disabilities.)

When symptoms imply one of these more serious problems may exist, parents with similar problems may be interacting negatively with their children because of their own feelings of anguish, despair, or worry. In these cases all family members may need to be involved and assessed before treatment can be successful. Medication may sometimes be necessary for effective treatment. However, many cases of anxiety and depression can be treated through counseling if they are properly diagnosed in the early stages. The clinician can then recommend effective strategies to be used by the parents and their children.

In some cases, the best choice is medication coupled with therapy. In most instances, children who require medication make excellent improvement, which is readily noticed and appreciated by the child and parents. At times the child's behavior is affected within a day or two. Generally, it requires a few weeks for the medication to build up to therapeutic levels. In some cases, adjustments may need to be made to the dosage or medication to achieve optimal therapeutic results.

COMMUNICATING EFFECTIVELY WITH ANGRY OR MOODY CHILDREN

Sometimes parents have become so frustrated with their child and the troubling behavior that they become ineffective and even antagonistic in communications with their child. Outside stressors can also increase the difficulty parents may encounter in their efforts to be effective communicators with their child.

Elder Marvin J. Ashton gave the following insights about communication in families:

> To be effective, family communication must be an exchange of feelings and information. . . . Time and participation on the part of all are necessary. . . . Differences should not be ignored, but should be weighed and evaluated calmly. One's point or opinion usually is not as important as a healthy, continuing relationship. Courtesy and respect in listening and responding during discussions are basic. . . . How important it is to know how to disagree with another's point of view without being disagreeable. . . . Try to be understanding and not critical. Don't display shock, alarm, or disgust with others' comments or observations. Don't react violently. Work within the framework of a person's free agency. Convey the bright and optimistic approach.[1]

As parents communicate with their angry or moody child or teen, they may wish to consider these related principles:

1. Do not expect children or adolescents to understand their problems entirely; they are only children. Firstborn children may be especially frustrating because they think they are adults.

2. Exercise patience in trying to listen to what your child or teen is really saying. A tense face, clenched fists, stern looks, and harsh voice convey impatience. Remember patience is merely a process of achieving a desired goal. You cannot force the goal. The problem may not go away immediately—it takes time.

3. Listen carefully to what the child or teen is saying in both words and behavior without "correcting" his or her feelings and concerns. Rather than telling your child what he or she is feeling, acknowledge and validate the expressed feelings. Frequently when parents do this they surprise themselves with how much more they can hear. While listening, they may find additional insight and inspiration about dealing with the problem.

4. Do not push your solutions on your son or daughter. Ask if he or she would like you to help or provide suggestions. Or ask what the child plans to do to resolve the problem. This method encourages cooperation and gives the child or teen ownership over resolving his or her own problems.

5. Provide examples of how you have coped with similar problems in your own life. Children and teens may respond positively to stories of how you have learned to cope with life's problems. They especially like it when they discover you are not perfect

and have had troubles as well. If your own resolutions to problems are humorous, then all the better.

6. Spare the criticism in your communications. If your child or teen feels criticized, he or she is much more likely to resist your assistance in resolving problems. Those suffering from depression already feel hopeless and worthless. Do not feed this with more criticism.

7. Remember to leave the emotion out of the conversation. Almost always a stern or frustrated voice will increase a child's resistance and will often result in explosive outbursts from adolescents.

8. People, including children and teens, dislike being controlled. Boundaries and limits are different from overcontrol.

9. Be direct in your communications. Talk about the problem or situation that concerns you. Be sure to pick your battles.

10. Timing is critical. If you cannot talk without shouting or raising your voice, wait until you can so the child or teen might hear you better.

11. Address issues before they become unmanageable. Small problems are much easier to address and the child or teen is more apt to cooperate in solving these problems before they get too big.

12. Remember, positive reinforcement for appropriate behavior is much more effective than punishment. Look for the good things in your children's behavior and let them know you notice. Those who hear only negative tones or information sometimes learn to seek negative parental responses for attention.

Know where you want to end up. Have a goal for how you would like your child's behavior to be, but don't expect to get there all at once. Little gains gradually accumulate and the goal will be realized.

Conclusion

Finally, it is important for parents to remember that rearing children in today's world is difficult. All parents make mistakes. If you make a mistake as you parent your child, remember to apologize and then prompt yourself not to repeat it. Children are resilient and they are forgiving. Never give up and do not hesitate to seek professional advice from a reputable child or adolescent therapist if your own thoughtful solutions have not yielded good results.

ABOUT THE AUTHOR

Kirk B. Thorn received his Ph.D. in clinical psychology from Brigham Young University. He has worked as a school psychologist and in a mental health setting, and he has been in private practice for the last 15 years. He and his wife, Debra, have four children.

ADDITIONAL READING

Sean E. Brotherson (2004, August), When your child is depressed, *Ensign, 34*(8), 52–57.

Mary A. Fristad and Jill S. Goldberg Arnold (2004), *Raising a Moody Child: How to Cope with Depression and Bipolar Disorder* (New York: Guilford Press).

Scott P. Sells (2001), *Parenting Your Out-of-Control Teenager: Seven Steps to Reestablish Authority and Reclaim Love* (New York: St. Martin's Press).

NOTE

1. Marvin J. Ashton (1976, May), Family communications, *Ensign, 6*(5), 52, 54.

E S S A Y   H 4

Learning Disabilities Can Be Learning Strengths

Christian Moore

Learning disabilities are sometimes referred to as "invisible disabilities." It's difficult to tell by looking at someone that he or she struggles academically. People with learning disabilities have average to above-average intelligence; they are creative problem solvers and often are very successful in the workplace—they just process information differently. Learning disabilities can be understood as a significant discrepancy between the individual's current academic performance and his or her intellectual potential. Some people with learning disabilities like to refer to their learning challenges as learning differences.

There is a broad spectrum of types of learning disabilities with an equally broad spectrum of impacts.[1] Although learning disabilities can be converted into an asset over the life span, the early academic years can be emotionally challenging. Also, the transition from high school to independent living and the search for a job with a livable income is often difficult, but not impossible. This essay will look at the emotional side of having learning disabilities and offer some strategies to help those with learning disabilities.

Just Think

There are two words that most people with learning differences hate to hear and would probably never say to another person: *just think*. The first time I remember hearing those two dreaded words was in the first grade while learning addition. Even now, twenty years later, I remember the teacher leaning over my shoulder and saying, "Just pay attention. Two plus two equals what? It's right in front of you." Then she repeated the dreaded words, *just think*: "If two plus one equals three then what would two plus two equal? Think about it." As I sat there looking at the paper, I was thinking, "What the heck do two twos have to do with four, and when is this teacher going to walk away from my desk and when is she going to stop tapping

her long, red fingernails on the number 4? I'm starting to wonder if the answer is in her fingernails, because *just thinking* is not helping me get the answer and as soon as she walks away everyone will stop smiling at me and looking at me like I am an alien because I don't see how a 2 and another 2 magically create a 4."

Third grade is my first memory of being around several other kids like myself who just needed to *think*; there were about five of us and we sat at the back of the room at a table. All the other kids in the class had individual desks. I also noticed that we had different math and reading books. The teacher explained things in what seemed to be a language that only the other kids could understand.

When I was a teenager, I was still struggling with telling time. I had a lot of doubt about my future. How can you be successful and make a living when doing something as simple as running a cash register at McDonald's seems impossible and terrifying? The feelings of fear and frustration in school made school miserable, with nothing to numb the pain except acting out enough to divert attention from the real issue: not being able to process information in a way that will bring you positive feedback, respect, and a passing grade. That experience of feeling left out is often with me still. Now that I am older, I can better keep it hidden, but inside I am often repeating to myself the words I heard all the way through school: *just think*.

Hard Work vs. Smarts

I have the opportunity to speak to many students and I often ask them what they think will take them farther in life, hard work or being smart? Often the students will yell at the top of their lungs, "Being smart!" I spend the next hour helping them understand that hard work is often the key to success. Now, being smart and working hard is a great combination—and I believe all people with learning disabilities are smart. I would like to share with you some strategies that helped me deal with and benefit from my learning disabilities.

CONVERT THE LEARNING DISABILITY INTO AN ASSET

When I was a therapist at a community mental health agency, I sometimes had to tell parents that their child had ADHD or learning disabilities. I would bring a cake into my office and say, "We need to have a party." I then told the family, "This diagnosis can become your best friend. Often people with learning disabilities are creative, great problem solvers, and can be positive risk takers; you can take the energy from ADHD and use it to work hard." I often work long hours and have been doing this for more than 10 years; I attribute this to my learning disability and the energy from my ADHD. There are many successful CEOs and business leaders who use their learning disabilities and ADHD as an asset

I encourage teens with learning disabilities to focus their energy on what they can control. I tell them they have no control over many things that frustrate them. They can't control their teachers, the homework assignments, the graduation requirements, or peers at school. I ask them to focus on their own response to these situations, which they can control. For example, they can work on their homework, show up to class, and be respectful to the teacher. It's liberating to focus on what you can control.

Find your talent, passion, or purpose, and then put your energy into that. For example, when I was in school I was sent to the principal's office for talking nonstop during class. Today I speak at more than 100 educational training meetings a year. My talent for talking got me into a lot of trouble as a child, but as an adult it's how I make a living. Convert the interest into a passion, then use that passion to serve others.

DEVELOP YOUR EMOTIONAL INTELLIGENCE

As an adult with learning disabilities I have not mastered reading, writing, or math, but I have found that much of my life satisfaction and success comes from how I treat myself and others. Character education consists of life skills, perseverance, empathy for others, ability to forgive others, communication skills, feelings of self-worth, honesty, hard work, problem-solving skills, and building a support system. Emotional intelligence is the greatest tool I know of for

HELPING A FAMILY MEMBER WITH A LEARNING DISABILITY

Parents can provide support as they make adaptations to help each child succeed. For example, a mother recognizes that her 10-year-old son with learning disabilities feels embarrassed when asked to read a scripture at family home evening without advance preparation. She chooses a scriptural passage that matches the level of the son's reading vocabulary and they read it through several times on Monday afternoon. This pays off when the child successfully participates that night in family home evening. A father recognizes that his daughter, diagnosed with ADHD, finds it difficult to clean her room because she is easily distracted. He hangs a white board in her room and writes on it three clear tasks. As the father checks on her progress, they can both admire the growing number of checks on her list. Parents can help siblings recognize that treating each child in the family fairly often means treating them differently.

It is helpful for parents to become familiar with legal rights and protective policies, obtain necessary testing to ensure appropriate diagnoses, and explore resources, such as one-on-one or small-group tutoring programs. Parents may request that teachers provide written descriptions of homework to help them accurately understand the teacher's expectations. Also, parents can encourage teachers to assign homework that provides the child with opportunities to practice skills that have already been taught and mastered in class rather than assigning homework that introduces new skills. Family members and educators, working together, can help the child begin to convert the learning disability into a learning strength.

Box H 4.1

overcoming many of the barriers that having a learning disability gives you. Along with improving your emotional intelligence, it is important that you learn about the learning disability laws. Public schools have an obligation to work with parents to create individualized education plans for students with learning disabilities. The plan focuses on your specific needs. Also, learn about the tremendous resources and advocates that most colleges and universities have—services for students with disabilities, with counselors who will help you get through the academic challenges.

CONCLUSION

It's important to remember that academics are only one of many aspects of life. You are literally a child of God; your Heavenly Father put you on this earth with many talents and abilities. The important thing is to maximize your talents and creativity and have humor when it comes to your weaknesses. Let the Lord help you convert your learning disabilities into your greatest strength (see Ether 12:27). Thankfully, our most important test on this earth is not an academic test, but a test of how we use our challenges to become more like our Heavenly Father.

ABOUT THE AUTHOR

Christian Moore, MSW, is a licensed clinical social worker and a speaker presenting at more than 100 conferences and workshops annually. He is the founder of the Why Try organization, whose aim is to help people overcome their challenges and achieve success in life. He and his wife, Wendy, have one child.

ADDITIONAL READING

Edward M. Hallowell and John J. Ratey (1994), *Driven to Distraction: Recognizing and Coping with Attention Deficit Disorder from Childhood through Adulthood* (New York: Simon & Schuster).

Edward M. Hallowell and John J. Ratey (2005), *Delivered from Distraction: Getting the Most Out of Life with Attention Deficit Disorder* (New York: Ballantine Books).

NOTE

1. For further information on various kinds of learning disabilities, visit http://www.ldanatl.org

REACHING TOWARD THOSE WHO ARE LESS ACTIVE

H. WALLACE GODDARD

Among the most painful struggles of life are disappointments that involve our highest aspirations. In a culture that teaches the vital, eternal role of family life, some of the most painful failures involve having family members who do not value and participate in the experiences that we consider sacred. Some members of the Church have spouses who choose not to participate in the Church. Some have children who have distanced themselves from family and spiritual traditions. For a person who has prized eternal family relationships above all else, the feeling of disappointment can be devastating.

A Latter-day Saint who has less-active family members has written the following: "These are serious issues, and there are no quick fixes. Week after week, declined invitation after invitation, poor choices are repeated again and again by those who seem to reject the gospel. Those continued rejections are extremely wearing on the loved ones who are waiting for their conversion. For me, continuing to hope and wait for change is just what I do. The Lord sustains me, and it seems to be my assignment. Don't assume that simply because I do have a strong testimony that this isn't a day-to-day test. It is, and it wears."[1] Fortunately, there are things that those who have less-active or non-member family members can do.

LET CHRIST TRANSFORM PAIN INTO PEACE

Jesus is the great healer. He can transform our pain and disappointment into meaning and peace. He can replace hurt with charity so that we see as He sees and love as He loves. Serenity even in the face of continuing difficulty can come when we put our trust in "him who is mighty to save" (2 Nephi 31:19).

It is certainly no accident that some of God's most faithful children have had the biggest challenges, even in their own families. Adam and Eve must have grieved at a son who was taken over by evil (Genesis 4). Abraham had a father who chose evil (Abraham 1). Isaac and Rebekah must have been saddened by some of Esau's choices (Genesis 25). Lehi and Sariah struggled because of Laman and Lemuel

(1 Nephi 2, 8). Alma the Elder sorrowed over his wayward namesake son (Mosiah 27). Heavenly Father weeps over His children who choose to follow evil over good (Moses 7). When we partner with Christ, He grants us compassion and strength to see us through the day and we have assurance of the ultimate triumph of His perfect purposes. "Come unto me, all ye that labour and are heavy laden, and I will give you rest" (Matthew 11:28). It is He who saves.

CHOOSE TO DWELL ON AND DRAW OUT THE GOOD

As a wise friend has recommended: "Don't just teach and promote the gospel. If you are in a discussion, ask questions to discover the other person's point of view. So listen to understand, not judge. Even though the inactivity of someone you love or care about can be deeply painful, don't make that the measure of your relationship. Focus on the blessing of having that person in your life. Remember that the Lord isn't going to give up on him or her."[2]

Our ability to look with redemptive compassion on those who seem spiritually dead is the measure of our spiritual maturity. The Prophet Joseph Smith declared: "The nearer we get to our heavenly Father, the more we are disposed to look with compassion on perishing souls; we feel that we want to take them upon our shoulders, and cast their sins behind our backs. . . . If you would have God have mercy on you, have mercy on one another."[3] Our compassion must also extend to family members of those who seem to have rejected the gospel.

Brother Carlfred Broderick, a nationally respected marriage and family therapist, told of a woman who appeared to have brought family misery on herself and her children-to-be by her choice in husbands. Soon after a temple marriage, the husband quit the Church and, as children joined their family, he lured them into his lifestyle. It appeared that all four of their children would choose a nonspiritual and nonreligious life. When Brother Broderick was called upon as stake president to give the woman a blessing, he made a great discovery. The Lord revealed to him that this good woman was experiencing these trials as part of her covenant to aid some of God's children who would struggle in mortality. With the help of a good bishop, the older son chose to serve a mission and he joined his mother in bringing a spiritual influence to the family.[4] Her story was a painful one with only partial victories, but she was doing the work of redemption. Any who have had fewer struggles might choose to honor her rather than scorn her. Those who have had similar challenges might choose to take hope in small victories.

RESPECT THEIR CHOICES WHILE OFFERING POINTS OF SPIRITUAL CONNECTION

Part of love is respecting agency. All of us must learn by our mortal experience to know good from evil (see Moses 6:56). Some choose a rocky path. Heavenly Father does not force His children onto the strait and narrow. Nor should we. The Master of righteous influence has declared, "No power or influence can or ought to be maintained by virtue of the priesthood [or any familial role], only by persuasion, by long-suffering, by gentleness and meekness, and by love unfeigned" (D&C 121:41).

Points of spiritual connection come most effectively into the lives of those who have made unwise choices when offered in a spirit of love. For example, family prayer is offered, but a less-active family member is not asked to pray unless he or she expresses a desire. Prayers involving personal matters, such as an individual's Church activity, are offered in private settings as faithful family members pour out their hearts to God. Providing a home atmosphere that brings the spirit of forgiveness, of love, of sincere concern, and of appreciation for the worth of souls can allow an individual who does not feel like going to church to feel a spiritual connection at home.[5] (See Box H5.1 for suggested points of spiritual connection.)

A mother created an inviting home, imbued with the Spirit, by faithfully having family home evening, telling scripture stories, and having family prayer.[6] In another case, a young adult convert to the Church was pressured by both parents to be dishonest and immoral. The parents were resentful that their counsel was not followed. But this new member observed that "I needed to express gratitude to my parents for all the kind things they had done for me. I began sending notes of appreciation to them as well as letters focusing on positive experiences from our lives."[7]

KEEP AN ETERNAL PERSPECTIVE

The Lord directs: "Therefore, dearly beloved brethren, let us cheerfully do all things that lie in our power; and then may we stand still, with the utmost assurance, to see the salvation of God, and for his arm to be revealed" (D&C 123:17). Sister Jacqueline Thursby shared her story of struggle and patience. She and her husband joined the Church as a young family. They were sealed in the temple. But her husband's interest waned. He left the Church and took their children with him. He and one of the children remain uninterested after many years of loving, praying, and ministering. Yet Sister Thursby finds joy in loving each member of her family. "We are sent to gently coax the light of Christ in each one of them until it becomes a steady flame of testimony," she wrote.[8]

We can take hope in Christ and partner with Him to assist in His work. While every effort we have made to influence family members may seem to have made little difference, we can seek the Spirit's continued direction and with faith and patience find the strength to remain steadfast. When less-active individuals do return to the fold on their own timetable, it is often the result of consistent effort on the part of loved ones, coupled with divine guidance. There is One who loves perfectly and has all power. He is able to do His work. We seek to become partners with Him in the great work of loving and blessing His children.

ABOUT THE AUTHOR

H. Wallace Goddard, Ph.D., CFLE, is a family life specialist for the University of Arkansas Cooperative Extension Service. He has written books for secular and Latter-day Saint audiences and contributes a monthly column to *Meridian Magazine*. He and his wife, Nancy, have three children and five grandchildren.

ADDITIONAL READING

Carlfred Broderick (2000), The uses of adversity; in *The Best of Women's Conference* (Salt Lake City: Bookcraft), 50–66.
Jaqueline S. Thursby (2004), *Begin Where You Are: Nurturing Relationships with Less-Active Family and Friends* (Salt Lake City: Deseret Book).

NOTES

1. J. S. Thursby, personal communication, June 4, 2004.
2. B. Keil, personal communication, June 4, 2004.
3. Joseph Fielding Smith, ed. (1972), *Teachings of the Prophet Joseph Smith* (Salt Lake City: Deseret Book), 241.
4. C. Broderick (2000), The uses of adversity; in *The Best of Women's Conference* (Salt Lake City: Bookcraft), 50–66.
5. Boyd K. Packer (1972, February), Begin where you are—at home, *Ensign*, 2(2), 70–71.
6. J. K. W. Frome (2004, June), Bringing church home, *Ensign*, 34(6), 25–27.
7. Names withheld (2004, October), Parents with different standards, *Ensign*, 34(10), 67.
8. J. S. Thursby (2004), *Begin Where You Are: Nurturing Relationships with Less-Active Family and Friends* (Salt Lake City: Deseret Book), xiv. See also Boyd K. Packer (2005, April), The light of Christ, *Ensign*, 35(4), 8–14.

Grandparenting and Extended Family Support

Richard B. Miller and Margie Egbert Edwards

*Grandparents are often the strategic reserve who can overlook dirty clothes and
untied shoelaces and sibling rivalries—not because they fail to see such, but rather, because their
unconditional love for their grandchildren is so irrepressible.[1]*
—Elder Neal A. Maxwell

Because people are living longer today than ever
before, grandparents and grandchildren are
able to enjoy their relationship for an unprecedented number of years. In earlier times, most grandparents died before or shortly after their grandchildren
were born, and it was unusual to have more than one
grandparent alive when a grandchild was an adolescent. However, today 97 percent of 20-year-old grandchildren have at least one grandparent still alive, and
nearly 40 percent have all four grandparents still alive.
Sociologist Peter Uhlenberg has observed that 91 percent of 20-year-olds in the United States today are more
likely to have a grandmother still living than were 20-
year-olds in 1900 to have their mothers still living (83
percent).[2] Grandparents are an important resource to
families, providing stability and support. And when
grandparents' health fails in later life, family members
have the opportunity to care for their needs.

The Role of Grandparents in Extended Families

Grandparents have substantial influence on their
extended families. They serve as role models to their
adult children and grandchildren, helping to promote
and maintain a family identity and essential family
values. They pass on the family's heritage by organizing family reunions, maintaining family traditions,
and recounting key stories and events in the family's
history. With their experience and wisdom, they are
an important source of support for their adult children, providing advice and information about child-
rearing practices. They also serve as mentors to their
grandchildren, supplying encouragement and counsel to them as they grow up.

Wise grandparents are careful not to interfere in
the lives of their adult children and grandchildren.
Generally, when their children become adults, grandparents should encourage and foster the independence of their children. President Spencer W. Kimball
stated: "Well-meaning relatives have broken up many
a home. Numerous divorces are attributable to the
interference of parents who thought they were only
protecting their loved children."[3]

His counsel to married children was to become
independent:

> Your married life should become independent of
> her folks and his folks. You love them more than ever;
> you cherish their counsel; you appreciate their associ-
> ation; but you live your own lives, being governed by
> your decisions, by your own prayerful considerations
> after you have received the counsel from those who
> should give it.[4]

The Family National Guard

Sometimes family circumstances make it necessary for the grandparent generation to provide

assistance to their adult children and grandchildren. Grandparents have been called "The Family National Guard."[5] During times of normalcy, grandparents are careful not to interfere in the lives of their children and grandchildren while they look for opportunities to foster relationships with them. However, if problems arise that require their help, grandparents change into their "uniforms" and play an active role in offering help and even financial assistance. Grandparents often have the resources, both of time and money, to provide significant help to younger, struggling generations. These family emergencies might include a health problem, death, unemployment, or divorce. In these situations, it is appropriate for grandparents to become more involved in helping their children and grandchildren. The help can be simple, such as helping prepare some meals, cleaning the house, or tending the grandchildren for a few days. In other cases, the help will be substantial, including having a child and grandchildren temporarily move into the grandparents' home.

Once the emergency is over, it is important that the grandparents adjust roles. They should change back into their "civilian" clothes and resume a less-involved relationship with their children and grandchildren. Although grandparents in their role as the Family National Guard do not frequently go on "active duty," they provide great strength and stability by simply being available. Knowing that their parents are there, if they are needed, gives security and

courage to adult children who are trying to establish and maintain independent lives.

PROVIDING ASSISTANCE TO EXTENDED FAMILY MEMBERS

Church leaders have taught that if a person isn't able to meet his or her own needs, family members should provide needed assistance. President Brigham Young said:

> Ever since I have been in this Church I have never suffered a relative to be maintained by the Church. . . . It is a disgrace to every man and woman that has sense enough to live, not to take care of their own relatives, their own poor, and plan for them.[6]

Although the obligation for the grandparent generation to provide needed help to children and grandchildren is clear, some of the most difficult decisions that grandparents will ever make will be concerning when and how to provide appropriate assistance. Every situation is different, making it impossible to have established rules about offering assistance. However, the principles that govern Church welfare are valuable guidelines for families who are faced with circumstances concerning family assistance. These principles were succinctly summarized by President Heber J. Grant when the Church welfare program was introduced in the 1930s. He said:

> Our primary purpose was to set up, in so far as it might be possible, a system under which the curse of idleness would be done away with, the evils of a dole abolished, and independence, industry, thrift and self respect be once more established amongst our people. The aim of the Church is to help the people to help themselves.[7]

Thus, help from grandparents to their adult children and grandchildren should, above all else, foster independence and self-reliance. Assistance that encourages long-term dependence, with no plan for eventual self-reliance of the recipient, is inconsistent with these principles. Instead, financial help should generally be a temporary bridge that helps children or grandchildren through a financial crisis and towards restored independence.

Grandparents must be clear about the conditions of the financial help. Is the money a loan, with expectations that it will be paid back? Are there expectations of reciprocal work, such as helping paint the grandparents' house, as part of the conditions for the

Asking for Assistance, Responding with Love

Grandparents can:

- Ask for help with specific needs.
- Express appreciation with thoughtful and genuine gratitude.
- Reciprocate in meaningful ways.
- Tell people how they can help. (Invite them to push the wheelchair; let them take your arm; ask them to speak into your "good" ear.)
- Find humor in situations—help others laugh with you.

Grandchildren and extended family can:

- Identify specific ways in which they would like to help.
- Make themselves available at a specific day and time. (Wash and set Grandma's hair each Friday morning.)
- Call or visit to share school events, successes, reports, or recent family photos.
- Include grandparents in family activities.
- Meet special needs. (Provide hearing and telephone amplification devices; large-print books, videos, books on tape; walkers, wheelchairs.)
- Visit with the caregiver.
- Provide respite care. Allow the caregiver to take a trip, visit friends, relax.
- Stay overnight. Perform nighttime duties.
- Call the caregiver daily.
- Bring in meals. Prepare meals ahead.
- Bring in a treat—a milkshake or fresh fruit.
- Bring your hobby or handiwork. Visit and complete your project.
- Encourage caregivers to talk about rewarding aspects of caregiving.
- Identify caregiving resources, such as hospital beds or wool mattress pads.
- Discuss caregiving challenges.
- Refer caregivers to a support group, if appropriate. Provide care for the family member while the caregiver attends the group.
- Be alert to possible caregiver stress, anxiety, and depression symptoms. Arrange for consultation with professionals, as appropriate.
- Encourage and support the caregiver's spirituality.

Box 36/2

financial help? How long will the financial assistance continue? Clarifying expectations will lead to less misunderstanding and subsequent frustration and resentment. (Essay 11 offers suggestions on helping children become independent adults.)

Some children expect continued financial support from their parents after they become adults. However, the perpetual dependence of married children on their parents is inconsistent with the Lord's command for married children to leave their parents: "Therefore shall a man leave his father and his mother, and shall cleave unto his wife: and they shall be one flesh" (Genesis 2:24). As President Spencer W. Kimball taught, part of leaving one's parents and becoming one with a spouse is to become financially independent.[8]

Consistent with the Church welfare principle of self-reliance, as well as the need for adult children to leave their parents and become independent, the grandparent generation should avoid having children "on the dole" of family assistance. How exactly to accomplish that task varies from family to family, and often is accompanied by significant concern and anguish. In these situations, grandparents are like bishops, who often struggle with similar long-term welfare concerns in their wards, trying to find the right balance between providing appropriate assistance without promoting inappropriate dependence. And like bishops, grandparents who ponder, fast, and pray for guidance from the Lord will be given direction concerning the proper way to resolve these concerns. In such important decisions, the Holy Ghost "shall teach you all things" (John 14:26) and "show unto you all things what ye should do" (2 Nephi 32:5).

Sometimes families do not have the blessing of having grandparents who provide stability and support. The grandparents may have died, or they may not be willing or able to serve as anchors in their families. In these cases, it is important to remember President Boyd K. Packer's counsel for families to adopt an older couple in their ward or neighborhood who can serve as a source of wise counsel and loving support.[9]

Providing Support for Aging Grandparents

In most families there will come a day when the health of grandparents will deteriorate and adult children and grandchildren will provide help and support for them. The commandment to "honour thy father and thy mother: that thy days may be long upon the land which the Lord thy God giveth thee" (Exodus 20:12) takes on new meaning, yet the commandment remains in force. Sister Barbara B. Smith said, "There is no better way to teach children respect for the elderly and the need for everyone to prepare for that time in life than by helping to care for their older relatives."[10] Elder Dallin H. Oaks observed that the caregiving provided to grandparents by children and grandchildren is "a worthy example [that] repeats itself from generation to generation."[11]

When elderly parents require assistance, President Ezra Taft Benson admonished families to "care for them to the very best of [your] ability."[12] Children and grandchildren can play beneficial caregiving roles in behalf of aging parents and grandparents by seeing to their needs for transportation, grocery shopping, housekeeping chores, home repairs, gardening, financial management, personal hygiene, nutrition, laundry, medications, medical attention, and church attendance. In addition, families provide emotional support in addressing and responding to elders' feelings, concerns, problems, hopes, and fears, while developing appropriate action plans. (Chapter 32 provides information on dealing with chronic illness.) Social needs do not diminish with age. Daily telephone calls, regular visits, and outings are appreciated. Telephone assurance services may be essential for frail elders.

Many elders enjoy being productive and independent. President Ezra Taft Benson encouraged us to "honor" our parents "by allowing them freedom of choice and the opportunity for independence as long as possible."[13] Encouraging participation in hobbies, reading, service activities, and sharing their talents contributes to positive self-regard and a zest for living.

CHALLENGES AND BLESSINGS IN PROVIDING SUPPORT FOR AGING GRANDPARENTS

Caregiving for grandparents and elderly family members has abundant rewards, but also presents many challenges. Emotional strain is often present in many caregiving families as caregivers seek to balance increased caregiving responsibilities with immediate family, career, community, and religious roles. Caregivers must make decisions regarding medical, social service, financial, and care-provider needs. These decisions may require consultation with other family members. (See chapter 32 for more about calling a meeting of the extended family to make caregiving decisions.)

In many cases, adult children caring for elderly parents and grandparents are older themselves, making physical strength limitations an important consideration. Assistance with bathing, toileting, feeding, and mobility require considerable physical strength. Fatigue and stress may accumulate and result in increased debilitation for the caregiver.

Relationship stress may also be problematic. The relationship between the caregiver and the grandparent can become tense, as unresolved hurts resurface in the face of the intense caregiving interaction. Relationships between adult children can become conflictual as they struggle with caregiving responsibilities and perceptions of equity.[14]

Interestingly, many grandchildren are currently assuming caregiving roles for their grandparents.[15] Like their parents, these younger caregivers experience both satisfaction and challenges in fulfilling these responsibilities. The challenges include less personal and social time, negative parenting and spousal relationships, negative impact on career advancement, and increased stress, depression, and physical health problems. Nevertheless, these younger caregivers also find that their lives are enhanced by fulfilling these caregiving responsibilities. They maintain close, reciprocal relationships with their elder family member and enjoy the companionship. They develop long-lasting positive memories. They acquire enhanced feelings of self-respect and provide valuable care that prevents nursing home placement.[16] For example, in many American Indian families it is considered a privilege to be asked to care for an elderly grandparent. Elder Bruce and Sister Marie Hafen recounted a story told them by Brigham Young University anthropologist Merlin Myers about his Navajo friend who, as a young boy, was told by his blind grandmother that his eyes and his hands were now hers—as she had cared for him, now he would have an opportunity to care for her. Both the grandmother and grandson were grateful for this reciprocal relationship.[17]

In addition, many caregivers have found spiritual satisfaction in their caregiving experiences. They have validated the meaning of their family member's life and have "[come] to appreciate the inner strengths . . . cultivated or learned in the caregiving struggle."[18] One study of caregiving grandchildren found that one-third of them reported increased church attendance as "an outcome of their caregiving roles" and acknowledged "their faith as a source of strength in dealing with the strains of the caregiving role."[19] In another caregiving study, prayer was identified by three-quarters of the caregivers as "a coping strategy."[20]

It is important for caregivers to address their own needs while attending to the needs of aging family members. When this is accomplished, caregivers are more likely to find satisfaction in providing caregiving services. (Box 36.2 provides ideas for meeting caregivers' needs.)

GRANDPARENTS ACCEPTING SUPPORT FROM EXTENDED FAMILY

Many elderly persons have an indomitable spirit that respects self and desires to be self-sufficient and contributing as long as possible. Research shows that "elders who consciously work to maintain even limited functional abilities and cultivate a positive attitude are less likely to become depressed." They also enjoy more positive relationships with their caregivers and are grateful for their life and experiences.[21] Wendy Lustbader has recounted many such examples from the people with whom she works. People who chose to wake each morning with a feeling of gratitude also acknowledged that "living requires courage under all circumstances."[22]

However, grandparents sometimes resist offers of help from their children and grandchildren; they do not want to be a burden. Unfortunately, at times "those who depend on others for daily survival often feel their very existence is an imposition."[23] Whatever caregivers and others can do to help grandparents feel important and useful is essential to their well-being. "Being of use makes being in need easier."[24] Grandparents may want to pay for transportation, a dinner out, a service rendered, and, when it is within the caregivers' ability to do so, accepting these payments can reinforce grandparents' worth and self-esteem.

Some grandparents may express regret about having to depend on others. Acknowledge that you understand: getting old is a test of courage, a new and difficult experience. Assure grandparents that being of service is enjoyable for you. Other grandparents may want to share their "treasures" with you, hoping that you will accept their keepsakes as an expression of appreciation. It is helpful to monitor this sharing behavior to assure that grandparents' needs are being met and that their feelings of generosity do not detract from their ability to be independent as long as possible. To prevent suspicions and jealousy among siblings, extended families may need to put in writing a system for tracking this sharing of treasures, possibly

with the intent to redistribute keepsakes at the death of the grandparent. The family should agree on who will pay for which needs, and how much money a family member may accept from the grandparent.

CAREGIVING SUPPORT THROUGH CHURCH RESOURCES

There are instances when the demands of caregiving, limited extended family resources, and the needs of grandparents are such that Church resources may be necessary. Visiting teachers and home teachers can provide important links between families and Relief Society and priesthood leaders. And, as President Benson reminded us, "When the elderly have no families to care for them, priesthood and Relief Society leaders should make every effort to meet their needs."[25] President Benson urged "priesthood leaders of the elderly to be sensitive to the Spirit of our Father in Heaven in assessing and meeting the spiritual, physical, emotional, and financial needs of the elderly."[26] In some circumstances 24-hour care in a care facility is warranted (see essay 12). On these occasions, "Relief Society and priesthood leaders may assist family members by helping evaluate the appropriateness of the institution."[27]

CONCLUSION

With people living longer, the Lord has blessed us with unprecedented opportunities to experience and enjoy extended family relationships. Grandparents have an important role in maintaining and passing on the family's heritage and traditions. If needed, they are a valuable resource in providing assistance to their adult children and grandchildren. As they grow older, most grandparents will eventually need help and care from their family, and Church leaders have made it clear that families have the responsibility to provide care to older family members. Despite the demands and stress of caring for older family members, this labor of love also brings significant blessings.

ABOUT THE AUTHORS

Richard B. Miller, Ph.D., is a professor in the School of Family Life at Brigham Young University and the director of the BYU Gerontology Program. He and his wife, Mary, are the parents of four children.

Margie Egbert Edwards, Ph.D., MSW, is a professor emeritus of social work at the University of Utah and teaches gerontology courses. She is the wife of Dan Edwards, mother of Megan, and grandmother of Aubrey, Erica, Justin, and Jonah.

ADDITIONAL READING

Ezra Taft Benson (1989, November), To the elderly in the Church, *Ensign, 19*(11), 4–8.

Dallin H. Oaks (1991, May), Honour thy father and thy mother, *Ensign, 21*(5), 14–17.

Susanne Frost Olsen, Alan C. Taylor, and Kelly DiSpirito Taylor (2000), Intergenerational ties, grandparenting, and extended family support; in David C. Dollahite, ed., *Strengthening Our Families: An In-Depth Look at the Proclamation on the Family* (Salt Lake City: Bookcraft), 135–141.

Boyd K. Packer (2003, May), The golden years, *Ensign, 33*(5), 82–84.

NOTES

1. Neal A. Maxwell (1997), *The Neal A. Maxwell Quote Book,* C. H. Maxwell, ed. (Salt Lake City: Bookcraft), 146.

2. P. Uhlenberg (1996), Mortality decline in the twentieth century and supply of kin over the life course, *The Gerontologist, 36*(5), 681–685.

3. Spencer W. Kimball (1978), *Marriage* (Salt Lake City: Deseret Book), 16–17.

4. Spencer W. Kimball (1977), Oneness in marriage, *Ensign, 7*(3), 5.

5. G. O. Hagestad (1985), Continuity and connectedness; in V. L. Bengtson and J. F. Robertson, eds., *Grandparenthood* (Beverly Hills: Sage), 31–48.

6. Brigham Young (1861), *Journal of Discourses,* 8:145.

7. Heber J. Grant (1936, October), in Conference Report, 3.

8. Spencer W. Kimball (1978), 16–17.

9. Boyd K. Packer (2003, May), The golden years, *Ensign, 33*(5), 82.

10. Barbara B. Smith (1978, May), In the time of old age, *Ensign, 8*(5), 85.

11. Dallin H. Oaks (1991, May), Honour thy father and thy mother, *Ensign, 21*(5), 17.

12. Ezra Taft Benson (1989, November), To the elderly in the Church, *Ensign, 19*(11), 6.

13. Ibid., 7.

14. N. P. Kropf (2000), Home, health, and community services; in R. L. Schneider, N. P. Kropf, A. J. Kisor, eds., *Gerontological Social Work: Knowledge, Service Settings, and Special Populations* (Belmont, CA: Wadsworth), 6:172–173.

15. M. Dellmann-Jenkins, M. Blankemeyer, and O. Pinkard (2000), Young adult children and grandchildren in primary caregiver roles to older relatives and their service needs, *Family Relations, 49*(2), 177–186.

16. Ibid., 183.

17. B. C. Hafen and M. K. Hafen (1994), *The Belonging Heart: The Atonement and Relationships with God and Family* (Salt Lake City: Deseret Book), 244.

18. K. J. Doka (2003–2004), The spiritual gifts—and burdens—of family caregiving, *Generations: Journal of American Society on Aging, 27*(4), 45–48.

19. Dellmann-Jenkins, et al. (2000), 182.

20. K. McInnis-Dittrich (2002), *Social Work with Elders: A Biopsychosocial Approach to Assessment and Intervention* (Boston: Allyn and Bacon), 318.

21. Ibid., 316.

22. W. Lustbader (1991), *Counting on Kindness: The Dilemmas of Dependency* (New York: The Free Press), 43.

23. Ibid., 18.

24. Ibid., 30.

25. Benson (1989), 6.

26. Ibid., 7.

27. Smith (1978), 86.

CREATING HEALTHY TIES WITH IN-LAWS AND EXTENDED FAMILIES

JAMES M. HARPER AND SUSANNE FROST OLSEN

*Therefore shall a man leave his father and his mother, and shall cleave
unto his wife: and they shall be one flesh.*
—Genesis 2:24

Nathan and Catherine had been married less than a year when it was time for the Thanksgiving and Christmas holidays. Because they lived close to both sets of parents, they had to decide how to spend the holidays. Catherine's parents told them they wanted them to come to their home for Thanksgiving dinner, Christmas Eve dinner, and on Christmas morning to open presents. Nathan's parents asked them to dinner on Thanksgiving and Christmas. Nathan and Catherine were presented with decisions they had never had to make before; they loved their families and wanted to be with them, but they also hoped to establish their own family traditions.

One of the major opportunities the formation of a new marriage offers is that of negotiating relationships between the families the spouses grew up in and the partnership they create through marriage. In this chapter we discuss the commandment that newly-married couples should leave their parents and cleave unto their spouses. We also discuss establishing a marital identity, accepting differences, and including new spouses in the extended family.

NEWLY MARRIED COUPLES SHOULD LEAVE THEIR PARENTS AND CLEAVE UNTO THEIR SPOUSES

One of the first scriptures in the Old Testament regarding family relationships is found in Genesis

2:24: "Therefore shall a man leave his father and his mother, and shall cleave unto his wife." The Oxford English Dictionary defines *cleave* as "to remain attached, devoted, or faithful to," and "to remain steadfast."[1] Thus, in cleaving to spouses, newly married couples are to be devoted, faithful, and steadfast to their new companions.

Elder Marvin J. Ashton, a member of the Quorum of the Twelve Apostles, clarified the meaning of this scripture as it relates to newly married couples:

> Certainly a now-married man should cleave unto his wife in faithfulness, protection, comfort, and total support, but in leaving father, mother, and other family members, it was never intended that they now be ignored, abandoned, shunned, or deserted. They are still family, a great source of strength. . . . Wise parents, whose children have left to start their own families, realize their family role still continues, not in a realm of domination, control, regulation, supervision, or imposition, but in love, concern, and encouragement.[2]

Elder Ashton reminded us that in cleaving to a spouse, married children should be faithful and supportive to their spouses, but not forget their parents. In turn, parents may need to give up previous roles they had with their children to allow the new couple to be independent. New husbands and wives must recognize that their spouses still have relationships with their parents.[3] President Spencer W. Kimball also cautioned parents and married adult children regarding their relationships:

> Frequently, people continue to cleave unto their mothers and their fathers. . . . Sometimes mothers will not relinquish the hold they have had upon their children, and husbands as well as wives return to their mothers and fathers to obtain advice and counsel and to confide, whereas cleaving should be to the wife in most things. . . .
>
> Couples do well to immediately find their own home, separate and apart from that of the in-laws on either side. The home may be very modest and unpretentious, but still it is an independent domicile. Your married life should become independent of her folks and his folks. You love them more than ever; you cherish their counsel; you appreciate their association; but you live your own lives, being governed by your decisions, by your own prayerful considerations after you have received the counsel from those who should give it. To cleave does not mean merely to occupy the same home; it means to adhere closely, to stick together.[4]

President Kimball identified some important points regarding family relationships. First, married children should confide in and counsel with their spouses. Second, if possible, they should establish their own household, separate from their parents. Finally, any counsel from outside sources should be considered prayerfully by both spouses together.

HELPING NEWLY MARRIED COUPLES CREATE A MARITAL IDENTITY

One of the great joys of growing older can be witnessing a child find a husband or wife and helping the couple create a strong marital identity. On one of the authors' walls hangs a saying: "Parents give their children two things: roots to grow, and wings to fly." What kind of husband or wife a child becomes and how he or she parents should give parents great joy, but it also requires sacrifice of time and effort, and adaptation on the parents' part to new roles.[5]

The first task of a newly married couple is to separate from the families in which they grew up.[6] One component of separating from families of origin involves creating a marital identity. It helps a newly married couple to think of themselves as existing together inside an invisible fence. They share information and behavior with each other inside that fence, and that information and behavior is not meant to be shared with others outside the fence—not with

future children and certainly not with parents or parents-in-law.

This may be difficult for daughters who have close relationships with their mothers. Marriage, to be successful, requires married daughters to share more with their husbands than with their mothers. This can be hard for mothers who want daily communication with their daughters and for daughters who feel guilty about limiting contact with mothers. Too much contact with the daughter could result in the son-in-law's feeling that his spousal relationship is being smothered. Mothers can help sons or daughters by not continuing to be their primary confidante after they are married. The same can be said for fathers who are overly involved with their married children. One of the great gifts parents-in-law can give to their married children is to recognize early that they must help define and protect the boundary of this new couple.[7]

Often the relationship between families can be like a tug-of-war, with the wife's mother giving the main tug on one end and the husband's mother at the other end.[8] If this is the case, it is important for both the husband and wife not to be in the middle. Research demonstrates that daughters-in-law who use husbands as mediators with mothers-in-law often make their own marriage and their relationship with the mother-in-law worse.[9] Parents must give the newly married couple time to adjust and allow them to be independent.

President Spencer W. Kimball, referring to Genesis 2:24, said: "She, the woman, occupies the first place. She is preeminent, even above the parents who are so dear to all of us. Even the children must take their proper but significant place. I have seen some women who give their children that spot, that preeminence, in their affection and crowd out the father. That is a serious mistake."[10] We might add that it is a serious mistake for newly married sons or daughters to put their parents in that first place and crowd out the new husband or wife.

Married couples should discuss what they will do to protect, maintain, and repair (if necessary) the invisible boundary or fence that guards their marriage. The husband needs to realize that strengthening his marriage and making certain that his wife feels secure with him is the biggest single thing he can do to help his wife and his mother develop a quality relationship.[11]

Newly married couples are often torn when it comes to special occasions and traditions such as Thanksgiving, Christmas, and birthdays. Sensitive parents-in-law recognize it is important for couples to develop their own traditions and have time together on special occasions. Parents can help by genuinely not pressuring their grown children to be at every family gathering, even though they will be missed. How much involvement should exist with extended family often requires negotiation and compromise in couple relationships until agreement on solutions can be reached. For example, one couple decided that they would alternate years between families for Thanksgiving, but would observe their own Christmas holiday traditions at home.

Understanding that expectations for family relationships have to change helps new parents-in-law help their children. Parents will do better to listen and not impose their opinions or feelings. Intrusion by in-laws, both physically by too many visits and phone calls, and emotionally by too many strongly held opinions, is a major concern of new daughters- and sons-in-law.[12] When parents have difficulty with this, they need to look at whether they are too enmeshed with their children. *Enmeshment* describes a process in which parents and children feel they always have to be together; to not be so is considered a personal affront. When enmeshment exists, it is difficult for family members to separate feelings, and loyalty issues are distorted. If a married child can't attend a family event, he feels like he is offending his parents, and his parents will be personally hurt.

For example, some parents insist that their married children live close by and expect that the entire clan get together weekly or sometimes daily for a dinner, family prayer, or family home evening. While there is nothing inherently wrong in this, if extended families are unable to create enough flexibility for a married couple to choose not to attend such activities, the result is often lowered marital satisfaction for the couple. Sometimes financial support is tied to how much participation there is in extended family activities. Giving priority to needs as a couple may be viewed by parents as betrayal. Moving away is seen as disloyal, and parents feel as though they cannot survive the distance. In such cases, the parents are holding too tight and may be failing to deal with their own emotional issues or needs.

Parents who are enmeshed with their children may be tempted to use coercive strategies, which at first glance may appear acceptable. For instance, a parent might discourage a married child from accepting a job offer which would move the couple far away by telling them that "the Spirit has revealed to us that

it's a bad idea." Perhaps such coercion would take the form of, "If you were listening to the Spirit, you would know (or do) . . ." rather than encouraging the married child and spouse to seek their own spiritual confirmations. Married children are entitled to receive revelation for their stewardship in guiding their families, and parents and grandparents should support and encourage their married children as they do so. This does not mean that parents and grandparents should always avoid giving spiritual guidance. When asked, they should offer their opinions, but even well-intentioned parents or other family members should use great caution in assuming that they have more powerful or immediate access to the Spirit than their married children. Rather than using coercive means to keep married children close, parents should realize that greater dependence on Heavenly Father will result when married children are encouraged to receive their own spiritual answers.

Closeness, on the other hand, is different from enmeshment. Parents who are secure in their relationships with their children understand that married children can be emotionally close without always having to be present. These children, in turn, have a sense of their parents' own security so they don't have to always be near them to take care of them emotionally. Parents who struggle with enmeshment will have difficulty helping their married children keep a strong marital boundary. Such parents feel they have to be inside the fence with their child and his or her new spouse. Parents need to learn to let married children have their own experiences and solve their own problems, except for situations when parents are invited to provide input and support.[13] If married children are having enmeshment difficulties with their parents and parents-in-law, they may want to (a) first express love to the parents for all that they do, (b) explain that they have a need to further strengthen their couple identity, and (c) explain how the expectations for being together with the family are getting in the way of their couple relationship. It is important to express that this is not betrayal or withdrawal of love and to assure the parents that the couple will participate in some family activities.

Parents who try to create a climate of safety in which children can express their feelings about how involved they want to be will have the greatest potential for positive influence in their children's and grandchildren's lives. When married children are treated with respect and love in this matter, they are more likely to want to spend more time with parents and extended family. Demands, expectations, manipulations, ultimatums, threats, and emotional blackmailing tend to strain or destroy relationships.

Triangulation is created when communication either builds a stronger relationship with the parent than with the spouse, or excludes the spouse. Parents should encourage children to discuss matters with their spouses. (Triangulation in families is described in chapter 28) For example, a mother who wants to know all the details of her daughter's marriage and tries to "fix" any problems would be wise to focus her efforts elsewhere. One of the authors' children, when newly married, came to him to complain about something the spouse had done. He kindly encouraged his child to talk to the spouse and suggested that such triangulating fails to solve the problem and weakens the marriage. Another parent in a similar situation suggested that his married child work through difficult spousal issues by involving a competent marriage counselor. In families where triangulation is common, information about children and their spouses shared with other family members could lead to gossip and subsequent estrangement. Diane Forbis wrote, "The potential for disrupting the family orchestration by talking about the unseemly behavior of a sister-in-law or the offensive language of a brother will *never* be worth any temporary satisfaction from voicing such indignation."[14]

Accepting Differences

Marrying into a family that is different from yours or has different values can be a challenge. Demonstrating humor, exercising patience, overlooking small irritations, and looking for the positive can help in dealing with differences.[15] One woman said: "When I met [his] parents . . . I didn't agree with them on religion, politics, or even on how to cook a pot roast. I really wasn't even sure if I liked them. But then I had to remember they had raised [my husband], and I loved him, so there must be something good about them. At that point, I began to enjoy their differences, and to love them, too."[16]

Mothers-in-law usually discover early that their daughters-in-law are not like them, and in some cases, this may be upsetting. Parents who are more enmeshed with their children hold expectations that their children-in-law will be like them. A more realistic expectation is that children-in-law will bring new perspectives into the family, and the family can learn from these differences and be complemented by

them. This may be especially difficult when a child marries someone who is less active or not a member, or a child marries someone who is the only member of the Church in his or her family. Parents who can work toward inclusion of a new son- or daughter-in-law and who show increased love and support have the best relationships with their married children and more influence in the lives of their grandchildren.[17]

Difference is something that can be anticipated and even looked forward to because of its potential for creating growth in family members. Prayer, fasting, and loving long-suffering are the best remedies when differences of children-in-law bother us.[18] Where there are strong differences, personality clashes, or even past offenses, it is important to lay those aside at extended family gatherings and treat each other with politeness, dignity, and respect. Paul's statement to the Corinthians is relevant: "For as the body is one, and hath many members, . . . and the eye cannot say unto the hand, I have no need of thee: nor again the head to the feet, I have no need of you" (1 Corinthians 12:12, 21–23).

Including New Spouses in the Extended Family

A primary issue for new spouses is how parents and other family members include a new person in their family system. Do they act like they do when people outside the family visit, or do they show the side that has heretofore been reserved just for family members? And if they act like they do around family, will this newcomer accept them? These inclusion and exclusion issues are present even when siblings have already married. In fact, the presence of other sons- or daughters-in-law can complicate inclusion issues because family members may make comparisons, and often sons- and daughters-in-law join in screening the potential in-law.

Research has shown that lack of marital approval, in-law blaming or triangulation, intrusion, forcing loyalty issues, holding grudges, and refusing to redefine one's role as a parent are related to poor in-law relationships and also jeopardize the marriage of the son or daughter.[19] In one study, 80 percent of couples in failed marriages had not gained the approval or support of parents to marry.[20] If parents are anticipating the marriage of their son or daughter, they should encourage the couple to ask both sets of parents for permission to marry, but parents should also find numerous ways to give messages that they trust the child's judgment and see him or her as fully capable of building a good marriage. The idea that good marriages are "found" is too prevalent in society (see chapter 7). Rather, strong marriages are built by what couples choose to do once they are married and by what parents and siblings on both sides do to help support them.

Jody and Jack came to my (James's) family therapy office a few weeks prior to their wedding date. It quickly became apparent that Jody's parents hoped I would talk them out of marrying. When Jack had visited Jody's home several months before, Jody's family all looked for any weaknesses he might have. Jody's mother's intrusive questions put Jack on edge, making it hard for him to talk comfortably. During the visit, Jody's mother told her that Jack was the wrong man to marry. He wasn't good enough and didn't treat her how she deserved to be treated. Jody's mother informed Jack that she was never wrong about people. She added that he and Jody were not good for each other. It would be a bad marriage. I gave them a typical battery of premarital tests and discovered that their relationship had many strengths. Their potential to be a happily married couple seemed better than average, except for the fact that Jody's parents and siblings were so down on Jack.

Jack wrote a letter, apologizing for anything he had done to offend them. It fueled the family fire even more. Jody's father even called Jack's mission president to ask what kind of missionary he had been. When Jack's parents got wind of this, they became distressed and asked Jack if he wanted to marry into a family who treated him so unfairly. Needless to say, Jack and Jody were bewildered. I eventually met with them and both sets of parents at different times. In time, the parents accepted that Jack and Jody would marry and pulled together to support them.

It is important for parents-in-law to find ways to personally build relationships with their children-in-law as individuals. Often interactions are with the newly married couple or the larger family group rather than with individuals. Mothers-in-law might consider inviting their daughters-in-law for a lunch and then work toward a balance of self-disclosure and acceptance in the conversation. Fathers-in-law could do something individually with their sons-in-law, again with the purpose of building a positive, accepting relationship. The burden of acceptance rests with parents-in-law in these situations. Children-in-law want nothing more than to be accepted and respected.

Communication is the key to mothers-in-law building good relationships with their daughters-in-law. While popular culture often suggests it is best to live far from parents-in-law, the results of one study demonstrated that the close proximity of daughters-in-law with their husbands' mothers did not add strain but provided opportunities for relationship development.[21]

A young wife married for more than a year told me (James) that her parents, who were not members of the Church, had never accepted her husband because they felt he had stolen her from them. When they called, they wanted to talk only to her, and they addressed letters only to her. Essentially, her parents were treating her as if she had not married.

Together we planned a celebration for their marriage that they as a married couple would throw when they visited her parents. They rented a hall and invited all of her family and friends. At this celebration, each talked about how much they appreciated being married and thanked her parents for contributing to who she was. She told me that after the celebration her parents asked to talk to her husband when they called, and they addressed letters to both of them. When parents not of our faith cannot witness the actual marriage ceremony, it makes it more difficult to redefine roles and boundaries, as was the case in this example.

When new roles are being defined for both parents and children, it helps parents to realize that they have to make adjustments that may not always be comfortable. This is normal and the discomfort may disappear with time and effort. Loyalty issues may come into play as new sons- and daughters-in-law struggle with what to call their new in-laws. Will they be comfortable if I call them Dad and Mom? How will my own parents feel? While awkward at first, stronger bonds are formed when in-law children call their in-law parents Dad and Mom and get past the idea that this somehow compromises their loyalty to their own parents.[22] It is also helpful to ask parents-in-law if it is all right to call them Mom and Dad, or what they would like to be called. Likewise, it means a great deal for an in-law to be referred to by siblings simply as "my brother" or "my sister" rather than always being labeled as in-laws.

Parents sometimes worry that sons and daughters will like their in-laws more than they like them. It is wise to see this new set of parents as complementary rather than competitive replacements. A married son or daughter now has an additional set of protectors who can appropriately provide help and support. Parents can be most supportive by encouraging their child's relationship with his or her in-laws, by inquiring sometimes about the well-being of the other in-laws, and by avoiding duplicating in a competitive way what the other set of in-laws does. For example, one set of parents gave a married couple money to finish their basement. While the other parents felt the temptation to offer a similar amount or even more money, they chose not to and avoided the competitive spirit that otherwise might have developed.

Even before they are married, couples begin to learn that their families are different. The more a person can learn and talk about the unspoken rules in the prospective spouse's family, the easier it will be to feel included. Examples of unspoken rules include how family members handle conflict, who is involved in making decisions, how emotionally expressive family members can comfortably be, how humor is demonstrated in the family, or what topics should not be discussed. The clearer family rules are, the better, because new sons- or daughters-in-law can't follow rules if they don't understand them.[23]

While the ideal is for extended family to be supportive, sometimes this is not the case. Especially hard are situations where parents have been abusive, even sexually abusive. The danger of interacting with parents-in-law in these circumstances is that even further abuse is possible. Elder Richard G. Scott stated: "Your Heavenly Father does not want you to be held captive by unrighteous influence, by threats of reprisal, or by fear of repercussion to the family member who abuses you."[24] In these cases, it is appropriate for spouses to counsel together and decide together how much contact, if any, to have with an extended family member who continues to be abusive. The supporting spouse must understand that his or her own anger about the past abuse does not help the spouse who has been abused, but may make it harder for the abused spouse to communicate openly. When spouses can be supportive and listen and not be emotionally reactive, they are better able to help the husband or wife who has experienced abuse decide how much contact the couple will have, together, with the family members who belittle or abuse.

One woman described how her mother-in-law ignored her letters and phone calls for years. She said, "I knew that the Lord wanted me to love my mother-in-law, yet how could I love her after all that happened?" She prayed that she would have endurance to continue to reach out and "dropped to [her] knees and asked the Lord to remove [her] long-held bitterness." She said, "I had been blinded by grudges and self-pity, but now I could see more clearly into my soul and the soul of my mother-in-law."[25]

If a married couple finds a parent or other extended family member to be disruptive or harmful to their marriage, they can approach the problem together. They will need to decide what limits to place on the type of contact and time they spend with that family member. If they decide they want to improve the relationship, they will need to decide together how to approach the other family member and what types of change they want to request. Then they should act together, with both married partners realizing their primary obligation is to be supportive of each other, regardless of how the extended family member responds. At times, the situation may be deemed serious enough to warrant cutting off contact with in-laws and extended family members who actively seek to harm family members or destroy relationships. However, couples can continue to pray for these family members from a distance, keeping their hearts soft and ready to forgive past offenses.

Gloria Horsley listed five things that every parent-in-law should avoid. They are giving advice, criticizing, pinning down children-in-law as to the specific reasons they are missing a family event, criticizing or taking over the disciplining of grandchildren, trying to control everyone and everything including children's beliefs, and unclear and indirect communication.[26] Conversely, when parents-in-law do things right, their influence is remembered and felt long after they are gone. Likewise, siblings can do much to help new in-laws feel included. Writing letters, making phone calls that include both sibling and new spouse, and doing activities with the new spouse increase feelings of belonging.

Adult married children can improve relationships with their in-laws by setting boundaries that help ensure their marriage is strong and happy. Having regular contact and communication with in-laws also sends messages that couples value their relationship with them.[27] Frequency of contact and communication that does not interfere with each other's being first in the marriage are important steps for building relationships with parents-in-law.[28] Research shows that when daughters-in-law disclose information about themselves, communicate openly, accept differences, use empathy, and push for a relational connection, they can have high-quality relationships with mothers-in-law. Being forceful, angrily avoiding in-laws, taking sides, and not accepting differences leads to poor in-law relationships.[29]

CONCLUSION

In summary, parents-in-law will do well to accept differences; encourage marital identity by helping develop and maintain the marital boundary of the children; avoid intrusion; offer advice only when it is sought; be accepting rather than critical; and work toward developing a personal, positive relationship with a son- or daughter-in-law by creating opportunities to spend time one-on-one. The good news is that when parents-in-law understand inclusion and exclusion issues, the necessity of monitoring and managing their need for control, the loyalty tugs, and the importance of helping a new couple establish a solid marriage boundary, in-law relationships are improved.[30]

If you are in an estranged relationship as a child-in-law or a parent-in-law, forgiveness may be necessary before you can do some of the things mentioned in this chapter. Forgiveness means you let go of consuming feelings of animosity, bitterness, and hatred.[31] Improved relationships will require time, effort, patience, and a willingness to communicate about issues and past offenses with love and concern. Some things may not be resolved in this life. Trusting in Christ and His timetable will help each prepare to do all they can do to mend troubled relationships.

Extended family relationships can do much to support and strengthen family members. The guidelines discussed in this chapter for relating to in-laws and for how parents should treat married adult children will help family members fulfill the proclamation's charge, "Extended families should lend support when needed."[32]

ABOUT THE AUTHORS

James M. Harper is director of the BYU School of Family Life, associate dean in the College of Family, Home, and Social Sciences, a Zina Young Williams Card Endowed University Professor, and a marriage and family therapist. He is a former president of the BYU 21st Stake and of the Korea Pusan Mission, and he currently serves as Gospel Doctrine teacher in the Timpanogos Park Second Ward.

Susanne Frost Olsen is associate director of the School of Family Life and a faculty member in the Marriage, Family, and Human Development program. She currently serves as Primary president in the Orem Utah Suncrest Tenth Ward.

ADDITIONAL READING

Extending family relationships (1986, October), *Ensign, 16*(10), 57.

M. O. Richardson (2005, April), Three principles of marriage, *Ensign, 35*(4), 20–24.

Patricia Russell (2000, March), Building good in-law relationships, *Ensign, 30*(3), 53.

NOTES

1. Oxford English Dictionary, 2d ed. (1989), s.v. "cleave."
2. Marvin J. Ashton (1974, January), He took him by the hand, *Ensign, 4*(1), 101.
3. Extending family relationships (1986, October), *Ensign, 16*(10), 57.
4. Spencer W. Kimball (2002, October), Gospel classics: Oneness in marriage, *Ensign, 32*(10), 40.
5. Extending family relationships (1986), 57.
6. J. S. Wallerstein and S. Blakeslee (1995), *The Good Marriage: How and Why Love Lasts* (Boston: Houghton Mifflin).
7. L. R. Fischer (1983), Mothers and mothers-in-law, *Journal of Marriage and the Family, 45*(1), 187–192.
8. P. Cotterill (1994), *Friendly Relations? Mothers and Their Daughters-in-law* (New York: Taylor and Francis).
9. B. H. Limary (2002), *The Mother-in-law/Daughter-in-law Dyad: Narratives of Relational Development among In-laws*; doctoral dissertation, University of New Mexico (Albuquerque, NM).
10. Spencer W. Kimball (1976, March), The blessings and responsibilities of womanhood, *Ensign, 6*(3), 70.
11. L. L. Ades (2003), *Predictors of the Quality of the Relationship between Daughters-in-law and Mothers-in-law* (marital), Dissertation Abstracts International–B, *63*(1), 4909.
12. G. C. Horsley (1997), *The In-law Survival Manual: A Guide to Cultivating Healthy In-law Relationships* (New York: John Wiley & Sons).
13. G. Lundberg and J. Lundberg (2000, January), The marriage balancing act, *Ensign, 30*(1), 54.
14. D. D. Forbis (1998, July), Harmony among grown children, *Ensign, 28*(7), 49.
15. P. Russell (2000, March), Building good in-law relationships, *Ensign, 30*(3), 53.
16. Horsley (1997), 46.
17. Name withheld (2000, July), The only member in my family, *Ensign, 30*(7), 16.
18. Forbis (1998), 49.
19. Horsley (1997); Limary (2002).
20. Horsley (1997).
21. R. Marotz-Baden and D. Cowen (1987), Mothers-in-law and daughters-in-law: The effects of proximity on conflict and stress, *Family Relations, 36*(4), 385–390.
22. L. S. Averick (1996), *Don't Call Me Mom: How to Improve Your In-law Relationships* (Hollywood, FL: Lifetime Books).
23. G. C. Horsley (1996), In-laws: Extended family therapy, *The American Journal of Family Therapy, 25*(1), 18–27; Horsley (1997), 47.
24. Richard G. Scott (1992, May), Healing the tragic scars of abuse, *Ensign, 22*(5), 31.
25. Name withheld (1994, October), Remove my bitterness, *Ensign, 24*(10), 66.
26. Horsley (1997).

27. M. J. Turner and T. S. Killian (2003), Factors related to the quality of relationships between sons- and daughters-in-law and fathers- and mothers-in-law, *The Gerontologist, 43,* 51.

28. Turner and Killian (2003), 51.

29. Limary (2002).

30. L. Berg-Cross and J. Jackson (1986), Helping the extended family: In-law growth and development training program, *Psychotherapy in Private Practice, 4*(1), 33–50.

31. For specific information about forgiving a family member, please refer to J. M. Harper and M. Butler (2000), Repentance, forgiveness, and progression in marriage and families; in D. C. Dollahite, ed., *Strengthening Our Families: An In-Depth Look at the Proclamation on the Family* (Salt Lake City: Bookcraft), 154–166.

32. First Presidency and Council of Twelve Apostles (1995, November), The family: A proclamation to the world, *Ensign, 25*(11), 102.

CHAPTER 38

FAMILY ORGANIZATIONS AND FAMILY HISTORY

CYNTHIA DOXEY AND DON NORTON

The divine plan of happiness enables family relationships to be perpetuated beyond the grave.
Sacred ordinances and covenants available in holy temples make it possible for individuals to return to the
presence of God and for families to be united eternally.[1]
—"The Family: A Proclamation to the World"

The proclamation on the family teaches that family relationships are important and that our connections in this life can continue through eternity.[2] "That same sociality which exists among us here will exist among us there," the Prophet Joseph Smith explained (D&C 130:2). This chapter focuses on helping relationships among family members—including extended family, ancestors, and descendants—endure through this life and into eternity.

One way to develop such relationships is through contact with extended family members. President Spencer W. Kimball taught that in our fast-paced world, people often lose a sense of continuity and connection with extended family members: "It is important for us also to cultivate in our own family a sense that we belong together eternally. . . . We ought to encourage our children to know their relatives."[3] Relationships with both immediate and extended family members can be maintained through involvement in family activities, reunions, and organizations, because, "after all, eternity will be but an extension of righteous family life."[4]

Another way to foster our relationships with past, present, and future family members is through family history and temple work. Joseph Smith taught that without all the ordinances of the temple we cannot be saved with "the fullness of salvation."[5] Learning about ancestors and keeping records for descendants helps to bind families across generations. Elder Dallin H. Oaks counseled: "We should understand that in the work of redeeming the dead there are many tasks to be performed, and that all members should participate by prayerfully selecting those ways that fit their personal circumstances at a particular time. . . . Our effort is not to compel everyone to do everything, but to encourage everyone to do something."[6]

FAMILY ORGANIZATIONS

Families can be organized at three different levels: the immediate family, the grandparent family, and the ancestral family. President Ezra Taft Benson taught that "through such family organizations, every family in the Church should become actively involved in missionary work, family preparedness, genealogy and temple work, teaching the gospel, and cultural and social activities."[7] In other words, each level of organization has important responsibilities associated with the threefold mission of the Church: proclaiming the gospel, perfecting the Saints, and redeeming the dead.[8]

Immediate Family

At the marriage of a husband and wife, the immediate family organization is formed. As this couple have children, their main concern becomes caring for, nurturing, and teaching their children, in addition to creating experiences that foster family love and happiness. In the immediate family, parents usually serve as the leaders, directing the work of the family and counseling with each other and with their children.

Grandparent Family

The grandparent family is formed as children from the immediate family mature, marry, and have children of their own. This level of organization is focused on continuing the work of the immediate family in terms of teaching the gospel and caring for one another, with the added dimension of maintaining contact with family members who no longer live in the same household. Because family members may now be geographically separated, organizing the family at the grandparent level requires more effort to develop and maintain close ties through regular meetings and reunions. In family councils and other meetings, support among parents, children, and grandchildren can be fostered and solutions to problems of families and individuals developed. Elder M. Russell Ballard and his wife, Barbara, emphasized that parents should "not overlook the potentially powerful asset grandparents can be. Grandparents can be welcomed and listened to in formal councils or on informal occasions. They've walked the road of life 30 or more years longer than anyone else in the council. Even if grandparents live far away, grandchildren can call or e-mail."[9]

Ideas for maintaining unity and close relationships with members of a grandparent family organization are as follows:

1. Plan regular reunions for social and spiritual activities.

2. Share newsletters or e-mail messages. By using the Internet, families may keep in touch more easily and quickly. One family uses a "chain letter": The parents send to one of the daughters an e-mail with information about what they have done. That daughter adds information about her life and family and sends it to the next daughter. The chain continues until all the children have added their own information and the letter returns to their parents, who update information in their portion of the letter and send the letter on.

3. Host occasional extended family home evenings. Some families arrange to have family home evening together with all children and their families once a month. The grandparents and their adult children each take a turn planning the lesson, activity, and refreshments.

4. Attend the temple together. This activity can be especially enjoyable when performing ordinances for deceased ancestors.

5. Organize family members to encourage a network of support for family members in need. One family regularly examines the needs of family members and joins together to help each other, both temporally and spiritually. This idea follows the counsel given in the proclamation: "Extended families should lend support when needed."[10] Although geographic proximity will influence many of these activities, frequent contact between family members is important.

Ancestral Family

The ancestral family, formed by descendants of a common ancestral couple, is generally marked by a more formal organization of appointed or elected leaders who manage and arrange the affairs of the family. Unlike the other two levels of organization, ancestral family organizations are more likely to be focused on issues other than social activities. The major purpose of ancestral family organizations "is to coordinate genealogical activity on common ancestral lines" and to "provide resource material from which the immediate and grandparent family organizations can draw to complete family histories."[11]

Creating and maintaining ancestral family organizations often becomes a challenge. A first step might be to use the Internet as a way to contact family members, perhaps creating a website where relatives can contribute information about themselves and their families. Many ancestral families can be organized informally by cousins contacting cousins and finding ways to share genealogical information and meet one another on occasion. Ancestral families may also be organized in a more formal way, by following these suggestions:

1. Call an organizational meeting, inviting all interested family members to participate.

2. Develop a statement of purpose and objectives for the organization. An objective might be to do genealogical research or to compose a history of a common ancestor. Another purpose might be to provide a central archive for family records, heirlooms, and other items of historical and sentimental value.

3. Elect or appoint leaders of the extended family organization: a president, vice president, secretary or treasurer, genealogy coordinator, family website coordinator, and other officers as needed. Leaders may write bylaws, or even formally incorporate, thus assuring direction of the organization over the years.

4. Periodically evaluate the usefulness of the organization by asking, "Are the goals of the organization

being met? Are family members staying connected? Is the family history and temple work being completed in a timely manner?"

Realize that at some point it may be wise to disband the organization if the needs of the families are not being satisfied, or if it has grown too large to maintain. At that point, smaller organizations created from within the larger organization may enable family members to become better acquainted and more effectively achieve their objectives.

FOSTERING FAMILY UNITY THROUGH GENEALOGICAL RESEARCH

Sometimes families feel that doing genealogical research is a difficult responsibility that they neither desire to accomplish nor know how to carry out. However, fulfilling our responsibility to redeem the dead can have a profound effect on the lives of our family members. One young adult stated: "Studying and researching my family history has deepened my respect for my ancestors and has increased my love for them. I feel much closer to my parents and grandparents because I now understand them so much better than before. Family history truly does bind generations together."[12]

Along with finding names of ancestors and extending pedigrees, family members are blessed by participating in temple ordinances for their ancestors. Elder Dennis B. Neuenschwander wrote:

> Family history research provides the emotional bridge between the generations. Temple ordinances provide the priesthood bridge. Temple ordinances are the priesthood ratification of the connection that we have already established in our hearts. . . . The promise of family history and temple work is eternal connection.[13]

As parents and children serve their ancestors by performing proxy ordinances, their eternal bonds and love for each other grow, as does their desire to continue as a family forever.

RECORD KEEPING

The term *family history* includes not only the activities described above, but also the writing of ancestral histories, keeping of one's own records, and the composing of one's own history. Personal and ancestral histories "turn [or bind] . . . the heart of the children to their fathers" (Malachi 4:6). President Kimball counseled Church members, "I urge all of the people of this church to give serious attention to their family histo-

ries, to encourage their parents and grandparents to write their journals, and let no family go into eternity without having left their memoirs for their children, their grandchildren, and their posterity."[14]

Because record keeping is a commandment, the work comes with promise—that our journals will be a source of inspiration to our families. President Kimball taught that "when our families are together in the eternities, we will already be acquainted" because of the journals and histories we have kept.[15] Following are some practical guidelines to achieving success in three different areas of family history.

Journal writing

President Kimball, himself an avid journal keeper, counseled the Saints: "Get a notebook, a good book that will last through time. . . . Begin today and write in it your goings and your comings, your deeper thoughts, your achievements, and your failures, your associations and your triumphs, your impressions and your testimonies."[16] The Prophet Joseph Smith regretted that many early events in the Church had gone unreported because records had not been kept consistently.[17] Journals (often called diaries) are personal records of our thoughts, feelings, and activities from day to day. Four basic guidelines will assure effective journal keeping.

First, entries should be made consistently. Some journal keepers jot down reminders each day and then, later in the week, write a page or so on each of those listed topics. Others set aside a regular time to write in their journals.

Second, the goal should be to focus on only one or two subjects at each writing. This helps the writer to explore the subject in meaningful detail. It's one thing to report that a prayer received an answer, but another to describe the context in which that answer came: the reason for the prayer, feelings about praying, and the answer or resolution. A journal should be much more than a simple list of important happenings.

Third, it's wise to write more than a few lines of description in each entry. One purpose of a journal entry is to bring back to the memory significant happenings in one's life so that they may be shared with posterity. Details help us and others re-create in an engaging and helpful way what we have thought, felt, or done.

Fourth, as President Kimball advised, "your journal should contain your true self rather than a picture of you when you are 'made up' for a public performance." Journal entries should not "paint one's virtues in rich color and whitewash the vices, but there is also the opposite pitfall of accentuating the negative."[18]

Traditionally, journals are handwritten in some kind of bound book, but today, many journal writers use an electronic medium, usually a word processor. The paper in a bound journal should be acid free so it won't yellow or otherwise deteriorate. Journals that were kept on acidic paper should be photocopied on acid-free paper, and the original stored in a safe place. Temperature and humidity should be temperate, and the storage area should not be susceptible to damage from water and fire. The pen with which you write should contain permanent black or blue ink; most ordinary ink will in time (several decades) fade from the page. Permanent ink pens carry such descriptions as *waterproof, carbon ink, accounting,* or similar guarantees of stability.

Three more guidelines are helpful as you write: have in mind a specific reader (your posterity, for example) as you write; give people's first and last names and their relationship to you at least once, so their identities won't be lost; and consider what you wish your ancestors had left you in the way of detail. In addition to the recording of timeless topics, ordinary detail can be interesting: what you did from hour to hour on a typical workday or Sunday; lists of purchases, school subjects, possessions, reading materials, and habits; patterns of exercise or daily routines. Such details reflect your character and lifestyle.

Some journal writers keep two journals: one that records significant daily happenings, as a reminder to self and to posterity of personal progress, and another confidential journal in which the writer records intimate and honest thoughts and feelings. This latter journal may be destroyed once it has served its purposes. Whatever kind of journal you keep, try to express yourself in your best writing style, not too casual.

One woman, who had begun to keep a journal at age ten, found it easy to compose her personal history. She interspersed her memories with many quotes from her journal, creating a fresh and authentic account. Another woman noted that her 26-year-old daughter still loves to read the journal entry recorded shortly after she was born. This entry reminds the daughter that she is wanted and loved. We can encourage our children to begin keeping a journal when they are young.

Ancestral histories

Histories of progenitors are ambitious but rewarding projects. Histories of living parents and grandparents are relatively easy to obtain; these people usually have kept records of various kinds. Histories of deceased relatives present special challenges. Many record sources may need to be consulted: family, church, community, legal archives, schools, the military, and others. Pamphlets and books on how to go about researching ancestral histories can be found in many libraries and bookstores, as can biographies of ordinary people, to serve as samples.

The tape recorder is a valuable resource in obtaining histories of spouses, parents, brothers and sisters, and living grandparents. Some general guidelines for writing an oral history follow.

Equipment. It is important to obtain clear sound, especially if you plan to preserve the tapes or transfer them to a more permanent medium (for example, digitized on a high-quality compact disk or DVD). It's best to use standard 60-minute cassette tapes (longer tapes do not preserve as well) and an extension microphone. Inexpensive digital recorders are now available.

The interview. Ask open-ended questions, and invite detail: "Tell me about . . . And then what happened? . . . How did you feel? . . . What were you thinking, and how did you react?" Interrupt momentarily to confirm or expand details, especially the spelling of unfamiliar names and places. Encourage the telling of stories.

Transcribing. Turning oral history into writing is a challenging and time-consuming but immensely rewarding process, well worth the effort. Speech and writing are different mediums, and thus a certain amount of editing is necessary to attain readability. You may wish to limit, or even omit, the interviewer's questions, so that the manuscript reads as if the informant has actually written it. The goal is an authentic voice—true to the expression of the person interviewed.[19]

One Latter-day Saint was prompted to interview his 60-year-old father in an effort to establish bonds with this very busy, somewhat emotionally distant man. Three hours of tape-recorded childhood recollections followed. The result was twenty pages of transcribed history, which the son sent to his father as a Christmas gift. The interviewer's mother reported that on opening the envelope, the father wept. She had seen her husband cry only one other time in their entire married life. Additional interviews resulted in a hundred pages of personal history, and father and son bonded closely.

Personal history

Personal histories can comprise many kinds of history: photographs, mementos (scrapbook-type materials), chronologies (simple or annotated), lists, letters, journals, and official documents. Some people tape record their life stories and have them transcribed into edited writing. Perhaps the most effective and comfortable approach to leaving a personal record is to write "episodes and essays"—brief narratives or thoughtful reflections on individual, memorable topics: a family pet, how the family celebrated a holiday, a memorable teacher, character sketches of family members. These shorter pieces are easier to write, and they usually include more details than they would if they were but part of a comprehensive life story. A goal of two to three pages a week would result in a substantial history within a year. These short pieces, when shared with other family members, create desirable bonds.

A chronology is simply a list of events in the order in which they occurred, and it is a good way to begin work on a life story. Compiling a chronology gets one to thinking about the order and meaning of life's events. Several topics lend themselves to separate chronological treatment: main family events, education, health, work, Church activity, and so on.

One benefit from composing chronologies is that you may have to consult family members about events and the dates when these occurred, and that kind of interaction has the effect of creating close ties. It's an especially good personal history activity for children and teens.

With the aid of personal computers and desktop publishing, a "complete" life history is within the grasp of many people. Though this kind of history is usually written by people toward the end of their lives, it can be written chapter by chapter by a person of any age. Older people sometimes have their autobiographies printed, bound, and distributed to posterity.

The impact of life histories on family members can be profound: "A personal history becomes a family treasure that enables children to emulate the virtues and personal characteristics of their forebears."[20]

CONCLUSION

The proclamation teaches that family relationships can endure beyond the grave through temple ordinances. In addition to the covenants made in the temple, we need to foster the love and concern that lead to a desire to be together for eternity. Frequent and regular contact among immediate and extended family members and active involvement in keeping records of ourselves and our ancestors is an important place to start.

ABOUT THE AUTHORS

Cynthia Doxey, Ph.D., is an associate professor of Church history and doctrine at Brigham Young University, primarily teaching and researching family history.

Don Norton, now retired from the Department of Linguistics and English Language at Brigham Young University, has taught the writing of personal history in a variety of settings for more than twenty-five years. His special interest is oral history.

ADDITIONAL READING

Janice T. Dixon (1997), *Family Focused: A Step-by-Step Guide to Writing Your Autobiography and Family History* (Wendover, NV: Mount Olympus).

Family History Library (1998), *Resource Guide: Preparing a Family History for Publication* (Salt Lake City: Intellectual Reserve). (Available at www.ldscatalog.com, item 36023000)

Marvin K. Gardner (1978, October), Getting—and keeping—the family together, *Ensign*, 8(10), 9–11.

NOTES

1. First Presidency and Council of Twelve Apostles (1995, November), The family: A proclamation to the world, *Ensign*, 25(11), 102.
2. Ibid.
3. Spencer W. Kimball (1974, November), Ocean currents and family influences, *Ensign*, 4(11), 112.
4. Ezra Taft Benson (1989, November), To the elderly in the Church, *Ensign*, 19(11), 5.
5. B. H. Roberts, ed. ([1949], 1962), *History of The Church of Jesus Christ of Latter-day Saints*, 2d ed., 7 vols. (Salt Lake City: Deseret Book), 6:184.
6. Dallin H. Oaks (1989, June), Family history: In wisdom and order, *Ensign*, 19(6), 6.
7. Ezra Taft Benson (1978, November), Worthy of all acceptation, *Ensign*, 8(11), 30.
8. Spencer W. Kimball (1981, May), A report of my stewardship, *Ensign*, 11(5), 5.
9. M. Russell Ballard and Barbara Ballard (2003, June), Family councils: A conversation with Elder and Sister Ballard, *Ensign*, 33(6), 18.
10. First Presidency and Council of Twelve Apostles (1995), 102.
11. Benson (1978), 31.
12. Lisa B. Hawkins and Cynthia Doxey (2001, August), Coming together through family history, *Marriage & Families*, 7.
13. Dennis B. Neuenschwander (1999, May), Bridges and eternal keepsakes, *Ensign*, 29(5), 85.
14. Spencer W. Kimball (1978, May), The true way of life and salvation, *Ensign*, 8(5), 4.
15. Spencer W. Kimball (1980, December), President Kimball speaks out on personal journals, *Ensign*, 10(12), 61.
16. Ibid.
17. Roberts ([1949], 1962), 2:198–199.
18. Kimball (1980), 61.
19. Machines and inexpensive computer software that facilitate transcribing are available.
20. Royden G. Derrick (1979, May), The heritage of royal families, *Ensign*, 9(5), 28.

CHAPTER 39

RESPONSIBLE CITIZENSHIP TO STRENGTHEN MARRIAGE AND FAMILY

ALAN J. HAWKINS

We call upon responsible citizens and officers of government everywhere to promote
those measures designed to maintain and strengthen the family as the fundamental unit of society.[1]
—"The Family: A Proclamation to the World"

Citizens of democratic governments enjoy great freedoms, but they also carry a burden of responsibility. Balancing strong individual freedoms and rights with personal and community responsibilities is a challenging task. I learned an important spiritual principle underlying responsible citizenship recently when I was reading from the Book of Mormon. In King Mosiah's sermon on government in Mosiah 29, Mosiah was trying to convince his people to accept a new form of government rather than rely on a monarchy. "And many more things did king Mosiah write unto [his people], unfolding unto them all the trials and troubles of a righteous king, yea, all the travails of soul for their people, and also all the murmurings of the people to their king; and he explained it all unto them. And he told them that these things ought not to be; but that the burden should come upon all the people, that every man might bear his part" (Mosiah 29:33–34).

There is a moral principle here. All citizens should bear the burden of good government. Thus, when the First Presidency and the Council of the Twelve Apostles of The Church of Jesus Christ of Latter-day Saints "call upon responsible citizens and officers of government everywhere to promote those measures designed to maintain and strengthen the family as the fundamental unit of society,"[2] they are not just suggesting that we get involved in good causes; I believe they are asking us to fulfill a moral

duty that rests on citizens of a free society. Moreover, they are inviting us to focus our citizenship in a crucial area: strengthening marriages and families. My purpose in this chapter is to encourage and facilitate such efforts.

There are many causes related to family life that need our involvement. One of the most crucial, contemporary challenges is the need to strengthen the institution of marriage. The divorce and sexual revolutions have diminished the institution of marriage and distorted its God-ordained purposes. But the good news is that in the United States and many other countries, the vast majority of people still value highly a good marriage, both as a personal goal and as an important element of a healthy society.[3] In fact, in the United States, public efforts at federal, state, county, and community levels to strengthen marriages are emerging in significant numbers.[4] Together, these efforts constitute a marriage movement.[5]

Opportunities to be involved are around us, and our strength is needed. I can think of no greater civic service that could be rendered by Latter-day Saints right now than giving time and resources to help this marriage movement grow. To encourage involvement, I recommend that readers obtain a valuable booklet, *Strengthening Marriages in Your Community: 101 Ideas to Get You Started*. (It can be ordered from www.smart-marriages.com for about $3; a portion of the booklet is available on-line.)

340

In the rest of this chapter, I address two common questions about involvement. My responses draw on my knowledge of the marriage movement, especially efforts related to opposing same-sex marriage and promoting divorce reform. Finally, I suggest some guidelines for involvement.

CAN A GROUP OF RESPONSIBLE CITIZENS REALLY MAKE A DIFFERENCE?

As responsible citizens come together, they can influence the direction of public policy and laws related to marriage. Groups of Latter-day Saints have influenced one of the most heated contemporary debates—same-sex marriage. In 1999, the state of Vermont changed state laws to allow all the civic benefits of marriage to be given to same-sex couples in a legal form called a "civil union." Soon after that change occurred, I asked an active, knowledgeable veteran in the debate on same-sex marriage why Vermont succeeded in making this change when previous, similar efforts in Hawaii, Alaska, and California had failed. Her response was quick and surprising to me. She said the difference was the lack of a large population of Latter-day Saints in Vermont giving their time and resources to defeat same-sex marriage proposals. Latter-day Saints were involved in large numbers in defeating these efforts in the other states. In May 2004, the Supreme Court of Massachusetts ruled that the state must issue marriage licenses to same-sex couples. Other states may follow suit (and a handful of Western countries have legalized same-sex marriages). I believe the involvement of Latter-day Saints, together with other responsible citizens, can make a decisive difference in how this legal and social debate plays out.

Same-sex marriage is only one of several important issues related to marriage, and may not be the most dangerous one. We have already seen a dramatic shift in the definition of marriage over the past 50 years with the divorce revolution. Personal happiness has become the defining purpose of marriage,[6] replacing the traditional defining purpose of complete commitment to another and to the children produced by that union. Changing attitudes were cemented by legal change that created unilateral, no-fault divorce—one person could end a marriage at any time for any reason. But this notion of ego-centered, no-legal-strings, deregulated marriage produces weaker ties. The safety and security of an "until death do us part" commitment—in good times and bad—

that vitally nourishes the kind of long-term love we yearn for has decreased. This loss of the central pillar of marital permanence profoundly weakens marriage and works against individuals' abilities to maintain a strong relationship.[7] The American author Judith Viorst put it this way: "One advantage of marriage is that, when you fall out of love with him or he falls out of love with you, it keeps you together until you fall in again."[8]

But there are fewer individuals and groups willing to challenge the current ideological and legal regime of divorce compared to the many who are stepping up to challenge same-sex marriage initiatives. I believe the voices of responsible, concerned citizens should be heard on this important public issue, too. Elder Dallin H. Oaks pointed at this issue in a recent address: "No society is so strong that it can support continued increases in citizen rights while neglecting to foster comparable increases in citizen responsibilities or obligations. Yet our legal system continues to recognize new rights even as we increasingly ignore old responsibilities. For example, so-called no-fault divorces—which give either spouse the right to dissolve a marriage at will—have obscured the vital importance of responsibilities in marriage." Elder Oaks suggested that no-fault divorce laws are leading our society down a dangerous path.[9]

Various policy and legal reforms have been proposed to help reduce divorce. For instance, "covenant marriage" legislation has been adopted in three states in the United States and proposed in many more.[10] Couples who choose covenant marriage in these states must receive premarital counseling and disclose anything to their future spouse that might reasonably affect the decision to marry; agree to get marital counseling if problems arise that threaten the marriage; and accept limited grounds for divorce (e.g., abuse, adultery, drug addiction, imprisonment) or a longer waiting period for divorce. Current research is exploring whether this more binding form of marriage can reduce the chances that couples will divorce.

Completely reversing unilateral, no-fault divorce laws probably is not possible, and I don't believe it would be wise to do so. But there are legal reforms that would address some of the problems created by current divorce laws and do more to reinforce marital permanence. For instance, in addition to covenant marriage, a handful of states have passed (and more are considering) legislation to encourage couples to get premarital counseling or education. Research suggests that this can increase marital quality and reduce the incidence of divorce in the early, riskiest years of marriage.[11] These kinds of modest policy changes to reduce divorce are possible when responsible citizens work hard to support them.

Our efforts to challenge divorce need not be limited to public, legal ones, however. One prominent marriage educator, Michelle Weiner-Davis, has spoken about "guerilla divorce busting."[12] She argued that the common response when someone tells you he or she is thinking about getting a divorce is to offer sympathy and support for the decision to go ahead. Instead, she urges us to challenge those thoughts (except in cases of abuse and the like) and to suggest ways of reviving and saving an imperfect relationship rather than casting it aside. She believes these natural, interpersonal interventions can make an impression on many people and prevent unnecessary divorces. Research suggests that most unhappy marriages become happy again when people hold on through the bad times.[13] In our interactions with others who are thinking about divorce, we can encourage them to take steps to revitalize their relationships.

CAN JUST ONE PERSON MAKE A DIFFERENCE?

Some responsible, concerned citizens think that just one person cannot make much difference, especially if he or she is not acting in some professional capacity, or given a prominent platform from which to urge action. But consider the case of Julie Baumgartner, a citizen of Chattanooga, Tennessee, who wanted to improve her community by strengthening marriage, promoting responsible fathering, and reducing unwed pregnancies. She began as just one person talking to other like-minded individuals. Over a few years, she built a vibrant coalition of religious, corporate, and civic leaders into a community-wide organization that promotes these goals with concrete opportunities for marriage and family life education. Her organization, First Things First (www .firstthings.org), is now the premier model of how to build a community healthy marriage initiative.

The scriptures teach us "that by small means the Lord can bring about great things" (1 Nephi 16:29) and "out of small things proceedeth that which is great" (D&C 64:33). President Gordon B. Hinckley quoted the latter scripture when he said recently: "Remarkable consequences often flow from a well-written letter and a postage stamp. Remarkable results

come of quiet conversation with those who carry heavy responsibilities."[14]

Speaking of troubling events occurring in cities, states, and nations that threaten what we revere, Elder Oaks reminds us that "we cannot afford to be indifferent or quiet We must be ever vigilant to ask 'Where will it lead?' and to sound appropriate warnings or join appropriate preventive efforts while there is still time. Often we cannot prevent the outcome, but we can remove ourselves from the crowd who, by failing to try to intervene, has complicity in the outcome."[15]

GUIDELINES FOR CIVIC (AND CIVIL) INVOLVEMENT

How we get involved as responsible citizens to strengthen marriages and families makes a difference in how effective we are and how the Lord can multiply our efforts, like the loaves and fishes in the New Testament (John 6:5–14). I suggest four guidelines for effective involvement.

First, we need to be informed. Our active participation in public life will be more effective when we take the time to study the issues, learn about relevant research, and stay current. Fortunately, this is easier to do than ever before with the widespread availability of the Internet There are many good websites to visit to gain current information and research about marriage and family issues (see Addition Reading and Suggested Websites at the end of the chapter).

A second guideline is to collaborate with other like-minded individuals and groups. Sometimes we need to strike out on our own and build our own initiative, especially when there is no activity in an area. But I think our efforts usually will be more effective when we join with other initiatives, especially when these initiatives are already farther down the same or a similar road. Occasionally I have students come to me with a passion to do something to strengthen marriages and families. They usually have an idea for a new organization or initiative that they want to start up. I have seen a couple of wonderful successes blossom from these personal efforts. But generally, I encourage them at least to start by adding their energy to similar ongoing efforts, rather than duplicate or divide efforts. Of course, joining with others sometimes will require compromise. But there are ways to compromise without abandoning basic beliefs. For instance, I actively participate with an organization making an impact at the national level promoting healthy marriages. But the leader of this organization will not allow it to take a position for or against same-sex marriage. She does this because she knows that members of the organization have different opinions about this, but all wish to strengthen marriage, however they define it. She does not want to divide the membership and dilute its effectiveness. Although she is getting pressure to change, I think she is making the right decision for this organization. Instead of fighting to change how this organization operates or divorcing myself from it, I have invested some energy in a different organization that is promoting passage of a constitutional amendment to prohibit same-sex marriages.

A third guideline is to strive to avoid contention and never promote it. This can be difficult when we are involved with moral principles to which we bring a lot of passion. But the Savior taught that "contention is not of me, but is of the devil, . . . and he stirreth up the hearts of men to contend . . . one with another" (3 Nephi 11:29). I don't believe this principle is limited to relations among the Saints; I think it applies widely. In Alma 1, Mormon describes how the faithful were being persecuted by nonbelievers in their communities. Most of the Saints "bore with patience the persecution which was heaped upon them" (v. 25). "Nevertheless, there were many among [the Church] who began to be proud, and began to contend warmly with their adversaries, even unto blows. . . . Now this was . . . a cause of much affliction to the church; yea, it was the cause of much trial with the church" (vv. 22–23). And in our day, President Hinckley has urged us to let our voices be heard, but he cautions: "I hope they will not be shrill voices."[16]

If we resort to contention to accomplish our public purposes, we risk hardening our hearts and losing that crucial, added strength that comes from the Spirit of God. When contention comes at us despite our best efforts to avoid it, the scriptures teach us to be patient (Alma 1:25), not to revile against our enemies (1 Peter 2:23), to turn the other cheek (Matthew 5:39), and to hold to the rod and ignore the mocking of the world (1 Nephi 8:26–30). If we shun contention, the Lord will fight our battles for us, and our efforts will be all the more fruitful for it.

I have been impressed with how Governor Mitt Romney of Massachusetts, who is a devout Latter-day Saint, has handled the struggle over same-sex marriage in his state. Based on his convictions of the sanctity of marriage, he has led his state's effort to nullify the state's supreme court ruling that legalized same-sex marriage. Yet the accounts that I have read and seen in the media suggest he has done this while striving to be respectful of the opposition and also respecting the constitutional processes operating in this struggle. He opened his testimony before the U.S. Senate Judiciary Committee on the Federal Marriage Amendment (which defines marriage as the union of a man and a woman) with these respectful words: "Like me, the great majority of Americans wish both to preserve the traditional definition of marriage and to oppose bias and intolerance directed towards gays and lesbians."[17] Similarly, Senator Gordon Smith (R-Oregon), also a devout Latter-day Saint, cast his vote in favor of the Federal Marriage Amendment while at the same time affirming his respect for gays and lesbians and his strong support for certain legal protections for a group that has experienced intolerance in our society.[18] In contrast, I have seen numerous leaders of pro-marriage groups, including Latter-day Saints, regularly speak disrespectfully and disingenuously about their opponents. All this seems to generate is media fodder; it does not advance the cause of right. The Lord is willing to bless our public efforts to strengthen marriages and families, but I believe that our civic efforts also must be civil if we are to claim that blessing.

A final guideline is that our desires to help strengthen other marriages and families in our communities should not come at the expense of our own spouses and children. Zeal has a way sometimes of overtaking our better judgment. "For what shall it profit a man, if he shall gain the whole world, and lose his own soul?" (Mark 8:36). I was impressed by how one young mother observed this principle. I called recently to ask her to consider accepting a job with a significant national organization dedicated to strengthening marriages. She brought experience and the ideal combination of qualifications to the job. I knew that she would want flexibility in work arrangements and could not give her full time to the work, so I said that we would accommodate her situation as much as possible. She was intrigued and flattered by the invitation, but asked for a few days to think about it. When she called back she politely turned the position down. She said it was her time now to focus on her young family; and even with job flexibility she didn't think she could do both jobs adequately. Although disappointed that an ideal candidate turned down the job opportunity, I deeply respected her decision. She continues to be involved in efforts to strengthen marriages and families, but she fits them into the temporal cracks of her busy family life rather than devoting herself fully to that cause at this time. "To every thing there is a season, and a time to every purpose under the heaven" (Ecclesiastes 3:1). In another season of her life, I'm confident she will bless others with more public labors to strengthen marriages and families.

When our seasons and opportunities come, we have civic and spiritual duties to bear the burden of responsible citizenship. Offering our public gifts in the service of the most fundamental units of a healthy society—marriage and family—will help to preserve our freedom.

ABOUT THE AUTHOR

Alan J. Hawkins is a professor of family life at Brigham Young University. He was a visiting scholar with the Administration for Children and Families, a member of the Utah Governor's Commission on Marriage, and head of research for the federal National Healthy Marriage Resource Center. He and his wife, Lisa, have two children and one grandson.

ADDITIONAL READING

Answering the Call: What Can I Do Now to Strengthen Marriages and Families? (2003), pamphlet (Provo: BYU School of Family Life and the Family Life Education Institute). Order from www.familylifeeducation.org or 1–800–452–5662.

Brent A. Barlow (2000), The marriage movement in America; in David C. Dollahite, ed., *Strengthening Our Families: An In-Depth Look at the Proclamation on the Family* (Salt Lake City: Bookcraft), 29–31.

Maggie Gallagher (2004), *Can Government Strengthen Marriage? Evidence from the Social Sciences* (New York: Institute for American Values); available at www.marriagemovement.org

Maggie Gallagher (2000). *The Marriage Movement: A Statement of Principles* (New York: Institute for American Values); available at www.marriagemovement.org

Theodora Ooms, Stacey Bouchet, and Mary Parke (2004), *Beyond Marriage Licenses: Efforts to Strengthen Marriage and Two-Parent Families, A State-by-State Snapshot* (Washington, D.C.: Center for Law and Social Policy); available at www.clasp.org

Strengthening Marriages in Your Community: 101 Ideas to Get You Started (2002), pamphlet (Washington, D.C.: Coalition for Marriage, Family and Couples Education). Order from www.smartmarriages.com

Linda Waite and Maggie Gallagher (2000), *The Case for Marriage* (New York: Doubleday).

SUGGESTED WEBSITES

Administration for Marriage and Families, http://www.acf.hhs.gov/healthymarriage

First Things First, http://www.firstthings.org

Institute for American Values, http://www.americanvalues.org

Institute for Marriage and Public Policy, http://www.marriage debate.com

Marriage Movement, http://www.marriagemovement.org

National Healthy Marriage Resource Center, http://www.healthy marriages.info

Smart Marriages, http://www.smartmarriages.com

NOTES

1. First Presidency and Council of Twelve Apostles (1995, November), The family: A proclamation to the world, *Ensign,* 25(11), 102.

2. Ibid.

3. Roper Center for Public Opinion Research (1998, February–March), The family, marriage: Highly valued? *The Public Perspective,* 17–18.

4. T. Ooms, S. Bouchet, and M. Parke (2004), *Beyond Marriage Licenses: Efforts in States to Strengthen Marriage and Two-Parent Families* (Washington D.C.: Center for Law and Social Policy).

5. M. Gallagher (2000), *The Marriage Movement: A Statement of Principles* (New York: Institute for American Values).

6. R. N. Bellah, R. Madsen, W. M. Sullivan, A. Swidler, and S. M. Tipton (1985), *Habits of the Heart: Individualism and Commitment in American Life* (New York: Harper & Row).

7. P. R. Amato and S. J. Rogers (1999), Do attitudes toward divorce affect marital quality? *Journal of Family Issues, 20,* 69–86.

8. Judith Viorst (2004); retrieved from www.brainyquote.com/quotes/quotes/j/judithvior146347.htm, October 14, 2004.

9. Dallin H. Oaks (2004, November 9), Where will it lead?, BYU Devotional Address; available at http://www.speeches.byu.edu

10. A. J. Hawkins, S. L. Nock, J. C. Wilson, L. Sanchez, and J. D. Wright (2002), Attitudes about covenant marriage and divorce: Policy implications from a three-state comparison, *Family Relations, 51,* 166–175.

11. J. S. Carroll and W. H. Doherty (2003), Evaluating the effectiveness of premarital prevention programs: A meta-analytic review of outcome research, *Family Relations, 52,* 105–118.

12. M. Weiner-Davis (2002, July), Guerilla divorce busting; keynote address presented at the Smart Marriages Annual Conference, Crystal City, VA.

13. L. J. Waite, D. Browning, W. J. Doherty, M. Gallagher, Y. Luo, and S. M. Stanley (2002), *Does Divorce Make People Happy? Findings from a Study of Unhappy Marriages* (New York: Institute for American Values).

14. Gordon B. Hinckley (2004, September), In opposition to evil, *Ensign, 34*(9), 5.

15. Oaks (2004).

16. Hinckley (2004), 5.

17. Mitt Romney (2004), Preserving traditional marriage: A view from the states, *Testimony before the U.S. Senate Judiciary Committee, June 22*; retrieved from www.mass.gov/portal/govPR.jsp?gov_pr=gov_pr_040622_WMR_gay_marriage_testimony.xml, accessed June 30, 2004.

18. Senator Gordon H. Smith (2004, October 14), The case for amending the constitution to defend marriage; address given at the College of Family, Home, and Social Science Honored Alumni Lecture, Brigham Young University.

Rearing Responsible Citizens

David B. and Linda W. Magleby

Parents have a sacred duty to [teach] their children . . . to be law-abiding citizens wherever they live.[1]
—"The Family: A Proclamation to the World"

Parents play a powerful role in orienting their children to government and establishing patterns of civic engagement. In this chapter we explore what scholars know about the role families and parents play in fostering active citizenship and also review what has been said on the topic in scripture and by Church leaders.

Importance of Citizenship and Civic Engagement

Many people take their citizenship for granted. Citizenship is defined as the legal status of a citizen with its attendant rights, privileges, and responsibilities. Among the rights of citizenship may be freedoms to vote, of religion and speech, of peaceful assembly, to petition for a redress of grievances, and to travel throughout a country. The responsibilities of citizenship include obeying and sustaining the laws of the country in which we live, participating in the political process, and serving in the community.

For members of The Church of Jesus Christ of Latter-day Saints, our responsibility as citizens is found in the twelfth article of faith: "We believe in being subject to kings, presidents, rulers, and magistrates, in obeying, honoring, and sustaining the law." Elder James E. Talmage commented on this teaching: "Among other virtues the Church in its teachings

should impress the duty of a law-abiding course; and the people should show forth the effect of such precepts in their probity as citizens of the nation and in the community of which they are part."[2]

Being a good citizen means learning to love and serve others, first in families, then in our communities, our countries, and the world. Because of the restored gospel, we understand that being a good citizen means "that when [we] are in the service of [our] fellow beings [we] are only in the service of [our] God" (Mosiah 2:17). Members of the Church are encouraged to participate as active members of the community by prayerfully studying the issues and exercising their privilege to vote. A First Presidency letter stated:

> We urge Church members to *register to vote,* to study the issues and candidates carefully and prayerfully, and then vote for those they believe will most nearly carry out their ideas of good government. . . . While affirming its constitutional right of expression on political and social issues, the Church reaffirms its long-standing policy of neutrality regarding political parties, political platforms, and candidates for political office.[3]

Social scientists describe the sense of social engagement and confidence in dealing with others in public activities as *social capital.* Political scientist Robert Putnam defines social capital as "connections among individuals—social networks and the norms of reciprocity and trustworthiness that arise from them."[4] Measures of social capital include political, civic, and religious participation, connections in the workplace, informal social connections, altruism, volunteering, philanthropy, reciprocity, honesty, and trust.[5] Putnam, among others, has documented that over time we have seen diminishing social capital. People are less involved in community groups and have not developed the communication and cooperation skills necessary for civic engagement. The concept of social capital is useful because it conveys the sense that individuals can acquire social capital out of their experiences and education. Among the most important transmitters of social capital is the family.

Research has demonstrated that Latter-day Saints are not only more likely to volunteer within their church but are also more likely to have "given a speech or presentation" and to have taken "part in making decisions" in the Church.[6] These same data also show that the more involved Latter-day Saints are in their church, the more likely they are to be involved in politics.[7] Latter-day Saints who are religiously active are more engaged in politics than religiously active Catholics or Southern Baptists. Obversely, Latter-day Saints with the lowest level of religious participation have a slightly lower rate of political participation than Southern Baptists and Catholics who have the same level of religious involvement.[8] The more social capital people have, the more effective citizens they are.

HOW CHILDREN LEARN ABOUT CITIZENSHIP AND CIVIC RESPONSIBILITY

The most powerful influence on how children view citizenship and civic engagement is their families.[9] In his classic study, *Political Socialization,* Kenneth P. Langton observed that "within the family the individual learns his first set of social roles . . . how he should relate to other people."[10] Children learn from their parents' knowledge about citizenship and government.[11] The orientation of the parents towards political participation "is shared by the children in many cases."[12]

The role of parents in raising children is clearly stated in scripture: "But ye will teach them to walk in the ways of truth and soberness; ye will teach them to love one another, and to serve one another" (Mosiah 4:15). "And they shall also teach their children to pray, and to walk uprightly before the Lord" (D&C

68:28). Modern prophets and apostles have also emphasized the central teaching role of parents. "The Family: A Proclamation to the World" states, "Parents have a sacred duty to rear their children in love and righteousness, to provide for their physical and spiritual needs, to teach them to love and serve one another, to observe the commandments of God and to be law-abiding citizens wherever they live."[13]

Elder M. Russell Ballard said, "Sooner, perhaps, than we realize, the fate of nations will be in the hands of today's children."[14] The family is the first community in which children learn to love and serve one another. In the family, children can learn about the blessings of belonging, of being loved, protected, and nurtured. They can learn to contribute to the family by their attitudes, their work, and their obedience. They can learn to be grateful for the contributions of others. With these family-centered principles as a foundation, children are prepared to love and serve in the community. Elder James E. Faust said, "Among the other values children should be taught are respect for others, beginning with the child's own parents and family; respect for the symbols of faith and patriotic beliefs of others; respect for law and order; respect for the property of others; respect for authority."[15]

CHALLENGES IN REARING RESPONSIBLE CITIZENS

There are challenges to rearing responsible citizens. One of the most formidable challenges is cynicism, a scorn for the motives or virtue of others. In the government setting, cynics believe that politicians are only interested in themselves and are not sincere. They believe that their votes cannot make a difference and that public officials don't care what "people like us" think. Cynicism is corrosive of citizenship and civic involvement because it fosters the myths that people don't matter, votes don't count, and the government doesn't listen to citizens. Statements such as "My vote doesn't make a difference," or "Politics is a lose-lose situation," or "Voting is just choosing the lesser of the two evils," when uttered in the presence of children, help to make them cynical. Children are also exposed to cynicism in the community and in the media.

A challenge related to cynicism is distrust. The view that "all politicians are corrupt" is an example of expressing distrust. Consider the impact of such a statement on a child who might later consider running for community office. Most politicians are not corrupt. They mirror the broader culture and are no more or less corrupt than business leaders, sports heroes, or others. And yet we do not express the view that all sports heroes cheat or take drugs. This increasing sense of distrust is one of the main causes of the decrease in social capital discussed above.

A common obstacle that parents can help their children overcome is a lack of self-confidence in dealing with government, bureaucracy, and complexity when facing community problems. The obverse of low self-confidence in dealing with these challenges is what social scientists call *efficacy*. Efficacy is the belief that one's actions within the political community can produce desired results. Families that foster civic engagement have children with more efficacy.[16] Rather than perpetuate the attitude that people cannot influence their surroundings, demonstrate the opposite to your children through your actions. Identify a local problem and then set about to solve it.

Another important lesson to teach children about government and civic engagement is that people do not always get their way. A remarkable feature of a constitutional democracy is the peaceful transfer of power from one party or candidate to another. In many a young democracy, the incumbent candidate behind in public opinion will either rig the election or disregard the election and hold power through force. The norm of accepting the outcome of free and fair elections is a mark of a mature democracy and responsible citizens. This attitude can be fostered in families by discussing that reasonable people can disagree on many topics and that government and politics often reflect these differences.

A useful additional step in this discussion of winners and losers in democratic decision making is to encourage children to consider why some people might not see things the same way they do. What about this individual or group influences how they think and what they support? Questions like this help foster the kind of tolerance we need to retain freedom and democracy. Note that this question and discussion does not diminish the view of the parent or child, but seeks to understand how reasonable people can disagree on a topic or policy.

OPPORTUNITIES TO TEACH CHILDREN ABOUT CITIZENSHIP AND CIVIC RESPONSIBILITY

The opportunities to teach our children about citizenship and civic responsibility are plentiful and include formal teaching moments like family home evening or talks we give on these topics and informal settings like holiday celebrations, conversations, and personal examples of civic engagement. Below are some possible teaching opportunities:

1. Show respect for the law by obeying traffic and other laws. We can teach children that obedience is the best choice, whether anyone else is there to see us wait for the red light to change or not. Our own integrity requires that we obey the laws. We can also show respect for the law by the way we talk about and address police officers or other officers of the law.

2. Vote. If you are blessed to live in a democracy, take the time to vote. Include your children in discussions about upcoming elections and take them with you to the polls when you vote. Explain the process, the election volunteers, the secret ballot, and so forth. Seeing how seriously you take voting will instill respect for the voting franchise.

3. Election campaigns provide opportunities to discuss elections and voting. You might watch a candidates' debate as a family and then discuss the process, the issues, and the strengths and weaknesses of each candidate. The purpose of the discussion is broader than just to see who the better candidate is. The discussion should foster gratitude that we have a process with choices, people who are willing to run, and that we have a voice in important issues to be decided. Perhaps take the discussion one step farther by considering the opportunity to run for office or become more involved in school and community efforts.

4. Talk about the news, especially examples of people who sacrifice to be able to live in a democracy. The news of nations frequently includes stories of people working to achieve freedom or to free themselves from a dictator. Use these current events as a contrast to the freedom your family experiences. Talk about why people yearn for freedom and are willing to sacrifice a great deal for it.

5. Provide community service as a family. While volunteering to pick up litter, help at a homeless shelter, or assist a candidate or party, explain how the service is linked to citizenship. Teach children that each of us has a responsibility to contribute to our society and government.

6. Volunteer in a campaign or attend a political event or rally. Encourage your children to become participants in democracy by meeting local candidates and volunteering to help in a campaign.

7. As you pay your taxes, take the opportunity to

explain why we have taxes, that the American Revolutionary War was waged over taxation without representation, and that all governments depend on raising revenue through taxes. An important link between taxes and civic responsibility is that we all benefit from such services as national defense, streets, police protection, and public education.

8. Make patriotic holidays teaching moments and integrate patriotic symbols where appropriate. National holidays provide an opportunity to reflect on the rights and privileges you enjoy as well as the responsibilities of citizenship. A family home evening lesson could focus on founders or others who have secured and defended your country.

9. Be positive when talking about elected officials. We can disagree with a policy or position an official takes without belittling motives or intelligence. If you live in a country where many ideas are tolerated, you have reason to celebrate. Better still, if you live in a country where you have the freedom to express your opinions, work to convince others of your ideas. Pray for elected officials, even if they are not from your political party. These officials are in need of our prayers, and including them in family prayers is a powerful teaching moment.

10. Consider taking family vacations that provide opportunities to teach children about history or visit a historical site. Visiting Washington, D.C.; the battlefield at Gettysburg; Colonial Williamsburg; or the Statue of Liberty can provide unforgettable memories for children. Before these trips, spend time talking about the significance of what you will be seeing. Allow time during and after the visit to answer questions and discuss the experience.

11. When a child makes a poor choice and breaks a law, teach responsibility and accountability. One of the most important things we can teach children is that choices have consequences. We are commanded to teach about repentance (D&C 68:25). When a civil law is broken, repentance includes confession to civil authorities, restitution where possible, and accepting the penalties or punishment that may be imposed.

Family traditions that include these elements reinforce children's sense of citizenship and encourage civic engagement.

CONCLUSION

Over the course of human history it is a relatively rare occurrence for people to live in freedom and gov-ern themselves. Countries sometimes experiment with democracy, but it rarely lasts more than a couple of generations before a depression, war, or dictator replaces it with authoritarian rule. Historically, people have tended to live more under totalitarian rule, monarchy, or in anarchy than to have governed themselves. To experience freedom and be able to retain it is remarkable and worth preserving. For that to happen, parents and other role models need to transmit the values and attitudes that foster active citizenship and civic engagement.

ABOUT THE AUTHORS

David B. Magleby is dean of the College of Family, Home, and Social Sciences at BYU. He is a distinguished professor of political science and senior research fellow at the Center for the Study of Elections and Democracy.

Linda W. Magleby is a wife, mother, and full-time homemaker. A graduate of the J. Reuben Clark Law School, she is active in civic affairs and served on the Primary General Board from 2000 to 2005.

ADDITIONAL READING

Sue Bergin (1988, September), Making a difference in your community, *Ensign, 18*(9), 12–15.

Alexander B. Morrison (1999, February), A caring community: Goodness in action, *Ensign, 29*(2), 13–19.

Dallin H. Oaks (1992, October), Religious values and public policy, *Ensign, 22*(10), 60–64.

NOTES

The authors express appreciation to Dustin N. Slade and Chad Pugh for their assistance in preparing this chapter.

1. First Presidency and Council of Twelve Apostles (1995, November), The family: A proclamation to the world, *Ensign, 25*(11), 102.

2. James E. Talmage (1965), *Articles of Faith,* 46th ed. (Salt Lake City: The Church of Jesus Christ of Latter-day Saints), 413.

3. First Presidency letter (2004, July 31), *LDS Church News,* Z05.

4. R. D. Putnam (2000), *Bowling Alone: The Collapse and Revival of American Community* (New York: Simon & Schuster), 19.

5. Ibid., 27.

6. D. E. Campbell and J. Q. Monson (2002, October 4), Dry kindling: A political profile of American Mormons; paper presented at the Conference on Religion and American Political Behavior, Southern Methodist University; available at http://www.nd.edu/~dcampbe4/dry%20kindling.pdf, 18–19. Campbell and Monson find that Mormons are more likely to volunteer within their church—60 percent report doing so over the past twelve months compared to 36 percent of Southern Baptists and 27 percent of Catholics. Fifty-three percent of Mormons "report having given a speech or presentation at church within the previous six months," while 14 percent of Southern Baptists and

4 percent of Catholics report the same. Mormons are also more likely to be trained in decision making, with 48 percent reporting attending a meeting where they had a role in the decision-making process within the last six months, compared to 28 percent of Southern Baptists and 8 percent of Catholics.

7. Ibid., 21.

8. Ibid., 22.

9. H. H. Hyman (1959), *Political Socialization: A Study in the Psychology of Political Behavior* (Glencoe, IL: Free Press), 85.

10. K. P. Langton (1969), *Political Socialization* (New York: Oxford University Press), 21.

11. R. G. Niemi and J. Junn (1998), *Civic Education: What Makes Students Learn* (New Haven: Yale University Press).

12. L. E. Thomas (1971, May), Political attitude congruence between politically active parents and college-age children: An inquiry into family political socialization, *Journal of Marriage and the Family, 33,* 376.

13. First Presidency and Council of Twelve Apostles (1995), 102.

14. M. Russell Ballard (1991, May), Teach the children, *Ensign, 21*(5), 78.

15. James E. Faust (1990, November), The greatest challenge in the world—good parenting, *Ensign, 20*(11), 34.

16. Langton (1969), 144, 155.

Preparing Children to Leave Home

Edy and Lynn Pehrson

During the often hectic and challenging process of raising children, the day our children would actually leave home to begin a life of their own seemed important, yet was so distant that it was seldom a cause of anxiety. We knew we needed to prepare ourselves and our children, but how? One thing that always seemed clear to us was that the process of preparing our children to be independent adults had to begin when they were young. We always planned to send our children out into the world to "seek their fortune," as they say. From the beginning we encouraged, and fully expected, our children to become independent and productive adults.

As our first child stood on the edge of the nest, ready to stretch his wings and fly on his own, we thought of all the things we had tried so hard to teach in preparation for this day. Had we adequately taught principles of responsibility, independence, spirituality, love of others, and self-confidence? Were our sincere efforts effective in his life? In this essay we describe the efforts that were most helpful in preparing our children to leave home.

Gospel living helped our family prepare. We taught our children to pay tithing. We were blessed with the inspiration and determination to read scriptures daily, and we are convinced that it helped each child to read better and feel comfortable reading aloud. Because we had no extended family living near us, we concentrated on our own family and had family home evenings with each child participating. Family activities led to an even closer family bond that has been valuable as each child has left home to be on his or her own.

We encouraged our children to get jobs when feasible. While we lived in Texas, our oldest child was able to secure a job working at a nearby stable. Later, we were blessed with the opportunity to purchase a horse and jointly rented some property with a man who became like a grandfather to our children as we worked and played together with the horses. The

work ethic our son learned has helped him become an independent, productive adult on his own farm. Later, we started our own business with the express purpose of providing jobs for our children. We were able to work together for a common goal and help our children prepare for future employment.

Another way to foster responsibility, motivation, independence, and self-worth is through the development of talents. This can be accomplished through participation in athletics, music lessons, part-time employment, or other worthy pursuits. In our case, we encouraged our children to find a sport they enjoyed and then give it their best. Some of our children excelled in track and field, others in high school wrestling. Our youngest child wanted to play volleyball, but she is only five feet tall. Her enthusiasm was contagious, and so we encouraged her to "go for it." She ended up being the cocaptain of her high school volleyball team and two club volleyball teams.

We taught the importance of education by pursuing education ourselves. Lynn earned his doctorate and completed a fellowship in child and family studies. After thirteen years of marriage and six children, Edy completed her bachelor's degree. We were pleased when several of the children adopted our desire for higher education. One of our children took thirteen years to complete a bachelor's degree, but was determined to do so even while raising her children.

Certainly everyone does not have the aptitude for or interest in a college education. Two of our children followed different but successful paths without university training. One started attending college but left to begin a family and later used her skills to become a legal secretary. Another followed a lifelong dream to become a skilled automotive technician. Other families may realize the goal of encouraging children to use their skills and follow their dreams in a host of other ways. Two keys that parents can use to help children find their own career paths are unconditional love and unwavering support.

For those in our family who chose to pursue a

college education, our family's agreement was that they would have to pay for their books and 50 percent of the cost of tuition and fees. They were welcome to live at home as long as they were single and lived in accordance with our values. This meant they would have to work hard in high school to even get into college, and they would either have to work or earn a scholarship to pay the balance. As our children enrolled in college or undertook other worthwhile directions, most of them preferred to attend the single adult wards instead of being involved with us in the "family ward." Though it involved scheduling challenges, we believe firmly that this was part of the emotional and physical separation that helped our children become healthy, well-balanced adults.

In today's world the ideal is often not the reality for all of our children. The process of leaving home and becoming independent for some is not immediately successful or realized without great challenge. In many families physical or emotional health problems make the process difficult and sometimes unrealistic. The realm of worldly attractions sometimes leads children to lifestyles that result in dependence rather than independence. We have experienced some of these things in our own home, and we are deeply sensitive to the realities many families face. Through our experience with such challenges, we, like so many other parents, have learned that comfort and solace come only when we humbly turn to a loving Father in Heaven for patience, understanding, and guidance.

In negotiating living arrangements when children are of sufficient age and maturity to leave home, it is important to show forth love while avoiding the pitfalls of inappropriate dependency. Ideas might include a sensitively timed heart-to-heart discussion of how a child might bear part of the family's financial obligations (i.e., paying for food, rent, car, utilities), share family work (preparing meals, helping with yard care), and take full responsibility for his or her own life (getting up on time for work, making appointments, keeping up a checking account). At some point, the message becomes, "We love you, but in the interest of your growth and development it is time for you to live on your own." Unfortunately, sometimes one or both parents are unable or unwilling to let go and thereby enable the dependency and lengthen the process of a child's leaving home.

On the other hand, a short-term return may require a different approach. We believe that in times of crisis it would be selfish to withhold our help when our child could greatly benefit and the sacrifices required by the situation are those we can gladly provide. For example, our daughter and her girls lived with us for a period of time until we could help her find a home. At other times when our children needed money for college or a new baby, we were able to pay them for work we needed done. However, even in these circumstances, it is important to establish boundaries and time lines to avoid ultimately damaging family relationships through inappropriate dependencies. (Chapter 36 describes the role of grandparents in aiding adult children without encouraging dependency.)

As our children have married (six out of seven are married at this writing), it has brought a new dimension into the family. We have seen significant growth as our children and their spouses work out financial, health, logistical, and time management problems, especially as they rely upon the Lord for strength and direction. We have tried to be available for consultation but not be overbearing, as we sense the main thing they need is a listening ear.

We still have meaningful ongoing contacts with the married children through family gatherings and individual relationships that mature and change as their life experiences parallel ours. It is our responsibility as the children mature and leave home for whatever reason to continue the connection through phone calls, letter writing, e-mail messages, regular dinners, parties, holiday celebrations, and family vacations. How often and how elaborate are the gatherings or vacations? They vary, based on the proximity of loved ones and circumstances with the other side of the family.

We have learned, sometimes the hard way, that preparing children for the inevitable day when they will begin a life on their own is a process that begins with less-than-perfect parents when that first child is born. Seeing our own children successfully leave the security of home to lead productive adult lives has been a source of great joy. We continue to play a meaningful but now different role in the lives of our adult children and our eleven grandchildren. If we as parents hope to be successful in preparing our children to leave our homes and become our peers as independent productive adults, we must be willing to foster the characteristics that lead to positive self-esteem, independence, family love, and a deep-seated knowledge that we can and will be together as a family forever. Only then can the seeds of eternal interdependence in families grow into a family tree that forever nourishes all of its branches.

ABOUT THE AUTHORS

Edyth (Edy) Pehrson is mother to seven children and grandmother to eleven. Since receiving her bachelor's degree at BYU–Hawaii in tourism and travel management, Edy has owned a travel agency. She has been happily married to her husband, Lynn, for 38 years.

Lynn Pehrson, DSW, has been a professor of social work at BYU and BYU–Hawaii for 22 years. He served 15 years as the Reserve Social Work Consultant to the U.S. Army Surgeon General. His marriage and children are the highlights of his life.

ADDITIONAL READING

Richard and Linda Eyre with Saren Eyre Loosli (2002), *Empty-Nest Parenting: Adjusting Your Stewardship As Your Children Leave Home* (Salt Lake City: Bookcraft).

Sarah Jane Weaver (2004, May 22), Finding a formula to parent adult children, *LDS Church News*, 706; available online at http://www.desnews.com/cn

E S S A Y   1 2

CARING FOR AGED PARENTS

CARRIE A. MOORE

Rosalynn Carter, former first lady of the United States whose work with aging issues has brought heightened public awareness, has said there are four kinds of people in the world: "Those who have been caregivers; those who currently are caregivers; those who will be caregivers; and those who will need caregivers."[1]

At its core, caring for aging parents is a spiritual stewardship, and those so entrusted know that the commandment "Honour thy father and thy mother" (Exodus 20:12) can be a stressful and time-consuming endeavor when advanced age, serious illness, dementia, or Alzheimer's disease necessitate regular intervention.

Mary knows her father well, but he no longer knows her. When she drives several hours to another state in order to visit, she often finds him non-responsive despite her mother's attempts to get him to speak. The situation is hurtful, Mary says, because she was so close to her father as a child. While she knows that Alzheimer's disease has stolen his memory, she longs for him to simply remember her name. Rather than dwelling on her sadness, Mary spends time with him recounting their shared memories.[2]

She recognizes that "self-pity doesn't make things better, but neither does being a Pollyanna" by pretending the situation isn't difficult. Her commitment to continue visiting frames their interaction as a positive personal choice, rather than a burdensome obligation. Determination to view the glass as "half full" rather than "half empty" sets the stage for everything else that caregivers will do, whether they live near or far.[3]

Sharon was forced to put her mother in a care center when repeated falls left her unable to care for herself. The decision was made despite guilt over a "promise" their mother had extracted from her and her siblings years earlier to "never put me in a home." They chose a facility in her mother's hometown so she would know some other residents. As the only sibling living in the same state as her mother, Sharon insisted that her brother and sister come to relocate their mother so she wouldn't be perceived as the "bad guy."

New challenges at the care center included resistance to the prescribed exercise regimen. Sharon began taking small chocolates with her during each visit as an incentive for her mother to walk a certain distance. When she completed the walk, Sharon would reward her with the candy—an arrangement that eased the power struggle between them and gave both Sharon and her mother something positive to look forward to.[4]

The decision Sharon faced to put her mother in a care center after making an earlier "promise" is one faced by many adult children, who make such vows lightly despite the long-term implications. Such promises often leave adult children so guilt-ridden that they make potentially harmful decisions in the face of changing circumstances.[5]

Rather than quit her job, relocate, and forfeit not only her current income, but her own future retirement, Sharon knew she would be creating undue financial and emotional hardship for herself by keeping the hasty promise. Because her siblings were not able to share responsibility for their mother's full-time care, Sharon weighed the facts and came to a decision that served both her and her mother best. As no two family situations are the same, there is no "one-size-fits-all" prescription for such decisions. Ideally, families will weigh all legitimate concerns and prayerfully formulate a plan.

One expert suggests substituting promises with the more realistic vow to "make sure you have the best care we can afford," and that "you will never go to any living situation that is not well suited to you." Doing what is best for the entire family, along with a commitment to treat the loved one with respect and dignity and to stay emotionally close, may be preferable. If such a promise has already been made, an alternative may be presented with a more realistic statement of what can be expected. Such actions risk anger, name-calling, and possibly even disinheritance, "but the price you would pay in guilt or in negative consequences for years . . . may well be worth this risk."[6]

Sharon's relationship with her siblings was also affected by her unwitting "election" as the primary caregiver. Often one person—by virtue of geographic proximity, sibling rank, resources, or marital status—is so designated. This is especially difficult when siblings assume that once the primary caregiver is designated, their responsibility ends and they fail to offer financial, emotional, and physical support. In such situations, resentment often builds despite a desire to do the right thing. Caregivers must realize—and make provision for—their own needs for emotional, social, and physical respite.

Sharon understood her own emotional needs and wisely involved both siblings in moving their mother to the care center with the gentle reminder that her role as sole care provider would be jeopardized if their mother became angry at her.

While Alzheimer's disease, dementia, and a host of debilitating physical or emotional conditions may necessitate full-time professional care, many adult children find they can successfully care for their aging parents themselves.

One woman recounts how her two aunts, busy women who lived in the same town, agreed to alternate 24-hour shifts caring for their mother. "One sister needed major surgery, and the other was a stake Relief Society president. Somehow they worked things out. Their experience was not unpleasant because their mother always kept up her spirits," serving as "a good friend, [and] a great listener."[7]

Another woman whose mother was left paralyzed by a stroke was willing to take on the caregiving role because, as a single woman without other family responsibilities, she felt she could devote herself to it. The decision was made easier by supportive siblings who were available and willing to offer respite when needed. Life changed in dramatic ways—her social life became nearly nonexistent and she had to seek permission from her employer to alter her work hours. Yet she learned much about living gracefully from a mother who was determined to find God's goodness amid suffering.[8]

Those who find great satisfaction in caring for their aging parents nearly always do so in part because they have prepared not only spiritually, but physically, emotionally, and financially. Such preparation is akin to being on an airplane when an emergency arises and "adjusting your own oxygen mask before you can help someone else. You can't give away what you don't have, even if your intentions are good."[9]

While concern for aging parents creates its own set of challenges, what may be less evident is the impact such circumstances have on relationships with spouses and children.

One family therapist predicts that caring for aging parents will be the number one challenge for marriages during the next 20 years, as partners struggle to maintain their own relationship while parenting not only their children, but often their own parents.[10] The number of adult children who find themselves a part of this so-called "sandwich generation" will likely continue to grow as advances in medicine and technology prolong life even as plagues, famine, war, and disease continue to sweep the earth.

Young children and teens whose parents are involved in caregiving can face their own challenges. One woman said that in hindsight, she felt she had been wrong to care for her mother at home for five years while her children were small. "She took over our home, our lives, the lives of our children. . . . My children stopped bringing their friends home. They never knew what she might do or say."[11]

Caregivers who become highly attuned to the

needs of everyone around them often fail to recognize their own needs, or to do anything about them. Denial, anger, social withdrawal, anxiety, depression, exhaustion, sleeplessness, and health problems often accompany the added stress of caring for aging parents. Yet free government-funded training programs, support groups, and materials for reference or referral are available, and often found by simply contacting state or county aging services agencies.

Informal networking is often helpful. For example, one man told of learning about baby monitors from a friend and putting one in his mother's room at night so he could hear any calls for help. Another was exasperated when his aging mother would wander away during the night, until another caregiver suggested he pin a length of elastic tape to his pajamas and pin the other end to his mother's nightgown so he would be awakened when she began to wander.

Despite the challenges, caring for one's aging parents embodies one of the ultimate expressions of Christlike love. Said one caregiving trainer: "The people I talk to every day are not the ones you read about in the newspaper or see on TV. They are the unnamed, unsung heroes in our communities and they're doing an incredible job that's very hard and long-lasting. They are just amazing. They're creative, have incredible strength, and most still keep their sense of humor. They keep their families together and I don't know how they do it. They are people I'm humbled to work with."[12]

ABOUT THE AUTHOR

Carrie A. Moore is religion editor for the *Deseret Morning News* in Salt Lake City. An award-winning journalist for 20 years, she has written curriculum for The Church of Jesus Christ of Latter-day Saints and has been a presenter at the BYU Women's Conference.

ADDITIONAL READING

Ezra Taft Benson (1989, November), To the elderly in the Church, *Ensign, 19*(11), 4–8.
Boyd K. Packer (2003, May), The golden years, *Ensign, 33*(5), 82–84.
Sarah Jane Weaver (2003, August 23), Fighting a battle to remember, *LDS Church News*, 207–210.

SUGGESTED WEBSITES

Aging with Dignity, www.agingwithdignity.com
Eldercare Locator, www.eldercare.gov
National Alliance for Caregiving, www.caregiving.org
National Association of Area Agencies on Aging, www.n4a.org
National Family Caregivers Association, www.nfcacares.org
National Organization for Empowering Caregivers, www.care-givers.com

NOTES

1. Sweet Briar College website, http://gos.sbc.edu/c/carter.html
2. Author interview with caregiver, name changed on request.
3. National Family Caregivers Association (2003), *Choosing to Take Charge of Your Life*, brochure for family caregivers; available at http://www.thefamilycaregiver.org/pdfs/TakeChrge.pdf
4. Author interview with caregiver Sharon Johnson.
5. M. Edinberg (2000), *Promises, Promises*, essay (ElderCare Online); available at http://www.ec-online.net
6. Ibid.
7. M. Richardson (2000), How do we help the folks?; in *The Arms of His Love: Talks from the 1999 Women's Conference* (Salt Lake City: Deseret Book), 328.
8. B. Hales and J. Nelson (2004, April 29), Honor thy father and thy mother: That thy days may be long upon the land; address at BYU Women's Conference, Provo, UT; unpublished, content of address as reported by author.
9. Author interview with Nancy Stallings, program manager for caregivers, Salt Lake County Aging Services.
10. T. Hargrave (2004, July 10), Caring for marriage while caring for aging parents; presentation at 8th Annual Smart Marriages Conference, Dallas, TX; notes of address as taken by author, in possession of author.
11. Richardson (2000), 328.
12. Stallings interview.

DEFENDING MARRIAGE

WILLIAM C. DUNCAN

Threats to marriage and family life intensified in the second half of the twentieth century and continue to develop in the twenty-first century in a world which increasingly, in the words of Elder Bruce C. Hafen, has "lost the plot" of family life.[1]

The institution of marriage faces many challenges, both cultural and political. Beginning in the early 1960s, the laws of every state were gradually changed to allow either husband or wife to argue that "irreconcilable differences," or something similar, were valid reasons to be granted a divorce, often even when the other spouse objected. The resulting ease in securing a divorce has led to a significant rise in rates of divorce (see chapter 4). There are circumstances when a divorce may be justified, such as, in the words of President James E. Faust, "a prolonged and apparently irredeemable relationship which is destructive of a person's dignity as a human being."[2] However, the current legal climate of no-fault divorce allows people to divorce because of reasons President Faust felt strongly were not cause to break the marriage covenant: mental distress, personality differences, growing apart, or falling out of love.[3]

While legal developments made divorce more prevalent, cultural trends have contributed to the creation of an atmosphere where extramarital sexual relations are less likely to be condemned. While marriage was once considered the only appropriate relationship for sexual intimacy, media and other influences encourage an ethic of promiscuity. Thus, between the ease of no-fault divorce and the cultural acceptability of extramarital sex, the number of couples living together without marriage has risen to the point where, for many young people, cohabitation is considered a prerequisite to marriage. Some do not plan to marry at all. Ironically, researchers have learned that couples who cohabit prior to marriage are more likely to divorce than married couples who did not cohabit.[4]

These dramatic changes in the legal nature and cultural importance of marriage have led to the contemplation of even more fundamental changes in marriage. Currently, one of the major sources of confusion and avenues for attack on the family is related to the definition of marriage. Since the 1970s, lawsuits have been filed in an attempt to force local governments to issue marriage licenses to same-sex couples.[5]

The work of many people to stop the movement supporting same-sex marriage has not interrupted its momentum. A suit in Vermont (1999) stopped short of redefining marriage, instead ordering the state legislature to offer the benefits of marriage to same-sex couples.[6] Then, in November 2003, the Massachusetts Supreme Judicial Court held that state's marriage law unconstitutional and later ruled that it would only be satisfied if the state began to issue marriage licenses to same-sex couples.[7] Massachusetts same-sex couples may now marry. This effort to redefine marriage threatens the family by legally endorsing a message that denies male-female differences and ignores the truth that "children are entitled to . . . be reared by a father and a mother."[8] This legal revolution would disconnect marriage from the ideal of children reared in a family headed by a married mother and father.

REAFFIRMING THE DEFINITION OF MARRIAGE

The effort to reaffirm marriage has taken many forms in the last decade. At the urging of concerned citizens, some states have passed laws specifying that those states will not recognize same-sex marriages contracted in other states.[9] In some, legislators have even proposed amendments to their state constitutions banning same-sex marriage (which were later approved in general elections).[10] In the 2004 election, voters in eleven states approved, by significant margins, amendments to their state constitutions that defined marriage as the union of a man and a woman.[11] Concerned groups and citizens have filed briefs supporting marriage in key court cases, engaged in debates, and written articles and letters to educate others about the importance of the issue.

The proclamation on the family calls on "responsible citizens . . . everywhere to promote those measures designed to maintain and strengthen the family as the fundamental unit of society."[12] Regarding the defense of marriage, the First Presidency has written, "We encourage members to appeal to legislators, judges, and other government officials to preserve the purposes and sanctity of marriage between a man and a woman, and to reject all efforts to give legal authorization or other official approval or support to marriages between persons of the same gender."[13] In 2004, the First Presidency issued a statement saying, "the Church accordingly favors measures that define marriage as the union of a man and a woman and that do not confer legal status on any other sexual relationship."[14]

Our individual efforts to defend marriage should honor, in content and tone, our prophet's plea for courtesy, thoughtfulness, and respect. In commenting on a successful effort to enact a ballot initiative to protect marriage in California, President Gordon B. Hinckley emphasized that "our opposition to attempts to legalize same-sex marriage should never be interpreted as justification for hatred, intolerance, or abuse of those who profess homosexual tendencies, either individually or as a group. . . . We love and honor them as sons and daughters of God."[15] President Hinckley has also written:

> I am not one to advocate shouting defiantly or shaking fists and issuing threats in the faces of legislators. But I am one who believes that we should earnestly and sincerely and positively express our convictions. . . . Let our voices be heard. I hope they will not be shrill voices, but I hope we shall speak with such conviction that those to whom we speak shall know of the strength of our feeling and the sincerity of our effort. Remarkable consequences often flow from a well-written letter and a postage stamp. Remarkable results come of quiet conversation with those who carry heavy responsibilities.[16]

We should work together with like-minded people of other faiths or who are not associated with any religious tradition. Because of the influence of the Light of Christ, there is a widely shared reverence for marriage and the family and a deeply felt need to defend them. Weight is added to the message when it is spoken by many different individuals and groups.

As much as possible, we should explain our position in a way that others can easily understand, even if they will not agree. While there is much scriptural and doctrinal authority for the idea that marriage should continue to be defined as the union of a man and a woman, there are other sources of authority that are widely appreciated and should not be ignored. For instance, social science research indicates that family structure matters to children's development and outcomes and that fathers and mothers make unique contributions to children.[17] In addition, many thoughtful commentators have provided helpful discussions of the threat posed by redefining marriage.[18] In terms of specific things we can do to defend the definition of marriage, this will depend on personal time and circumstances. (Chapter 39 discusses several ways to advocate for the family.)

Of course, we can all work to provide examples of strong families and of the value of family life "founded upon the teachings of the Lord Jesus Christ."[19] One of the major reasons that arguments for redefining marriage resonate with some is that they have witnessed the failure of many families to live up to their ideals. As a result, they no longer understand the value of the ideal.

A time in which fundamental assumptions about the nature of marriage and family life are being questioned and challenged is a difficult time for us and our families. However, it is also a time of opportunity. Some confusion is genuine, and as we work to defend marriage, our effort may be what is needed to point others in the direction that will lead to a resolution of their honest search. Ultimately, we may also be able to fortify our society so that the good work of families everywhere can continue.

ABOUT THE AUTHOR

William C. Duncan, JD, is the director of the Marriage Law Foundation. He and his wife, Catherine, are the parents of five children.

ADDITIONAL READING

William C. Duncan (2004), The state interests in marriage, *Ave Maria Law Review, 2*(1), 153–182.

Maggie Gallagher (2004), Rites, rights, and social institutions: Why and how should the law support marriage? *Notre Dame Journal of Law, Ethics and Public Policy, 18*(1), 225–241.

Lynn D. Wardle (2000), Legal and moral issues of same-sex marriage; in David C. Dollahite, ed., *Strengthening Our Families: An In-Depth Look at the Proclamation on the Family* (Salt Lake City: Bookcraft), 347–352.

NOTES

1. Bruce C. Hafen, remarks at the 1999 Spring Convention of the Association of Mormon Counselors and Psychotherapists; quoted in J. Swensen (1999), World has forgotten how to be husband, wife, Elder Hafen says; available at http://archives.his.com/smartmarriages/1999-April/msg00005.html

2. James E. Faust (1993, May), Father, come home, *Ensign, 23*(5).

3. Ibid., 37.

4. J. Teachman (2003), Premarital sex, premarital cohabitation, and the risk of subsequent marital dissolution among women, *Journal of Marriage and Family*, 65, 444–455.

5. See L. D. Wardle (2000), Legal and moral issues of same-sex marriage; in D. C. Dollahite, ed., *Strengthening Our Families: An In-Depth Look at the Proclamation on the Family* (Salt Lake City: Bookcraft), 347–352.

6. *Baker v. Vermont*, 744 A.2d 864 (Ver., 1999).

7. *Goodridge v. Department of Public Health*, 798 N.E.2d 941 (Mass., 2003).

8. First Presidency and Council of Twelve Apostles (1995, November), The family: A proclamation to the world, *Ensign*, 25(11), 102.

9. In 1995, Utah became the first state to enact such a law. There are currently 39 states with statutes or constitutional amendments that would prevent the recognition of an out-of-state same-sex marriage.

10. Four states have constitutional amendments: Haw. Rev. Stat. §572–3 (1999); Alaska Stat. Ann. §25.05.013 (1998); Neb. Const., Art. I, sec. 29; Nevada Const., Art. I, sec. 21.

11. B. Knickerbocker (2004, November 29), Political battles over gay marriage still spreading, *Christian Science Monitor*, 1–5.

12. First Presidency and Council of Twelve Apostles (1995), 102.

13. First Presidency statement opposing same-gender marriages (1994, April), News of the Church, *Ensign*, 24(4), 80.

14. Statement from the LDS First Presidency (2004, October 20), *Deseret News*, A9.

15. Gordon B. Hinckley (1999, November), Why we do some of the things we do, *Ensign*, 29(11), 54.

16. Gordon B. Hinckley (2004, September), In opposition to evil, *Ensign*, 34(9), 5.

17. Craig H. Hart (2000, August), Parents do matter: Combating the myth that parents don't matter, *Marriage & Families*, 2–8; available at http://marriageandfamilies.byu.edu; C. T. Warner (2004, October 5), How the order of marriage shapes us all, and what we lose if we change it; presented at Families under Fire 2004, Brigham Young University, Provo, UT; transcript available at http://familiesunderfire.byu.edu. See studies recently summarized in B. H. Maher, ed. (2004), *The Family Portrait: A Compilation of Data, Research and Public Opinion on the Family*, 2d ed. (Washington, D.C.: Family Research Council).

18. For example, S. Kurtz (2004, March 10), Death of marriage in Scandinavia, *Boston Globe*, A23; M. Gallagher (2003, July 20), Stakes are high: Gay marriage, the end or the beginning? *Pittsburgh Post-Gazette*, C1.

19. First Presidency and Council of Twelve Apostles (1995), 102.

E s s a y   1 4

INTERNATIONAL EFFORTS TO DEFEND MARRIAGE AND FAMILY

A. SCOTT LOVELESS

Each July since 1998, the World Family Policy Center at the BYU Law School has hosted the World Family Policy Forum, a quiet gathering of international diplomats and government officials. During several days of meetings and presentations, the Forum acquaints these influential people with philosophy, legal developments, and recent findings from the social sciences demonstrating the importance of parents in the lives of children and families in the life of the broader society.

These days together also facilitate a professional level of friendship and mutual confidence, rapport and trust, both between host and guest and among the guests. On occasion, guests will sometimes briefly open a window into their cultures. A woman from one of the former Soviet republics surprised us by saying, "I'm going to return to my country and tell my president that what we need is faith." A representative from Scandinavia admonished the other delegates, "Whatever you do, don't follow our model. Tonight in my country, over half the adults in the country will go home and be alone." And a representative of China drew kind and appreciative smiles, implicitly acknowledging what many had wanted to ask but had been too polite, when she said, "Despite China's one-child policy, we really do understand the value of the family."

The Forum is a two-way street We get to share the information from the resources provided by a university: science, demographic statistics, comparative studies, and philosophy. But our guests bring their real-life experiences from their home countries and from their policy backgrounds in their countries and at the United Nations. Together we find the family to be a crossroads of mutual understanding, a commonality shared by all world cultures.

Supporting and advocating for the family necessarily encompasses a constellation of issues surrounding the family's natural and essential role in society: issues relating to marriage, procreation, the raising and instruction of children, moral values, and the value of life itself. Marriage is important to human society for many reasons. Perhaps its major contribution is its role in binding man and woman together in a way whereby the powerful forces of the human sexual drive are harnessed for constructive purposes rather than destructive ones.

A core feature of morality is that it entails a voluntary assumption of responsibility for the effects of one's actions on others, directly and even indirectly. Marriage is an assumption of mutual responsibility for each other between spouses and an assumption of responsibility for the children born to that union. All involved benefit, including the larger society, which is renewed with a new generation of responsible citizens trained well from birth. The culture of "me first, then who cares?" or in the German idiom, *Nach mir die Sinnflut* ("When I'm done, let Noah's flood come again") is directly countered by strong families. Who cares? We care—about each other and about everyone in the family. Having learned to care, and not with mere "head knowledge" but with the learning of experience and habit, family members are then equipped to enter society as kind, compassionate, diligent citizens. This is what families can and should do, and what they actually do in most cases, even in the face of duress, hardship, and sacrifice.

Whether our forum provides government officials with their first instruction on these principles, clarifies or reawakens their own teachings and experience from childhood, or simply helps them put words to their instincts, we hope to either kindle or rekindle the spark to do what is needful when such issues are raised in political forums around the world, from the UN through national and subnational bodies, down to the local school board and PTA. On occasion, we receive heartening feedback.

One of the good friends we have made at the UN who has attended our forum several times is a member of the diplomatic corps of a major Islamic country. He once related to us that after attending the forum,

he had returned home and said to his father, "These people are doing what we should be doing!" Later, this same friend learned of a proposal being introduced before the United Nations Human Rights Commission in Geneva to officially recognize homosexual behavior as a fundamental human right, with all of the protections in law that such rights enjoy. When he inquired of his ambassador, he learned that his country had not planned to send a representative to the Geneva meeting. He asked to be assigned. His request was refused. He asked if he could represent his country officially if he took his personal vacation time and traveled at his own expense. At this, he was given authorization.

He traveled to Geneva and single-handedly worked nonstop for more than two weeks raising procedural objections and introducing major amendments to the proposal, while also working behind the scenes to raise the awareness of other countries to the dangers of the proposal. The session ended with no resolution of the issue, a victory for our friend's valiant efforts. Had he not been present, the resolution almost surely would have been approved. The following year, a similar attempt was made, but this time the pro-family, pro-life governments and nongovernment organizations (NGOs) were prepared to act in concert, and again the proposal was defeated.

We have made a network of friends among the diplomatic corps of many countries and among the people of many faiths and private organizations. Many people around the world respond instinctively to threats and challenges to the family.

A wonderful recent example is the events of 2004, the tenth anniversary of the United Nations' 1994 International Year of the Family (IYF), an event that many felt had actually contributed to the decline of the traditional family. In the fall of 2003, we were approached by the UN ambassador from Qatar with a request for cooperation in arranging a series of conferences around the world to celebrate IYF's tenth anniversary. The object, as he explained it, was to put forward good family scholarship that might undo much of the damage from the original IYF in 1994. In 2004, Qatar was the UN chair of a large negotiating block of countries at the UN known as "G-77" and was therefore in a position to assist at the intergovernmental level. They were asking us to provide them with scholarly support from around the world and logistical assistance. We swallowed hard several times, then determined to do what we could with our limited resources to help Qatar's effort succeed.

In 2004, family conferences were held in Mexico City, Stockholm, Cotonou (Benin), Geneva, Riga (Latvia), Baku (Azerbaijan), and Kuala Lumpur prior to the culminating conference in Doha (Qatar) in late November. Our level of involvement and participation varied with the location, but we were able to locate scholars throughout the world whose work demonstrated the critical role of family in every human society. Through the combined efforts of our many friends, the conferences were successful beyond any realistic expectations. On December 6, 2004, the United Nations General Assembly officially "noted" (i.e., accepted) the Doha Declaration in support of policies recognizing and supporting the family as the fundamental unit of society.

The struggle is far from over, but we have established a beachhead. It is our hope that by working together with and extending the cooperating network of like-minded people throughout the world, we can help preserve the precious but delicate place of marriage and family in all world cultures for many more generations.

The struggle is no less vital here at home, and it is no less a struggle of ideologies. In this respect it recalls the urgency of Alma's step in giving up the judgment seat to preach the word of God among the people to overcome the relativistic, supposedly amoral effects of the doctrine of Nehor (see Alma 1–16). It will take informed, calm, insistent, involved, and caring voices in every legislature, every professional association, city council, library, school board,

and PTA meeting. These sessions are just as important to families and children, if not more so, than meetings of the Congress and the United Nations, for it is at the local level that ideology and policy are implemented and have their effects. We must not only recognize and react to the subtle social forces eroding family and faith—we must work, like Alma and Amulek, to counter them. Every married couple, every family member, every informed and concerned citizen should find a way to let their voices be heard. If everyone does his or her part, remembering President Gordon B. Hinckley's counsel to be calm, informed, and not "shrill,"[1] we will succeed. God bless your efforts.

ABOUT THE AUTHOR

A. Scott Loveless, JD, Ph.D., serves as executive director of the World Family Policy Center and on the faculty of the BYU J. Reuben Clark Law School. He and his wife, Cheri, are the parents of eight children and grandparents of four (so far).

ADDITIONAL READING

Gordon B. Hinckley (2004, September), In opposition to evil, *Ensign, 34*(9), 3–6.

C. S. Lewis (1996), *The Abolition of Man* (New York: Simon & Schuster).

James Q. Wilson (2002), *The Marriage Problem* (New York: HarperCollins).

NOTE

1. Gordon B. Hinckley (2004, September), In opposition to evil, *Ensign, 34*(9), 3–6.

E S S A Y   1 5

SHARING THE PROCLAMATION

ADRIAN T. JUCHAU

As I have "go[ne] forth with faith to tell the world the joy of families,"[1] I have learned a number of lessons. This essay will describe some of my experiences, as well as experiences of others, as we have tried to live and share principles of the proclamation on the family. As you read, you may wish to ask for divine guidance and prayerfully con-

sider what you can do to share the principles of the proclamation with others.

GO FORTH WITH COURAGE[2]

When sharing the proclamation with others, courage causes us to step into the unknown, enables us to face our fears, and leads us to act in defense of truth. As a family advocate, I was asked to give a series of firesides while traveling out of state. The first night did not go well. The room was filled with married couples who didn't believe that an unmarried college kid could share much of anything that would help them strengthen their marriages—and I wasn't sure I could either. As I look back on that night, I realize that I am the one who learned the most from that experience, both in preparing for my presentation and in reflecting upon that nearly catastrophic event. I humbled myself and sought the help of my Heavenly Father. I knew that I must rely upon His word and not upon my arm of inexperienced flesh. With renewed hope and courage, I was ready to make my next attempt.

A few days later I was to speak on parenting. Before the fireside began, I was approached by a man who had long finished his parenting years. "How many kids do you have?" he asked.

"Well, none," I reluctantly replied.

"Oh, I see. How long have you been married?"

"I'm not married."

"Hmmm. Well, what did you get your degree in?"

I was flustered. "I don't have my degree yet."

"Very well, it was nice to meet you. Good luck tonight. I'm going home now. You haven't got anything to offer me."

At first, I was discouraged. Then I remembered Paul's counsel to Timothy: "Let no man despise thy youth; . . . Neglect not the gift that is in thee. . . . Take heed unto thyself, and unto the doctrine; . . . for in doing this thou shalt both save thyself, and them that hear thee" (1 Timothy 4:12–16). I determined to press forward, filled with a brightness of hope and a deep desire to make a difference. At the conclusion of my presentation, that same man came up to me with tears in his eyes and apologized for what he had said. His wife had convinced him to stay, and he said he was glad, as he had learned much. I was grateful that on this occasion I had the courage it took to be an instrument in the Lord's hands.

I have a friend who also stepped out of her comfort zone and found the courage to share the proclamation with others. She had always wanted to share the gospel but was afraid to try. She accepted my challenge to look for opportunities to share and defend proclamation principles, and her chance came when she least expected it. While undergoing a medical procedure, she became friends with the nurse who cared for her. She had the impression to give the nurse a copy of the proclamation along with her testimony of its truths. The nurse graciously accepted the gift, and in time wanted to know more about the teachings of Jesus Christ upon which happy and successful families are established and maintained. After meeting with the missionaries, this woman was baptized and now other members of her family are learning more about Heavenly Father's plan of happiness for families. I am confident that countless lives could be changed for good if more of us would look for ways in which we could share the principles of the proclamation.

GO FORTH WITH LOVE

Our potential to influence the lives of others for good is significantly hindered if we are not filled with the love of God and our fellowman.[3] Pure love helps us to see one another as God sees us and helps others to embrace the truths of the proclamation. This love also helps us to be bold but not overbearing and enables us to endure the opposition we might face as we share and defend these sacred truths.

I have come to learn that as we try to share proclamation principles in the spirit of love, the Spirit will testify of their truthfulness. I remember a friend of mine who was struggling with her feelings of individual worth. As we talked about her difficulties, the words of the proclamation echoed in my mind: "Each [human being] is a beloved spirit son or daughter of heavenly parents, and, as such, each has a divine nature and destiny."[4] In an unforgettable way, I was filled with God's love for my friend as the Spirit bore witness to me that God was mindful of her, that she indeed possessed the attributes of deity, and that great things were in store for her. As I shared these profound truths with her, the Spirit enlightened her mind and comforted her troubled heart.

When sharing and defending the proclamation, we may find ourselves addressing sensitive issues. Being filled with Christlike love can help us do so in a meaningful but nonthreatening way. One of my acquaintances recently circulated a petition that defended traditional marriage. This act unintentionally offended one of her friends who claimed to have homosexual tendencies. We must understand that even when we are thoughtful in our approach, many will take these truths to be hard (see 1 Nephi 16:2; 2 Nephi 9:40), so we must remember to show forth an increase in love (D&C 121:43). My acquaintance responded to this young man's reproach by sincerely expressing her love for her friend. She did not waver on her moral position, but she lovingly told her friend that she wanted him to enjoy the same happiness that she has found through living the principles of the proclamation. As the saying goes, others probably won't care much about what we know until they know how much we care.

ANSWER THE CALL

Perhaps the best way for the proclamation to bless the lives of others is for us to internalize its message and practice its principles beginning within the walls of our own homes. As we do so, this inspired document will become more than a decoration on our walls—it will be etched upon the fleshy tables of our hearts (2 Corinthians 3:3). Our desires to share the proclamation will increase (see 1 Nephi 8:10–12). Furthermore, when others see the fruits of proclamation principles in our lives, they "will inevitably come as a flood to where the family is safe . . . and know that the gospel is the great plan of happiness."[5] As I have studied the proclamation and made an effort to share it with others, precious truths have been reaffirmed and the blessings of heaven have flowed into my life and spilled into the lives of others. This experience can be yours as you make a sincere effort to respond to the Lord's invitation.

I do not know what you can specifically do to make a difference, but God does. Relying on the Holy Ghost helps our efforts to be more effective and enables us to accomplish things beyond our own natural capacity. We would be wise to seek more diligently and listen at all times for the promptings of the Spirit, and when they come, we must be sure to act upon them. While our measure of success cannot be contingent on another's agency, we can gauge our success by the degree to which we involve the Spirit of the Lord in our efforts. Elder Henry B. Eyring taught:

As we read what the proclamation tells us about the family, we can expect—in fact, we must expect—impressions to come to our minds as to what we are to do. And we can be confident it is possible for us to do

according to those impressions. . . . We can start now to "promote those measures designed to maintain and strengthen the family." I pray that we will. I pray that you will ask, "Father, how can I prepare?" Tell him how much you want what he desires to give you. You will receive impressions, and if you act on them, I promise you the help of the powers of heaven.[6]

I witness the truthfulness of this apostolic promise. I invite you to answer the call to "promote those measures designed to maintain and strengthen the family."[7] May the Lord bless you with courage, love, success, and joy as you faithfully act upon the quiet whisperings of the Spirit to bless the families of the earth.

ABOUT THE AUTHOR

Adrian T. Juchau is a certified family life educator and a graduate student at BYU. He recently graduated as valedictorian in the School of Family Life. He enjoys speaking and writing about families in a gospel context. He recently married Lisa Funk.

ADDITIONAL READING

Henry B. Eyring (1998, February), The family, *Ensign*, 28(2), 10.
Family Life Education Institute (2002), *Answering the Call: What Can I Do Now to Strengthen Marriages and Families?* pamphlet (Provo, UT: BYU School of Family Life). To order the pamphlet, visit www.familylifeeducation.org or call 1-800-452-5662.

NOTES

1. R. M. Gardner and L. J. Gardner (1985), Go forth with faith, *Hymns* (Salt Lake City: The Church of Jesus Christ of Latter-day Saints), 263.

2. Ibid.

3. The scriptures teach us that if we lack this love, we can pray for it with all the energy of our hearts (see Moroni 7:48).

4. First Presidency and Council of Twelve Apostles (1995, November), The family: A proclamation to the world, *Ensign*, 25(11), 102.

5. Boyd K. Packer (1994, May), The father and the family, *Ensign*, 24(5), 19.

6. Henry B. Eyring (1998, February), The family, *Ensign*, 28(2), 10.

7. First Presidency and Council of Twelve Apostles (1995), 102.

INDEX

335; organizations, 335–37; genealogy and, 337–39; strengthened through citizenship, 340–44; as community, 346; international efforts to defend, 357–59. *See also* Blended family, Children, Home

"Family, The: A Proclamation to the World," reprint, xi. *See also* Proclamation to the World

Family history. *See* Genealogy

Family home evening: as safeguard for family, 3; made known to Lord's servants, 10; survey on, 41–42; as tool to strengthen marriage and family, 89; as spiritual pattern, 153–54; in single-parent home, 180; as strengthening family process, 251; children and, 255–56; Gordon B. Hinckley on community events and, 265; reserving Mondays for, 268

Family prayer: as safeguard for family, 3; survey on, 41–42; as tool to strengthen marriage and family, 89

Family scripture study: as safeguard for family, 3; survey on, 41–42; as tool to strengthen marriage and family, 88

Family therapy, coping with addiction through, 100

Fanaticism, 16–17

Fasting, 211–12

Fast offerings, 63–64

Fathers: Gordon B. Hinckley on priorities of, 6; succumbing to false teachings, 8; Gordon B. Hinckley gives advice to, 144; preside over family, 167–68; provide for family, 168–69; protect family, 169–70; partner with spouse, 170; Gordon B. Hinckley on, 171, 252; custodial, 179–80; single, 179–80; non-custodial, 180;

Fault-finding, in marriage, 52, 58

Faust, James E.: defines families, 1; on disintegration of family, 3; on choosing when to divorce, 120; on emotional infidelity, 128; on sacrifice in parenting, 131; on children's different temperaments, 138; on parenting as partnership, 146–47; on disciplining children, 147; on families and devotion to God, 185; on sanctity of life, 190; on finding modest prom dresses, 210; on grief for rebellious children, 223; on parents with rebellious children, 223; on successful parenting, 224; on influence of extended family, 232–33; story of wayward son, 233; on family home evening, 251; on family time, 265; on teaching children citizenship, 346; on justified divorce, 355

Favoritism, 22

Fear: of marriage, 46–47; of failure, 125; as effect of violent media, 216

Feinauer, Leslie, 300

Feminism, radical, 8–9

Ferre, Richard, 234

Fiery darts, dream of, 152

Financial assistance, extended families and, 322–23

Financial decisions, 64–65; marital harmony and, 65–66; as reflection of values, 66–67

Financial hardships, importance of paying tithes and offerings during, 63–64

Financial management, 246–47; Thomas S. Monson on

living within our means, 63; Gordon B. Hinckley on, 169

First Presidency: on giving priority to spiritual patterns, 153; on adoption, 198–99, 238–39; on modesty, 207; on temple garment and modesty, 209; on desensitizing effect of violent media, 216; on counteracting media violence, 219; on marriage and unwed pregnancy, 238; on home, 243; on family home evening, 251; on teaching children gospel, 251; on immoral behavior, 295; on voting, 345; on same-sex marriage, 356

First Things First, 342

Flom, Helen W. and Ross, 195

Flor, Douglas, 251

Food, managing, 246

Forbis, Diane, on triangulation, 330

Forgiveness: charity and, 52; growth in marriage and, 52–53; for premarital sex, 69; for physical abuse, 94; after pornography, 106; after infidelity, 114–15; abuse and, 305–6

Forsaking, as first step to healing from infidelity, 110–12

For the Strength of Youth, 207

Foundation: building home's solid, 9–10; building children's spiritual, 132–33

Foundational truths, 7–8

Fowers, Blaine, on how to have a good marriage, 58

Freeman, Patti, 264

Friends: keeping, at a distance, 125; teenagers' need for good, 231–32; as community influence on family, 265

Friendship, as marital value, 58

Fronk, Camille, 78

Frustration, parenting and, 148

Fun, as tool to strengthen family and marriage, 88–89

Funerals, 286

Gallagher, Maggie, 32; on finding happiness in marriage, 121

Gamblers Anonymous, 99–100

Gardner, Howard, on different types of intelligence, 136

Gay. *See* Same-sex attraction

Gender: false teachings about, 8–9; as essential characteristic of eternal identity, 31

Genealogy, 337–39

General Social Survey (GSS), 33

Generosity, 58

Gifts: Marvin J. Ashton on children's, 136; children as, 203

Goals: setting family and marital, 88–90; overcoming addiction and, 104; supporting children's, 158; family and, 248

God: Gordon B. Hinckley on desire of, for our happiness, 1; Neal A. Maxwell on love of, 3; foundational truths of, 7; establishing close relationship with, 9–10; seeing power of, in leaders of Church, 10; teaches us to be family, 14; opportunities to please, 18; perceived favoritism and, 22; can help with addictions, 104; marriage ordained by, 119; gives us stewardship over children, 136; nurturing children as work of, 174–75;

world affecting mortality, 135; on violence, 215; on judging wayward children, 224; on same-sex attraction, 295, 298; on caring for elderly, 324; on redeeming dead, 335; on citizen responsibilities and divorce, 341; on community involvement, 342

Oaks, Stella Harris, on dealing with family transitions, 73–74

Objectification of women, 162

Olsen, Susanne Frost, 73, 327

Olson, Paul, 78–79

Olson, Terrance D., 73

Opposition, 153–55

Optimism, 185

Ordinance, temple marriage as essential, 48

Outcome, focusing on process instead of, 27

Overprotectiveness, 145

Packer, Boyd K.: on balancing family and church, 4; on scheduling children, 6; on marriage as partnership, 58; on marrying later in life, 79; on trials in marriage, 83; on addictions and hearing Holy Ghost, 97; on family as core of Church, 132; on letting society place limits on family life, 134; on fostering Light of Christ, 146 (Box 17.2); on building shield of faith, 155–56; on parenting as partnership, 170; on disabilities, 189; on disabilities as punishment, 190; on restoration of disabled children, 190; on salvation of disabled, 190; on chastity and plan of salvation, 211; on temple covenants and children, 226; on dealing with rebellious children, 234; on same-sex attraction, 295; on acting on same-sex attraction, 297

Pain, Thomas S. Monson on comfort from, 288

Palmer, Gary K., 272

Papernow, Patricia, 186

Parable: of talents, 131–32; of prodigal son, 225–26

Parental monitoring, 211

Parent–child interviews, 89

Parenting: as transition, 75; effect of addiction on, 97; sacrifice and, 131; Gordon B. Hinckley on joy of, 132; children learn through, 133; Gordon B. Hinckley on love in, 135; understanding children's development and, 135–36; understanding differences in children's talents and, 136–37; reducing sibling rivalry, 137; understanding differences in temperament and, 137–38; adapting in, 138; as learning process, 141; authoritative, 143; encouraging and filling creative needs and, 143–44; connecting with children and, 144; setting limits and, 144–45; overprotective, 145; as partnership, 145–47, 170; coercion in, 146 (Box 17.2), 148–49; differing personalities in, 147; discernment and, 147–48; punitive, 148–49; praying for help in, 149; teaching children and, 159–60; teaching appropriate attitudes to children, 165–66; helping children develop social skills, 166; challenges of single, 174–75, 178–82; stepchildren, 186; children with disabilities, 190–91; infertility and, 195–96; teaching modesty and, 210; teaching chastity and,

211–12; successful, 224; judging and, 224–25; setting boundaries for teenagers and, 228–29; rebellious teenagers with love, 229–30; effect of contention on, 250; Robert D. Hales on, 252; role of community in, 264–65; with music, 275; coping with angry children and, 313–15; newly-wed children, 328; teaching citizenship and, 345–48. *See also* Aging parents, Children, Family, Fathering, Mothering, Teenagers

Parents: pass characteristics to children, 24; role of, in development of children's self-esteem, 26–31; attitudes on marriage of, 46; children learn about money from, 63; appropriate intimacy between children and, 68

Partnership: marriage as equal, 57–58, 85–87; parenting as, 145–47, 170

Patience, in nurturing children, 175–76

Patterns: Richard G. Scott on changing, 95; altering addictive, 99

Peace: after suicide, 242; after death of child, 279–80; through Jesus Christ, 318

Peck, M. Scott, on children's need to feel valued, 230

Peer pressure, 211, 228

Pehrson, Edy and Lynn, 350

Perfection: Richard G. Scott on seeking, in potential spouse, 48; Joseph Fielding Smith on, 126; progress as, 126; families and, 153; eating disorders and, 310–11

Perry, L. Tom: on fathers' providing for home, 167; on fathers' presiding in home, 168; on protecting homes, 169; on home as refuge, 243

Personal histories, 338–39

Personalities, in parenting, 147

Pessimism, 45

Physical abuse. *See* Abuse

Physical body, 2

Piaget, Jean, 136

Piano: playing, during family dishes time, 12–13; Patricia Holland encourages daughter at, 138–39

Pinegar, Ed J. and Patricia P., 88

Pioneers, 21–23

Planning sessions, 88–90

Plan of happiness: as family-centered plan, 1–5; Elder Ballard on understanding, 4; gender roles in, 31; marriage as part of, 44; role of transitions in, 75–77; chastity and, 210–11; role of illness and death in, 286

Play, 273

Poduska, Bernard, 63

Pornography: protecting families from, 102–3; fidelity and, 103; suggestions for overcoming addiction to, 103–5; suggestions for spouses coping with, 105–6; signs of, 106 (Box 13.1); women and, 106–7; man overcomes addiction to, 123–24

Porter, Chris L., 135

Possessions, finding satisfaction with current, 15

Pratt, Parley P.: on our developing traits of heavenly parents, 24; on love and charity, 52

Prayer: decision making in marriage and, 47; for strength to deal with infidelity, 117–18; to love as God loves, 118; for help in parenting, 149; after September 11,